From the Balloon to the Moon

by

H. V. Pat Reilly

A Chronology of New Jersey's Amazing, Aviation History

**THE MANUSCRIPT FOR THIS BOOK WAS MADE
POSSIBLE THROUGH A GRANT FROM THE
AVIATION HALL OF FAME & MUSEUM OF NEW JERSEY**

From the Balloon to the Moon
First Edition, 1992

HV Publishers

285 Genther Avenue

Oradell, N.J. 07649

201-261-4845

ISBN 0-9632295-0-8

The publisher offers discounts on this book when ordered in bulk quantities

Printed in the USA

Editor Carol Suplee

Design & production by Joyce Huber, PhotoGraphics

Special Photography, Jon Huber

Introduction

New Jersey's role in the science of flight is a remarkable story. In every chapter of aviation history, New Jersey pilots, engineers, explorers and scientists have left an indelible imprint.

We know that mankind's accomplishments must be judged in the context of their time. The first hot-air balloon flights, to 18th century onlookers, were as much a miracle as space walks and moon landings are to modern observers.

Let us step back in time to the first untethered hot-air balloon flight--Nov. 21, 1783. Thousands of Parisians stood in stunned silence as Francois Pilatre de Rozier and Francois Laurent, Marquis d'Arlandes, proved they could soar above the rooftops of Paris and return safely. The worldly citizens of Paris watched in wonder, certain they had seen the marvel of the millennium.

A decade later, another Frenchman, Jean-Pierre Blanchard, sailed his balloon over the rooftops of Philadelphia. The young city, capital of a new nation, was a sophisticated center of learning and science in the New World, and citizens would surely have heard of the French balloonist's exploits.

But imagine how simple farmers in Deptford Township, NJ, might have greeted Blanchard's floating apparition as it drifted over the broad Delaware River and settled with a thump on their green fields. Would they have heard the news from Paris, even ten years later, of men who soared where no humans had ever ventured? Tied to earth, would they have even dreamed about flight?

No. Blanchard's balloon flight was an unequaled phenomenon, a central event in their bucolic lives to be recorded and discussed for generations to come.

Ballooning dominated the collective imagination during the 1800s. Those early pilots were held in such reverence that they were addressed as "Professor." New Jersey was again in the forefront of the fledgling science when Charles F. Durant of Jersey City flew a balloon of his own creation and became America's first native-born aeronaut.

Then, men of vision, like Dr. Solomon Andrews of Perth Amboy, developed non-rigid airships powered by primitive engines. No longer a slave to the prevailing winds, man could now direct his flight. Visionaries began to glimpse its enormous potential for civilian and military use.

The age of fixed-wing flight had begun with the Wright brothers at Kitty Hawk in 1903. Soon, flying became a popular sensation exploited by entrepreneurs, including the Wrights, as a new and exciting form of entertainment. It was show business — a couple of hundred feet in the air. By 1910, Atlantic City had become a leading aeronautical center, its beaches filled with sunbathers and sky-gawkers.

With the coming of World War I, aviation fulfilled its serious potential and, for the first time in history, airmen's feats of daring-do were a factor the strategies of a global conflict.

For a time in the post-war period, aviation returned to its novelty status and reckless barnstormers en-

Amelia Earhart

Charles Lindbergh

thralled onlookers — and risked their own necks — with their aerobatic high-jinks. It took a young American midwesterner to prove once again that the flying machine held untapped possibilities for the human race. Flying his small, silver plane, "Spirit of St. Louis" which was powered by an engine developed in Paterson, NJ, Charles Lindbergh crossed the treacherous North Atlantic. In one dramatic day and night, he changed forever the attitudes of skeptical government and business leaders who had been reticent about supporting the budding aviation industry.

The industry took off with a roar. Developing airlines found that the best and most reliable airplanes and engines were built in New Jersey. In short order, major towns and cities across the United States were building airports. Air mail and passenger service became commonplace. Newark Municipal Airport was the busiest in the world in the 1930s.

The science of aviation reached new heights during World War II. And though the cost in lives was terrible, its worth was proved beyond any shadow of doubt. For the first time in history, air power was decisive in the Allies' victory in both the European and Asian theaters of war.

By the late 1940s rocket engines designed in Denville and Paterson, NJ, opened a new vista of space to the world. In 1969, a New Jerseyan landed the first vehicle on the moon.

These events, accomplished by men and women of great vision, are outlined in this chronicle. Here you will find the stories of New Jersey aviation pioneers whose inventiveness and daring cleared the skies for the astronauts of today. Here also, the genius of New Jersey scientists and manufacturers is revealed. Their aeronautical products — from powerful engines to parachutes to delicate navigational aids — propelled the industry's progress and helped the world's famous aviators accomplish their celebrated deeds.

In each era, the pioneers of flight have inspired veneration among their earth-bound compatriots. Jean-Pierre Blanchard, surprising New Jersey farmers as his balloon sailed by; Charles Lindbergh, pushing his body and his plane beyond reasonable limits of endurance; Amelia Earhart, determined to prove women could equal the aeronautical feats of men; Chuck Yeager, breaking the barrier of sound; and American astronauts, in the ultimate human achievement, walking on the earth's silvery moon — all of these in their time can be called miraculous.

As science presses forward, pushing back barriers that are yet to be imagined, surely more miracles are waiting to capture our imagination. And like the Parisians of 1783, we will stand looking heavenward, stunned and silent.

Wally Schirra

Arthur Godfrey

FOREWORD

I recall enjoying Buck Rogers' comic strips as a child, but never enjoying the movie versions of that comic strip about space. My first memory about leaving earth was watching aircraft at Teterboro Airport. Finally, one day, I left earth on my first flight, as a passenger, from Teterboro.

I had to settle for movies about aviation until flight training, during 1947, at Pensacola, Florida as an Ensign graduate of the U.S. Naval Academy. So many events in aviation happened before and during my lifetime as a New Jerseyan.

This book helps to fill that void with factual tales from the 18th century to the 20th century of Buck Rogers and my contemporaries.

I was one who really left Earth three times. In these pages you can share my experiences, as well as those of other New Jersey astronauts, aviators, aviatrix and ballooners.

You will lift off with "From the Balloon to the Moon"!

Wally Schirra

Astronaut

Mercury 8 Gemini 6

Apollo 7

ACKNOWLEDGMENTS

Thanks to the generous support of the Emil Buehler Trust, a New Jersey-based foundation dedicated to the advancement of aviation science, technology and education, this historical chronology was made possible.

Emil Buehler, the founder of the trust, was born in 1899 in Alpirsbach, a small Black Forest village in Germany. He first flew at age 17 for Kaiser Wilhelm's Navy during World War I.

Following the war, he graduated from the University of Stuttgart with degrees in architecture and engineering and immigrated to the United States. Working for prestigious U.S. architectural firms, Buehler garnered national recognition for his designs of the Daily News building in New York City and the Washington, DC, Greyhound Bus Terminal.

During that period he remained active in the field of aviation. In the late 1920s, he and aviation pioneer Clarence Chamberlin purchased farmland in Paramus along what is now Route 17, and planned to establish an airport there. Protests by local residents caused the men to scrap the idea and Chamberlin sold his interest in the land to Buehler. That was the first of a number of similar farms bordering the highway that Buehler purchased. He sold the original acreage to the developers of the Garden State Plaza, then the largest shopping mall in the United States. He developed the other plots of land as office complexes that still remain part of the Trust.

While his entrepreneurial talents were aimed at land development, he established the Buehler Aviation Research Corp. and the Emil Buehler Trust. During World War II, he founded and operated an aviation school for mechanic training in Newark and later ran a seaplane base on the Hudson River. He personally designed and supervised the construction of an aviation facility at the Executive Airport in Fort Lauderdale, FL, where he and his staff rebuilt antique and experimental aircraft.

His legacy of philanthropic commitment extends to a number of leading educational institutions. Donations from the Emil Buehler Trust have led to the establishment of the Buehler Planetarium at Broward Community College and the funding of the development of a wind tunnel with Mach 3 capability at Rutgers University. In 1974, the university conferred on Emil Buehler the title of Eminent Engineer.

Since his death in 1983, projects that have been funded by the Emil Buehler Trust include the restoration of a Grumman G-21 "Goose" amphibian airplane for the Smithsonian's National Air and Space Museum; the Emil Buehler Aerodynamic Analog, a unique experimental teaching facility donated to the Mechanical Engineering Department of Texas A&M University; and a Pilot Decision-Making Training Research Program by the AOPA Air Safety Foundation. The Trust has provided financial support to the following organizations. The Eagle Flight Explorer Post in East Orange, NJ; the Sky- Life Flying Camp in Upstate New York; the Aviation Hall of Fame & Museum of New Jersey; the Broward Community College to establish the Emil Buehler Aviation Center and Achievement Awards; and the Musee America in Ver-sur-Mer, france.

FURTHER ACKNOWLEDGMENTS

The author would be remiss not to acknowledge the contributions of various aviation historians, pioneers and friends who enriched this chronology by their recollections and outstanding collections of logs, diaries, memoirs, media accounts and personal writings which they graciously shared. They include: William Rhode, David Winans, William Ryan, Arthur Raymond Brooks, Edward and Julia Gorski, Paul Garber, Edith Durant Censier, Robert B. Whitman, Olive Simmons Ussery, Mrs. Helen Boland Scherff, William Chestnut, Mary Jean Martin, John L. Dorrothy, Paul Wittemann, Silvio Cavalier, Adiel Strang, Louise Chamberlin, John Hadley, Robert Noorduyn, Mrs. Audrey Balchen, Mrs. Anne Morrow Lindbergh, Vincent Carson, William Conrad, John Dickerson, George Williams, Gloria Acosta Yarhouse, Richard Switlik, Gerard Abbamont, Mrs. Ruth DeGarmo, Mrs. Lee Reichers, Scott Scammel III, Walter Hartung, Mrs. Frances Forsythe, Susie Solberg Nagle, Frank Romano, Karl Woeppel, Carol Greene, Ben Rock, Louis Ranley, David Van Dyke, Gregory F. Weidenfeld, Raymond Compari, David Wahlberg, Harry Liming, Charles Dimmick, Robert Mahler, Joseph Rosen, and Richard E. Byrd III.

The original manuscript may never have been completed without the professional editing talents of Carol Suplee, the work processing skills of Dorothy Gulino and Karen Careri and the determination of Faye Guglielmo to keep the chronology on track throughout the two-year period it took to complete. The production skills of Joyce Huber have gotten us through the labor pains of birthing this volume. Their dedication and professionalism are deeply appreciated.

Table of Contents

Barnaby glides from dirigible; Chamberlin and Ruth Nichols set records; Teenage record setters — Garofalo, Goldsborough, Buck and Schneider; Woman jumps at 17,000 feet; Reichers flies Atlantic; Wilson, first state aviation director; *Akron* and *Macon* crash; First nonstop Pacific flight; Earhart flies Atlantic solo; Teaneck has first high school aviation course; Gorskis operate Teterboro; Luscombe moves to West Trenton; Mail rocket flies; Hindenburgh explodes; Seaplane bases abound; Bendix moves to Teterboro; Decker, national glider champ.

Civil Air Patrol founded; Home front prepares for war; New Jersey airmen at war; Castle, McGuire and Walsh win Congressional Medal of Honor; McGuire second all-time American flying ace; New Jersey WASP contribute to war effort; Tuskegee Airmen leave their mark; Lewis, co-pilot on Atom bomb run; First electronic flight simulator; Wehran's Teterboro Air Terminal, world's busiest; New Jersey rocket engine breaks sound barrier; Two Piper Super Cruisers fly around the world; Odom flies nonstop Hawaii to Teterboro in a Bonanza.

Powder Puff Derby headquartered at Teterboro; Newark Airport expands; Godfrey buzzes Teterboro tower; Stroukoff builds New Jersey's largest airplane; First air-cushioned flying machine.

Wally Schirra flies in all three generations of spacecraft; Schweikart tests space suit; Aldrin lands on the moon; Wisely, Howarth and Meade Vietnam heroes.

New Jersey Aviation Hall of Fame founded; Forbes establishes transcontinental balloon records; Eagle Flight established.

PEOPLExpress flies at Newark Airport; Loudenslager wins World Aerobatic Championship; Campbell flies Ultralight coast -to-coast; Around the world in 47 hours; first all-woman military flight crew; First woman aviation director; First woman to walk in space; Stealth fighter crashes; Artist, writers and historians abound.

Frenchman, Jean-Pierre Blanchard

1793
First Balloon Flight
Jean Pierre Blanchard

Even the majestic eagles that soared over the New Jersey countryside were dwarfed by this giant, floating apparition that skimmed the treetops and settled to the ground before the incredulous eyes of a Gloucester County, NJ, farmer.

Any 18th century man, even the most worldly, would have counted himself lucky to have seen such a sight.

As the huge round ball with its wicker basket dangling below approached the earth, the farmer, quelling with what must have been pure terror, dropped his tools and rushed across the field through thickets and brambles toward the landing spot.

It was a moment that even this uneducated farmer could recognize as history-making. As he watched, the huge cloth bag atop the basket began settling to the ground while a small man tugged on the guy wires and his little black dog ran about, barking in excitement.

This farmer was later to confirm that the event truly did occur. The date was January 9, 1793 and the daring young man aloft was Jean-Pierre Blanchard, a noted French balloonist who had just completed the first manned flight in the Western Hemisphere.

It was a delicate moment. The balloonist shouted a welcome in a tongue the farmer didn't understand and showed him a letter which might just as well have been in a foreign language, for the farmer could not read.

But these barriers fell quickly when Blanchard shared the wine which had been packed aboard the gondola.

No such event could have gone unnoticed in the tiny community of Deptford. Within minutes, the two were joined by neighbors. Two men and two women arrived on horseback. Another, who found the site on foot, came with gun in hand.

But there was no violence. Fortunately, the armed man had the ability to read and he triumphantly announced that the letter was from none other than President George Washington.

Blanchard's handwritten journal contains this description of that moment:

"In the midst of profound silence was it read with a loud and audible voice. How dear the name of Washington is to this people! With what eagerness they gave me all possible assistance, in consequence of his recommendation."

One startling fact piled on another. The welcoming party learned that the balloonist had traveled from Philadelphia, more than 15 miles away, in less than an hour. For them such a trip would have taken three or four hours by carriage or horseback and required crossing the wide, rushing Delaware River.

Blanchard's wicker basket with the balloon stuffed inside was hoisted on the men's shoulders and carried to a nearby farmhouse where the momentous events were set down on paper. A letter certifying the descent was written and signed by witnesses.

"These may certify, that we the subscribers saw the bearer, Mr. Blanchard, settle in his balloon in Deptford Township, County of Gloucester, in the state of New Jersey, about fifteen miles from Philadelphia, about 10 o'clock 56 minutes, a.m. Witness our hands the ninth day of January, Anno Domini, 1793."

Everard Bolton

Joseph Griffith

Joseph Cheesman

Samuel Taggart

Amos Castell

Zara North

After a brief rest at a local tavern and a hearty country dinner, Blanchard was taken back to Philadelphia in the carriage of Jonathan Penrose, Esquire. They arrived at 7 p.m. and the diminutive French aeronaut went immediately to the home of President Washington to present the unusual flag he had carried on his aerial journey. The flag had the French tricolor on one side and the Stars and Stripes on the other. Jean-Pierre Blanchard was one of the early professional balloonists in Europe. He first flew in 1784, just a year after the world's first balloon, developed by two French brothers, Joseph Michel and Jacques Etienne Montgolfier, was flown at Versailles, France. Blanchard saw ballooning as an easy way to make a living by promoting flying exhibitions, first in Europe and then in the United States.

In 1785, he and Dr. John Jefferies, an American expatriate, were the first aeronauts to fly across the English channel. After 44 successful flights in France, Germany Holland Belgium, Switzerland, Poland and Austria, Blanchard set his sights on the American continent. He arrived in Philadelphia in December 1792, and began promoting the first manned flight in America.

The normally staid Pennsylvanians were enthusiastically awaiting the flight even though Blanchard was selling tickets at the astronomical price of $5 each. Those fortunate enough to afford the fare crowded into the walled yard of Philadelphia's Walnut Street prison to witness the event.

On the day of the ascent, Philadelphia was in a festive mood. Cannons were fired several hours before the flight, a signal to all that Blanchard would take off at 10 a.m. President George Washington himself wished the Frenchman well and personally presented him with a letter of safe conduct. At nine minutes after ten o'clock with a band playing, cannons roaring and thousands of people cheering madly, the balloon ascended from within the prison walls and began to drift southeast toward the Delaware River.

Blanchard described the scene in Philadelphia from his loftly perch: "...yet I could not help being surprised and astonished when, elevated at a certain height over the city, I turned my eyes toward the immense number of people which covered the open places, the roofs of the houses, the steeples, the streets and the roads, over which my flight carried me in the free space of the air. What a sight! How delicious for me to enjoy it!"

Although his American adventure had been an artistic success, it was a financial failure. So Blanchard decided to return to Europe to develop his fortune.

Jean-Pierre Blanchard did not find his pot of gold when he returned to France. Aerialists were becoming a rather common sight in the skies over Europe and audiences willing to pay to watch them fly were dwindling with each performance.

The small Frenchman did manage to support himself and his flotilla of balloons for the next eight years, until tragedy struck in 1808. While on a flight over Paris, Blanchard suffered a heart attack and fell unconscious in his gondola. The balloon landed roughly on its own and amazingly, he was uninjured in the

fall. But his health declined rapidly after the attack and, on March 7, 1809, he died in Paris.

The place where Jean-Pierre Blanchard landed near Bib Timber Creek in Deptford Township is marked by a bronze plaque. It proclaims that his epic aerial voyage in 1793 brought the age of flight to America and the Garden State.

1818
First Parachute Jump
Louis-Charles Guille

Twenty-six years after Blanchard's maiden flight, another Frenchman, Louis-Charles Guille, made ballooning history in New Jersey. On Nov. 20, 1819, his balloon lifted off from Jersey City, rose to an altitude of about 500 feet, then he cut the cord that linked his basket to the balloon. He descended by parachute as an astounded crowd cheered. Guille is credited with the first parachute jump in the western world.

1830
First American Aeronaut
Charles Ferson Durant

Inducted Aviation Hall of Fame of New Jersey, 1981

Although they had been dramatically introduced to air travel in 1793, Americans did not immediately rush to conquer the skies. Perhaps they were too busy trying to tame the land they had fought so hard to win, or were too preoccupied with resolving their differences with Great Britain to dedicate valuable time to what was considered an expensive, dangerous and useless novelty.

But, on September 9, 1830, an excited crowd, estimated at more than 20,000 people, swarmed in and around the southern tip of Manhattan island at Castle Garden, now know as Battery Park. They had been arriving since before noon to witness an amazing feat. Charles Ferson Durant, a 25-year-old Jersey City resident, had announced that he would become the first native American to fly.

The spectators who were fortunate enough to find a spot inside the Castle Garden walls (they paid 50 cents each, half-price for children) spent the afternoon watching Durant inflate his five-story balloon with hydrogen gas and load the wicker gondola with instruments, supplies and several carrier pigeons. The birds were tó be used to carry messages back to

Castle Garden concerning the progress of his flight. As a military band played rousing marches and cannons were fired to signal the launch hour, Durant climbed into the wicker basket, just a few minutes before 5 p.m.

The *New York American* reported: *When Mr. Durant took his station in the car, he was carried round the Garden, so that the numerous spectators might have a full view of him and his arrangements. The Aeronaut showed perfect composure, and distributed to those around copies of a poetical address, written for the occasion.* "About half past 5 o'clock, three guns were fired; immediately thereafter, the cords were cut, it [the balloon] cleared the Garden, till it descended within 30 feet of the river and we entertained for a moment strong fears, that the car would touch the water, but with much presence of mind Mr. Durant threw out a considerable part of his ballast, when he again ascended majestically the Aeronaut waved his flags, then with hat in hand, he bowed to the large concourse of spectators in the Garden, as if in token farewell. The multitude loudly cheered the intrepid voyager.

Some of the crowd stayed in Castle Garden until midnight awaiting word from Durant but no carrier pigeon arrived. It wasn't until Sept. 11, two days after his ascent, that word was received: Durant had landed safely near South Amboy, NJ, about 30 miles from Manhattan. He had released the carrier pigeons on schedule but the normally reliable birds never returned to their roost. So, for more than 24 hours, there was fear that Durant had perhaps disappeared over the Atlantic Ocean. The flight had lasted approximately one hour and 40 minutes and no harm had come to either the aeronaut or his balloon. Durant, with balloon in tow, returned to New York City late on Sept. 11 aboard the steamboat "Thistle."

It is not known at just what age Durant's passion for flying began to develop. It is known that in 1828, he went to Paris, then the ballooning capital of the world, to study under the famous French aeronaut Professor Eugene Robertson. All early balloonists were accorded the title "professor" because ballooning was considered a science. Durant remained in Paris for two years studying aeronautics and flying with Robertson.

The January, 1918, edition of *Air Travel Magazine* described a particularly adventurous flight Durant and Robertson made on Aug. 3, 1829:

He [Durant] made several ascensions with Monsieur Robertson, and on one of them had an opportunity to display his nerve and daring. At 2,000 feet, something went wrong near the top of the silk bag and the balloon began to leak. For a moment, the two men looked at each other in stern silence. The American whipped out his jackknife, placed it with blade open between his

THE FIRST AMERICAN TO FLY A BALLOON—1830

Charles Durant

teeth and climbed the ropes to which the basket was suspended.

Up and up he climbed to the side of the swaying balloon. No circus athlete could have displayed a more marvelous performance. Slowly, he reached the top of the drifting gas bag and located the seat of trouble and quickly made the necessary repairs, descending to find Robertson pale as a ghost, but with no end of praise for his fearless pupil.

A Natural Showman

Although Durant claimed he had become a balloonist for the sake of science and had, in fact, detailed his discoveries of air currents and other atmospheric phenomena in articles that were widely published in newspapers and scientific journals, he also seemed to have a natural flair for showmanship. Prior to each of his flights, he would compose a poem — some were as long as six verses — and then drop them to his adoring fans as the balloon lifted from earth.

The heavenly subjects on which he dwelled in the following poem written for his 1830 trip from Manhattan to South Amboy must have seemed mystical to the simple people who watched in awe and cheered his every move.

The Aeronaut's Address
To the inhabitants of the lower world, assembled at
CASTLE GARDEN

To witness the Ascension of a Balloon Good bye, to
you—people of earth,

> *I am soaring to regions above you:*
> *But much that I know of your worth,*
> *Will ever induce me to love you.*
> *Perhaps I may touch at the moon,*
> *To give your respects, as I pass, Sirs,*
> *And learn if the sphere are in tune,*
> *Or if they are lighted with gas, Sirs.*
> *I will measure those mystical things*
> *That encircle the spherule of Saturne,*
> *With Jupiter's belts and his rings*
> *And draw out a chart from a pattern,*
> *Then take my departure for Mars*
> *Perhaps I'll look in upon Venus,*
> *Than mount to the galaxy stars,*
> *And leave all the planets between us.*

Construction of balloons was an expensive proposition and Durant needed whatever funds he could extract from the fascinated public to finance his scientific projects. The balloon he constructed for his third flight in August of 1831 was described in the January 1918 issue *Air Travel* as the largest ever built in America. It stood 47 feet tall and had a diameter of 28 feet. Six-hundred yards of "China Levantine silk" were pieced together by 37 seams. The balloon's lifting power was between 500 and 600 pounds. The silk was coated with "a varnish of turpentine, linseed oil and gum elastic."

Although Durant's first flight was history-making, his sixth flight on June 14, 1833 from Castle Garden was his greatest success. It was estimated that more than 100,000 people witnessed the ascension. The entire park and surrounding wharfs, piers and houses were swarming with eager onlookers. The Upper Bay was covered with sailing vessels of every description. They were drawn to the Garden not only by the peerless aeronaut, but by the promise that President Andrew Jackson and the celebrated Indian Chief Black Hawk would be among the spectators.

At 5 p.m. the President arrived, briefly acknowledged the cheers of the crowd, and then left before Durant's ascent. Black Hawk and his Indian entourage had sailed from Philadelphia to the tip of Manhattan on a steamboat. They stayed aboard the boat, anchored a few yards from the shore, where they could view the flight and be clearly seen by the spectators.

Later in a dictated autobiography entitled *Life of Ma-Ka-Tai- Me-She-Kia-Kiak* or *Black Hawk*, the chief commented on his travel experiences:

"We had seen many wonderful sights on our way—large villages , the great national road over the mountains, the railroads, steam carriages, ships, steam boats and many other things; but we were now about to witness a sight more surprising than any of these.

"We were told that a man was going up into the air in a balloon! We watched with anxiety to see if it could be true; and to our utter astonishment, saw him ascend in the air until our eyes could no longer perceive him."

Although Black Hawk doesn't mention it in his text, a New York City newspaper reported that the Chief asked if Durant might pay a visit to the Great Spirit while aloft.

Between 1830 and 1834, Durant made 12 balloon ascensions; six from Castle Garden, one in Albany, two in Baltimore and three in Boston. He never had a serious accident, although on his last flight in Boston on Sept. 13, 1834, he was carried out to sea on one air current and back to shore on another, an event which resulted in an unscheduled splashdown in Boston Harbor. He was rescued by a passing boat.

Durant gave up flying in 1834, the year of his marriage. One must assume that Mrs. Durant did not look favorably on aviation. Three years later, the American Institute presented him with a medal for his invention of a portable barometer, the first of its kind that could be taken aloft.

He was a man of tremendous vision and had the capability to grasp matters that took others years to master. He became a well-known printer-lithographer, developed the first silk produced in the United States and made an in-depth study of seaweed culled from New York Harbor.

On March 2, 1873, halfway through his 68th year, Charles Durant died in his home at 103 Hudson Street, Jersey City, where he had resided for 39 years. Located in a prestigious section of Jersey City known as North Point, the building had historical significance. It was called the "White House" and had been owned by Colonel Richard Varick, a former mayor of New York. Four years before Durant bought the property, Aaron Burr, a Newark, NJ native and U.S. Vice President under Thomas Jefferson, had boarded there while writing his memoirs. The White House was demolished in 1899.

During the few short years Durant thrilled Americans with his aeronautic exploits, he insisted that neither spherical nor dirigible balloons would ever be made practical for flying through the Earth's atmosphere. What was necessary, he said, was to invent a device that could be steered.

He missed seeing that device flown by just 30 years.

1835
Father of
American Ballooning
John Wise

The year after Charles Durant gave up flying for matrimony, John Wise, a 27-year-old piano maker from Lancaster, PA, made his first public ascension in a small, home-made hydrogen balloon. Like Jean-Pierre Blanchard, Wise took to the air from Philadelphia. He floated about for an hour and 15 minutes before landing easily in a Haddonfield, NJ, some nine miles from his starting point.

That was the beginning of a ballooning career that spanned more than 40 years and some 446 free balloon flights. Wise's many aeronautical experiments and later attempts to fly the Atlantic Ocean rightfully earned him the title of the "Father of American Ballooning."

By the mid-1800s most of the prominent aeronauts in Europe and America had come to the conclusion that a wind current blows constantly from west to east at an elevation of 12,000 feet. The revelation spurred many balloonists to plan for a flight across the Atlantic Ocean.

But, as with any revolutionary project, finding a financier willing to invest money in another man's dream was a major stumbling block.

In 1859, at age 51, Wise convinced a Vermont business man, O. A. Gager, to underwrite his carefully planned Atlantic flight. Wise designed and produced a 60-foot-high balloon with a diameter of 50 feet that was christened *Atlantic*. Wise, Gager and aeronaut John LaMountain, who built the balloon, took the sphere to St. Louis and with George Hyde, a reporter with the *St. Louis Republican*, Flew it eastward 809 miles in 19-plus hours to a safe landing in the northern New York State village of Henderson.

Although high winds and drenching rain had forced Wise and his companions to shorten their flight, they did prove that it was possible to fly on the jetstream blowing from the west across the treacherous North Atlantic. They had also established a flight distance record that wasn't surpassed until the end of the 19th century.

The advent of the Civil War changed Wise's plans to attempt to fly the Atlantic. He did again become involved in a transatlantic attempt with Washington Harrison Donaldson, a circus stunt man, but withdrew from the project because of a carnival atmosphere that Donaldson and their backers, the *New York Daily Graphic,* created each time the balloon was exhibited. The dramatics were more than the conservative Wise could take. He decided to withdraw before his well-earned reputation was damaged by the showman.

Angered by Wise's refusal to anticipate further, an editorial in the newspaper stated: "Mr. Wise's course from the outset was marked by incapacity, cowardice, and excessive demands for money."

The debonair, mustached Donaldson, who once walked across Niagara Falls on a tightwire, continued with the project. In early October 1873, he and two companions headed out over the Atlantic in the Wise balloon. After six hours in the air, they crash-landed in New Canaan, CT, just 60 miles from where they had begun.

Later that same month, Donaldson flew a balloon from Newark over New York Bay and on to Brooklyn, NY. The balloon's descent was described in the *Illustrated Daily Graphic* as "quite exciting and dangerous," which was a gross understatement. The huge free-flying air bag dragged the aeronaut in his small wicker gondola on a jouncing journey across Brooklyn farmlands for half an hour before being smashed against a heavy post and rail fence. Donaldson climbed from the basket suffering just a few minor cuts and bruises.

1846
Military Interest

The Smithsonian Institution was established in 1846, and a New Jersey professor of physics at Princeton University, Joseph Henry, became its first secretary. At the outbreak of the Civil War, President Lincoln appointed Henry as the chairman of a committee that was to make commendations for using balloons as military aerial observation stations.

1855
First Woman to Fly
Miss Lucretia Bradley

Little is known of Miss Lucretia Bradley who became the first American woman to fly alone in a gas filled balloon from Easton, PA to Still Valley, NJ (now a section of Phillipsburg).

In his book, *Through the Air*, published in Philadelphia in 1873, aeronaut John Wise told of meeting Lucretia Bradley in 1854, presumably in Philadelphia:

In the fall of 1854, I sold an old balloon, considerably worn to Miss Lucretia Bradley for one hundred dollars and cautioned her at the same time concerning its condition and the necessity for handling it carefully. To all of which she replied, 'If it was strong enough for you, it is strong enough for me.' In January of 1855 she made an ascension with it from the town of Easton, Pennsylvania.

Dr. Charles A. Waltman, a historian from Easton, tells us that Bradley was in his city in the fall of 1854 giving lectures on the subject of Phrenology. Her attempt to fly her balloon from Easton is verified by the lead paragraph of an article that appeared in the Feb. 1, 1855 edition of the *Easton Argus*.

"Balloon Ascension by a Lady—Frightful Accident—Miraculous Escape of the Lady."

Miss Lucretia Bradley, whose failure in October last, to make an ascension from our Borough, was announced in the Argus—*adding our opinion at the time that it was not from any cause within control of the lady, though the public were disposed to think differently—made another attempt on the Thursday last, (Jan. 24, 1855) with very different success.*

The article then went on to recount how Miss Bradley ascended in her balloon more than two miles (certainly an estimate) and that "its journey through the

Lucretia Bradley

mid-air, was really sublime, and filled every heart with admiration."

As the balloon drifted toward the southeast, it suddenly exploded and the *Argus* reporter wrote: "The witnesses of this frightful catastrophe simultaneously felt a thrill of horror impossible to describe. It was apparent to every beholder that the balloon was torn to shreds, and no longer under the control of the voyager."

That Lucretia Bradley survived that flight is a miracle, but survive she did, landing safely on the opposite side of the Delaware in Still Valley, four miles from where she had ascended.

When she returned triumphantly to Easton, the citizens paraded her through the streets in a carriage drawn by two prancing horses. The *Argus* states, "There was not a single person in our whole community whose heart was not relieved of a heavy depression and rejoiced as for their own safety."

Bradley's personal account of her flight appeared in three Easton area papers: *The Argus, The Northampton Farmer* and a German publication, *Der Unabhangige Demokrat.*

I rose with perfect calmness and great velocity to a height of over two miles, my whole feelings being those of indescribable tranquility and gratified delight.

There was no perceptible breeze until I reached the highest point of my voyage, directly over a bend of the Delaware, when four heavy currents struck my balloon on all sides with equal force. Finding my balloon full, I opened the valve three times in succession, and while letting off gas as fast as I could (the balloon at the same time rapidly emptying itself from the mouth), a very strong undercurrent forcing up into the mouth of the balloon caused a roaring like the ocean in a heavy storm, followed by a noise like the discharge of a cannon, and sudden fall of about a hundred feet.

Had there not been witnesses to her misadventure, Lucretia Bradley's account of her flight would have been thought a fabrication.

She believed that Divine Providence guided her safely to the clover field and the horrified witnesses could not dispute her belief. The *Argus* stated: "Considering all the circumstance of the case, we regard this balloon ascension as the most surprising event of the kind in the history of aeronautics."

And who would doubt that even today?

In further discussing Bradley's flight, John Wise stated emphatically, "The balloon was brittle, should have been oiled." He also reported that the daring lady purchased another balloon of Irish linen that was properly treated and made three other ascents. He does not say from where she ascended or where she landed. A search of the *Easton Argus* archives of the next three years turned up no reference to the lady in the vicinity.

Like Jean-Pierre Blanchard, the first aeronaut in the United States, Lucretia Bradley established her place in history by ascending from Pennsylvania and landing in New Jersey.

1860
Atlantic Challenger
Thaddeus S.C. Lowe

A gangling, young New Englander with the impressive name of Thaddeus S.C. Lowe also looked longingly across the seas. Lowe built a long balloon, called "The City of New York," in Hoboken, NJ to pursue his dream of transatlantic flight. It took the entire summer to complete the 125-foot-high gas bag. The balloon was exhibited in late fall at the burned-out site of the Crystal Garden, Fifth Avenue and 42nd Street in Manhattan.

The following year, Lowe decided to test the constant west-to-east air currents by flying from Cincinnati to Unionville, SC on April 19, 1861, seven days after the Civil War had begun. When Lowe landed, he was arrested as a spy. Only the intervention of a local merchant, who had flown with Lowe at one time, saved him from being shot as a Union operative.

When the aeronaut returned to the North, he enlisted in the Union Army and eventually became the commander of the Army's observation balloon corps. Lowe took German Count Ferdinand von Zeppelin, who toward the end of the century designed and flew the first large rigid airship, for his first balloon flight during those war years.

1863
America's First
Dirigible Balloon
Dr. Solomon Andrews

Inducted Aviation Hall of Fame of New Jersey, 1980

The tall, distinguished man stood ramrod straight in the 12-foot-by-16 inch wicker basket attached by a gaggle of wires to three cigar-shaped balloons floating above his head. The 80-by-13-foot balloons were fastened together in tandem. A slight June breeze ruffled his greying hair as he motioned to those around him to release the restraining ropes. Immediately, the three cylindrical, highly varnished cloth bags lifted the wicker basket into the air and Dr. Solomon

Andrews of Perth Amboy, NJ was airborne for the first time in his 57 years.

Andrews was a medical doctor and surgeon, a three-time mayor of Perth Amboy, collector of the Port of Perth Amboy (which at that time rivaled New York City) and a prolific inventor.

As a young man, he had conceived the idea that a balloon might be steered by natural forces. He dwelled on the problem for years and in 1849, at the age of 43, he constructed a building 100 feet long, 46 feet wide and 36 feet high in Perth Amboy. This was America's first hangar. He then built a cigar-shaped balloon with wooden supports in the lower half.

In the January, 1932 issue of *Popular Science Monthly*, Roger B. Whitman, the great, great-grandson of the doctor described his grandfather's theory of flight:

Andrews proposed to apply to a balloon the same principles that drive a sailboat. With a cross wind, the pressure on the sail is resisted by the pressure of the water against the opposite side of the hull, and the boat moves ahead when the hull is held at an angle that will bring these forces together to give forward motion.

Similarly, the downward pull of gravitation on a gliding airplane is resisted by the air pressure under the wings. These forces combine to give forward motion as the plane is set at the gliding angle; and descent, instead of being in a straight drop, is on a long slant.

Until Dr. Andrews' time, most balloons were spherical, and met equal air resistance when moving in any direction. His idea was to shape the balloon so that there would be less resistance to forward motion than to motion up or down. To do this he made a balloon in the form of a fat cigar or, as he called it, 'a flattened oblate spheroid.'

From this bulging cylindrical envelope with pointed ends, he suspended a basket containing a weight that could be moved from end to end. The shifting of this weight would tilt the entire machine and thus give the skipper control over the angle of flight. He calculated that an angle of from 10 to 15 degrees would result in satisfactory forward progress.

To fly, the bow would be tilted upward and ballast discharged to make the craft lighter than air. She would then rise; but with the lift opposed by the air pressure against the broad upper surface, her movement would be forward, at the angle established by the tilt. Once in motion, it could be steered with an ordinary rudder. Arrived at the desired height, the pilot would discharge gas to make the ship heavier than air, and with the angle reversed she would descend on a slant that would carry her farther ahead. In this manner, flight could continue until, through the discharge of gas and ballast, the ship would be brought to earth.

Dr. Solomon Andrews dirigible-balloon

Andrews built an airship 80 feet long, 20 feet wide and 10 feet deep. he inflated it in the summer of 1849, but never took it from the building, although he conducted a number of experiments that were helpful in later years.

The development of a flying model of his "Aereon," as he called the strange contraption, didn't begin until the outbreak of the Civil War in 1862. Although he was then in his 56th year, he volunteered as medical officer with the Union Forces. While serving in Virginia, he observed the efforts of the balloon corps to make observations over enemy positions in a tethered balloon. He realized that his controlled flight airship not only could fly straight up like the balloons, but could also fly over enemy positions and return with a great deal of vital information. He attempted to interest President Lincoln and Secretary of War Edwin M. Stanton in his venture, but his efforts were rebuffed at all turns.

Determined to prove the usefulness of the Aereon, Dr. Andrews left the service and immediately began constructing an improved airship at his own expense. He was certain that the war could be shortened by his "spy-in-the-sky."

There were problems on the first ascension in June of 1863, but by August the Aereon was flying exactly as the doctor had predicted.

Although he gave several successful demonstrations of controlled flight and his invention was highly praised by newsmen and other observers, including Professor Joseph Henry, Secretary of the Smithsonian Institution, the government would not or could not accept the idea that a man-made flying object could be controlled in flight.

Then, too, the war was grinding down to a sad conclusion and Congress was reluctant to allocate funds for new military contraptions.

In November of 1865, Dr. Andrews formed the Aerial Navigation Company which is considered the first incorporated organization in the world dedicated to commercial aviation. Andrews planned to fly passengers regularly from New York and Philadelphia in his Aereon dirigibles. The company's charter authorized "the transportation of passengers, merchandise, and other matter from place to place" and can be seen today in the offices of the County Clerk of New York County, New York City.

The first Aereon built by Dr. Solomon Andrews' Aerial Navigation Company was 80 feet long, 50 feet wide and 36 feet deep. It had a gas capacity of 60,000 cubic feet.

Late in May 1866, Andrews took the odd-shaped gas bag up from a lot in lower Manhattan, where it had been constructed. There were three passengers, all officers of the company. The *New York World* reported that it flew against the wind "with tremendous velocity."

The news story concluded optimistically: "Navigation of the air was a fixed fact. The problem of the centuries has been solved." The Aereon landed safely in Astoria, Long Island.

Just when it seemed the airship business would become successful, the company's capital was lost in a bank failure and Andrews could not find backers to bail it out.

On Oct. 24, 1872, Solomon Andrews — physician, civic leader, prolific inventor and the designer of the first dirigible-balloon flown in America — died at his Smith St. Perth Amboy home.

During his 66 years on earth, he had proven that it was possible to fly against the force of the wind. The year of his death was almost 37 years before the first successful powered dirigible was flown, and four years before Wilbur, the elder Wright brother, was born.

Shortly before he died, Dr. Andrews wrote that he had answered to his satisfaction a question that had nagged him for 40 years: "Who knoweth the way of an eagle in the air?"

1890

Kites Aloft

William A. Eddy

In the 1985 edition of the New Jersey Aviation Hall of Fame's annual publication, Bill Rhode of Wayne, NJ, aviation historian and author, told of the kite flying adventures of William A. Eddy:

The very first flying machine of any kind, manner or form was the ancient Chinese kite. These kites were invented before the birth of Christ and their science, performance and sport spread out across all of Asia. Variations of the Chinese kite were the Malay and Korean kites. Marco Polo brought the sport of kite flying back to Europe from China.

A tremendous interest in ancient kite flying, and in particular the Malay Kite, projected William A. Eddy of Bayonne, NJ, into a rather spectacular early aviation career.

Starting about 1880, Eddy flew his kite from a vacant lot at 30th Street and Avenue C in Bayonne. He further perfected the Malay kite into a triangular piece with a dihedral incorporated into a high cross-bow. Eddy's kite would rise high into the air out over the Kill Von Kull and could be seen directly above the shore of Staten Island, NY.

He raised one of his kites to a height of 2,400 feet with 3,000 feet of line. On another occasion, he made a train of five kites that rose to a height of 4,000 feet. In 1891,

Eddy's train of kites carried a record thermometer into the sky. He wrote a number of articles on his experiments for the respect publication, Scientific American Weekly.

In the summer of 1893, at the old amusement park on Bergen Point at the southern tip of Bayonne, Eddy built a model plane consisting of six stacked flat surfaces and attached it to his kite train by a ring and hook release. He launched it five times from his kite train. It succeeded in gliding about a quarter mile from a height of 1,000 feet. On another occasion, it glided about a half mile and landed in Newark Bay, 1,500 feet from shore.

The notoriety attending Eddy's kite flying caused the English gliding pioneer Percy Pilcher to visit him in 1883 at his Bayonne home and witness his feats.

In August, 1884, the Blue Hill Observatory near Boston, MA, induced Eddy to perform some experiments. Eddy's kite train, consisting of seven Eddy and two Hargreave-type kites, carried an aluminum thermograph weighing one and a quarter pounds to a height of 1,500 feet.

A few days later, Eddy's kite train carried aloft an automatic camera that photographed the city of Boston. It next carried a meteorgraph that weighed three lbs. to a record height of 7,441 feet.

In 1896, Eddy's kite train, consisting of kites six to nine feet wide, reached a height of 9,385 feet. The flight was carried on in conjunction with government observers at Blue Hill.

On still another occasion, an Eddy kite train stayed aloft for 12 hours and carried instruments that recorded a progression of temperature changes and barometric readings. Records also indicated that winds aloft were often in a different direction from those on the ground. Subsequently, an Eddy kite train at Blue Hill reached a record altitude of 12,000 feet, establishing an official world record.

A short time later, the U.S. government weather stations all over the country were equipped with large instrumented kites to record the weather.

On the evening of July 5, 1897, by pre-arrangement, Eddy lofted his kite train from the New Jersey Oval at Bergen Point while a Lieutenant Wise of the U.S. Army garrison on Governor's Island, NY, eight miles to the east, raised a similar kite train. The men signaled each other with red and green lanterns that were run up the kite train by pulley-lines. They communicated using Morse code via the lanterns till midnight. Eddy's part of the experiment was witnessed by a large summer picnic crowd at the park.

Back at the Blue Hill Observatory on July 19, 1900, more than three years before the flight of the Wright brothers, an Eddy kite train carrying a complement of instruments, and tethered by a leash of piano wire, rose to a height of 15,900 feet.

CHRONOLOGY OF OTHER AERONAUTICAL EVENTS AND ACHIEVEMENTS
1793 to 1899

1809
* Jean Pierre Blanchard dies in Paris of heart failure.

1838
* William Paulin, a professional aeronaut, ascended from the Eagle Race course in the Chambersburg section of Trenton, NJ to the pleasure of 3,000 spectators.

1866
* John Woonton of Boonton, NJ, obtained a patent for a steam-powered helicopter. History does not record that Woonton ever flew his novel contraption.

1872
* Dr. Solomon Andrews — physician, civic leader, inventor and aeronaut died in Perth Amboy.

1873
* Charles Durant, the first American to fly, died at age 68 in Jersey City.

1880
* America's greatest inventor, Thomas A. Edison of Menlo Park, NJ spent some time experimenting with a steam-powered helicopter. He mounted his huffing and puffing device to a scale to test its lifting ability, during a demonstration for James Gordon Bennett, publisher of The *New York Herald.*

1890
* M.L. MacDonald, a daredevil Scotsman, nicknamed "Daring Donald, " flew in a hot air balloon from El Dorado, an amusement resort atop the Hudson Palisades at Weehawken, NJ, and parachuted safely down.

1903
First Powered Flight
Wilbur and Orville Wright

In 1969 at a special ceremony in Atlantic City, Mayor William T. Somers presented the key to the city to a 73-year-old Bringantine woman in recognition of her long and warm relationship with Wilbur and Orville Wright.

Irene Tate Severn, operator of a clam wholesale business in Brigantine, was six years old when she witnessed the first powered flight over the dunes at Kitty Hawk, NC. At that time, Irene's father, Capt. Bill Tate, was a fisherman and her mother, Ettie, was the Kitty Hawk postmistress.

"It always reminded me of a skeleton, the ribs of a great big animal." — Irene Tate Severn.

In 1900, Mrs. Severn recalled, the Wright brothers were looking for a place to conduct glider experiments, and they wrote to the Kitty Hawk weather station among other places.

Capt. Tate delivered the letter himself. The Weather Bureau man read the request and said: "Some damn fools want to come down here and fly kites."

Tate fished the letter out of the trash can where the weatherman had tossed it and answered it. He told of the dunes, the steady high winds on the Carolina coast and gave enough news to interest the Wright brothers in going to Kitty Hawk.

"I was a scary sort of child," Mrs. Severn was quoted in the *Atlantic City Press*. "and when the Wright brothers had their queer looking equipment stored in our barn, I used to be afraid to go near it. It always reminded me of a skeleton, the ribs of a great big animal.

"Kitty Hawk, at that time, was practically inaccessible. Kill Devil Hill, where the fliers were making their experiments, was a high peak of sand—constantly moving. They say it has shifted nearly 300 yards. I don't think there's a hotel in Atlantic City as high as that hill.

"They explained to father what they were trying to do. Of course, everybody thought they were crazy. They stayed at our house the entire time they were there and kept everything under lock and key. Some Dayton people were interested in what was going on and a lot of others were trying to steal their ideas. Everything was guarded, watched constantly, and father

had to be the detective. Someone broke into the little cabin they had built down at the foot of Kill Devil Hill and once a man, dressed as a fisherman, was seen prowling around the barn.

"The Wright brothers were very quiet-spoken men. Orville prophesied that by the time I grew up, the air would be full of flying machines. Father laughed at him and said it would never be, but I've lived to see it and I've been up hundreds of times myself. I remember well how Wilbur Wright was desperately afraid of catching typhoid fever. We boiled all his drinking water for him. It's strange that he died of that very disease.

"When they got their first plane ready they found that the covers were too large for the wings. Mother made a new set for them out of cream colored sateen. They thought the silk cotton mixture would be best, it never occurred to them to use linen. When the covers were finished there was some of the material left over and mother made me a dress out of it. I remember it well because it had funny little ruffles over the sleeves.

"I think mother kept some scraps of the material, I'm sorry the dress wore out, but we didn't think it would ever be of any importance."

The brothers from Dayton became well known in the small North Carolina coast town of Kitty Hawk, having spent several seasons on the dunes testing their gliders and tinkering with their winged machine that was supposed to fly.

They returned to Kitty Hawk in the fall of 1903, determined to get their machine aloft with the aid of a gasoline engine and a whirling propeller. Most people believed propelled flight couldn't be accomplished. "If the good Lord wanted man to fly, he would have given him wings." was a common admonition.

On Dec. 17, the air machine was brought from its hangar and placed on a 60-foot rail track that was to become the world's first runway. With five men from the Kill Devil Lifesaving Station watching, the engine was started. It made a terrible racket.

Orville Wright positioned himself on his stomach in the center of the machine, released the restraining wire, and the bi-winged wood and sateen frame began to inch forward into a 27-mile wind. Two-thirds of the way along the track, the man-made bird lifted off the ground to a height of about 10 feet, stayed airborne for 12 seconds and then settled smoothly back on the sand. Man had flown without the aid of a balloon to lift him skyward.

When a white granite monument, commemorating man's first conquest of the sky in a fixed-wing vehicle, was erected at Kitty Hawk, a piece of the granite was sent to Mrs. Severn. It was a lasting souvenir of her childhood brush with history.

1906
Balloon Records Set
Alan Hawley

Alan Hawley

A Perth Amboy native and New York stock broker, Alan Hawley, defeated 15 competitors in a balloon race across the English Channel in 1906. He had ascended from Paris on Sept. 30 and landed in England the following day, 402 miles from the starting point.

A year later, the gentlemen aeronaut took Wilbur Wright aloft at St. Cloud, France for the pioneer inventor's first and only balloon flight. The two men remained in the air for more than three hours and finally landed in Orleans, France, 80 miles away.

Hawley again captured the headlines in September of 1910 when he won the first U.S. national championship balloon race that began at the Indianapolis Motor Speedway. Hawley was then 41 years of age, having been born in Perth Amboy on July 29, 1869.

On Oct. 17 in St. Louis, he and Major Augustus Post, a founder of the Aero Club of America, participated in the annual James Gordon Bennett International Balloon Race.

Flying the America II inflated with illuminating gas, the two men, standing in an open basket, soared upward from St. Louis and were carried on gale-force winds to the northeast. Forty-six hours later, they landed in a wilderness near Lake Tschotogama, 85 miles northeast of Chicoutimi, Quebec, Canada. They had flown a distance of 1,171.13 miles.

Despite an injury to Hawley's leg and lack of adequate food or survival equipment, the aeronauts tramped through the dense Canadian forest for nine days before they were discovered by fur trappers and taken back to civilization by canoe.

When Hawley and Post arrived in New York, they received a tumultuous reception, a forerunner of the Broadway parades that followed historic events in succeeding decades.

Hawley's free balloon flight established a distance record that stood for more than 40 years. His unprecedented achievement earned him the James Gordon Bennett Trophy.

In addition, the Perth Amboy native became the permanent holder of the Aero Club of America's Lahm Balloon Cup for setting balloon flight records in the United States on three occasions.

Alan Hawley's ballooning skill and his support of aviation advancement were the prime reasons he was elected president of the New York City-based Aero Club of America in 1913. A founder of that organization, he predicted at his installation that "certainly and speedily we are coming to the day when the aviator will cross the Atlantic in a heavier-than-air machine."

In 1912, he and his fellow club members, which included many leaders of industry, played an active role in the establishment of the Aerial Reserves of New York . The military reserve fliers were equipped with aircraft at the expense of the private sector.

As it became more apparent that the United States would become an active participant in World War I, Hawley and his fellow club members helped organize our nation's first air arm.

First Private Airfield
Robert J. Collier

Inducted Aviation Hall of Fame of New Jersey, 1984

Robert J. Collier, editor-publisher of *Collier's Weekly*, established the first private airfield with a hangar in New Jersey on his estate "Rest Hill" in Wickatunk (near Marlboro). The field was also used for polo matches by his friends.

Collier was among the first directors of the Wright Company, incorporated with a capital stock of $1 million on Nov. 22, 1909. Among the other prominent founding directors were: Russell A. Alger, August Belmont, Andrew Freedman, Cornelius Vanderbilt and P.W. Williamson. Collier, Alger and Vanderbilt ordered the first three airplanes from the company.

In April of 1911, Collier, then the president of the Aero club of America, loaned his Burgess-Wright flyer to the Army Flying Service to patrol the border along the Rio Grande River in Texas. Philip O. Parmelee, an Army pilot, made a record flight from Laredo, Texas to Eagle Pass in the Collier plane. When the maneuvers were concluded, the airplane, then christened *Laredo*. was shipped back to the Collier estate at Wickatunk. Oliver C. Simmons, a graduate of the Wright school in Dayton, who had also flown in Texas, became Collier's personal pilot.

In March of the following year, Simmons outfitted the biplane with floats. He and Collier then established a hydro-aeroplane base at Seidler's Beach (Keyport) on the Raritan Bay. The base was officially recognized by the Aero Club of America as the first of its kind in

America. A small hangar and workshop were constructed at that location

Walter Brookins, the Wright's chief pilot, visited the Collier estate in April 1912 and gave Robert Collier about eight hours of flying instructions over the Raritan Bay.

Just before the opening of the Aeronautic International Exposition at the Grand Central Palace in New York City (May 9-18, 1912), the Aero Club decided to extend an invitation to Rear Admiral Hugo Osterhaus, in the hopes of interesting the Navy in aeronautics. With pilot Brookins, Collier flew the Laredo from Seidlers' beach 35 miles north to a landing beside the U.S.S. Washington anchored in the Hudson River and personally delivered the invitation to the Admiral. That stunt was another "first."

Grover Loening, who spent a lifetime developing flying boats, told how he first met Collier in his book *Our Wings Grow Faster* published by Doubleday, Doran & Co.

As a young engineer, he had designed and built his first flying boat and attempted to fly it off Newark Bay in Bayonne. A split propeller ruined the test. He then took the repaired "aeroboat" to Collier's hangar at Seidler's Beach and flew it in the late summer of 1912. Here's how he remembered Collier.

The Collier personality is vividly recalled. The generous hospitality, the craze for playing tricks on everyone, the high-powered consumption of liquor, the polo parties, the hangovers—all pretty tall stuff for a young engineer to get mixed up in—but a liberal education and a rare opportunity to make friends. There is a tender spot in my heart for Robert J. Collier, and a profound respect for his forthright sincerity and courage and his brilliant energy, which magnetized everyone who came in contact with him.

Loaning built a large flying boat the following year, and again took it to Seidler Beach for a test flight. He described what happened:

It had been nursed, watched over, every part tested. Even the hull was launched and carefully tested for water tightness before it was finally finished. The balance was correct. The flotation was correct. So I gingerly started out one afternoon on the first hop. The plane flew after several long take-offs, but the lateral control system, which involved a warping of the wings, was very hard to move, and I did not dare turn it. So back to the beach to see what could be done to develop easier warping. All in all, I was elated at the results and confident we could lick the bugs in it.

Then a big mistake was made. A thunderstorm was rapidly coming up, and we would not have time to trundle the plane up the beach on the crude rollers we were using, and yet I knew that if it was left at the water's edge the seas would pound the craft to pieces.

So we decided to anchor it out with what looked like a plenty big enough anchor.

The storm broke—just an ordinary afternoon thundershower—but the wind gusts just took the poor little plane, with a wing area giving loading of only four pounds per square foot, and lifted it bodily out of the water and smashed it in again, first on one side, then on the other; and there was I, standing helpless on the shore, forced to witness what to me was a terrible calamity and actually hearing the crunching of my dream plane echoed in a sickly sinking of my heart. I admit I cried.

Some of the onlookers claimed the plane had been struck by lightning. I doubt it. But, a hopeless wreck it was, finally washed up on the beach and lay at my feet, a shapeless mess.

Never again did I return to Seidler's Beach. It still to this day is to me a tragic graveyard.

It's ironic that in 1921, Grover C. Leoning was the winner of the Collier Trophy for his "design, development and demonstration of the Loening Flying Yacht."

In March 1913, before water was first released into the Panama Canal, Robert Collier sent his Wright-Burgess land plane down to Panama by boat, along with photographer James H Hare, and pilots Al Welch and Oliver Simmons. Hare had boasted to Collier that they would take off from the beach on the Atlantic Ocean and photograph "both oceans at once." But Al Welch had surveyed some of the terrain on which they might have to set down on the 90-mile flight and could find no obvious clear fields.

On the way to the hotel from one of these pedestrian surveys, they passed the local telegraph office where unclaimed telegrams were posted. There was one for Hare. It read: "Don't do it if it's dangerous," signed, Collier.

Then the following day came a similar wire that convinced Welch that the venture was too hazardous, so the airplane was shipped back to New Jersey.

Robert Collier (left), with pilot Oliver Simmons.

Robert J. Collier died on Nov. 19, 1918 at the age of 42 following World War I service in Europe. He had energetically promoted aviation throughout his lifetime. The first private airfield in the Garden State still remains on his hill-top estate in Wickatunk where he is buried beside his father and mother. The Collier estate is now occupied by the Collier School for the Care and Training of Girls, conducted by the Sisters of the Good Shepherd.

In 1922, the Aero Club of America trophy established by Collier was renamed in the donor's honor by the National Aeronautic Association, the predecessor organization to the Aero Club of America. The name did not become official until 1944.

1909
First Soldier to Fly
Lt. Frederic E. Humphrey

A New Jerseyan was the first of three army aviators taught to fly a Wright Flyer. Lt. Frederic E. Humphrey, a native of Summit, NJ, Lt. Benjamin D. Foulois and Lt. Frank Lahm were detailed by the Army Signal Corps to study aviation at College Park. There they received flying instruction from Wilbur Wright aboard the Army's Wright plane.

In October of 1909, Humphrey made three solo flights of three minutes each. Historians claim he was the second military man in the world to fly. A Capt. F. Ferber of the French Army had flown an aeroplane of his own design on July 25, 1908 at Issy-les-Moulinous, the park of Paris.

Humphrey, a 1906 graduate of the U.S. Military Academy at West Point, was 26 years old when he made his epic flight.

Following a long, distinguished career in the Army Air Corps, General Benjamin Foulois retired to Ventnor, NJ.

First New Jersey-built Aeroplane
Frank, Joe and James Boland

Inducted Aviation Hall of Fame of New Jersey, 1980

"Frank didn't care about anything but flying. He was a great pilot," said James Boland in describing his older brother in a feature article that appeared in the Nov. 6, 1965 issue of the *Elizabeth Journal*. James also remembered his other brother, Joseph, as something of a mechanical wizard who built the engines for Frank's "flivver airplanes."

Frank and Joe Boland built and flew the first fixed-wing aircraft in New Jersey on the large Correja estate in Iselin in November 1909. Frank flew the flimsy craft; Joe was the co-pilot.

There was another flight demonstration in February of 1910 on the Correja estate. This time photographers and members of the New Jersey Aeronautics Society were present to observe. The account of the activities that day appeared in the *Sunday Call*, Feb. 13, 1910.

When the visitors reached the experimental grounds, they found the aeroplane housed in a portable iron shed. It had been sealed up for the winter months and it required a good hour's work to loosen the frozen bars and gain access to the machine.

Resembling in some respects the planes of the Wrights, yet on account of its wheels and absence of rear rudder more like the Curtiss machine, the big white-leaved flier was indeed a strange looking sight to the uninitiated. Wheeled from its shed, one found himself looking upon a graceful aircraft which upon examination proved to be more stable and stronger than it appeared at a distance.

The biplane measured 44 feet from tip-to-tip and the plane's wings were six feet in width. The front elevation planes were greatly similar to those of the Wright machines, being controlled by a tiller leading to the pilot's seat.

In the meantime, Frank Boland had pulled down his furlined cap, for the air was chilly, and had taken his seat before the tiller, while his brother [Joe] had climbed into the seat above him, grasping both tiller ropes.

At last the motor gave three or four preliminary spurts and started off with the noise of a rapid-fire gun. The propeller churned the air with such force that it seemed as though those holding the machine would be dragged from earth. suddenly Frank Boland raised his hand and the assistants let go of the plane.

Immediately the aeroplane picked up speed, heading directly toward a clump of trees. Just when it seemed as though the flight would end in destruction, before the craft had ever left the ground, Joe Boland pulled up the ropes leading to the warped fins, and in less time than it takes to tell, the flying machine swerved away from the dangerous trees and a minute later, as Frank Boland turned the elevating planes upward, it soared in the air, gracefully rising to the height of about 15 feet and maintaining this altitude until it reached a rather steep hill, where it came to the ground, alighting easily.

On the return flight, Clarence E. Fisher, a leading spirit of the Aeronautics Society, took Joe Boland's

L to R, Joe Boland, Clarence Fisher, Frank Boland

seat above Frank. Twenty-five years later Fisher described the flight:

"I don't remember a great many details of the day, but I do recall how sensitive the tiller controls were. If you barely touched them the ship would respond.

"Of course that flight was a tremendous thrill. The passenger seat was rather high off the ground, and as soon as the ship took off, we may have been only 15 feet up but it seemed like a hundred."

Fisher never did learn to fly. Like James Boland, he was to become a Cadillac dealer.

The Boland brothers had opened a bicycle shop on Grand Street in their home town of Rahway in 1902. They had been tinkering with the design of a fixed-wing airplane during the same period that the Wright brothers were developing their fliers. The Bolands built several planes before getting one to successfully climb into the air.

James Boland's Remembrances

"On the first flight, Frank flew it pretty high because he landed in a big tree." James Boland related. "He didn't know how (to fly) that first time. He just drove it like a car."

James Boland didn't fly, but he did finance his brother's aerial adventures.

"I was the youngest, so my brothers bossed me," he said. "I financed them. We almost went bankrupt a couple of times. Frank and Joe didn't care about money."

James Boland became an automobile dealer in 1904, one of the first in the Union County. He sold Cadillacs on Westfield Avenue in Rahway for more than 50 years until he retired in 1955.

In late 1908, the three brothers founded the Boland Airplane and Motor Company in Newark, near the mouth of the Passaic River.

The Boland Tailless biplane was indeed a unique craft. The editors of *Harper's Aircraft Book* of 1912 were lavish in their praise of the strange flying machine:

When first flown by its inventor, the machine absolutely amazed all beholders, for it performed evolutions and flew in a manner apparently contrary to all laws of aviation, and its intrepid owner drove the odd creation with the same facility and ease with which he would handle an automobile. The machine is so unusual and so distinct from all others that a detailed description and plans are of value to all interested in aeroplanes.

The article went on to describe the size, shape and aerodynamics of the biplane and the Boland "V" engine that generated 60 horsepower.

In November of 1911, Wilbur Wright visited the Boland plant to determine whether the unusual means of controlled flight designed by Frank and Joe Boland infringed on any of the Wright Brothers' patents. It was reported that Wilbur found no infringements and had praise for the Boland tailless biplane. He was quoted as saying:

"The turns in flight by this aircraft are the smallest in radius that I have seen."

That praise was further supported by an April 26, 1913 article in the *Aero and Hydro Magazine*. In a two-page story dedicated to the Boland design, the magazine stated "...distinctive in its method of aerial control and in the entire absence of a tail."

During the three-year period of 1910-1912, the Boland Company built seven different airplane models. Six flew; one was solely a show piece. All the models featured the Boland tailless design and were powered by 60, 70 and 100 hp eight cylinder "v" type engines designed by Joe Boland. The Boland Tailless Flying Boats were priced at $5,000, F.O.B. Newark, fully equipped and could carry two passengers.

In 1911, Frank Boland, looking for a financial backer, formed a partnership with Ella Uppercu, wife of Inglis Uppercu, a leading Cadillac dealer, which gave them equal rights to all of Frank's airplanes and designs but not Joe's engines.

Frank Boland and his tailless biplane.

Frank Boland's adventures continued to attract media coverage during this busy period. Descriptions of the aircraft were the subject of numerous articles in aircraft publications of the day and each new aeronautical achievement made headlines in the local media.

First in South America

A significant headline appeared in the *Elizabeth Journal* in late August, 1912. "Build Airship on Rush Order." And the subhead read: "Rahway Men to Ship Machine to South America."

The article said the Bolands were working night and day in the old Gordon shop on Seminary Avenue on two aircraft that were to be sold to a Central American Government, but "some secrecy attaches itself to the place where the machines are to be used, and it is possible that the aeroplanes are being purchased for war purposes by some private individual in the service of one of the Central American republics." The conjecture made good reading, but as far as can be ascertained, no war was planned. There was only a desire to bring the age of flight to the southern hemisphere.

By late September 1912, Frank Boland and Charles Hoeflich, a Rahway mechanic Frank had taught to fly, were in Caracas, Venezuela, making demonstration flights. A cablegram sent Oct. 6 told of enthusiastic crowds watching the two machines make "lofty ascensions," but no "fancy work."

A letter from a F.E. Sniffen to the Boland Company dated Sept. 30, 1912, described how Frank Boland was received by the South Americans:

Gentlemen:

Frank went up yesterday and made a very successful flight. Off the ground in 16 seconds, height 5,000 ft., *25 minutes in the air, going about 35 miles. Flight witnessed by all of Venezuela. The surrounding mountains were black with people, and the inhabitants went nearly wild.*

After the flight all hands were taken to the President's box and presented in due and ancient form. The President was delighted, as well as everyone else. There is nothing too good for the bunch now. After the finish we were wined and dined at the Venezuela Club, being guests of several millionaires etc.

Through the courtesies of the Governor and Commander-in-Chief of the Army, we had the grounds policed by three thousand soldiers, and one thousand police, they were all in brilliant uniforms, and the sight was indeed beautiful.

For the remainder of the year, Boland and Hoeflich continued their flying demonstrations in various Venezuela cities and towns. The Boland Tailless Biplane was not only the first to fly in South America, but also the first to fly over the towering Andes Mountains. Frank received a silver cup from the Venezuelan government for that feat.

The aviators had invitations to fly on the island of Trinidad and the Central American countries of Costa Rica and Panama. The Panama flight was to be in conjunction with the 1913 opening of the Panama Canal.

In January 1913, Boland and Hoeflich left Caracas with their aeroplanes aboard a cargo ship bound for Trinidad. They were accorded a hero's welcome in Port-au-Spain, the island's capital. It was a fateful trip for Frank Boland, as his brother James related years later.

"The governor of Trinidad wanted to see Frank fly, but was leaving before the scheduled demonstration flight. To oblige the governor, Frank decided to demonstrate before he left, although it made it necessary to fly in the dim evening light. The flimsy craft crashed after circling the field several times, and Frank was killed instantly. The date was Jan. 23, 1913.

CHRONOLOGY OF OTHER AERONAUTICAL EVENTS AND ACHIEVEMENTS
1900 TO 1909
1902

- Mr. S.D. Mott, of Passaic, NJ, designed and patented a helicopter that was featured in the revered *Scintific American Magazine*

1905

- "Early gas-filled baby blimps piloted by Frank Goodall and powered by early crude gasoline engines made featured flights out of Palisades Amusement Park for the edification of thousands of trolley borne pleasure seekers. They soared out over the river on calm days and returned to the park.

1911 Sales Brochure for Boland Engines

A WORD TO THE WISE.

OUR AERONAUTIC MOTOR is not built with the object in view of simply making as light a motor as possible, but of making one as light as possible that is able to meet all the requirements of designers of aerial craft of the present day.

A few years ago all that was required was an extremely light engine that would run for five minutes, but today one is needed which will develop its full power for as long a time as the Aviator cares to remain in the air and be able to do it every day if necessary.

That we have succeeded in building the latter kind of motor, we would be pleased to demonstrate to you if you care to visit our factory and see one of them at work.

Boland Brothers,

613 St. George Avenue,
28 Westfield Avenue,

Tels., 125-R
2-J

Rahway, N. J.

1910
Fixed-Wing Feats

The flying of fixed-wing aircraft suddenly caught the public's imagination in 1910. In the seven years that had passed since Orville Wright made the first powered flight at Kitty Hawk, motor-driven flying machines designed by other men throughout the world had progressed slowly. In Europe in 1906, Brazilian-born Alberto Santos-Dumont became the first man to fly in a winged craft propelled by an engine on the continent, and advancement of the art was equally slow in the United States. Glenn Curtiss, who eventually became the Wright's greatest competitor, did not fly his first aeroplane until 1908.

It is generally agreed that the slow development of fixed-wing flyers was caused by the reluctance of the Wright brothers to share their discoveries with others. Although they were the first to fly, they remained secretive concerning their aircraft designs and they patented all of their drawings so others could not infringe on them.

Each new Wright flyer built by the Dayton brothers exceeded the performance of previous models, but their wondrous machines were considered nothing more than novelties until other designers created their own versions of the motor-driven gliders.

It was the competition the Wright brothers tried to stymie that eventually thrust the aeroplane into the headlines and garnered the support of governments and industry.

While 1908 and 1909 were the years that aviation began to develop beyond the perimeters of the Wright brothers' invention, it was in 1910 that the daring young men in their flying machines became the international rage. On either side of the Atlantic, promoters were offering healthy cash prizes for various aeronautical accomplishments. The hucksters of the day had discovered that men and women willing to risk their necks in flimsy motorized gliders could attract huge crowds of thrill seekers eager to pay to see speed, distance and altitude records broken or to watch breathlessly as the dashing aviators performed loops and rolls in their wood, wire and cloth contraptions.

While more famous names in the infant aviation business like the Wrights, Curtiss and Bolands, were making headlines with their new advancements in aerodynamics, there were others throughout the United States and Europe attempting to develop the perfect flying machine. New Jersey had its share of dreamers in a year when aeronautical inventions were finally beginning to be noticed.

Jack Holden

An early New Jersey flying enthusiast was Jack Holden of Lyndhurst, NJ. Holden had designed and built his own motorized kite which he flew from the high ground down along Riverside Avenue toward the Passaic River.

In a book entitled *Lyndhurst Historical Essays*, published by the town of Lyndhurst, Holden's early flights were described:

Came the day for Holden to soar into the air for a bird's eye view of the town. He checked the motor and wings of his motored kite, placed the device atop of his chosen slope so as to add momentum and starting power. He donned his helmet, rechecked everything, started the motor 'put putting' with brakes off and down the hill he flew hoping that the wings would glide him upward to soar like a bird in the air. To his amazement everything seemed to go according to plan, except the wings, which did not support him aloft, and dunked him into the Passaic River, as though the flying machine were a submarine.

Years later, Roland G. Rosslip, now retired and living in Saddle Brook, NJ, recalled as a child seeing Holden flying in 1911 and 1912. "I would go to school using a short cut across the Post Farm, which also happened to be a flying field used by Jack Holden for his experimental flights. The Post farm extended from Stuyvesant Avenue to River Road (now Riverside Ave.). At the east end (of the farm) there was a hill which he used to gain momentum to take off, now known as Post Avenue.

"He would go down the hill and travel on flat ground for about 400 feet, and then try to take off. He would rise off the ground about 10 or 15 feet, and then crash to the ground. His friends would then surround the plane to see how much was still in one piece."

Charles Grieder

Charles Grieder of Paterson wanted to fly, too. Although Grieder had a basic design for an airplane, he didn't have the money or the mechanical skill to get the project off the ground. To resolve his problem, Grieder asked his brother John, who owned a silk mill on Straight St. in Paterson, to finance his aeronautical project, and Henry Lehr, also of Paterson, an expert silk loom mechanic, to help build the airplane. An agreement was struck and construction began in the attic of a house on Madison Avenue, located one block behind St. Anthony's Roman Catholic Church.

The Grieder brothers and Henry Lehr built the biplane in five sections—four wings and a tripod fuselage. Work proceeded on schedule until it was time to remove the various parts from the house. The wings fit through the attic windows, but the body of the plane was too large, so the innovative men removed a portion of the building in order to rescue their creation.

The plane was a pusher type, powered by a Curtiss engine, purchased in Buffalo by Lehr. It was first flown at Clay Street (now 21st. Ave.) and 26th St. in Paterson.

Charlie Grieder made numerous test flights in the biplane. After each time in the air, he would suggest changes in the basic design of the machine that Lehr would implement. By early 1913, Grieder had become a familiar figure flying over Paterson and Clifton. On many Sundays, he flew out of Olympic Park in Clifton prior to a semi-pro baseball game sponsored by the Dougherty Silk Mill, next to the park.

Then Grieder and Lehr went in search of a place with better flying conditions, and discovered that the wind currents above Bath, NY (near Corning), were particularly well suited for flying. Grieder spent hours soaring over the New York farmlands.

One day in June, the pusher engine began to sputter at 500 feet over the rural New York countryside and Grieder was forced to make an emergency landing in a wheat field. The owner of the farm, on which Grieder had torn up 100 feet of the crop, sent his automobile (a rare possession at that time) to pick up the aviator.

Grieder and the gentleman farmer soon became friends. The farmer was impressed with Grieder's interest in improving his flying machine, and agreed to finance the pilot's future experimental flights.

The airplane was moved to Bath. Grieder and Lehr commuted by train from Paterson. To have a few hours of flying and maintenance time, the Paterson boys had to catch a "milk run" train that passed through Paterson at 1 a.m., then make the long trek home in the early evening. The farmer's support of the flying project lasted for almost a year, but as the U.S. began supporting the British and French in their war effort, he turned his interest in that direction.

Grieder down in a wheat field near Bath, NY.

In the spring of 1914, while Grieder and Lehr were performing an engine check on the airplane, the pilot was hit in the legs by the whirling propeller. His legs were almost severed and local doctors wanted to amputate. Grieder refused to let them. Eventually, he found a surgeon in Philadelphia who repaired his damaged limbs, although the doctor wouldn't guarantee he would ever walk again. Through shear determination, Grieder did walk and attempted to enlist as a pilot early in World War I. He was not accepted as a flier but did give Army Air Service recruits ground school training.

During the entire period that the Grieders and Lehr were involved with flying, John Grieder never had an interest in becoming airborne. Henry Lehr only left the ground once, and that was an accident.

According to his son Henry Jr. of Ramsey, the senior Lehr's "flight" took place at Olympic Park during an engine test.

Lehr was perched on a wing while he revved the motor. Unknown to him, someone had removed the blocks from in front of the wheels and as the propeller spun faster, the plane began to roll. Almost immediately the tiny craft and its startled occupant were airborne. When the plane's altitude had reached two feet, Lehr slid down off the wing and dragged his feet along the grassy field while holding desperately to the flying machine.

A number of spectators realized what was happening, grabbed the plane's wings and pulled it back to earth, much to Henry Lehr's great relief. Only minor damage was done to the plane during the two-foot-high flight. Charles Grieder flew it considerably higher later that day.

Henry A. Hettinger

In South Jersey, Henry A. Hettinger, the owner of a successful business manufacturing gasoline engines of his own design in Bridgeton became an early flying enthusiast. According to Bill Chestnut of Bridgeton, who wrote an in-depth article on the career of Hettinger for the spring, 1989, edition of the *South Jersey Magazine*, Hettinger might have had a dual interest in the advancement of aviation.

"One has to wonder what the motivation was for Henry Hettinger to turn his interest to aviation." Chestnut wrote. "I can venture several guesses. First, I feel it was his truly inventive nature to get involved with a totally new technology. Second, he saw the possibility of a vast market for the airplane engine he was to invent, and thereby he would not have to be so dependent on the whims of the oyster business [he had invented a gasoline engine powered dredge winding machine for use aboard oyster schooners]. Third, the local newspapers, particularly the Bridgeton Pioneer, were filled with the exploits of early aviators and this fired his imagination."

Hettinger joined the newly formed Aero Club of Pennsylvania in 1910 and was one of its first members to build his own airplane. The flying machine was built under a tent near the Hettinger engine plant on Grove Street, Bridgeton. In June of that year, taxi tests were made on the west side of the Cohansey River in a meadow south of the former South Jersey Institute. While running the plane up and down the meadow the propeller hit a piece of driftwood and broke, bending the shaft at the same time. In an article that appeared in the *Pioneer* the planes engine was described:

The engine was especially designed and manufactured by Mr. Hettinger, and is believed to be of a character that will be in demand in aerial machines. It is not likely that any further tests will be made upon the meadow.

Hettinger's first flight took place at the Cumberland County Fairgrounds in southwest Bridgeton, and it was almost his last. Chestnut found the following description in the Sept. 20, 1910 edition of the *Bridgeton Evening News.*

Henry Hettinger, head of the Hettinger Engine Company, and a daring amateur aviator, made a dip of death Saturday afternoon which resulted in destruction of his aeroplane and he himself miraculously escaped severe injury or death.

The attempted flight had not been announced, but before the second heat of Class D at the Bridgeton Driving Association's [harness racing] track Saturday afternoon Mr. Hettinger approached the device and after looking at several details took his seat in the front of the plane.

The engine was started and the propeller passed through air with such rapidity that the seven-foot blade could not be seen. The wind which had been brisk from the northwest subsided. The daring aviator swung the lever and the plane shot forward. At the same time a gust of wind swept across the track. The plane had risen possibly 12 feet when caught in the wind. It was dipped as a boat on a tack and barely escaped touching the ground on its port side. The presence of mind of the aviator sent the plane again on its right course.

It had but straightened when the crash came which startled the crowd. Women screamed and men left their seats. All feared the aviator had met the fate of his machine.

A second seemed as minutes and Mr. Hettinger was underneath the pile of wreckage. It could not be seen whether he still held his position or not as the plane had struck on its port side which cut off all view.

Before assistance could reach the scene Hettinger crawled out and stood stunned from his experience

looking at the ruins. When rescuers reached him, it was found that he had received no injuries more than a severe shaking up.

A month later, Hettinger was flying again, this time without mishap. The *Evening News* said: "Never before has the local aviator shown such complete control of his power bird. The weather conditions were very favorable and it was an ideal day for an experiment of this nature."

Hettinger flew regularly for the remainder of that year and in 1911 added pontoons to his biplane and flew off the Cohansey River. For whatever reason, Hettinger then gave up flying the following year. In 1988, his daughter, Elizabeth Hettinger Garrison, then in her 80s, told Chestnut the plane was put in storage behind the factory. It was dismantled in the late teens.

Hettinger died of cancer in 1931 at age 56.

Harry Bruno

In Verona, NJ, on Nov. 25, 1910, Natalie Ebbets, 16, of Montclair raised a beribboned bottle of Sandeman's port and smashed it with some trepidation on a bicycle wheel attached to a strange contraption and said meekly, "I christen you the Brumah!"

The group of youngsters standing in a small half-circle around her cheered and congratulated each other. The flying ship, designed and built by Harry Bruno and Bernie Mahon, two 17-year-old Montclair residents for whom it was named, was now ready to fly.

The young aviation enthusiasts attached ropes to the monoplane and began hauling it onto the roof of a barn on which a wooden track had been built. The job took over an hour, and when the wood, wire and cloth plane was in place and tied securely to the chimney near the peak of the roof, the young inventors decided it was too late to fly that evening.

Bright and early the next day, the two were back at the barn with their friends. They tossed a coin to decide who would be the first to fly. Bernie Mahon won. He climbed nervously into the open cockpit and carefully tested the elevator lever and the rudder bar.

Once confident that all was well with his creation, he told Bruno to cut him free. The 14-foot glider rolled swiftly down the 30-foot track and jumped into the air. It climbed slightly and then glided smoothly toward the earth. As it neared the ground, Bernie pushed the controls forward and the tiny plane crashed to earth, shattering the left wing.

Mahon was catapulted from his seat and tossed roughly to the frozen earth. He suffered a sprained arm and a nasty gash above his left eye, but his injuries couldn't dampen his enthusiasm. He and Bruno congratulated each other and immediately made plans to rebuild the damaged Brumah.

The building and flying of the Brumah had not gone unnoticed in the press. The *Montclair Times* praised the inventiveness of the young men and the *New York Evening World* covered the event. People were so certain that the boys would succeed in flying that a justice of the peace in Cedar Grove erected a sign beside his house that read:

Notice:

All Aviators are Hereby Warned not to Fly Their Machines over This House Under Penalty of Imprisonment.

It took almost a month to repair the Brumah and when it was again airworthy, the owner of the barn fearing that on a second try someone would be killed, refused to let the boys use his roof as a ramp. The mid-December weather was cold and snowy and it seemed that the next flight would not take place until spring. Then someone remembered a sand pit out in the country between Caldwell and Pinebrook that had a steep 40-foot cliff and a leveled landing area below.

Harry suggested they replace the bicycle wheels with runners from a sled so that the Brumah could slide down the snow-covered hill like a toboggan. When the alterations were completed, the boys called their new ship the Brumah II and prepared for their second flight on Christmas night. They and their faithful friends poured buckets of water down the 60-foot slope. It froze instantly, forming a slick toboggan slide along the cliff's slanting edge.

On the morning of Dec. 26, Harry Bruno climbed into the cockpit, checked the controls and signaled his friends to release their hold on the Brumah. The frail glider sped down the icy runway directly into a strong head wind and within seconds, it was airborne.

Having learned from Mahon's mistakes, Bruno sat perfectly still, holding the controls in a stable position. The glider performed perfectly. It flew 265 yards and landed smoothly on the snow-covered floor of the sand pit. That flight was the beginning of Harry Bruno's aviation career that would span more than 50 years.

Two Flying Records Are Set

Glenn Curtiss and Charles Hamilton

With interest in aeronautical events hitting a fever pitch of excitement, the *New York Evening World*, a leading newspaper of the time, offered a prize of $10,000 to the first person to fly from Albany to New York City with a maximum of two stops for refueling. The prize was first tendered in 1909 as part of the Hudson-Fulton Celebration, and when no one took the challenge that year, the newspaper let it stand for a second year.

On a clear Sunday in April 1910, the prize was won by Glenn Curtiss. New Jerseyans, with a view of the river, watched in amazement as the man, who was to become a dominant force in aeronautical development, sped by their shoreline astride a giant wood and canvas bird that flew at an incredible speed of more than 50 miles per hour. Curtiss had flown the 137 miles in just 152 minutes.

In June, another member of the Glenn Curtiss flying team, Charles "Daredevil" Hamilton, a lanky, jug-eared pilot with flaming red hair, became the first man to fly from New York to Philadelphia and return in one day. The round-trip flight covered a distance of 149 miles.

It was on the return trip to New York that Hamilton found it necessary to set his Curtiss aeroplane down in a North Amboy, NJ, pasture to refuel before the final jump across New York's Lower and Upper Bay to a safe landing at Belmont Park. For his record-setting efforts, Hamilton also received a $10,000 prize that had been offered jointly by the *New York Times* and the *Philadelphia Ledger*.

It is interesting that Charles Durant, the first American aeronaut, also landed in the section of New Jersey, just south of Staten Island known collectively as the Amboys in 1830.

Early Air Meet Held

Aviation came early in the 20th century to Atlantic City because of its prominence as the leading summer resort in the northeast. Wealthy families from New Jersey, Pennsylvania, Delaware and New York would pack their large steamer trunks in late June and move into the magnificent hotels that lined the famous Boardwalk. They'd stay a month or even the entire summer for sun and fun. The social whirl was endless, although proper Victorian etiquette prevailed.

Each summer a new fad was introduced to titillate the young debutantes and their swains. The fad might have been as mundane as the latest bathing suit fashion or the arrival of the newest model of Mr. Ford's horseless carriage. In 1910, the talk of the Boardwalk was the flying machine called an "aeroplane."

Because the aristocratic clientele who spent their summers at the New Jersey resort were people who had the means to underwrite the development of new technologies, the pioneering inventors and airmen viewed the city as the perfect location for one of the earliest air meets in the United States. The Atlantic City Air Carnival began over the beachfront between Young's Old Pier and the Million Dollar Pier on July 2, 1910. Several aerial records were established during the 10-day event.

Walter Brookins, a Wright trained pilot, flying a Wright biplane, became the first aviator to fly to a height of one mile. In one hour, two minutes and 35 seconds, Brookins rose 6,175 feet above the white sand beach of the posh Garden State resort to win a $5,000 prize from the Atlantic City Aero Club.

Glenn Curtiss, fresh from his successful Albany to New York flight, set another world's record by flying 50 miles back and forth along the Atlantic shoreline in one hour and 14 minutes in full view of the fascinated beach crowds.

Curtiss also gave the first demonstration of aerial bombing. At an altitude of 100 feet, he flew his frail machine over the yacht of John K. Mehrer II and dropped oranges on the moving target. The bombing was so accurate that water was splashed on the squealing female passengers aboard the yacht. A witness, Brig. Gen. William A. Jones, later stated: "The trial shows absolutely that the day of the battleship for attack on foreign cities is nearing its end." Certainly a profound statement for that period of time.

Asbury Park Air Meet

A 10-day air meet was held at Asbury Park, in early August of the same year. On the first day of the meet Aug. 10, Walter Brookins was almost killed in a serious accident. Brookins later described what happened:

"I was scheduled to take the Wright ship up for the first flight on opening day. A crowd of 50,000 was there to see the show. They had stands on four sides of the field. There was about 50 press photographers on the field, all of whom insisted on standing in front of my ship to get a picture as I was taking off. I had to stop the motor three times to keep from running over them.

"Finally after warning them to keep the field clear when I landed, I managed to take off. I flew for about 20 minutes and then started down.

"Of course I had to land into the wind which was blowing diagonally across the field. This brought me in over one of the stands and the hospital tent. And then, right where I intended to land, were the 50 photographers. My motor was off so I couldn't fly over them. I did the only thing possible — nosed down from an elevation of 50 feet and tried to land in front of them.

"Well, all they had to do was raise the flap of the hospital tent and drag me in. I had a broken nose, a broken ankle and several teeth knocked out. And the ship was a complete wreck.

"As I said, that was the first day of the meet. They sent another ship by express from Dayton and on the sixth day they carried me out of the hospital, set me

Curtiss aeroplane on Atlantic City beach.

in the new ship and I flew every day for the rest of the meet."

Wilbur Wright himself attended the meet and watched some spectacular flying exhibitions by two of his top aviators, Archie Hoxsey and Ralph Johnstone.

It was at Asbury Park that wheels were first used on a Wright flyer. Up until that time, the Wright brothers had stubbornly refused to replace the skids on their airplanes with wheels. When the decision to use wheels was made, Frank Coffyn of the Wright exhibition team was the pilot.

"I remember that very well," Coffyn said, "because it just happened that when Orville made any changes in the plane, he always wanted me to test them in public flights. At Asbury Park they just put wheels on the skids. I made the first flight in public with the Wright plane with the wheels. At the same meet, Ralph Johnstone made his first flight with wheels on the skids. He didn't judge his landing speed well enough and cracked into a lot of automobiles. He broke the plane up considerably and smashed the headlights on the automobiles. We all laughed at him."

At the same meet parachutist Benny Prinz, jumping from a hot air balloon, was killed when his cotton parachute failed to open properly.

All types of airplanes, rigid balloons and free balloons took part in the show. They were competing for $20,000 in cash prizes. New Jersey Governor John Franklin Fort presided on Governor's Day, Aug. 12, and all during the long 10-day meet state and local dignitaries sat in the spectator stands that accommodated 10,000. To keep visitors off the field and to make them pay 50 cents to see the show, a 10-foot high canvas wall was erected around the entire field. They used one mile of canvas for the enclosure.

On Aug. 19, Ralph Johnstone and Arch Hoxsey made the first public night flight in Wright flyers on a moonlit night over Asbury Park and Interlaken, where the meet was actually held.

Hoxsey and Johnstone were dubbed the "Heavenly Twins" by newsmen of the day. They were the stars of the Wright Air Show team. They enjoyed chasing each other around the sky and their aerobatics quickly won the hearts of the public across the United States.

Their careers were meteoric, but like a meteor they faded quickly. By their mid-20s, they were both dead.

Less than three months after the Asbury Park meet, Johnstone crashed in Denver when the wingtips of his Wright flyer folded and the plane fell 800 feet into Overland Park.

On the last day of 1910, Hoxsey was killed in Los Angeles while attempting to better his altitude record of 11,474 feet, established five days earlier. Gusting winds drove his Flyer down from 7,000 feet.

The deaths of so many famous aviators in a two-year period promoted Robert Collier, then president of the Aero Club of America, to call for safer aircraft and less recklessness in the skies.

"An Issue on which the Aero Club of America should take a resolute stand is that which has cost America so many priceless lives during the past year." he stated. "Hoxsey, Johnstone, Moisant, Ely, St. Croix and others were too heavy a toll to pay for the morbid curiosity of a public which is often indifferent to scientific results, so long as it may be thrilled by sensational glides and dips and attempts for altitude. Every meeting sanctioned by this club, and every aviator holding its license, should be held strictly accountable for permitting such useless and reckless exhibitions." At the same time, Collier outlined his platform for the club, attempting to appeal to the entire community of aviators throughout the United States, many of whom didn't feel adequately presented by the Aero Club, controlled predominately by easterners.

The planks in his platform for 1912 were:

"To make this club the representative of American aviation in fact as well as in name. To make its interest truly national in character, so that it represents San Francisco as truly as it does New York, the west as adequately as it does the east. To recognize that our representation of America abroad carries with it certain responsibilities, among them the duty to listen with equal respect to every section of this country."

He then pointed out. "One of the most important duties of this organization should be to assist in building up a strong public opinion in favor of aeroplanes for the Army and Navy. The figures show that while we are second or third in naval strength, we are sixth or seventh in naval and military aviators. This is a poor showing in view of the fact that we have the mechanical genius, the men, the courage and the money to equip the finest naval and military aviation corps in the world. Both branches of the service have given this club generous cooperation in making our pilot license their standard. The least we can do is to help them by every means in our power to secure adequate equipment."

First Attempt
to Fly the Atlantic
Walter Wellman

A crowd of 75 people gathered at 5 a.m. on Saturday, Oct. 15, 1910 on a sandy beach in front of a large, odd-shaped building overlooking the inlet at Atlantic City. For more than two months, most of the people in the fashionable resort had eagerly awaited this day.

The group had come to witness and help launch, a 4,700-pound dirigible that was to be the first flying machine to attempt a flight across the Atlantic Ocean. The ambitious project had been widely discussed in Atlantic City since the spring of the year when Walter Wellman, a newsman/explorer, in cooperation with the Atlantic City Aero Club, first built the huge, $112,000 wooden hangar on the beach to house his dirigible *America*.

Wellman and his airship had captured headlines in 1909 with an aborted flight to the North Pole. His daring attempt to become the first to fly to the Pole had been sabotaged by a fierce Arctic storm that left the *America* in complete disrepair. While Wellman's attempt to locate the Pole was unsuccessful, Admiral Robert E. Peary culminated more than 20 years of arctic exploration when he reached the Top of the World by sledge on April 6, 1909.

The Peary discovery was not made public until the Admiral and his team again reached civilization in September of the same year.

With the discovery of the Pole by Peary, Wellman turned his attention to other challenges. An aerial Atlantic crossing seemed to be the perfect alternative.

The preparation for the Atlantic flight had taken all summer and many skeptics were saying that the newsman would never begin the flight and was using the attendant publicity as a means of attracting sponsors for other adventures. Wellman flatly denied the accusations, but all through August, September and early October, he seemed content to enjoy the luxury of his Hotel Chalfonte suite overlooking the bustling Boardwalk, while his crew, led by Melvin Vaniman, a

Walter Wellman

mechanic and early American balloonist, tinkered with various bits and pieces of the dirigible.

Weather conditions were blamed for the delays and one reporter editorialized: "All Mr. Wellman wants of the weather is a dead calm around the hangar and a brisk west wind blowing everywhere else. That's all he's been asking, and the dinged weather can't seem to get to it."

That Wellman was apprehensive concerning the flight was indicated by a statement he made during the seemingly endless waiting period: "The combination of a ton of inflammable hydrogen, nearly three tons of gasoline, sparking motors, electric lights and wireless, is not one to inspire perfect confidence."

In the meantime, the general public was invited to enter the hangar for a fee and to stare up at the canvas underbelly of the large, cigar-shaped airbag.

By the time the canvas tarpaulins that covered the seaward end of the balloon house were removed on Oct. 15, and the two-ton equilibrator, a 300-foot steel cable strung with gas cans that dangled like a great serpent below the *America*, was hoisted out into the water, hundreds of spectators were on hand to view the proceedings. The equilibrator was intended to keep the airship at a comparatively uniform elevation above the ocean and compensate for variations in the airship's buoyancy that would be affected by atmospheric conditions and changes in temperatures. Although the theory had merit, in practical application the equilibrator proved to be more of a hindrance than a help to the intrepid flyers.

Once the sandbag ballast was removed from the restraining ropes inside the beachfront hangar, and a 27-foot lifeboat was attached, it took 100 men to guide the airship across the beach and down to the water's edge. There, ropes were attached to the motor yacht *Olive* so it could tow the historic vessel out to the open sea. The yacht and airship disappeared into the mist at 8:05 a.m., cheered on by an enthusiastic audience that numbered several thousand. A short time later, the tow line was thrown loose, the primitive engines started, and the *America* had begun what was to become a record shattering flight.

There was a crew of six aboard. Wellman was the commander, assisted by Vaniman. The wireless operator was an Australian, Jack Irwin; the navigator, Murray Simon. Both men had extensive experience working aboard steamships, and Wellman considered

them highly qualified. Louis Loud and Fred Aubert rounded out the crew.

There was, however, one more passenger aboard the "America"—a cat named Kiddo that had been brought aboard by Simon. Vaniman didn't want the cat aboard so he ordered a wireless message sent to Leroy Chamberlin, Wellman's secretary and son-in-law, who was back at the hangar. The message stated: "Roy, come and get this goddam cat."

That, simple, but pointed message concerning a stray cat was the first wireless message ever received from an aircraft on the high seas.

The *America* and her crew flew over the churning Atlantic for almost three days, getting as far north as New Hampshire. The flight was bedeviled by one calamity after another — dense fog, gusting winds, an overheating engine, contracting and expanding hydrogen and the dragging equilibrator — all caused aggravation and concern for the *America's* crew.

By noon on Monday, Oct. 17, the winds had blown the airship to the southeast, and navigator Simon estimated that they were again off the coast of Atlantic City. After more than 60 hours of sleepless struggle to keep their inadequate engines running, Wellman decided that the venture should be aborted. But it wasn't until 5:07 a.m. on Tuesday that the Royal Mail Steamship company's *SS Trent* was spotted and signals were exchanged asking for help. The crew of the *America* crowded into the lifeboat that hung below the huge airbag. Vaniman pulled a long rope attached to a hydrogen escape valve and the dirigible gently descended toward the water. When they were only a few feet above the waves, Simon and Loud released clamps that bound the boat to the airship and the small craft splashed into the water. Within minutes, they were aboard the *Trent*.

Although Wellman and his valiant crew had not accomplished what they had set out to do, they did establish two records for manned flight in a powered aircraft. They flew for 71.5 hours and traveled 1,008 miles, eclipsing the previous records of 38 hours and nearly 1,000 miles set by Count Ferdinand Zeppelin of Germany in 1909. New Jersey had again played a leading role in the progress of aviation history.

Dirigible "America"

1911

New Jersey's First Aerodrome

Frederick Kuhnert

Inducted Aviation Hall of Fame of New Jersey, 1990

Fred Kuhnert

A successful florist in Hackensack, Fred Kuhnert was bitten by the "flying fever" that swept the nation in 1909. He began working on sketches of a passenger carrying airplane at his home at 73 Pink Street, Hackensack, and became so caught up in the excitement of flying that in 1911, he and a partner, Matthew Andronico, bought a 20-acre parcel of land near his home to be used as an airfield.

The field was enclosed with a nine-foot plank fence and christened, *Kuhnert's Aerodrome.* It was the first of its kind in New Jersey.

In those days professional baseball teams didn't play on Sundays, so Kuhnert hired well-known players or contracted with entire ball clubs to play exhibition games. Crowds as large as 2,000, traveling mostly on foot or bicycle, attended the games. When the game was over, the crowd anxiously awaited the additional entertainment Kuhnert had planned, normally a flying demonstration. If the wind was not right for flying, trick bicycle riders or other circus acts were performed.

Many of the great aviators of the day appeared at Kuhnert's Aerodrome. Frank Boland flew his tailless biplane over the marshlands of South Hackensack, as did the noted Frenchman Louis Bleriot. Stunt flier Charles Hoeflich and Ruth Bancroft Law, one of the first women aviators in the world, were also engaged by Kuhnert to perform.

Alfred Kuhnert, then 13 years old, remembered the excitement that his entrepreneur father generated each weekend from early May to September. Fred Kuhnert, who obviously enjoyed the spotlight, acted as his own announcer for the aerial demonstrations. Following a ball game, he would walk toward second base carrying a megaphone and then hold his handkerchief high over his head. If the material didn't flutter, he would raise the megaphone to his mouth and announce: "Ladies and gentlemen, we will have our flight this afternoon and you will be entertained." He would then name the pilot who would fly and assure his rapt audience, "You will be astounded at some of the things he's going to do in the air."

While Kuhnert ran his weekend extravaganzas, he and his family worked on his airplane in a tar paper barn next to his home. He envisioned a winged vehicle that would carry as many as 14 passengers, an ambitious undertaking considering that in 1911 no fixed-wing aircraft could carry more than three aloft.

Kuhnert built a frame with seats and perched it on bicycle wheels. The engine in the middle of the frame powered three propellers—one on each side and one in the rear. The wings were flat on the bottom and cylindrical on the top. The carefully bent wood ribs were covered with Irish linen and highly lacquered. Photographs of the Ferryboat seem to give it the quality of a ghostly apparition.

Although the aircraft had been ground-tested, it had never flown. Then one sunny Sunday afternoon before a capacity crowd, Kuhnert climbed aboard and opened the throttle. The delicate, big bird picked up speed but would not lift off the ground. Embarrassed, Kuhnert told his audience that he would make necessary changes in the airplane's structure and be ready to fly a few weeks later. But at that point Mother Nature shattered Kuhnert's dream.

Early one August morning, a violent tornado-like storm swept through Hackensack, blowing down trees and lesser buildings in its path. Alfred Kuhnert remembers Julius Hoffman, the watchman at the aerodrome, running to the Kuhnert house yelling: "Help! The field is gone. The field is gone. Everything is gone!"

"There was nothing left of the buildings," Alfred reported. "The airplanes had disintegrated, there were parts all over the field of the big ship. Everything was torn apart. It was all destroyed."

Fred Kuhnert never tried to rebuild his Aerodrome or his Ferryboat. Quite possibly the freak storm that had blown away his dream had also saved his life, for most people who saw the Ferryboat believed that if it had gotten off the ground, the results would have been more disastrous than the storm.

Ruth Law

First Coast-to-Coast Flight

Calbraith Perry Rodgers

Although Calbraith Perry Rodgers was not a Jersey native, his courageous flight from coast to coast in an early Wright flyer, set the stage for a similar flight by a New Jerseyan 75 years later in a more modern Wright flyer.

The miles of interwoven railroad tracks that line the Hudson River shoreline in Hudson County played a small but vital role in the dramatic race for a $50,000 prize offered by newspaper publisher, William Randolph Hearst, for the transcontinental flight in an elapsed time of 30 days.

In September 1911, three men set out to be the first to fly from ocean to ocean. Robert Fowler, a Wright-trained pilot, began his flight from San Francisco on Sept. 11. James Ward, piloting a Curtiss airplane, flew from New York westward on Sept. 13. Both pilots planned to follow the course of the railroad across the country, as that was the only viable means of aerial navigation at the time. Following a single track in California, Fowler had no trouble on his first day in the air and managed to fly 85 miles, landing near Sacramento. Ward, on the other hand, became confused by the profusion of tracks in the Jersey freight yards and couldn't locate the one that would eventually lead him to Chicago. He flew only 20 miles the first day.

The third contestant, Calbraith Perry Rodgers, a raw-boned, cigar-smoking giant of a man, who was a descendant of Commodore Oliver H. Perry, the commander at the battle of Lake Erie in the War of 1812, also began his flight in New York but he had learned a valuable lesson from Ward's misadventure.

Flying a special Model EX Wright flyer, christened *Vin Fiz* to advertise a soft drink produced by his sponsor, the Armour Company, Rodgers took off on Sept. 17 from a race track at Sheepshead Bay, Brooklyn and headed for the New Jersey freight yards. Once over the vast intertwining net-work of steel, he easily spied the Erie railroad tracks that would lead him across New Jersey and on to Middletown, New York, more than 80 miles from Brooklyn.

Rodgers had overcome the track confusion by simply having friends aboard the special train that would escort him to California, drop white strips of canvas along the track. At an altitude of 500 feet, the strips were clearly visible from his pilot's perch which protruded from the frail pusher plane.

He expected to be in Chicago in four days, but on takeoff from Middletown the following day, he hit a tree and crashed — the first of many such mishaps.

By the time he reached Chicago, Rodgers had consumed 28 of the required 30 days and he still had two-thirds of the country to cross. Determined to be the first to fly coast-to-coast, he kept on his course and on Dec. 10, following a four-week hospital stay, he arrived in Long Beach, CA. During the grueling 84-day flight, he had five serious crashes, several mid-air engine failures and numerous take-off and landing problems.

He didn't win the Hearst prize and used all the expense funds provided by Armour, but he had accomplished his mission. In early April, 1912, while on an exhibition flight over Long Beach, a seagull became lodged between the *Vin Fiz's* rudder and tail causing the plane to crash into the sea. Rodgers was killed instantly.

Although they survived their flights, neither Fowler nor Ward reached their destinations.

Other Early Flights

George N. Boyd

On Long Island, George N. Boyd, a Paterson native, became a member of the Early Birds of Aviation when he flew his home-built flyer, powered by a 60-hp engine of his own design, at the Nassau Boulevard Field. He stayed airborne for about five minutes and flew approximately 10 miles over Jamaica and New Hyde Park before landing successfully.

His first plane had no definite specifications. "We didn't have any measurements. It was just guesswork," he explained years later. "Anything you wanted, you had to make yourself."

In describing his initial flight on July 14, 1911, Boyd said: "I was surprised when I saw the trees pass under me." He hadn't expected his six-cylinder engine to get his frail machine off the turf strip.

The plane, held together by piano wire, was constructed of steel tubing, bamboo and pine strips. His mother sewed the cloth to cover the wings.

Although there were early flying instructors, Boyd didn't bother with lessons. "Nobody knew much about it. What they did tell you, they were only guessing anyway. Instructors used to charge $250 for two-and-a-half hours of lessons. If you couldn't fly in 150 minutes, you were no good," he said.

Boyd admitted he had numerous flying accidents, but he managed to escape with nothing more than a sprained ankle. Like so many other young men of the day, Boyd joined a barnstorming team at age 22 and for two summers flew at county fairs in New Jersey and New York.

"There was good money to be made at that time at the fairs," he recalled. "All you had to do was get off the ground, no stunt flying then. The planes would fall apart if you tried any maneuvers."

Boyd gave up flying in 1913. During World War I he tested airplane engines. He later went to work for the Cadillac Division of General Motors as a foreman and a supervisor. When he passed away at age 92 in 1981, he was listed among the 242 members of the Early Birds of Aviation, those men and women who flew before Dec. 17, 1916. His Early Bird plaque was donated to the Aviation Hall of Fame & Museum of New Jersey by his daughter Alberta with whom he lived in Brielle, NJ.

William Gary

On a clear, crisp early February day, Totowa residents lined the banks of the Passaic River to watch William Gary attempt to fly his cylindrical-shaped "aeroplane" off the frozen water. For seven hours in the biting cold, the determined pilot practiced take-offs and landings before climbing to an altitude of 15 feet and flying successfully from the Hilary Street bridge to the bridge that crossed the river at Cumberland Avenue. The bystanders cheered and Gary waved in appreciation of their fortitude.

Gary's unusual aircraft was well known to most Totowa residents. He called it the *Garyplane;*" they dubbed it the "hoople." He had built the first Garyplane in 1908 from a mail-order design he considered feasible. The aeroplane had a giant circular wing, measuring 20 feet in diameter, that was covered by a special Irish linen called Niad. It was powered by a 50-hp gasoline engine which hung in the center of the hoop. The pilot sat behind the engine. A tail wing and flaps that ran across the hoop stabilized the unusual-looking flying machine.

The first hoople was destroyed by a June windstorm in 1910 because it was not securely tied down, so the industrious designer attached a large peak-roofed shed to his home for his next creation.

At 8 a.m. on Dec. 28, 1910, Gary flew the second hoople along Totowa Road, near Grove Cemetery. The event attracted a large crowd that applauded enthusiastically as the Garyplane became airborne, but when it achieved the altitude of four inches above the pavement, the motor stalled and the second hoople crashed.

Undaunted, Gary built an improved model of his strange craft and installed a more powerful engine. It flew in April 1911, achieving a height of 110 feet before it, too, came tumbling down.

While a less-determined person might have become disheartened by constant adversity, Gary remained resolute, rebuilt the Garyplane, and then fully tested

Gary's Hoople

it on the frozen Passaic River before attempting his triumphant flight on that cold February day in 1912.

Gary gave up flying until after World War 1. Then when the U.S. Postal Service began using planes for air mail service, he decided to design a suitable air mail plane. The new Garyplane was a monoplane with Spanish cedar wings, an aluminum fuselage and a 90 hp OX-5 engine, the best then being built in the U.S. In 1922, it was successfully tested in the Massachusetts Institute of Technology's wind tunnel, and proved to be more efficient than the German Junkers and Fokkers of that period.

Gary obtained a United States patent on his new creation, formed a partnership and sold stock to interested parties. He seemed ready to become an aviation entrepreneur, but it was not to be.

The day chosen to flight test his new aircraft at Murchio Airport in Preakness was wet and windy, so Gary decided to get the "feel of the air" by taking up an old JN-4 "Jenny" prior to flying his new machine. Over Barbour's Pond, which was about the size of a large puddle, the Jenny was caught in a down draft, went into a stall, and crashed. Badly injured internally, Gary had 72 hemorrhages in 36 hours. It took several years for him to recover.

While he lay incapacitated in the hospital, souvenir hunters stripped his plane. It was never flown.

1912
First Air Mail Flight
Oliver Simmons

Inducted Aviation Hall of Fame of New Jersey, 1987

Mayor Ferd Garretson of Perth Amboy, a staunch advocate of early aviation, promoted the idea of a "Safe and Sane Fourth of July" for the city's 1912 celebration by arranging for the first air mail flight in New Jersey. Working with Edwin C. Roddy, the assistant postmaster in South Amboy, Garretson contacted his friend, Robert J. Collier, and requested that Collier lend his Wright B. flyer, *Laredo,* and pilot Oliver Simmons for an air mail flight from South Amboy across the Raritan Bay to Perth Amboy. Collier, who kept the plane on his estate in Wickatunk, enthusiastically endorsed the idea.

On July 4th, Simmons flew the flimsy craft to the Collier hydroplane base at Seidler's Beach, and from there, with a young newspaper reporter, Harold Hoffman, as a passenger, he flew to South Amboy, where Hoffman deplaned at the coal docks.

Much to the chagrin of pilot Simmons, Mayor Garretson insisted on accompanying him on the historic flight.

"The pilot was not too happy to have me along," Garretson recalled years later. "Every extra pound of weight added to the danger."

The mail bag weighed 18 pounds, leaving some leeway for a passenger. Garretson remembered: "After 90 minutes of instruction and cautions as to what I could not touch and how I was to behave in case of a mishap, I was allowed to take a place next to him."

A few minutes past noon, Simmons and the mayor were ready to take off, but by then the bay was alive with small boats filled with enthusiastic passengers eager to be near the flying machine. Three times Simmons began his run across the water but was forced to shut off the engine to prevent ramming some craft that crossed his path.

Finally at 12:22 p.m., the *Laredo* became airborne near the "new dock" at the foot of Henry Street, South Amboy as an estimated 20,000 Fourth of July celebrants cheered. Mayor Garretson, holding the sack of mail between his knees, clung to the wing struts of the tiny amphibian for dear life. The aeroplane fought a strong crosswind which kept Simmons too busy at the controls to appreciate the ovation from the crowd.

In three minutes, the "Laredo" had crossed the wide expanse of the Raritan and gently touched down off the easterly end of Lewis Street, Perth Amboy.

Garretson and Simmons were greeted by Postmaster William H. Pfeiffer, Assistant Postmaster John H. Tyrell and two members of the city's water sports committee, Harry R. Wilson and Garret V. Evens. Simmons handed the mail bag to the postmaster, then reached in his back pocket and pulled out two picture postcards that he said had missed the regular mail and had been handed to him by a young girl as he was preparing to leave.

The fliers were taken to the Packer House where Dr. F.C. Henry, chairman of the water sports committee, had arranged for a luncheon. Simmons was presented with a diamond-studded scarf pin. Later at a similar affair in South Amboy, he received a silver cup commemorating the flight.

One of the first letters flown in New Jersey was from Mayor Michael Welsh of South Amboy, addressed to Mayor Garretson. It read:

"My dear Mayor Garretson:

"Greetings to the people of the County metropolis from those of the infant City of Middlesex.

"The conquest of the air having been accomplished, we must look for new worlds to conquer. As the first communication between our cities by the most modern contrivance is thus held on the anniversary of the nation's natal day, so may it be the precursor of an increased and harmonious relationship between our municipalities. Permit me to express my sincere wish for your continued welfare and the prosperity and happiness of your city.

"Sincerely and respectfully,
Michael Welsh, Mayor"

It should he noted that the obscure newsman, Hoffman, went on to become a governor of New Jersey.

More Mail Flights

At an aero meet held at the racetrack and aviation grounds in Ho-Ho-Kus, NJ, a second mail flight was undertaken in 1912. A Wright single-engine biplane flown by Joseph Richter lifted off from the old racetrack (near Race Track Road and what is now Route 17) on Aug. 3, carrying 1,662 pieces of mail. Richter circled briefly and turned toward Ridgewood, about a mile away.

Six minutes later the airplane flew over the area that is now the YMCA athletic field on Oak Street in Ridgewood and the pilot dropped the mail sack. It was retrieved by post office employees W.P. Spreitzer and Walter Van Emburgh. Each envelope bore a special circular cachet with the words "Aerial Special Dispatch."

On the same day, a young Philadelphia aviator, Marshall Earl Reid, flew his Wright Flyer from Ocean City to Stone Harbor carrying the first air mail in the

A W.A.T.E.R. photo

Simmons (in cap) ready to fly mail held by Mayor Garretson.

southern part of the state. He flew at an altitude of 1,500 feet which no doubt took longer to reach than the flight across the water to Stone Harbor. Reid was hired by the postal authorities to make seven round-trip flights between the two resort towns. Altogether he transported 15,645 pieces of mail.

In the next few months after their historic flights, two of those New Jersey air mail pilots were involved in life threatening accidents.

In late August, the Red Bank paper reported that Oliver Simmons had shocked a large crowd attending a carnival in Keansburg when his plane plunged into Raritan Bay

The article read:

Keansburg—August 26. R.J. Collier's hydro-aeroplane was totally destroyed Saturday afternoon near Keansburg and the occupants aviator Oliver G. Simmons and James H. Hubbard, a passenger of Red Bank, injured. The machine was up about 200 feet and being watched by a record-breaking crowd attending the [Keansburg] carnival. The accident happened at the conclusion of the baby parade.

Simmons seemed to have perfect control of the aircraft and started to bank preparatory to making a circle above the huge throng. A heavy gust of air caught the machine and it descended to the water with great rapidity. People on shore stood aghast expecting to see the men dashed to death on the shore by hitting one of the fleet of boats near the place. Simmons tried his utmost to swerve the craft and right it. His efforts were futile and the aeroplane landed sideways in four feet of water.

Hubbard, a garage man of Red Bank, slid from the seat in the descent and was buried under the broken craft and heavy engine. Simmons also slid from his place, but presence of mind saved him from falling into the water. He grabbed a guide rope and held onto the machine. As soon as the plane hit water, Simmons feared for the life of his passenger when he saw him pinned under it. At the risk of his own life, he crawled under the debris and brought the injured man from his perilous position. As Simmons carried Hubbard to shore he was cheered by the hundreds who saw what he had accomplished.

Several physicians were summoned. Hubbard is suffering from a badly sprained neck, a deep gash on right side of his face near the ear and severe bruises about the body. Simmons escaped with a few slight cuts and was bruised.

As soon as the aviator and his injured passenger left the beach, hundreds of curio seekers started to strip the machine. Simmons when informed of what was taking place hired several men to tow the broken machine to shore and call a halt on the souvenir seekers. The engine was taken back to Seidler's [beach] yesterday morning.

Simmons and his passenger [had] left Seidler's beach at 4:15 o'clock Saturday afternoon and arrived over Keansburg six minutes later. The machine is a total wreck according to the pilot, but it is probable that the engine will again be used. A sixty-horse power engine will supplant the thirty-five horse power type now used by Mr. Simmons. The aviator says when more power is obtainable then he can rise in a dead calm and prevent accidents similar to the one occurring Saturday.

Members of the Raritan Yacht Club of this city when informed of the accident were much grieved as Mr. Simmons was expected to make flights off the club house later during the afternoon.

As Mr. Simmons was flying over the boardwalk prior to the accident, he dropped several circulars, which bore the following:

While we are heartily in sympathy with Roosevelt's Bull Moose movement, we believe it will result in the election of our governor, Woodrow Wilson, as president."

> Signed.

> *R.J. Collier's Aeroplane, Simmons, Aviation,*

A week later, Simmons received a letter of sympathy from the governor.

Dear Mr. Simmons:

I was indeed sorry to learn that you had met with a serious accident in Sandy Hook Bay on Saturday last, and desire to express to you my sincerest sympathies, and the hope that you will soon be well again.

I have learned of your kindly interest in me and my candidacy, and I wish to express to you my appreciation of your support and good feeling.

> Cordially yours,

> Woodrow Wilson

Two months later, Marshall Reid and his passenger, Lt. Commander Henry C. Mustin of the Philadelphia Navy Yard, were forced by engine trouble to land their hydro-aeroplane on the Delaware Bay and wait 16 hours to be rescued.

The problem occurred just 24 minutes after the two men had left Cape May Point on their planned 93-mile flight to Philadelphia. While flying at 100 feet, the motor suddenly exploded, almost jolting the men from their seats. Reid later described what happened:

"Four cylinders blew out in rapid succession. Then we shot downward. What was left of the engine caught fire. When we struck the water it swept over us, but didn't quench the flames. I beat the flames with my cap, while Mr. Mustin cut off the supply of gasoline.

"If that accident had happened over land there is nothing in the world that could have saved us. The pontoons saved our lives and proved how much safer hydro-aeroplanes are than the land flying machines."

Either the explosion or the hard landing split the plane's pontoons and the two men spent 16 exhausting hours incessantly bailing water from the broken floats. They were picked up near Maurice Cove.

Over the next eight months, Reid kept busy flying at various South Jersey resorts. During July 1913, he and his Curtiss flying boat were engaged by the Wild-

wood Board of Trade for a week to make daily flights from the beach front.

During that period, his machine was damaged when he landed on land, preventing him from flying on to Atlantic City for a similar engagement. By August, he announced he was giving up flying because of the unusual number of accidents that seemed to be catching up with him.

Read returned to flying at the outbreak of World War I and served with General Pershing along the Mexican border and then became a Naval aviator.

Oliver Simmons too left the aviation business complaining that he couldn't make a decent living as an aviator or aeronautical mechanic. In 1921, he founded the Simmons Method Hob Co. in Philadelphia and six years later he became president and general manager of the National Tool Co., Cleveland, OH. Simmons was a prolific inventor and held 32 patents in the machine tool field.

He retired in 1936 and moved to his country home, Clifton Farm in Davidsonville, MD. He suffered with heart problems in the early 1940s, and died at Bethesda Naval Hospital, MD in 1948. He is buried at Arlington National Cemetery.

Following Simmons' death, Paul Garber, the curator of the Smithsonian Institution's aeronautical collection, asked Mrs. Simmons to donate the silver cup the aviator had received from the South Amboy businessman's association after the first air mail flight. It was commonly believed at that time that the New Jersey flight was the first of its kind in the nation.

The cup was donated, and for several years proudly displayed at the Smithsonian. When the National Air and Space Museum opened, the cup was relegated to storage where it remained for almost 20 years.

When Oliver Simmons was inducted into the New Jersey Aviation Hall of Fame 1987, Olive Simmons Ussery, the pilot's daughter, asked Hall of Fame officials if they would request NASM to loan the trophy to the New Jersey museum so that it could be on display for public interest. It took nearly two years to arrange the loan.

Once the handsome trophy was back in the Garden State, the author created a six-minute slide show concerning the important aviation events in which the Amboys were involved, and arranged with the Perth Amboy Chamber of Commerce to present the show at the city schools along with the trophy.

Instant Heroes

Barnstormers

By the middle of the 20th century's second decade, airplanes doing aerobatics or offering passenger rides were a must in every town or village planning a special celebration. The Wright and Curtiss airmen were the most popular, but their fees to perform and busy schedules made it almost impossible for a low budget group to hire.

There were, however, any number of freelance male and female barnstormers from various states who were available to entertain. In the summer of 1913, pilots George Gray, Miss Ruth Law, 0. E. Williams, George Dyott, Fred Hild and Harry Atwood were appearing throughout New Jersey at such events as the opening of the Gloucester Country Grange at Pitman, the Mount Holly Fair, the Byberry County Fair, the Shark River Carnival, the Belmar and the Sussex County Fairs, Newton. Hild, flying a Bleriot-type monoplane, was even giving weekly exhibitions in the skies over Secaucus.

A Garden State native on the barnstorming trail was George W. Beatty of Whitehouse. He began flying in 1911 at age 24 and immediately set an American altitude record while carrying a passenger.

Before taking up flying, he was a linotype operator and general mechanic. His first flight was made at Belmont Park. He entered a small competitive flying meet held by the Aero Club of New York, just two days after he won his pilot's license.

Arthur J. Lapham

One of the unsung heroes of early aviation was Arthur J. Lapham, a native of Dover, NJ, whose family moved to Union City, NJ, when he was just a toddler.

Lapham was the first man to jump from an airplane using the "Stevens Safety Pack" parachute, developed by A. Leo Stevens. The parachute was the first free fall manually operated pack ever designed. It permitted airmen to jump clear of a disabled plane and release the parachute from the pack on the way down. Prior to that development, the parachute packs were attached to the plane's wings and were pulled free when the pilot jumped. If, however, the plane began spiraling down, the pilot wouldn't drop faster than the plane and they'd both crash together.

Lapham, at age 20, was already an experienced jumper when he made his initial jump with the new self-contained parachute pack. He was taken aloft in a Wright flyer, piloted by Harry Bingham Brown at Oakwood Heights, Staten Island, NY, on May 30, 1913. The drop was not a success for Lapham's parachute did not open fully and he plunged 400 feet into a marsh. The spectators and fellow aviators believed

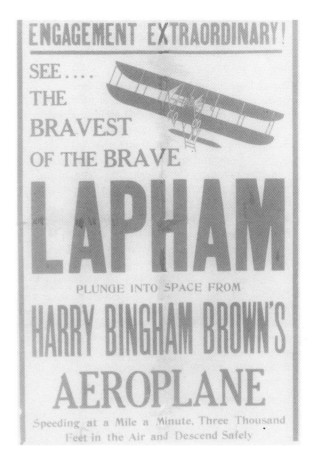

he was dead, but when rescuers got to him, they found him buried so deeply in the mud that shovels were needed to dig him out. A boat was poled through the marsh and Lapham was taken to a local hospital. There, they found he was suffering from shock, but otherwise nothing else was broken.

Other aviators on the scene told the press that they believed Lapham had jumped from an inadequate height. There was a treacherous wind blowing as he and Brown ascended in the fragile plane and it seemed from the ground that the ship could not attain any greater altitude.

Many of the spectators attempted to reach the downed airman and were caught in the swamp. The *New York Times* reported in its May 31 edition that "at least half the number who tried to get through were wet to the knees."

The lucky jumper was back entertaining the crowds the following day.

Lapham began his parachuting career at the age of 18. He joined Arthur W. Marsh, who headed The New England Balloon and Airship Co. and they jumped together as the "Two Arthurs." Lapham made approximately 200 jumps from below a hot air balloon.

He then went with Leo Stevens, who was a well known aeronaut of the day, and made many jumps with the Stevens parachute. It was during that same period that Lapham went to Puerto Rico and demonstrated his jumping skills and the efficiency of the new parachute.

When Lapham married and settled down in Union City, he put his career as a jumper behind him. He established a successful automobile dealership and became a Union City Commissioner.

In 1950, he was presented with the A. Leo Stevens Medal, sponsored by the Stevens Memorial Fund, headquartered in New York City. The medal was presented by Lyman H. Ford, vice president of the Pioneer Parachute Co., and Col. Augustus Post, secretary of the Stevens Memorial Fund.

In 1906, Post had established a balloon flight record of 1,171 miles, with New Jerseyan Alan Hawley.

At the award ceremony, Col. E.V. Stewart, who was in charge of training paratroopers at Wright Field, Dayton, OH, paid tribute to Lapham and other early jumpers. "The pioneer work done by the men who risked their lives in those early days, blazed the way for saving the lives of countless pilots and passengers who have used parachutes," he said. "It also led to the creation of airborne troops, one of the most important arms of the military forces."

A poster used to advertise Lapham's jumps in 1913 was on display at the ceremony. It read: "See the bravest of the brave plunge into space from Harry Bingham Brown's aeroplane, speeding at a mile a minute 3,000 feet in the air."

First Akron Disaster
Melvin Vaniman

Melvin Vaniman, who had been Walter Wellman's second in command on the aborted flight in 1910, was not discouraged by the failed attempt of the airship *America* to fly across the Atlantic Ocean. He obtained backing from Frank Sieberling, president of the Goodyear Tire and Rubber Co., to build another dirigible for a second attempt. Like the huge airship that would be built by the Navy 20 years later, Vaniman named his the *Akron* in honor of Goodyear's headquarter city in Ohio.

The aerostat being assembled of cotton and rubber at the Goodyear plant was the largest ever built in the United States. The 268-foot, cigar-shaped bag was designed to lift the weight of 80 people, a carrying capacity greater than most of the Zeppelins being built in Germany. It would be powered by three gasoline engines, have a wireless aboard and carry a lifeboat slung below its control car.

The huge gas bag, constructed of three layers of cotton

Airship hangar on Atlantic City inlet.

cloth and rubber, weighed 4,400 pounds when it left Akron in a large box on a freight train in mid-September 1911. Its destination was Atlantic City.

Upon its arrival, Vaniman and his crew immediately assembled and inflated the dirigible and by early November, a flight test was made over the resort's beach. *Aero Magazine*, a weekly aviation publication of the day, told of a test flight in its Nov. 11, 1911 issue:

The craft is equipped with a new form of steering propellers, which seemed to give Vaniman better control of the craft than has ever been exhibited in a dirigible before. He made sharp turns, and performed evolutions, it is said, which might properly be classified with those of an aeroplane. At one time the dirigible was racing with an express train and succeeded in distancing it after a dash of a little more than a mile. For a finishing touch Vaniman drove the ship along Atlantic Avenue, the principal street of this city, not 200 feet above the house tops.

Then when he had fully succeeded in arousing the whole population, and bringing it out on the streets to watch and cheer, he suddenly guided the balloon toward the marshy district behind the city, in the direction of Pleasantville. An anxious three hours followed with no sign of the airship. Finally word came that Vaniman had landed on a mud flat near Pleasantville and had been unable to rise, owing to a sudden chill which came over the atmosphere and contracted the gas in the already partly deflated aerostat.

Those aboard the *Akron* on that test flight included: Vaniman, Louis Loul, chief engineer; Jack Irwin, wireless operator and Louis Blotcher, a mechanic. Vaniman's brother, Calvin, and Frank Sieberling, Jr., the son of the sponsor rode along as passengers.

The *Akron* was housed for the winter in the same hangar on the Atlantic City inlet used by the "America" the year before. In the late spring of 1912, additional flight tests were made in preparation for the Atlantic flight on a then unannounced date.

On one such trial flight tragedy struck. At 6:15 a.m. on July 2, the dirigible lifted off from the inlet beach heading due east toward the Atlantic. Within minutes it had flown two miles and risen to a height of 1,000 feet. Calvin Vaniman, who was at the controls, then maneuvered the ship left and right as the shoreside crowd applauded.

It was on the third turn that the onlookers first noticed a thin curl of smoke from the stern, and an instant later an explosion was reported that sounded like a car backfire. The *Akron* trembled for a short moment, silhouetted against the rising sun, and then began to drop gradually toward the inlet waters.

The onlookers were stunned into silence, not sure of what they were seeing. Then the upper half of the balloon exploded, collapsing the forward section, and the entire structure plunged into the inlet's 18 feet of mud and water, burying four of the five crewmen beneath tons of metal, cotton and rubber. Calvin Vaniman had been thrown clear of the car at the time of the first explosion. It was reported that thousands of spectators and three wives of the crewmen witnessed the disaster.

Aside from Melvin and Calvin Vaniman, those who dropped to their deaths aboard the ship were George Brilliant, a French engine expert; Frederick Elmer, a mechanic and Walter Guest, an assistant mechanic.

The explosion was blamed on leaking gas that was ignited by a spark from one of the engines.

1913
First Rocket Flight
Frederick Rodman Law

New Jersey historian David Winans of Colonia told this amusing story of an early rocket launch attempt.

A unique chapter in New Jersey's long history of aviation was nearly written in Jersey City when parachutist Rodman Law attempted to blast off in a huge skyrocket over the waters of Newark Bay.

Frederick Rodman Law was a professional stunt man and early parachute jumper who had dropped from most of New York City's bridges, several large buildings and even from the Statue of Liberty. To cap his many other daring jumps from airships, balloons and airplanes, Law conceived the idea of parachuting from a large manned rocket of his own design. Somehow (accounts vary) Law managed to obtain funds for his lunatic project. His many friends, including aircraft builder Charles Wittemann, thought that Law was crazy, and they insisted that he have a dry run of his rocket. Law complied by launching a test shot with a sandbag as a payload. His bird went high enough to convince him that a manned shot would be successful.

And so it was on the afternoon of March 13, 1913 that Law made final preparations for his launch. Contemporary photographs (published in Scientific American two weeks later) showed first, a procession of men carrying the heavy rocket motor (accounts again disagreed as to the weight of the black powder contained inside). Law had his solid rocket motor casing, some 10 feet long by 30 inches in diameter, filled by the International Fireworks Company of Jersey City. The casing was bolted to a hollow cylinder capped by a hinged nose cone. A 24-foot, four by four timber was attached through the motor casing to add stability to the rocket in flight. The whole contraption, some 44 feet in length, was raised upon its timber tail and allowed to lean against a triangular gantry aimed toward Elizabeth. Law planned to parachute from his bird at 3,500 feet and drift toward Elizabeth for a successful landing. However, Murphy's law took over at the launch.

Rodman Law attired himself in padded clothing and donned his aviator's heavy helmet. He climbed up the timber ladder attached to the gantry and lowered himself into the rocket's nose section. After attaching the harness of his Stevens parachute within the nose section, he leaned out and shouted to Sam Surplee (manager of the fireworks company) "Fire when you are ready". From behind a heavy timber bulwark, Surplee lit the long fuse that was attached to the rocket motor, and then something went awry.

Instead of the smooth lift-off Law expected, a mighty explosion occurred. Observers, who had not had the sense to duck, were knocked off their feet and Law was unconscious at the base of the gantry, but aside from a few burns on his hands and face, Law survived to die in bed six years later.

The First Controlled Glider
Leland E. Dorrothy

Like so many boys of that day, Leland Dorrothy and Charles Meyers of Bloomfield were determined to fly. They poured over plans of the simple aircraft of their time and eventually designed a flyer of their own. Theirs would not be a powered flight, but they saw no reason why a glider should not be controllable.

Over the winter months of 1912 and '13, the two 18 year olds worked on a twin set of gliders that would have wide wing and tail surfaces, a simple cockpit with a steering wheel that would permit them to control the direction of their flight. All materials used were readily available. The landing gear utilized baby carriage wheels and the wings were covered with Irish linen. All the bolts, turnbuckles and screws were purchased at the local hardware store.

On June 29, 1913, the boys with the help of friends took the gliders to the crest of the hill below Ridgewood Avenue in Glen Ridge on the site of the Glen Ridge Country Club and prepared for their flight tests. A rope was attached to the nose of Dorrothy's glider and when the young airman gave the signal, his friends grabbed the rope and ran full tilt down the hill towing the glider behind them until it lifted off the ground.

The flight of the first controlled glider was near perfect. The boys were elated.

Moments later Meyers sat aboard his similar glider ready to be launched. The boys again ran down the hill toward Broad Street, Bloomfield, with the glider in tow and almost instantly Meyers was airborne. Then suddenly, two front support wires broke and a

Dorrothy ready to fly the *Bald Eagle*

spar failed causing the wing to collapse. The craft dropped like a rock. Miraculously, the boy pilot escaped with only a black eye.

Neither boy gave up flying. Charles Meyers joined Eastern Airlines and eventually became a captain. He retired as Chief Pilot in 1961.

In 1929, Leland Dorrothy organized Flights Interstate, Inc. which primarily operated between Asbury Park and Newark Airport. The company had a contract with the *Newark News* to fly the Wall Street edition of the paper to the resort city where it was distributed to various shore points by truck. The flying paper delivery was 55 minutes faster than the train. Flying a Ryan monoplane, pilot Albion Brooks flew through a heavy cloud cover on the first flight from Newark to Asbury Park on Monday, Aug. 14, 1929. The flight took 27 minutes, but the company's general manager Frederick M. Shaw confidently predicted that the normal transit time would be 20 minutes on clear days.

The company eventually owned 10 aircraft, both Ryans and Bellancas. During the summer racing season, newspapers would be flown to Saratoga, NY. It is believed that Flights Interstate was the first air cargo line and the first feeder passenger line in the United States.

It was in 1929, that Dorrothy obtained his private pilot's license (#8601) after he soloed at Red Bank Airport. He never flew for his company. The Depression and a series of accidents forced Dorrothy's airline to declare bankruptcy and close shop in 1932.

Dorrothy died in 1966 after a long career with the Metropolitan Insurance Co.

First Airboat Commuter
Alfred W. Lawson

In the Nov. 16, 1913 issue of The *World Magazine,* a headline read: "New York's First Airboat Commuter." The subhead declared: "Alfred W. Lawson Sails the Air Lanes from His Home at Seidler's Beach on Raritan Bay (NJ) to West 130th Street, Making 30 miles in About 37 Minutes—Plans a Flying Boat to Hold Ten Guests to Cruise in Next Summer."

Wing assembly plant at Newark Airport

In 1908, Lawson was the founder of the popular aeronautic magazine *Fly*. His publishing office was located on 28th Street in Manhattan.

His airplane was a Thomas flying boat which he piloted himself. He had learned to fly at Hempstead Plains, Long Island early in 1913. He took lessons from two different schools at the same time. He learned to pilot a Sloane Deprudusen monoplane and a Moisant-Bleriot monoplane alternately in order to gain broad experience rapidly.

He had coined the word "aircraft" in 1908 and was responsible for putting it in the dictionary in 1912.

In 1910, he founded and edited *Aircraft Magazine*.

Lawson not only wrote of the present and future of aviation in his magazine, he expended a great deal of time, energy and money attempting to prove that "the future" is now.

In 1919, he flew the 18-passenger Lawson Airliner, powered by two 400-hp Liberty engines, from Milwaukee, WI, via Cleveland to New York and Washington, DC, and returned to demonstrate the use of an airplane as a passenger carrying vehicle. The flight covered a spectacular 2,500 miles without a problem.

The Lawson Airliner was the first such plane built in the United States. Vincent J. Burnelli, who later designed and built his aircraft at Keyport, NJ, was the engineer of the Lawson project.

1914

Wittemanns to New Jersey

Charles, Paul and Walter Wittemann
Inducted Aviation Hall of Fame of New Jersey, 1973

The Wittemann-Lewis Aircraft Company moved from the Wittemann family estate on Staten Island to a large building on the north edge of the Newark meadows, where Newark Airport is now located.

In 1905, Charles Wittemann and his brother Adolph had founded the C. & A. Wittemann Company, one of the earliest aircraft manufacturing plants in the world, on their parent's estate at 17 Ocean Terrace, Staten Island. They had been experimenting with flying machines as early as 1900 and their small business flourished immediately. Captain Thomas S. Baldwin, a prominent exhibition airman, was among the Wittemann's early customers.

The Staten Island plant was expanded several times until it became apparent that a larger work area was needed and the Newark meadows seemed ideal for aircraft experimenting. At that time, Adolph, a marine engineer, returned to the sea, and his brother Paul began taking a more active role. Just before moving to Newark, the Wittemanns joined forces with Samuel C. Lewis, and the company name was changed in order to give both principals equal billing.

Orders for aircraft of all sizes poured in, and the Wittemann's craftsmanship continued to attract customers with important projects. Early in 1915, Captain Hugo Sundstedt of South Bayonne brought the Wittemanns his plans for a five-ton seaplane in which he expected to fly across the Atlantic Ocean. Because of the size of the plane, the company moved to a temporary building on the edge of Newark Bay where it could be flight tested.

War had broken out in Europe in 1914, and by the following year most aircraft plants in the United States were kept busy filling government orders for Army and Navy training planes.

By mid-1916, Wittemann-Lewis had more private and government contracts than they could handle in the Newark facility and felt the necessity to expand again. It was ascertained that the marshy Newark meadow would be too costly to fill in order to construct a larger plant and its needed airstrip, so Charles and Paul went in search of a new location.

They found a tract of land below the Hasbrouck Heights hill in Bergen County that belonged to Walter C. Teter of Montclair, NJ. The property was managed by Henry Hollister, who also served as the mayor of the small community of 18 farming families.

The marshy land was criss-crossed by drainage ditches. A sod airstrip was cleared, and in the latter part of 1916, Charles Wittemann and Capt. Stewart A. Morgan flew a Wittemann model "TT" biplane from Newark to Teter's meadow to discuss the land purchase deal with Hollister.

When a deal was struck, the Wittemanns moved from Newark to Teterboro. Helen Aitken Boesch, now an Oregon resident who had lived in Hasbrouck Heights at that time, was employed as a stenographer. She remembered that Paul Wittemann held the position of president, Charles was vice president, but she didn't recall Walter Wittemann's title.

Mayor Hollister's office was a square concrete block building, about the size of a two-car garage, on the perimeter of the marsh. He vacated it, and the Wittemanns moved in.

"It contained two private offices in the rear and an open room across the front of the building." Mrs. Boesch explained. "One private office was occupied by the Wittemann brothers. Mr. A. Francis Archier, chief engineer and designer, occupied the other. The large, front room was used by two draftsmen and I had a desk and typewriter in one corner next to the president's door.

"There was a huge stove in the center of the front room and a clothes line strung across its width nearest the stove. This line was necessary because someone was forever missing his step en route from the temporary office to the building under construction and falling into a ditch.

"We were singly honored on one occasion to drape the soggy cloths of Postmaster General Egge who had come to Teterboro on an inspection tour. I was dispatched up the road to the railroad station until our guest dried out." Mrs. Boesch recalled with a chuckle.

At the first Pan-American Aeronautical Exposition held in New York in February 1917, the Wittemanns exhibited their tractor biplane. *Aerial Age Weekly* reported the plane "was admired for the simplicity of its construction and business-like appearance in its coat of battleship gray." Following the exposition, the airplane was put through its paces by Eddie Stinson and greatly impressed the military representatives on the scene.

A project begun at the Newark plant was the design and construction of a pilot-less war plane that could deliver a large quantity of TNT on a pre-set target. Work on the robot-guided aircraft continued at the new Teterboro facility. Although test flights were successful, World War I ended before it could be put into production.

The new Teterboro plant opened for business in late 1917. The building had an open assembly floor span of 120 feet by 200 feet and 30 feet of headroom. Small work shops were located in separate buildings on either side of the central hangar. It was the largest airplane assembly plant in America at that time. In addition to the runway, a road was cleared to the Hackensack River for the testing of amphibious planes. During that time, Samuel Lewis resigned from the company and the name was changed to the Wittemann Aircraft Corporation.

Wittemann employees were kept busy producing and flight testing military training planes designed by Charles W. Hemonn who was recognized nationally as a leading aeronautical authority. (See 1920)

Aeromarine Plane
and Motor Company
Inglis Uppercu

Following the tragic death of their brother Frank in 1913, Joseph and James Boland continued building flying boats of Frank's design at the Boland Aeroplane and Motor Co. plant in Avondale, NJ, but they lost control of their company. Frank Boland's widow claimed her husband's share of the business and im-

Inglis Uppercu

Smithsonian Institution

mediately sold it to Inglis M. Uppercu whose wife already owned a piece of the business.

The company was re-incorporated by Uppercu as the Aeromarine Plane & Motor Co., with a factory in Nutley, NJ, and executive offices at 1818 Broadway, New York City, where Uppercu had a thriving Cadillac dealership. Plans to build hydro-aeroplanes, powered by Joe Boland's light, powerful 100-hp, V-8 engines, moved ahead.

A year later, the company opened a second plant at Broad Street in Newark and a "floating hangar" was built on an old barge anchored in Newark Bay, opposite Jersey City. From there, company engineers flight tested their flying boats. The hangar provided shelter for the aircraft and space for Joe Boland to make mechanical adjustments to the engines.

Although Inglis Uppercu became the premiere entrepreneur of early commercial aviation in the United States, it was his ongoing automobile business that supported his aviation undertakings.

Born in 1875 in North Evanston, Il. where his father practiced law, Uppercu and his family moved to New York in 1888. Upon graduation from high school in Bay Ridge, Brooklyn, and from the Brooklyn Polytechnic Institute, Uppercu entered Columbia University Law School. Despite his family's desires to have a second generation lawyer in the family, Uppercu left Columbia and became involved in the budding automobile industry. He began by doing experimental work with the Neostyle Company and, later, the Duryea Automobile Co.

At the age of 27, he founded the Motor Car Company of New Jersey in 1902 and within six years had the Cadillac franchise for the metropolitan New York area. That led to his acquaintance with James Boland, who had opened a Cadillac dealership in Rahway. His association with Boland's two older brothers, Frank and Joe, piqued his interest in aviation.

By 1917, the Newark facility became too small for the production of both land and sea planes, so the operation was moved to a 66-acre plot of land on Raritan Bay at Keyport. There were 16 fireproof buildings on the property with a total floor space of 130,000 sq. ft. To flight test both land and sea aircraft a 2,000-foot air strip was created beside the buildings, and a ramp was built into the calm waters of the bay.

More than 70 years later, in his kitchen at 180 Washington St., Keyport, 91-year-old Adiel "Mitzie" Strang, a former Aeromarine mechanic, recalled the move from Nutley to the little fishing town on Raritan Bay.

"In Feb. 1917 more than 100 of us came to Keyport on a special train that stopped at Second and Walnut Streets. From there we walked to the new Aeromarine plant.

"The town of Keyport will never forget the good citizens who came here with Aeromarine Company. Among those in the original group were Joseph Boland, Joseph Morley, Ed Riley, James Delaney, George Ayers, Richard Griesinger, George Fritz, Elmer Straub, Harry Martin, Kenneth Stone, Ed Musick, Paul and Cy Zimmermann, Paul Ash and many others.

"In June 1917 the plant was going strong. People from all over Monmouth County came to work there. And today no matter where you go if you mention Keyport, someone will say, 'Keyport. My father or grandfather used to work there with Aeromarine.'"

With WW I creating a need, the company's 1,200 employees, under general manager Hugh Robinson, went into wartime production of various models of seaplanes to fulfill a $2 million Navy contract. By the war's end, Aeromarine had produced more than 300 single-float seaplanes and Model 40 flying boats used by the Navy as trainers.

Robinson, an aviation pioneer who had been associated with Glenn Curtiss, hired Paul G. Zimmermann as the company's chief engineer. Following the war, Zimmermann would develop the first metal flying boat in America, the first metal-fuselage mail plane and the first commercial flying boat flown from New York to Puerto Rico by Aeromarine's chief pilot C.J. Zimmermann (no relation). (See 1920)

Preparing For War

Just prior to America's entry into World War I, 24 states were anxious to organize National Guard and Naval Militia detachments. Many of them applied to the Aero Club of America, then led by New Jerseyan Alan Hawley, for assistance in acquiring airplanes and equipment from the private sector.

Edward MC. Peters, Commander of the Naval Reserve in New Jersey wrote the following letter to the Governors of the Aero Club.

Gentlemen:

It is desired to bring to the attention of the Aero Club of America the fact that the First Battalion, Naval Reserve of New Jersey, is organizing an aviation section.

This has received the approval of the Navy Department and I have appointed Ensign-elect J. Homer Stover to the immediate charge of organizing the section.

The Division of Naval Militia Affairs of the Navy Department has been requested to state what aeronautic equipment the Government would supply for this section.

It has replied that clothing and equipment for the enlisted men in accordance with the funds available would be furnished.

In regard to furnishing an aeroplane or other special equipment it is advised that steps will be taken to render such assistance as may be possible with the Federal funds available.

There is, however, no definite assurance that an aeroplane, hangar, etc., will be provided before some remote date from that source.

Knowing the aid that the Aero Club of America, with the assistance of the Aeroplane Fund, is giving in the promotion of military aeronautics, it is asked what assistance, if any, and in what form the Aero Club of America will give this organization in its work of obtaining an aeroplane and other necessary equipment for the aeronautic section.

So it was that a few farsighted civilians could envision the importance of air power in time of national emergency and were willing to support the development of an air arm of the Army and Navy while the bureaucrats in Washington did little to encourage the movement.

At about the same time the Naval Reserve Commander was requesting assistance in organizing an air arm, Robert J. Collier, a past president of the Aero Club of America, was organizing a large aircraft show on his Wickatunk estate, to spark interest in aviation's potential. Those who were invited to the private show were the Who's Who of New York and New Jersey high society, people wealthy enough to buy the aeronautical equipment needed to outfit the National Guard aviation units.

In response to Commander Peters' request, Inglis Uppercu presented one of Aeromarine's latest model hydroplanes to the Naval Militia of New Jersey. Uppercu said he was donating the machine as a demonstration of his patriotism.

Before going to the Navy, the plane was exhibited at the Newark Automobile show in February 1916. The gift was officially recognized at a ceremony aboard the *U.S.S. Adams* docked in Hoboken. Ensign Stover was in personal charge of the prized gift.

Alan R. Hawley continued the club's efforts to generate support in the U.S. Congress for military aviation to be used by General John J. Pershing and his troops along the Mexican border in their battle with Pancho Villa and his band. In March 1916, he wrote to President Wilson and a number of Congressmen urging their help:

"An immediate appropriation of $1 million to at once equip four aero squadrons with the necessary high powered aeroplanes may save lives of 10,000 American soldiers on the Mexican border. Army Aero squadrons at the border has only six low-powered scouting aeroplanes. Signal Corps has no funds available at present to get necessary equipment.

"There should be three aeroplanes available for every aviator now at the Mexican border which is the number of aeroplanes allowed to each aviator in Europe, and three more squadrons should also immediately be put in readiness. The Aero Club of America is training 50 aviators to place at the Army's disposal to make up shortage of Army aviators. To prepare to meet a need does not mean to wait until hundreds of men have lost their lives. We ought to prepare to preserve the lives of our soldiers. An aeroplane is worth a thousand soldiers in such a campaign as the American forces are about to undertake. A hundred high-powered aeroplanes would make it possible to round up Villa and his band in a very short time where it might take thousands of men a long time with considerable losses to attain the same end."

Sincerely,

Alan R. Hawley

Shortly after Hawley's letter was sent, he received a surprising reply from Major Samuel Reber of the Signal Corps, who was in charge of the Army aviators.

"The Chief of Staff directs me to state that the expedition which is going into Mexico will be there for a short time and that it has all the aeroplanes necessary. Your patriotic offer placing your services at the disposal of the government is greatly appreciated and every effort will be made to utilize them if possible."

S. Reber

It wasn't until the late summer of 1917 that Congress appropriated $640 million for military aeronautics. By then, Americans were dying in the skies above the trenches in France flying British and French fighter planes.

John E. Sloane, the son-in-law of inventor Thomas A. Edison, was one of the first executives to volunteer his company's services to train officers for the militia of states interested in forming aviation sections.

The Sloane company had been building flying boats at a small plant in Garden City, Long Island, for several years. In addition, Sloane ran a flying school in the same city and planned to open another at Sheepshead Bay Speedway, Brooklyn.

In March 1915, Sloane's company transferred its operation to Bound Brook, NJ, and later in the year moved to larger quarters in Plainfield. There, under the direction of designer Charles Healy Day, several training and racing planes were produced.

To reinforce Sloane's offer, the Aero Club agreed to pay the travel and living expenses for out-of-state militiamen.

Exactly a year after the move to Plainfield, the Sloane Aeroplane Co. was dissolved and the Standard Aero Corp. was formed. John Sloane had lost his interest in the company to Mitsui and Co. a Japanese investment firm. At that time, the company had an order from the war department for 12-Day designed tractor H-2 biplanes. The H-2 had established an altitude record of 13,500 feet the previous April with DeLloyd Thompson at the controls. In addition, a prototype of the Standard-J biplane, also designed by Day, was underway.

Late in the year, the Standard-J prototype was taken to Daytona Beach, Fl, and extensively test flown for several months. The U.S. Army placed an order for 23 to be delivered in 1917. To keep on schedule, Ralph Barnaby was hired as a project engineer.

The name of Wright first came to New Jersey in February 1916 when the Wright Company of Dayton, merged with the Glen L. Martin Co. and received an order to build the popular 140 hp Hispano-Suiza (Spanish-Swiss) engine. The new company set up shop in a former automobile plant owned by the Simplex Motor Car Co. of New Brunswick. As the war in Europe escalated, the original order of $2 million for engines grew to $50 million.

Wright-Martin was one of five aircraft and engine companies in New Jersey that significantly contributed to the war effort. The others were: Aeromarine Aircraft and Engine Co. of Keyport; Maximilian Schmidt Aeroplanes of Paterson; Standard Aircraft of Bayway and Plainfield and the Wittemann-Lewis Airplane Co. of Newark and Teterboro. Between them, the companies combined to build more than 2,500 aircraft and thousands of engines over a two year period. A total of 13,984 airplanes were built throughout the United States prior to Nov. 1, 1919.

The formation of a military flying service that the Aero Club of America had so diligently campaigned for became a reality in the summer of 1916. Officers of the New York National Guard were mustered into Federal service to form the First Aero Company. Robert Collier and Alan Hawley, two New Jerseyans who between them held the presidency of the Aero Club for some eight years, were the men who spearheaded the program to educate Congressional and military leaders to the importance of air power.

Many of those National Guardsmen and hundreds of other men from every state in the Union went off to France to fight in the "dirty war." Some died in air battles against the hated "Hun," while others returned home heroes.

When the majority of the Ivy League colleges organized "aeroplane corps," Princeton was among the first. The students' interest in flying had been piqued in 1916 when a National Guard cross-country flight was organized. Led by Capt. R.C. Bolling, the unit flew from New York to Princeton and return from November 18 to 20.

An aviation program under the guidance of Dr. Joseph Raycroft was established and the alumni equipped it with a Curtiss plane. When the chance to learn to fly was announced more than 200 undergraduates applied for the training. Only 60 could be accepted.

A training field for pilots was set up on the outskirts of Princeton on the east side of the old Route 206. And at the same time, an airship station was established at Cape May to accommodate blimps designed to patrol the waters along the New Jersey Coast.

1917-1918
The "Great War" Years

Prior to the United States' entry into the conflict that became known as the "Great War" many Americans looking for adventure went to Europe to fight on the side of the French. One of those was Ronald W. Hoskier of South Orange, who volunteered in the French ambulance service early in 1916.

In April of that year, Hoskier transferred to the French Service Aeronautique and took pilot training at the Bleriot School at Buc. He finished his training in the early winter, and on Dec. 11, 1916, was sent to serve with the l'Escadrille Lafayette, Squadron 124, the first significant organized group of American combat pilots. The Escadrille was operating from the aerodrome at Cachy on the Somme front.

In less than five months, Hoskier made a deep impression on his fellow aviators. Paul Rockwell, whose brother Kiffin flew with Hoskier, wrote at the time.

"From the day of his departure for the Front, every time I've met one of the pilots or have received news from the Escadrille Lafayette, Hoskier has been mentioned as one of the most active members of the unit. Since his arrival, the Squadron has not made a single sortie in which he has not taken part. He had innumerable combats and I have heard so much of these that I am always afraid of receiving the news that he has been killed."

The day of Sergeant Ronald W. Hoskier's death was April 23, 1917. His Morane Parasol monoplane was shot down in a cloudy sky over France, killing him and his machine-gunner, Dressy, instantly. The last few minutes of their fateful flight were described in the book *The Lafayette Flying Corps* edited by James N. Hall and Charles B. Nordhoff:

Evidently Hoskier saw a German beneath him, and apparently he dove on him, and at the same instant several other enemy machines appeared. They encircled him and opened fire. He hadn't a chance. Suddenly his Morane was seen to dive straight down, full motor. The wings folded up and that was the end. Poor Dressy was thrown clear of the machine in the fall. It is some comfort to us that both men fell within our lines. Their bodies were brought to Ham and buried here, with full military honors, close to little Genet [Belgium].

Although Hoskier was the only New Jerseyan to fly with the original Escadrille 124, a number of other young men from the Garden State joined a later organization called The Lafayette Escadrille. They all held non-commissioned officer ranks and came from the northern portion of the state. They were Cpl. John R. Adams of Jersey City, Cpl. Stuart E. Edgar and Sgt. Robert B. Hoebner, both of Nutley, Sgt. Charles M. Jones of Red Bank, Sgt. Elmer B. Taylor of Cedar Grove and Sgt. Stephen M. Tyson of Princeton. Milton W, Holden of Camden joined the Lafayette Flying Corps but was injured in training and never flew in combat. Edgar and Tyson were killed in action.

When the United States declared war on Germany, April 6, 1917, the official personnel strength of the Aviation Section, Army Signal Corps, was 131 regulars and reserves. Of that number 112 were pilots. The number of Army aircraft was reported to be "less than 300."

New Jersey's Flying Aces

Leslie J. Rummell, Kenneth B. Unger, James W. Pearson, Oliver C. LeBoutillier and Arthur R. Brooks

The men who flew in combat during World War I saw themselves as knights-errant traveling in search of adventure. It was not uncommon for both Allied and German pilots to salute the opponent they had just conquered as the poor devil went spinning down in flames. To these 20th century knights, the dogfights over the Marne were, in many cases, just an extension of a polo match or any other team sport — only the stakes were higher.

New Jersey had four native born flying aces in World War I, Lt. Leslie J. Rummell and Lt. Kenneth B. Unger both of Newark, Capt. James W. Pearson of Nutley and Capt. Oliver C. LeBoutillier of East Orange. Rummell was the only one who flew with the American Expeditionary Forces. The other three were fighter pilots with the British Royal Air Force. Capt. Arthur Raymond Brooks, born in Massachu-

setts, spent more than 60 years in the Garden State, mostly in Summit, also flew with the United States Air Service.

Rummell served with the 93rd Aero Squadron, Third Pursuit Group. He was shipped overseas on Christmas Day 1917. During 11 months of combat flying, he was credited with downing seven enemy planes and was awarded the Distinguished Service Cross in September of 1918. The citation read:

"Lieutenant Leslie J. Rummell, leading a patrol of three planes, sighted an enemy biplane which was protected by seven planes (Fokker type). Despite tremendous odds, he led his patrol into battle and destroyed the De Nash plane. By his superior maneuvering and leadership four more planes were destroyed and the remaining three retired."

A graduate of the Newark Academy and Cornell University, Rummell was about to enter Harvard Law School when he decided to apply for the air service. He never did return to the United States to finish his schooling for in January of 1919, he died of pneumonia at the Colombey les Belles Base Hospital in France. Ironically, two days before the official word of his death reached his family, his mother received a letter from him stating that he was recovering.

In September of 1919, Rummell's parents, Mr. and Mrs. Jacob Rummell, dedicated a memorial stained glass window in their son's memory at the Church of the Redeemer on Broad and Hill Streets in Newark, opposite City Hall. In October, an American Legion Post was organized in Newark and named the Leslie J. Rummell Post No. 164.

At age 19, **Unger**, who had learned to fly under the auspices of the United State Aero Club, attempted to enlist in the U.S. flying service and was refused, so he joined the U.S. Navy. But the urge to fly was all consuming, so in June 1917, he went AWOL, made his way to Canada and joined the Royal Flying Corps. Following intensive flight training, Unger was sent to England in April of 1918 and was assigned to the veteran 210 Squadron.

In less than ten months, the New Jerseyan had distinguished himself as a flying ace with 14 confirmed "kills." In one day, June 26, he shot down four German fighters during a prolonged dogfight over the French countryside.

By the war's end, Unger was the fifth ranking ace of Squadron 210 which scored more victories and produced more aces than any other Royal Air Force unit.

Pearson received his commission in the Royal Flying Corps in November of 1917. He was assigned to the RFC's 23rd Squadron and downed his first enemy plane on May 30, 1918. He received credit for the conquest of a German fighter in both June and July, and his two victories in August qualified him as an "ace."

Over the next two months he raised his total victory count to eight and on November 1, 1918, ten days before the Armistice, he won his last aerial battle.

Pearson returned to the United States in March of 1919 on medical leave, and the following September resigned his commission and returned to Nutley.

The Red Baron's Last Flight

Early in 1917, **LeBoutillier** joined the Canadian Flying Corps. He had learned to fly in Mineola, NY, the previous year, so the Canadians gave him an additional 29 hours of flying instruction and then sent him to France to do battle against Germany's crack flying aces. Among his opponents was the famous German ace, Manfred von Richthofen, known as the "Red Baron."

Richthofen personally destroyed more than 80 Allied planes before he was shot down April 21, 1918, over France. LeBoutillier took part in the dogfight in which the Red Baron was finally conquered.

In 1970, at his home in Las Vegas, NV, he remembered that adventure with absolute clarity:

"It was the greatest fight of any war under any circumstances," he said. He noted that Australian ground forces claimed credit for killing the Baron, but LeBoutillier felt it had been a fellow pilot, Capt. Roy Brown, who dealt the coup de grace to the German ace. The Canadian RAF officially credits Brown with the kill.

"By God, I saw Brown's tracer bullets hitting into the fuselage around the cockpit area," LeBoutillier exclaimed. "The Baron turned his head, knew he had been fired on, and continued chasing another Canadian pilot, Lt. Wilfred May."

It had been a lopsided aerial confrontation from the beginning. Eleven Allied Sopwith Camel fighter planes were badly outnumbered by Richthofen's 27 planes of the so-called "Flying Circus".

"We all came back that day on both sides except Richthofen," LeBoutillier recalled. The red triplane that Richthofen flew in that last battle was designed by a young Dutchman named Anthony Fokker. It was considered one of the most maneuverable aircraft of the time. As the Camels and German fighters mixed together in deadly combat, LeBoutillier recalled, "I never saw so many German triplanes in my life!"

He described the last minutes of the Red Baron's final flight: "Brown made his pass on the red triplane near the tower of Vaux [France]. When Richthofen's plane passed over the 53rd Battery it made, more or less, a flat turn, wobbled a bit, then glided to the ground. From all reports, it's a good possibility that von Richthofen was dead before his plane hit the ground."

LeBoutillier said he dropped from 2,000 feet to approximately 300 feet, witnessed Richthofen's last minute in the air and returned to his base. It was

hours later that his squadron learned that the pilot of the red triplane was Germany's ace of aces.

The 24-year-old American had his share of aerial victories. From April 1917 to May of 1918, LeBoutillier was credited with destroying seven enemy aircraft and had a shared victory with a fellow squadron member.

He returned to the United States in 1919 and barnstormed around the country. In the classic films *Hell's Angels and Wings*, he was hired to fly the aerial combat footage.

LeBoutillier was proud of the fact that he gave Amelia Earhart her first twin engine instruction. It was in the Lockheed Electra in which the aviatrix and her navigator disappeared in 1937.

After a stint as a test pilot for Howard Hughes and as a CAA inspector, LeBoutillier founded a wholesale drug company in the 1950s. He died in 1983.

Ray Brooks, a graduate of the Massachusetts Institute of Technology, joined the air service in December of 1916. He trained with the Royal Flying Corps in Canada, and when the United States went to war, he was commissioned a 2nd Lieutenant with the American Expeditionary Force.

"I was an eager beaver to die for this country," Brooks said years later. "Don't ask me why, that's just the way I felt. I had a Guardian Angel to whom I prayed often, daily in fact. I also had another physical angel named Sister Mary Magdalene of the Assumption. She promised to pray for me while I was overseas. I credit my life to those two angels."

Brooks did his initial combat flying with the 139th Aero Squadron and shot down his first Fokker in July, 1918. He was then transferred to the 22nd

Capt. Arthur Raymond Brooks

"I was an eager beaver to die for this country," Brooks said years later. "Don't ask me why, that's just the way I felt. I had a Guardian Angel to whom I prayed often, daily in fact. I also had another physical angel named Sister Mary Magdalene of the Assumption. She promised to pray for me while I was overseas. I credit my life to those two angels."

Brooks did his initial combat flying with the 139th Aero Squadron and shot down his first Fokker in July, 1918. He was then transferred to the 22nd Pursuit Squadron and destroyed five more enemy aircraft before the Armistice.

The day he remembered most vividly was September 14, 1918 when he inadvertently came under attack by eight Fokker D-7 aircraft baring the markings of Richthofen's Flying Circus fighter squadron.

"It was a helluva scramble," he reminisced. "We were about three miles deep in German territory. We had the sun behind us and a cloud cover beneath us. Suddenly, I detected a formation of Fokkers above us and saw we were going to be jumped! I figured I was a dead bunny. I was plenty scared and yelling to no purpose at the top of my lungs. I figured I'd do as much damage as possible before the inevitable.

"Twice I tried to ram them. One red-nosed nightmare came in from my right and I had just time enough to see his feature before I let him have a few incendiary bullets. I turned upon another and after a short burst was satisfied a second had quit."

At that point, Brooks decided he had pushed his luck to the limit and turned back toward friendly lines now some 10 miles away. But one of the Red Baron's pilots was persistent and hung on the American's tail.

"He began trailing me and I figured he had me cold," Brooks continued. "My plane had taken more than 100 bullets. A wing spar was shot away. One of my rudder controls was gone. He was firing bursts at me. I was side slipping by using the toe of my boot on a severed control wire regulating the rudders. I was able to dodge his gun bursts in this way. Eventually he broke off contact and I was able to alight on a grassy strip just within the Allied lines. I had escaped death again."

Brooks' Spad XIII biplane, *Smith IV*, now belongs to the Smithsonian Institution in Washington, DC. The Smith one, two and three had been so badly damaged during Brooks aerial battles, they had to be scraped. As he explained, all of them were named for his girl friend back home.

"Well, you see, I had this girl, Ruth Connery, that I had met while attending M.I.T. before I joined the Army and started flying in France. I didn't want to call my plane *Ruth* because someday I might have to say that *Ruth* got shot in the tail and that wouldn't be nice. So I called my planes *Smith* after the college she went to."

Ridgewood's DeGarmo Brothers

The DeGarmo brothers of Ridgewood, NJ, all served with the Army Flying Service. Lindley, the oldest, graduated from Cornell University with an engineering degree. He was killed in England when the motor of his Spad biplane failed while in flight. He made a successful forced landing on a rough field, and although the plane survived with only light damage, the jolt broke Lindley's neck. He was 27 years old and had been living in Coconut Grove, FL. The Lindley DeGarmo American Legion Post in Coconut Grove is named for him. He was the first Ridgewood native to lose his life during the first world war.

Elmer DeGarmo was also a wartime pilot assigned as a flight instructor at the old Homestead Airport in Florida. He never served overseas. In post war years, Elmer worked as a road engineer in Florida and supervised the construction of the "Overseas Highway" to Key West.

When George DeGarmo followed his brothers' footsteps, he was too young to be a pilot. He served overseas for 22 months in England and France with the 341st Aero Squadron, and achieved the rank of sergeant. After the war, George went on to a distinguished aeronautical career in New Jersey.

Walter Avery of Maplewood flew as a combat pilot and was awarded the Distinguished Service Cross and the French Croix de Guerre for his efforts. Following the war, he remained in aviation. He helped locate the first beacon sites needed to establish air mail routes for the Department of Commerce. In the 1940s, he was the supervisor of Passenger Service for Eastern Airlines. He retired in 1955.

A number of Early Bird Pilots were pressed into service as civilian instructors. Those whose aeronautical achievements touched the Garden State before and after the war were Bert Acosta, Billy Diehl, Ed Musick and James Hill.

Edwin F. Kingsbury, a long time Rutherford resident, served with the U.S. Army Air Service, Bureau of Aircraft Production and attained the rank of Captain. Kingsbury, a physicist, was engaged in the development of aerial camera and the testing of the first successful aerial cameras using large-sized film. During his service, he invented a flicker photometer, that measured lights of different colors. It replaced a German instrument that had become unobtainable during the war years.

In October of 1918, **Major Frederic E. Humphrey** of Summit, the first American military man to fly an airplane in 1909, was appointed commander of the Massachusetts Institute of Technology's School of Aeronautical Engineering. He headed the Department of Practical Airplane Design from October 1918 to January 1919, when he was assigned to McCook Field, Dayton, OH, to become one of the founders of the Research Center of Aeronautical Work.

The Armistice, Nov. 11

William Dolan

Lt. William Dolan of Boonton was based at Issoudun, France , then the largest flying school in the world, with the First Reserve Aero Squadron. On Nov. 10, 1918, when it became certain that the Armistice would be signed, he and his fellow airmen hopped in their planes and made a mad dash to Orly Field, outside Paris. They wanted to be in the City of Lights for the big celebration.

"Everybody who could take off, took off, and, in anything that could fly." the veteran said 40 years later at his Ridgewood home. "Once we got there it was bedlam. A great celebration. Everybody was in a festive mood, and we had quite a few drinks. It's hard to put into words."

Dolan explained that he and his buddies believed they were celebrating the end of warfare for all time.

"We thought it was the war to end all wars. I was glad it was over because so many wonderful young men were getting killed. We were glad it was over, but I regretted I didn't get a chance to get to the front and test my skills."

As an enlisted man, Dolan took flight instruction at Issoudun, and won his pilot's wings in Sept. 1918. He was commissioned as a 2nd Lieutenant.

"Eddie Rickenbacker [the leading American ace] was the first U.S. enlisted man to become a pilot, and yours truly was number two." Dolan said proudly.

In discussing the enemy, Dolan claimed, "We had no animosity against the Germans. There was actually a sort of chivalry in those days, at least in some ways. If a man was killed over their lines, they'd fly over and drop his boots."

At the outbreak of World War II, Dolan volunteered for service in the Air Corps. Although he served as an intelligence officer with the 384th Bombardment Group of the 8th Air Force, he did fly nine bomber missions over occupied France and Germany. At age 48, his young compatriots called him "Pop," although he held the rank of Lt. Colonel.

Having been born on the 4th of July 1894, Dolan was truly a Yankee Doodle Dandy who had strong patriotic beliefs. When he was 89 years old he commented on how Americans have changed since World War I.

"Young people today are entirely different. In World War I, you had the top young men of the country clamoring to get in [the service]. They were college boys—Harvard, Yale, Princeton, Dartmouth. You had people paying their own way over there. We had the richest bachelor in America as our mess cook. We had one old guy, Bruce Wayman, I say old, he was 37 and we wanted to take care of him, so we made him the dog-robber [orderly] for Hobie Backer. One day I came into Hobie's tent, and Hobie was polishing his own boots while Bruce sang for him.

"We had this feeling, back in 1917, of love of country, pride in our branch of service, pride in our family and pride in ourselves. Today, if you stood up and talked about those things, you'd be considered a square."

"Pop" Dolan stayed active in the 384th Bombardment Group Association, and in 1983, went to England to help dedicate a stained glass window in the Parish Church of St. James the Apostle in Grafton Underwood, Northamptonshire in honor of those airmen who lost their lives during the war. The airfield used by the 384th was on the outskirts of the pristine village.

Dolan died in Ridgewood in 1987.

First Commercial Aircraft

Charles Healy Day

Inducted Aviation Hall of Fame of New Jersey 1981

Along with the establishment of an Army Air Service, another project the Aero Club of America vigorously promoted was a nationwide air mail service. In order to demonstrate the feasibility of carrying mail by air, in 1916 Alan Hawley, the club president, flew from New York to Washington DC, carrying a heavy bundle of newspapers, representing the mail. Victor Carlstrom was the pilot. The trip in an open cockpit biplane took three hours and seven minutes. The flight was hailed a great success by the Aero Club, but considered nothing more than a publicity stunt by the Washington bureaucrats.

The idea did not die completely. Almost two years later, while most Americans were absorbed in an all-out effort to win the war in Europe, the Post Office Department and the Army agreed to join forces to establish an air mail service between New York and

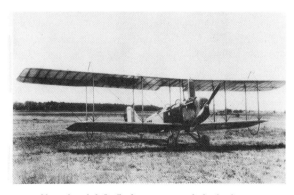

Standard J-1, first commercial airplane

Washington. Airfields were hastily cleared at Belmont Park race track on Long Island, in North Philadelphia and at the old Polo Grounds in Washington Heights' Potomac Park.

Curtiss JN-4s (Jennies), military training planes, were chosen for the first experimental flight. The plan called for one Jennie to fly from Belmont Park south to North Philadelphia, while another of the biplanes would fly north from Washington. At Philadelphia, the mail from either direction would be transferred to other airplanes with fresh pilots, and continue on its journey north or south.

The flights began in May of 1918 with Army pilots at the controls. They continued with moderate success until July. During the trial period, there were no major accidents but the service was not as dependable as the Post Office had hoped, due to poor weather conditions that frequently grounded the aircraft.

That summer, the Post Office Department and the Army severed their partnership, although the Army Air Service agreed to share the know-how it had gained during the months its airmen flew the mail. Ironically, the first superintendent of the Aerial Mail Service, as it was then called, was a Captain Benjamin 0. Lipsner, who had been discharged by the Army so that he could assume his new position. Working with an advisory staff, Lipsner established a list of specifications for prospective air mail planes and then proceeded to ask manufacturers to submit their aircraft for testing.

Within a few months, the Standard JR-1, built by the Standard Aircraft Corporation in the Bayway section of Elizabeth, NJ, was the aircraft of choice. The prototype of the airplane, designed by Charles Healy Day, had first been flight tested just as the United States entered the war by a subsidiary company, Standard Aero Corp. of Plainfield.

Day converted the pilot's front cockpit into a mail compartment and the rear observer's pit became the pilot's control cockpit. The newly revamped machine was called the JR-1B and sold for $13,500.

In August 1918, the Post Office Department received six new JR-1Bs. They had the same 150 hp engines as the "Jennies," but could fly at greater speeds, were more fuel efficient and were designed to carry 200 pounds of mail.

The new mail service began on August 12, 1918, flown by experienced civilian pilots, between Bayway and Washington. Within the first few months, it became apparent that the Bayway Field was unsuitable for regular air mail service because of a poor approach pattern over Morse Creek and a tendency to flood. So operations were transferred back to Belmont Race Track.

Those six Standard airplanes designed and built in New Jersey, became the first commercial aircraft flown on a regular basis in the United States.

In less than a year, air mail service became considerably more reliable between Washington and New York, and new routes were established as far west as Chicago.

In those formative years, air mail pilots became romantic heroes. Although their job seemed routinely repetitious, hardly a day passed without a challenge for an air mail pilot to overcome.

The Washington-New York route seemed tranquil when compared with the flight from New York to Chicago via Bellefonte, PA, and Cleveland, OH. The major obstacle on that route was the treacherous Allegheny mountain range that spawned changing weather conditions. Heavy ground fog, sudden rain squalls, unpredictable wind patterns and low-hanging clouds were a constant threat to the safety of the planes and airmen. That rolling Allegheny terrain was dubbed "Hell Stretch" by the postal pilots.

The first group of civilian Post Office pilots included: Ed Gardner, Maurice Newton, Max Miller and Robert Shank. They were soon joined by Leon "Windy" Smith, Mike Eversole, E. Hamilton Lee, John Miller, Charles Anglin, Dean Smith, James Edgerton, John Charlton, Harry Scherlock, Frederick Robinson, Randolph Page and Jack Webster.

During the war years, a total of 1,601 Standard Js were built as Army trainers, although those fitted with Hall-Scott 4-Banger engines were banished from the service due to excessive vibration that caused fuel line fractures and resultant fires.

Following the war, the Curtiss Corporation bought almost 1,000 surplus SJ-1s, fitted them with their own OX-5 engines and sold them to private pilots and early barnstormers. When Standard Aircraft closed in 1919, other versions of the biplane were built from surplus parts purchased from the New Jersey factory. Because of their greater weight-carrying capability, the SJ-1 became more popular with barnstormers than the famous Curtiss "Jenny".

1919
Atlantic Skies Conquered

At the conclusion of War World I, aviators from all nations were seeking new worlds to conquer. The most challenging feat for pilots of the period was a flight across the Atlantic Ocean. To make the challenge more enticing, Lord Northcliffe, owner of

London's The *Daily Mail*, offered a prize of £ 10,000 (approximately $50,000) to the first airman to conquer the Atlantic skies.

Just a month before the Armistice was signed on November 11, 1918, the U.S. Navy tested the first of four large flying boats designed and built by Curtiss Aeroplane and Motor Co. They were designated as Navy-Curtiss (NC) flying boats.

"If there is to be no fight for these fine ships of both sea and air, then let us at least give them a chance to display their ability at long-distance flying," said the Aircraft Committee of the Navy. Under the direction of Commander John Tower, plans were made for an adventurous undertaking while the last two NC ships were still under construction.

It was decided that the flying boats, each with a six-man crew, would fly from Far Rockaway, L.I. to Trepassey, Newfoundland, then make the long, overwater hop to the Azores to refuel before flying on to Lisbon, Portugal and on up to Plymouth, England. To help assure a reasonably successful venture, the Navy strung 41 destroyers between Trepassey and the Portuguese islands as navigational landmarks.

In March 1919, a severe storm badly damaged the NC-1's wings. In order not to delay the flight, it was decided to fit the NC-1 with the wings of the NC-2, thus eliminating one flying boat from the journey. It wasn't until May 8 that the three remaining aircraft left Far Rockaway and headed north to Trepassey, 1,150 miles away. The NC-3, with Cmdr. Towers aboard, led the pack followed by the NC-1 and 4.

Off the coast of Cape Cod, the NC-4 had engine trouble forcing it to land on the open sea and taxi for five hours to the Chatham Naval Air Station. She arrived in Newfoundland four days later.

On May 16, all three boats were ready to start across the unpredictable ocean. They flew in a loose formation for many hours, then were separated by heavy rains and fog. The NC-1 and NC-3 made forced landings on heavy seas. The ocean was so rough that the NC-1 crew abandoned their flying boat and were rescued by a cargo ship. The NC-3, rode out the storm for more than 24 hours before she taxied into port at Ponta Delgada in the Azores.

Although their fuel supply was dangerously low, the NC-4 flew on. Through a break in the clouds, the crew spotted the northern portion of the Azore Island of Fayal. When they landed on Horta harbor, they had been in the air for more than 25 hours.

On May 26, with the crew of the NC-3 cheering her on, the NC-4 began the 900 mile flight to Lisbon. Later in the afternoon of May 27, the Navy flying boat landed on the Tagus River. Albert C. Read, the tired but happy flight commander and navigator, radioed his superiors a message, terse and to the point:

"We are safely on the other side of the pond. The job is finished."

But the job wasn't finished. The next day the NC-4 set off for Plymouth, arriving at 9:26 a.m. on May 31,1919. Cmdr. Read and his crew had flown 3,936 nautical miles in a flying time of 52 hours and 31 minutes.

All Americans were proud of the accomplishment of the six brave men and their sturdy, American-built flying boat, but none more than Parmenus R. Southard, a prominent boat builder in Freeport, NY. Southard and a crew of six had constructed the floats used on the NC aircraft. Lou West of Wanaque, NJ, the grandson of Southard, takes pride in the fact that the brave men who flew aboard the NC ships were well-educated for that time but the man who expertly supervised the construction of the strong pontoons had only a third-grade education.

West also remembers that the pontoons on the NC-4 had begun to leak from the pounding they had taken on the ocean and when the biplane was returned by ship to the United States, his grandfather's men rebuilt them.

John Alcock and Arthur Brown

Individual American and British flyers were hot in pursuit of the *Daily Mail* prize money. One of the first to announce his intentions was Hugo Sunstedt, who had designed a huge biplane flying boat that had been built by the Wittemann brothers. He named it "Sunrise" and on early tests, the ship seemed capable of making the flight. But during a test flight early in 1919, the big plane crashed into the waters off Bayonne and sank from sight. It was Sunstedt's "sunset" instead.

Two British teams shipped aircraft to St. John's, Newfoundland, in the spring of 1919, determined to be the first to fly non-stop between the continents. On May 18, Harry Hawker and Ken Grieve took off from St. John and set a straight course of 1,925 miles toward the Irish coast. After covering a trifle more than 1,000 miles, engine trouble forced them to alight on the sea where they were rescued by a passing ship.

An hour after Hawker and Grieve departed, they were joined in the race by Fred Raynham and Fairfax Morgan. On takeoff an axle broke and two months later, when they tried again, a crosswind wrecked the machine as soon as it rose from the ground.

The next two planes brought to Newfoundland in order to take advantage of constant westerly winds, were a Handley Page V/1, 500 bomber, under the command of Adm. Mark Kerr, and a Vickers-Vimy bomber and its crew, Capt. John Alcock, a former Royal Air Force pilot, and Lt. Arthur "Teddie" Brown, who had been a wartime aerial observer and a self-taught navigator.

Both groups worked feverishly to reassemble and flight test their aircraft. The Handley Page was based at Harbour Grace and Adm. Kerr had refused to let Alcock and Brown use his field until he was through occupying it. Angered by the admiral's attitude, the two Brits moved onto the rough field on which Raynham and Morgan's plane had broken its axle, determined to be first in the air.

And first they were. On the morning of June 14, Alcock gunned the twin-engine bomber across 600 feet of rough turf before it became airborne. Spectators watched as the biplane hung about 200 feet off the ground, fighting a gusting head wind that seemed determined keep it from climbing to a higher elevation. Finally the plane's altitude increased and the two men pointed its nose toward Galway Bay.

Sixteen hours later, their ice-scarred and weather-beaten Vickers-Vimy was circling over Clifden, Ireland, its pilot looking for a safe place to land. Alcock spotted what appeared to be a level field and glided down gently. When the bomber was only 50 feet above the ground, the pilot realized his landing place was a bog. It was too late to pull up so down they went. As the wheels hit the muck, they dug in up to their hubs, pitching the bomber's nose into the mire and all but hurling the aviators out of the open cockpit.

No matter, the *Daily Mail* prize had been won.

British Dirigible R-34

The successful transatlantic flights of the NC-4 and Alcock and Brown's Vickers Vimy didn't dampen the enthusiasm of Brig. Gen. Edward Maitland the British Air Ministry's Director of Airships and his competent crew of airshipmen.

They had been prepared to fly the Atlantic from the east to the west in the rigid airship R-34 months before the two airplanes had accomplished the feat from west to east, but a test flight mishap altered their plans to cross in April.

The impressively large dirigible—643 feet long—left East Fortune, Scotland on July 1, 1919, under the command of Maj. George Scott. A total complement of 30 crewman and passengers, and one stowaway (an airman who had been dropped from the crew prior to the flight to save weight) were aboard. The stowaway wasn't discovered until the R-34 was over the ocean or he would have been dropped from the dirigible by parachute.

The one non-Brit on board was Lt. Cmdr. Zachary Lansdowne of the U.S. Navy, who had been invited along as an observer. Four years later, he would take command of the U.S.S. Shenandoah, the Navy's first airship.

The ship flew through fog and low cloud cover during the first two days of the voyage. Capt. Scott purposely kept the dirigible out of the hot sun to avoid expansion and loss of the highly flammable hydrogen gas.

The skies cleared on the third day and the crew had their first look at the vast ocean dotted with glistening icebergs. Later that day, July 4, the Newfoundland coast was crossed and the R-34 turned south toward its final destination, Mineola, New York.

In his personal logbook, Gen. Maitland wrote:

"As we skim over this American countryside, I confess to a delightful glow of satisfaction at gazing on American soil for the first time—from above. It brings home to me more than anything else could ever do, what a small place this world really is, what an astonishing part these great Airship Liners will play in linking together the remotest places of the earth; and what interesting years lie immediately ahead!"

The following day, the weather turned ugly and the airship was buffeted by gusting winds, dangerous up and down drifts and frightening lightning flashes. The situation became so ugly, Maj. Scott asked U.S. Navy vessels to stand by in case of an emergency landing.

The weather cleared during the night and although dangerously low of fuel, Scott pushed on toward Long Island. At 9:54 a.m., Sunday, July 6th, the first rigid airship to fly over America soil landed at Mineola. The flight had taken 108 hours and 12 minutes.

After three days of parties and ceremonies honoring their unprecedented flight, Capt. Scott and his crew began the return flight to England. A strong tail wind helped the airship complete the journey in just over three days. As the third decade of the 20th century began, a total of 39 men had flown across the forbidding Atlantic Ocean.

Wrights Moves to Paterson
Frederick B. Rentschler

When defense contracts dried up after the Armistice in 1918, many manufacturers of aircraft, engines and accessories were forced to shut down their operations. The civilian market was limited mainly to air service veterans who became barnstorming nomads, flying inexpensive war surplus aircraft.

Despite their prestigious name, the Wright-Martin Company of New Brunswick, which had built approximately 10,000 Hispano-Suiza engines between 1917 and early 1919 at a total cost of more than $50 million in the large Simplex automobile plant, found themselves in the same position as other, less well-known manufacturers — business was drying up. So work-

United Technologies archives

Frederick Rentschler

ers were laid off and in October 1919, the Wright-Martin Corp. was dissolved.

Frederick B. Rentschler, a former officer of Wright-Martin believed that the aviation business had a sound future beyond the hoopla of spectacular flights and entertaining barnstormers. So when Wright-Martin closed its doors, Rentschler and other officers involved with Wrights, before the Martin merger formed the Wright Aeronautical Company and moved into a new plant in Paterson, NJ. The space available was on the third and fourth floors of a building in which a phonograph cabinet maker occupied the first two floors. In less than a year, however, Wrights Aeronautical took over the lower floors.

Through his personal contacts in Washington, Rentschler immediately secured Navy contracts for additional Hispano-Suiza engines to keep his small work force occupied. At the same time, he and his engineering staff threw their efforts into improving various models of water-cooled engines. The first new engine developed in Paterson was designated the Model E-2 and it immediately established a reliability record in Army tests.

In 1922, the "T" engines were created. They were called the Wright Tornado and Typhoon. The same year, the company decided to build airplanes for their engines and enter them in various prestigious races around the country. Soon Wright engines were delivering speeds of more than 200 mph and attracting the attention of both military men and other aircraft manufacturers. The company was on the way up. (see 1923)

Pilot's Nightmare
Heller Field

In order to be nearer vital rail links and to eliminate the need to fly over Manhattan Island, the Post Office Department decided to move its New York air mail landing site from Belmont Park race track to an odd-shaped piece of land in North Newark owned by Paul Elias Heller. The new facility was named Heller Field (now part of Branch Brook Park).

One has to wonder who chose the Heller site. Certainly it wasn't the pilots. They would not have chosen to fly in and out of the triangular-shaped field encircled by obstacles that made landings and take-offs risky for even the most seasoned airmen.

The simple 1,800 foot turf runway had the Morris Canal along one side, a converging set of railroad tracks on another and the large Tiffany Silversmith Co. building, with a jutting red brick chimney, on the third side.

Although the dedication of the field was set for Dec. 15, 1919, the first mail plane arrived on Dec. 6. The plane was flown by Walter H. Stevens, with Victor Nain, a mechanic, in the front seat. Carrying 700 lbs. of mail from Washington, Stevens nursed the open cockpit plane through a snowstorm before landing easily at Heller Field. In his book, *The Seat of My Pants*, Dean C. Smith, one of the country's most talented air mail pilots, described the new terminus:

Heller Field was probably the worst of all. Situated as it was between Tiffany's factory and a canal, approaching planes had to glide between the factory building and a steep hill, make a sharp bank over a gully filled with debris and quickly set down, right out of the turn, to land at the edge of the field. It was so small that they had bulldozed a mound of earth for the plane to run into. When a new pilot would come in for his first landing, the employees of Tiffany's would line up on the ramp to observe; they were usually rewarded with a spectacular splash in the canal, a wild ground loop or a nose-up into the mound.

A number of pilots learned to play it safe and landed on the adjacent Forest Hill golf course, rather than risk the dangers at Heller Field.

Almost immediately after the formal dedication, it became obvious that the North Newark facility was a death trap. On a cold, snowy Friday, in late January 1920, U.S. Mail plane #203 crashed landed in the mound of earth. The pilot escaped with only minor injuries. But in March, pilot Harry Sherlock was not as fortunate. As he approached the field, he misjudged the banking radius of his World War 1 Martin bomber and crashed into the Tiffany chimney. The

A Heller Field landing.

plane broke into several sections and the top half of the stack tumbled to the ground. Sherlock was found dead still strapped in the cockpit.

Just 12 days after Sherlock's dramatic accident, pilot Fred Robinson took a Heller Field mail clerk up for a spin in his Curtiss Jenny. When they reached an altitude of 1,000 feet, the Jenny went into an unexplained dive and fell to the ground like a stone. The clerk was crushed and died instantly, but Robinson survived, only to be killed five months later in a plane crash near Millersburg, PA.

In October, on his third day on the job, John P.Carlton Jr. was killed instantly when his frail plane smashed into a nearby Essex County hillside on a foggy morning.

In all, 26 air mail employees died in airplane accidents between December 1919 and May 1921, when the airfield was closed. It was a sad period in the history of the Post Office Department.

Murchio Airport
Tom Murchio

Inducted Aviation Hall of Fame of New Jersey, 1983

Tom and Joe Murchio of Haskell, NJ, leased a 70-acre section of the Van Orden farm on Hamburg Turnpike in Preakness (Wayne Township) and began flying two World War I Curtiss "Jennies" from a makeshift runway. They took earthlings on short flights for $10 or on the grand tour of Passaic and Bergen counties for $25.

The brothers were expert mechanics and had owned and operated an automobile repair shop in Pompton Lakes, NJ, since 1914. But like so many other early automobile enthusiasts, Tom and Joe lifted their sights skyward and developed a fascination for airplanes.

The airplane passenger business was better than the two men had anticipated, so they purchased the "airfield" in 1922, built a fieldstone hangar and named it Murchio Airport. Business remained brisk throughout the 1920s, especially on Sundays. Crowds estimated at 3,000 to 4,000 would walk, drive or ride their bicycles to the sod airfield, line up on either side of the runway and watch as stunt flyers and parachute jumpers perform their aerobatic tricks. The Murchios and their pilots sold rides for a dollar or two.

In 1924, a new form of aerial advertising originated at Murchio's. A Standard J-1 biplane with an electric sign mounted under its bottom wing flew at night over towns and cities in New Jersey and New York advertising the highly acclaimed motion picture *Iron Horse*. Although the lighted aerial signs became popular in the next decade on the large billboard-size sides of blimps, the limited space beneath an

The Murchio gang - top: Joe Pavlick, Tom Weir, Fred Weiss, Bill Beach, Bill Markey, Tom Murchio. middle: George Kotteles, Fred Jansen, Jim Durren, Bob Golem, Warren Wanamaker, Irv Fullard. bottom: Henry Bragga, Hank Murata, Pete Kinney.

airplane's wings and the greater speed of the craft made the idea obsolete before it had a chance to prove its worth.

When Joe Murchio was married in 1927, his wife Helena insisted he give up flying, so he opened an auto repair shop in Greenwood Lake, NY, and began collecting and restoring antique cars. His collection became so well known, he was asked to put 25 vintage cars on display in the Asbury Park Convention Hall each summer.

That same year, 1927, the aviation industry boomed following the successful flights across the Atlantic by Lindbergh, Chamberlin and Byrd. Tom Murchio built two wooden hangars beside his runway. He also designed and built four airplanes that he used for "passenger hopping" (a phrase used for short sightseeing flights), and became a dealer for Air King biplanes.

The Sunday air show business went well until 1931 when an aviation board was established in New Jersey to regulate pilots and the aircraft they flew. Neither the war surplus or Murchio's wooden planes could get ATC (stress analysis) ratings, so Tom was out of business temporarily.

Always known as a tough taskmaster with the pilots who used his field, Murchio was forced for the first time to open the airport to itinerant pilots and to rent tie-down space. Those early Depression years were bleak for everyone.

When ATC-rated Taylor Cub monoplanes were introduced to the market, Murchio purchased several and was back in business.

Many well-known New Jersey pilots and parachutists flew into Murchios or worked for him as weekday instructors and Sunday stunt fliers. They included Bill Rainey, Ed Gates, Pete and Bill Beversluis, George Wanamaker (of the department store family), Buddy and Bob Golem, Bruno Vitale and his brother "Esso," who was an instructor. Riggy Braga and George Lambros, (who in later years had a successful float plane base on the Hackensack River) and Pete Kinney, (remembered as entertainer Arthur Godfrey's mechanic at Teterboro) were also Murchio regulars. The first woman pilot in the area was Mary Reifschneider. Bill Rhode and Frank Hammond were the regular parachutists. Rhode established a parachute jumping record there just prior to World War II (see 1940.)

Rhode related a conversation he had with pilot Bruce Huppert, who flew one the large Curtiss Condor biplanes, used by transatlantic flier Clarence Chamberlin to hop passengers from various airfields around the United States in the 1930s:

"Clarence Chamberlin purchased three Curtiss Condors, built in 1929 for the airlines, and reconditioned them at Teterboro Airport. They originally carried 18 passengers, but by removing the rest rooms and kitchen, Chamberlin was able to increase the capacity to 25. He then formed Chamberlin Air Tours and barnstormed around the country with the three airplanes taking passengers on short hops for one dollar each.

"Chamberlin and Huppert spent a very profitable weekend at Murchio's in July 1937, although the runway was a bit short for the large planes. When landing, they had to float in over the highway and parking lot, and then taxi back to load and unload their passengers. Chamberlin told Huppert, 'You're bringing it in too fast. You're using up 2,000 feet of runway for your landing. The time it takes you to taxi back to the passenger corral could be used in another trip.' Huppert replied, 'If I bring it in any slower, it'll fall out of the sky.'

"Chamberlin was resolute and decided to demonstrate what he meant. He took the giant Condor around the field, and on the final approach, he slow-flighted it in with power. As the big bird pancaked briskly to earth, Chamberlin yanked the control column back and the Condor kissed the grass very lightly. He rolled about 1,200 feet and was back at the passenger corral almost immediately.

"'Oh! That's how you do it,' Huppert said, smiling at his boss. The two pilots carried 1,200 that day at $1 each."

Rhode remembered other pilots who spent happy times with him at Murchio such as Alden Russell, John Syrek, Ralph Baker, Len Herman, Frank Reiser, Roy Van Houten and Al Boyd. All of them were competing for a chance to make a few dollars on the busy weekends.

"When the war came it changed everything," said Rhode. "Airplanes were no longer a novelty. The circus days were over."

Until Tom Murchio died in 1950, the airport was used mostly as a flying school. The G.I. bill provided the money for young men and women to take flying lessons and Bill Rhode estimates that several hundred veterans were taught aeronautics at Murchio's.

Bruno Vitale of Wayne recalled: "The flying school charged $6 an hour. Today it's up to around $30."

The airport continued to operate until 1956 when it was sold to developers. It cost Gerrard Berman $2,000 an acre, a high price in those days. "You know what that land is worth now?" Rhode asked in 1990

World's First Air-Port
Bader Field, Atlantic City

Glen Curtiss, who had introduced the first practical flying boat in 1911, returned to Atlantic City in 1915 and established a sightseeing service flying the early wooden-winged boats off the inlet. Flying over the South Jersey resort became the "in" thing to do among the summer residents.

In 1918, a movie producer named Jaccard also set up a flying boat base on the inlet. The competition, the heavy waves and windy days caused Curtiss to envision a land operation on a nearby marshy sandbar that had been partially filled over the years by the dumping of cinder from the resort hotels' furnaces.

The idea gained momentum when it was announced that the Second Pan-American Aeronautical Congress would be held on the Steel Pier beginning May 2, 1919. Under the leadership of an Atlantic City businessman, Henry Woodhouse, a group was formed to finance the creation of an airfield on the island, just 2,000 feet from the Boardwalk. In a 1978 interview in the *Atlantic City Press*, the former airfield project manager, John Rutter, then 88, told how the runways were laid out.

"A fella named J.W. Cuthbert had streets all cleared and lots set up because he was going to build a housing development there." Rutter remembered. "But nobody wanted to live there because there was no bridge to the island except around Virginia Avenue. In those days that area was 'the sticks.' So the city took the land back for taxes. Then, when they were going to put in an airfield, we just put the runways in where the streets were supposed to go."

Atlantic City proudly proclaims that it had the first "air-port" in the world. It was not the first municipal air facility in the United States, but it was the first to call itself an air-port. The word "air-port" reportedly was coined by Henry Woodhouse, who reasoned that Atlantic City was a wonderful place for a seaport so why not an "air-port?" Local newspapermen, however, claim the honor of coining the word "air-port" for William Dill, then editor of the *Atlantic City Press*. No matter whose idea it was, the first "air-port" in the world was in New Jersey.

The program published for the Second Pan-American Aeronautic Convention, Exhibition and Aerial Contests listed eight specific contests to be held each weekend from May 1 to June 1, with 14 daily activities. Some substantial prizes (for those days) were up for grabs. Most were underwritten by newspapers from various cities for flights of considerable distance. For instance: Boston to Atlantic City, Cleveland to A.C., Detroit to A.C.— everyone got into the act.

Lt. Roland Rohlfs of the Curtiss organization was the first pilot to land at the new facility. He had flown 125 miles from New York City and won a $500 Pulitzer prize for his efforts. Eddie Stinson was second. Stinson also landed eight consecutive times in a 15-foot circle. Lt. Omar L. Locklear, the renowned aerobatic pilot, gave an exhibition of climbing a rope ladder from one plane to another in mid-air. In addition, a crate of eggs was dropped by parachute. None were broken and they brought 25 cents each as souvenirs.

One serious accident marred the Aeronautical Congress. A plane carrying pilot Beryl H. Kendrick and passenger James H. Bew, Jr., overturned in a spin on May 24, killing both men.

The printed program also declared that the Atlantic City air-port was the official aviation field of the Aero Club of America, the Aerial League of America, the Atlantic City Aero Club, the Pan American Aeronautic Federation and the Aerial Coast Patrol Commission.

It went on to outline the purposes for which the facility was created. Among the expressions of purpose provided by Augustus Post, secretary of the Aerial League of America, indicated the belief that Atlantic City would be a leader in aviation development throughout the United States:

—To supply an air-port for trans-Atlantic liners, whether of the seaplane, land aeroplane or dirigible type."

—To establish a model airport which shall serve as a model for other American cities to follow in establishing municipal or public air-ports or aerodromes."

—To set an example which, if followed by approximately 100 cities in the United States in the near future, will supply the aerial transportation which this country needs; will keep American aeronautics in the forefront; will give employment to a large number of American Army and Navy airmen, aeronautic engineers and mechanics who have been demobilized; will permit the utilization and salvage of war aeronautical material worth tens of millions of dollars; and will insure the United States from again being caught unprepared in the event of war.

In September 1919, Joseph H. Shinn of the *Atlantic City Press,* flying with Earle Ovington, the president of the Curtiss Flying Station at Atlantic City, dropped 10,000 cards over the city announcing the arrival of the Navy plane NC-4 on its return from the first transatlantic flight by a fixed-wind aircraft.

To whet the appetite of seashore visitors every conceivable aeronautic stunt was attempted.

Ovington raced his Curtiss "Seagull" flying boat against high powered speedboats. Racing from a standing start, the seaplane was outdistanced by the speedboats at the beginning of the unique contest, the first of its kind in yacht racing.

Ovington had to be cautious not to let the "Seagull" become airborne for he would have been disqualified had the plane lifted off the water. The boats had a 50-yard lead heading into the home stretch, but Ovington correctly estimated the distance to the finish line, gave his plane the gun and finished nine seconds ahead of the boats. The plane became airborne 10 feet over the line.

At the far end of the gravel airport, Captain Hugh L. Willoughby, who, in 1890, had begun to experiment with aircraft models based on photographs and observations of birds, was constructing a seaplane known as the Willoughby Type H. He had built his first plane in 1909 in Atlantic City shortly after helping Orville Wright to make his first official flight in Washington, DC

The Third Pan-American Congress

From May 20 to May 30, 1920, the Third Pan-American Congress was held on the Steel Pier in the South Jersey playground. It was proclaimed the "greatest aeronautical event ever held." Alberto Santos-Dumont, pioneer Brazilian inventor and aeronaut, was named chairman of the Congress committee. He had spent more than $500,000 to develop the sport of aeronautics since 1901, when he first piloted a dirigible of his own design around the Eiffel Tower in Paris.

Thirty-two countries, 400 aero clubs and 5,000 other organizations and industrial representatives were invited to send delegates to the Congress.

Santos-Dumont stated at the time:

"Aerial transportation and aerial sports will knit the states of the Western Hemisphere into an integrally united, co-operating and friendly combination, allied for well-being in sport, trade and commerce, as well as for strength in time of possible war."

Two major events took place at the Congress. The inauguration of a plan for awarding private mail contracts was announced by Assistant Postmaster General Otto Praeger and an American record was set by the Larsen all-metal, six-passenger monoplane flying non-stop from Atlantic City to Philadelphia and return in 59 minutes.

Although aerial sightseeing remained popular among the approximately 10 million people who visited Atlantic City each year, the new air facility did not attract a great deal of commercial or private aircraft.

By 1922, Woodhouse and his group concluded that the airport was not the investment bonanza they had envisioned and on July 8 sold it to the city. An athletic field was created there and named for Edward L. Bader, then mayor of the resort. From that time on the first "airport" has been referred to as Bader Field.

The city fathers had invited Bevan "Bev" Baldwin, who had supervised the construction of Franklin Field in Philadelphia, to move to Atlantic City and lend his expertise in the building of the athletic field. Baldwin eventually had both the athletic field and airport under his jurisdiction.

Harry A. Nordheim

Inducted Aviation Hall of Fame, of New Jersey, 1988

Harry Nordheim

Atlantic City native, Harry "Knock" Nordheim remembered the inlet island before an airport was even considered. "It was nothing more than a place to dump furnace cinders." he said. "Ed Bader's father owned the trucks that collected the cinders so the Baders had it coming and going for them."

The first three 200 X 200 hangars Nordheim remembered had been moved from the beach where they had been used as train round-houses. In those early days, the trains from Philadelphia ran right to the water's edge.

"I thought the city was going to use them for storage and then Bader suggested an airport." he said. "The hurricane of 1944 knocked down one of the hangars. The entire field was under two feet of water. Another of those original hangars was demolished after the war. There is only one left now."

Nordheim claimed to be the first Atlantic City native to receive a mechanics Air Frame and Power plant license in 1929 and a year later the first to earn a private pilot's license. He received his commercial license late in 1930.

Following his historic solo flight from New York to Paris in May of 1927, Charles Lindbergh visited Atlantic City as part of the 82 city cross country tour the American hero undertook in the fall of that year. The purpose of the tour was to promote aviation and encourage future pilots. His comments concerning Bader Field were recorded in the *Boardwalk News*.

"Yes, the Atlantic City airport has good possibilities, and is in an ideal location to the city proper. In fact, it's the best situated in that respect, I think, than any I have yet encountered."

That opinion was seconded in March of 1928 when Capt John Heywang, of the New York-based American Society for Promotion of Aviation, addressed the A.C. Lions Club at the Breakers Hotel. He said the airport was "superior to landing places in most cities" but he deplored the lack of publicity given to it.

Newspaper clips of those years indicate that the airport was a political football. The local Chamber of Commerce and the Atlantic City Aero Club wanted the field to be open to all comers, while the politicians were looking to lease the airport to one operator.

In 1928, Mayor Anthony M. Ruffu, who succeeded Bader in office, convinced his council to approve a ten year lease to New York Airways. The action caused a roar of protests, but public opinion didn't alter the vote.

About two years later, the lease was broken and the debate on how the airport should be operated continued. Eastern Airlines became the operator in June of 1931. The opening of the new service was not taken lightly by Eastern's president, Captain Eddie Rickenbacker, the popular leading American flying ace of World War I. He arrived at Bader Field in a Curtiss Candor biplane with a host of celebrities including Lindbergh, Amelia Earhart and heavyweight boxing champion Gene Tunney.

But by October 1933, Eastern had removed its equipment and vacated the offices and hangar at the airport.

An *Atlantic City Press* headline best told the story: "Loss of Mail Causes Eastern Air Transport to Move Out, City Holds the Bag."

Throughout the '20s and '30s, the two greatest advocates of an "open" airport were Erwin L. Schwatt, president of the Aero Club of Atlantic City and A.T. Bell, the Chamber of Commerce aviation committee chairman.

In 1935, Schwatt was quoted in *The Press* as saying:

In the spring of 1919, about 16 years ago, a private flying field was successfully operated by the Curtiss Company, one of the pioneer aviation organizations. Today this same field, now the Atlantic City Municipal Airport, is still controlled by private interests, although apparently not so successfully operated. In the interim the city recognized the advisability of purchasing this field for municipal purposes, offering to the public and all airline operators the facilities of an open airport.

But after the field was acquired and new hangars built, runways improved, fences erected, bulkheads constructed and floodlights installed, providing satisfactory accommodations for visitors to the resort as well as to encourage the operation of airlines to other points in the United States, the municipal airport was practically ruined as such by a lease to private and selfish interests.

Aside from the ups and downs of the airport's operation, there was some excitement to stir the adrenaline of the summer guests. On June 5, 1931 at Bader Field, a crowd of about 2,000 watched as William G. Swan became the first man to fly a rocket powered aircraft. Swan used a primary glider in which he sat out on the skid just under the wing. He equipped the glider with ten rockets. When the first rocket was fired, he was propelled forward so violently that it almost catapulted him off his perch. The ship became airborne in 40 feet and climbed to 100 feet. The violence of the first rocket burst made him decide not to fire the others for fear of being propelled out over the water. Swan soared 1,000 feet and made a perfect landing. The flight was considered a gimmick to be used regularly as an attraction on the Steel Pier. Hindsight now indicates it was an historic accomplishment and another aviation first for Bader Field.

Silvio Cavalier

Inducted Aviation Hall of Fame of New Jersey, 1987

Silvio Cavalier, an itinerant pilot who had learned to fly at Teterboro Airport in 1929, first arrived at the Jersey shore in the fall of 1933. That summer and the next, he carried sightseeing passengers and staged small air shows at Ocean City, NJ, for the Reich Flying Service, based at Roosevelt Field, Long Island. Following his second summer, Irving Schwatt asked Cavalier if he'd be interested in moving to Atlantic City. Although the crowds had been good in Ocean City, a tragic accident in July, 1934, gave Cavalier cause to wonder if it wasn't time to move to another location.

During that summer, Cavalier had been joined at Ocean City by pilot Gus Michaelson and parachute jumper Art Sousa. In the late afternoon each day, Sousa would be taken up 2,000 feet over the resort's beach and he'd jump to attract a crowd of vacationers to their small landing strip, where Cavalier and Michaelson would be waiting to carry them aloft for a few dollars on a quick sightseeing flight.

One late afternoon, Cavalier was hired to fly a local businessman from Ocean City to Atlantic City. As he was about to leave, he noticed dark, ominous clouds on the horizon, and warned Sousa not to jump if the breeze picked up and the weather turned bad.

When the time came for the nightly jump, a brisk wind was blowing in from the ocean, but both men knew that without the jump the evening's crowd would not be as large as usual, thus cutting down on their profit. So the decision was made to jump, despite Cavalier's admonition to be careful.

Michaelson took Sousa up over the Atlantic, a quarter mile off the Ocean City beach, and the parachutist jumped, fully expecting to drift back into shore. But just at that moment, the swirling wind shifted direc-

Silvio Cavalier

tion and Sousa was blown farther out to sea where he splashed down still strapped in his parachute. Despite valiant efforts by local yachtsmen and the coast guard, Sousa was dead when he was dragged up onto the beach.

"I was just returning from Atlantic City when I saw those two fools flying out over the ocean," Cavalier said years later. "I'd warned them but they didn't listen. When Michaelson heard Gill Robb Wilson, the state director of aeronautics, was coming to investigate the incident, he took off. I never saw him again."

With that bitter memory still fresh in his mind, Cavalier asked operator Steve Reich about wintering in Atlantic City.

"Give it a try. If we don't make it, we can store the airplanes down there and save hangar rent," Reich replied.

When Cavalier arrived at Bader he found little more than seagulls occupying the island. "Knock" Nordheim had a Waco and Tom Davis owned a Curtiss pusher, that's all they had on the airport." Cavalier recalled.

For permission to use the facility, Cavalier was told to see "Bev" Baldwin, who sent him to Joseph Paxson, a city commissioner. Paxson wondered why anyone would want to fly out of Bader in the winter months, but he was more than willing to let Cavalier try his luck. Paxson said:

"Young man, that airport is the biggest headache in my department. Nothing I'd like to do better than put a lock and key on it. Give it a try. If you don't make any money don't pay us. We already had four or five operators there. They all pulled out and nobody paid us. Even the Governor of Pennsylvania owes us $400 for gas."

"I was never the manager of the airport. They had no money for a manager." Cavalier explained. "What I get credit for is getting it going. By the time I left, we had three operators there."

The winter of 1934 was hard on Cavalier. His first student was Tom Davis, but before he could pay for lessons Davis had to sell his Curtiss pusher. Several other students Cavalier had that winter kept the wolf away from the door.

"I had a room for $2.50 a week," the pilot laughed. "I ate at a local diner and owned a $20 car. I owed my sister $300. I had no money at all, so that's when I decided to start banner towing."

During that summer, his banner towing operation and his charter work paid off handsomely and by the season's end he had returned the $300 to his sister and had $2,600 in the bank. The following summer, he had purchased a Stearman bi-plane from Reich and went into business for himself.

In the meantime, the politicians kept signing leases with various air carriers. East Coast Airways, Pan American and Licon Airways were among those passenger carriers who tried their luck at Bader through the 1930s and failed to make a profit. Knock Nordheim worked for most of them.

The Post Office Department celebrated its 20th anniversary of air mail service on May 19, 1938. Gill Robb Wilson, was asked by Postmaster General James Farley to arrange for one private operator in New Jersey to fly the mail from one point to another. Cavalier was chosen. He flew in an open cockpit plane from Atlantic City to Camden, NJ, where the mail was transferred by autogyro to Philadelphia.

In June of 1939, Commissioner Joseph Paxson proclaimed that banner towing would be eliminated over Atlantic City. "Airplanes towing advertising banners above the city will not be tolerated this summer and must be stopped," Paxson said. "They are a constant menace to the lives of the crowds on the beach and boardwalk and the noise of the motors due to the load they pull, is objectionable to our residents, particularly on Sunday.

"Further," he continued, "unlike a newspaper, where stories are edited and advertisements checked before they are published, the planes carry uncensored, and in some cases, objectionable advertising."

The *Atlantic City Daily World* reported the following day that Silvio Cavalier and the Commissioner had met after the news of the ban was published and later Paxson said: "Don't worry about Cavalier. I took care of him. If you see his ship towing banners, let me know and that will be the end of it."

The paper reported that another source alleged that what actually transpired was the renewal of Cavalier's license. The following weekend Cavalier was again towing banners in defiance of the ban.

Perhaps anticipating further harassment, Cavalier got his instrument rating and applied to Eastern Airlines for a pilot's position. In 1940, he was hired by Eddie Rickenbacker himself. Because there was a 15-month probationary period, Cavalier had Chester Ship run his business at Bader until he was established at Eastern. He stayed with the airline for 28 years.

Like all airports along the east coast of the United States, Bader Field was taken over by the military during World War II. It also was used by the Civil Air Patrol.

Harry Nordheim remembered those days:

"The FAA came along and had us take motors out and wings off (the planes), we couldn't fly for six years."

Following the war, Nordheim established the Atlantic City Aerial Service at Bader Field and became the leading banner towing company in South Jersey. During the company's peak years, Nordheim had 15 airplanes towing banners, doing charter work and being used for flying lessons. The company was housed in the last of the original hangars that had been moved from the beach. Nordheim recalled that the corrugated steel outer walls of the building were peppered with pin holes and every time there was a blustery rain storm the water would spray like a shower into the hangar. That original hangar now has a concrete block facade.

Nordheim purchased a tract of land in Margate, NJ, and in 1967 opened the Flying K (for Knock) Airport which he was still operating in 1989.

In 1963, Maurice "Curt" Young moved his company, Southern Jersey Airways, from Cape May County Airport to Bader Field. Although the company had begun as a crop dusting operation in the late 1940s, the new emphasis was on charter service with a fleet of 15 single and light twin engine aircraft.

Young began scheduled service as an Allegheny Commuter commenced on June 15, 1970 and operated until 1987 when the agreement was not renewed. On March 15, 1988, Southern Jersey Airways began operating the Eastern Express in conjunction with Eastern Airlines. They flew between Atlantic City and New York, Washington and Philadelphia. Then on May 3, 1988 the Continental Express inaugurated regular service to Newark Airport. Over the years of expansion of its commuter service, the company disposed of the aerial application business and slowly cut back on the FBO services it had at Cape May, Ocean City and the terminal at the A.C. International Airport.

"Curt" Young died in 1975 and was succeeded by his son, Don, as president and CEO. Don grew up in the business, working in every department at one time or another. He is a licensed pilot with almost 4000 hours, but, as he likes to say, his license is now only current in "flying his desk."

In the late 1980s, Southern Jersey Airways was operating three Dash-7 and five Twin Otter aircraft.

When Atlantic City became the gambling mecca of the U.S., air traffic—fixed wing and helicopter—significantly increased at Bader Field and a temporary air traffic control tower was installed. In 1983, a permanent tower was opened, and a year later banner towing was eliminated. ACE Aviation, a banner towing operation, continued to assemble their banners at Bader, but they were flown from smaller airports in the area.

Other operators serving Atlantic City's booming gambling community in the late '80s were Jet Express Charter and Atlantic City Air Taxi which did charter work and had a flight school. Butler Aviation was the fixed base operator.

The city managed the airport from the early 1960s to the mid-80s. Paul Argus was the manager for more than 10 years, but as traffic increased and the operation became more sophisticated, the city fathers decided that the public could be better served if the airport were run by a professional management organization.

On June 1, 1986, Pan Am World Services assumed management of the field and passenger terminal at the international airport at Pomona. Edward O. Goddard was the Bader manager in 1989.

CHRONOLOGY OF OTHER AERONAUTICAL EVENTS AND ACHIEVEMENTS
1910 to 1919

1912

- Maxmillian Schmidt received a number of orders for his flying machines built and tested in Paterson.

1916

- Charles W. Meyers of Glen Ridge, NJ, established a new world's record for a model airplane flight. The Aero Science Club of America member's handmade model flew 178 seconds, beating the previous record set by a British modeler by nine seconds. The contest was held Sept. 30, 1916 in Glen Ridge.

1917

- George F. Russell, of East Orange, NJ, designed and patented a radio-controlled winged torpedo plane and built a lifesize seven-foot model of it.

1918

- A large Handley-Page English bombing plane was built at Elizabeth, NJ, by Standard Aircraft Corp. and test flown off the factory field at Bayway.

1919

- Brothers William and Donald Garretson established an airport in Perth Amboy on land leased from the Maurer Brick Co. Early Garretson Field flyers were John Bogett, John Yellen, Harry Edwards, Frank Seesock, Stan Solby, and Leonard Cockuski. The Garretson boys were the sons of Ferd Garretson, the former mayor of Perth Amboy, who organized the first New Jersey mail flight in 1912.

- Ex-military pilot Edwin E. Ballough landed his biplane on top a Newark Quartermaster's Depot building and then successfully took off. It was the first time in history that such a feat was accomplished. A Newark News photographer, Chris M. Wagner was a passenger on the flight.

- The first regular aerial delivery service in the nation was inaugurated May 25, 1919 between the L.S. Plaut stores in Newark and Asbury Park, NJ. Paul Micelli and Louis Goldberg made the first 25-minute flight between the two cities. The Plaut company was also the first commercial organization in the U.S. authorized by postal officials to carry air mail.

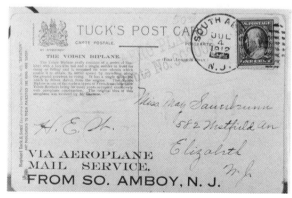

1920
Aviation Comes of Age

The 1920s had begun with great hope. The war in Europe had ended 14 months before and industry had completed the conversion from producing weaponry to products for the betterment of mankind.

Possibly the most important event of 1920 took place on Jan. 16 when the National Prohibition Act banned the use of beer, wine and liquor by all Americans. The stage was set for a decade of decadence. Words like "speakeasy" and "flappers" became part of the English language.

It also was the year that American women won the right to vote and Babe Ruth was sold by the Boston Red Sox to the New York Yankees. Republican Warren G. Harding was elected president and former president Woodrow Wilson received the Nobel Peace Prize. And, too, it was the first year an Austrian named Adolf Hitler and his German Workers' Party made the headlines.

The decade of the '20s marks the transition of aviation in the United States from a series of scattered, itinerant ventures to an industry of national scope, built on a solid financial foundation. This development was made possible by the steadily increasing number of municipal airports nation-wide and spurred on by an awareness that European countries had surpassed the United States in putting the airplane to work.

By mid-decade, President Calvin Coolidge had signed a measure which not only established definite programs for Army and Navy air development, but also instituted a comprehensive plan for the expansion of commercial aviation.

As the decade progressed, New Jersey became the mecca for those airmen and women who challenged themselves and their machines to the outer limits.

The aviation industrial complex in North Jersey comprised of the Fokker Aircraft Corp. and the Wright Aeronautical Corp. dominated the industry throughout the decade. Most aviation records during that happy era were accomplished either in Fokker-designed planes or in aircraft powered by Wright engines. This dominance attracted most every nationally prominent aviator of the decade to the Garden State.

Throughout the '20s, New Jersey pilots, airports, entrepreneurs and corporations continued to play a leading role in the advancement of the aeronautical industry.

First Passenger Airline
Aeromarine West Indies Airways, Inc.

Aeromarine West Indies Airways, Inc. was hastily formed in the fall of 1920 when a fledgling company, Florida West Indies Airways, a contract mail carrier between Key West and Havana, was unable to finance the project. Regularly scheduled passenger service had been the dream of Inglis M. Uppercu from the time he had founded Aeromarine Plane and Motor Co. in 1914. World War I had briefly sidetracked his plans, but it also provided him with surplus Navy aircraft suitable for conversion to passenger planes.

After the wartime contracts dried up in early 1919, the Aeromarine firm had been forced to layoff a large number of workers and to scramble for both military and civilian business to keep the large Keyport, NJ, plant operational. (Editor's note: At that time it was considered the finest airplane plant in the nation). Some small jobs came in, and in February 1920, the first of the Navy's twin engine F-5L biplanes was purchased and its conversion to an 11-passenger airliner begun.

When Uppercu discovered the predicament Florida West was facing, he arranged a merger thus creating a subsidiary of his Keyport company.

Three newly converted Model 75 Navy Cruisers—the *Nina, Pinta* and *Santa Maria*—were used during that first winter season of service to Havana. They were flown by Durston Richardson and Ed Musick.

Aerial Age Weekly magazine featured the historic event on its front page. The Nov. 8, 1920 headline read: "Key West-Havana Air Line Inaugurated."

The text cheered:

Monday, November 1, 1920, will go down in history as an epoch-making date, one that will fully rank in significance with the trials of Fulton's steamship and the inauguration of the first railway between New York and Albany; for on that day the first American passenger air line came into existence, to operate on a daily schedule between Key West and Havana. Three Aeromarine cabin flying boats of the largest size ever used for the transportation of passengers were put into service between the extreme tip of Florida and the Cuban Capital. These big boats, which have a span of 104 feet and are fitted with two 400 horsepower Liberty engines, afford luxurious accommodations to eleven passengers who will be agreeably surprised to find there, all the comforts a private yacht or a high-class limousine offers.

The article went on to describe the front and rear passenger cabins and the open cockpit "to give the crew the greatest possible visibility in thick weather."

The time was right for a U.S./Cuban connection. Congress had passed the Prohibition Act earlier in the

Adiel "Mitzie" Strang

year and Americans were looking for a legal place to party. None could have been better than Havana, where wine, women and song dominated the scene.

Business was surprisingly good that first winter. Three more 11-passenger model-75s were added to the fleet—the *Columbus, Balboa* and *Ponce de Leon.* It took the twin-engine planes 96 minutes to fly the 110 miles between Key West and Havana. By winter's end, 1,100 passengers had paid the one-way fare of $75 to cross the straits of Florida without a mishap.

In September of 1921, Aeromarine began twice-a-month service between New York and Havana, a distance of 1,521 miles. The six-passenger HS-2L flying boat, Presidente Zayas, took 19 hours with stops in Atlantic City, Beaufort, SC, Miami and Key West.

All along the way, Aeromarine aircraft and pilots were making headlines that helped promote new business.

On March 4, 1919, Cyrus J. Zimmermann flew an Aeromarine Model 40 flying boat out to sea to greet the *SS Leviathan* returning from Europe with the men of New York's 27th Division. When the flying boat passed over the huge ship, a packet of letters for the soldiers was dropped on the deck as a special air mail surprise.

Impressed by Zimmermann's pinpoint flying, Thomas A. Patten, the New York City Postmaster, requested a demonstration of a mail drop aboard a ship. Although the weather conditions were extremely unfavorable for August, Zimmermann and Richard Greisinger, a mechanic, flew off the choppy waters of the Hudson River at 86th Street and headed out over the Atlantic. Shortly, the flying boat was circling above the White Star liner *Adriatic*, which had sailed an hour and 45-minutes earlier. A bag of mail was effortlessly dropped on board.

In October, 1919, Zimmermann and Greisinger flew from Keyport to Havana in 20 days. The flight had been delayed 10 days in Key West while an engine was repaired. They then became the first airmen to make the round-trip flight arriving at the Hudson River dock on Dec. 3, 1919.

Pilot Edwin Musick made a stir in March, 1920, when he flew a Aeromarine flying boat off the ice in Raritan Bay carrying provisions to the *SS Princess Anne*, a passenger ship stranded off Rockaway, Long Island.

The flight proved the viability of using flying boats for emergency purposes.

In October, 1919, a wealthy Cuban businessman, Hannibal J. de Mesa, formed the Campania Cubana Americana and purchased four Aeromarine single-engine flying boats to transport passengers from Key West to Havana, and for sightseeing flights over the Caribbean Island.

Durston Richardson was assigned to pilot the Cuban plane with Adiel (Mitzie) Strang as his mechanic. In 1989, 91-year-old Strang remembered the part he played in those early attempts to create interest in flying:

"Every flight had to carry a mechanic as there were no self-starters. The mechanic had to crank the engines by hand. Since there were only one or two seats for the crew in the plane, the mechanic had to sit on the gas tank under the engine in the open. We also helped the pilot land the plane, because we could see both sides of the ship and he could only see one.

"We mechanics wore sailor suits aboard the flying boats. When we were at the dock it was my job to help the passengers aboard and get them seated before I cranked the propeller. Looking back now, I realize it was a great adventure."

Strang recalled one trip to Havana that was almost his last. He and Richardson had flown back to Key West to do required maintenance on their airplane. On the return flight to Cuba, they encountered foul weather and were blown off course. Poor visibility forced them to fly just above the turbulent sea and with less than 15 minutes of fuel left in the plane's tank it seemed certain that they would have to ditch the flying boat in the water. To do so would have surely resulted in destroying the craft.

They had just about given up hope of reaching Cuba, when Strang saw land on the horizon. As they neared the shoreline, a small cove came into view and Richardson set the plane down as the last drops of gasoline were consumed.

The village of Jaruco at the mouth of the Jaruco River overlooked the cove. No one there spoke English and there was no gasoline or communication system. In Key West and Havana, the two flyers were given up for dead, until they walked cross-country to a telegraph station and sent a message to Havana. Upon returning to Jaruco, they agreed to help load sand on a coastal schooner in exchange for being towed to Havana.

The two airmen received a royal welcome as the schooner entered Havana Harbor in the shadow of El Morro Castle. Of their experience, Strang said:

"The mosquitoes along the Jaruco River were the biggest I've ever seen. We have nothing in New Jersey to compare with them. I lost enough red blood to those man-eaters to fill a good-sized beer barrel."

The Richardson-Strang adventure made headlines in both the United States and Cuba and their brush with disaster possibly cooled the ardor of wealthy Cubans for air travel. Six months later the company went out of business, and the airmen returned to Keyport.

On June 22, 1920, the first of the converted flying boats was christened by New Jersey's governor Edward K. Edwards. Charter flights from New York to Newport, RI, Southhampton, Long Island and Atlantic City were popular that summer.

Over the next three years, Aeromarine became the leading promoter of commercial aviation in the country. Flying both their own flying boats and the converted Navy models to key mid-west and southern cities east of the Mississippi River, the company's president, Charles F. Redden, with advertising manager Harry Bruno and pilots Richardson and Musick, attempted to interest businessmen and the general public in flying. Bruno was the Montclair boy who had attempted to fly his home-built glider off a barn roof in 1910.

While on tour, the imaginative Bruno arranged numerous stunts to tie in with local events, all designed to focus attention on the airplanes. In every city they visited, he was a marathon talker. From a public relations standpoint, the tours were outstanding successes. But no matter how glamorous or exciting Bruno made flying seem, the public remained reluctant to leave terra firma.

Back on the east coast, the fledgling air service was also attracting newsprint. In June 1922, an Aeromarine flying boat flew off the Raritan Bay at Keyport carrying 27 passengers. That flight to the Hudson River at 84th Street in Manhattan established a record for the largest number of passengers carried in one aircraft.

In July, a passenger service across Lake Erie was inaugurated between Detroit and Cleveland using two 11-passenger flying boats. In the first month 624 passengers flew the new route and there were 150 charter flights. Soon, advanced reservations were necessary for those wishing to make the 90-minute flight.

The manager of operations for the Great Lakes Division was Roland Rohlfs, the former Curtiss pilot who, in 1919, had been the first to land an airplane at Bader Field. Harry Bruno was also attached to the division along with pilots Zimmermann, Musick and Richardson.

Late in 1922, the company sent its second annual report to Admiral W.A. Moffett, Chief of Naval Aviation. It showed that the three divisions— New York, Southern and Great Lakes—had carried a total of 9,107 passengers, chalking up 739,047 passenger miles without a single accident.

An Aeromarine 50-B Flying Boat

That perfect safety record was shattered early in 1923 when the flying boat *Columbus* with seven passengers aboard, ditched in the Straits of Florida about 20 miles from Havana because of engine problems. Two adults and two children drowned when the plane was hit by 10-foot waves. It was surprising that the resulting press coverage did little to slow passenger traffic.

Despite excellent passenger figures, mail and freight contracts, the company could not make a profit and new avenues of finance were drying up. The Keyport plant had been kept busy building 25 Martin Bomber-2NBS-ls for the Army and upgrading low-compression Liberty engines, but none of these projects were profitable enough to erase the red ink.

In August 1923, Harry Bruno resigned from the company to form his own promotional firm with R.R. "Dick" Blythe, an insurance man with a flare for public relations. The new company became H.A. Bruno & Associates. Over the next three decades, the partners promoted some of America's leading aviation personalities and corporations.

It was becoming obvious to Inglis Uppercu that an airline could not support itself, even with air mail contracts, because the Congress had decreed that carrying mail by plane should not cost more than the same service provided by the railroads. His support of commercial aviation had won the respect of the nation's aviation community which culminated in his election in 1922 as president of the Aeronautical Chamber of Commerce. However, the $500,000 he had invested to stimulate commercial air travel had not brought the expected orders for aircraft. The Keyport plant was working with a skeleton staff. Larger buildings were being used to build buses for the Healy-Aeromarine Bus Co.

By mid-January 1924, the Aeromarine Plane and Motor Co. was out of business. The company was ahead of its time by five years when government regulations and subsidies helped fledgling airlines establish their services. Those airlines, however, owed a great deal to the Keyport company for the education it had provided to the general public on the safety and reliability of aircraft.

Until the early 1930s, Inglis Uppercu continued to back aviation projects. Vincent Burnelli, the prolific aircraft designer, used the Keyport facility to build a number of experimental aircraft, including his famous "flying wing." In 1928, Uppercu obtained a license from the German Klemm Company to build the German two-seat, open-cockpit, low-wing monoplane at the Keyport plant. One of the frail planes had just been flown around the world by Baron von Koenig-Warthausen. It had taken 15 months for the 22-year-old Baron to accomplish the historic flight in the small plane, powered by only a two-cylinder engine.

The American version of the sport plane was known as the Aeromarine-Klemm AKL-26A with a French nine-cylinder Salson engine that produced 40 horsepower. The imported engines proved too costly so they were replaced by a 65 hp five-cylinder LeBlond radial engine. The diminutive planes with a large wing area proved popular but buyers became scarce as the Depression of the 1930s tightened its grip on the nation, and in 1931 the company closed. That was the last aircraft business in the small Raritan Bay town famous for its clam diggers.

In his book, *The Flying Years*, Lou Reichers of Kearny, a prominent aviator of the 1930s and 40s, remembered Uppercu's support of aviation:

Mr. Uppercu was one of aviation's earliest philanthropists, all the old-timers in aviation must remember him with nostalgia. Anyone with an idea or invention that might advance the science of aeronautics could be sure of a sympathetic ear, and more often then not, enthusiastic financial support. Probably most of the money he made in his Uppercu-Cadillac Corporation he sank into Keyport ventures. His most notable contribution was the inertia starter, and it was an important one, too. Old-timers won't easily forget the cold days when it took two and sometimes three men, with their hands clasped in a chain, to pull through a Liberty engine propeller, trying to start the balky machine.

Uppercu retired in 1938 and spent the final years of his life sailing his yacht in the Caribbean.

First Itinerant Pilot
William "Billy" Diehl

Inducted Aviation Hall of Fame of New Jersey, 1973

"I saw the field down there, so I just landed my little English Avro on the grass." Billy Diehl told the author 50 years after the event. "Charles Wittemann and a couple of his boys came running across the field toward me. I thought he was going to yell at me and tell me to get off his field. Instead he treated me real nice."

From that moment in the early spring of 1920 until he died in 1974, Diehl claimed he was the first pilot to land on the Hasbrouck Heights meadow. In 1960, he asked Charles Wittemann to write him a letter veri-

Billy Diehl

fying the fact, much to the chagrin of Wittemann's younger brother, Paul, who felt Diehl was using his brother to make a name for himself.

As Paul pointed out "We had been flight testing our mail planes from the field for almost a year before Diehl showed up."

In his letter to Diehl, Charles Wittemann diplomatically appeased the aviator. "Your landing was unexpected and naturally created a great interest, since it was the first landing, from outside, at our new airport," he wrote. "Unfortunately, my record does not show the exact day, but apparently it was early in the summer. Possibly you have a memo of the exact date."

Because the letter emphasized "from outside," historians credit Diehl with being the first "itinerant" pilot to use the Wittemann facility.

Although Diehl had an exciting career in aviation, he never felt he received the recognition he deserved, and after retiring from flying, he spent his every waking hour attempting to enhance his image.

For the majority of aviators of yesterday or today, Diehl's exploits would have been most fulfilling. Here are a few high points of his career:

—He was a member of the *Early Birds*, a select group of approximately 500 pilots who flew solo before Dec. 17, 1916.

—During World War 1, he served as a civilian instructor in the Signal Corps, teaching future combat pilots to fly.

—In 1919, he operated a flying taxi, thus becoming one of the first pilots of passenger planes.

—He was a stunt pilot in the era of silent movies having been seen in Pearl White's movie serial *The Perils of Pauline* and a silent flick starring Irene Castle.

—In the 1930s, he taught Martin and Osa Johnson, the famous African game trekkers to fly.

Born in North Bergen in 1891, Bill Diehl developed an early love for automobiles and was a self-taught mechanic.

At the age of 22, he became fascinated with aviation and decided to build a plane. To finance the project, he sold his motorcycle and purchased a Fox-Deluxe, six-cylinder 60-horsepower engine and began work on a flying machine from plans he found in a magazine. At that time, he was employed as a plumber's assistant, but for a year, his hours away from pipe repair were devoted to his airplane.

When it was finished, he and a group of friends pushed the strange looking contraption about a mile through the streets of North Bergen to a park in Guttenberg, where he tested it. After taxiing back and forth across the field, he then began flying just a few feet from the ground .

"That was an exciting experience!" he recalled enthusiastically. He had become an *Early Bird* in 1914.

Throughout his life, Diehl believed the World War 1 civilian instructors never received the recognition they deserved.

"We didn't fly in combat and make a name for ourselves," he said, "because they needed the few experienced pilots of those days to teach others how to fly."

As late as the 1960s, Diehl was soliciting congressmen and senators in an effort to gain official recognition for the cadre of civilian flight instructors. When he died, he willed money to have three bronze plaques produced with the names of all the civilian instructors. One went to the Air Force Museum in Dayton, Ohio, another to Paul Garber at the Air and Space Museum in Washington, D.C. and a third to the New Jersey Aviation Hall of Fame and Museum at Teterboro.

One of his most memorable experiences occurred while he was flying for the Pathe Movie Studio in 1920.

"The script called for me to dip the plane under the Brooklyn Bridge with a stunt man standing unsupported on the top wing," he recalled matter-of-factly. "We went under the bridge just fine, but we couldn't rise with the stunt man on top. The motor was turning at only 1,100 revolutions that very hot day."

"So we went under the Manhattan Bridge, then the Williamsburg Bridge. I headed for Jersey, but we still couldn't rise. We went below the tops of skyscrapers, with the stunt man still standing on top, waving to people who had their heads outside windows to watch us.

"Luckily, when we got to the Hudson River, the stunt man lay on the wing, reducing the resistance. We just made it over the Palisades and landed in a field about 1,000 feet from the cliff."

Another of Diehl's great disappointments was that no one would finance the production of an aircraft engine muffler he had invented. He installed his prototype in an OX-5 powered American Eagle airplane at the Arcola airfield in Rochelle Park. The muffler reduced exhaust noise drastically. Later the muffler was successfully used on a large Wright J6-300 engine with equally satisfactory results.

His invention was ahead of its time. In 1928, no pilot wanted a quiet airplane. Just imagine buzzing the hangars and no one hearing you! Or flying over your girl friend's house at 75 feet and having her be completely unaware of your presence. In those barnstorming days it was unthinkable.

In 1973, Billy Diehl received special recognition. In May, he was inducted into the New Jersey Aviation Hall of Fame, and in the fall a street on Teterboro Airport was named in his honor. A year later, he died.

Not long after Billy Diehl first landed at Teterboro, the Wittemann brothers announced a new moneymaking scheme — a passenger sightseeing service. A July edition of the Hasbrouck Heights newspaper, *The News-Letter*, proclaimed: "Mrs. David Levy, First Local Aviatrix"

A Major Smith, billed as a *British Ace,* piloted the airplane described as a British Army Training plane. The newspaper classed Mrs. Levy as a *nervy* passenger because she was flying at 90 mph and several thousand feet above sea level.

Harold M. Hecht, Mrs. Levy's guest, was the second passenger of the day. After a 15-minute flight, the plane landed on the wet, sod airstrip and its wheels sank in the mud, causing it to tip over on its back. Both the pilot and Hecht jumped out unscathed, and the newspaper assured its readers:

"The plane likewise was undamaged, and the field having now thoroughly dried, there is not the slightest chance for such a mishap again."

First Coast-to-Coast Air Mail Flight
John Ordway Webster

Inducted Aviation Hall of Fame of New Jersey, 1974

During the war years, Charles Wittemann's reputation had grown in government circles, and in 1918 President Woodrow Wilson appointed him to the President's Aviation Commission as an aeronautical adviser. In addition, he was asked to collaborate with

"Jack" Webster

Otto Praeger, the second assistant Postmaster General, to plan and lobby for a Congressional appropriation to establish an official transcontinental air mail service for the U.S. Post Office Department.

In early 1919, the Wittemanns had received a contract from the U.S Postal service to convert unused Army Air Service DH-4 airplanes with Liberty engines into air mail planes capable of carrying 400 pounds of mail. The Wittemanns redesigned 100 DH-4s to accommodate weights of 400, 800 and 1,000 pounds. John Ordway Webster, a World War I test pilot, was assigned by the Post Office Department to test fly the converted planes as they were completed at the Teterboro plant. Much valuable information and many design changes were the result of Webster's test flights.

In the late spring of 1921, government officials invited the Wittemann company to demonstrate its converted DH-4s, called DH M-2s. Charles Wittemann and "Jack" Webster flew from Teterboro to Bolling Field, outside of Washington, DC, in two hours and 45 minutes. They were met by Postmaster General Hayes, his assistant Otto Praeger and their corps of experts.

The larger capacity airplane was accepted by postal officials following a competitive demonstration against crack U.S. Army Air Service planes. The DH-M-2 outdistanced the Army planes, one of which was flown by General "Billy" Mitchell.

Seven Days Coast-to-Coast

On the return two-hour, eight-minute flight to Teterboro, Wittemann and Webster mulled over a proposal for a transcontinental test fight that had been suggested by the postmaster.

A month later, under the direction of postal officials, Webster prepared for the coast-to-coast jaunt. The flight was designed as a performance test of the DH-M-2 carrying 1,000 lbs. of mail; not a speed test.

Webster left on the trail-blazing flight from Hazelhurst Field, Mineola, L.I. at 6:20 a.m. on Aug. 25, 1921. The DH-M-2, designated #250, carried 825 lbs. of mail. Webster flew side by side with an earlier model DH-M (capacity 440 lbs.) carrying only 350 pounds.

The two planes reached Bellefonte, PA. in 2 hours and 2 minutes. The fuel consumed by the DH-M was 25 gallons per hour. The #250 used only 23 gallons per hour.

On the next leg, Bellefonte to Cleveland, the DH-M carried 300 lbs. and consumed 33 gallons per hour and #250 used only 31 gallons carrying 825 lbs.

Webster's plane again out performed the smaller model on the Cleveland to Chicago leg of the journey. He then flew on alone to the west coast, stopping at Iowa City, Omaha, North Platte, Cheyenne, Salt Lake City, Elko and Reno, Nevada. He ended his solo journey at the Army Air Service base in San Francisco. The flight had taken seven days.

Several weeks later Webster flew back to Teterboro in easy stages.

Ankledeep Aircraft Company

A 28-year-old former Army pilot and barnstormer from Denison, IA, Clarence D. Chamberlin, and a partner Bob Stroop, established an airplane assembly business in an unused barn and small concrete block building, on the high ground adjacent to the Hasbrouck Heights railway station. The small buildings were situated a few hundred yards west of the large Wittemann factory.

Chamberlin and Stroop had found financial backing to purchase 40 surplus World War I English biplanes still in their crates for $100 each. In return for the money advanced, Chamberlin and Stroop were to assemble, test fly and sell the aircraft and receive 50 per cent of the profits.

They called their small business the *Ankledeep Aircraft Company* because the entire marshland area was subject to the whims of the tides. Interviewed 50 years later, Roger Q. Williams, who had been working for the Wittemanns at that time, remembered how he flew off the soggy field:

"We parked our planes on high ground near the railroad station. When we planned to fly, it was a regular routine to see any one of us, with the tailskid of our plane on our shoulder, trucking our plane across the narrow, rickety wooden bridge covering a deep ditch. Then we would taxi down wind to the take-off point. The need to fly was in our blood."

During the winter of 1921 and into the spring and summer of 1922, the two partners, assisted by Lou Foote and Bill Davis, worked from morning until night assembling the wood and fabric English Avro airplanes that they sold to aviation enthusiasts for $750 to $1,000 each.

In his book *Record Flights*, Chamberlin recalled how the first reconstructed Avro with its temperamental 130 hp Clerget rotary engine was tested. He and Stroop were reluctant to fly the plane because neither of them had experience with the Clergets. As they mulled over the test, Bert Acosta, even then one of the legendary figures of American aviation, walked by and commented on the fine appearance of the Avro.

"Take a hop in it if you like," one of the men said, casually. "You know how to handle the motor, don't you?"

Bert fell into the trap. If the temptation to fly the ship had not been enough, the inference that he did not know all about the Avro and its power plant would have decided him.

In the next 15 minutes, he treated us to a convincing demonstration of what he knew about Avros and Clerget motors. What Bert didn't know and doesn't yet, was that he also gave a brand-new ship a thorough flight test. After the things he did, we worried no more about our Avros. And the humorous part of it all was that when Bert finally landed, he thanked us for the flight.

During that year, Chamberlin and his wife Wilda, whom he called "Bill," had been living in Manhattan and on many nights he slept in the block building rather than make the long journey back to the city via the 125th Street ferry. In June 1922, the couple moved into an apartment in a Victorian house in Hackensack.

Although he had been drawing money to cover his living expenses while he worked for Ankledeep, Chamberlin's 50/50 split was not to come until all the aircraft were sold. And when that time came, his financial backers conveniently forgot the 50/50 agreement — never put in writing — and Chamberlin was cut off without a cent. That was the first of many successful projects the trusting "Iowa farm boy", as he referred to himself, let slip through his fingers.

For the next two years, Chamberlin explored every avenue in aviation to support his household. His principal income came as a pilot-photographer for several New York and New Jersey newspapers. On off days, he'd supplement his earnings by taking people on sightseeing flights from airfields as far south as Camden, or by giving flying lessons.

Chamberlin taught Basil Rowe to fly in 1923. Rowe went on to become the chief pilot for Pan American World Airways.

"In early 1923," Chamberlin wrote. "Basil Rowe came to my place at Teterboro straight from the hay fields of Sidney, NY. He bought a DH-6 with an OX-5 engine and I gave him about three hours of flight training. He said he couldn't wait longer because he wanted to get to work earning money. He was going to barnstorm from a field outside of Binghamton, NY, which he had surveyed before buying the plane. But while he was gone, some contractor had excavated a cellar for a house on the spot Basil had picked. Basil was so intent on looking at the excavation that he ran right into it.

"He wasn't hurt but the plane was a pile of rubbish sitting in the bottom of the hole. Basil took a good look at it, left it there and caught the next train back to Teterboro. He bought another DH-6, took a few more hours of lessons and off he went barnstorming. He made about $5,000 that summer and came back and bought half interest in my business. We were partners for about two years. Basil wanted to try his luck in Florida or thereabouts and I wanted to stay up north. During those two years, we assembled and sold 238 converted war-surplus English, French and Italian planes."

One of the many projects Clarence Chamberlin undertook to make money, was to fly two black men associated with Marcus Garvey, the would-be *leader extraordinary* of his race, on fund-raising promotions.

The two men would publicize their flights in black neighborhoods and then parachute into the area and solicit funds from the admiring throngs that greeted them for Garvey's dream of a *United States of Africa* based in Liberia.

The most famous of the two black jumpers was the dapper Col. Hubert Julian, known as the "Black Eagle". He and his partner made several successful jumps from Chamberlin's airplanes using the standard balloon type parachutes.

One day, Julian showed up at Teterboro with a new type of 'chute. It was a pull-off type, meaning that the rip cord was pulled while the jumper was still on the wing, and once it billowed open, it pulled him into space.

Julian and Chamberlin went up in an old de Haviland biplane. Once over the jump site, the Black Eagle climbed out to the end of the wing and held onto the strut with one hand, pulling the rip cord with the other. At that moment, Julian's sense of daring do took a nosedive. When the parachute grabbed at the rushing wind, Julian grabbed for the strut, wrapping both arms and legs around it. Fully opened, the parachute became a powerful brake and the airplane gave a sickening lurch.

The spruce struts were strong and especially designed to take stresses from fore and aft. But as the parachute, acting as a giant rudder, pulled the plane around, the strut gave way and the erstwhile jumper was launched sideways, kicking and screaming, still clinging to the piece of broken strut.

He landed safely, however, and soon regained enough composure to accept accolades and donations from his fans.

Chamberlin was understandably disgruntled. Not only had the Black Eagle crippled the ship by his sudden attack of indecision, but it was all Chamberlin could do to keep the plane steady and nurse it back to a safe landing. There is no record of Julian's having offered to share his windfall in order to pay for the damage.

By the mid-1920s, Clarence Chamberlin had developed an outstanding reputation in the field of aviation and although he never enlarged his small facility on the Hasbrouck Heights' marshland that had become Teterboro, he had earned the title "Mr. Teterboro". In 1926, he was elected Recorder of Teterboro, equivalent to Justice of the Peace.

Jumping Brothers

Another jumper who gave Clarence Chamberlin fits was Granville "Granny" Smith of Paterson. Smith and his brother Dan had built solid reputations as daring jumpers and wherever they appeared the promoters would expect large crowds.

"Daredevil" Dan Smith

In the summer of 1924, Chamberlin contracted to stunt fly and drop a jumper at the New York and New Jersey Firemen's Fair at Westwood, NJ. The aerobatics were scheduled for late in the day. Following the stunt flying, Chamberlin began to climb to a height of several thousand feet. His plane was a war surplus English Avro biplane with a long nose skid protruding in front of the propeller to prevent it from nosing over on landing.

Historian Bill Rhode described what happened in an article that appeared in *Propwash*, the publication of the Aviation Hall of Fame of New Jersey.

At sunset over the Westwood fairgrounds, Smith climbed out of the front cockpit, attached himself to the 10-foot rope leading to the parachute and dropped off the wing. Instead of pulling free, the parachute remained stuck in the bag and Granny Smith dangled 10 feet below the plane. Chamberlin, seeing the problem, rolled the plane sideways until his jumper could swing up onto the landing gear. Smith then clung to the nose skid while Chamberlin headed back to Teterboro. With the parachute still jammed in its pack and the long rope flowing backward over the Avro, Chamberlin had to negotiate his landing in darkness.

Smith, down under the engine and holding on for dear life, was coated with burned castor oil (commonly used as an engine lubricant) that blew back from the revolving cylinders of the LeRhone rotary engine. As Chamberlin landed on the rough sod in darkness, Smith bounced off the long nose skid. He and the rope caught in some high grass and threatened to flip the Avro nose over. The skid prevented it, and they rolled 200 feet just short of a deep drainage ditch. Smith was bruised, but unhurt.

"Daredevil" Dan Smith, as he billed himself, was not as lucky at the New York City Police Games held at the Jamaica racetrack on Sept. 19, 1925.

That day, he announced that he would attempt to break the world's record for a delayed parachute jump. He dropped 1,800 feet before pulling his ripcord. When he hit the ground, he was rendered unconscious. Later, he told the press:

"My iron muscles let me flirt with death. I live cleanly, keep on a strict diet and get plenty of exercise that develops my tough iron muscles and strong constitution that saved my life."

Daredevil Dan's last jump was at an airshow in Matamoras Airport in Pennsylvania, just across the Delaware River from Port Jervis, NY, on April 27, 1929. The melting winter snow had swollen the river to flood stage, which didn't at first seem to be cause for alarm.

While hundreds watched, Smith and his barnstorming partner pilot, Andy Stinis, flew up over the airport. Smith jumped from the biplane, but gusting wind carried him over the river and he dropped into the swirling rapids. The weight of the wet parachute pulled him under as spectators stood by. They were powerless to help because no boats were available. Smith's wife, Patsy Kelley, also a professional parachutist, witnessed her husband's death.

Smith, a native of Plainfield, NJ, had made his first jump in 1918 at the age of 15.

Granville Smith gave up parachuting several years later and went to work as a bartender in the Paterson area.

World's Largest Aircraft
Barling NBL Bomber

Charles Witteman

The day was comparatively cool for August in Dayton, OH, as the huge tri-wing aircraft rolled out of its open-sided, temporary hangar at McCook Field. It had taken almost 11 months for the engineers and mechanics at the Army air facility to complete the assembly of the Night Bomber, Long Range, Model 1 (NBL-1) designed by Englishman Walter H. Barling and built by the Wittemann Aircraft Corp. at Teterboro Airport.

The maiden flight of the flying Goliath was scheduled for August 22, 1923. There had never been a flying machine so large. Its three wings had a span of 120 ft. Its fuselage was 65 ft.long and it stood 27 ft. high. There were eight wheels and six 400 hp Liberty engines. It had been designed to carry a crew of six, 2,000 gallons of fuel and 5,000 pounds of bombs.

Lt. Harold Harris, the test pilot, pushed the throttle forward and the *Barling* began to roll across the turf field. In 14 seconds, the aircraft reached a speed of 60 hp and in a run of only 360 ft. became airborne. In six minutes, the giant bird had climbed 2,000 feet, as Harris flew in circles and figure eights above a team of Army Air Service experts on the ground. That successful flight lasted 28 minutes.

Although years later, Gen. Harold Harris, USAF-ret., said he had found the *Barling* to be exceptional in many aspects, the performance tests didn't impress those watching. The top speed had been 100 mph and service ceiling 10,000. At that height, however, the plane would be able to cruise for 12 hours, an endurance comparable to the B-24 and B-17 aircraft developed more than a decade later.

Harris established several weight-carrying records with the bomber, but those accomplishments didn't alter the negative attitude of the Army brass.

It had been June, 1920, that Charles and Paul Wittemann announced they had been awarded a contract by the Engineering Division of the U.S. Army Air Service to construct two bombing planes designed by Walter Barling. When completed they would be the largest aircraft in the world, the brothers proudly proclaimed.

The contract for the airplanes was awarded to the Wittemanns not only for their manufacturing experience and expertise but also because of the large aircraft assembly space inside their Teterboro hangar.

Although A. Francis Arcier, a British subject, was the Wittemann's chief engineer and designer, he had little input concerning the construction of the bomber. Walter Barling had an office in the plant and his own crew of draftsmen. Arcier kept busy making design changes and overseeing the work that continued on the conversions of the DH-4s.

Fuselage sections of the *Barling* were constructed of wood, two layers of 3/16th-inch spruce strips, glued at right angles to each other, then pressure-formed around a circular jig. The four sections were then bolted together. The wings and tail surfaces were fabric covered.

One of the young engineers on the job was Roger Q. Williams, who in later years recalled the financial struggle that faced the Wittemanns during that period.

"Cost overruns caused by Walter Barling's constant design changes during the construction of the bomber

Barling Bomber

and the Army's slow payment of bills were draining the Wittemann's treasury. Their two financial backers, Lorilard Spencer and a Mr. Sands, who had kept the Wittemann factory operational over the years, refused to advance additional funds. Plans to build a second prototype were scrapped, and in order to complete the first machine, the employees agreed to defer their pay until the funds came from Washington."

According to Williams, in order to make ends meet the Wittemanns took on other contracts.

"My first assignment was a secret project in a dark corner of the factory," Williams told the author. "I was the adviser and test pilot of a strange boat, already being built by Carl Batts and Bill Hartig."

The flat-bottomed vessel was equipped with a 6-cylinder, 220 hp Liberty engine and a large wooden propeller attached to a six-foot tripod in the rear of the boat. Williams said it was "the grandfather of the swamp buggies used in the Florida Everglades today." It had been designed for the use of bootleggers to haul contraband liquor from ships anchored at sea to hidden coves along the shore so shallow that Coast Guard boats could not follow."

After many tests on the Hackensack River, the boat seemed to lack power, so a 12-cylinder, 410 hp Liberty engine and even larger propeller was installed.

"It did not take too long to learn that the huge, wooden propeller, mounted so high above the boat's keel was a handicap to performance and safety." Williams explained. "Up to a certain point of power output, the hull's nose rose neatly out of the water in a pleasing manner. But when more power was applied, the entire boat began to 'porpoise' dangerously. I concluded too dangerously for safety—my safety. I had a strong hunch that more power would cause the boat to pitch uncontrollably and nosedive into the river's bottom. In desperation, a few changes were made to enlarge the fins on the hull to create more buoyancy.

"During a test, the boat almost took a dive and that scared the hell out of me, so I quit the project. One of our mechanics, who thought I'd lost my nerve, volunteered to take over the test trials. When he applied more power than I had, there was a loud explosion, a sudden dive, and splinters from the wooden propeller flying everywhere. The mechanic lived to regret his folly. He had two broken legs and other injuries."

Meanwhile, back at McCook the Barling tests were completed. Although it hadn't suffered even the slightest of problems, the big bird couldn't win the heart of even one Army Air Service decision maker. So it was grounded and dismantled and shoved out of sight at Fairfield Air Depot, at Wright-Patterson Air Service Base.

Roger Q. William remembered his last vision of the bomber:

"The last I saw of the Barling Bomber, it was being loaded on 11 flatcars at the railroad station in Hasbrouck Heights for shipment to Dayton for test flights. Each day we'd show up at the factory waiting for our pay. In due course, word came from Dayton that Lt. Harris had tested the Barling and refused to accept it as it only made 90 miles-per-hour, empty, despite its 2,600 horsepower engines. We're still whistling for our pay."

Mrs. Helen Boesch, Paul Wittemann's secretary, had nothing but sympathy for the struggling Wittemann brothers. She wrote:

"After years of strife on the part of the Wittemanns to keep this infant industry going, it was forced into bankruptcy. To witness the smashing of the dreams of these men for an airport only six miles from New York City, the loss of their plant and a great deal of their family fortune was truly heartbreaking. Of course, the members of the Board, all wealthy men, were equally affected.

"The Trustees in Bankruptcy took over the operation of the plant. The work force, reduced to skeleton size, was employed at completing existing work to finish contracts. I was the only female 'skeleton' in the whole plant."

1921
World's Largest Hangar

At the conclusion of World War I, the United States Navy turned its attention to the development of a lighter-than-air program. Airships seemed to be the ideal vehicles for sustained flights over the oceans of the world.

Although the transatlantic flight of the R-34 airship in 1919 gave a big boost to the airship industry in Great Britain, it was still widely agreed that the most experienced craftsmen in the construction of large rigid airships were the Germans. So arrangements were made with the Germans to build a dirigible with a gas capacity of 2,475 million cubic feet as part of the reparation the Germans were supposed to pay to all the Allied countries they had fought.

The giant ship was designated the ZR-3. It was to be 650 feet long, 90 feet in diameter and 101 feet high from below the control car to the top of the hull.

To prepare for this new age of aviation in the United States, the Navy acquired 1,500 acres on the outskirts of Lakehurst, NJ, in Ocean County. The site was occupied during the war by Camp Kendrick, an Army chemical warfare proving grounds. The Navy called the new facility the Naval Airship Construction and Experimental Station, later changed to the Naval Air Station. By air, Lakehurst was 40 miles east of Philadelphia and 50 south-west of New York City.

In December 1919, the Secretary of the Navy announced that the Navy planned to erect a hangar unprecedented in size at Lakehurst. It would be 804 feet long, 318 feet wide and 200 feet high. The frame would be of structural steel built on the three-hinged arch principle, each arch supported on steel towers 62 feet high. The entrance door would be double, consisting of two leaves, each 177 feet high and 136 feet wide, framed in structural steel and braced to a thickness of 76 feet at the bottom.

Construction began almost immediately and in August 1921, Hangar #1 at the Naval Air Base, Lakehurst was completed. The 36 million cubic foot structure was the largest in the world and cost almost $3 million. It was designed to house two five million cubic foot, hydrogen inflated rigid airships (each more than twice the size of the British R-34) side-by-side. There were overhead trolleys to assist in the construction of airships, and three docking rails of tracks of special design for landing, releasing and mooring purposes that extended throughout the length of the building and for 1,500 feet in front. The hangar also had working areas and living quarters for some personnel.

At the dedication ceremonies, Lt. Alford J. Williams flew a DeHaviland through it with ease.

The LTA operation at Lakehurst became the Navy's principal base for airship operations, and in the 1930s, it was the first transatlantic air passenger terminal in the United States.

Although the Germans were busy building the reparation prize at the large Zeppelin Works in Friedrichshafen, the Navy convinced Congress to appropriate funds for an American built airship. Within six months of the establishment of an air station at Lakehurst, work was begun on the superstructure of the ZR-1.

In December 1922, three balloons arrived at Lakehurst to be used for training flights for Navy personnel assigned to the LTA program. From that time until after World War II, balloons were a common sight flying across the mid-section of the Garden State.

U.S.S. Shenandoah

In the early summer of 1923, ZR-1, the first dirigible built in the United States, was completed in Hangar #1. Sections of the massive airship had been constructed at the Naval Aircraft Factory in Philadelphia and shipped to Lakehurst for final assembly.

On Aug.13, the ZR-1 became the first dirigible in the world inflated with helium, the non-inflammable gas. A week later, it became airborne with a full gas capacity of 2,115,000 cubic feet.

Its design was based on the German Zeppelins used during World War I. It was 680 feel long, 78.74 feet in diameter and was constructed of a German-produced alloy called duralumin, reputed to be "as light as aluminum, as strong as steel "

The airship was powered by six Packard 300 hp engines, significant at a time when automobile engines averaged 25 hp. It also contained the first water recovery apparatus to produce ballast from engine exhaust gasses.

On September 4, the ZR-1 made its maiden voyage over southern New Jersey under the command of F.R. McCrary, a Navy commander, the watchful eye of R.D. Weyerbacker, manager of construction, and Captain Anton Heinen, a former German test pilot employed by the Navy. The airship made test flights to Philadelphia and New York on Sept. 11 and to Washington DC, on Sept. 22. Early in October, the large silver dirigible flew cross-country to show off the Navy's air might at the International Air Races in St. Louis.

Mrs. Edwin Danby, wife of the Secretary of the Navy, christened the airship the *U.S.S. Shenandoah* (an Indian name meaning "Daughter of the Stars") on Oct. 10. The vessel was immediately commissioned a ship of the U.S. Navy, based at Lakehurst.

The Navy had ambitious plans for its new recruit—a flight over the North Pole. The program called for the construction of mooring masts in appropriate places across the United States and Canada and aboard a ship in the Arctic, so the *Shenandoah* could be conveniently supplied and serviced on her journey north. It would be the first to fly over the Pole.

The flight tests continued right into 1924 with crews making extensive trials of mooring, riding and casting off from a mooring mast at Lakehurst.

On Jan. 16, with winds gusting from the south at 63 mph, the sailors had difficulty holding the ship steady above the mast so it could moor properly. By late afternoon, the winds abated and the emergency seemed to be over. Then at 6:44 p.m., a sudden 74-mph gust struck America's pride and joy at an angle that twisted it on the longitudinal axis and ripped off the nose, leaving it dangling from the top of the mooring mast. The *Shenandoah* began to sink toward the ground, and only a rapid discharge of ballast by the crew kept it airborne. Slowly, it lifted, stern first, and then drifted off into the winter darkness with half the crew aboard.

News reports stated that the nation's first airship was lost. Americans were horrified. Later in the evening, a message was received at Lakehurst that the *Shenandoah* was still alive, drifting aimlessly in the stormy darkness. Reports of sightings poured into newspaper offices and radio stations. Many observers said they saw the huge hulk floating directly above their rooftops and feared it would soon settle on some unsuspecting home. By late night, the crippled dirigible had been pushed by the winds as far north as Middlesex County.

In those days, radio stations signed off the air at midnight, but Station WOR, then based in Newark, was asked to continue broadcasting throughout the night to keep the public abreast of the situation. Millions of Americans got very little sleep that night.

Finally, at 3:30 a.m., the *Shenandoah* limped back to its Lakehurst base and the entire nation breathed a sigh of relief. A long night's vigil had ended happily.

The accident prompted the Navy to postpone the Arctic flight. Following extensive repairs, the *Daughter of the Stars* went back into service under the command of a new skipper, Lt. Cmdr. Zachary Lansdowne. To prove he wasn't gun shy, Lansdowne successfully attached the nose of the *Shenandoah* to a mooring mast erected on the fantail of the Navy oiler *U.S.S. Patoka* while the ship was underway in Narragansett Bay.

Just a week later, the *Shenandoah* joined in Naval exercises for the first time, scouting for the fleet over the Atlantic Ocean. It flew continuously for 40 hours, 300 miles at sea.

On Oct. 7, 1924, the dirigible left Lakehurst for a round-trip transcontinental flight to Tacoma, WA, via Fort Worth, TX and San Diego, CA. The highly successful and visible flight took 19 days, 19 hours and

Shenandoah's last flight.

covered 9,317 miles — the most extended operation by an airship of any nation up to that time.

While the airship was away, the German-built zeppelin, *ZR-3,* arrived at Lakehurst on Oct. 15, 1924. It had taken less than three days to fly from Friedrichshafen, Germany. U.S. navy Captain George Steele commanded a crew which included a Commander Klein, Lt. Cmdr. Krause and Major Kennedy. Dr. Hugo Eckener, president of the Zeppelin Works, was the official navigator and the remainder of the crew was German.

The *ZR-3* was shorter than the *Shenandoah* but had a larger gas capacity (2,475,000 cubic feet) and a greater diameter (90.75 feet). Her five 400-hp, Maybach engines provided a cruising speed of 71 miles per hour. There were 31 passenger berths aboard.

Although they encountered quite a bit of fog on the transatlantic crossing, it was, overall, uneventful.

Once over Manhattan, the captain flew in five large circles to show off his prize to the citizens of the New York boroughs and New Jersey municipalities bordering the Hudson River.

Within minutes the streets, parks and roofs were alive with excited spectators shouting, "It's the *ZR-3!*" over and over again. Along the river, the roar of ships' whistles was deafening as the crews of passenger and cargo vessels at the Manhattan, Brooklyn and New Jersey piers paid homage to their sister ship in the sky. Then the airship turned south across Staten Island and the Jersey communities along the Atlantic Shore. At 9:16 a.m., it arrived over the Lakehurst Naval Air Station. Lines were dropped, engines stopped and more than 350 sailors pulled the giant cigar-shaped balloon to the ground.

On Nov. 24, the *ZR-3* flew to the Anacostia Air Station at Washington DC, and the following day was christened the *U.S.S. Los Angeles* by Mrs. Calvin Coolidge, the president's wife.

When the newly commissioned Navy vessel returned to Lakehurst, it was towed into Hangar #1 and berthed alongside its sister ship *Shenandoah.*

The arrival of the *Los Angeles* grounded the *Shenandoah* for almost a year. The Navy had only enough helium to fill one airship at a time and in order to test fly the Los Angeles, the helium had to be pumped from the Shenandoah.

The lifting gas was not returned to the Shenandoah until the late summer of 1925 in preparation for a demonstration flight to St. Louis, Minneapolis and Detroit. It was cast off from the Lakehurst mooring mast on Sept. 2 under the command of Zachary Lansdowne. The navigator was Lt. Cmdr. Charles E. Rosendahl.

The 35-year old Lansdowne was one of the Navy's most experienced airship officers. He had flown as an observer on the British R-34 dirigible crossing of the Atlantic in 1919 and had taken part in experimenting with helium as a useful lifting gas for airships.

He lived at 634 Sixth Street, Lakewood, NJ, with his wife Betsy, a son, Falkland, and daughter Betsy. Lakewood, then primarily a summer resort town, was the most convenient to Lakehurst. Many naval officers and their families resided there while on duty at the Naval Air Station.

The autumn had been chosen for flight Number 57 in order to avoid the violent summer weather common to the central states.

Sept. 3 was a warm, sunny day, and an unusually large crowd of relatives and friends of the crew gathered at the foot of the mooring mast. They separated respectfully as Lansdowne approached the ladder that led up to the control car. After receiving ready reports from his officers, Landsdowne gave the command to cast off.

At four o'clock in the afternoon, the giant vessel slipped from its mooring mast and headed out across the Allegheny Mountains toward Wheeling, WV, at an altitude of 2,500 feet. The flight was routine until the "silver arrow" was over the flat farmlands of Ohio. At 3:30 a.m., Sept. 4, a severe weather front was sighted to the northeast and several course changes were ordered by Cmdr. Lansdowne.

No matter in which direction the airship moved, the storm followed relentlessly, and, at about 5:30 a.m., foul weather hit the ship, causing it to rise. Cmdr. Lansdowne ordered the engine speed increased to slow its ascent, but it was now in the firm grip of the squall. At 4,000 feet, the sudden rise was momentarily checked, only to begin again until the ship had reached its "pressure height" (the altitude at which decreasing atmospheric pressure allows the helium to expand beyond the pressure capacity of the bag). Helium vents were opened for five minutes to relieve the gas pressure.

Finally the ship reached its crest and began to fall rapidly. Ballast was discarded to slow the descent, but to no avail. Within two minutes, the dirigible dropped 2,800 feet. Then it rose again, and to compensate for the next fall, the aluminum gasoline tanks were readied for dumping.

Cmdr. Lansdowne sent Lt. Cmdr. Charles Rosendahl from the control car to check on the men and the tanks. As Rosendahl began climbing the ladder leading from the control car to the keel, the *Shenandoah* shot upward to approximately 7,000 feet. Then he heard a sharp cracking noise. The wooden struts holding the control car snapped. The car began swinging freely on its cables. Col. Hall, a U.S. Army observer on the flight, yelled a warning to Lansdowne and the other men in the control car, and then began climbing the ladder to safety.

At that moment, there was another ear-shattering report and the control car, with its eight occupants, was hurled to the earth, 7,000 feet below. The huge silver bag held aloft by the helium within its steel frame was completely without controls.

On the ground, an Ohio couple, Mr. and Mrs. Andy Gamaras, watched as the giant ship performed its fateful dance in the lightning-filled sky above their home. They saw the *Shenandoah* almost stand on end, twist and come apart. They ran to the control car and found seven crushed bodies, all beyond help. One of the crew lived for a few moments after being dragged from the wreck by Andy Gamaras.

Two sections of the airship were now being whipped about by the storm. The aft section, with Lt. Bauchaand and 24 men aboard, was carried away like an autumn leaf, and eventually landed 12 miles from where the control car had hit the ground. Three men died and one was badly injured in the crash.

Meanwhile, the lightened bow section climbed like a spinning rocket to nearly 10,000 feet. Lt. Cmdr. Rosendahl clung desperately to a girder in order to avoid being thrown into the dark night. When the nose section finally reached the apex of its climb and stabilized a bit, Rosendahl remembered feeling very alone.

"Then I shouted forward and found that there were six other men stationed at strategic positions along the nose. I knew then we could make it," he recalled.

Under Rosendahl's direction, the surviving crewmen alternately vented helium and dumped ballast to bring the derelict section safely to the ground. Rosendahl remembered that the process took "an eternally long hour" as the strange vehicle circled in a 10-mile radius around the crash site. They finally landed two miles north of Ava, OH, in the farmyard of Ernest Micholas.

Miraculously, 29 men survived the ordeal. The majority of the 14 men who died were with Lt. Cmdr. Landsdowne in the control car. Lansdowne and three of his officers were buried in Arlington National Cemetery with full military honors.

Other New Jerseyans who lost their lives in the crash were Charles Broom, aviation machinist mate, Toms River; Celestino P. Mazzuco, aviation machinist mate, Murray Hill; James A. Moore Jr., machinist mate, Jersey City and George C. Schnitzer, chief radioman, Tuckerton. The injured New Jersey residents were chief gunner Raymond Cole, Beechwood and John F. McCarthy aviation chief rigger of Freehold.

During World War II, a Navy destroyer was christened the *U.S.S. Lansdowne*. On Sept. 2, 1945, the *Lansdowne* carried the Japanese delegation to the surrender ceremonies aboard the battleship *Missouri*.

It wasn't until 1947 that then Rear Admiral Charles Rosendahl was awarded the Distinguished Flying Cross for his heroics aboard the *Shenandoah* 22 years earlier.

U.S.S. *Los Angeles*

With the demise of the *Shenandoah*, the German-built *Los Angeles* was the only rigid airship in the Navy's fleet. Over the next seven years, it became the workhorse of the Navy's lighter-than-air program. Early in 1925, it cruised to Bermuda and back, and in May flew to Puerto Rico where it was moored between flights to the *U.S.S. Patoka*.

Lt. Cmdr. Charles Rosendahl relieved Captain George Steele of command in June of 1926 and stayed on as commander until 1929.

In August, 1927, a rapid change of temperature brought a stiff, cool summer breeze ashore and caused a strange phenomenon to overtake the *Los Angeles* at Lakehurst.

Anchored to a mooring mast, the airship's tail was enveloped by the cool air, causing it to rise. Within minutes, it rose tail first to a vertical position. It stood on its nose for a brief moment, then swung around in a 180-degree arch and dropped slowly down until it was parallel once again. None of the 24-man crew aboard were injured during the dirigible's strange dance in the wind.

Throughout the 1920s, the *Los Angeles* was used to train personnel and develop new flying and berthing techniques. In January 1928, Rosendahl landed the ship on the deck of the aircraft carrier *Saratoga*. A month later, it made the first roundtrip flight to the Panama Canal Zone and back

That summer Chief Petty Officer Lyman Ford made a parachute jump from the belly of the Los Angeles while flying over Lakehurst. That was the first jump ever made from a dirigible.

Lt. Cmdr. Herbert V. Wiley assumed command of the airship in April, 1929, and immediately became involved in the planning and construction of a "trapeze" that was to swing down below the airship's wide hatch in the lower portion of its superstructure to "catch" small fighter planes equipped with large hooks protruding above their upper wing.

The first attempt to catch a plane took place on April 3, 1929. Cruising at 48 knots, 2,500 feet above Lakehurst, a small UO-1 airplane piloted by Lt. A.W. Gorton hooked onto the trapeze and was then released. The UO-1 made a number of successful test flights as did the sparrow-like Curtiss F9C aircraft until the airship was ready to join the fleet.

In 1931, the *Los Angeles* participated in fleet exercises testing the defenses of the Panama Canal. The airship's part in the maneuvers was as a scout vessel in search of enemy convoys. Before it was declared "destroyed," the *Los Angeles* had found an "enemy" convoy and reported its location to the fighting ships below. When it finally returned to Lakehurst, the *Los Angeles* had set a record for extended operations.

In the late spring of 1932, the *Los Angeles* was towed into her hangar and decommissioned, never to fly again. She remained at Lakehurst until 1939 when she was dismantled for scrap.

The *Los Angeles* had flown 4,320 hours on 331 flights. She was the only Navy dirigible that didn't come to a tragic end.

Smithsonian Collections
Paul E. Garber

Inducted Aviation Hall of Fame of New Jersey, 1987

Paul E. Garber

A 20-year-old man, small in stature but bursting with ambition, joined the staff of the Smithsonian Institution in Washington, DC, as a preparator, a person who prepares objects for display. Paul Edward Garber was ideal for the position; innovative and doggedly determined.

Aviation was his great passion, but at that time the Smithsonian didn't have an aeronautical collection even though the Institution's secretary (director) during the early 20th century had been Samuel P. Langley, who had attempted to fly his *Langley Aerodrome* off a boat in the Potomac River in 1903.

Garber's first "flight" happened on the beach at Atlantic City where he was born in 1899. At age five, his uncle built him a kite with his name and a large "5" on its surface, and they flew it from the beach. The young boy, always small for his age, became completely entranced by the flying object that began dragging him across the sand.

"I was pulled splashing into the surf, clutching that string, and headed for Europe, when my uncle hauled me back," Garber explained almost 70 years later. That wetting in the Atlantic, whet his appetite for flying, a hunger that continued for a life time.

Garber's mother, the former Margaret Sithens of Millville, NJ., met his father, a Philadelphia art dealer, when she applied for a job as a secretary. Until Paul's 10th birthday, the family lived in Millville, Plainfield and Tenafly, before moving permanently to Washington in 1910 where his father opened an art gallery.

It was that year that Garber saw his first airplane fly. He took a trolley to Fort Myer, VA, to watch Orville and Wilbur Wright demonstrate what became the Army's first aeroplane.

"I never got over the thrill of seeing that airplane —this marvelous creation, it looked like an enormous kite, flying about 200 feet high with two men in it—the noise, its engine and revolving propellers."

Throughout his formative years, Garber built and flew kites. When he was 13, he organized the "Capital Model Aero Club." At 15, he and the club members made a glider with a 20-foot wing-span. He flew it.

When Garber joined the Smithsonian staff on a three-month trial basis, Charles Doolittle Walcott was the Secretary of the institution, but Garber's immediate boss was Carl Mitman who headed the Mechanical Technology section.

After two months on the job repairing and preparing objects for display, Mitman went on vacation and Garber decided to "create something in aviation of my own making." His creation was a scale model of Da Vinci's Manual Ornithopter.

"I made a label for it with my name on it and presumptuously decided to put it on display." he recalled." While I was up on the ladder, a nice old gentlemen came along and said, 'What do we have here?' I was looking down on his bald head. I said, 'Sir, this is my copy of a manual ornithopter conceived by Leonardo Da Vinci.' I then told him what it was and who Da Vinci was. Then he wanted to know who I was, I told him and said I made the model. He thanked me and off he went.

"I put away the ladder and went back to my shop which was then in the Arts and Industries Building. I thought I'd sweep the floor once more and sharpen my tools again — I really didn't want to leave. Then along came Harry Dorsey, the Secretary's chief clerk. He asked if my name was Garber and I said 'Yes sir.' He asked if I could take a civil service exam in this kind of work. I said 'Yes sir.' He said, 'Come up to my office and I'll give you the forms. If you pass you'll have a job.' I asked 'How is that Mr. Dorsey?' he said, 'Secretary's orders.' I said, 'Dr. Walcott? I don't even know him. How does he know me?' He said, 'He's been talking to you for the last half hour.' So that's how I got my job."

Over the next three decades, that job grew from preparator to Associate Curator of the Division of Mechanical Technology.

When asked about the aircraft he helped to acquire for the Smithsonian, now exhibited in the National Air and Space Museum, perhaps the most popular museum in the world, Garber modestly credited all the Institution's Secretaries under whom he had served during his 70 years with the Institution. However it's common knowledge among those who know him best, that Garber was directly responsible for the most important exhibits in the aviation collection.

Some of the principal ones include:

—General Billy Mitchell's French Spad-16;

—the NC-4, the first plane to fly the Atlantic;

—the Fokker T-2, which made the first coast-to-coast nonstop flight in 1923;

—the Douglas World Cruiser *Chicago*, one of the first planes to fly around the world in 1924;

—Charles Lindbergh's *Spirit of St. Louis*;

—Wiley Post's Lockheed Vega, *Winnie Mae;*

—the rocket-powered Bell X-1, the first to surpass the speed of sound;

—two Mercury space capsules, Alan Shepard's *Freedom 7* and John Glenn's *Friendship 7*, just to name a few key examples.

Garber enjoys telling of a visit Charles Lindbergh made to the Air and Space Museum just a few years before the *Lone Eagle's* death.

"He came to my office and asked if it could be arranged for him to sit in the *Spirit of St. Louis* which is now hung from the ceiling of our Milestones of Flight Gallery," Garber explained. "I told him of course it could. So when the museum was closed that evening I got him a ladder and up he went into the *Spirit.*" Garber said that after Lindbergh was safely ensconced in his airplane, he never looked up, but moved away and sat quietly waiting for Lindbergh to finish his business.

"The hall was reverently silent and I became lost in thought. Perhaps a half hour passed before I heard someone quietly call my name. I looked up and there was the legendary Charles Lindbergh looking down at me from his *Spirit of St. Louis* in flight. I'll never forget that moment."

During World War I, Garber had served as a sergeant in the air service. The Armistice was signed while he was in flight training and the flight school closed down.

"I guess the Kaiser heard I was on my way and decided he'd better quit." he laughed.

He achieved the rank of Commander in the Navy during the World War II. His principle assignments were developing scale models and methods of identifying enemy aircraft, inventing a kite and control system used as targets for Navy gunners and a two-kite-supported assembly whereby an airplane with a hook could engage a horizontal line and thereby deliver material and information to headquarters.

When he left Navy service in 1946, the National Air and Space Museum was established as a separate bureau of the Smithsonian and he became curator, then head curator and senior historian. Under the leadership of this New Jerseyan, the Air and Space Museum was opened in July of 1976 with the finest collection of historic aircraft in the world.

Garber "officially" retired in 1969 at the age of 70. He then received an honorary assignment and has maintained an office at the National Air and Space Museum for the last 20 years. A popular speaker, Garber has traveled frequently throughout the United States "selling" the importance of preserving our nation's aeronautical treasures. When not traveling, he is in his office by 7:30 a.m. five days a week,

He spends the majority of his days at a typewriter or on the telephone answering the public's mail and telephone queries. Now in his 90s, he can still spill out statistics on speed and distance records, personalities and events as though he were a computer.

In 1980, the NASM's preservation, restoration and storage facility in Suitland, Maryland, where the museum's reserve collection of historically significant air and space craft is housed, was named for Paul E. Garber, as Historian Emeritus and Ramsey Fellow of the National Air and Space Museum.

1923

Wright J-1 Whirlwind Engine

Charles Lanier Lawrance

The United States Navy's desire to power their aircraft with air cooled engines resulted in an historic merger. The Wright Aeronautical Corporation of Paterson purchased the Lawrance Aero-Engines Company of New York City in May of 1923, for $500,000. Frederick Rentschler, president of Wrights, named Charles Lanier Lawrance, the designer of an air cooled engine, a vice-president of the company.

Rentschler then ordered George J. Mead and Andrew Van Dean Willgos, his two most talented engineers, to work on improving the engine. What eventually emerged was the Wright 200hp J-1 air-cooled engine called the *Whirlwind.*

In 1924, Charles Lawrance was named president of the company and Frederick Rentschler resigned.

During the first World War, Lawrance was engaged in Aeronautical research for the Navy Department. Despite opposition from the experts of the day, who preferred water-cooled aircraft engines, Lawrance began work on an air-cooled motor in his small Manhattan factory. Within a year, he had developed a two-cylinder, 60-horsepower air-cooled engine. In 1918, the engines were used by the U.S. Army to power an airplane called *Penguin* because it was designed **not** to fly.

The idea for the Penguin came from France. In order to teach men to fly World War I airplanes, the French let their pilots teach themselves to fly by starting them out in low-powered, clipped-wing airplanes that could not get off the ground. In these, they learned to taxi a plane, get a feel of the controls and become familiar with the instruments. That low-powered, air-cooled engine was the great-great-grandfather of the Whirlwinds and the later Cyclone engines that powered the leading aircraft over the next four decades.

To prove the efficiency of the revolutionary engine, Lawrance and his staff concluded that they needed the perfect airplane in which to install it. On the advise of Clarence Chamberlin, who Lawrance highly respected, company officials contacted Giuseppe Bellanca, a frail Sicilian engineer who had immigrated to the United States prior to World War I. Bellanca had designed a biplane that Chamberlin had flown during his barnstorming days and the pilot remembered how well it handled compared to other aerobatic planes of those times.

Bellanca was hired by Wrights and moved into the Paterson plant to supervise the construction of a Wright-Bellanca single-engine, high-wing monoplane, designated the WB-1. What emerged was a squatty, fat-bodied cabin aircraft that derived its lifting power not only from its long wing but also from the wide airfoil-shaped struts that supported the wings. It cruised at 100 miles per hour and flew further on a gallon of gasoline than any airplane of that time. Years later, Chamberlin said: "It was the most efficient plane of its day, and possibly of all time."

Wright Aeronautical had entered the airplane building field in 1922 when they introduced the so-called *Mystery* plane. Known officially as the "N," the plans had been drawn by a Commander Hunsaker for the Navy. A large seaplane of somewhat unconventional design, the airplane was powered with a T-2, 600hp engine when it was entered by the Navy in the Pulitzer Prize race. During preliminary tests it showed speeds in excess of 200 miles an hour, but there was not sufficient time for proper testing , and while racing it developed oil problems and had to drop out.

The following year, a racing seaplane, the NW-2, was built as a Navy entry for the Schneider Cup race. It was powered by a new T-3A, 675 hp engine which made it the most highly powered single-engine seaplane in the world. The NW-2 flew at 197 miles an hour during tests, but like the "N", an accident prevented the plane from competing.

At the same time, two Navy-Wright fighters, the F-2-W, were built for the 1923 Pulitzer race and they finished third and fourth.

The Wright-Bellanca WB-1 of 1925, equipped with the Lawrance air-cooled J-4 Whirlwind engine, was

Charles Lanier Lawrence

the first in the efficiency races and second in the speed races at the National Air Races held at Mitchell Field, LI. But again, fate turned against Wright's aircraft program when the WB-1 crashed during an attempted endurance flight.

That year the Wright engineers also designed and built the *Apache*, designated by the Navy as the WF-1, a single-seated, shipboard fighter. In July 1927, Navy Lieutenant Charleton Champion set a new altitude record of 37,000 feet over the Anacostia Naval Station in Maryland flying the Wright-Apache plane.

The second Wright-Bellanca monoplane was the last built by the Wright Company. It was equipped with the highly efficient J-5 Whirlwind engine and won several races at the National Air Races at Philadelphia and took first place in the Detroit New Transport Trophy contest. Over the next five years, the plane out flew all others built at that time.

In 1926, Clarence Chamberlin became Charles Lawrance's personal pilot which finally afforded him the opportunity to fly the WB-2. Flying out of Teterboro, Chamberlin and Lawrance showcased the plane to potential buyers. Quickly, the Bellanca and its Whirlwind engine became the leading contender for the $25,000 Orteig prize as the first plane to fly nonstop from New York to Paris.

When the WB-2 was eventually sold to Charles Levine, a wealthy scrap dealer from Brooklyn, NY, Chamberlin went to work for him. That was the beginning of a stormy, but rewarding relationship.

Charles Lanier Lawrance stayed with Wright Aeronautical through the remainder of the 1920s. In 1928, he was awarded the Collier Trophy for his achievements in 1927, when his engines powered three airplanes across the Atlantic and one from California to Hawaii, the longest over-water flight up to that time.

He was modest about his engine. When associates bemoaned how little credit he received for his creative genius, he asked with a smile: "Who ever heard the name of Paul Revere's horse?"

In 1930, the inventor organized the Lawrance Engineering and Research Corp. in Linden, NJ.

He served as president of the Aeronautical Chamber of Commerce from 1931 to 1932. During his first year in office, he was the commodore of the first amateur air cruise in the country. He led 15 seaplanes, amphibians and flying boats on a four-day air tour that ended in formation at Montauk Point, LI.

He retired as president of his company in 1944 and became board chairman. He died in June 1950 at age 67 at his home in East Islip, LI.

Fred Rentschler

After Fred Rentschler resigned from Wrights, he decided to form his own engine company and asked George J. Mead and Andy Willgos to join him. They established a partnership with the Pratt & Whitney Company in West Hartford, CT. There they began building an air-cooled engine that had been first designed in a residential two-car garage behind Willgos' home at 22 Wellesley Road in Montclair.

The first Pratt & Whitney *Wasp* engine was tested in a Wright Apache airplane for the Navy which led to an order for 200 of the new motors. Over the decades, Pratt-Whitney became one of the most highly respected engine builders in the world.

Rentschler was born in 1887 in Hamilton, OH. He graduated from Princeton University and during World War I worked for the Wright-Martin Company in New Brunswick. In 1919, he and other Wright-Martin executives formed the Wright Aeronautical Corp. that moved to quarters in Paterson. Ten years later, he helped create and became the president of the United Aircraft and Transportation Corp. He directed the corporation's divisions that produced Pratt & Whitney engines, Hamilton Standard propellers, Sikorsky helicopters and Chance Vought *Corsair* fighter planes during World War II.

In 1931, he was instrumental in organizing United Airlines, that sprung from a merger of several small airlines based across the United States

Frederick B. Rentschler was considered a living legend when he died in 1956.

Giuseppe Mario Bellanca

Known affectionately as G.M. to his friends, Bellanca arrived in America in 1911 with an engineering degree. He spoke no English but taught himself the language by going to the nickelodeons and matching subtitles with the spoken word.

Living in Brooklyn, he formed the Bellanca Aeroplane Co., and in 1912, opened a flying school. His brother, August, had turned to the local Italian community for financial backing, and the lawyer who drew up the papers was Fiorello LaGuardia. Bellanca taught LaGuardia to fly in an airplane of his own design. On their first flight, the plane landed in a tree. Following the jarring stop, LaGuardia asked his instructor good-naturedly "how do you stop an airplane if you can't find a tree?"

Bellanca stayed with Wrights through the historic year (for aviation) of 1927 and then formed his own company near New Castle, DE. For the next two decades, he built his reputation as an aircraft designer and builder to such an extent, his portrait appeared on the cover of *Time Magazine*.

He sold the New Castle plant in 1956 and retired to develop a new plastic plane in his private workshop. He died in 1960 at age 70, a wealthy man.

1924
Hadley Field

There was great excitement on a cold bright December morning in 1924 as air mail pilot James D. Hill prepared to fly the mail from the Post Office Department's newly established airport terminus located on a farm operated by John R. Hadley Sr. in Piscataway Township, NJ

Finally ready for his historic flight, Hill climbed into the open cockpit of the fragile biplane, adjusted his goggles, and at 9:45 a.m., Dec.16, the small airplane lifted off the sod runway. It circled the field once before turning westward on the first leg of the New York to Chicago air mail run. The new air mail facility for the New York metropolitan area was then officially open.

In September of the previous year, John E. *Pink Whiskers* Whitbeck and his assistant, Charles F. Devoe, both Post Office Department officials, appeared at the home of John Hadley to inquire if Hadley's 114-acre farm could be used by the government as an air field for the postal department's fledgling air mail service.

At that time, the mail was being flown from Belmont Race track on Long Island, but poor weather conditions and the necessity of flying over New York City, had prompted the postal department to again look for a suitable airfield in New Jersey. Hadley's farm seemed to fit the bill perfectly. Not only was it level and unobstructed, but it was convenient to a major rail terminal in New Brunswick.

After reaching an agreement with the Hadley family (John's brother actually owned the property), the field was plowed into a smooth landing strip and a single hangar was built. John Hadley became a Postal Department employee.

Whether from New York or New Jersey, the flight to Cleveland and Chicago, with a refueling stop in Bellefonte, PA., entailed traversing the Allegheny Mountains. Although the Alleghenies can't compare in majesty to the mighty Rockies, flying over them — in World War I open cockpit planes powered by 12-cylinder, watercooled Liberty engines with no radios and only a simple compass for navigation—was a tremendous challenge.

The menace of the Allegheny range wasn't its elevation, but rather the unpredictable weather patterns that seemed to change on an hourly basis across the rambling mountains. If a pilot found himself in trouble, there were very few places level enough to set a distressed plane down without risking the pilot's life. It is no wonder that the valiant men who regularly flew the route christened it *Hell Stretch*.

In 1925, the first night air mail was flown from Hadley Field. New Jersey historian Dave Winans of Colonia described the historic event.

Hadley Field had its biggest moment on the night of July 1, 1925, when pilot Dean C. Smith took off for Cleveland in his DH-4, The Fastest Dollar (Smith kept a dollar bill taped on the fuselage next to the cockpit). In view of a crowd of about 15,000 people, Smith took aboard some 87 pounds of mail and lifted off the floodlit field at 8:47 p.m. (He had attempted to leave a few hours earlier but carburetor trouble forced him to return to Hadley for repairs).

Postmaster General Harry S. New, who was hurrying to the scene by train from Washington missed Smith's takeoff. Two hours later, pilot James D. Hill loaded another 250 pounds of mail aboard his ship and was speeded on his way by the Postmaster General. These flights inaugurated the first coast to-coast night air mail service.

Ironically, Dean Smith did not finish his run to Cleveland. Two forced landings, ending with a crackup 12 miles from Cleveland forced Smith to transfer his load to another plane for the last leg to Chicago. James Hill actually arrived in Chicago before Smith's mail was delivered there.

Two eastbound pilots left Chicago's Maywood Field for Hadley that same evening. Paul "Dog" Collins landed at Hadley with 135 pounds of mail at two o'clock the next morning, followed by Charlie Ames with 180 pounds at 4:37 a.m. The mail was trucked to nearby Stelton railroad station for delivery to the New York Post Office.

A month later, the Hell Stretch created problems for Harry A. "Jiggs" Chandler, a Highland Park, NJ, resident. Flying the regular night route, Chandler ran into fog over Wilkes-Barre, PA, and landed in a field of oats. He lit a flare in order to inspect the condition of the field and found no obstructions in his path, so he taxied across the field to prepare for a takeoff. As he gunned his engine and the DH-4 began to roll, oats became tangled in his landing gear impeding his takeoff and causing the plane to hit a tree along the bank of the Susquehanna River. The ship landed in the water. Chandler was pinned in the cockpit, water up to his chin, when two campers rescued him.

In the true tradition of the early air mail service, Chandler reported to post office officials that there were 14 sacks of mail submerged in the river before he collapsed and was rushed to a hospital. Following his recovery from a skull fracture, Chandler resumed flying the mail.

As did many of his fellow air mail pilots, Chandler moonlighted as a barnstormer, flying stunts to attract potential passengers and then taking them on short flights for $5 per person.

While barnstorming on the afternoon of Aug. 30, 1927, the Jupiter engine that powered Chandler's Bristol biplane suddenly sputtered and cut out. Chandler attempted to land on the Schenk farm in the Randolphville section of Piscataway, but this time Lady Luck deserted him. The plane crashed, killing him and his passengers. He had logged 4,132 hours flying the mail.

The Hell Stretch claimed another victim in the fall of 1925. Charlie Ames left Hadley Field with a load of mail at 10 p.m. on Oct. 1, heading west toward Bethlehem and Allentown, PA. The weather was overcast, with a 5,000 foot ceiling, when he left New Jersey. But, as so often happened over the Alleghenies, he was soon surrounded by fog. The 31-year-old pilot was due in Bellefonte at 11:30 p.m. and by 12:30 a.m.,

Major air mail terminal.

Charlie Gates, the Bellefonte field clerk, began searching for Ames. For the next 24 hours, air mail officials at Hadley and Bellefonte awaited word of Ames' whereabouts, but none came. Search parties were organized and, three days later, a reward of $500 was offered by the Post Office.

The search for Charlie Ames became front page news. Dozens of people claimed they had heard the plane flying overhead on the night it disappeared, but such reports led nowhere. Then, an ugly rumor circulated that Ames had absconded to Canada with his important air mail cargo.

It took searchers 10 days to locate Ames' crumpled De Haviland in the Kittatinny Mountains with the dead pilot still propped at the controls. Apparently he never realized how low he had been flying because his altimeter had not accurately compensated for the difference in barometric pressure between New Jersey and the Bellefonte area.

John Hadley Jr., who was nine years old when Hadley Field first opened for business, recalled the efforts his father and other Post Office workers exerted to deliver the mail:

"From Hadley Field, the mail was taken by truck to New Brunswick where it was loaded on the train for New York,"

Hadley said in an interview years later.

"I can remember one winter day when the roads to New Brunswick were drifted full of snow. My brother and I had large Flexible Flier sleds. They were tied together and the mail bags were stacked on and tied down. Henry Joho, my father and Dean Smith, pulled that load of mail all the way to the New Brunswick train station through the snow on foot. Have you ever heard the slogan ' The mail must go through?' "

Early barnstormers John Hadley remembered seeing at the South Plainfield airport were Basil Rowe, Clarence Chamberlin's partner at Teterboro, and Johnny Miller. They flew from a section of the farm away from the air mail hangar.

Once the air mail routes had been established, the federal government decided to turn over mail transport to private carriers.

It was hoped to accomplish two goals. First, the government eliminated the need for pilots and planes and second, the mail contracts would stimulate the aviation business and eventually lead to nationwide passenger service.

A newly formed airline, Colonial Air Transport headed by Juan T. Trippe, was awarded the first of these contracts in 1926. The firm was to fly the mail between Hadley, Teterboro, Hartford and Boston. The majority of the government pilots then joined the airline ranks and flew more sophisticated aircraft than the World War I open cockpit DH-4s.

Colonial flew Fokker F-7 trimotors; National Air Transport used Douglas N-2 planes, and Pitcairn Airways operated Pitcairn PA-5 Mailwings. Those early Jersey-based carriers later merged with other regional airlines to form American, United and Eastern Airlines.

On a rainy September day in 1927, Dean Smith flew the first air express packages from Hadley Field to Cleveland and on to Chicago.

The pioneering service was inaugurated on September 1 by American Railway Express, precursor of the Railway Express Agency (REA). The packages were shipped by train from New York to New Brunswick, then carried by Model T Ford trucks to Hadley for flights to western cities. The airlines initially participating in the program were Colonial Air Transport, National Air Transport, Boeing Air Transport and West Air Express. The transcontinental package service took 32 hours.

The air mail pilots were a breed apart. They took great pride in the job they did and their dogged determination to deliver the mail on time took its toll. During the seven years the government ran the air mail service, 34 pilots and nine assistants died. But those who survived were revered by their fellow aviators.

Those pilots who regularly flew out of Hadley Field included: Wesley Smith, Bill Hopson, Verne Treat, Lloyd Bertaud, Brooke Hyde-Pearson, Warren Williams, Jack Webster, in addition Dean Smith, Hill, Ames and Chandler.

Early Aerial Communications

Arthur Raymond Brooks

Inducted Aviation Hall of Fame of New Jersey, 1980

In 1928, Bell Telephone Laboratories moved onto Hadley Field with experimental communications aircraft. Their chief pilot was World War I flying ace Arthur Raymond Brooks. At first, he and Phil Lucas had two Fairchild monoplanes to fly and later a 14-passenger Ford trimotor, dubbed the *Flying Laboratory,* was added to the fleet.

"My job was to fly and fly and fly," Brooks said 60 years later. "I put in more than 2,800 hours for Bell Labs."

Brooks was originally hired by Bell Labs (then Western Electric Engineering headquartered in New York City) in December of 1916, but when he graduated from the Massachusetts Institute of Technology the following June, Uncle Sam called. Soon he found himself flying combat missions over France with the likes of Billy Mitchell, Toohy Spaatz, Reed Chambers and Eddie Rickenbacker.

Historian Dave Winans, Arthur Raymond Brooks and
John Hadley Jr.

After the war, Brooks barnstormed around the country for a few years. Then Chambers and Rickenbacker secured government air mail contract #10 and formed an airline to fly mail and passengers between Florida and Cuba and points north. They asked Brooks to join them in the enterprise. In less than a year, the airline proved a bust and Brooks and his wife moved to Washington, DC. He was hired by the Bureau of Aeronautics as an airways extension engineer, responsible for the installation of beacon lights from Boston to Bellefonte and on into Washington.

He joined Bell Labs in 1928 and founded the company's aviation department, working with a team of engineers who tested airborne radio equipment and instruments. He not only flew the test flights, but traveled with Bell Labs' marketing staff exhibiting products at airshows across the country.

"We'd set up displays and show the latest equipment." Brooks explained. "I knew the air crowd — there was no way I couldn't have known them — and they were fascinated by what we were doing."

Lockheed, Boeing and Douglas installed Bell equipment in their new planes. United, American and TWA airlines purchased altimeters, radios and directional finders first tested at Hadley.

Among Brooks' more memorable adventures was establishing a communication system for the *Graf Zeppelin's* visit prior to her round-the-world flight in 1929.

The coverage of the historic event was described in the Bell Labs publication:

The radio transmitting and receiving apparatus on our airplane was one terminal of a network which extended to press association offices and to broadcasting stations of the Columbia chain. In the plane were A. R. Brooks, pilot; F.S. Bernhard, in charge of the radio apparatus; and for the occasion, a representa-

tive of International News Service; the Columbia announcer; and a representative of the Associated Press.

When word came that the Graf Zeppelin *was nearing the coast, the plane took off from Hadley Field and flew for some time between Lakehurst and Barnegat. On the dirigible's arrival, they accompanied it to Lakehurst while the speakers described the scene to their associates in New York, all talks being broadcast. The ground force at Hadley Field included R.S. Blair, W.C. Tinus, W.E. Reichle and R.J. Zilch.*

In December of the same year, the *Flying Laboratory* became the first plane to make radio contact with a ship at sea. The *SS Leviathan* was 200 miles from the coast when contact was accomplished. On the same flight, newsmen spoke to their counterparts on the ground and were then transferred to correspondents in London, England.

On another occasion, Brooks was invited to attend an MIT reunion, but his work schedule did not permit. So he made arrangements with the management of the Massachusetts restaurant where the dinner was held, to broadcast greetings from his airplane flying over New Jersey, a miraculous achievement for that time.

By the late 1930s, Bell was phasing out aircraft radios and Brooks, seeing war clouds on the horizon, decided to join the military again. But it wasn't to be. Three spinal surgeries prevented him from serving, but not from participating. Brooks, the engineer-pilot, wrote 18 secret technical manuals—one a hundred pages thick—and worked with the anechoic chamber at Bell's Murray Hill, NJ, plant.

After the war, he joined the company's publication department and became its manager in 1957. He retired in 1960.

In his later years, he became a national treasure. Although badly crippled and sightless, Brooks remained alert and active into his 95th year. He regularly attended functions around the nation with his close friend Ed Lawlor, a businessman and former World War II B-17 pilot.

When Ray Brooks died in July, 1991, he was the last World War I flying ace who flew for the United States.

A New Era Dawns

Ken Unger

Inducted Aviation Hall of Fame of New Jersey, 1981

When Newark Municipal Airport opened in October, 1928, the air mail carriers were ordered to move to the new facility. Colonial Air Transport was the first to go in 1929, but the others, National Air Transport (NAT) and Eastern Air Transport stayed on, a decision that proved a mistake.

Ken Unger rides "shotgun" for Gen. Robert W. Johnson

In mid-March 1930, a fire swept through a hangar at Hadley causing an estimated $200,000 in damage. The entire building and contents were lost including four Eastern Air Transport mail planes, an NAT plane fitted with special government experimental instruments and eight privately owned machines. Eastern immediately moved to Newark and NAT followed suit a few months later. Hadley was no longer in the airmail business.

In the late '20s, Ken Unger, the Newark native who had flown with the Canadians during World War I, and had served as an air mail pilot after the war, moved his flying school and aircraft sales operation from a farm field outside of Morristown, to Hadley Field. For the next three decades, Unger became a leading force at South Plainfield airport.

Throughout the 1930s, Unger's business flourished. He was recognized as one of the most versatile pilots in the country, serving as test pilot, teacher, stunt and racing pilot and personal pilot for prominent men and women in government and industry. Among his clients were Gen. Robert W. Johnson, Doris Duke and Bernard Baruch.

Those airman who worked for him over the years included J. Morgan Harding, a New Brunswick native; Elliot "Dutch" Underhill, born in Spotswood, NJ; Matthew G. Zeleski, the police chief of South River, NJ, and Johnny Perri, a parachute jumper, who worked with Unger at weekly summer Sunday air shows.

One Sunday, Perri set a free fall record by jumping from a plane, piloted by Unger, at 12,000 feet. He delayed opening his 'chute until he was less than 2,000 feet from the ground. Like so many of the jumpers of those days, Perri earned the title *daredevil* whenever his name was mentioned in the local media.

Henry E. Apgar became the "voice" of Hadley in the 1930s. Apgar was an unlikely candidate to succeed Nat Brittingham on the Hadley mike because he stut-

tered. "I could barely get a word out at school. I stuttered so much," Apgar said. "But once I got behind a microphone I didn't stutter any more."

Apgar's job was to coax spectators into taking airplane rides and to describe the various aerobatic feats that took place throughout the day. He remembered a Sunday afternoon in 1932 when Unger was circling his airplane above him. "Then suddenly he wasn't," Apgar said. "He was floating down in a parachute. A wing had separated from the rest of the airplane. The wing landed here, the rest of the plane landed there, and Unger came down someplace else. The following week, the crowds were bigger than ever. It's amazing how much people got out of something simple back in those days. They loved it and I loved it."

Apgar never stopped promoting the history of Hadley and later he became mayor of South Plainfield.

In 1934, Ken Unger expanded his business by acquiring the flying school and maintenance base at Westfield Airport that had formerly been operated by the Fonda Aviation Corp. The manager at the new facility was Carl Rasmussen, an ex-naval pilot.

Douglas Fonda had been the chief pilot of the Newark Air Service branch at Westfield before starting his own company. He had made a stir in the aviation community in 1931—when the country suffered in the Depression—by offering flying instructions at the rate of $5 per lesson. In the first five months of the program, 40 students, including nine women, signed up for the program. Fonda's planes flew 10 hours a day. But like so many other businesses of those unhappy years, he was forced out of business by the nation's financial crunch.

Unger also expanded to the Jersey shore during the summer months. Matty Zeleski ran a sightseeing service based at Brielle, NJ, for him.

During World War II, Ken Unger enlisted in the Navy at the age of 43. He is thought to be one of the oldest men ever to complete the Navy's flight training and earn his wings.

Following the war, he returned to Hadley and became the head of the Johnson & Johnson aviation department. J & J had one of the first corporate aircraft in the nation because of the interest of Gen. Robert Johnson in aviation. Unger retired to Florida in 1958.

A New Owner and Manager
Thomas W. Robertson

Inducted Aviation Hall of Fame of New Jersey. 1983

Thomas W. Robertson was named the manager of Hadley Airport in 1933. He had been the assistant manager of the Curtiss-Wright Airport in Caldwell, NJ, for a year before the C-W Corporation transferred him to Hadley, which it also operated. In 1935, he

Tom Robertson

purchased the airport lease and continued on as owner/operator of the field until the property was sold to developers in 1968.

During World War II, the Bendix Corp. leased two Hadley hangers in order to do research work on molded plywood for aircraft construction. Robertson managed the project. The Andover-Kent Co. of New Brunswick built 10 Navy training planes of the material and tested them at Hadley.

They were jokingly called "Flying Pianos" because their plywood frames were covered with a mahogany veneer, much like a piano.

Under Robertson's tutelage, the airport was a place where aeronautical experiments became realities. Among them were the radio terrain clearance indicator, the forerunner of modern radar, and John Doe's sturdy fin-type blower, designed to reduce parasitic wing drag. The device was used on DeHaviland planes and others. The Curtiss-Wright Co. developed the Tanninger airplane which was the first vertical take-off and landing aircraft.

Of all his activities, Robertson recalled field maintenance as his toughest challenge. "We had a sod field," he explained, "and the hardest job was keeping it usable. When it rained, it took five to 10 hours to dry. Ruts in the sod were constantly being filled, and several times a year we'd roll the runway."

In 1946, Robertson operated the largest aircraft repair station in New Jersey. The leading operator at the field at that time was a former Air Corps pilot Rick Decker, who owned 20 airplanes and ran the most active flying school in New Jersey.
Born in Newark, Robertson lived in Plainfield until he retired to the seaside resort of Lavalette, NJ.

The last aircraft to land at Hadley Airport in 1968 was a Cessna 180 flown by Capt. John Hicks, a former flight instructor at the field and, later, an American Airlines pilot. John Hadley Jr. was there to greet him.

All that remains of Hadley Airport today is a granite monument installed near where the original hangar stood, now the site of a Holiday Inn along Stelton Road.

John Hadley Jr. learned to fly in 1940 under the watchful eye of Ken Unger. After the Pearl Harbor attack, he enlisted and flew for the Navy for five years and another five in the Naval Reserve.

At war's end, he decided to give up flying and went to work for Johnson & Johnson in New Brunswick where he and his wife Mary Lou raised their family. When he retired as a J&J marketing manager, he and his wife moved to Sarasota, FL.

Fokker Comes to America

Anthony Herman Gerard Fokker

Inducted Aviation Hall of Fame of New Jersey, 1974

No one had a greater influence in developing American commercial aviation than the Dutch aircraft designer, Anthony H.G. Fokker. His large three-engine aircraft dominated the aviation industry throughout the 1920s and were the aircraft of choice among the budding airlines of that decade.

Fokker's reputation as an aircraft designer for the German Air Service during World War I had gained him worldwide attention. His fighter planes, especially the three-winged Dr.I flown by Manfred von Richthofen, the "Red Baron," were highly respected by both German and Allied airmen.

After the Armistice in 1918, Fokker returned to Holland and established a successful aircraft manufacturing business in Veere, Zeeland. He and one of his bright young engineers, Robert B.C. Noorduyn, first journeyed to America in 1920 to attempt to sell his aircraft to U.S, Army Air Corps officials Although he was cordially received and taken on an inspection tour of Army facilities, no immediate orders were forthcoming.

The trip did lead to the formation of the Netherlands Aircraft Manufacturing Company of Amsterdam, a sales organization based in New York, under Noorduyn's management. Over the next two years, both the Army and Navy ordered various Fokker military planes, and in 1921 one of his commercial models, the F III, made demonstration flights around the U.S. with Bert Acosta at the controls,

In 1923, a large Fokker monoplane with a wing span of 79 feet, was flown non-stop across the United States by two Army Lieutenants, John A. Macready and Oakley G. Kelly. Participation in the first non-stop transcontinental flight focused a great deal of media attention on Fokker and the two officers.

One of Fokker's strongest boosters was the legendary General Billy Mitchell, the man credited with revolutionizing air warfare. Mitchell and the Dutchman had met in Holland in 1922, and upon the General's return to the U.S., he urged the Army to ask Fokker to rebuild 100 De Havilland DH-4s, replacing the wooden fuselages with welded steel tube. In addition, Fokker received an order for 30 new airplanes.

In order to fulfill the contracts, an American corporation was formed in May of 1924 and the Wittemann plant at Teterboro was leased. One of the former Wittemann financial backers, Lorillard Spencer, became president of the new Atlantic Aircraft Corp., the American Fokker Company. A. Francis Arcier, another Wittemann alumnus, was named technical manager. To watch over Fokker's interest, Noorduyn became the general manager.

Robert B.C. Noorduyn

Inducted Aviation Hall of Fame of New Jersey, 1978

Noorduyn was an excellent aircraft designer in his own right. Two of Fokker's most popular aircraft, the Universal, accommodating four passengers, and the Super Universal, which carried six, were Noorduyn creations.

Noorduyn had spent the war years of 1914 to 1918 working for British aircraft manufacturers, before joining Fokker in 1919. While Fokker was the flamboyant promoter and salesman, Noorduyn was the faithful, hard-working manager who kept the American company on course. Well liked by all employees, he spent as much time in the plant as he did in the office.

Noorduyn left Fokker in 1929, worked for Bellanca and Pitcairn for a few years, and then went to Canada and founded Noorduyn Aircraft Ltd. at Montreal in 1935. His Noorduyn *Norseman* became the workhorse of the flying community in Canada's frozen north. There were more than 1,000 built. The *Norseman*, a sturdy, high-wing, single engine jack-of-all-trades, was a rough and tumble creation suited for wheels,

Bob Noorduyn and Tony Fokker.

floats or skis. During the World War II invasion of Normandy, France, the *Norseman* was used to land at the beachhead to evacuate wounded Allied troops.

The Noorduyn Canadian company also built nearly 3,000 North American Harvard all-metal advanced trainers for wartime service.

At the time of his death in 1959, the *Montreal Star* ran an editorial tribute to his career. It read in part:

Of course, it is testimony to aviation's tremendous growth and advance that thousands of our keenest young air enthusiasts may not even know his name, geared as they are to thinking in terms of jets and supersonic speeds. But among bush pilots of another day, among many existing non-scheduled operations and to thousands of Canadian and United States service veterans, his contributions can never be forgotten.

1926
Flight To the North Pole

Richard E. Byrd and Floyd Bennett

Henry Ford, then America's leading car manufacturer, became interested in aviation and in 1925 decided to organize the Ford Reliability Tour, an extensive crosscountry air rally that would be open to all types of aircraft flying a predetermined 1,500 mile route. Fokker, determined to show off his product, put in a rush order to his Veere plant in Holland for a Fokker F.7 trimotor. The component parts of the plane were completed in eight weeks and shipped to the Teterboro plant for assembly. Three Paterson-built Wright Whirlwind engines were installed —one in the nose and two under the large wings.

Late in September, the large monoplane with the *Flying Dutchman* (as Fokker liked to be called) at the controls, flew to Detroit to begin the tour. On every leg of the tour, the F.7 placed first. The publicity-minded Dutchman took members of the press from each major city along the route on familiarization flights. The tour was a great triumph for Fokker aircraft in America. Two men with plans to fly to the extreme end of the earth, noted explorer, Sir Hubert Wilkins and little-known Navy Lt. Cmdr. Richard E. Byrd, both journeyed to Teterboro to inquire about obtaining a Fokker F.7. to explore the Arctic.

Richard Byrd was a young, ambitious Navy navigator and explorer from a prominent Virginia family, who had just arrived back in the United States from a surveying mission in northern Canada with explorer Donald MacMillan. The expedition had been sponsored by the National Geographic Society. His desire

Richard Byrd and Floyd Bennett.

to be the first to fly over the North Pole brought him to Teterboro, prepared to buy the large Fokker plane.

Fokker, then using the plane as a demonstration model, wasn't anxious to sell, so he asked an astronomical $40,000 for the Reliability Tour winner. Byrd convinced Edsel Ford to purchase the plane and christened it *Josephine Ford* in honor of Ford's daughter. Realizing the historic importance of the first Polar flight, Fokker insisted the sales contract provide that the word "FOKKER" be painted in large letters on the fuselage and under the wings.

With the plane in his possession and with the help of Ford, Byrd convinced a number of wealthy men to back his project, including Vincent Astor, Rodman Wanamaker, John D. Rockefeller Jr. and Dwight Morrow, an Englewood resident and a partner in the renowned financial House of Morgan.

In late April, 1926, the supply ship *Chantier*, with the *Josephine Ford* and a 50-man expedition force aboard, commanded by Byrd and pilot Floyd Bennett, arrived at Kings Bay, Spitsbergen, Norway. They established a camp adjacent to one headed by the renowned Norwegian explorer Roald Amundsen. Amundsen had plans to fly the dirigible *Norge* (Norway) over the Pole to Alaska. However, the Italian-built airship was still in Leningrad, Russia, after an overland flight from Italy.

The Byrd crewmen were looked upon as interlopers by Amundsen's group, but the veteran explorer was cordial to Byrd. He instructed his 25-year-old protege, Bernt Balchen, to be helpful in any way possible to Byrd and Bennett.

Balchen, a blond, handsome, athletic youth, was an expert pilot and navigator, a combination that was rare among the aviators of that time. The rugged Norwegian was very much at home in the frozen north country and would become one of the world's leading experts on Polar survival.

The Norge arrived at Spitsbergen on May 7, commanded by Italian General Umberto Nobile, who was upset by the presence of Byrd's expedition, and urged Amundsen to hurry preparations for their flight in order to be the first to fly to the Pole. Amundsen, unwilling to make the important exploration into a race, vetoed the idea.

After several test flights of the *Josephine Ford* by Byrd and Bennett, with a great assist from Balchen, the Fokker was ready to attempt the long, dangerous voyage.

They waited until after midnight on May 9, when the northern sun was closer to the horizon and the icy runway was solidly frozen for takeoff. The Fokker lifted into the air at 12:37 a.m. and headed from Kings Bay to the Pole.

Byrd expected the 1,535 mile round-trip flight to take approximately 24 hours. The Fokker flew at an average speed of 70 mph, which did not take the wind factor into consideration. Late that same afternoon, the *Josephine Ford* was spotted on the horizon and received a rousing welcome as it gently settled onto the ice of Kings Bay. Odd Arneson, the aviation editor of an Oslo newspaper *Aftenposten*, cabled a message to his editor:

"Byrd over Cross Bay (adjacent to Kings Bay) after 15 hours of flying. Ten minutes later the two courageous fliers landed in good condition. The fliers themselves insist they were over the Pole but on the basis of the time they could hardly have been there. Probably no farther north than Amundsen (Amundsen had flown north in 1925)."

A great controversy raged over Byrd and Bennett's accomplishment and officials in both Oslo and Rome publicly denounced the record flight. President Calvin Coolidge, on the other hand, was overjoyed and sent a message of congratulations to the two fliers:

"The President sends his heartiest congratulations to Commander Byrd on the report that he has flown to the North Pole. It is a matter of great satisfaction that this record has been made by an American."

Later Byrd's charts were turned over to the National Geographic Society's experts who verified the flight.

Whether Byrd and Bennett reached the North Pole or not, the employees at the Fokker plant in Teterboro and those at the Wright Aero Corporation in Paterson were thrilled by the positive publicity their aircraft and engines received. Byrd's flight was just the beginning of the engineering accomplishments of New Jersey designers and craftsmen.

When the aviators and their plane returned to the United States, Bennett and Balchen flew the Josephine Ford on a nationwide tour. Balchen questioned Bennett concerning the flight. The Norwegian noticed that the plane was flying at an average speed of 70 mph with a normal landing gear and not the cumbersome skis the airmen used on the Arctic flight which would have reduced the speed. When he asked Bennett how the plane could have flown to the Pole in 15 hours, the pilot replied, "We had a tail wind." Balchen pointed out that the wind would have been against them on the way back to Spitsbergen.

"We're both cockeyed somewhere," Bennett shrugged. "Well, it doesn't matter now. We won't be flying this bucket across the Atlantic or anywhere else. You'll be working in the Fokker factory, and I'll be looking for a job."

The Josephine Ford was left in Dearborn, MI, as a permanent exhibit in the Ford museum where it still rests.

Gates Flying Circus
Ivan R. Gates

Inducted Aviation Hall of Fame of New Jersey, 1976

The Gates Flying Circus arrived at Teterboro Airport in the summer of 1926. It was led by Ivan Gates, a large, burly man who had been promoting air shows since before World War I, and Clyde Pangborn, a pilot who had earned the nickname *Upside-down Pangborn* by flying that way in an open cockpit plane on coast-to-coast tours.

The Gates boys were arguably the best-known of all the barnstorming teams in America. The flying troupe had seasoned pilots, daring aerial acrobats and talented promoters who kept the crowds coming to see the boys risk their lives in all manner of breathtaking stunts.

Gates was barnstorming in the west and southwest with a cadre of several planes, pilots and wing-walkers when he was joined by Pangborn in 1923. Gates named himself president and director. Pangborn was chief pilot and general manager. At that time, they had two planes and two additional employees.

By the time it set up shop at Teterboro, the circus had seven planes, mostly modified Standard J-1 biplanes, designed by Charles Healy Day and first built in Plainfield in 1916. They were painted bright red with a "Texaco" logo on each side of the fuselage and under each lower wing. For the publicity, the oil company supplied the fuel and oil for all the ships.

In order to keep the wood, fabric and wire planes in working order, Gates leased an old two-story factory in Lodi, NJ, as an overhaul base. Charles F. "Slim" West became the foreman of that shop.

Although the Gates Flying Circus spent less than three years at Teterboro, its presence in North Jersey left a mark on impressionable youngsters who were fascinated by airplanes. With the busy Fokker plant and the Wright Aeronautical test hangar already at the field, Teterboro was a beehive of activity. It is fair to say that a majority of the most famous aviators of that period could be found at Teterboro at one time or another by awed youngsters who spent all their spare time at the airfield. But those pilots who were preparing for historic flights to various parts of the world had precious little time or inclination to talk to local kids.

On the other hand, when the circus troupers weren't performing, they would chat with the youngsters, bribing them with airplanes rides if they'd clean the mud off the planes and run errands. Many of New Jersey's prominent pilots of the next three decades had their first plane rides with Gates pilots.

They were a dashing group in their boots and riding breeches, caps, goggles and flowing scarfs. Their devil-may-care attitude and rowdy flamboyance made them particularly attractive to young ladies who watched them perform in the south during the winter months and up north in the summer.

The pilots during that period at Teterboro, in addition to Pangborn, were Bill Brooks, Floyd Clevenger, Jack Ashcraft, Ives MacKinney, Buck Steele, Bill Stultz, Harold McMahon, Erret Williams, Joe James, Lee Mason, G.P. Nagle, Roy Ahern, Warren Smith, Hank Tallman, Freddy Lund, "Okey" Bevins, Chet Vogt and Homer Fackler.

The stuntmen included Aron "Duke" Krantz, "Shorty" Bittner, John Runger, "Happy" Johnson, Mickey Efferson, Jack Parks and George Babcock. The advance man was George Daws.

The Gates Flying Circus staged a huge New York National Airplane Show and Monster Air Circus at Teterboro in late August, 1927. Thousands of spectators came to see static displays of the latest aircraft and to watch the stunt flying, parachute-jumping, wing-walking and mid-air plane changing.

As a special event, a Broadway stage actress, Anini Hendricks, starring in *A Night In Spain*, made her first parachute jump at the air show.

The show was a tremendous financial success as the Gates pilots carried passengers aloft well into the night for a dollar a piece.

It was the job of the advance man, George Daws, to arrange for locations to hold the flying circus and to publicize it in every way possible. When the circus was scheduled to appear in Atlantic City, Daws knew that the flyers would be performing to a rather jaded audience, accustomed over the years to spectacular aeronautical performances. So, when he called on the editor of the *Atlantic City Press*, Daws was prepared to impress him.

"Our pilot, Clyde E. Pangborn, will fly the length of your Boardwalk upside-down," Daws bragged.

"He'll fly upside down?" the editor repeated. "You mean with his head hanging down out of the open cockpit the full length of our Boardwalk? That's preposterous! It's two miles long."

GATES FLYING CIRCUS

Gates Flying Circus

"Preposterous? No! Astounding? Yes!" Daws replied confidently. "He does it every day."

When the circus arrived a few days later, the planes flew in formation, then the pilots looped and stunted their old Standards above the Boardwalk. As they neared the far end of the two-mile wooden strip, Pangborn spun his biplane over at 3,000 feet and glided upside down along the entire length of the "boards." He then easily recovered 1,000 feet above the inlet.

Even sophisticated Atlantic City was impressed and the circus drew twice the number of spectators it had expected,

The successful transatlantic flights of Lindbergh, Chamberlin and Byrd, during the early summer of 1927, proved the reliability of Wright engines and the sturdiness of new aircraft design. This stimulated the public's confidence in air travel, and throughout the United States new airlines sprung up overnight. It became obvious that in the interest of public safety, the aviation business would have to be regulated. Organizations like the Gates Flying Circus became a principal target of government agencies.

Inspectors were constantly checking the airworthiness of World War I vintage planes like the Standards the circus flew. In order to forestall the grounding of his planes, Ivan Gates found Charles Healy Day, the Standard designer, in South Jersey and asked him to join the troupe. He wanted Day to make alterations to the Standards in order to pass inspection.

Shortly thereafter, Day and Gates formed a partnership to build a Standard biplane that would conform to the new government regulations. For more than a year, Day worked in the Lodi plant making vital adjustments to the old Standards while he worked on his new design, similar to the original Standard, called the Gates-Day (GD) Standard.

In April 1928, Ivan Gates resigned as a principal in the Gates-Day Aircraft Corp. and the company was reorganized as the New Standard Aircraft Corp. Charles L. Augar Jr. was president of the new firm in partnership with Day. Work continued on the Standard G-D-2 biplane.

In February 1930, Rueben H. Reiffin, the managing director of the corporation, announced that his company had received a $50,000 order from the U.S. Navy for New Standard training planes.

But no matter what change they made, daredevil aviators were coming under constant attack by the media. In editorials across the country, writers emphasized that the aircraft were constructed of nothing more than wood and fabric, held together by a series of guy wires. Some of the planes, the writers pointed out, were more than 12 years old.

Many tricks that had become standard fare at all air shows were now restricted by new regulations. The stunt men were not permitted to change planes in mid-air. For that matter, aircraft were required to fly a minimum of 300 feet from each other. Explosives and fireworks could not be carried aloft and night flying without navigation lights was prohibited.

By the early winter of 1928, it became apparent that the end was near for the Gates venture. New laws, ready for implementation in 1929, not only put a crimp in stunt flying but also outlawed commercial flights in wooden planes or any aircraft that did not carry an Approved Type Certificate.

The last four-plane group of Gates flyers, left Teterboro in late November of 1928 heading toward the south. They made their way into Tennessee, Alabama, Louisiana and Mississippi led by "Whispering" Bill Brooks. Others in the squadron were among Gates' top pilots Ives MacKinney, Jack Ashcraft and Homer Fackler.

Their stay in the south was cut short by devastating Mississippi River floods throughout the area and continued harassment by government inspectors. They returned to Teterboro on a cold February day in 1929.

In his book *Baling Wire, Chewing Gum and Guts*, published in 1970, historian Bill Rhode poignantly described the last flight of the circus.

They roared over Teterboro from the southwestern end of the field. How proud they flew with the same devil-may-care flair they had always had. Several hundred pairs of eyes were on them. The mechanics in the Wright Service hangar laid down their tools and came out. The hundred men who worked in the

Fokker factory poured out the big open-sided hangar door to watch them.

Brooks, Ashcraft, MacKinney and Fackler flew them, each with one or two stunt men or mechanics in their front pits. It was the usual noise made by a squadron of planes, but this time it seemed more ominous. When they reached the middle of the field they were wing to wing. At Brooks' signal, they all looped side by side. They were at 2,000 feet.

Pangborn swallowed hard as he watched them. They looped side by side one after another. It was their swan song. The hard shelled Gates, tough as he was, then revealed himself as a soft sentimentalist. Tears bristled in his eyes.

After five loops, they broke off in a fleur-de-lis and went into their own bag of tricks. Each one ended by spinning down close to the ground and then making a three point landing on the soil. Brooks was the last one down. He made one final loop.

The famous Gates Flying Circus had given its last show. It had played every state in the union. It had carried over 750,000 passengers, but now it had to fold its wings in the interest of progress.

They taxied over to the rail fence at the south end of the field, flipped back their goggles and cut their switches. A new era in aviation was beginning. In a few days they would all be paid off and new plans made.

As they left the back room that night, many of them were to go on to greater glory and some were destined to pay the supreme price for being a pilot.

Some of the Gates troupe stayed on at Teterboro while others returned to their home states. Most stayed in the aviation business. About three-fourths of them died young, caught up in the thrill of flying, willing to go beyond the bounds of safety to find it.

Ivan Gates simply moved across the Hudson River to a plot of land in Jackson Heights that he leased from an investment broker, E.H. Holmes. They called the place Holmes Airport. Business thrived during the first nine months of 1929. Then came the crash on Wall Street and Gates' investments were wiped out. He had become almost penniless overnight.

Over the next two years, the famous aviation entrepreneur organized a few air shows that were only moderately successful during that depressed era. He

Planes of the circus.

was certain that a show he planned in 1931 in Jersey City would be a smashing success. As a favor, many of his old friends appeared including Major DeSeversky, Betty Lund, Art Davis, Clyde Pangborn, Clarence Chamberlin and Ruth Nichols.

The show was billed as the Frank Hague Air Meet in honor of Jersey City's iron-fisted mayor, but Gill Robb Wilson, the newly appointed New Jersey director of aviation, forbade the promoter to use the mayor's name. Hague, the supreme politician, was incensed, but Wilson explained he was only protecting him (Hague) from the possibility of unwanted publicity. As it turned out, a small boy crawled under the rope separating the crowd from the flight line and walked straight into a whirling propeller, killing him instantly. Then in one of the races, a participant hit a waterfront building and another ditched in the Newark Bay.

Wilson also canceled the scheduled women's race because Betty Lund was entered and refused to withdraw. Lund's husband, Freddy, had been killed several weeks earlier and Wilson felt that Betty was in no mental condition to fly. His decision did not sit well with the women aviators at the show. He was called an anti-feminist by Amelia Earhart.

Following the show, Mayor Hague thanked Wilson for keeping him out of the resultant bad publicity. What had appeared to be an upturn in fortunes for Ivan Gates, ended under a dark cloud.

Early in 1932, tragedy again struck. A storm of hurricane force blew down all the hastily constructed hangars at Holmes Airport leaving Gates with nothing but a pile of uninsured rubble.

The once highly respected promoter was reduced to running a penny arcade on Times Square. It was more than he could tolerate, and in November 1932, he committed suicide by jumping from his sixth floor Jackson Heights apartment. He was 42 years old.

Aron F. "Duke" Krantz

Inducted Aviation Hall of Fame of New Jersey, 1973

Arguably, the most colorful character of the Gates circus troupe was Aron F. Krantz, known affectionately as "Duke". He was billed as the "Daring Diavalo" (Devil in Spanish) and "Sky High Krantz", the parachute jumper.

Actually, all the Gates' aerial acrobats had been named *Diavalo*. Ivan Gates realized that the mortality rate of the aerial acrobats was terribly high, and in order to avoid having new billboards, posters and fliers printed each time a wing walker fell to his death, Gates created one name to fit all.

Krantz beat the odds and died of natural causes 40-plus years after the Circus disbanded.

He had just turned 27 when he decided to give up his secure job at the U.S. Post Office in Houston, TX, to join the Flying Circus as a mechanic and part-time acrobat. A natural showman, he was looking for the limelight. It came sooner than he expected when the Gates' wing walker was killed while performing. Krantz thrived as *Diavalo*. He played the role to the hilt. Men envied his apparent devil-may-care bravado and women flocked to him as they would to a movie star. Soon he was the highest-paid circus performer. Years later he said:

"In all, I guess I gave about 1,000 performances, sometimes three a day. I made about 255 parachute jumps and received a $25 bonus for each. My monthly base salary was $300; the other members got $100.

"For each plane change — I did about 500 of those — I got a $5 bonus. I got a $2.50 bonus for every wing-walking performance."

His wing-walking performances included standing on his head on the wings, hanging by his heels and teeth from below the undercarriage, standing on the wing with arms outstretched while the plane looped and a raft of other tricks.

Why did Krantz survive while other *Diavalos* perished?

"I was careful. I had my stunts all figured out before I'd do it. For instance, for standing on top of the wing I had a lot of little secret devices. I wore a belt under my sweater that nobody could see. I had cables—full cables, not wires—made up with snaps on them, and they were hidden in the airplane all the time. So when I got up in the air, I would stand up, hook the cables to the belt and take one in each hand. As I reached up, I was snapping these fittings that nobody could see. Then I would straighten up and, with no hesitation at all, stretch out the cables good and tight. The pilot would go into a dive and come around in a loop. That was, of course, one of the spectacular stunts."

After the Gates circus folded, life was no less exciting for the daredevil who had come to America from his native Sweden in 1915. Having taught himself to fly in 1927 at Teterboro Airport in an airplane he'd built himself, Krantz became the pilot for the *New York Daily News* air photography section in 1932, a job he held until the United States declared war on Japan and Germany in 1941.

During those years, Krantz covered, such stories as the Lindbergh baby kidnapping and the burning of the ocean liners *Morro Castle* and *Normandie*. He was under the dirigible *Hindenburg* when it blew up at Lakehurst.

"I saw a flash of light, looked up, then came a series of explosions as each chamber went. People started jumping like flies. Then the flaming mass came down on them. It was horrible," he recalled.

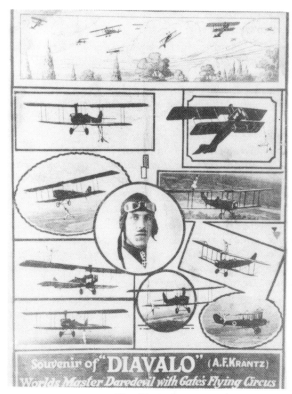

The "Duke"

It was while flying for the *Daily News* that Krantz found entertainer-pilot Harry Richman and Eastern Airlines' pilot Henry T. "Dick" Merrill after their plane *Lady Peace* had gone down in Newfoundland while attempting to fly the Atlantic from England. Not satisfied with pictures from the air, he landed the News' white Waco on very rough terrain to get a first-hand story. The *News* had pictures and story on the streets long before the crash site had been located by Eastern president Eddie Rickenbacker and the crew in the DC-2 rescue plane.

In 1942, Krantz became the head of the test pilot operation at Willow Run, MI, where B-29s were assembled.

"More than one B-29 burst into flames on me, or an electrical system went on the blink. I always managed to get them down safely anyway. In some 15,000 hours of flying, I only had two accidents, and they were flukes. I was never injured," he said.

After the war, he returned to his Hasbrouck Heights home and joined the Bendix Corp. at Teterboro as the head of the company's flight operation. Pilots Roy Ryder and Paul Arnold were members of his staff.

Prior to retiring from Bendix in 1962, Krantz and his second wife, Hetty, moved to Closter, NJ. They spent their retirement years traveling to the southwest

United States and Alaska, and among aviation friends in New Jersey.

Duke Krantz died while on a Florida vacation in 1974. Time had caught up with the last—and most famous — Diavalo.

First Air Mail Contract
Juan Terry Trippe

Inducted Aviation Hall of Fame of New Jersey, 1975

On the evening of July 1, 1926, a crowd of more than 5,000 spectators gathered along the sod runway at Teterboro Airport awaiting the arrival of the first commercial airplanes, under contract with the government, to carry mail between the Greater New York area and Boston. The central figures in the group were Second Assistant Postmaster Irving Glover, who had jurisdiction over air mail operations, Anthony Fokker, the aircraft designer and builder, Charles Lawrance, president of Wright Aeronautical Corp., Col. Benjamin Foulois, commandant of Mitchel Field, and Juan T. Trippe, the 27-year-old vice president and general manager of Colonial Air Transport, the company which had out bid three others in November 1925 for the postal department's Contract Air Mail (C.A.M.) Route No. 1.

Three aircraft, two Fokker Universals, built at Teterboro, and a Curtiss Lark, had left Hadley Field in S. Plainfield at 6:45 that morning and flown to Boston via Hartford with the first sacks of mail. Following a lengthy official reception and luncheon, the three planes lifted off Boston's gravel runway to the resounding roar of a 17-gun salute by the 101st Field Artillery, Massachusetts National Guard. Army and Navy training planes escorted them to the Connecticut border. At Hartford, the tired airmen found another enthusiastic crowd eager to meet them.

Daylight Savings Time had not come into vogue in the 1920's, therefore the last vestiges of sunlight disappeared at 8:15 p.m. and Trippe realized his aircraft would have difficulty locating the New Jersey strip, which was unlighted. Hurriedly, he asked his friends and workers at the field to park their cars along the perimeter of the runway and turn on their lights to illuminate the field. At 8:55, the crowd heard the planes overhead and two minutes later, Major Talbot O. Freeman landed his Fokker Universal.

A band struck up a rousing march as Hustis I. Wells in the Lark and LeRoy Thompson, piloting the second Fokker, pulled up in front of the Fokker hangar and waved to the crowd. Glover and Trippe made a few short remarks praising the new service before the three planes headed back to Hadley Field. Once there the mail was sent by train to Manhattan or transferred to other aircraft for transcontinental delivery.

Although his ancestry was pure English and his family background nautical — a schooner named the *John C. Trippe* fought in the battle of Lake Erie in the War of 1812 — Juan Terry Trippe, born in Seabright, NJ, was named for his favorite aunt, Juanita Terry.

Trippe was expected to follow in his father's foot steps as an investment banker but young Juan became intrigued with aviation and left Yale in 1917 to join the Navy as a pilot. Following World War I, he returned to college and organized the Yale Flying Club.

While in school his friends were the progenies of the wealthy Whitney, Vanderbilt and Hambleton clans, an association that would be invaluable throughout his life.

Upon graduation from Yale in 1923, Trippe entered the field of investment banking and in less than a month became restless and decided to try his hand at aviation. He purchased nine surplus Navy seaplanes for $500 a piece and founded Long Island Airways. Trippe was president, sales manager and mechanic. He often flew charter flights when one of his airmen went off barnstorming. The charter service lasted less than a year.

Undaunted, Trippe founded Eastern Air Transport with financial help from his friends Cornelius Vanderbilt and "Sonny" Whitney, and began lobbying in Washington for the New York to Boston air mail contract that had just been approved by Congress. Discovering the only real competition for the mail route was the Connecticut-based Colonial Airways, headed by the state's governor John H. Trumbull, Trippe met with Trumbull and his wealthy backers and came away with a merger.

Juan Terry Trippe

Although Major General John F. O'Ryan was president of Colonial Air Transport, Trippe ran the operation. In the first three months the fledgling airlines' three aircraft, powered by Wright Whirlwind engines, flew 44,000 miles in 486 hours without a mechanical problem, an outstanding record in those early days of commercial flying.

Once the business of carrying the mail was firmly entrenched, Trippe began planning to upgrade the service as a passenger airline. His directors did not share his enthusiasm for expansion, so without their approval, he ordered two new 12-passenger Fokker trimotors from Tony Fokker at Teterboro and when the bill for $37,000 was presented to the Board, he was fired.

At the time of his induction into the Aviation Hall of Fame of New Jersey, Trippe explained in a letter to this writer dated March 31, 1975, why he left Colonial. "I well remember the first Colonial Air Transport flight from Boston via Hartford to Teterboro which inaugurated the U.S. contract air mail route No. 1," the pioneer wrote. "The equipment was single-engine Fokker Universal. This was a four-passenger and pilot cabin aircraft with the already well known Fokker monoplane wing. Our company soon became a profitable operation and Colonial submitted bids for the New York-Chicago and New York-Atlanta mail contracts when they were advertised a year later.

"Colonial was the successful bidder on both routes and would have been awarded the contracts had some of our Directors, particularly those from Boston and Hartford, not decided later that the new routes were too ambitious for the company as then constituted. An agreement was made between the shareholders permitting all to vote on whether to expand or remain only on the Boston-Hartford-New York route. If the Colonial expansion program was voted down the so-called 'New York' shareholders of the company were to acquire the three-engine Fokker cabin monoplanes already on order for Colonial. The losing shareholders were also to be reimbursed for the full value of their investment. The Colonial shareholders meeting took place, I recall in Hartford. The final vote was 50 ½ in favor of continuing only the Boston-Hartford-New York route, against 49 ½ who favored the Colonial expansion program."

The Colonial Company withdrew its bids for the new Chicago and Atlanta routes, and the New York shareholders, led by Trippe, walked away with the contracts for the two 12-passenger Fokker trimotors.

Colonial continued to fulfill its contract with the government, and when Newark Municipal Airport opened in 1928, the airline was one of the first to transfer from Hadley Field to the more modern Newark facility. In the early 1930s, Colonial merged with other carriers and became American Airlines.

1927
Pan American Airways

Having sold theirs shares in Colonial Air Transport, Trippe and several other former Colonial shareholders founded Pan American Airways.

Never one to be caught short, Trippe had flown to Havana with Tony Fokker in the early months of 1927 while still employed by Colonial and, with characteristic foresight, he obtained a letter in which Cuban President Gerardo Machado granted him exclusive landing rights in Cuba. With what he later described as "a simple two-or-three-page letter" in hand, Trippe was ready for business.

He hurried off to Washington and secured an air mail contract that stipulated service would begin between Key West, FL, and Havana just 16 days later. Tony Fokker's crew at Teterboro was busily constructing two F-IOA trimotors for the new international service, but as the starting date grew nearer, it became obvious that they were not going to be ready for the first flight.

On Oct. 19th, J.E. Whitbeck, the infant airline's Key West manager, had seven bags of mail but no airplanes. The day was saved when Cy Caldwell, later to become a well-known aviation journalist, flew into Key West in a Fairchild floatplane owned by West Indian Aerial Express. Whitbeck paid Caldwell $175 to fly the 90 miles to Cuba to deliver the mail. A few days later, a Fokker piloted by Ed Musick landed on the primitive Key West runway and a regular schedule of flights was begun.

At age 28, Trippe had founded what would be the world's most renowned airline. And as he had planned to do with Colonial, Pan Am carried its first passengers on an international flight on Jan. 16, 1928.

For Trippe, Havana was just a stepping stone into the Caribbean and Central and South America. He hired Charles Lindbergh to make survey flights over the various islands and countries in the southern hemisphere to find likely land and sea bases where aircraft could set down. Within five years, Pan Am had mail routes running south from Panama to Chile and then across the Andes to Buenos Aires and Montevideo.

Pan Am's accomplishments in international air travel under the direction of the Seabright native are legendary:

1929—Pan Am's first big flying boats, Sikorsky S-40s, begin serving South American ports;

1935—The *China Clipper*, a Martin M-130, inaugurates trans-Pacific mail and passenger service between Alameda, CA and Manila. Ed Musick is the inaugural pilot;

1939—The *Dixie Clipper*, a Boeing 314, completes the first transatlantic passenger flight, New York to Marseilles, France;

1947—A Lockheed Constellation, *Clipper American*, completes the first commercial round-the-world flight.

1949—Double-decked Boeing Stratocruisers were introduced on Atlantic and Pacific routes;

1958—A Pan Am 707 flies the U.S. into the jet age by inaugurating New York to Paris service;

1970—The first Boeing 747 jumbo jet flies from New York to London bearing the Pan Am colors.

Although Trippe retired in the mid-1960s, he was the visionary who foresaw the need for larger aircraft and placed the initial orders for the jumbo jets. He also saw a need to develop "reliever airports" to accommodate the growing number of business and private aircraft that were clogging the runways of major commercial airports throughout the world. To that end, he began negotiating a lease with the Port of Authority of New York and New Jersey for the operation of Teterboro Airport. He envisioned Teterboro as the ideal location for a reliever airport in the greater New York metropolitan area because of its proximity to Manhattan and the expanding industrial centers in northern New Jersey.

In a 1944 speech, Trippe correctly predicted the route commercial aviation would travel in the last half of the 20th Century:

"The true objective is to bring to the life of the average man those things which were once the privilege of only the fortunate few. The average man's holiday has, in the past, been the prisoner of two grim keepers—money and time. His enjoyment of the world has been circumscribed by the high walls of his economic jail. We can level these prison walls only by bringing travel costs down, and by shortening travel time."

Captain Edwin C. Musick

After the Aeromarine West Indies Airways folded in the mid-1920s, pilot Eddie Musick joined Pan Am as the airline's most experienced transport pilot. His no nonsense approach to flying made him an immediate favorite of Juan Trippe, who chose him to fly the first official Pan Am Fokker trimotor from Teterboro to Key West and on to Havana.

Three years later, Musick became the chief pilot of the company's Caribbean Division and for the next seven years he commanded the famous Pan Am Clippers on pioneering flights which opened South and Central America and the Pacific to passenger aviation.

The Caribbean operation, an important service in its own right, was also the flying laboratory for the development of the special techniques of over-ocean flying. Out of those experimental flights came the development of multi-engine aircraft, better flight control, improved communications and meteorological service and improved crew scheduling.

When the first of the ocean-going flying boats, a Sikorsky S-42, was ready for Pan Am's acceptance tests, Musick was at the controls. In the course of those tests he set ten world records for seaplane performance.

Christened the Pan American Clipper, Musick flew the Sikorsky to the Pacific Coast, and in April 1935, began flight surveys for a transpacific service. Due to the limited range of the aircraft, the flight made stops in Hawaii, Midway, Wake and Guam islands before arriving in Manila. In November of that year, Musick and a crew departed San Francisco in another famous flying boat, the Martin-built *China Clipper*, with the first Pacific air mail. The early flights terminated in Manila but within a year, the service pushed on to Hong Kong and Singapore.

In early 1937, again flying the Sikorsky Pan American Clipper, Musick left San Francisco on a survey flight to New Zealand. The round-trip flight was a great success. In December of the same year, he again set out on another survey over the Kingman Reef-Samoa route with a crew of six. It proved to be his last flight. Some 75 miles from Pago Pago the plane exploded and plunged into the Pacific. There were no survivors.

Eddie Musick had flown an estimated 1,500,000 miles for Pan Am, more than any man before him. No passenger ever suffered death or injury in a plane he commanded during the nearly five years he'd spent in the sky.

In 1944, a Liberty ship built at the Henry Kaiser shipyard in Richmond, CA, was christened the *Edwin C. Musick* by his wife Cleo. A fitting tribute to a pioneer of the transoceanic flight.

They Conquered the Atlantic
Lindbergh, Chamberlin, Byrd

By 1927, a number of brave aviators had attempted to fly across the Atlantic Ocean from New York to Paris in quest of the $25,000 prize offered by hotelier Raymond Orteig and the instant fame that would come to them. Each in his turn had failed; many, tragically. The prize remained unclaimed.

Aviation engineers believed that the development of the air-cooled Wright Whirlwind engine, proven reliable on the flight of Byrd and Bennett to the North Pole in 1926, combined with either of two well-designed aircraft — one built at Teterboro by Anthony Fokker and the other by the Wright Aeronautical Corp. of Paterson — could fly successfully between New York and Paris.

A Fokker C-2 trimotor monoplane, an improved version of Byrd's North Pole trimotor, was being readied at Teterboro for Byrd to fly to Europe, and a number of aviation personalities were interested in the Wright-Bellanca airplane being test flown at Teterboro.

The strange hand of fate prevented both planes from becoming the first to achieve what, until then, had been the impossible dream. It was a year marked by many significant milestones.

1927: January: An unknown but determined midwest air mail pilot, Charles A. Lindbergh, made several trips east with an offer to buy the Wright-Bellanca airplane from the Wright company. Although he had a certified check from his backers in St. Louis, Wright officials were reluctant to sell to an unknown. Lindbergh had mentioned he intended to fly the Atlantic and the Wright people were dubious concerning his chances of achieving his goal. They reasoned that if Lindbergh failed, the resulting negative publicity would hurt future engine and aircraft sales.

Lindbergh refused to be discouraged. He went to San Diego to have an airplane specially built for his flight by the Ryan Company. It would be powered by a Wright Whirlwind engine.

February: Wright Aeronautical sold their Wright-Bellanca (WB-2) plane to the Columbia Aircraft Corp., headed by Charles A. Levine, a flamboyant millionaire, who had made his fortune selling war surplus material, and Guiseppe Bellanca, who resigned his position as aircraft designer at Wright. Clarence Chamberlin also left Wright's employ to continue as pilot of the WB-2.

April: Pilots Clarence Chamberlin and Bert Acosta, flying the WB-2, established a closed-course world's endurance record over Roosevelt Field, LI.

On the morning of April 12, the two men filled the aircraft's fuel tank to capacity (451 gallons) then took off and climbed to 2,000 feet. They began flying in lazy circles above the airfield, taking turns at the controls. They twice watched day merge into night and stayed in the air until the Whirlwind engine sputtered and died. Chamberlin made a dead-stick landing back at Roosevelt Field on April 14—51 hours, 11 minutes and 25 seconds from the time they had gone aloft. The amazing feat of endurance proved the plane was capable of flying from New York to Paris and beyond. Only the vacillations of Charles Levine stood in the way of their transatlantic flight.

Lindbergh, Byrd and Chamberlin

Two days after the Chamberlin-Acosta endurance flight, Anthony Fokker decided to personally test fly Byrd's Fokker C-2 trimotor at Teterboro Airport. As he prepared to taxi the plane onto the sod runway, Floyd Bennett, who was scheduled to pilot the ship on the Atlantic flight, asked to go along. While Bennett climbed aboard the large monoplane, George Noville, the prospective radioman, and Byrd himself also asked to join the flight.

Although it was against his better judgment because of the small amount of fuel in the rear of the plane to counter balance the weight in the cockpit, Fokker agreed to take them aboard.

For an hour, the large three-engined craft flew over the meadowlands of the Hackensack River and as Fokker tried to land back at Teterboro, he discovered the big ship was even more nose-heavy than he had expected. The special fuel tanks that had been installed in the rear of the plane permitted only one of the men to crawl into the back to help offset the weight up front.

Fokker gunned the engine and continued to circle the field until the fuel tanks ran dry. He then glided down toward the marshy runway. As the wheels touched down on the soft turf, the heavy plane dug in and the ship nosed over and slammed down on its back.

For a long moment, the stunned men hung upside-down in the cockpit. Then Fokker broke the silence and called to the others. Bennett, in the co-pilot's seat, couldn't move. His right thigh was broken and a fragment of the nose propeller had punctured his lung. Byrd complained of a painful wrist (it was broken) and Noville, like Fokker, reported that he had only been shaken up.

A few days after the accident, Byrd announced that the damaged plane would take at least three weeks to repair and that Bennett would be hospitalized for a month, obviously unable to fly the Atlantic.

On Sunday, April 24, the Wright-Bellanca monoplane was christened *Columbia* by Charles Levine's nine-year-old daughter, Eloyse, at Roosevelt Field.

Following the christening, Eloyse asked to be taken for a flight with her friend Grace Jonas, the 15-year-old daughter of Ralph Jonas, president of the Brooklyn Chamber of Commerce. Clarence Chamberlin agreed to fly the girls and took mechanic John Carisi along for the ride.

As the plane bounced across the unpaved runway and lifted into the air, a pin in the left shock absorber sheared off and the left wheel dropped down under the fuselage. Airmen on the ground immediately recognized the problem and realized Chamberlin didn't know anything had gone wrong. Since there was no radio in the *Columbia*, Dean Smith, the air mail pilot from Hadley Field, borrowed an airplane, scribbled a message on its side, and flew up beside the Bellanca. Chamberlin understood the message and knew he had trouble. He prepared for an emergency landing.

There were 350 pounds of sand bags in the rear of the plane to keep it from nosing over when landing as the Fokker had at Teterboro a few weeks earlier. In order to lighten the load, Chamberlin instructed Carisi to drop the bags one at a time as he circled over Roosevelt Field.

In his book, *Record Flight*, Chamberlin described what happened next:

What happened thereafter was chiefly a matter of luck and the Bellanca's amazing controllability at stalling speed. I was, of course, headed into the wind, and as I leveled off for a landing, I banked the Columbia over to the right, so that when she finally touched on the slick, wet grass, it was in a 'three-point' landing — tail skid, right wheel and right wing tip. The drag of the wing caused the ship to 'ground loop' slightly to the right. Then, as it lost speed, it settled gradually on the unsupporting left wheel which came up and cracked the left front strut extending from the fuselage out of the wing. The left wing tip dropped, touched and slid along, causing the plane to swerve in that direction as it slid to a standstill without further damage. Eloyse and Grace were lifted from the plane and started toward a car that had driven on the field to pick them up. Half way to the car, they turned and ran back to where I was inspecting the plane.

"Thank you for the ride, Mr. Chamberlin," they said, being a little disappointed, for I had promised them a crash and then didn't give it to them.

Just two days after Chamberlin set the *Columbia* down on one wheel, Lt. Cmdr. Noel Davis and Lt. Stanton Wooster made a transatlantic flight attempt in a Keystone biplane named the *American Legion*. The overloaded plane took off from Langley Field at Hampton, VA, but couldn't maintain altitude. It dropped nose first into a swamp and sank. The aviators became trapped inside and were suffocated by fumes and mud.

It appeared that the only plane that could fly to Paris ahead of the *Columbia* had been tragically eliminated from the competition.

May: Meanwhile, Levine haggled over who would pilot the *Columbia* to Europe. Chamberlin, the plane's original pilot knew the airplane best, but Levine didn't think he had the stature or was charismatic enough to be a flying hero. Bert Acosta, one of the most dashing pilots of the day, decided to leave the *Columbia* camp following the record-shattering endurance flight with Chamberlin. He joined the Byrd team. So Levine chose Lloyd Bertaud, a tall air mail pilot, who flew regularly on the mail run between Hadley field and Cleveland, to fly the *Columbia* with Chamberlin.

While Byrd's Fokker and Levine's Wright-Bellanca were hastily being repaired for their transatlantic flights, word was received on May 8 that two Frenchmen, Captain Charles Nungesser, a World War I flying hero, and Captain Francois Coli, had taken off from Paris and were well on their way to New York. Reports had the Frenchmen's plane *White Bird* spotted off the coast of Newfoundland long before it could have possibly neared the North American shore. Paris papers reported a safe arrival in Manhattan and the City of Lights went wild. But the actual fact was that the two men were never heard from again.

May 12 was marked as a day that the transatlantic competition really began to heat up.

Early in the day, Bernt Balchen ferried Byrd's rebuilt Fokker from Teterboro to Roosevelt Field and taxied up to a hangar with the sign "The America Trans-Oceanic Co., Inc." above the doors. That company was headed by department store tycoon, Rodman Wanamaker, the sponsor of Byrd's flight.

Balchen, who was highly respected by Fokker, had become the Dutchman's chief test pilot and performance engineer. The handsome Norwegian tested and delivered a multitude of aircraft being built at the Fokker plant.

In the afternoon of May 12, Charles Lindbergh, the 25-year-old former air mail pilot, arrived at Curtiss Field in the Ryan monoplane, *Spirit of St. Louis,* built to his specifications in San Diego. The frail ship was named for the home city of his backers.

Lindbergh's flight from San Diego to St. Louis on May 11 had established a new record for a 1,500-mile run—14 hours and five minutes. He flew on to New York the following day, averaging an amazing 120 miles per hour.

Now that all three of the remaining U.S. planes in the Trans-Atlantic derby were in one place, a New York Times reporter wrote: "What promises to be the most spectacular race ever held 3,600 miles over the open sea to Paris—may start tomorrow."

Certainly the race would be spectacular, but the Times was a bit optimistic concerning the date of departure.

It was anybody's ball game. The bets were still riding on the *Columbia* being first or perhaps Byrd's Fokker *America*. Few thought Lindbergh would be first off the line.

The flights were dependent on the weather which was not being cooperative that month of May. Meteorologist Dr. James H. Kimball was the weather authority for all the contestants. He was highly respected by the men who would pit their skills against the elements.

Other tireless workers who could be found with the *Spirit* and *Columbia*, fine tuning the Wright Whirlwind engines, were the engineers from the Wright Aeronautical Corp. The group, headed by Harold "Doc" Kinkaid, never stopped tinkering with their "babies." Edward J. Mulligan was officially assigned to Lindbergh's Whirlwind, and Kenneth J. Boedecker worked nonstop on the big radial engine in the nose of the *Columbia*. Kenneth Lane, who was in charge of Wright's airplane division, was concerned with the success of all the aircraft, but especially the *Columbia* which had been built by Wright.

Mulligan remembered his association with Lindbergh:

"During this period (May 1927), what was to me the most remarkable thing in connection with the flight was occurring continually. Lindbergh landed at Curtiss Field practically unknown here in the East, his undertaking regarded as fool-hardy even by those who had met him once or twice. During the weeks of preparation his personality, fineness, ability and awareness of what he intended to do, and his preparedness for the job, so impressed itself not only on those who were closely associated with him, but also on all those with whom he came in contact, particularly the 'hard boiled' newspapermen (he was news with a capital 'N') who put him over to the general public so well that I believe seventy-five per cent of the people of the country were not only wishing him success but were more than half sure he would make it. To me, considering man, engine, plane and all, it seemed impossible to fail."

Boedecker also recalled those exhilarating days:

"It so happened that at the time of Lindbergh's arrival, Chamberlin's ship and engine were all ready to go. Early in the evening (May 12) it looked as though the weather might be satisfactory for an early morning take-off and knowing that Mulligan had only a limited amount of time in which to get Lindbergh's engine checked, I pitched in and helped him into the wee small hours of the morning. This really proved unnecessary as the weather turned bad over various parts of the route and the actual departure was delayed for about two weeks. This, of course gave us the opportunity of making some flight tests, the recollection of which can never be erased.

"If a little vanity (or something) can enter here, these test flights made Mulligan and myself two of the very few who have had the privilege of flying in the *Spirit of St. Louis*.

The interest shown in Lindbergh by the Wright Aeronautical Corp. went beyond simply tuning the engine of the Ryan.

Guy Vaughan, company president, assigned his public relation consultants, Harry Bruno and "Dick" Blythe to protect the young aviator from "the exploiters and the mob." Blythe became Lindbergh's constant companion until the airman took off for Paris.

Both the *Columbia* and *America* might have been the first to fly New York to Paris if it hadn't been for foot dragging on the part of Charles Levine and Richard Byrd. Levine thrived on controversy and publicity. After settling on Clarence Chamberlin and Lloyd Bertaud as pilot and navigator, he had a "manager" contract drawn up, putting the two fliers under his wing for 12 months after the successful conclusion of their flight. He told the men if they didn't sign the contract, paying them $150 per week during the life of the document, they wouldn't fly.

He also agreed to underwrite a life insurance policy payable to the wives of both men. He then reneged on the insurance deal. Bertaud became furious at Levine's high-handed tactics, and obtained a temporary injunction prohibiting Levine from easing him out of the project, and barring the *Columbia* from flying without him.

In the *America* camp, Byrd continued to order additional test flights, while Wanamaker milked the project for as much publicity as possible. As early as May 15, in the midst of all the testing, Byrd announced that the *America* would be ready soon to face the Atlantic challenge.

Throughout this period, Tony Fokker was showing the effects of the frustrating delay. He would drive his Lancia sports car from the Teterboro plant to Roosevelt Field several times a week, trying to pressure Byrd into action. On May 17, the Atlantic weather report seemed ideal for the flight but nothing happened—except a Fokker outburst.

In his book, *Come North with Me*, Bernt Balchen quoted Fokker as saying, "If we don't get going soon, I myself will buy the plane and fly it over the ocean, by Gott! Look at the sky! Just a little mist only. Any fool could fly it blindfold with both eyes shut!"

During one of Fokker's visits to Roosevelt, he had Balchen and Acosta take him up in the *America* for another test flight. When they flew into the clouds, Fokker asked Balchen to turn the controls over to

Acosta. Within minutes the plane went into a sharp banking turn. Fokker urged Acosta to use his instruments to correct the plane's flight. Acosta admitted he didn't know how to fly with instruments. "I'm strictly a fair-weather boy." he said. It was obvious that if the *America* was ever to get airborne, the co-pilot was going to do the bulk of the flying through the treacherous Atlantic weather patterns. Until that time, Balchen was not an official member of Byrd's crew. Fokker told Byrd of Acosta's short-comings as a pilot and insisted that Balchen go along. Byrd told the Dutchman that Wanamaker would only sponsor the flight with an all-American crew. Fokker immediately stated that would be no problem. He sent Balchen to the Bureau of Naturalization to declare his, intentions of becoming an American citizen.

Lindbergh Flies Alone

May 19 was another rainy day, unfit for flying so Charles Lindbergh drove from his hotel on Long Island to Paterson to visit the Wright engine plant. After returning to Long Island that afternoon, he asked Dr. Kimball for the latest weather report and discovered there was a clearing trend over the Atlantic. Immediately the die was cast. Lindbergh decided to go at dawn the following day.

Through an early morning fog, Charles A. Lindbergh raced the fuel-laden *Spirit of St. Louis* down the runway at Roosevelt Field. The tiny plane struggled to become airborne, barely clearing the telephone wires at the end of the field. When the *Spirit* was a few hundred feet off the ground, it began to fade from the sight of those who had gathered to wish the pilot a bon voyage. The most publicized flight in history had begun.

Not to be overshadowed, Charles Levine announced that the *Columbia*, piloted by Chamberlin with a "mystery" navigator aboard, would take off at dawn of the following day.

Flying through weather fair and foul, Lindbergh successfully landed at Le Bourget Airport outside Paris on May 21, 33 ½ hours after leaving New York. He immediately became "the hero of the age." His solo exploit caught the imagination of people throughout the world. In Paterson, the Wright Company employees were given the day off to organize a parade.

In a *Time* magazine article that appeared after the flight the *Lone Eagle* was quoted as saying just before he took off for Paris: "When I enter the cockpit it's like going into the death chamber. When I step out at Paris it will be like getting a pardon from the governor."

Unlike the feasts requested by others who are condemned to die, Lindbergh's rations for the flight consisted of four sandwiches, emergency army rations and two canteens of water.

His first words to the crowd of 25,000 at Le Bourget were: "Well, here we are. I am very happy."

Time magazine predicted that Lindbergh would make a fortune upon his return to the United States. "Not only did Capt. Lindbergh win the $25,000 prize offered by Raymond Orteig, Manhattan hotelman, for the first New York-Paris non-stop flight, but he established for himself the immemorial right of extracting dollars from the hero-gaping U.S. public by appearing on the vaudeville stage, in the cinema etc." That prediction clearly indicated how little the press and public knew of their new shy hero.

Although the long New York to Paris route across the Atlantic had been conquered by Lindbergh, and his exploits had dominated the front pages of newspapers all over the world, there was still considerable interest in the activities of the two also-rans—the Fokker *America* and the Wright-Bellanca *Columbia*.

At Teterboro, Tony Fokker fumed. Due to Byrd's procrastination, Fokker's big trimotor had not been the first to fly the Atlantic. And despite Levine's bravado, the *Columbia* sat in its hangar at Curtiss Field.

Even before word of Lindbergh's safe arrival had been received, Levine had the optimistic legend, "New York-Paris" painted on the side of the *Columbia*. And when Guiseppe Bellanca became fed up with Levine's antics and quit his job with the Columbia Aircraft Company, Levine had the Italian's name obliterated from the aircraft's tail.

It appeared that the *Columbia* might never get off the ground because Byrd's backer, who had leased the entire Roosevelt Field complex, wouldn't let Levine use the airfield's long runways.

Columbia Flies to Germany

Almost daily, Charles Levine made headlines by announcing various aviation projects that he seemed to have little intention of undertaking. He and Clarence Chamberlin continued flight testing the plane, and on one occasion, Levine took the controls for more than an hour.

On June 3, Byrd and his crew—Balchen, Acosta and Noville—test flew the *America* with more than 6,000 lbs. of fuel and ballast aboard. Carrying a total weight of more than 11,000 lbs., the three-engined Fokker easily lifted off Roosevelt Field's runway and cleared the telephone wires at the far end. At the same time, Chamberlin flew the *Columbia* from Curtiss Field to Teterboro to have a new carburetor heater installed at the Wright service hangar.

As of midnight, June 4, Levine had not named a co-pilot to accompany Chamberlin, but he had received Byrd's permission to use the Roosevelt runways. Thereupon, the always enthusiastic Chamberlin announced that he planned to take off at dawn—alone, if necessary,—and establish an endur-

Smithsonian Collection

"Columbia's" rough landing.

ance and distance record. He wouldn't say where his final destination would be.

Just before dawn, the *Columbia* was towed from Curtiss Field to Roosevelt Field and its gas tanks were filled. As the sun rose in the east, Charles and Grace Levine arrived in a limousine to wish Chamberlin well.

The Whirlwind engine, run up under the watchful eye of the Wright engine expert Harold *Doc* Kinkaid, roared steady and strong. The Bellanca was ready to go.

Chamberlin, alone in the cockpit, revved the engine, awaiting the appearance of a co-pilot. Suddenly, Charles Levine darted through the crowd surrounding the plane and without looking back, jumped into the enclosed cockpit with Chamberlin. Within seconds, the small plane began to taxi down the runway. Grace Levine anxiously wondered what "her Charlie" was doing in the plane, and was assured by John Carisi, Chamberlin's dedicated mechanic, that it was only a test run.

The plane began rolling down the turf strip at an escalating speed, but was forced to stop because spectators blocked the way. When Chamberlin spun the plane around and taxied back to the starting point, Mrs. Levine was much relieved. She had told Chamberlin the week before that she would burn the plane if her Charlie ever planned to fly the Atlantic.

Her relief was short-lived. Chamberlin again gunned the engine and the *Columbia* easily lifted off the runway. This time he and his sponsor were on their way to Europe. As the small silver plane disappeared over the horizon, Mrs. Levine fainted dead away.

Prior to takeoff, Chamberlin and Levine had decided to fly to Berlin rather than Paris, a distance of 3,905 miles (295 miles further than Lindbergh). In later years, Chamberlin told the author that Berlin was chosen because it was the second part of his surname.

On the morning of June 6, the Columbia's fuel gauge read empty as Chamberlin made a dead-stick landing on a wheat field near the village of Mansfeldt, Ger-

many. They managed to get about 20 gallons of gas from the friendly villagers and flew on toward Berlin. They never did find the fog-bound German capital and when their fuel again ran out, they landed in a soggy field near Cottbus, Germany. As the plane's momentum slowed, its wheels caught in the soft turf and it tipped up on its nose, breaking the propeller.

The two Americans had flown 42 hours, 45 minutes, the longest flight recorded up to that time. Except for one short period when Levine took the controls and accidentally put the airplane in a dangerous 16,000-foot dive, Chamberlin had piloted the Bellanca for the entire journey.

They spent the night in Cottbus and when repairs were made to the *Columbia*, they flew on to Berlin, 110 miles away. There, they were accorded a tumultuous welcome.

After a whirlwind tour of European capitals, Levine suggested they fly back to the U.S., but Chamberlin demurred. He had become fed up with the quirks of the "junk dealer," a derogatory nickname applied to Levine.

Although he went on to have a distinguished aeronautical career, Clarence Chamberlin never received the recognition and adulation accorded to Lindbergh. He had flown farther, for a longer period of time and had transported the first passenger across the Atlantic Ocean, but he was the second man to accomplish the non-stop Atlantic crossing, and therefore was considered an also-ran by the hero-worshipping public.

The sturdy Paterson-built Bellanca wasn't through with its European adventures. Levine recruited pilot Walter Hinchcliffe and flew off to Rome (one of the capitals he and Chamberlin had missed). On the flight south, the ship was damaged on a rough landing and never reached the Italian capital.

Once the seemingly indestructible plane was repaired, they flew back to Paris. Then on a whim, Levine flew solo across the English Channel and bounced down near London. His thirst for adventure finally quenched, Levine shipped the Columbia back to the United States.

California to Hawaii

Maitland and Hegenberger

While numerous transatlantic flying records were being established in airplanes powered by Wright Whirlwind engines, two Army pilots, Lieutenants Lester Maitland and Albert Hegenberger, convinced their supervisors that they could fly nonstop from California to Hawaii. They chose an Army Fokker trimotor, similar to Cmdr. Byrd's plane *America*. On June 28, they took off from the Oakland Airport in the overloaded Fokker, *Bird of Paradise,* and followed a radio beam out of the San Francisco Area. The Army had arranged for a similar beam to lead them into Hawaii, but their radio receiver went dead, so they had to depend on Hegenberger's considerable navigational skills. Considering the minute size of their target, Hegenberger did an excellent job and the two men reached the islands in 25 hours and 50 minutes.

The flight was considered a great triumph. Although the flight from the mainland to Hawaii was 1,200 miles shorter than Lindbergh's, the two men flew 600 miles further over water and against strong west-to-east headwinds. Several months later, they and the Atlantic flyers were honored by national, state and city governments.

First Intercontinental Airmail

The *America*

On the day that Maitland and Hegenberger arrived in Hawaii, the *America* stood poised on a dirt incline that had been constructed at the end of the Roosevelt Field runway to provide the big Fokker with an added boost on takeoff. It had been a frustrating seven days for the crew members, Bert Acosta, Bernt Balchen and George Noville, for this was the fourth time in less than a week that the *America* had been readied to fly. On the previous three occasions, Lt. Cmdr. Byrd had canceled for various reasons. Tony Fokker was particularly disheartened by the delays. Had it not been for the flight-test accident at Teterboro in April, the *America* might have been the first to fly the Atlantic. Actually, the airplane had been ready to fly at the time of Lindbergh's flight, but for reasons best known to himself, Byrd seemed in no hurry to challenge the Atlantic skies. Many newsmen were openly questioning Byrd's intestinal fortitude, and at one point Acosta became so frustrated, he sat down and cried.

But now the time and date was firm and, prior to boarding the airplane, Byrd handed the waiting reporters a statement that outlined his expectations of the flight.

The text read: "Whereas I am attempting this flight for many reasons, I hope our countrymen will appreciate the fact that my shipmates — Noville, Acosta and Balchen — are flying over the top today totally for the progress of aviation to which they are devoting their lives. There is, they realize, little glory in the undertaking. There are no prizes awaiting them."

Acosta piloted the plane on take off and it used 3,270 feet of runway to become airborne through the morning mist. The flight, uneventful for the first 12 hours, suddenly took a frightening turn.

The *America* was flying through a constant gray mist at 6,500 feet with Balchen at the controls and Acosta sleeping fitfully beside him. Balchen became hungry and remembered the chicken sandwich under his seat. He asked Acosta to take the controls and relaxed for the first time in more than four hours. Bending down to pick up the sandwich, he felt himself being pulled against his seat belt, and realized the plane was spiraling downward. A quick check of the instruments proved him right, so he dropped the sandwich and grabbed the wheel from Acosta. He managed to get the plane level again at 5,000 feet above the sea. Acosta was chagrined and asked Balchen to pilot the plane as long as they were fog bound. As Fokker and Balchen had discovered at Roosevelt Field, Acosta had never learned to fly by instruments.

As they approached the Normandy coast 38 hours into the flight, the skies cleared, boosting the airmen's spirits. But their joy was short lived. When they reached the outskirts of Paris, a dense curtain of fog obscured the City of Lights.

For nearly an hour, Balchen flew in circles through the impenetrable mist, dropping lower with each turn, ever mindful of the Eiffel Tower. Finally, they had no choice but to turn back toward Normandy, where they had last seen clear skies. After another hour of blind flying, Balchen nosed down to 1,500 feet and suddenly saw a flashing sign advertising the resort city of Deauville. The fuel gauge quivered on empty as the Fokker flew along the dark coast toward a distant lighthouse beacon. Byrd ordered Balchen to ditch the *America* near the light.

The crew braced themselves as the pilot lowered the monoplane to four feet above the whitecaps, cut the engines, and let the big bird splash into the foaming water. They had unceremoniously arrived in Ver-sur-Mer, France. It was 2 a.m. on July 1. Their flight had taken 42 hours and covered more than 4,200 miles.

Once ashore, the aviators dragged themselves up the dunes toward the lighthouse, roused the keeper and his family from their beds and in fractured French, explained they had come across the ocean in an airplane from the United States. Welcoming them, keeper, Jules Lescope, and his wife and daughters, gave the men warm food and dry clothing. Acosta, who had injured his collarbone during the rough landing, was offered a bed while the others returned to the plane to retrieve their personal belongings and the first sack of mail ever flown between the continents.

They reached the beach at the first light of day. A crowd of villagers had gathered around the crippled Fokker, which now stood high and dry on the sand. Although the villagers enthusiastically offered to help the aviators remove the contents of the plane their generosity soon got out of hand. In their quest for souvenirs, they stripped the *America* of its fabric covering and hauled off pieces of equipment. The fliers were too tired to protest.

"America" splashed down.

Discouraged, Byrd and Noville accepted an invitation from the deputy mayor, Joseph Coiffier, to sleep in his home, while Balchen returned to the lighthouse to join Acosta as a guest of the Lescopes.

At the Coiffier house, Byrd met Mrs. Estella Tanugi de Jongh and her son Emile. Mrs. Tanugi de Jongh was an American from New Orleans who had married a French businessman and moved to Paris. She and her son spent the summers by the sea in Ver-sur-Mer, joined by her husband on the weekends. On that early July morning in 1927, she and her son were the only people in the channel village who spoke English and they were immediately recruited by the village officials as interpreters.

Mrs. Tanugi de Jongh accompanied Byrd to the village post office and helped him send a cablegram to Rodman Wanamaker, the sponsor of the flight. The cable read:

Mr. Rodman Wanamaker

Wanamaker Store, New York City

Deeply sorry didn't reach Paris. Will report details Forced landing dark night unavoidable. America will be repaired. Crew Safe. Will deliver flag and mail when reach Paris. Regards you and Whalen [Grover Whalen, the official greeter for the City of New York]

Byrd then returned to the Coiffier house and went to sleep in the bed of Louis Coiffier, the family's oldest son, until Samuel H. Wiley, the United States consul from Cherbourg, arrived to officially accept the international mail. The mail was then delivered to the Ver-sur-Mer post office for cancellation.

The following day, the four men were welcomed in Paris by French Premier Raymond Poincare and 20,000 cheering spectators. It didn't seem to matter to the French that the first commercial transatlantic air mail flight had not been a complete logistical success. Days later, the four airmen, accompanied by Clarence Chamberlain, sailed home aboard the *SS Leviathan* to another rousing reception in New York.

Back in Ver-sur-Mer, the steel-tube skeleton of the *America* were trucked to Cherbourg, and then shipped back to the United States. No one knows what happened to the remains of the Fokker once it arrived in the U.S. Some historians say that

Wanamaker shipped sections of the plane to his various stores as an exhibit, but there is no proof of that. Fifty nine years later, the author went to Ver-sur-Mer in search of the remains of the famous New Jersey plane that might still have been in the villager's possession. (See 1986)

Flies off the *Leviathan*

During their return voyage from Europe aboard the United States Lines' steamship *Leviathan* in mid-July, Commodore Herbert Hartley, the ships's captain, asked Cmdr. Byrd and Clarence Chamberlin for their opinion of the possibility of flying the mail from ship to shore in order to expedite special letters and packages.

Both pilots agreed that it could be done. They pointed out that floatplanes could also overtake ships at sea and either land beside them on the water or fly over them and drop mail bags on the open decks.

At the time, these conversations seemed like nothing more than interesting cocktail chatter to the two airmen. Then, less than a month after his return to the U.S., Chamberlin received a telephone call from a U.S. Lines' official asking him to undertake a ship to shore demonstration flight. Chamberlin agreed, and while the *Leviathan* was in dry dock for her yearly overhaul, a 118-foot by 24-foot "runway" was mounted atop the ship's superstructure at an angle of about 45 degrees, extending from starboard to port in front of the forward funnel and out over the bridge. Then a Fokker biplane with a Whirlwind engine, was taken apart at Teterboro, trucked to the Manhattan pier and reassembled by Ed Gorski, Bill Hartig and Chamberlin on the make-shift runway.

The *Leviathan* sailed on the night of July 31. The following morning, off the shore of Fire Island, Chamberlin began the demonstration which he described in his book *Record Flights*.

I tried the motor thoroughly and then had the big blocks in front of the wheels removed, leaving only a small pair in their place. The tail came up as I opened the throttle and I 'jumped,' both wheels over the restraining blocks. There was no stopping now, even if I had wanted to.

The plane gathered headway quickly from the wide-open motor and the slight incline in the wooden runway. I had expected to use all of the platform with the heavy plane and perhaps drop a part of the 100 feet between the end of the runway and the water. Instead, the ship took the air three quarters of the way down the plank path that had been built for her, and was flung high in the air by the uprushing wind which was turned skyward by the sides of the big liner as she passed the jumping-off place.

Chamberlin reported that the flight was a complete success, although the Coast Guard cutters *Wilkes* and *Humphries* and a Navy destroyer *Lawrence* stood by "in case I didn't have it figured out just right."

Fog forced him to land at Curtiss Field, but as soon as it lifted, Chamberlin flew the mail to the Wright hangar at Teterboro, where he officially delivered the first mail flown from a ship to shore. Later Chamberlin said: "I was sworn in as an honest-to-goodness air mail pilot."

"Old Glory" Disappears

Lindbergh had won the Ortig prize; Chamberlin had flown further and longer than any other man and Byrd had successfully carried the first sack of air mail between the continents. Still, promoters felt there was notoriety to be gained from challenging the Atlantic skies.

One of those was Philip Payne, a Union City, NJ, resident, and managing editor of the New York Daily Mirror, a Hearst newspaper. The plane he planned to use for an Atlantic flight was a specially built Fokker, with a single Bristol-Jupiter engine, that belonged to William Randolph Hearst. Its destination would be Rome, Payne had announced.

In a patriotic gesture he christened the plane *Old Glory*. James Hill, a veteran air mail pilot, with more than 200,000 miles in open cockpit planes, and Lloyd Bertaud, who had been scheduled to fly with Chamberlin in the *Columbia*, were chosen as pilots.

As the preparations neared completion, Payne announced that he was going along on the flight. His pilots protested that his weight was equivalent to 100 gallons of fuel and that he would be nothing more than useless dead weight. Payne was insistent and on Sept. 2, *Old Glory* was flown to Orchard Beach, Maine, the proposed starting point.

Despite protests from Hearst on the west coast, the overloaded *Old Glory* took off from the beach at 12:53 p.m. and headed out over the ocean toward the Eternal City—Rome. Having a radio aboard, the airmen could contact ships below.

The first was the *SS George Washington*, at about 800 miles from New York. At 12:41 a.m. the passenger liner California heard a plane overhead, but no radio contact was made. Three hours later, a number of ships heard an SOS signal, then a message: "Five hours out of Newfoundland east." Ships rushed to the area but found no sign of the plane.

On Sept. 12th, the *SS Kyle,* a Canadian ship chartered by Hearst to search for the flyers, found a section of *Old Glory's* wing and landing gear, but there was no sign of the men. Aeronautical experts were of the opinion that the plane was doomed when the 225-pound Payne insisted on going along.

Old Glory's landing gear is in the Union City library.

The Lindberghs

Charles and Anne Morrow Lindbergh

Charles Inducted Aviation Hall of Fame of N.J, 1973

While others attempted to conquer the treacherous New York-to-Europe air route, Charles Lindbergh was busy writing his book, *We,* at the home of Capt. Harry F. Guggenheim at Sands Point on Long Island. Capt. Harry, who was born in West End, NJ, had been a World War I Navy aviator. He was the son of one of America's richest families and had convinced his father to establish the Daniel Guggenheim Fund for the "Promotion of Aeronautics" which he, Harry, would preside over.

When the manuscript was completed and turned over to G. P. Putnam's and Sons for publishing, Lindbergh began a 48-state, 71-city tour of the United States in the *Spirit of St. Louis* with the full support of the Guggenheim fund. *Lucky Lindy,* as he was popularly known, flew more than 22,000 miles, made 147 speeches promoting aviation and participated in countless dinners and parades in his honor.

The importance of the goodwill flight to the future of commercial aviation was simply stated in an article entitled, *The Aerial Tour of We*, that appeared in the September 1927, issue of The Wright Engine Builder, a Wright Aeronautical employee publication.

The country-wide tour of Colonel Lindbergh is keeping alive as nothing else could, the recently awakened interest of the general public in aviation. Although less than half of the proposed itinerary has been covered so far, the intense interest shown everywhere in the visits of the renowned flier and his plane is already bearing fruit in the constantly increasing number of airports now being laid out or planned for the cities visited.

At every city, Col. Lindbergh urges the necessity for more and better airports and points out the advantages of patronizing existing facilities. His well-known simple brevity of speech is making a lasting impression. He is doing much to foster the growth of commercial air traffic, and by actual demonstration is bringing home to "the man with his feet on the ground" the fact that flying is not merely a source of thrilling adventure for the Lindberghs, Chamberlins and Byrds of the world, but is also a safe, quick and practical method of transportation for the average citizen in pursuit of business or pleasure.

Visits Central America

Lindbergh's long distance flights were far from over. At the request of Dwight W. Morrow, the U.S. Ambassador to Mexico and the chairman President Coolidge's committee to investigate the state of American aviation, Lindbergh agreed to make a good will flight to Mexico City and then on into Central America. The flight began in December, 1927, and America's hero did not return to the states until February of 1928. Newspapers estimated that the aviator had spent more than 40 days and nights in the air from the time Lindbergh left San Diego on May 10, 1927 to the time he returned from the Central American tour on February 12, 1928. The Tour had taken him to Mexico, Panama, Venezuela, Trinidad and Havana, a total distance of 8,286 miles.

To be certain that the Whirlwind engine in the nose of the *Spirit of St. Louis* was properly tuned along the route, the Wright Corporation sent J. Russell Voorhees, one of its leading engine experts, to Panama by ship to service the engine there. Voorhees, a Midland Park, NJ, resident, left for Colon, Panama in late December 1927 to await the arrival of the historic plane on Jan. 13, 1928. Once the airman left Panama, Voorhees hopped aboard an island steamer and made his way to Havana, arriving just before the *Spirit* landed.

The Panama and Cuban trips were not the first for the Wright motor expert as his letter from Cuba, dated February 4, 1928, indicated.

"Arrived here from Panama at 10 o'clock this A.M. Went out to the flying field as the factory sent some mail out there for me. While there I saw some of the boys from Pan American Airways, the planes I flew to Key West with. They sure were surprised to see me come walking in the hangar. I have some other work to do for the Cuban government so I will not have to hang around and wait for Lindy to arrive this time. It is not quite as warm here as it was in Panama but it isn't cold by any means ."

In 1929, Voorhees turned down a chance to go to the South Pole with Cmdr. Richard E. Byrd and instead went to San Antonio, TX, as an engine instructor at the U.S. Army Aviation school. In February 1930, Voorhees accepted the position of service manager with Varney Air Lines in Portland, OR.

Two months after his Latin American trip, Lindbergh presented his sturdy plane to the Smithsonian Institution in Washington, DC. Paul Garber was at Washington's Bolling Field to accept the historic gift.

Morrow, a partner in the banking firm of J.P. Morgan & Co., had a family estate in Englewood, NJ. When Lindbergh returned from the tour, Morrow invited him to his home to meet his wife and three daughters. Almost immediately, Lindbergh and Morrow's second oldest child, Anne, became fond friends. On their first date, Lindy flew Anne in a rented plane from the Guggenheim estate. Following their third date, they became engaged.

On May 27, 1929, Anne Morrow and Charles Lindbergh were married in the Morrow family's Englewood home on Next Day Hill Road. That union lasted until his death in 1974.

The Morrow home is now the Elizabeth Morrow School and the room in which the couple were wed is being used as a sixth-grade classroom.

A museum has been established at the Guggenheim estate at Sands Point. The room in which Lindbergh wrote *We*, and where he and Anne spent many enjoyable hours as the guests of the Guggenheims, is now open for public viewing.

Lindy, Pan Am Consultant

Prior to his wedding, Lindbergh had agreed to become a consultant to Juan Trippe, the young, dynamic president of the burgeoning Pan Am Airways. Four months after their marriage, Charles and Anne, accompanied by Juan and Elizabeth Trippe, were on the Pan Am inaugural flight from Cuba south to Trinidad and Dutch Guiana. Lindbergh flew the Sikorsky amphibian over the 9,000-mile route.

That was just the beginning of the aviation adventures the Lindberghs would share.

In March, 1930, the couple made their first glider flights above San Diego. They both earned first-class glider licenses. Anne Morrow Lindbergh, on a solo flight, stayed aloft for six minutes and became the first woman in the United States to earn a first-class license.

A month later, clad in electrically heated flying suits in anticipation of a transcontinental high-altitude flight, the Lindberghs roared down the runway at Grand Central Airport outside Los Angeles in their new Lockheed Sirius monoplane. They climbed above 10,000 feet and turned toward the east, arriving at Roosevelt Field, 14 hours, 45 minutes and 32 seconds later, breaking the 1929 transcontinental record of Capt. Frank M. Hawks by almost three hours.

Later in the year, the Lindberghs flew the Sirius into Teterboro to have the plane's engine serviced at the Wright hangar in preparation for a flight to the Orient. During those months of preparation, the Lindberghs lived in the Morrows' Englewood home.

By the spring of 1931, Anne Lindbergh had soloed and earned her radio operator license. The couple were ready to leave on an extended flight to the Orient on behalf of Pan Am. Juan Trippe wanted to begin passenger service to the Far East and asked Lindbergh to survey the route via Canada, Alaska, Siberia, Japan and China. With pontoons installed on the Sirius, the couple left from Flushing Bay, NY, on July 29, 1931, and arrived in Nanking, China on Sept. 19. The flight was an outstanding success and an unparalleled adventure for a woman of that time. The 25-year-old Smith College graduate later wrote a best-selling book, *North to the Orient*, that vividly described their adventure.

One of the many human interest stories contained in the book concerned the naming of the Lockheed Sirius. Their arrival in Alaska had amazed the local Eskimos population who pointed to Lindbergh and his float plane and said "Tingmissartoq," which means, "The man who flies like a bird." That Eskimo word became the name of the Sirius.

While they were away, a large stone home was being built for them on 320 secluded acres in Hopewell, Hunterdon County, NJ. Shortly after they moved in, a son was born to the couple, Charles A. Lindbergh, Jr. Their parental joy was short-lived. On the night of March 1, 1932, young Charles was kidnapped and later found dead in a shallow grave on the property. The trial of Bruno Richard Hauptmann, accused of the kidnapping and murder, became a nightmare for the Lindberghs. They found they had no personal privacy after their son's death except when they were in the air.

In an attempt to avoid the spotlight's glare, the Lindberghs agreed to survey a north Atlantic route for Juan Trippe and Pan Am.

On July 9, 1933, the couple headed north again. Their flight carried them across the North Atlantic to the Scandinavian countries and Russia. Then across Europe and Africa, back over the South Atlantic and home on Dec. 19, via South America and the Caribbean Islands.

The flight covered 30,000 miles and the couple visited 21 countries and four continents without a major incident. They faced a wide range of flying conditions from the frigid wastes of Greenland to the tropical jungles of South America.

Charles and Ann Morrow Lindbergh

Powered by a single Wright Cyclone 710 hp engine, the Sirius averaged 500 miles a day. The Lindberghs' shortest flight was 150 miles and the longest 1,834 miles between Bathhurst, Cambia (in Africa) and Natal in northern Brazil. In all, they made 53 stops along their route.

Col. Lindbergh did the majority of the flying. Anne Lindbergh relieved him at the controls to permit him to take sextant observations, work on charts and make notes. At the same time, Anne sent and received all radio messages in code, made all drift and ground speed observations and kept their flight log. The flight again clearly demonstrated that a Paterson-built Wright engine was dependable and had exceptional stamina.

Following the conviction of Hauptmann in 1935, the couple, with their small son Jon, who had to be guarded around the clock, felt compelled by the constant harassment of the press, to move to England. Their secret journey to England was accomplished by two other New Jerseyans.

At the time of his New York ticker tape parade following his solo flight to Paris, Lindbergh had become friendly with Charles Hand, then New York Mayor Jimmy Walker's official greeter. When Walker left office, Hand joined the United States Steamship Lines as the head of public relations. He had, as his assistant, Walter H. Jones of Hasbrouck Heights.

Hand and Lindbergh had stayed in touch over the years, and when the *Lone Eagle* and his family were looking for a way to escape from the press unnoticed, he called Hand for help. It was arranged that the Lindbergh family would sail from New York aboard the U.S. Lines' cargo ship the *American Importer* from the Chelsea piers on the Hudson River on Dec. 21, 1935. The plans for the crossing were so secretive that even the ship's master, Capt. John W. Anderson of Belleville, NJ, wasn't told who would occupy connecting rooms 101, 103, and 105. He later said he thought the occupants would be John Jacob Astor and a small party.

At 7:30 p.m., just a half hour before the vessel's scheduled departure time, Walter Jones brought the Lindberghs to the ship and introduced them to Anderson. The family went immediately to their rooms where a light supper was served. The *American Importer* didn't sail until 2:53 a.m., almost seven hours late, but by then her celebrated passengers were sound asleep.

At 37, Capt. Anderson was the youngest skipper of the United States Lines' fleet and when his vessel returned to the New York almost a month later, he discovered that he was a celebrity. He told the press that Anne Lindbergh knew "plenty" about navigation and was a dotting mother. And Charles Lindbergh "is the kind of a guy who doesn't worry." The six foot two, slim sea captain, like Lindbergh, was noted for his taciturnity. He went on to become the Commodore of the United States Lines and master of the *SS United States,* the world's fastest passenger liner.

The Lindberghs lived in England and France for several years, a period Mrs. Lindbergh described in the *New York Times* Magazine, 50 year later. "We were very happy in England and France. It was so marvelous to be able to go out in public without being mobbed, to have our privacy."

The couple fought for that cherished privacy throughout the remainder of their married life, and today more than 60 years after his historic solo flight across the Atlantic Ocean, members of the Lindbergh family continue to live extremely private lives.

Most historians would agree that Charles A. Lindbergh was the greatest American hero of the first half of the 20th Century, and although he was born and raised in Little Falls, MN, he will always be linked to New Jersey, personally and professionally. Of his universal appeal, Lindbergh said in 1969:

"I've had enough fame for a dozen lives; it's not what it's cracked up to be."

The Dole Race

James Dole, the Hawaiian pineapple king, was impressed by the publicity generated by hotel-man Raymond Orteig's $25,000 prize to the first person to fly non-stop between New York and Paris. So on May 25, while Lindbergh was being honored in Europe, Dole offered a similar prize to the first person who would fly non-stop from the Pacific Coast and Hawaii. To make the race more appealing, Dole offered a $10,000 second prize. In hopes of attracting Lindbergh to participate, he set a starting date of Aug. 12. Maitland and Heggenberger had already jumped the gun and accomplished the feat in June of that year, but because of their military status, they were not permitted to accept the money.

So the race for the Pacific prize was on and it proved to be almost as tragic as the Atlantic race had been. Eight planes, most of them old single-engine biplanes flown by barnstormers with limited experience in long distance flying, left Oakland, CA. Two crashed on takeoff, one turned back to Oakland because of structural problems and three were lost at sea. Only two made the flight safely.

Art Goebel, a movie stuntman, with Lt. Bill Davis as navigator, flew the Travel Air *Woolaroc* to Hawaii in 26 hours, 17 minutes and 33 seconds to win the race. Two hours later, Martin Jensen and Paul Schluter, flying a Breese monoplane named *Aloha,* arrived in Honolulu to claim the second prize. Like the successful transatlantic planes, both the *Woolaroc* and the *Aloha* had been powered by Whirlwind engines.

On a Wing and a Prayer

While heroic airmen were setting new records and making headlines all over the world in 1927, their exploits were inspiring others back home to become involved in aviation.

Like so many boys of the 1920s and '30s, Vincent Taylor was an airplane enthusiast. He spent every waking hour planning his next bicycle trip to Teterboro Airport from his home in Ridgefield Park, NJ, so he could mingle with the famous aviators who flew for the Gates Flying Circus, the Fokker Aircraft Corp. and Colonial Air Transport. But on Sept. 12, 1927, Taylor's enthusiasm for aviation almost cost him his life.

Late that afternoon, Taylor was at Teterboro to greet Colonial's mail plane on its final run of the day from Boston to Hadley Field. As usual, the high wing monoplane landed at the airfield, discharged a small bag of mail and taxied back down the turf runway in order to turn into the wind for takeoff to Hadley. Because the plane had a tail skid instead of a rear wheel, it was impossible for the pilot, Ponton D'Arce, to spin the plane around on the soggy field without having someone pick up the plane's tail and walk it around.

Knowing the problem from past experience, the eager Taylor stood by the end of the runway to help. He grabbed onto a four-inch welded rod that protruded from each side of the lower fuselage and pushed the plane in a 180-degree circle. Then, not satisfied that he had pushed it far enough, he gave it a second shove just as D'Arce gunned the engine. Taylor, suddenly caught in the prop wash, was flung over the leading edge of the stabilizer and found himself trapped on the plane's tail as it streaked down the runway.

In the open cockpit ahead of the Fokker's thick wing, D'Arce could not see the tail assembly and the roar of the engine drowned out Taylor's cry for help. Seconds later, the plane was airborne and heading south toward Hadley Field, 20 miles away.

The teenager resisted hysteria. He grabbed the brace wire that ran from the stabilizer to the vertical fin and jammed one foot against the welded rod just below him. There he clung for what seemed to be an eternity. Then, to his relief, D'Arce throttled back the engine and began banking around Hadley to line up with the grass runway. Taylor tightened his grip on the wire as the pilot made a perfect three-point landing, taxied to the mail room and cut the switch.

It was only then that D'Arce realized he had a stowaway riding on the tail of the plane. With a typical pilot's bravado, he said "I thought the damn airplane got unusually tail heavy. I had to push almost full forward on the stick. Come on kid, I'll drive you home."

For that day Vincent Taylor dominated the aviation news in the metropolitan New York area. His parents were not all that pleased about his celebrity status and forbade him to go near airplanes again.

The *Hamza* Flies

One morning in June, 1927, the citizens of Union City, NJ, were surprised to see a large sausage-shaped cotton bag resting on the roof of a three-story building owned by Morris F. Hamza, a textile manu-facturer. The object was a lighter-than-air flying ma-chine that Hamza had dreamed of creating for years. The cotton fabric had been specially treated to make it airtight.

Hamza's blimp was 94 feet long, 15 feet in diameter and had the capacity to hold 15,000 cubic feet of gas. It was to be powered by a motorcycle engine with a gas tank capacity of eight gallons. Twenty additional gallons would be carried in five-gallon cans to be transferred into the main tank. With just the weight of a pilot, Hamza estimated that his creation would travel at 60 mph and could fly 8,000 miles.

The inflated bag sat atop Hamza's building for a week in order to ascertain if the fabric was airtight. The Hudson county newspapers gave his project a great deal of skeptical space which Hamza ignored. Satis-fied with the tightness of the material, the textile man deflated the bag and stored it in his building.

In August, Hamza along with Tony Hensler and a number of assistants, including his son Fred, trans-ported the fabric bag and an open gondola to a field in Secaucus, and inflated it with gas. Once it stood high in the air, straining at its ropes, the Union City blimp was christened *Hamza*. Hensler then climbed aboard the gondola, started the engine, and signaled for the ground crew to release the ropes.

To everyone's amazement (except Hamza's) the blimp rose rapidly over the Jersey meadows and turned toward New York City. It followed a zigzag course over Manhattan and Queens that ended with the aeronaut pulling the rip cord that released the gas to save himself from being blown over the Long Island sound. Landing lightly in a marsh between College Point and Flushing, Long Island, the fabric bag was badly torn.

The Hamza blimp never flew again, but Morris Hamza had the satisfaction of making his dream come true and creating a novel piece of aeronautical history.

Perhaps inspired by his father's dedication, Fred Hamza became a pilot and taught flying for many years at Teterboro Airport. He died in 1987.

1928
Wind Sock Blows West
Floyd Bennett

Inducted Aviation Hall of Fame of New Jersey, 1973

Two Germans, Herman Kohl and Baron Guenther von Huenefled, and an adventurous Irish flier, James Fitzmaurice, were the first to fly across the Atlantic Ocean from east to west. They took off from an air-strip near Dublin, Ireland in the German-built Jun-kers monoplane *Bremen,* and were forced down on Greenly Island, off the east coast of Labrador on Friday, April 13, 1928.

Like the transatlantic flights of the previous year, the *Bremen* adventure was international news. The other successful aerial crossings of the Atlantic had been from west to east with a strong tail wind to boost them along, the *Bremen*, on the other hand, had bucked that same wind every mile of the way from Ireland. Their safe arrival just off the American continent, even though the stalwart crew had been expected to land at Mitchel Field, was another momentous step in aviation progress.

On Greenly Island, the crew was safe and unhurt and cared for by the local populous. They were unable to leave because the Junkers' undercarriage had been damaged while landing on the packed Labrador ice. Canadian and U.S. newspapers leased aircraft to fly their reporters and photographers to Greenly Island for first hand interviews and pictures of the plane and crew. The Canadian icebreaker *Montcalm* was di-verted from its normal duties to plough through the ice to rescue the adventurers. On April 18, the *Montcalm's* captain called off his attempt to create a channel through the treacherous ice about 50 miles short of his goal.

At that point, only small single-engine planes had successfully flown to Greenly Island, and it was obvi-ous that an airplane capable of carrying a greater load of spare parts and supplies was necessary for a suc-cessful rescue. C.B. Allen, the aviation editor of the New York World, contacted Cmdr. Richard E. Byrd and suggested that Byrd's Ford trimotor, being read-ied for a South Pole flight, be sent to Greenly with the equipment needed. Byrd saw the suggestion as an excellent way to attract publicity for his planned South Pole adventure and asked his pilots, Floyd Bennett and Bernt Balchen, to fly from New York to Dearborn, MI, in a borrowed Bellanca, to pick up the trimotor for the flight to Canada and Greenly Island.

Both pilots were suffering with influenza contracted on recent flights to northern Canada, but they were eager to take part in the rescue effort. Bennett, whose lung had been pierced in the *America* accident at Teterboro the previous April, had spent several days in bed, just prior to the Dearborn flight, attempting to recuperate from the heavy congestion in his damaged lung. As he and Balchen flew west he remarked, "We're a fine pair to go rescuing anybody."

At Dearborn, Edsel Ford noticed immediately that the pilots were not well and insisted they spend a few days in his company's hospital while the trimotor was equipped for the flight.

On April 20, the airmen left the hospital and took off immediately for Lac Ste. Agnes. Accompanying them was Charles Murphy, a New York World reporter, Thomas Mulroy, one of Byrd's Antarctic team, and Carl Wenzel, a Ford workman, who would install skis and winter gear on the Ford trimotor in Canada before it left for Greenly Island.

The heater in the Ford did not work properly and Bennett slept in Balchen's flying suit for the entire flight. At Lac Ste. Agnes, Bennett had to be helped from the plane and was put to bed in a local home. A doctor from an adjoining town was called and did what he could to make him comfortable.

Herta Junkers, the daughter of the famous German aircraft designer and an accomplished pilot, had lived several years in New York as a representative of her father's company. When the Bremen had gone down on the ice in Labrador, she immediately took charge of the rescue effort. She was in Lac Ste. Agnes when the Ford arrived and was shocked by Bennett's condition. She made arrangements to have him flown in one of the Junkers smaller planes to Quebec City, 75 miles away.

Balchen visited Bennett in the clapboard farmhouse before they both left on different flights. Bennett, looking drawn and pale wished Balchen good luck.

"I'll see you when I get back, Floyd." Balchen told his friend.

Bennett smiled weakly. "That depends on how the wind sock blows," he said. Then he added with more enthusiasm "One thing I want you to promise me, Bernt. No matter what happens, you fly to the South Pole with Byrd." Balchen nodded glumly and left. An hour later, Bennett was on his way to Quebec where his condition was diagnosed as lobar pneumonia.

Bennett's wife, Cora, was told of her husband's condition at their home in Brooklyn, NY, and with Dr. Alvan L. Barach of New York's Presbyterian Hospital, took the train to Quebec City. When Mrs. Bennett arrived in Canada she was suffering from a severe case of tonsillitis and Dr. Barach put her in a hospital room adjacent to her husband.

Dr. Barach found Bennett deathly ill and asked John D. Rockefeller and Harry F. Guggenheim in New York to send a special serum by air to the Quebec hospital. Charles Lindbergh who was a guest at the Guggenheim estate volunteered to fly the needed drug to Quebec in his new Ryan B-1 monoplane. But at the last minute, the Army Air Corps offered a fast Curtiss Falcon that had the range to fly directly to Quebec City without a refueling stop in Montreal. Within hours, Lindbergh was airborne and three hours and 40 minutes later, he landed the Falcon on Quebec's historic Plains of Abraham.

As happened everywhere he went, Lindbergh was greeted by the media and a large crowd of autograph seekers. He pushed through the crowd and went immediately to visit Bennett. The expression on his face as he left the sick pilot's room clearly indicated the severity of Bennett's condition.

That same day, Byrd arrived by train from Boston and spent the next two days by his friend's bedside as Bennett's life slowly ebbed. He died on April 25, 1928 at age 37.

The Canadians gave Bennett full military honors and put his remains on a special car aboard the Montreal Express for the sad journey back to New York. Thousands of people lined the streets from Manhattan's Grand Central Station to the Seventy-first Regiment Armory where Bennett's body lay in state. Two days later, the body was sent to Washington, DC, and President Calvin Coolidge declared that the chief warrant officer should be accorded an "admiral's funeral."

Bennett was interred at Arlington Military Cemetery. Several years later, the Naval Air Station in Brooklyn was named Floyd Bennett Field to honor his aviation achievements.

Mexico's Hero Killed

Captain Emilio Carranza, Mexico's premier flying ace, crashed in the Pine Barrens of Burlington County, NJ, on Friday night July 13, 1928. He was killed instantly.

Captain Carranza had been on a goodwill flight in the United States in response to Charles Lindbergh's flight to Mexico and Central America earlier in the year. Carranza, 23, flew a Ryan monoplane similar to Lindbergh's. He had attempted to fly nonstop from Mexico City to Washington, DC, in early June, but unfavorable flying conditions had forced him down at Mooresville, NC. Although the flight was not a complete success, Carranza was given a hero's welcome in Washington, and was hosted at dinner by President Calvin Coolidge.

Carranza then flew on to Roosevelt Field in New York and the red carpet was rolled out by Mayor Jimmy Walker. He was an instant darling of New York's social set.

During his visit to the United States, Carranza and Lindbergh flew in separate planes from New York to

Detroit. The event was described in the July 14, 1928 edition of the *New York Times:*

One of the most beguiling episodes of his visit [to the U.S.] was the occasion when Captain Carranza had the duty of rescuing Colonel Lindbergh in a disabled plane. The two flyers had started off together from Curtiss Field, L.I., bound for Detroit. Lindbergh was flying a big Curtiss Falcon biplane and Carranza was at the joystick of the Colonel's own new Ryan Brougham.

Over Oak Harbor, Ohio, Lindbergh's gas mechanism failed, failing to supply the motor from either the regular or the spare tanks. He landed in a cornfield. Carranza, seeing his companion take to the earth, circled back. The biplane was left behind, and Captain Carranza took his illustrious host on board the Ryan as a guest. Thus, they reached Detroit.

By the time Carranza left New York on his return flight to Mexico, he had become a nationally known figure. When his plane plunged into a dense forest near Chatsworth, NJ, about 20 miles from Mount Holly, the county seat, his death was mourned in the U.S. and Mexico.

Large cranberry picking machines were used to penetrate the thick undergrowth where the pilot and his shattered plane had fallen. Fierce thunderstorms and poor visibility were blamed for the disaster.

Carranza, who had been married just four months before his flight to the United States, was anxious to return to his bride in Mexico. His decision to leave was sudden. The weather reports for New York state were not favorable but it is supposed that the young aviator felt he could outrun the storms by flying south. He left Roosevelt Field at 7 p.m. and crashed in the Pine Barrens about an hour later.

In the *Times,* most of the leading aviators of the day lavishly praised Captain Carranza's modest and unassuming personality, his ability as a pilot and what his flight had meant in the terms of goodwill between the U.S. and Mexico.

The American Legion of Mount Holly took an active part in the funeral services before Carranza's body was returned to Mexico for a hero's burial.

On July 17, the Mexican government gave $500 to John H. Carn of Chatsworth who had found Carranza's body and $250 to Arthur Carabine, the Burlington County detective who had led the rescue party.

In 1935, the Mount Holly American Legion Post convinced the State Commission on Historic Sites to set aside 10 acres of land in the Pine Barrens surrounding the Carranza crash site as the Carranza Memorial Park. Later the same year, school children in Mexico gave pennies to provide a fund for the erection of a monument at the place where Carranza's body was discovered. The monument was built of stones quarried near Mexico City.

Every year since then, the Mount Holly post has held a memorial service at the crash site. Representatives of the U.S. and Mexico, in addition to state officials, participate in the service.

Fokker Popularity Soars

The popularity of Fokker aircraft was at its peak during the last three years of the 1920s. New aircraft were being developed and in late 1927 orders were backlogged at the Teterboro plant so the factory was enlarged and another was opened in Brighton Mills, NJ (near Passaic), where subassemblies were produced. In addition, a third factory was opened at Glendale, WV, 10 miles south of Wheeling.

During that year, Bob Noorduyn introduced his Super Universal monoplane that could accommodate six passengers, and the first Fokker F-10 powered by three 425 hp Wasp engines rolled off the production line. Built under the supervision of chief engineer Alfred A. Gassner, the airliner carried 12 passengers. An F-10a, an improved model that seated 14, was used by Pan American Airways for its first passenger flight to Havana.

A twin-engine Fokker military bomber was flight tested in Aug. 1927. The plane was distinctive in that it had a single wing, in contrast to the tremendous biplane bombers that had been used up to that time. Fokker was again ahead of his time.

One of the company's trimotor F-7s was being used by a company called "Voice of the Sky." The firm flew its airplane over the New York metropolitan area broadcasting the voices of opera and popular singers and advertisements to an amazed audience below.

Late in the year, the Atlantic Aircraft Corp. was reorganized and renamed the Fokker Aircraft Corporation of America.

The many aviation successes of 1927 became the catalyst for more achievements in 1928. Right in the center of all this aeronautical excitement were the Fokker Aircraft Corp. and the Wright Aeronautical Corp.

There was a waiting list of commercial customers for the new F-10a deluxe trimotor. Canadian Colonial Airlines, Western Air Express, Universal Air Transport and Pan American Airways were just a few of the carriers who wanted the giant-winged passenger planes. In addition, the Richfield Oil Company ordered an airplane designed especially for corporate flying. It was the first of its kind.

At the same time, Richard Byrd, now a Navy commander, was back at Teterboro overseeing the construction of a new trimotor in which he planned to fly to the South Pole.

Just a few hundred yards from the busy Fokker Teterboro hangar, the Wright Aeronautical engineers were busily testing their new Cyclone engine in a large, single-engined XO-3 Mohawk biplane called *The Iron Horse.* The sturdy craft was flown by test pilot Leon Allen. The Cyclone soon would replace the Whirlwind engine in popularity with aircraft manufacturers. It became the workhorse of the 1930s and through the war years of the 1940s.

California to Australia

Two Australians, Capt. Charles Kingsford-Smith and Charles Ulm, had purchased a Fokker F-7 from Sir Hubert Wilkins, the polar explorer. The plane had been damaged while landing in Fairbanks, Alaska and its three Whirlwind engines had been removed. The two men rebuilt the plane for a planned 7,000-mile flight from Oakland, CA, to Brisbane, Australia. The planned route was divided into three huge hops across the largest of all oceans, the Pacific.

The Fokker, rechristened *Southern Cross,* with Kingsford-Smith at the controls, Ulm in the co-pilot's seat and two Americans, Harry Lyon, navigator, and James Warner, a radioman, lifted off the runway at Oakland on May 31 heading toward Hawaii, 2,400 miles away. The next hop, and the longest ever accomplished over water, was to Sava in the Fiji Islands. As Kingsford-Smith landed on the tiny spot of land in the mid Pacific, 3,200 miles from Hawaii, the Fokker's fuel gauge read "empty."

On June 9, more than 15,000 people greeted their countrymen as the *Southern Cross* touched down at the Eagle Farm Aerodrome, Brisbane, Australia after the final 2,200 mile flight through a severe tropical storm.

The courageous journey was considered to be on a par with Lindbergh's transatlantic flight the year before.

Kingsford-Smith and the *Southern Cross* weren't content to rest on their laurels. In June, 1930, with Evert Van Dyck as copilot, Capt. J. Patrick Saul, navigator and John Stannage, radio operator, Kingsford-Smith flew the sturdy Fokker 12,000 miles across Asia and Europe to Croyden Airport, near London, England. The ambitious flight took 12 days.

They then flew across the Atlantic and arrived in New York on June 25. During their stay in New York, the *Southern Cross* crew visited the Fokker plant and, following a tour of the facilities, were honored at a large banquet.

Later that week the *Southern Cross* was flown across the United States to its original starting point, Oakland, CA, thus completing a circumnavigation of the world.

The hard working Fokker trimotor is now on display in Australia.

Woman Flies Atlantic
Amelia Earhart

Inducted Aviation Hall of Fame of New Jersey, 1973

By the end of 1927, a total of seven men had successfully flown nonstop across the Atlantic Ocean on the long route from New York to Paris and beyond, but no woman had made the treacherous crossing. Several had tried, but their attempts had met with failure.

The first was Ruth Elders, an attractive southern lady. She captured the headlines in October, 1927, when she and pilot George Haldeman, flying a Stinson-Detroiter named *American Girl,* took off from Roosevelt Field and headed out over the Atlantic. They flew for more than 28 hours, but were forced down in the Azores by a faulty oil line.

A few weeks later, a leading feminist of the day, Frances Grayson, with pilot Oscar Omdahl, navigator Brice Goldsborough and a Wright engine expert, Fred Koehler, left Roosevelt Field in a Sikorsky amphibian destined for Harbour Grace, Newfoundland. They were never heard from again.

Another early feminine challenger in 1928 was an alleged heiress from Rochester, NY, Mabel Boll. She had met Charles Levine in Paris and offered $25,000 to be aboard the Wright Bellanca *Columbia* on the proposed flight from Europe to the United States. When the flight was canceled it was reported in the press that she became hysterical.

Once back in the U.S., the stylish brunette, who wore a huge diamond and was characterized in the press as the "Queen of Diamonds," convinced Levine to lend her the *Columbia* so she could fulfill her ambition to become the first woman to fly the Atlantic. A former Gates Flying Circus pilot, Wilmer Stultz, was hired to flight test and ready the plane for the flight.

As a preliminary to the big event, Miss Boll, Charles Levine and Stultz made the first nonstop flight from New York to Havana, Cuba, in the indestructible *Columbia.*

In the meantime, Mrs. Frederick Guest, the American wife of the British Secretary for Air, purchased the Fokker trimotor that Commander Byrd was having tested at Teterboro Airport for his Antarctic expedition. Henry and Edsel Ford had agreed to back the Byrd expedition, but insisted that the principal aircraft used on the exploration be a Ford trimotor that Ford Motors had just begun to produce.

The Guest Fokker was christened *Friendship* and unbeknown to Mabel Boll, Wilmer Stultz was hired to test fly the ship, equipped with pontoons, off the Charles River in Boston.

Fokker F-32 flies over Teterboro plant

It was at that point that Mrs. Guest's determined family and the hand of fate brought another aviatrix into the Atlantic race. Bowing to family wishes, Mrs. Guest withdrew as a flying candidate, but immediately asked her friend, book publisher George Palmer Putnam, to find the right woman to fly the Atlantic in her place. Putnam turned up Amelia Earhart, a Boston settlement house worker, who had a pilot's license.

Within days of her agreeing to fly, Earhart, Stultz and navigator Louis "Slim" Gordon flew the Fokker to Trespassey, Newfoundland, in preparation for the Atlantic flight.

At the same time, Mabel Boll, distressed over losing Stultz as her pilot, hired Oliver Le Boutillier of East Orange, NJ, a World War I fighter pilot, and navigator Arthur Argles, to fly her to Harbour Grace, Newfoundland in the Columbia.

Inclement weather kept both planes grounded for several days. Then, on June 17, well before dawn, the *Friendship* climbed into the air and flew to Wales. The first woman had flown across the ocean, although she never touched the controls during the entire 21-hour flight.

Earhart later described herself as nothing more than "baggage" in the back of the plane. She was determined to again fly the Atlantic at the controls of her own plane.

Once the deed had been accomplished, Miss Boll gave up her chase for glory and married a Count of questionable pedigree.

The executives and workers at the New Jersey Fokker and Wright plants were overjoyed by the accomplishment of their products. They had played a direct role in establishing another first in aviation history.

Fokker Sold

Aviation trade publications reported that the Fokker Aircraft Corp. had 906 employees and was the leader in passenger aircraft construction. Together the Fokker factories in Teterboro and Passaic were producing an airplane a week, and the Glendale plant turned out a three-engined Fokker every two weeks. The orders placed by Fokker for 350 Pratt & Whitney Wasp and Wright Cyclone engines was the largest in America for civil aircraft. Orders for airplanes came from around the world and the majority of budding airlines in the United States flew various Fokker models. The company had a 40 per cent share of the transport aircraft market.

In May, the General Motors Corp. acquired a 40 per cent interest in the Fokker Corp. Anthony Fokker, who owned 20 per cent of the company's shares, was appointed Technical Director for a five year period at a salary of $50,000. T. Whalen, a General Motor's vice president, became general manager, and Edward V. Rickenbacker, the flying "ace" of World War I, was appointed vice president for sales. Tony Fokker had great hopes for the new partnership.

Contributing to Fokker's optimism for the future was his newest creation, the Fokker F-32, test flown in Sept. 1929 at Teterboro. The huge plane had four 525 hp Pratt & Whitney Wasp engines, a 100-foot wingspan and could accommodate 32 passengers. The fuselage was divided into four compartments with eight seats each. It had a plush art deco interior and could be converted to handle 16 sleeper berths if it was flown as a nightliner.

Universal Air Lines ordered five of the new ships, but unfortunately, the prototype crashed on takeoff at Roosevelt Field destroying several homes. Universal canceled its order.

Western Air Express bought five F-32s for its Los Angeles to San Francisco route. In a flamboyant fashion for which he would become famous, Capt. Eddie Rickenbacker arranged to fly 60 passengers, among them Western Air officials, in two F-32s to the west coast on what was described as an "aerial house party."

During 1930, two F-32s were in the air five hours a day, a great improvement in aircraft utilization over other aircraft of the period which averaged only two flight hours a day. Introduced during the year the Stock Market crashed, Fokker produced only 10 of the large planes because airlines discovered it was difficult to find 32 people who wanted to fly to the same place at the same time.

Sadly, in the mid-30s a fuselage of one of the aircraft was set up as a gas station on Wilshire Boulevard in Los Angeles.

The F-32 was the last Fokker transport built in America until the *Friendship* class 28 years later.

In May 1930, General Motors' officials announced that the Fokker name would be replaced by the title General Aviation Corp. Tony Fokker, then just an employee of the company, was dismayed by the name change but was powerless to oppose it.

In February 1931, a new Fokker mystery plane was unveiled at Teterboro. The center wing, twin-engined bomber, powered by two Curtiss-Wright Conqueror engines, was flown to Washington, DC, for demonstration flights for Army officials. Although Tony Fokker didn't know it at the time, that airplane, designated the XA-7, was the last major contribution to aviation built at the Fokker Teterboro plant.

Knute Rockne Killed

April 1, 1931 newspaper headlines across America screamed the news "Knute Rockne Killed In Air Crash."

The legendary Notre Dame football coach and six other passengers were aboard a TWA Fokker F-10 airliner on March 31, when it crashed during a thunderstorm over Kansas. Government inspectors found that a wing had collapsed on the three-engined airplane. Due to Rockne's enormous popularity, the crash caused a national shock wave that made front page news for seven successive days. Five weeks after the accident, it was announced that all 1929 trimotored Fokker planes built at Teterboro, were not considered safe and were ordered grounded for inspection.

The airlines hardest hit by the groundings were Pan American Airways, Western Air Express and American Airways for they had 35 of the planes. Although it would happen numerous times in the future, this was the first time aircraft had been grounded for structural failures and it made a profound impression on the traveling public.

Weeks later, Fokker planes were declared safe, but the damage had been done. Within a year, the plants at Teterboro, Passaic and Glendale were closed. On July 10, the Board of the General Aviation Corp. announced that Anthony Fokker had retired as director of engineering. Fokker fought his forced retirement and in the end retained his yearly $50,000 for the five years of the contract, and the unrestricted right to use his trade-name "Fokker." He did, however, lose all the physical assets of his company in America.

On Dec. 23, 1939, Anthony Fokker died of meningitis in New York's Murray Hill Hospital. He was 49 years old.

Fokker, was a lonely, wealthy man at the time of his death. He had begun doubting the importance of his total commitment to the development of aircraft. His two marriages and several love affairs had ended he said "because I thought there was nothing more important than my aeroplanes. I suppose I was too self centered."

The American Fokker Aircraft Corp., which had its beginnings at Teterboro Airport, was the foundation for the General Aviation Corp that transferred in 1934 to California and became the manufacturing division of North American Aviation. Today, the company is known as North American Rockwell, a leading supplier to the nation's aerospace program.

In the Netherlands, the Fokker company manufactures short to medium haul airliners called F-27

Friendship (the name of Amelia Earhart's 1928 Fokker trimotor) and the F-28 Fellowship.

World's Busiest Airport

Newark Metropolitan Airport

In August 1928, a four-passenger Ryan monoplane, similar to the one Lindbergh flew across the Atlantic a year earlier, landed on a short stretch of an unfinished 1,600-foot, hard-surfaced runway in the meadows adjacent to the city of Newark. That was the first landing at the new municipal airport and the first plane in the U.S. to use a hard-surfaced runway.

The airport's first international passengers arrived on Oct. 17, 1928. Capt. Frank Hawks, with seven passengers aboard from Montreal, landed a Niagara Airways Ford trimotor, then among the largest transport planes in the world. They were welcomed by hundreds of cheering spectators. A year later, Hawks began flying for Texaco and went on to be a renowned record-setting airman.

For several years, the Aeronautical Club of New Jersey, headed by John J. Bergen of South Orange and Atlantic flyer Clarence Chamberlin, had urged the construction of an air facility for the state's largest city. At the time, the city fathers were intent on improving Port Newark and were reluctant to use land near the waterfront for aviation.

In 1926, to prove the feasibility of an airport, Chamberlin landed a small Italian SVA-9 biplane on a road leading to a garbage dump in the meadowlands, a site which is now the northeast corner of the present airport. Although the stunt attracted media coverage, it didn't alter the thinking of Newark councilmen.

The three successful transatlantic flights of Lindbergh, Chamberlin and Byrd in the spring of 1927 clearly indicated a practical commercial use for airplanes, so the project was again considered. Newark Mayor Thomas L. Raymond announced support of the idea in July 1927 and the plan won the endorsement of the U.S. Assistant Secretary of Commerce for Aeronautics William P. MacCracken, and Herbert C. Hoover, the Secretary of Commerce.

The enthusiasm of city officials was not shared by the entire community. The *Newark Evening News* printed a letter from an irate reader:

"There is no commercial aviation in sight. Forget the airport! The craze will soon die out."

Despite objections, construction began in January 1928 on the 68-acre site where Chamberlin had landed two years earlier. Preparing the swamp land for an airport was a tremendous under-taking. The level of the land had to be raised six feet to avoid flooding. Sand from Newark Bay was hydraulically pumped into the area. Within nine months the swamp was transformed to what the pilots called the "Newark Cinder Patch," because of the hard packed cinder runway. It officially opened Oct. 1, 1928.

The first employee hired to work at the new air terminal was William "Whitey" Conrad of Manasquan, NJ. Sixty years later, Conrad reminisced about those formative days of the airport:

"I was working at Hadley Field and heard Mayor Raymond was looking for someone with aviation experience, so I made an appointment for an interview. He looked at me and was surprised I was so young— maybe 22 or 23, I don't remember—but he was impressed by the experience I had in the aviation business, so he gave me the job as night manager under a then unnamed manager. I began work on Aug. 8, 1928. My one-year contract lasted 40 years."

Robert L. Copsey, vice president of the Newark Air Service which occupied the only hangar on the field, was the airport's first manager. Copsey had been a World War I bomber pilot, a barnstormer and one of the first inspectors for the Bureau of Air Commerce (BAC), predecessor to the Civil Aeronautics Administration (CAA). He carried the 29th pilot's license issued by the BAC.

The president of Newark Air Service was Capt. John O. Donaldson, a World War I flying ace who was born in 1898 at Fort Yates, ND, where his father served as an Army Officer. Donaldson had stayed in the service for several months after the war and won the Mackay Gold Medal for taking first place in the Army's transcontinental air race in October 1919.

He resigned his commission in 1920 to enter the business world. Subsequently, he founded the Newark Air Service but continued to fly in air races along the East Coast. He was a handsome man with a devil-may-care personality which made him popular among his peers and his fans.

In 1930, at an American Legion air meet at Philadelphia's Municipal Airport, he was killed while stunt flying. He lost control of his plane at 1,800 feet and crashed in full view of 40,000 spectators.

Following his death, he was promoted posthumously by the Air Corps to the rank of major. In 1951, the Air Force Base at Greenville, SC, was renamed Donaldson Air Force Base. Copsey succeeded Donaldson as president of the company.

Aldworth Named Superintendent

In 1929, Richard Aldworth became the airport's superintendent, as the manager was called in those days. A former airport reporter with the *Newark Sunday Call,* E.B. "Mannie" Berlinrut said of Aldworth:

"He had an astonishingly accurate understanding of the long-range potential and requirements for commercial aviation."

Whitey Conrad also had great respect for his superintendent. "He was a terrific man. Very fine. Very much military. He wanted us to be in uniform and that was a good idea. We went out and bought our own uniforms and they reimbursed us. I still think they should be in uniforms. That separates the airport people from the passengers." Aldworth was responsible for setting up landing fees for the airlines and private aircraft. Once it was done at Newark it became routine everywhere. He was smart, and a good pilot too."

Aldworth's vision and creative supervision made Newark Municipal Airport the innovative leader in commercial aviation throughout the 1930s. Vincent Bonaventura, the manager of Newark in 1989 when the airport celebrated its 60th anniversary, noted:

"Our airport had the first paved (with cinders) runway in the nation; it was the first with night lighting and we had the first air traffic control tower. Newark also had the first weather station and the first airport post office was established here."

He might also have mentioned that Newark had the first instrument landing system (Lindbergh tested it in 1933) and the first airport police department, organized in 1935.

Two other professionals who dedicated their life to the growth of aviation in the New York-New Jersey metropolitan area were Archie H. Armstrong and Vincent A. Carson. Like Conrad, they were there when it all began and stayed on the job when the Port Authority of New York and New Jersey assumed control of the facility in the late 1940s. Before they retired, they had witnessed the tremendous growth of the airport in the 1930s, the decline in the early '40s and '50s, and the rebirth in the late '60s.

Born in Newark, Armstrong, a professional engineer, worked for the city in 1927 when the decision was made to develop an airport in the meadows beside Newark Bay. He recalled that the initial cost of the field was about $2 million and, at this writing, was worth more than 100 times that amount.

Throughout the '30s, he served as airport engineer and was responsible for the design of many of the early buildings. He also supervised the maintenance department.

"In the old days I'd get a fellow with a telegraph pole chained to a truck to clear an 18-inch snowfall from the runway," he chuckled. "Now they use an $80,000 snow blower driven by men who have gone to school to learn the intricacies of snow removal"

He became airport superintendent after World War II and held the position for almost 20 years — first for the City of Newark and then the Port Authority.

Armstrong was succeeded as superintendent by Vincent Carson, who had also been hired in 1928, as a member of the operations and maintenance crew. He

Special mail delivery at Newark Airport.

rose to assistant manager before entering the Army Air Corps in 1941. He served in North Africa and the China-Burma-India theater during World War II. Upon discharge, he held the reserve rank of Lt.Colonel.

He returned to Newark, and when the Port Authority assumed the management of the field in 1948, he was named manager of La Guardia Airport. In 1956, Carson took the same position at Idlewild Airport (now John F. Kennedy Airport) and served there during the period of massive construction that created one of the largest and most modern air terminals in the world.

He returned to Newark as general manager in 1963 and participated in the planning of the major airport expansion that would come in the next decade.

In 1964, he served as president of the American Association of Airport Executives and was named Airport Manager of the year in 1968. A year later, he received the Port Authority Distinguished Service Medal.

Carson, a Newark native, resided for many years in Livingston, NJ, where he died in May of 1990.

Early Corporate Aircraft
Edwin E. Aldrin Sr.

Inducted Aviation Hall of Fame of New Jersey, 1990

Three new hangars were completed in 1929. The municipal hangar was the largest. Passengers looking for a flight prior to scheduled service, went to either the Eastern Aeronautical Co. hangar or the Newark Air Service facility to contract for a plane and pilot.

The fourth hangar belonged to the flight department of Standard Oil Company of New Jersey (now EXXON). The department was organized and managed by Major Edwin E. Aldrin Sr., a World War I

Smithsonian Collection

Edwin E. Aldrin Sr.

veteran. In order to facilitate the development and testing of new aviation products, two aircraft were purchased to supplement a Buhl Special "Air Sedan" operated by the company's sales promotion department. They were a Lockheed Vega and a Curtiss Robin.

The Standard Oil testing department was called "Stanavo," a word coined by Aldrin that stood for Standard Aviation Oil. It was inscribed atop a drawing of a huge eagle that covered the entire fuselage on both sides of the planes.

Company aviation personnel were based in the east, south, and midwest. Those who lived in New Jersey were Shep Dudley and Bob Ellis from Essex Fells and Frank Kline of Mountain Lakes.

Ed Aldrin was born in 1896 in Worcester, MA. He attended Clark University, where his physics professor was Dr. Robert H. Goddard, the pioneer rocket researcher. In 1917, he joined the Coast Artillery as a second lieutenant and, within months, transferred to the aviation section of the Signal Corps.

As chief of the education section in the engineering division at McCook Field, Dayton, OH, Aldrin founded the Air Service Engineering School, now the Air Force Institute of Technology at Wright-Patterson Air Force Base outside of Dayton.

Under his direction, the Standard Oil aviation department became one of the most efficient in the country. He and his fellow pilots did not participate in air races and other dangerous flying events, but their distinctively decorated aircraft could be found conspicuously parked on the airfields where major air shows were being held.

In 1929, Aldrin demonstrated Standard Oil products in Europe, flying the Vega 6,000 miles and visiting 12 European capitals. He was the first U.S. businessman to pilot his own plane on the European continent. While he was at it, he set several city-to-city speed records.

That same year, the Montclair, NJ, resident set a U.S. cross-country record by flying the 2,700 miles from Glendale, CA, to Newark in 15 hours, 45 minutes, surpassing the old mark by three hours. To take advantage of a strong tail wind, he flew at 11,000 feet, an exceptionally high altitude for a pilot with no oxygen or radio.

He played a small but significant role in the U.S. space program. In the late 1920s, Aldrin was able to arrange a meeting between Professor Goddard, his Clark University physics teacher, and Harry Guggenheim, the administrator of the Guggenheim Fund. That meeting resulted in the professor receiving necessary funds to continue his rocket propulsion experiments which eventually led to men landing on the moon in 1969. One of those men was Edwin E."Buzz" Aldrin Jr.

Aldrin Sr. left Standard Oil in 1938 to become an aeronautical consultant. In 1940, he was named manager of Newark Airport.

He was recalled to active duty in the Army Air Force during World War II, and left the service as a full colonel in 1946. He returned to the business world and became involved in a spectacular product promotion flight for the Atlas Supply Co. At Teterboro Airport, he helped organize an around-the-world flight of a DC-4 for Atlas executives and sales personnel in January 1948. The airplane was named the *Sky Merchant* and carried the full line of Atlas automotive products to be introduced and sold in 46 cities and 28 countries in South America, Africa, the Middle East, Asia and Australia. The flight covered more than 50,000 miles.

Aldrin and his family moved to Brielle, NJ, when he retired in 1961. He died in that Jersey shore community in 1974 at the age of 78.

Airline Service Begins

The first airline based at Newark was Transcontinental and Western (now TWA). In 1929, when the U.S. Post Office Department moved its air mail operation from Hadley Field to Newark, Colonial Air Transport (predecessor of American Airlines) was the first air mail carrier to follow. By early 1930, National Air Transport (became United Airlines) and Pitcairn Airways (became Eastern) moved to Newark.

That year, Newark was the busiest airport in the world, handling 44 daily passenger flights and 22 all-mail flights. In addition, 13,956 people were taken on sightseeing flights. From Jan. 1 to Dec. 31, there were an unprecedented 21,767 aircraft movements.

First Air Traffic Controller

William "Whitey" Conrad

Inducted Aviation Hall of Fame of New Jersey, 1990

Newark's first tower was a wooden structure erected in the middle of the field. The tower had no telephone or radio. Air traffic controllers used red and green signal lights to direct aircraft movements. Although the light system might seem primitive by today's standards, according to Whitey Conrad it was a vast improvement over the previous method — an airport official standing at the head of the runway waving planes in and out with signal flags.

Conrad became the first air traffic controller at Newark. "Back in the early 20s," Conrad recalled, "there was no such thing as controlling traffic. It was a real free-for all. It wasn't until 1928 when Newark Airport opened that anything resembling control came into being. In 1929, I developed a flag system for visual control, which was followed by my 'bisquit-gun.' That was a hand-held flashlight with reflectors and a 21-candle power bulb. I guess that was the real beginning of air control — so they tell me."

His innate modesty crept through in that statement, because the Conrad bisquit-gun is still in use today for emergency purposes.

"Then it wasn't long before we saw the need for elevated lights," Conrad continued, "so I got an old oil derrick-type structure rigged and I'd climb up there with two big searchlights to signal the aircraft."

That was the first control tower.

In 1931, more than 90,000 passengers used Newark, an amazing figure considering that the commercial aircraft of those days, such as Fokker and Ford trimotors, carried an average of 12 passengers on each flight.

Those early travelers flew to places only dreamed of five short years earlier — across the nation with Transcontinental and Western or on international flights to Canada with Canadian Colonial.

As traffic increased phenomenally at Newark, the federal government established rules for controlling air traffic, many at Conrad's suggestion. When controllers were licensed, Conrad was issued ticket number four. He was still upset about that 60 years later.

"The first three numbers went to fellows out in Cleveland because they were the first with radio control, so even though we had the first tower in Newark, we had to bow to the guys with the first radios."

By 1934, Newark's control system was as automated as any in the nation. A group of former pilots called airways traffic controllers were installed at Newark by the airlines to control the altitude and speed aircraft flew across the nation. When a plane was approaching Newark the airline radioman would call Conrad who would then direct the plane into Newark.

"It was the beginning of today's large air traffic control centers," Conrad explained.

Before he retired, he supervised the construction of the modern 14-story steel, glass and concrete tower now in use at Newark. The distinctive structure is an electronic marvel. Controllers are able to track aircraft by the use of computers from take-off to landing from any part of the world. When he left for the quiet life in Manasquan, Whitey Conrad was as comfortable with the modern technology that will take New-

Newark air traffic controls 1933: L-R back: Chris Raucher, Mike Murphy, Ed Rehise: front: Richard Aldworth, airport superintendent, "Whitey" Conrad and Newark deputy mayor William Fox.

ark Airport into the 21st century as he had been with his bisquit-gun in 1930.

"I saw aviation grow from Jennies and Stinsons to the super jets and, though I'll always love it, I really feel it now belongs to the younger men," he said. "I miss the excitement of the tower, but...."

119th Observation Squadron

The 119th Observation Squadron of the New Jersey National Guard, commanded by Major Kellogg Sloan, moved to Newark Airport in 1929. Major Robert L. Copsey was named operations officer of the unit.

The squadron's Douglas 02H biplanes were housed in hangar #10 and an administration headquarters was in building #9.

Copsey took command of the squadron in the early 1930s and stayed active in the military throughout his career.

The 119th was federalized in 1940 becoming part of the U.S. Army Air Base at Newark, under the command of Maj. Chester A. Charles. Two fighter squadrons were based at the airport as an air defense unit for the New York area. In 1942, jurisdiction of Newark Army Air Base was assigned to the Air Service Command. Brig. Gen. William E. Farthing was in charge when the unit's name was changed to the New York Air Service Post Area Command.

The Air National Guard remained at Newark following the war. In 1950, units of the 119th were activated for the Korean Conflict, and in 1960, the unit became an Aero Medi-Vac squadron flying C-119s and C-121 Super Constellations.

In 1965, the air guard moved to McGuire AFB and a year later building #9 was destroyed by fire. As the airport expanded in the late 1960s, both the building and hangar 10 were razed.

David Morris, the Newark Airport historian, said:

"The old 119th Observation Squadron lives on as the 119th fighter Interceptor Squadron of the New Jersey Air National Guard. The 'Jersey Devils' fly F-4 Phantoms from Atlantic City and are an integral part of our nation's air defense command. Many of our state's best known military aviators have commanded the New Jersey Air National Guard unit. They include two World War II flying aces, Maj. Gen. Donald Strait and Maj. Gen. Frank Gerard.

"Each time the 119th 'scrambles,' they take part of Newark Airport with them."

Records by the Dozen

Newark's modern facilities attracted adventurous men and women who were pushing aviation to its limits and setting new standards almost monthly. Many of them became legends in their own time and, even today, their names are spoken with reverence.

On February 14, 1930, Army Lieutenants Will White and Clement McMullen lifted off from a Newark runway in a Lockheed Vega on the first lap of a flight to Buenos Aires. They broke the existing records for each segment of the trip as well as for the entire flight.

The 6,780-mile flight was achieved in five days and five hours elapsed time, of which 52 hours and 15 minutes were spent in the air.

A month later, Capt. R.A. Ellis, a Standard Oil pilot, flew his Lockheed Vega from Miami to Newark in eight hours at an average speed of 160 mph. That flight broke the record of eight hours and 30 minutes, set by White and McMullen the previous month.

In October, the Transcontinental & Western Airways inaugurated the first all-air passenger service from Newark to Los Angeles. The trip took 36 hours.

Bill MacLaren, a flight instructor at Newark, announced that he and Mrs. Beryl Hart, one of his students, would fly the Atlantic in a Bellanca floatplane, christened *Tradewind*.

They planned to follow a southern route and make the flight in four stages—Newark to Hampton Roads, VA, to Bermuda, then on to the Azores and into Paris.

Hart, a well-to-do-widow, sponsored the undertaking. To further help finance the flight, MacLaren made arrangements with a local stamp dealer to carry first day covers imprinted with a commemorative cachet celebrating the flight.

On Jan. 7, 1931, the two adventurers, the pert, smiling lady and the dapper, mustached pilot, decked out in boots and breeches, left Newark and flew to the Naval Air Base at Hampton Roads. The following day, they plunged through heavy storms and fog to a safe landing in the sheltered harbor of St. Georges, Bermuda.

While they awaited fair weather in Bermuda before setting out on the next leg of their journey, MacLaren sent a postcard to his friend, a Mr. Roessler of East Orange, NJ. It read: "First stage made—more difficult than expected — a series of unfortunate accidents — next jump our big test — the last stage Azores to Paris will be easy."

A large crowd gathered along the shore of St. Georges harbor to watch the Bellanca lift off the water and turn eastward over the Atlantic toward the Azores, more than a 1,000 miles away. Those Bermudians were the last to see MacLaren and Hart alive. The two aviators were never heard from again.

On June 6, 1931, Amelia Earhart, the first woman to fly across the Atlantic Ocean in 1928, completed the first cross country flight in a Pitcairn autogiro from Newark to San Francisco. Later in the month, she flew back to Newark.

The previous April, Earhart had established an autogiro altitude record of 18,415 ft. over Willow Grove, PA, in a Wright Whirlwind-powered Pitcairn machine.

In September, James H. "Jimmy" Doolittle won the 1931 Bendix Trophy race flying the Laird *Super Solution* from Burbank, CA, to Cleveland, OH, in nine hours, 10 minutes, and 21 seconds, arriving a full hour before the second place winner. Doolittle then flew on to Newark, establishing a new transcontinental speed record of 11 hours, 16 minutes, and 10 seconds. Doolittle earned $10,000 for his half-day effort.

Earhart and Doolittle returned to Newark in July of 1932. First, Earhart established a new women's solo trans-continental record when she landed at Newark with an elapsed time of 19 hours and 15 minutes. The flight also set a new long distance flying record for women of 2,435 miles.

Doolittle's flight was described in the September issue, of *Aviation* Magazine:

From dawn to dusk on July 25, Maj. James H. Doolittle flew his Lockheed Orion monoplane, with [George] Washington's great-great-great-grandniece and a representative of the Aeronautical Chamber of Commerce as passengers, over all the points visited by Washington during his career. General Washington would have needed four years to travel by stagecoach and saddle the 2,610 miles which Maj. Doolittle covered in 15 hours and 40 minutes. To celebrate the 157th anniversary of the Postal Service, 30 packages of letters with air mail stamps were dropped at as many points of historical interest along the route. Though the yellow monoplane did not conclude its flight at Newark until 9:15 o'clock in the evening, by 10 o'clock the next morning 29 of the 30 letters were in the hands of those to whom they were addressed in New York.

Mail Contracts Canceled

In February 1934, stemming from a Congressional investigation by Alabama Senator Hugo Black, President Franklin D. Roosevelt canceled all private carrier air mail contracts and ordered the Army Air Corps to fly the mail.

The investigation had uncovered an alleged bid-rigging plot on the part of the major U.S. air mail carriers — American, Trans World, Eastern and United Airlines — with the knowledge and consent of former Republican president Herbert Hoover's Postmaster General, Walter Folger Brown. Democrat Roosevelt viewed the domination of the mail routes by large corporate airlines as another example of how big business had brought on the worst economic depression in the history of the United States.

Airline executives were certain that the Army could not fly the mail as safely or efficiently as their larger more powerful planes. To prove the point, Jack Frye, president of TWA, called his friend E.V. "Eddie" Rickenbacker, then a vice president of Eastern Airlines, and arranged for a graphic demonstration of the capabilities of the still budding airline business.

On February 18, 1934 in Los Angeles, the two executives had every compartment of a DC-1 crammed with sacks of mail. Then at 10 p.m., two hours before the air mail cancellation order went into effect, the DC-1 lifted off the L.A. runway with Jack Frye at the controls and Rickenbacker as co-pilot. Thirteen hours and four minutes later (three hours ahead of schedule), the last load of transcontinental private contract mail arrived at Newark Airport. The record setting flight was a final dramatic gesture by the two airmen to show what American ingenuity and free enterprise had accomplished.

In May, 1934, after a disastrous 78 days of flying the mail in open-cockpit planes, flown by inexperienced Army pilots, air mail contracts were again awarded to private carriers. It had been an expensive lesson for the bureaucrats. The army lost 57 airplanes and 12 pilots in less than two months. On May 14, to celebrate the return of postal revenues to the airlines, Jack Frye broke his own air mail speed record for a coast-to-coast flight. In a powerful Northrop Gamma, he flew from Los Angeles to Newark in 11 hours and 31 minutes. Once again, New Jersey was the focal point of a dramatic aviation achievement.

In the 1920s, William John Frye flew stunts in Hollywood. During that period, he and friends created an air service for the stars. Standard Air Lines specialized in carrying motion picture personalities on vacation flights. The small airline was acquired by Western Air Express and merged with Transcontinental Air Transport, which became TWA. Frye, a hard worker and dedicated airman, was named president of TWA in 1934. He was 30 years old.

Not to be outdone by Frye's flight, on Nov. 8, Rickenbacker, Silas Morehouse and Capt. Charles W. France flew from Los Angeles to Newark in a twin-engine DC-2, the most modern airliner of the day, in 12 hours and three minutes to set a new record for passenger transport planes.

The next year, D.W. "Tommy" Tomlinson and J.S. Bartles flying a TWA DC-2 broke Rickenbacker's record by almost an hour.

When Eastern Airlines began flying the Douglas DC-2 transport from Newark to Miami the move brought about the transfer of many well-known commercial airmen to Newark Airport. The list included Everett Chandler, Gil Waller, Gene Brown, Don Johnston, Bob Minick, Larry Pabst, Johnny Armstrong, Earl Potts, Pete Bransom, Walter Wipprecht, Pete Parker, John Gill and a man who would become perhaps the best-known airline pilot of that era, Capt. H.T. "Dick" Merrill.

During that first year of operation from Newark, Eastern's DC-2s established several speed records. Capt. Potts flew from Washington to Newark in 47 minutes and Capt. Johnston set a new mark from Miami to New Jersey of five hours and 30 minutes.

Newark Expands

In 1935, an "art deco" administrative building with a control tower perched on top, was opened. It provided passengers with the convenience of transferring from one airline to another without trudging along cinder ramps toting their luggage from one hangar to another. The airport was then handling 50 to 60 flights an hour.

Major "Jimmy" Doolittle was back at Newark in January 1935 when he dashed nonstop in the Shell Oil Company's Vultee from Los Angeles to Newark in exactly 12 hours.

A month later, Leland Andrews, flying a Vultee similar to Doolittle's, bested the major's record by a half-hour.

On Jan. 19, 1936, Howard Hughes, a dashing California millionaire who had produced the epic film *Hell's Angels* in 1930 for a then staggering $4 million, flew his lightweight experimental airplane "H-1" from Burbank, CA, to Newark in seven hours, 28 minutes, and 25 seconds at an incredible 327 mph. The flight established the eccentric millionaire as a national hero, and the "H-1" captured the interest of aviation experts everywhere, including Japan.

Later that year, Hughes suggested that the U.S. Army adopt the "H-1" as a fighter plane, but his proposal was rejected. In typical Hughes fashion, he mothbailed the sleek monoplane in a California hangar.

In Japan, the government commissioned Mitsubishi Ltd. and Jiro Horikoski, a top aeronautical engineer, to develop a superior fighter plane. From that pooling of talents came the "Zero," a sleek, fast low-winged monoplane that had many of the H-1's characteristics.

Hughes believed that he had unwittingly contributed to Japan's dominance of the skies over the Pacific during the early years of World War II. He made his feeling known to a Senate committee in 1947: "I am told that the Japanese copied the Zero from this airplane."

In April of 1937, Capt. Frank Hawks flew his new Granville Racer *Time Flies* from Miami to Newark in four hours and 21 minutes. On landing, Hawks overshot the Newark runway and damaged the plane slightly.

The following September, Hawks was killed while demonstrating the Gwinn Aircar near East Aurora, NY. After a successful take off, the little ship ran full tilt into electric and telephone wires that were practically invisible in a background of trees.

As Texaco's flying goodwill ambassador, Hawks had established 214 inter-city flight records, both in the U.S. and aboard. He was widely mourned.

That same month, a commercial airliner record between Newark and Miami was set by Eastern's Dick Merrill. The flight of the DC-3 transport, powered by two 1,000-hp Wright Cyclone engines, covered 1,192 miles in five hours and 26 minutes.

Newark to Miami and Return

On May 17, 1938, Kenny Kress and Glenn Englert, two Lock Haven, PA, pilots, took off from Newark on a most unusual flight. They planned to fly a small Piper Cub non-stop to and from Miami. The flight was to prove that light aircraft of the day were not just airport toys. The tiny Cub was a flying gas tank as it lifted off the Newark runway at 4:06 a.m. and headed south.

The pilots had practiced for weeks refueling in the air. At specified airports along its route, the Cub was brought down within 15 feet of the runway. Then, flying steadily at that height, a rope was dropped from the plane to a car speeding along below. Five-gallon cans of gas were tied to the rope as the plane and car sped along a parallel route at more that 50 miles per hour. The procedure was repeated five or six times at each airport, until 30 gallons were lifted aboard the plane.

The aviators ran into foul weather in both directions throughout most of the flight. Their steady nerves, endless stamina and the fine cooperation of ground crews eventually brought them success.

The Piper Cub landed back at Newark some 63 hours and 55 minutes after it had departed.

The flight established a new distance record for small aircraft of 2,420 miles on a point-to-point basis. It was estimated, however, that the gross distance flown was in excess of 3,500 miles.

The power plant of the Piper was a 50 hp Lenape "Papoose," an evolution of the three-cylinder Aeromarine engines designed by Joe Boland, one of the New Jersey brothers who built the first fixed-wing airplane in the Garden State. Boland owned the Lenape Engine Company in Matawan, NJ.

During the summer of 1939, the Japanese demonstrated their aviation capability to the world. They sent a low-wing, twin engined Mitsubishi monoplane, designated J-BACI, around the world on a "goodwill air mission." Unbeknownst to the citizens of the free world, the flight was a show of aeronautical strength that would soon be brought to bear on United States' armed forces.

With a crew of six, the plane, christened "Nippon" (Japan), flew across two oceans to five continents and more than 30 nations. Starting toward the east, the Japanese airmen arrived at Newark Airport on the seventh day of the flight.

The tour was sponsored by two Japanese newspapers, the *Osaka Mainichi* and the *Tokyo Nichi Nichi*. Following the flight, the publisher of both papers wrote Newark tower chief William Conrad the following letter of appreciation.

Dear Sir:

On October 20, the Nippon glided to its final stop at the Haneda Airport of Tokyo to complete the longest circle around the world ever achieved by one airplane and one crew on one continuous journey.

First on the lips of the fliers upon their arrival home, were the words of thanks for the unfailing courtesy you so readily accorded them when their welfare was left in your care. As the sponsors of the flight, we wish to assure you that your warm friendship will long remain among our most dearly cherished prizes of the entire project.

During the total elapsed time of 55 days, the Nippon was actually in the air for 194 hours, flying 32,845 miles over foreign lands and waters. Two great oceans and five continents were crossed and the equator twice. Twenty-nine landings were made in 16 different countries while the wings were dipped in salute from the sky to a dozen more.

Many are the honors given and new records credited to the Nippon fliers. They all serve to deepen our appreciation of your kind cooperation which we are most eager to reciprocate at the first opportunity.

Cordially yours,

Shingoro Takaishi, Chairman, Board of Directors

LaGuardia Airport Opened

Throughout the decade of the 1930s, Newark led all the world's airports in passenger traffic. In 1938, 355,123 passengers passed through Newark's terminal, one-quarter of the total number of passengers carried in the world. They were heady times, but a dark cloud from across the Hudson River hung over the airport.

Fiorello H. LaGuardia, New York City's dynamic mayor and a staunch advocate of aviation, was determined to have a major commercial airport in New York. In 1936, he flew into Newark on a Transcontinental and Western Air DC-2 and refused to debark from the plane claiming, "My ticket says New York, and that's where I want to go." To accommodate his honor and garner a great deal of free press coverage, the airline flew LaGuardia to Floyd Bennett Field in Brooklyn.

The airfield, named for the Navy pilot who flew Lt. Cmdr. Byrd over the North Pole, was the site LaGuardia hoped would be New York's commercial airport. The Post Office Department ran mail truck speed tests and found Newark to be much more convenient to New York's central post office than Floyd Bennett, so the mail service continued from New Jersey.

Nothing could dampen LaGuardia's determination, so in 1938, he began building an airport at North Beach on Jamaica Bay. In the meantime at Newark, the major airlines were bickering with the city fathers over new long-term leases. Before agreements could be reached, LaGuardia's North Beach Airport was certified by the Civil Aeronautics Authority as "an adequate, safe and convenient landing terminal" and three airlines moved their operations to the new facility.

By 1940, Newark Airport had been closed. Perhaps, only the advent of World War II saved it as a major commercial terminal.

Reporter "Mannie" Berlinrut remembered what Dick Aldworth (who became stricken with the Hodgkin's disease that would take his life in 1944), told him during that dark period, "Look, son, they've won a big one. But we've got to hang in, for the day will come when it won't make much difference. We'll need all the airports we've got in the New York area."

The visionary man who had developed Newark as the leading commercial air terminal in the world never lost sight of the future even when his empire was crumbling around him.

As Aldworth predicted, the airport's future would again be bright, Perhaps brighter than he ever could have imagined, but first there was a war to win. (See 1940)

1929

Great Hope, Then Despair

At the dawn of 1929, the United States had a new president, Herbert Hoover. The roar of the '20s continued unabated and the Garden State's aviation industry flourished apace. While adventurers were still breaking barriers of time and distance, others were establishing aeronautical businesses, many of which would endure for decades.

It was a year when two of aviation's greatest names, Curtiss and Wright, merged to form an aviation empire unequaled in its scope; new avionic instruments and safety equipment were developed and tested; new aircraft were introduced and previously unexplored areas of our planet were conquered.

Several new airports were opened. In Mercer County, Scudder's farm, on a site north of the present interstate highway I-95, was selected by the U.S. Department of Commerce as the site for a landing field midway between New York and Philadelphia. A beacon light, so essential to early navigation, was erected and a portion of the farmland cleared for a runway. Governor Morgan Larsen officially dedicated what was to become Mercer County Airport before an air show that featured pilots Jimmy Doolittle and Amelia Earhart.

The airport remained active during the Depression due, in a large part, to the presence of the Luscombe Aircraft Company, a leading aircraft builder.

One of two major General Motors aircraft plants operating in New Jersey during World War II was built adjacent to the airfield along with a Naval Air Station. By March, 1942, the old Mercer Airport was closed and development continued on the site of the present airport. At the end of the war, 7,000 Grumman torpedo bombers built by GM had been delivered to the Navy.

The airport became the property of Mercer County in 1952 and opened for public use. Some of the more prominent corporate users have been Johnson & Johnson, RCA, U.S. Steel and Ronson Aviation. In the 1980s, a modern passenger terminal was constructed and the airport was serviced regularly by the Allegheny Commuter line, operated by Southern Jersey Airlines of Atlantic City.

Ronson Aviation became a principle tenant and trained the helicopter pilots of the New Jersey State police.

American Cirrus Engines, Inc., which produced 4-in-line air-cooled engines at a plant in Belleville, NJ, built a single runway airport at Pine Brook, NJ.

To instill a spirit of caution and precision among their employees, the American Cirrus management encouraged them to learn to fly. The company officials believed that the men who created the engines should experience how much airmen depended on their products. The flying school was run by a Capt. William N. Lancaster.

The Camden Central Airport was officially opened on Sept. 21,1929. The 180-acre facility served Philadelphia as its official air mail depot. The airfield had two runways, one 2,500 feet long and the other 3,600 feet. The Curtiss-Flying Service occupied one of the two concrete and steel hangars on the field. The Ludington Philadelphia Flying Service opened a ground school there.

During the opening day celebration, Army and civilian pilots participated in an air show. But the star of the show, was the Fokker F-32, the largest transport plane in the world.

Earlier that year, Consolidated Aircraft Co. introduced the Admiral Flying Boat which had been designed by Isaac Laddon, a Garfield, NJ native. The innovative machine was the first in a series of Consolidated's highly respected amphibians.

In November 1929, at Keyport, aircraft designer Vincent J. Burnelli, president of the Uppercu-Burnelli Corporation, announced an agreement with Societa Trans Adriatica of Italy to begin manufacturing 20-passenger Burnelli airplanes within 90 days. The agreement called for the Italian company to produce not less than 50 aircraft a year for a five year period. It was the first time rights for the manufacturing of an American-designed plane aboard had been granted. Renator Morandi, president of the Italian company, visited the United States with members of the Italian Air Commission led by Gen. Italo Balboa, to investigate American transport planes for use as airliners. Burnelli's plane was chosen by the commission.

At about the same time, Bert Acosta, who had piloted the Fokker C-2 monoplane *America* across the Atlantic in 1927, founded the Acosta Aircraft Corp. with a capital investment of $300,000. The corporation had offices at 225 Broadway, NYC. Acosta planned to build aircraft of his own design in which anyone could learn to fly. His company motto was typical of the flamboyant airman: "I spent a quarter century telling you that you must fly -- now I'm going to give you a ship in which you can do it."

By the early fall of the year, his multi-purpose, all metal amphibians, called "Amanda A's" were being built in the former Mercer Automobile factory at Trenton.

Then came "Black Thursday," Oct. 24, the day the stock market crashed. The first Acosta planes hadn't been completed when the crash came and within days the airman's financing disappeared along with his dream of a people's airplane. It was the beginning of the end of a great aviation career.

Bertrand Acosta

Inducted Aviation Hall of Fame Of New Jersey, 1976

Bert Acosta was widely applauded for his daring victories in air races in the early 1920s. Often censored for his capricious buzzing of New York City skyscrapers or flying under East River bridges, Acosta earned the title of "Aviation's Bad Boy."

He began building his reputation for aeronautical fearlessness at age 14, flying in a wobbling, patchwork, homemade plane at Imperial Beach, CA. In 1911, at age 16, he became an instructor for Glenn Curtiss on the Jack Rabbit flats on North Island near San Diego where he was born. Over the next three years, he worked for Curtiss and barnstormed along the West Coast from Canada to Mexico.

When war broke out in Europe in 1914, Acosta flew to Toronto and enlisted in the Royal Canadian Air Service. He was 19 years old. With a strong recommendation from Curtiss, the Canadians promoted the young American to chief flight instructor. When the United States entered into the war in 1917, Acosta applied for a commission and asked to be sent to Europe. His request was refused and he was sent as a civilian to Hazelhurst Field, Long Island, NY, to become the chief instructor at the Army Air Service base there. He then joined Col. E.J. Hall, Chief Technical Director of Aircraft Production, and worked as a development team member on the Liberty engine. At the same time, he became Director of Flying and Testing for the Air Service. He put his life on the line many times testing frail, untried aircraft. In 1918, he set an American altitude record, climbing to 22,500 feet over Dayton, OH without oxygen.

After the war, Acosta participated in several memorable adventures. In June 1920, he broke the American nonstop distance record in a German Junker JL-6, a flight of 1,200 miles from Omaha, NB, to Lancaster, PA. A year later at the Omaha International Aero Congress, he won the Pulitzer Trophy Race flying a Curtiss CR-1. He finished third the previous year. He had, at that point, flown more varied aircraft than any man in the world.

According the those who knew him best, Acosta lived on the ground as recklessly as he did in the air. Following the Pulitzer race, his friends confided that he was "even faster than that with women." The handsome airman was adored by the flappers of the Roaring '20s as a nonstop party boy, big spender and lover. And at age 26, there was no end to the parties.

Smithsonian Collection

Bert Acosta and Clarence Chamberlin

A crash in a Sperry Messenger, a single-seat biplane, and six weeks of delirium in a hospital seemed to spur Acosta to even more daring feats. He flew under the Brooklyn, Williamsburg and Manhattan Bridges that span New York's East River. He buzzed the tops of skyscrapers and took any dare placed before him. Only his innate flying skill kept him from killing himself. And when the authorities grounded him, he went on a drunken spree that latest for weeks.

In 1927, Acosta, at age 32, was perhaps the best known civilian pilot in the world. When his license was returned, he joined Clarence Chamberlin on a record-setting endurance flight. He was then hired by Lt. Cmdr. Richard E. Byrd to pilot the third nonstop flight across the Atlantic Ocean in the Fokker trimotor *America*.

Over the next two years, Acosta's reputation as an aviator and playboy was at its zenith, but when the stock market crashed and he lost his aircraft business, his life began falling apart. His public behavior made headlines on a regular basis. He was jailed for buzzing Naugatuck, fined $2,000 for buzzing Roosevelt Field, had his license suspended for five years for stunt flying with an expired license, and was sent to the Elmira Reformatory for six months for deserting his second wife and two sons. But even as he was being led away in shackles, he was seen waving at a young lady in the courtroom who was identified as Mrs. Dorothy Walker, his most recent love. Despite all his flamboyance, his eventual fate seemed predestined.

Over the next five years, Acosta hit rock bottom. He was sleeping in flop houses and getting his daily calories from a bottle. When his license was returned in 1935, he taught flying for awhile, but couldn't shake his alcoholism and soon was back in the gutter.

It was then that his daughters by his first wife who he divorced in 1921, Bertina Dolores and Consuelo Gloria, moved to New York and dragged their father up from the depths. Just as it seemed Acosta was ready to settle down, he boarded the *SS Normandie* in October 1936 and sailed for France on the first leg of a journey to Spain. There, he joined in the Loyalists' struggle against Gen. Francisco Franco's "Nationalist" forces.

He was now a mercenary ready to fly in combat for $1,500 a month and $1,000 bonus for each Nationalist plane destroyed. Other New Jerseyans attracted by the deal offered were Eddie Schneider, the teenage record-setter from Jersey City and Albert Baumler, known as "Ajax," of Bayonne, who became a World War II flying ace.

Acosta and his fellow Americans flew out-dated airplanes against new German-built models but managed somehow to survive. On one mission, Acosta and his Spanish gunner shot down two enemy planes, but was rebuffed when he asked the authorities for his bonus. "What proof do you have?" he was asked. The answer was of course "none," so he received no bonus. Again badly stung, Acosta quit at the end of the first month and asked for his $1,500, only to discover that the Loyalists paid in pesetas that could not be taken out of the country.

Once back in the United States, Acosta's physical and financial condition declined. He had contracted tuberculosis and couldn't afford proper care. Richard Byrd heard of his plight and made arrangements to have him placed in a sanitarium in Denver, CO. His daughters visited him there and for a while it seemed his health was improving. But Bertrand Acosta died in 1954 at the age of 59—both a legend and a tragic figure in his own time.

First Transcontinental Passenger Service
Turner Wills

The first transcontinental passenger air service combined daylight flying and nighttime traveling aboard a Pullman train. The two-day, two-night journey from Los Angeles to New York was sponsored by the Pennsylvania and Santa Fe railroads and Transcontinental Air Transport, the predecessor of TWA. The Airway Special train arrived at the Pennsylvania Station in New York City on July 10, 1929 with just two paying passengers who had completed the entire journey — Albert Hitchen, a Los Angeles insurance broker, who held ticket No. 1 and Turner H. Wills of Neptune, NJ. Hitchen carried a letter from Los Angeles Mayor John C. Porter to Mayor Jimmy Walker of New York City. Wills had greetings for Mayor Walker from the All Year Club of Los Angeles.

In 1929, primitive navigational aids both aboard the aircraft and on the ground made night flights a precarious undertaking. Air mail pilots had been flying across the nation around the clock since 1925, but no airliner was ready to risk the lives of passengers in the dark skies above America. So, in order to expedite coast-to-coast travel, a railroad and airline combination ticket was introduced. The total transcontinental travel time was 48 hours, as compared to almost five days by rail.

The cross-country air route involved 12 stops, enough ups and downs to cause Belva Darling a Los Angeles newswoman, to leave the party in Winslow, AZ., because of air sickness.

The legendary actress, Mary Pickford, christened the 12-passenger plane with a bottle of grape juice because Prohibition was then the law of the land.

The first leg of the flight between Los Angeles and Winslow had been piloted by Charles Lindbergh. His bride Anne Morrow Lindbergh of Englewood, accompanied him.

In a letter to his bride-to-be, Turner Wills described his flight:

"We left Los Angeles yesterday and at once climbed to 12,000 feet. I cannot describe to you the beauties of the trip, and wish that you had been with me to enjoy them. It was just like riding in a great big automobile."

Forty years later, Mrs. Wills remembered how she felt when she received the letter.

"I was mad as hops. He plunked down $351.94 for the ticket from Los Angeles to New York, and all I could think about was that the money should have been spent for furniture," she said.

Born in Stanhope, NJ, Wills was working for a lumber company in Los Angeles when he started the historic trip east aboard a Ford trimotor. In the intervening years, he and his wife logged hundreds of hours aboard commercial airliners on business and pleasure trips.

The Wills had been married 57 years when he passed away in October of 1986.

First Round-The-World Airship Flight

The most successful rigid airship was appropriately named the *Graf Zeppelin* in honor of Count Ferdinand von Zeppelin, the father of the Germany's lighter-than-air industry (Graf in German means "Count"). It

was the largest yet built —775 feet long, 100 feet wide and 110 feet high. In order to demonstrate the comfort and dependability of the new airship, Dr. Hugo Eckener had skippered the *Graf Zeppelin* across the Atlantic in 1928. Landing at the Lakehurst Naval Air Station on Oct. 14, it made history as the first paying transatlantic passenger flight. Among the 20 passengers was Lady Hay-Drummond-Hay, a correspondent for the Hearst News Service, who thus became the first woman to arrive in America by air.

The trip had not been a smooth one. It took 111 hours and 44 minutes to fly 6,200 miles, no faster than the ocean liners of the day. Nevertheless, Eckener and his crew of 40 were welcomed as heroes wherever they went. Their stay in America included a ticker tape parade up Broadway and breakfast with President Calvin Coolidge.

Once back in Germany, Eckener sought financial backing to establish a regular air service between the continents, but none was forthcoming. So, again, he planned demonstration flights, one of which was an ambitious flight round the world. With backing from William Randolph Hearst, the flight was scheduled to begin at Lakehurst on Aug. 7, 1929. In exchange for his support, Hearst nsisted that the flight begin and end in the United States.

Lt. Cmdr. Charles E. Rosendahl, captain of the *Los Angeles* and hero of the *Shenandoah* tragedy, and Lady Hay-Drummond-Hay, again representing Hearst, were among the passengers who were aboard the *Graf Zeppelin* when it flew back across the Atlantic to its German base at Friedrichshafen. The crossing took 55 hours and 24 minutes to set a lighter-than-air transatlantic speed record. Additional passengers, all of whom were paying $2,500 to be part of the great adventure, joined the flight there.

Although the circumnavigation of the world was a monumental undertaking for that period, the flight itself turned out to be rather routine. Wherever the giant silver ship flew, it was welcomed with enthusiastic fanfare. Dr. Eckener couldn't have asked for better publicity for his pride and joy.

On Oct. 29, the *Graf Zeppelin* returned to Lakehurst following its transcontinental flight across the United States. The global adventure, covering 20,500 miles, had taken 12 days of flying time, or 21 days in elapsed time.

This time, following another Broadway parade, the airmen were greeted at the White House by a new president, Herbert Hoover.

When the *Graf Zeppelin* again returned to Germany, it began regular flights to South America and had a successful career until dictator Adolph Hitler had it torn apart in 1940—an ignominious end for a great lady of the sky.

A mobile mooring mast for dirigibles had been installed and tested at Lakehurst before the *Graf Zeppelin* returned from its circumnavigation of the globe. Developed under the direction of Lt. Cmdr. Rosendahl purely for naval purposes, the mast was hailed as a boon to commercial airship flights. The mobile mast, which ran on steel tracks, made it possible to move a dirigible in and out of the huge hangar at Lakehurst with fewer ground crew members.

At that time, dirigible development had begun to exceed that of fixed-wing aircraft.

Innovative Parachutes

Stanley Switlik

Inducted Aviation Hall of Fame of New Jersey, 1989

Stanley Switlik

In the early summer of 1929, Floyd Smith, a prominent early aviator, in cooperation with Stanley Switlik, president of the Switlik Parachute Company in Trenton, demonstrated his aircraft safety seat for representatives of the Army, Navy and Department of Commerce at Mercer County Airport.

The device was a parachute built into an aircraft seat that, in case of emergency, could be quickly strapped on in anticipation of leaving the ship. When the passengers were ready, the pilot pulled a lever and the floor of the plane sprung open dropping the passengers out the bottom of the fuselage.

The first test flight of the specially constructed monoplane was flown by Stuart Reice and the new seat was occupied by R. B. "Doc" Taylor, the Switlik parachute test jumper. Reice took the plane up 4,000 feet and then deliberately put it into a dangerous spin. As the small craft spun wildly, Reice pulled a lever and Taylor immediately dropped through the floor.

Centrifugal force was found to be sufficient to throw Taylor clear of the plane and a few seconds later the 'chute opened easily, without a shock. The experiment was deemed a great success.

Several weeks later, Marie Smullen, an employee of the Naval Aircraft factory in Philadelphia was dropped from the Smith seat at 1,000 feet and landed without a scratch. It was Ms. Smullen's first airplane ride and parachute jump.

"I got a big kick out of the drop," she said afterward. "I did it just for the love of thrills. I didn't know what

happened until the chute opened. Really there is nothing to it"

Although the tests were successful, Switlik's ejection seat idea didn't catch the fancy of the military or industry representatives who witnessed the tests and no business materialized from the seat project.

Switlik's firm was originally named the Canvas Leather Specialty Co., based in Trenton. A Polish immigrant, Switlik founded the company in 1920. At first it specialized in the production of golf and mail bags. By 1924, the company was making safety belts for aircraft and the following year began producing parachutes. The name was then changed to the Switlik Parachute Company.

Stanley Switlik became acquainted with the leading aviation personalities of the day, and in 1930, hired Parker D. Cramer, a pilot for the Sir Hubert Wilkin's Antarctic Expedition, as sales manager. In the late 1920s, the company had begun developing equipment that would help explorers survive in extreme cold climates. For Cmdr. Richard E. Byrd, Switlik designed an insulated flying suit to be worn on his first South Pole expedition. Four quick-detachable seat parachutes made in Trenton went along on Byrd's second antarctic expedition in 1933.

First Jump Tower Constructed

In 1934, when Amelia Earhart returned from a goodwill visit to Russia, she described parachute jump training towers she had seen the Russians using. Stanley Switlik, in partnership with Earhart's husband, George Palmer Putnum, developed the first U.S. parachute tower on Switlik's estate in Prospertown, NJ. In 1940, the nucleus of the first parachute corps in the United States Army received its initial jump training from a second Switlik tower built at Windsor, NJ. There were 48 enlisted men and two officers who were being trained as instructors for the 501st Parachute Battalion at Fort Benning, GA. Taller towers were erected at Fort Benning and Fort Bragg, NC, and are still used for paratrooper training.

With the outbreak of World War II in 1939, plans were drawn to expand the Switlik plant. In April 1940, a new 50,000 square foot building in Trenton was opened. It was estimated that 200 parachutes a week could be produced for both the Army and Navy. The company was then among the largest producers of parachutes in the world. .

When silk became scarce at the outset of World War II, Switlik used a revolutionary product called nylon for the first time. During the war, almost a million airmen and paratroopers worldwide used the Switlik detachable chest pack. And for the cramped quarters of ball-turret gunners aboard B-17 Flying Fortresses, Switlik designed and produced a compact parachute in 1943.

Stanley Switlick and his clever crew of inovators developed dummy parachutists, weighing about 40 pounds each, which were used successfully to create an entire bogus airborne division during amphibious landings in southern France and the Philippines. The dummies were equipped with demolition packs that simulated automatic rifle fire as they descended and then destroyed the dummy when it reached the ground.

During the Korean Conflict, American paratroopers jumped with especially heavy loads, so Switlik developed a 'chute that was less bulky. He sold the rights to that parachute and the detachable chest pack to the U.S. government for $1.

In 1947, in cooperation with Boeing Aircraft, the Switlik Company designed and produced the first parachutes for missile recovery.

The company moved to Hamilton Township in 1951. Into the 1980s, it continued to produce life vests and life rafts for the shipping and airline industries and parachutes for special purposes.

For those who had successfully bailed out of aircraft in a real emergency, Switlik organized the Caterpillar Club. Membership served as a tangible form of recognition for those jumpers and helped establish camaraderie among them. The best-known survivors of an emergency jump are Eddie Rickenbacker, Jimmy Doolittle, Charles A. Lindbergh and President George Bush.

Stanley Switlik died in 1981 at age 91. His son Richard assumed the ownership of the company, and his sons Richard Jr., Gregory and Stanley have held executive positions over the years.

Few companies in the world have done more to save aviators' lives than Switlik Parachute of New Jersey.

New Standard Aircraft

The New Standard Aircraft Corp., under the direction of Charles Healy Day, began to manufacture five-place, open cockpit biplanes in an old silk mill in Paterson. The aircraft were updated versions of Day's popular Standard J-1 used as trainers during World War I, the postal air service in 1919 and by barnstorming pilots throughout the 1920s.

Business was brisk for the new company. Orders were received for planes to carry mail and passengers, tow banners and to use as Navy trainers. The aircraft parts were built in Paterson and assembled at Teterboro by Aron "Duke" Krantz and R.J. Mathews on the damp sod at the south end of the field. Clyde Pangborn test flew each of them.

At the same time, the New Standard Flying Service was organized at Teterboro to operate the airfield, teach flying and carry passengers. Another Gates alumnus, Ives MacKinney, headed the operation.

In October, the corporation announced the appointment of Lt. Frederick Schauss as a sales and demonstration pilot in the south. He had been the operations manager of Congressional Airport, Washington, DC. With the addition of Schauss, the corporation had a staff of six demonstration salesmen—Clyde Pangborn, Carl Dixon, Hugh Herndon, Homer E. Fackler and George Daws.

As a promotional stunt for the new company, Pangborn and Dixon planned to attempt an endurance flight at the New York State Fair at Syracuse using one of the new biplanes. Their goal was to stay aloft more than 500 hours. Pilot Hugh Herndon , who had inherited family wealth, financed the project and supplied the chase plane that was to be used to refuel the Standard, christened *Empire State Standard.* Practice refueling runs were made in the skies over Bergen County. Herndon, Warren B. Smith and Fackler flew the chase plane, while 17-year-old Sam Barnitt of Hasbrouck Heights, worked night and day with the pilots keeping the chase plane airworthy. In August, Pangborn and Dixon flew for several days above the Syracuse fair grounds, but eventually engine trouble forced them down before a new record was established.

First Aerial Police

Many pilots who had migrated to Teterboro during the 1920s became important citizens of the northern New Jersey area. They contributed their time and effort to charitable causes and others assisted in times of emergency.

When Bergen County's flamboyant police chief Peter J. Siccardi organized the first aerial police force in the United States, he was able to recruit some of the nation's best known aviation personalities to participate. Anthony Fokker donated an airplane and Bernt Balchen, Clyde Pangborn, Leon Allen and Hugh Wells joined county patrolman Charles LoPresti, a licensed pilot, as deputy county officers.

To demonstrate the use of the police plane, Siccardi kept traffic moving prior to the 1929 air show for the benefit of the Elks Crippled Kiddies Fund. To help raise money for the children, aviators volunteered their services. Warren Smith, flying a New Standard biplane, astounded the crowd by making an outside loop, putting him among the first five pilots in America to achieve that feat. Duke Krantz gave his last wing-walking exhibition, and Charles Massa of Paterson attempted to set a new parachute altitude record when he bailed out at 15,000 feet.

After its initial burst on the scene, the flying police force became dormant when the plane was damaged and the county Freeholders refused to provide funds for its repair.

In 1931, mechanics at the Fokker plant decided to repair the plane and in August, Billy Diehl, accompanied by patrolman LoPresti, took it up for a test flight.

Siccardi announced that no designated patrols would be flown, and that the plane would be used only when there was a special need.

The plane proved its worth a few months later, when Pangborn flew a deathly sick patient from Teterboro Airport to Bergen Pines Hospital in Paramus for emergency treatment. Pangborn was forced to land on a small farm that bordered the hospital grounds. For his heroic humanitarian efforts, the Bergen County Chamber of Commerce awarded him a gold watch.

First To Rome
Roger Q. Williams

Inducted Aviation Hall of Fame Of New Jersey, 1975

For almost a year, Roger Q. Williams had planned a flight from the United States to Rome. In the late fall of 1928, his first attempt to fly a pontoon-equipped plane named *Roma* over the 4,000-mile route had been aborted because of engine trouble. But the worldwide publicity given the unsuccessful flight aroused the attention of William Randolph Hearst, the newspaper publisher, who offered Williams his plane *Green Flash* in exchange for exclusive rights to the story for his newspaper syndicate. Williams described what happened in a personal memoir written for the Aviation Hall of Fame of New Jersey:

This offer was like a gift from Heaven, so I readily accepted without a moment of hesitation. The Green Flash, *by the way, was a Bellanca J plane similar to the* Columbia *(flown by Chamberlin and Levine to Germany in 1927).*

I took possession of the Green Flash *in its hangar at Curtiss Field, LI. Piero Bonelli [his co-pilot] and I looked it over preparatory to a flight test. Then bad news arrived in the form of an urgent request from Mr. Hearst that he would like me to consider Lou Yancey as my navigator in lieu of Bonelli. I felt sorry for Piero but something told me it was for the best. On the flight I found Yancey to be a better co-pilot than a navigator and myself a better navigator than I had expected to be.*

The Green Flash *was ready and reliable for a long flight because Martin Jensen has tested its worthiness on a solo endurance flight of longer duration than our proposed flight to Rome from New York.*

"A short flight from Curtiss Field to Teterboro Airport found the [engine of] Green Flash *being hurriedly groomed for its mission by Ken Boedecker, Ben Zabora, Ted Sorensen (Wright Corp. engineers) and myself. Then we were off for Old Orchard, ME, for the take-off to Rome.*

Roger Q. Williams and Lewis Yancey.

History now records the attempted take-off of the Green Flash *carrying a world record of two-and-one-half times its empty weight that bright May day. At the last few yards of the actual take-off, the right wheel struck a deep bleeder hole in the run way sand and collapsed. Down went the right wing tip to scrape the sand. Down dipped the nose to shatter the wooden propeller. Up went the tail high into the air. When the tail dropped with a bang onto the sand, two top longerons were bent beyond repair. Luckily for Yancey and myself, neither of us was hurt or even bruised. But our hopes were gone with the wind. We were without a plane.*

Fate must have been watching over us on that Memorial Day for the phones from New York were ringing like mad to reach us. Hearst's happy voice asked me. 'Do you still want to make that flight to Rome? Can you get another plane for it?' I said, 'Yes if Mrs. Stillman will sell us her Bellanca 'North Star'. To make a long story short, we contacted Mrs. Stillman and bought her North Star.

We flew it to Teterboro Airport. We gave the North Star a new name —The Pathfinder—*and proceeded to repaint the silver fuselage light green to provide a fine background for its new name in large letters. It did not take Boedecker and Zabora long to tune up the engine and see that everything was ready for its venture. A short farewell to friends and well-wishers, and we took off for Old Orchard for my third attempt to make the flight from New York to Rome, which must have been destined for me.*

The Pathfinder *and its crew made the archives of aviation on July 8th, 9th and 10th, 1929 reaching Rome in 41 hours.*

Williams didn't mention that because of strong headwinds, he and Yancey ran out of fuel off the coast of Spain and had to land at Santander, about 3,400 miles from Old Orchard and 1,000 miles west of Rome. They had flown 31 hours and 41 minutes. The following day they flew on to the Italian capital. They had encountered fog for a greater portion of the Atlantic crossing necessitating blind flying for the most part.

First Blind Flight
Lt. James Doolittle

A small company specializing in aviation communication devices located in Boonton Township, NJ played a leading role in the first "blind flight" of an aircraft. The Aircraft Radio Corp, a division of Radio Frequency Laboratories developed a homing radio. It was one of three instruments needed by a young Army Air Corps officer, Lt, James Doolittle, to become the first man to take off and land an airplane by the use of instruments alone. The other instruments were a Kollsman "sensitive" barometric altimeter and a Sperry artificial horizon.

The successful test flight, sponsored by the Guggenheim Fund for the Promotion of Aeronautics led to the development of the all-weather flying capabilities now taken for granted.

Doolittle, who had built a solid reputation as a talented racing pilot, was on leave from his army duties to work with Harry Guggenheim in the establishment of the Guggenheim Laboratory at Mitchel Field, LI, The task was to perfect instrument flying of which the majority of airmen in the 1920s had little knowledge.

On Sept. 24, 1929, accompanied by Lt. Benjamin S. Kelsey as the safety pilot, Doolittle took off and landed a Consolidated NY-2 military trainer while flying under a light-proof hood stretched over the rear cockpit. The flight lasted 15 minutes over Mitchel Field. During the entire test, Lt. Kelsey never touched the NY-2's control stick.

Radio Frequency Laboratories (RFL) was founded by several young industrial scientists in the rural township of Boonton. Under the leadership of Richard W. Seabury Sr. and Lewis H. Hull, who held a doctorate in physics from Harvard University, the young scientists were intent on creating inventions and acquiring patents in the new field of radio receiver equipment.

Hull was able to attract a few capable inventors in radio circuitry and as their list of patents grew, business prospered. Leading broadcast receiver manufacturers were using their inventions.

In the late 1920s, Seabury and Hull decided to create a subsidiary of RFL to develop aircraft radio equipment. The new company, called Aircraft Radio Corporation (ARC), began to develop lightweight receivers

to work in conjunction with radio-range beacons that would guide air mail pilots from one airport to another. The first beacons were installed at Hadley Field, Bellefonte, Cleveland and College Park, MD. The initial tests of the new equipment were conducted at Hadley by ARC's test pilot, former Army Captain Russell Luff Meredith.

The logistics of getting new equipment to Hadley and installing and testing it soon became burdensome. Meredith suggested they establish an airstrip in Boonton on a 105-acre apple orchard. The runway was laid out on the flat land. A hangar and two other buildings housing a laboratory, an instrument shop and offices were constructed along the west side of the strip.

As business grew, the company acquired a Berliner parasol-winged monoplane and eventually a Fokker Super Universal.

Jimmy Doolittle would often hop over to Boonton in his Vought Corsair for installation or adjustments of his radio equipment. On a number of occasions, he'd spend a weekend at the home of Lewis Hull and his family in the township. Hull recalled a particular Saturday that his wife flew with Doolittle:

"One Saturday, Jimmy asked my wife to fly with him and they rushed over to ARC (where Doolittle's Corsair was hangared). After tightly strapping her in the rear cockpit, he zoomed up and looped 13 times, the last one being an outside loop, of which he had been the inventor. His passenger temporarily lost her taste for this flying game."

Colonial Air Transport was ARC's first passenger airline customer. Colonial had Model B radio-beacon receivers installed in all its planes.

In the early 1930s, Hull and his engineers worked closely with U.S. Army Air Corps personnel to develop a pilot-operated, two-way voice radio command set. The project had the backing of Gen. Benjamin D. Foulois, then the Assistant Chief of the Corps. The final product was a first in military aircraft, one of many important communication devices developed by ARC over the next decade.

From 1934 to 1940, ARC remained entirely in the military communication field. Sales steadily grew and the facilities in Boonton were enlarged to accommodate the increased staff. During World War II, ARC employed more than 1,100 people. Gross sales reached a peak of more than $22 million in 1944.

Following the war, ARC began to cultivate the civil aviation market. After two lean years, 1946-47, the company attracted a fair share of the market for communication-navigation equipment in business aircraft.

In 1952, Laurence and David Rockefeller acquired a substantial block of ARC stock and Lewis Hull, who had served as president since 1930, became chairman

Russell Luff Meredith

of the board. William F. Cassidy, Jr., an able engineer/administrator was elected president of the company.

In 1959, the Rockefeller interests arranged a merger with the Cessna Aircraft Company of Wichita, KS, one of ARC's oldest and most valued customers. The company was renamed the Aircraft Radio & Control Division of the Cessna company and remained in business at its original base in Boonton Township until 1984 when Sperry Flight Systems purchased the company and moved it to Phoenix, AZ.

Two Legends
Curtiss and Wright

On July 5, 1929, the Wright Aeronautical Corporation of Paterson and the Curtiss Aeroplane & Motor Corporation of Buffalo, NY, merged to form the Curtiss-Wright (C-W) Corporation. Thus, two legendary names in aviation were welded together as a single giant entity. Included in the merger were the Keystone Aircraft Corp. of Bristol, PA, an aircraft manufacturing company, the Curtiss Airplane Co. of Wichita, KS and the Curtiss Airport Corp., which leased airports from coast to coast through the Curtiss Flying Service, a teaching and charter organization. The merger couldn't have come at a less opportune time. Three months after the agreements were signed, the stock market crashed and sales of aircraft and engines plummeted. The 1929 Wright Aeronautical stockholders report announced net profits of more than $900,000 as compared to almost $2.5 million for the previous year. Richard F. Hoyt became the chairman of the new corporation; Thomas A Morgan, president and Charles Lawrance was named a vice president. Guy Vaughan assumed the position of president of Wright Aeronautical. Within a year, Lawrance resigned to establish his own research company in Linden.

Wright-powered aircraft continued to set records. In January of 1929, the Whirlwind powered Fokker *Question Mark,* an Army transport plane, under the command of Maj. Carl Spaatz, set a refueling endurance record of 150 hours and 40 minutes. In April, Elinor Smith, flying a Whirlwind-powered Bellanca, established a new world's endurance record for women of 26 hours, 21 minutes.

A Wright Apache plane, flown by Lt. Apollo Soucek, USN, set a new world altitude record of 39,140 feet over Washington, DC, on May 8, 1929. Less than a month later, he flew the same plane, with pontoons attached, and established a seaplane altitude record of 38,555 feet. In June of 1930, the lieutenant broke his own land plane record, flying to a height of 43,166 feet.

In June of 1929, Leon Allen, the Wright test pilot set a record of sorts himself. Flying the Wright-built AO-3 Mohawk plane, called the *Iron Horse,* that was used as a test-bed for new engines, Allen suddenly found himself sitting in the quiet fuselage as the engine began to fall earthward. He explained what happened in the *Wright Engine Builder,* the Curtiss-Wright house publication:

As I was taking off over the Navy Yard buildings [Philadelphia] and the Delaware River I throttled the engine a little as soon as the speed was up to about 80 miles per hour and climbed slowly in a large circle. Intending to check all the instruments for a minute before leaving the field, I leveled out at 2,500 feet and opened the throttle full. In a few seconds there was a terrific explosion. My head hit something and I sat down in the seat so hard that my spine felt as though it was being telescoped. My vision seemed to fade out for a few seconds. My first thought was that the stabilizer had let go but I soon realized that if that were the case the ship would be doing a nose dive and not what it seemed to be doing, a very tight loop. My next thought was that the engine had let go.

By that time, things had slowed up enough so that I could get my head up out of the cockpit and look over the side. There was no engine in sight and wires, thermometer connections and tachometer shafts were streaming back along the cockpit.

Allen had no alternative but to jump for his life. When he tried to stand up in the cockpit he found that the G-force created by the rapidly descending plane had him trapped in his seat. With a great effort, he pushed himself up and slid out over the fuselage until he fell clear of the plane. He parachuted safely to the ground, suffering only a wrenched back and a few cuts and bruises. The *Iron Horse* was a total wreck and never rebuilt.

In 1930, the Curtiss Corp. transferred its entire engine manufacturing division to Paterson and the Buffalo plant assumed the total responsibility for aircraft design and construction.

At the same time, the company announced it would begin production of two new Cyclone engines—the R-1750-E, that produced 525 hp and the R-1820-E, rated at 575 hp. The latter had nearly three times the power of the Wright Whirlwind used on Charles Lindbergh's *Spirit of St. Louis* just three years earlier.In Caldwell, NJ, the new Curtiss-Essex Airport was dedicated that same year and a large air show was held. As thousands watched, Frank Hawks, Al Williams and Reginald Pete Brooks performed. In addition, all the new Curtiss aircraft models were demonstrated, including the big, 18-passenger Curtiss Condor airliner.

Guy W. Vaughan

Thomas Morgan was named chairman of the Curtiss-Wright Corp. in 1935, and was succeeded as president by Guy W. Vaughan.

Vaughan, a Bay Shore, Long Island, native, had begun his engineering career in 1898 with the Desberon Motor Co. of New Rochelle, NY. Two years later, he joined the Standard Automobile Co., eventually rising to the office of vice president and chief engineer.

During that period, he began racing cars and won many events behind the wheel of a French Decauville race car. His racing activities greatly enhanced his reputation as a driver and automotive engineer.

In 1909, he designed and developed the Vaughan Car, which was marketed with moderate success by the W.A. Woods Co. of Kingston, NY. About 80 Vaughan cars were sold at a time when the automobile was still considered a rich man's toy.

He worked for several other automotive companies until the outbreak of World War I when he joined the Wright-Martin Co. in New Brunswick, as quality manager. Later, he became the factory manager for both the New Brunswick and Long Island plants. Under his management, the production of Hispano-Suiza aircraft engines jumped from 12 engines a month to 35 engines a day.

Following the war, Vaughan returned to the automotive business and held high administrative positions with several companies before joining the Wright Aeronautical Corp. of Paterson in 1925 as vice president and general manager.

Throughout the next two decades, Curtiss-Wright became the most dominant name in the aircraft engine field. The accomplishments of Whirlwind and Cyclone engines on both commercial and military aircraft from 1935 to 1940 cover the entire spectrum of aviation's most historic events. Some of the more noteworthy included:

Cyclone engines powered the first all-metal, stressed skin, low-wing, commercial aircraft by Boeing and Douglas. They were the forerunners of today's modern airliners.

A Cyclone-powered Loening amphibian was flown by Thor Solberg, with radio operator Paul Oscanyan, from New York to Norway in 1935.

Howard Hughes flew his Northrop Gamma, with a single Cyclone engine, from Burbank, CA, to Newark in a record time.

Louise Thaden and Blanche Noyes set the women's east-west transcontinental record in 1936 in a Whirlwind-powered Beechcraft monoplane.

In 1938, six B-17 Flying Fortresses, each with four Wright Cyclone engines, made a goodwill flight to Buenos Aires and return, then the longest non-stop mass flight in the history of the U.S. Army Air Corps.

Howard Hughes and four crewmen flew a Cyclone-powered Lockheed monoplane around the world in three days, 19 hours and 8 minutes on July 10-14, 1938.

In May 1939, the first Pan American Airways transatlantic flight was accomplished by the Boeing flying boat, *Yankee Clipper*, with four Cyclone 14, 1,500 hp engines. See 1940

South Pole Conquered
Byrd and Balchen

At 8:55 a.m., Friday Nov. 29, 1929, the *New York Times* received a message from Antarctica:

"My calculation indicates that we have reached the vicinity of the South Pole, flying high for a survey. The airplane is in good shape, crew all well. Will soon turn north. We can see an almost limitless polar plateau. Our departure from the Pole was at 1:25 p.m."

South Pole pilots, Harold June, Dean Smith, Bernt Balchen.

The brief historic report had come from Cmdr. Richard E. Byrd, who, with three companions, had become the first man to navigate a flight over the South Pole, The men had flown 1,600 miles in 18 hours, 59 minutes.

Bernt Balchen, who had been one of two pilots aboard the *America* on Byrd's 1927 transatlantic flight, piloted the Ford trimotor "Floyd Bennett," named in memory of the Commander's late friend and pilot on their 1926 flight over the North Pole. The co-pilot was Harold I. June. The fourth member of the party was photographer Ashley C. McKinley.

The Floyd Bennett was powered by two Wright Whirlwind engines slung under each wing and a more powerful Wright Cyclone engine in the nose of the plane.

Although Byrd's epic announcement to the world had been terse and devoid of dramatics, the flight, and for that matter the entire two-year expedition, had been filled with excitement, beyond the imagination of any Hollywood writer.

The flight to the South Pole had left the base camp at 3:29 p.m., Thursday, Nov. 28 (Thanksgiving Day). The trimotor Ford flew about five hours before the Queen Maud mountain range loomed on the horizon. Balchen guided the monoplane toward a narrow glacier pass 10,000 feet above sea level, but when the ship was 1,000 feet below the crest of the glacier, he realized the fuel-heavy craft was not going to make it over the top. He signaled Byrd to drop weight from the plane, and as McKinley slid two 125-pound bags of food through the Ford's trap door, Balchen struggled with the controls and managed to clear the gleaming ice ridge by less than 500 feet.

Smiles lit the faces of the four airmen for they knew the greatest hazard was past and the South Pole now lay dead ahead. Nine hours and 45 minutes after lift-off, Byrd's terse message was relayed to the world.

The previous March, Balchen, June and geologist Lawrence Gould flew a Fokker Universal to the foot of the Rockefeller mountain range to allow Gould to gather rock specimens. A violent Antarctic storm caught the men on the ground and blew the Fokker about a half mile from the explorer's camp, smashing it on the ice. When the storm subsided, Byrd, pilot Dean Smith, and radioman Malcolm Hanson flew to their rescue in a single-engine Fairchild monoplane. The men had been marooned in the Antarctic wasteland for 15 days.

Byrd's Antarctic expedition had sailed from Hoboken aboard the square-rigged *City of New York* in late August, 1928. There were 32 men on the ship. The remaining 51 expedition members sailed on the *Eleanor Bolling,* named for Byrd's mother.

When they arrived at the Rose Ice Shelf in late November, the Antarctic summer was just beginning to bloom. The expedition's members worked throughout December creating the underground home that would be known as "Little America".

In June, 1930, the South Pole expedition returned to New York and was welcomed by a half-million people along the lower Broadway ticker-tape parade route. Although Byrd was lionized, he took the greatest pride in the fact that not a single man had been lost on the expedition.

Byrd would become an admiral and lead three more Navy sponsored expeditions to the Antarctic over the next decade. The Fokker trimotor, *Josephine Ford,* used on the flight to the North Pole, and the Ford trimotor Floyd Bennett, that flew over the South Pole, are preserved today in the Henry Ford Museum at Dearborn, MI.

Dean C. Smith

Inducted Aviation Hall of Fame of New Jersey, 1986

When Dean Smith left the Postal Service at Hadley Airport, a tribute to him was published in the October 1928, issue of the airport's monthly publication. It read:

Commander Richard E. Byrd selected Hadley Airport's oldest pilot in the person of Dean Smith, to accompany him to the South Pole, where vast aerial explorations will take place.

Dean Smith is the oldest pilot stationed at Hadley Airport in number of hours in the air and was one of a group of intrepid aviators which included the late Harry Chandler, who was killed in a deplorable accident about a year ago; James DeWitt Hill, a graduate engineer, and Lloyd Bertaud, pilots of Old Glory which carried these two splendid pilots to their death in the ocean somewhere east of St. Johns, Newfoundland, where the ill-fated flight to Rome was started; Wesley L. Smith who is now operations director for National Air Transport, Inc., contractors on the air mail route to Cleveland; and Charles Ames who died when his plane crashed into a mountain in Pennsylvania during a heavy fog.

Smith was known about the airport as a general good fellow, with a pleasant personality and extensive knowledge of the upper air current. He was a World War I flyer with a fine record and while stationed here displayed his knowledge of how to handle all types of aeroplanes.

For more than two years, Smith made his regular trips to and from Cleveland with from 50 to 2,000 pounds of mail and express. His record as an airmail pilot is a brilliant one, as he never had a 'crash', although weather conditions prevented him from getting through to the terminal several times.

The best wishes of those who knew him and worked with him accompany him on his trip to the South Pole.

Commander Byrd selected him to take the place of the late Floyd Bennett. Smith's experience is expected to be a great asset to the Byrd expedition.

Throughout the 1930s, Smith flew for both National Air Transport (forerunner of United Airlines) and American Airlines as a Senior Captain. Just after Germany attacked Poland and World War II began, he joined the Curtiss-Wright Corp. airplane division as director of sales in Buffalo, NY. In 1942, he advanced to director of transport.

A year later, he was employed by the Fairchild Engine and Airplane Corp. with offices in New York City. That was followed by post war positions with Hughes Aircraft and the Douglas Corp. When he retired in the late 1950s, he wrote an autobiography, *By the Seat of My Pants*, that received critical acclaim.

During his years of flying air mail from Hadley Field and commercial aircraft from Newark Airport, Smith and his wife Beth lived in the New Jersey towns of Summit, East Orange and Maplewood. Smith died in Easton, MD. in 1987.

CHRONOLOGY OF OTHER AERONAUTICAL EVENTS AND ACHIEVEMENTS
1920 to 1929
1920

- A large dirigible hangar was built at Cape May as a supplemental field for Lakehurst. It was 800 feet long.

1921

- On State Highway 35, a few miles south of Long Branch, NJ, Lt. John Casey, a World War I army pilot, established a small airfield. In the Winter of 1923, he flew passengers off the frozen Shrewsbury River, near Red Bank, NJ, in ski-equipped planes. He then established Red Bank Airport which he operated until 1938.

- 1924: Army pilot Leslie Arnold, a long-time Leonia, NJ, resident, was one of eight Army pilots who became the first to fly around the world in Douglas World Cruisers. They flew 27,553 miles in 175 days and spent 371 hours in the open cockpit planes.

- A young lady from Trenton, made a splash along the French Cote d'Azur flying her Curtiss flying boat over the Promenade des Anglais in Nice. Eleanor Van Vredenburgh was the first woman to fly a seaplane in Europe. Upon her return to the United States, the adventurous lady married her flight instructor Paul Micelli of Sea Girt.

1924

- Brothers, John and "Beans" Hunter crash-landed in a cornfield along Passaic Street in Rochelle Park, NJ, and an airport was born. They convinced the Trautwein family to use the field as a private landing site in exchange for teaching their 16-year-old son, Fred, to fly. Once young Trautwein learned to fly, he and his father established an airport on a portion of the 100-acre farm. Trautwein's airport became a favorite with many local pilots until it closed in the mid-1930s.

1926

- Leo Stevens of Englewood who built a reputation as a balloonist, took off in a small balloon from his home town and flew northeast the entire night. He landed in New York State 350 miles north of New Jersey.

- Colonial Air Transport pilot Le Roy Thompson of Hackensack one of the three pilots who flew the first air mail between Hadley Field and Boston in 1926, was killed Oct. 30, when his five-passenger Fairchild monoplane crashed in a field a few miles from Hadley Field. Thompson was ferrying the plane to Teterboro to be used for weekend sightseeing flights. Flying with the 32-year-old pilot were his fiancee, Elizabeth McGowan of Westwood, NJ, George Haubner of Hillsdale, NJ, and his roommate Wesley Hubbell. Two hunters who were almost hit by the falling plane said it dove at full power into the field as it was making a turn at approximately 200 feet above the ground.

1928

- January - Clarence Chamberlin and Roger Q. Williams, flying a Bellanca monoplane, set an endurance record of 51 hours and 52 minutes over Mitchel Field, NY.

- Flying from Teterboro Airport, Lt. Royal V. Thomas and Vaughn Weatherby, a mechanic, were killed when their Bellanca monoplane, *Reliance,* crashed in Moonachie, NJ. The two men were flight-testing the aircraft at Teterboro, prior to attempting an endurance flight. Thomas, a former Army flier from Durant, OK, had ambitions to fly solo across the Atlantic Ocean. He had bested Lindbergh's flying time to Europe during his first endurance flight over Roosevelt Field on Long Island, staying in the air 35 hours, 24 minutes and 59 seconds. Just prior to the crash, witnesses reported that they saw a wing come loose from the plane.

1929

- In early January, an Army Fokker C-2A established a flight endurance record of 150 hours and 40 minutes. The big trimotor was refueled in flight by a hose from another plane. The two planes made 37 contacts and 4,190 gallons of fuel were transferred from one plane to the other. The crew, commanded by Carl "Toohy" Spaatz, included: Capt. Ira C. Eaker, Lt. Elwood Quesada, Lt. Harry Halverson and Sgt. Roy Hoe.

Newark Airport--1930s.

in Moonachie, NJ. The two men were flight-testing the aircraft at Teterboro, prior to attempting an endurance flight. Thomas, a former Army flier from Durant, OK, had ambitions to fly solo across the Atlantic Ocean. He had bested Lindbergh's flying time to Europe during his first endurance flight over Roosevelt Field on Long Island, staying in the air 35 hours, 24 minutes and 59 seconds. Just prior to the crash, witnesses reported that they saw a wing come loose from the plane.

1929

- In early January, an Army Fokker C-2A established a flight endurance record of 150 hours and 40 minutes. The big trimotor was refueled in flight by a hose from another plane. The two planes made 37 contacts and 4,190 gallons of fuel were transferred from one plane to the other. The crew, commanded by Carl "Toohy" Spaatz, included: Capt. Ira C. Eaker, Lt. Elwood Quesada, Lt. Harry Halverson and Sgt. Roy Hoe.

- Flight Interstate, Inc., a feeder airline based at Newark Airport and headed by Leland Dorrothy, received the first air freight issued in the United States.

- Mrs. Keith Miller was named chief test pilot of the Victor Aircraft Co., Mount Holly, NJ. It was a

position held by very few women in the United States at that time.

- Catherine C. Barton of Englewood, designed a flight medal requested by the Navy Department to commemorate the first transatlantic flight of the NC-4 in 1919.

- Major George A. Vaughn, president of Eastern Aeronautical Corp., based at Newark Metropolitan Airport, announced the purchase of the General Aviation Co. operating at New York Airports in Syracuse, Elmira and Geneva.

- Vincent J. Burnelli, president of the Uppercu-Burnelli Corp. in Keyport, announced that the Societa Trans Adriatica of Italy would begin manufacturing 50 of the 20-passenger aircraft designed by Burnelli. It was the first time manufacturing rights for an American plane were granted to a European company.

- A plane owned and piloted by William Taff, with Mrs. William Jeannine and Roger James Ryan as passengers, crashed through the roof of Governor Morgan F. Larson's bedroom in the Little White House in Sea Girt, NJ.

Amazingly, no one was hurt. The governor was not home at the time, but his elderly mother had been in his bedroom just moments before the crash.

1930
Wild Glider Ride
Ralph S. Barnaby

Inducted Aviation Hall of Fame of New Jersey, 1981

Capt. Ralph Barnaby

Except for those tycoons whose fortunes rose and fell with the fluctuation of the stock market, the full impact of the 1929 crash did not strike at most Americans' pocketbooks until the early 1930s. Although money belts were tightened, there was still enough cash about to finance experimental and record flights.

During the first month of the new decade, Captain Ralph S. Barnaby of the U.S. Navy proved that a glider could be successfully launched from beneath a dirigible in flight. The date of the daring experiment was Jan. 31, 1930.

Fifty years later, Barnaby, then the aviation exhibits consultant for the Franklin Institute in Philadelphia, PA, described his flight in the 1980 issue of the *Franklin Institute News.*

It's fifty years now since I made a newspaper headline with a glider flight I made from the Navy's dirigible USS Los Angeles. This flight — a "first"— was undertaken ostensibly to determine the feasibility of using a glider for tactical purposes. I suspect, however, that the timing of my flight was somewhat influenced by the publicity Frank Hawks had received in the fall of 1929 by his glider tow across the country. Whatever the motive, the idea was not mine, it was Admiral Moffett's. The admiral, then Chief of the Navy Bureau of Aeronautics, was always quick to recognize opportunities to bring Naval Aviation to public notice.

During the summer of 1929, I had become the first American ever to obtain a Federation Aeronautique Internationale Soaring Certificate.

One day in the late fall of that year—after Hawk's feat—I got a call that the admiral would like to see me. When I walked into his office, Admiral Moffett said, Barnaby, would it be possible to launch a glider from the Los Angeles ?" As I gasped, he said, "Think it over and come in to see me tomorrow, because if your answer is 'yes,' you are going to do it!"

I slept very little that night. By morning, however, I had the answer. It was 'yes' provided the Navy could obtain a glider of the type with which I was most familiar, the German-built "Pruefling."

Things started to move immediately. The glider I had used that summer was purchased and shipped to Lakehurst, NJ, where assembly proceeded rapidly and according to my plans. On Jan. 28, 1930, I was ordered to Lakehurst to await suitable weather for the drop.

Since the weather forecast for Jan. 31 was favorable, the glider was attached to the airship in the hangar on the afternoon of the 30th. I made a few practice descents down the ladder from the airship into the cockpit. This descent into a cramped glider cockpit, in itself, was no small feat with a seatpack parachute dangling against my legs.

The 31st dawned clear and cold —16 degrees F, to be exact — and plans were made to walk the Los Angeles out of the hangar at 7 a.m.. But the hangar doors wouldn't open, the tracks had iced up. Next, while preparing the ship, the ground crew poked a hole in the nose of the envelope. By the time this had been repaired, the hangar doors had been freed and we were ready to go. It was around nine o'clock when we finally took off. I rode in the airship's control car during the takeoff, while we cruised down toward Atlantic City and the coast, gradually climbing to the 3,000 foot altitude requested. As we approached the Lakehurst Naval Air Station, again, I went back through the ship, along the catwalk to the station where Lt. Cal Bolster was standing by the glider release gear, and prepared to climb down the ladder to the glider.

Though the ship's engines were idled, it was an icy blast which hit me as I climbed down the ladder, removed and handed up the control-locking mechanism, folded myself up into the tiny cockpit, secured the cockpit cover around me, and watched the ladder being drawn up.

The engines roared again and the airspeed indicator needle climbed slowly toward 40 knots as the town of Lakehurst slid slowly under us.

Many thoughts flashed through my mind as I sat there waiting, cold and a little scared. I wondered how I had ever let myself be maneuvered into this position. Oh yes, I was the Navy's glider expert. Don't I hold the No. 1 Soaring Certificate? Actually, my total glider time as of that moment totaled about 45 minutes, of which 15 minutes and 6 seconds had been in one flight — the certificate flight six months before.

It must have been quite a sight from the ground. The huge Los Angeles flanked on either side by two of the Navy's larger non-rigid blimps, trailed by the little ZMC-2, the Navy's metal-skinned dirigible, and a number of miscellaneous airplanes, all carrying news photographers, reporters, and observers.

As the hangar slid under the nose, I looked up at Cal Bolster and gave him the thumbs-up signal. A moment later, he gave me a goodbye wave and pulled the release.

My chief concern had been the possibility of being slammed against the bottom of the airship or into one of the five whirling propellers. I might well have spared myself the worry. The glider dropped away like a shot! If I hadn't had a well-tightened safety belt, it might have left me behind. I leveled off about a hundred feet below the airship, and let the glider slow down to 30 miles per hour — its normal gliding speed — breathed a sigh of relief, and settled back to enjoy the ride. The descent took a little over thirteen minutes.

I probably could have stayed up longer, but by that time I was thoroughly chilled and the prospect of some hot coffee spurred me on. After several circuits of the field, I headed the glider in toward the group of people gathered alongside the hangar. The skid on the bottom of the fuselage touched, slid smoothly along the snow-covered field, and the flight was over.

It was in the landing that my lack of practice showed up. I undershot the designated spot by a couple of hundred yards, much to the annoyance of the movie men, who were unable to get any good close-ups of the landing. I was also a little annoyed for, if I do say so myself, it was a good landing — except photographically speaking.

A few minutes later I was in the hangar drinking the coffee and answering questions.

Barnaby was born in Meadville, PA, in 1893. His family moved to New York City in 1900 where he attended local schools and eventually graduated from Columbia University with a mechanical engineering degree.

His first job in 1915 was with the Elco Company in Bayonne, NJ, builders of cabin cruisers and speed boats. In early 1917, he joined the engineering department of Standard Aero Corp. in Plainfield, working under the direction of Charles Healy Day and his assistant Jean A. Roche, a former college classmate of Barnaby's.

With America's declaration of war, he joined the Navy, attended the Naval Aviation Inspectors School and was commissioned an Ensign. He served in Europe for six months, and at war's end, returned to the United States in time to help ready the Navy's Curtiss flying boats for the first transatlantic flight.

Throughout his 30 years in the Navy his assignments were related to his engineering background from the construction of the Navy's first airship, the *U.S.S. Shenandoah*, to the development of remote control aircraft and missiles. When he retired in 1947, he held the rank of captain.

He immediately joined the staff of the Franklin Institute as head of the Aeronautics Section, and in 1963 suffered a heart attack. When he recovered he became an exhibits consultant to the director of the science museum with the title "Keeper Emeritus of the Hall of Aviation."

Barnaby died in 1986 at age 93.

Jersey City Airport
Ruth Nichols

Inducted Aviation Hall of Fame of New Jersey 1988

Ruth Nichols

A few months after the Jersey City Airport was officially dedicated in April, 1930, by Arthur Potterton, the city's commissioner of Parks and Property, Clarence Chamberlin was induced by the Jersey City Flying Club to establish his airplane manufacturing plant in the city.

The club offered Chamberlin the use of its hangar in exchange for hours of free flying time. Club members flew mostly with Chamberlin's instructors, "Waspy" Sherman and Hunter Zeth, in either a Kinner Swallow or an OX-5-powered Swallow.

Chamberlin called his company the Crescent Aircraft Corp., and his planes were designed for Navy use on photographic missions.

A young and talented aviatrix, Ruth Nichols, joined the Crescent sales department and began her record-shattering career under the tutelage of Chamberlin.

In her book, *Wings for Life,* Nichols described the Jersey City flying facility:

The little, improvised airport was only a thousand feet in one direction and little more in the other, with, of course, the usual obstacles of telephone wires and tall buildings on three sides and the bay on the fourth.

Nichols had built a reputation as a competent aviatrix working for Aviation Country Clubs and participating in the Powder Puff Derby. In 1929, she and Amelia Earhart were the driving forces behind the organization of the "Ninety-Nines," the worldwide women aviators organization.

Chamberlin and Nichols immediately planned a stunt to demonstrate how slowly Chamberlin's eight-place cabin Crescent monoplane could glide to the ground. Nichols took a parachute jumper up 2,000 feet in the Crescent, and when he jumped, she cut the plane's switches and drifted down more slowly than the jumper.

Immediately following the first stunt, Chamberlin asked Nichols to participate with him in another first—a midnight flight from New York to Chicago to make the first air delivery of New York newspapers to the Windy City. Nichols flew the entire route and later Chamberlin told the *New York Evening Post*:

She has an uncanny feeling for drift and held her course much more accurately, for instance, than I do. We started out at night for Cleveland. After she had flown for half an hour, I saw she was so good that I went to sleep. and didn't wake up until we had arrived. She not only is a fine pilot, but has the rare gift of common sense, the kind of horse sense that means everything in an emergency.

In November of 1930, Ruth Nichols flew from the Jersey City Airport to Burbank, CA, in 16 hours, 59 minutes and 30 seconds, eclipsing the previous transcontinental record for women set by the Australian "Chubby" Miller, by eight hours. The Lockheed Vega with a Wasp engine in which she flew, belonged to Powell Crosley, president of the Crosley Radio Corp. of Cincinnati. In December, Nichols became the first woman to set a one-stop transcontinental record flying from Los Angeles to New York in 13 hours and 21 minutes. The record surpassed one established six months earlier by Charles Lindbergh.

All the planning and preparation for Nichols' flights was done under the watchful eye of Clarence Chamberlin and his master mechanic Bill Hartig.

In her book, Nichols described what Chamberlin's know-how and experience meant to her many record-breaking flights:

It was a lucky day for me, I realized, when I first met Clarence Chamberlin. Seldom, if ever, have I known any pilot so prolific in ideas, enthusiasm, experience and know-how. He had a superb flying (feel) with which great pilots are born, plus a practical engineering background and the sort of personality that kept everyone around him keyed up to a high pitch of enthusiasm. There were plenty of laughs interspersed with the serious work of plotting my future course.

In January of 1931, the effects of the deep Depression gripping the nation took their toll on the aircraft business in New Jersey. Both Chamberlin's Crescent Aircraft Corp. and The New Standard Aircraft Corp. of Paterson declared bankruptcy. Both companies announced that they hoped to reorganize.

The bankruptcy proceedings didn't stop Chamberlin and Nichols from continuing to challenge altitude, speed and distance records.

In March, 1931, flying her Lockheed Vega from the Jersey City, Nichols set a new world's altitude record for women of 28,743 feet, breaking the mark previously held by Elinor Smith.

Nichols' accomplishment brought a great deal of national media attention to New Jersey as a center of aviation activity.

A few months later, she set a new woman's inter-city speed record between Newark and Washington that tied the existing record of Frank Hawks.

Following extensive upgrading of the Vega, including the installation of a 600 hp Pratt and Whitney supercharged Wasp engine, the young aviatrix was ready for her most daring flight—the transatlantic challenge. As part of her pre-Atlantic preparation, Chamberlin arranged a dinner party with Charles Lindbergh and his wife Anne, so that Nichols could share the advice of two men who had conquered the turbulent Atlantic airways in 1927.

Nichols christened her Vega *Akita*, an Indian word meaning "to discover," and by the first week in June, she and Chamberlin decided she was ready to become the first women to fly the Atlantic alone. The Vega was heavily loaded with emergency equipment and Nichols had a difficult time getting it off the short Jersey City runway for a hop to Floyd Bennett Field in Brooklyn. On landing in Brooklyn, the lightweight landing gear Chamberlin had designed for the Vega gave way and broke the main bulkhead. Within a week, the Navy mechanics at Floyd Bennett (then a Naval air terminal) with an assist from Chamberlin and Hartig, rebuilt the landing gear and *Akita* was ready to fly again.

The second leg of her flight was even less successful than the first. Heading for Newfoundland, the jump-off point for her transatlantic crossing, Nichols flew to St. Johns, New Brunswick, where she expected to find an airfield with adequate runways to accommodate her high-powered Vega. Instead, she found two small runways surrounded by wooded hills and cliffs. After circling the field a number of times, Nichols decided to attempt a landing, and that's when trouble struck. She described her almost fatal landing:

I slid in over the trees and edged through a narrow ravine. So far so good. Maybe my luck was holding. Dead ahead was the runway. I made an S turn for the proper approach and headed straight into the blinding rays of the setting sun. I couldn't look ahead to gauge the length of the runway, because ahead was the fiery glare. Only by staring straight down through the cockpit window could I see even the edge of the runway. This was indeed coming in on a wing and a prayer.

In that split second, I realized if I could touch the wheels on the ground before the intersection of the two runways, then I could clamp down on the brakes to stop the plane in time. I couldn't risk a short dropped stall with the fragile landing gear, which required a feather-light landing. Cautiously, I eased back on the stick and kept my eyes glued to the edge of the runway. Now we were skimming the ground. Now the wheels must be about to touch.

Suddenly, the dazzling blaze of the sun was doused by the shadow of the cliff and I saw to my horror that I had passed the intersection and still had flying speed. Akita was tearing straight toward an approaching cliff at eighty miles an hour. There wasn't a chance of stopping her in time to avoid destruction. Only one thing to do. I gave her the gun, pinning my last desperate hope on the chance that the speed of the ship at full throttle would pull her up and over the wooded crag.

You are not conscious of thought processes or even of fear at a time like this. There is only the awareness of more stark necessity for lightning action. You act by conditioned reflex."

Akita shrieked at the suddenness of the climb, roaring toward the onrushing rocks. She lurched upward and I eased up on the stick to avoid dropping her into a power stall. The jagged edge of the cliff rushed at us. Here it was. I got set for the crash and it didn't come. By some miracle we had cleared the top of the crag by a hair. Even as I breathed a prayer of thanks, I saw another ridge ahead. 'Come on, Akita! Good girl, Akita.' She struggled, quavered, made one last desperate effort—then came a splintering crack as the tail broke through the treetops. More rocks ahead — a deafening C-R-A-S-H — then paralyzing silence. From 70 miles an hour minimum climbing speed, the motor impacted to a dead stop. The whole back end of the ship must be coming over on top of me, relentlessly bearing down, pushing my head and shoulders down between my knees.

Splintering pain, and the silence of catastrophe.

Nichols suffered five broken vertebrae that grounded her for several months. The Vega was salvageable and again Clarence Chamberlin was there to return the ship to Jersey City and piece it back together.

On Oct. 25, flying in a steel corset, Nichols and her Vega broke the women's nonstop distance record, flying nearly 2,000 miles in about 14 hours from Oakland, CA, to Louisville, KY. She became the first pilot in history to top established marks in three different maximum international categories—altitude, speed and distance — flying the same airplane.

The following day, Oct. 26, as she was about to take off from the Louisville airport, her airplane caught fire and burned. Nichols again missed death's cold hand by tumbling from the cockpit, steel brace and all, just before the gas tank exploded.

Despite all of Nichols' trials and tribulations, the International League of Aviators, in making its annual awards in 1932, gave her a special medal as the outstanding pilot of the United States for 1931, the first such honor extended an American woman.

When Amelia Earhart flew solo across the Atlantic in the spring of 1932, Ruth Nichols gave up the quest, but continued to fly and promote aviation.

That year, she helped launch the New York and New England Airways Co. by flying one of their planes from New York City to Bristol, CT, thus becoming the first woman airline pilot in the United States.

In 1935, the Jersey City Airport was closed and Chamberlin moved his base of operations back to Teterboro. He then operated three 25-passenger Curtiss Condor biplanes, originally flown by Eastern Airlines, on barnstorming tours around the United States. He offered Ruth Nichols the opportunity to fly with Harry Hublitz as co-pilot of one of the big planes.

On a flight out of the Troy, NY, airport, one of the Condor's two engines stalled on takeoff. Hublitz attempted to get back to the field, but the Condor crashed short of the runway killing Hublitz and badly injuring Nichols. Four passengers survived with severe bruises. It was Nichols third scrape with death.

Unlike the majority of her contemporaries in aviation, Ruth Nichols was born in silver-spoon comfort in Rye, NY. Her sportsman father was a member of the New York Stock Exchange. She graduated from Wellesley College in 1924. That same year, she received a flying-boat pilot's license — the first such license issued to a woman by the Federation Aeronautique Internationale, the only official licensing agency at that time. Eventually she flew every type of licensed aircraft — glider, autogiro, land planes, seaplanes, flying boats, monoplanes, biplanes, triplanes, piston and jet-powered craft.

In 1939, with war breaking out in various parts of the world, the need for air ambulances was uppermost in her mind, so she founded "Relief Wings." Serving as national director, Nichols and three other women toured 36 states in five months to raise funds to launch the project. When the United States declared war on Japan and Germany, Nichols turned the basic structure of her mercy flying operation over to the government sponsored Civil Air Patrol, then joined the C.A.P. and eventually held the rank of Colonel.

Two years before her untimely death in 1960, Nichols flew as co-pilot in the Air Force supersonic TF-102A Delta Dagger. She became the first woman to fly faster than 1,000 mph and as high as 51,000 feet.

Although Ruth Nichols endured numerous injuries in aircraft accidents, she never gave up flying. In later years she said:

"Flying has nearly killed me many times; it has never made me rich. Yet from the challenge of the skies, I have reaped humanity's most treasured reward—life in its fullest meaning for myself and in relation to others."

Nichols was found dead on the bathroom floor of her plush suite in New York City. Discovered notes indicated that she had taken her own life at age 59.

Clarence D. Chamberlin

Inducted Aviation Hall of Fame of New Jersey, 1973

Aviation pioneer Clarence Chamberlin often told young admirers:

"There were all kinds of ways to make a living with an airplane in the old days. We barnstormed, did every stunt we could think of, hopped passengers for one dollar each, taught flying, and anything else we could dream of in order to make enough money to stay alive until we were ready to take on bigger challenges like flying the Atlantic Ocean."

During his first decade as an aviator (1919-1929), Chamberlin had accomplished more than most other aviators did in a lifetime. He had established an endurance record; become the second pilot to fly across the Atlantic and the first to carry a passenger. He had flown farther and longer than any man before him and had performed the seemingly impossible stunt of flying an airplane off an 80-foot-long ramp of a steamship.

By 1930, Chamberlin was an entrepreneur, having founded the Crescent Aircraft Company in Jersey City. His close associate was master mechanic Bill Hartig. The two men and a small staff worked long hours constructing the little planes they called Baby Crescents. At the same time, Chamberlin continued to do whatever he could to keep the wolf away from his door.

In September of 1930, the *Jersey Journal* reported a Chamberlin stunt that made his airplane a favorite at that year's aviation show in New York City.

Colonel Clarence Chamberlin, who made history when he flew to Germany after Lindbergh's epochal transatlantic flight by plane, performed a brand new stunt today when he piloted a Baby Crescent plane through the Holland vehicular Tunnel from Jersey City to New York.

This new baby plane, a creation of the flying colonel's own as a duel-control training ship, was manufactured at the Crescent Aircraft Company's plant on Lembeck Avenue, Jersey City, and was delivered by Chamberlin today at the Aviation Show at Grand Central Palace.

As he taxied the plane from the factory on Lembeck Avenue through the streets of Jersey City to the south tube of the Holland Tunnel, Chamberlin's stunt attracted much attention.

A permit had been obtained from the Tunnel Commission to allow the baby plane to go through the under-river tube. Traffic at the tunnel was held up for a few minutes while mechanics folded back the wings of the plane to allow it to proceed.

The plane has a wing spread of 30 feet, is 20 feet, six inches long and stands seven feet high. Its wheel tires are 28" by 4" and it weighs 975 pounds, and the usual load is 600 pounds. It's high flying speed is 160 miles an hour, and its climbing rate 1,000 feet a minute. The cruising speed is 100 miles an hour and it carries 30 gallons of gasoline.

After a successful passage through the Holland tunnel, the plane proceeded through the streets of New York to the Grand Central Palace.

Chamberlin's rank of "colonel" was bestowed in a rather round-about fashion. He had learned to fly in the Army Signal Corps during World War I and held the rank of second lieutenant in the Signal Corps Reserve upon leaving the service in 1919. Following his transatlantic flight to Germany in 1927, New Jersey's governor made him a major on his staff. He then returned to his home town of Denison, IO, for further honors. Not to be outdone, the Iowa governor appointed him a lieutenant colonel on his staff. Later on a visit to Kentucky, the governor of that state named him a "Kentucky Colonel," the rank he used for the remainder of his days.

On Thanksgiving Day 1931, Chamberlin was hopping passengers out of a New York airport when he spotted a large animal- shaped balloon that had been released in the Macy's Day parade. He deftly dived at the rubber animal and punched a hole in the gas bag with his wing. As the leaking balloon began to sag toward the ground, Chamberlin forced it to land on a empty lot by sideswiping it with his landing gear and wings. He then landed in a small field a block away and hurried to claim the $25 reward that Macy's had established for retrieving free-flying balloons.

Macy's did not expect an aviator to claim the reward and had hoped to capitalize on the publicity when the balloon was found miles away from the parade site. Reluctantly, the store moguls paid Chamberlin. Immediately after the incident, the Department of Commerce issued a bulletin that balloons could not be released again because they were considered to be a hazard to air navigation.

On Jan. 10 the following year, as part of a real estate promotion, Chamberlin landed his diesel powered Lockheed Vega on Route 4 in Teaneck before the highway was opened to vehicular traffic. He was greeted by more than 2,500 people who crowded so tightly on the roadway that Chamberlin feared for their safety as the plane rolled to a stop.

The nine-year-old daughter of Teaneck Mayor Karl D. Van Wagner christened the aircraft *Miss Teaneck* by smashing a champagne bottle filled with ginger ale on the plane's propeller. (Prohibition forbade the use of real champagne.)

Mayor Van Wagner said, "Such an auspicious occasion as this called for the key to the city, however, we in Teaneck do not need such ornaments. It is well known to our residents that everything in this town is open but the safe in city hall."

With the Depression at its peak in 1932, perhaps Teaneck couldn't afford a symbolic city key.

In the meantime, real estate salesmen moved among the crowd and tried to interest them in plots of land adjacent to the highway.

In March of 1932, Chamberlin added a high-altitude flight to his exploits with the diesel-powered Lockheed. He flew to an altitude slightly in excess of 19,000 feet, which was considered a record for a compression-ignition-engined aircraft.

He went into the barnstorming business in a big way during that last half of the '30's decade. He purchased used, 20-passenger Curtiss Condor biplanes from Eastern Airlines and flew the length and breadth of the United States, taking passengers on short sightseeing flights above their towns and cities. His second wife, Louise, acted as his advance person. She would travel by car to the next location they had decided to visit and scout landing sites. Then she'd visit the local newspapers to interest them in publicizing of the world-renowned aviator's appearance in the town.

Fifty years later, Mrs. Chamberlin told the author:

"I did the advance work for him. I found a lot of hayfields for him to land on. I tested the field for his use by driving 40 miles per hour across it. If the back seat didn't come up and hit me in the head, then it was OK for him to land. We kept traveling from 1936 until we had to stop when wartime restrictions prevented us from flying within 50 miles of the ocean."

At his induction dinner into the New Jersey Aviation Hall of Fame, Clarence Chamberlin pointed to his wife and said, "That's the best advance man I ever had. Without her hard work, we would have starved."

When World War II began, Chamberlin established an aviation technical school in Manhattan that was eventually switched to Newark. The enrollment was good, but the management left much to be desired.

"Clarence had great imagination and ambition," Mrs. Chamberlin remembered. "But he'd lose interest in a project once it was established. The schools would have been very successful if they had been run by academic administrators. Instead, Clarence hired old aviation friends, who knew nothing about running a school and the business failed."

Throughout his life, Chamberlin was a popular speaker. He'd traveled countless miles lecturing on the importance of aviation to high schools, colleges and civic groups. In the 1950s, he suffered a severe heart attack that slowed his activities. He moved from New Jersey to Connecticut and he and Louise became realtors. They spent their winters in a small home on the Gulf of Mexico in Fort Myers Beach, FL. He died in 1974 at the age of 81.

William A. Hartig

Inducted Aviation Hall of Fame of New Jersey, 1974

Clarence Chamberlin called Bill Hartig "the greatest aircraft mechanic I have ever known."

Like Chamberlin, Hartig learned about the maintenance of aircraft airframes and power plants by trial and error. There were no aeronautical schools to attend when he first went to work for the C & W Wittemann Company on Staten Island in 1910 at the age of 15. Even his boss, Charles Wittemann who designed and built his first airplane in 1906, was still experimenting with "flying machines" when Hartig joined the budding concern.

He moved with the Wittemanns, first to Newark and then to Teterboro in 1918 as chief mechanic. He supervised the construction of the Barling Bomber and numerous experimental aircraft.

In 1925, after the Wittemanns left Teterboro, Hartig signed on with Anthony Fokker as maintenance supervisor. Two years later, the Kearny, NJ, resident joined Bellanca Aircraft Co. in Staten Island but left in 1928 to work for Chamberlin's Cresent Aircraft Co. in Jersey City. He moved to Teterboro in the early 1930s to maintain the planes for the Chamberlin Flying Service.

Hartig and Chamberlin worked together for 14 years. While Chamberlin barnstormed, flew in air races and

Bill Hartig & Clarence Chamberlin

organized flying schools, Hartig, with sweat, tears and grass roots experience, kept the airplanes flying.

During World War II, Hartig taught at an industrial trade school in Harrison, NJ, and then joined the Brewster Aero Corp. at Newark Airport and assembled combat planes.

After the war, he rejoined Chamberlin in various ventures until both men decided it was time to retire. William Hartig died in 1973.

Teenage Record Setters

Garofalo, Goldsborough, Buck and Schneider

In 1930, four New Jersey teenage pilots gained prominence. Trained and encouraged by Charles R. Dann, who operated the Atlantic Air College at Westfield Airport, the four boys learned to fly in their mid-teens and immediately began to establish flying records.

In April 1930, 18-year-old Alex Garofalo established a new national altitude record of 19,246 feet above Westfield exceeding the previous mark by 1,000 feet. A month later, Frank H. Goldsborough, 19, established both the westward and eastward junior transcontinental flight records when he arrived back at Westfield on May 11 making several overnight stops along the way. He flew from Los Angeles in 28 hours, 12 minutes, smashing his own record of 34 hours, 3 minutes set on the east-west hop from Newark the previous week. His plane was named *American Boy*.

Goldsborough was the son of Bryce "Brick" Goldsborough who had flown as the navigator/radioman aboard Mrs. Frances Grayson's Sikorsky amphibian *Dawn* on an ill-fated attempt to fly the Atlantic in 1927. The plane and crew were lost on the initial flight from Roosevelt Field to Harbour Grace, Newfoundland.

Ironically, Frank Goldsborough was killed just a month after his record-setting transcontinental flight when he crashed into a mountain near Bennington, VT.

Robert Neitzel Buck

Inducted Aviation Hall of Fame of New Jersey, 1981

Robert Neitzel Buck, 16, became the youngest licensed pilot in the United States when he received his ticket upon graduating from the Atlantic Air College. Buck's instructor, C.D. "Pa" Bowyer, soloed the teenager at Westfield on May 15, 1930 in a Kinner Fleet biplane.

On July 6, 1930, the Elizabeth, NJ, native, established a new junior altitude record of more than 15,000 feet.The record flight was the climax of a

Bob Buck and "Pa" Bowyer

Westfield Airport air show and took nearly two hours of circling and climbing in a small "Air Cub" biplane, designed and built by Peter Abeille in the National Aircraft Co. plant in Plainfield.

The young flyer had hoped to reach 25,000 feet to set a new world's senior light plane record that had been set the previous February by a Lt. Zimmerly over St. Louis, MO. Rain storms and heavy mist prevented the tow-headed boy from climbing higher into the heavens, although he was bundled in heavy Arctic-type clothing and carried oxygen to keep him alive at those heights.

"The ship was climbing in great shape when I decided to come down," Buck said after the flight. "I'm sure I'll be able to take it more than 25,000 feet into the air the next time I get the opportunity."

A year earlier, Bob Buck had assisted William Mumford in building a glider that was test flown at Westfield. The glider, known as the *Diving Dottie II* was, as its name indicates, the second of its kind built by the boys and was extremely air worthy. The glider, with Mumford aboard, was towed behind Dr.A.0. Buck' car along the north/south runway at Westfield. During the afternoon, the fragile aircraft flew at more than 40 feet above the ground. The boys were congratulated by pilots and officials at the field for their fine design and workmanship.

Mumford, an 18-year-old graduate of Westfield High School, had learned the basics of flying from Hilary Watts of Westfield and went on to get his private pilot's license. He flew for pleasure for more than 50 years.

Junior flying records fell like ten pins in 1930. Flying a Cessna monoplane, Edward Schneider, an 18-year-old Jersey City high school student, flew from coast-to-coast at speeds exceeding those established by Frank Goldsborough earlier in the year. Schneider flew from Westfield to Los Angeles in mid-August in 29 hours and 55 minutes. On the return flight to

Roosevelt Field, he flew for 27 hours and 19 minutes, besting Goldsborough's time by an hour and 36 minutes.

Schneider was greeted by his father, Emil A. Schneider, a Jersey City butcher, and 2,500 enthusiastic Sunday visitors at the historic Long Island airfield.

Schneider's record was short lived. On Sept. 29, Bob Buck flew from Newark Airport to Los Angeles in an elapsed time of 28 hours, 33 minutes. He returned to Newark in 23 hours, 47 minutes.

In July 1931, Buck flew a Pitcairn Mailwing round-trip between Newark and Havana, Cuba, a feat never accomplished by a teenager. Later in the year, he set another standard for young airmen by flying from Newark to Washington, DC, in one hour and 40 minutes. His time was just 35 minutes longer than that of Frank Hawkes, holder of the senior record.

Buck's accomplishments were nationally acclaimed and he was received by President Herbert Hoover at the White House. He flew back to New Jersey in one hour and 36 minutes.

In May 1932, Buck completed a 10,000-mile air odyssey from Newark to the Yucatan, Mexico, and return in a Lambert 90 Monocoupe. The 18-year-old had established another record.

Between his many flights, Buck authored two books for G.P. Putnam's Sons publishers.

In 1936, at age 22, Buck left Union Air Terminal, Burbank, CA, and set a course for Newark. Immediately upon taking off, he dropped his landing gear. Two thousand miles later, he skidded to a landing on the belly of the plane at Columbus, OH, to break the light plane distance record.

The following year, Buck joined TWA as a co-pilot and was promoted to captain two years later.

During World War II, he flew for the Air Transport Command over the North and South Atlantic. From 1943 to 1945, he flew a Boeing B-17 on weather research flights across the North American continent and around-the-world.

Following the war, he continued to fly TWA international routes. At the time of his retirement in 1974, he was TWA's chief pilot rated to fly the latest jet equipment, B-747s.

He became an avid sailplane pilot while living in retirement in Fayston, VT, and continued his atmospheric and weather research.

Eddie Schneider Jr.

In 1933, Eddie Schneider became the principle operator of the Jersey City Airport at Droyer's Point. The airport, a popular general aviation field, was ordered closed by the city council, under the iron fist of Mayor Frank Hague, on Dec. 31, 1935. Money was available through the Work Project Administration (WPA) to build a baseball stadium on the airport site, and the Hague was not one to turn down a gift from the federal government.

In a mass protest of the closing, a fleet of planes flew over Jersey City's annual Holy Name Parade to bring the plight of the airport to the attention of the spectators who lined the city's streets. The lead plane towing a banner declaring "Save the Jersey City Airport," was followed by aircraft flown by Bill Picune, Dick Freeland, Al Clemmings, Bob Hurley, Ed Aherns, Bruce Huppert and Schneider. Although the Jersey Journal gave the demonstrators wide coverage, it made no impression on the mayor and council.The ball park would be built. It became the home of the Jersey City Giants, the AAA farm club of the New York Giants.

Scurrying to find a new base of operations, Schneider planned to establish a flying school at Floyd Bennett Field in Brooklyn, but first joined Bert Acosta and other American pilots to fly for the Loyalist cause in the Spanish Civil War. When money promised to the mercenary airmen was not forthcoming, they returned to the United States and picked up their flying careers.

Schneider's Brooklyn flying school afforded him a living in the late Depression years. Then tragedy struck in December 1940. While giving a flying lesson to George Herzog of Brooklyn, Schneider's plane collided with one flown by a Naval Reserve pilot Ensign Ken Kuehner, and crashed killing him and his student. The Navy plane landed safely. Eddie Schneider was only 28 years old.

Around South America
Emile H. Burgin

On May 14, Emile H.(Eddie) Burgin of New Egypt, NJ, began a 20,000-mile airborne odyssey, the first flight around South America in a land plane. Capt. Lewis A. Yancey was the commander/navigator aboard the high-winged Stinson-Detroiter, christened *Pilot Radio*. Zeh Bouck was the radio operator.

A magazine of the day, *Radio News,* in conjunction with IT&T sponsored the flight. Burgin was described in the magazine as follows:

Eddie Burgin is a veteran of well over 3,000 hours in the air and prominent among our transport flyers. Burgin, you may recall, came in first in the New York-Los Angeles air race a few years back. His plane was a Stinson, powered with a Wright Whirlwind J6, 300-horsepower motor.

Burgin, Yancey and Bouck left from Roosevelt Field on the good will tour to Cuba, Mexico, Central and South America. They successfully flew down the west coast of South America to Buenos Aires.

While in the southern most part of the continent, Burgin flew his plane up to 5,000 feet and called his wife, Clara Tantum Burgin, in New Egypt, 5,838 miles away, via a radio and telephone hookup. They spoke for eight minutes.

"I held level at 5,000 feet over Buenos Aires," Burgin explained. "There was no static or any disturbance. It was like I was talking to her in the next room."

While in South America, he also made the first radio contact from a plane to a ship, the S.S. *Majestic*.

During the trip, the plane visited the principal cities in Central and South America and had 17 forced landings due to engine failure. It was the first to land in Cayenne, French Guiana, better known as "Devil's Island." It also was the first to land in a South American jungle and successfully take off again.

After leaving Puerto Rico on the last leg of its historic flight, the Pilot Radio developed engine trouble over the ocean at least 40 miles from the nearest land. Zeh Bouck described what happened.

"With a glance at his chart, Yancey told me to raise someone quick, and I went aft again. A quick juggling of coils, neon tubes, dials and the antenna reel, consuming exactly one minute, I was back on the Pan American calling wave. CMM was my best bet, but to make sure that some one would reply, I interspersed the call with S.0.S. Before the roar of the dynamotor died down in the ear phone, CMM was back at me with a quick 'K' (go ahead). I told him we were having motor trouble, and please stand by for position report."

The engine kept running until they reached Great Exuma Island in the Bahamas where Eddie Burgin spotted a wide expanse of white. Thinking it was a sandy beach he began his descent.

"Eddie straightened out the plane," Bouck continued, "and as the wheels touched, the Atlantic Ocean poured over the motor and windshield. Things happened. There was a queer grinding noise, discordant cymbals and drums, two dull thuds, and I was lying on my back, on top of the plane."

The white beach Burgin had seen turned out to be a salt marsh and when the wheels finally hit the wet sand two feet beneath the water, the plane came to an abrupt halt and flipped over on its back. Although shaken up, the three men crawled out unharmed. Within minutes, one of the gas tanks blew up and the *Pilot Radio* was consumed in flames.

Even the disappointing end to the record setting flight had a singular accomplishment. The S.0.S. had been the first successful one sent from an airplane.

Years later, Clyde Pangborn flew to Great Exuma, found the remains to the *Pilot Radio* and brought the compass back to Burgin as a souvenir. The compass is now on display in New Jersey's Aviation Hall of Fame & Museum.

Burgin learned to fly in 1919 in a seaplane at Port Washington, NY. In 1920, he took further instructions in flying seaplanes at Keyport.

He was a daily visitor to the Jersey Shore from 1936 to 1940, flying late editions of metropolitan evening and morning newspapers from Newark Airport to Red Bank and Belmar.

"I remember that I landed on a little sand strip on the Shark River at Belmar," he said. "Later I flew the papers to the National Guard Camp at Sea Girt." He recalled landing at Red Bank at an airport operated by the Casey Brothers.

During his flying career, Burgin was a barnstorming pilot with air circuses. He dropped the first parachute jumper over Portland, ME, in 1925.

In June, 1929, he received wide publicity for successfully refueling a plane in the air off Long Island's South Shore near New York. The plane he refueled was attempting an endurance record.

"It didn't make it, though," he said.

During his 31 years of flying, he logged 10,000 hours in the air and carried over 22,000 passengers on sightseeing and charter flights out of Roosevelt Field and Newark Airport.

He made his last flight on April 8, 1950, in Santo Domingo where he was a pilot for the Barahona Sugar Company.

"I was a private pilot for the executives," he said. "It kind of broke my heart to quit."

Burgin contracted malaria in 1949 and then developed pneumonia. After he recovered his health, he found that he had lost his equilibrium.

"After I regained my balance," he said, "I returned to flying. But I had difficulty in keeping my balance during night flights and when flying with instruments, so I decided, all-in-all after 31 years, I had better quit."

He said doctors believed large doses of penicillin may have caused his loss of equilibrium.

Emile Burgin died in 1970.

A Race With No Winner
Ives MacKinney

In March of 1930, the New Standard Aircraft Corp., headed by Ivan Gates and Charles Healy Day, sold its subsidiary, the New Standard Flying Service, Inc. at Teterboro, to Capt. Ives MacKinney, a popular former Gates Flying Circus stunt pilot.

Although the Depression had brought a downturn in the aviation business, MacKinney's dashing personality attracted potential aviators to his new business.

MacKinney ran a benefit air show for the Veterans of Foreign Wars over the Memorial Day weekend. The aerial activities, in which MacKinney participated, included an air race around pylons. It was his last race.

Bill Rhode, chronicler of the Gates Flying Circus, described MacKinney's last flight in his book, *Baling Wire, Chewing Gum and Guts.*

On the final day of the show, Mac took part in a race for all OX-5-engined planes. Okey Bevins was leading with an OX-5 Travel-Aire and Mac was third with a TP Swallow. As Mac rounded the pylon on the northern end of the field, he was just 50 feet in the air. The wind caught him and he spun into the ground.

MacKinney's fiance, Grace Ayers of Ridgefield Park, was among the thousands of spectators who witnessed the shocking crash. Mechanics and pilots rushed to the scene. Silvio Cavalier was the first person to reach the crumpled plane. "Ives head had crashed through the Swallow's dash board," Cavalier later reported. "He was in terrible shape. 'I'm okay,' he said, as I took his helmet and goggles off."

David Miller and John Sargent, both student flyers, helped Cavalier drag MacKinney from the wreckage. He died at 8:30 that evening in Hackensack Hospital.

Aron "Duke" Krantz, the former Gates stunt pilot who was working for MacKinney that day carrying passengers in a 20-passenger Sikorsky biplane, said the accident occurred when MacKinney's craft was flipped over by the blast from the propeller of one of the other four planes in the race. Homer E. Fackler, a test pilot for New Standard, John Miller, Robert Wolfe and Okey Bevins were the other participants.

Fackler said, "Mac, who always worked hard and played hard regardless of the stakes or the odds, was flying low, cutting sharp corners in a desperate endeavor to win the cup offered as a trophy. All I could see from above was Mac's left wing tip hook into the ground and the plane followed."

Cavalier remembered that MacKinney had been in another accident the summer before. "Ned Smith asked Ives to test fly a homebuilt he (Smith) had put together. Ives took it up and when he tried to put it in a spin, the tail dropped and it began a flat spin. Ives couldn't get it out of the spin and it crashed straight down. He was pulled out of that wreck with a broken leg."

As happened so often in those formative years of aviation, a fine airman lost his life seeking a bauble—this time it was a $12 trophy.

In July of that year, Roy Ahearn, another Gates pilot returned to Teterboro to visit with old friends. He immediately became fascinated by three little Belgian-built Albert monoplanes that a William Davis of Ridgewood had purchased from Charles Levine. The planes were lightly built of veneer-covered wood and

Ives MacKinney

had a one piece wing. Ahearn asked Davis if he could put one of the little craft through its paces. Davis agreed, perhaps hoping that Ahearn's test flights would attract buyers for his planes.

Ahearn took it up and went through the standard Gates aerobatic routine to the delight of those on the ground. When he landed the crowd roundly congratulated him and while in a euphoric mood, he told them he'd push the plane through an outside loop, a difficult and dangerous maneuver.

Bill Rhode described Ahearn as "one of the most callously cool pilots who ever flew with the Circus. It seemed at times that he did not possess a nerve in his body. He was completely oblivious to danger. Perhaps his feeling of immortality, was too strong for his own safety." On that mid-July day in 1930, it certainly was.

Strapped into the cockpit by four safety belts, Ahearn flew up 4,000 feet over Teterboro and three times put the plane into a dive and attempted to bring it up on the outside to complete the loop. Each time, the small 60-horsepower engine failed to produce the power necessary to complete the difficult stunt.

On the fourth attempt, he flew a little higher, nosed the plane over and opened the throttle wide. At 2,000 feet, he tried again to negotiate the loop. The strain was more than the plane could endure and the wing lifted off in one piece.

The fragile fuselage plummeted to the ground with Ahearn strapped inside. The crash sight was the golf course across old Route 6 at the north end of the airport. Ahern died instantly.

Aerial Photography
George Jay DeGarmo Jr.

Inducted Aviation Hall of Fame of New Jersey 1976

Following Ives MacKinney's fatal crash, George J. DeGarmo Jr. purchased the New Standard Flying Service from MacKinney's estate. DeGarmo, born in 1898 in Flushing, NY, was raised in Ridgewood, NJ. Upon returning from service in World War I, he grad-

Bob Golem, Billy Diehl and George DeGarmo

uated from Tulane University in 1926 with a BM in Mechanical and Electrical Engineering. He worked for several engineering firms in the south including the city of Miami in the late 1920s.

DeGarmo's continued interest in aviation brought him back to New Jersey where he became immersed in attempting to make a living in aviation during the Depression years. He and a small staff of pilots including Billy Diehl and Bob Golem, taught flying and offered charter and short sightseeing flights. He also became interested in aerial mapping and photography. With a Col. Maxwell, he set up a lab for developing film in back of the Fokker hangar.

Early in 1931, DeGarmo and Maxwell won a contract with the U.S. Department of Agriculture to map the Superior National Forest north of Duluth, MN. It was the first aerial survey ever done for the Department of Agriculture. The project was almost scuttled before it began when DeGarmo was involved in a near-fatal crash at Teterboro. On takeoff, with three passengers, the engine of a New Standard biplane quit cold at 100 feet and the plane spun into the ground. Miraculously, they all survived.

In 1932, DeGarmo formed the Standard Aerial Surveys Company in Hackensack and in early 1933 sold the New Standard Flying Service to Ed Gorski. He then moved his business to Newark where, for 17 years, his company specialized in aerial surveying and photogrammetric engineering.

After he and his wife, Ruth, moved to Freehold, NJ, DeGarmo flew out of Monmouth County Airport (now Allaire).

He joined the Navy in 1941 as a lieutenant and, due to his civilian flying experience, he received his Navy wings after just two months of flight training. He served as the officer in charge of aerial surveys in Photo Squadron #2 and spent two years in the Pacific doing intensive aerial mapping. He left the Navy in 1945 as a commander and joined the reserves. He commanded the Patrol Photographic Squadron 956

for three years before joining Wing Staff 93 as the Officer in Charge of Photo Interpretation. He retired from the Naval Reserve as a captain in 1959 after 20 years of service.

Following the war, DeGarmo sold his business to Robinson Aerial Surveys of Dover, NJ, and continued to be active in various forms of engineering.

He died in 1971 in Red Bank, NJ.

A 17,000-Foot Jump
Bernice LaBalter

In the 1920s and 1930s, aviation records were set on almost a daily basis only to be broken the following day. Of all the records being set, those that most fascinated the public were established by parachute jumpers, the daring young men and women of the aviation community.

One of the early women parachutists at that time was Bernice LaBalter of Pompton Plains, NJ, who had become involved with aviation through her relationship with Ralph Baker of Wayne, a seasoned jumper. LaBalter and Baker had met in 1929, and soon, Bernie, as she liked to be called, became Baker's protege.

LaBalter and Baker jumped professionally at Murchio and Teterboro Airports throughout 1929 and '30. It was prior to a large air show at Teterboro in September 1930, that Baker convinced LaBalter that she should attempt to establish a parachute altitude record for women. George DeGarmo, enthusiastically endorsed the idea and offered one of his planes to LaBalter for the stunt. He knew that advertising an attempt by a woman to break a parachute record would draw a larger than usual crowd to his air show.

On the day of the show, LaBalter pulled on a heavy flying suit, strapped on two parachutes, and was taken aloft by Billy Diehl. For 20 minutes the small plane circled above the anxious crowd below, climbing higher with each turn.

Without oxygen aboard, their breathing became labored at 12,000 feet, but they continued to climb. When the altimeter strapped to LaBalter's leg read 17,000 feet, Diehl signaled her to jump. She opened the cabin door, laboriously dragged her equipment through the small opening while clinging to the wing strut, and then jumped. She immediately pulled the parachute's ripcord and the billowing, white canopy slowed her rapid descent through the thin air. When she landed safely on the soft Teterboro turf, she was mobbed by well-wishers and newspaper photographers. She had established a new parachute jump record for women and for a brief moment was famous throughout the country.

In addition to Baker and LaBalter, there were a number of men and women who gave parachute demon-

Frank Hammond

strations each Sunday at various Garden State airports during the '20s and '30s. They were Bill Rhode at Murchio's and Teterboro, "Daredevil" Johnny Perri at Hadley Field, Freddy Ross at Nelson Airport in Franklin Lakes, Elwood Wester at Murchio, Frank Hammond at Caldwell Airport, Sherwood Cole at Mercer Airport in Trenton and Ralph Voorhis and Bill Picune at Teterboro.

Other jumpers who worked regularly in the tri-state area included Art Sousa, Charles Massa, William "Chippy" Coniry, Ralph Penley, Harry Dalrymple, Al Ulrick, Elwood "Ike" Webster and Harry "Doc" Kornhiser.

In an article entitled "Fanfare and Foolishness" by New Jerseyan H.E. Brennert that appeared in the April 1949 issue of *American Helicopter* magazine described the exploits of Frank Hammond.

Frank Hammond of Caldwell, NJ, who at one time held the rather aimless record for making the greatest number of parachute jumps in a single day, was a good all-round stuntman and was among the first to do the wing stand while looping. That was in 1933. He used a Fledgling biplane, and his equipment was much the same as his 1949 successors.

Hammond was a barrel-chested, robust fellow with a good sense of humor and the most enviable control over his imagination He loved to parachute jump, and I've seen him jump just as readily for $3.25 as he did a week previously for $150. Incidentally, Frankie and I used to crow quite loudly at one time about the fact that it was we who packed Lindy and Anne's parachutes for their trip to the Orient.

One day, Hammond got an idea about two men jumping with the same parachute at the same time. It had never been done before, and he felt it might go well at an air show we were running soon at the Curtiss-Caldwell Airport.

After some high-pressure persuasion, Frank interested one Paul Doto, another jumper in the idea. Paul had spun in and crashed his plane into the greenhouse of a nursery adjoining Murchio Airport at Preakness, only a few months previously. And while he escaped with only a broken arm, the experience did his nerves no good. Consequently, when jumping time drew near, Paul was visibly jittery. He wore a specially made harness with snap-hooks for attachment to the harness of the parachute that Hammond was wearing— the one that was supposed to let both of them down together. In addition, Paul wore an Irvin seat-pack chute, just in case something went wrong.

And it did! Hammond pulled the rip-cord just after clearing the ship, but the strain was too great on the makeshift harness, and Doto broke clear and fell away from his partner. Not at all surprised, for as he later confessed, he had been expecting the worst, Doto got hold of his rip-cord and was soon drifting safely down under his parachute. Paul joined the Caterpillar Club that day, but I have never found it in Irvin's records. No doubt they never heard about it because I'm quite certain that this is the first the story has appeared in print.

Nonstop To Bermuda

In late June, 1930, Roger Q. Williams again undertook a perilous flight. This time he flew Charles Levine's venerable Paterson-built Bellanca monoplane *Columbia* (in which Levine and Clarence Chamberlin had flown nonstop to Germany three years earlier) from Roosevelt Field, L.I., to the tiny island of Bermuda and back. The flight covered 1,600 miles and took 17 hours and two minutes to complete.

With co-pilot Errol Boyd, a former British Royal Air Force aviator, and a Navy-trained navigator, Harry E. Connor, Williams had again accomplished an aeronautical feat never attempted before. When the trio reached Bermuda, the return flight was almost aborted because of a balky magneto. But after circling the island and not finding a level place to land, Williams decided to return to Long Island.

Except for a forced landing on Bermuda by Lew Yancey and his crew earlier in the year, the flight of the *Columbia* was the first to the British isle.

Although he and his crew were the first to fly nonstop from New York to Bermuda and return, Roger Q. Williams had his transport pilot's license suspended for seven days by Gilbert G. Ludwig, the U.S. Director of Air Regulations. Williams was chastised for flying over British territory without first having obtained permission from the Bermuda authorities.

Williams wasn't the first pilot disciplined by the Aeronautics branch for flying violations. The popular Bert Acosta had his license suspended for stunt flying and later revoked for flying during the period of suspension. Texaco's pilot, Frank Hawks, was also fined for stunt flying over Roosevelt Field. Anthony Fokker was once fined for flying without a license.

Williams, born in Brooklyn in 1891, was orphaned at the age of eight and sent to live with foster parents in Park Ridge, NJ. In a personal letter written 50 years later, he described his train ride from Jersey City to Park Ridge:

"I caught my first glimpse of the now-modern airport at Teterboro as an eight-year-old orphan lad being a passenger on the New York and New Jersey local of the Erie Railroad on my way to a new home at Park Ridge. The first sight that greeted me was a huge swamp, extending from the bay waters of Hackensack — a dismal sight that did not bolster my prospects of a new home and new life with strangers. The sadness of my journey was only broken when the local stopped at such depots as Carlstadt, Wood Ridge, Hasbrouck Heights, Anderson Street, Hackensack, Westwood, Hillsdale, Woodcliff Lake and Park Ridge.

"Nestled amid this swamp at Hasbrouck Heights, and owned by a native swamp dweller named 'old man Teter', was an obscure high spot dubbed 'Moonachie' by Mr. Teter. He was a self-claimed mayor and shared the high ground with his family of thirteen. They all escaped being marooned by a long lane, high and dry, beginning at the so-called Moonachie to the Hasbrouck Heights railroad station. At full-moon tide, this avenue of egress and exit was under two feet of water."

Williams was 84 when he dictated his remembrances of those days. The time was almost 17 years before the Wittemanns, had established an airfield on Teter land, so he can be forgiven for perhaps giving Walter Teter more credit than he deserved in establishing southern Bergen County communities.

Williams served as an aviator in World War I. The troop ship carrying him to Europe was turned back in mid-ocean because the Armistice had been signed. He barnstormed for several years after the war and then went to work for the Wittemann brothers in the very swamp he describe earlier.

In addition to his record flights, Williams flew one of Clarence Chamberlin's three Curtiss Condor biplanes hopping passengers at various airports in a four state area.

One Sunday, flying out of Teterboro, he flew for 14 hours and carried 1,013 passengers in the 25-seat Condor.

In 1938, he was hired by Reader's Digest to travel around the country on an aviation lecture tour to promote aviation to the "crossroads of our country." In almost two years, he talked to more than 150,000 people, attending 457 meeting held in 177 towns and cities throughout the nation. He also appeared on 27 radio talk shows.

During World War II, he served at supply bases in Fairbanks, Alaska, as commander of the 6th Airodepot Group.

In 1947, he joined Transocean Airlines at Oakland, CA, to establish the Taloa Academy of Aeronautics. Four years later, he went to work for the Naval Air Station at Alameda, CA, on the engineering staff.

Williams, a writer and inventor, was inducted into the Aviation Hall of Fame of New Jersey in 1975. Failing health prevented him from attending his induction dinner, but he sent a personal tribute to the dinner guests present:

"I doff my hat in admiration for each pilot who helped to lay a cornerstone for the Teterboro Airport and its Hall of Fame.

"It gives me a heart full of joy to recognize your many silent contributions to the progress of aviation when it needed a friend.

"God be with you and may He enter your name on His GOLDEN SCROLL to hang on the walls of our GOLDEN AIRPORT where all aviators GONE WEST will someday meet in happiness and fun."

"Warm regards,

"Roger Q."

The following year, Roger Q. Williams "went West" at the age of 85.

Bernt Balchen

Inducted Aviation Hall of Fame of New Jersey, 1975

On July 2, 1930, an estimated crowd of more than 3,000 was on hand at Teterboro Airport to welcome explorer/pilot Bernt Balchen back to Bergen County. Although he had been in the United States for just four years and the majority of that time was spent flying to remote places of the world, the handsome, shy Norwegian had become one of New Jersey's most popular aviation heroes. Now he was returning from two long years in Antarctica as the first man to have piloted a plane over the South Pole.

The welcome home was sponsored by the Bergen County Chamber of Commerce and attended by such aviation notables as Capt. Eddie Rickenbacker, Clarence Chamberlin, Roger Q. Williams and Anthony Fokker, Balchen's employer when he wasn't off exploring the world.

Former State Senator Edmund W. Wakelee, president of the chamber, organized the celebration assisted by J. W. De Baubien, chairman of the chamber's aviation committee. Jacob W. Binder, executive secretary of the chamber, was the master of ceremonies.

The highlight of the day was a presentation to Balchen of a specially designed gold medal. On one side of the medal was a giant eagle with outspread pinions touching icebergs that represented the North and South Poles where Balchen had spent so many years of his young life. The inscription on the face of the medal read: "To Bernt Balchen, commemorating the joining of the Poles and his other achievements in the world of aviation."

From the Royal Norwegian Vice-Consul for New Jersey, Johannes Randulf Bull, Balchen received the Knighthood of the First Class Order of St. Olav, conferred on him by the King of Norway. In his brief remarks, Bull noted that Balchen's flight to the South Pole from the expedition base Richard Byrd had named *Little America* had followed the path beaten earlier across the frozen wasteland by "that other great Norwegian, Roald Amundsen."

In his formative years, Bernt Balchen had been well-trained by the Royal Norwegian Air Force and his boyhood idol, Roald Amundsen, in the field of aeronautics and exploration. He was an accomplished mechanic, pilot and navigator, a rare combination for those early years of aviation.

On that clear July day, the Chamber was not just honoring an heroic pilot, but rather a man who, in his brief career in the county, had become an active citizen. When he was in New Jersey, Balchen worked as the chief pilot for Fokker and participated in Bergen County Chamber activities as a member of the aviation committee. In February of 1931, he became the chairman of that committee and led a campaign by the Chamber to have Bergen County assume ownership of Teterboro Airport.

With all of the aeronautical notoriety that had been focused on North Jersey because many of the world's historic aviation achievements were being accomplished in Teterboro-built Fokker aircraft and almost all of them were powered by Wright Whirlwind engines built in Paterson, it was appropriate for the Bergen County Chamber to become active in the expansion of aviation in the area. Many Chamber members believed that Teterboro should have been the principle commercial airport in the greater New York metropolitan area. They were disappointed when Newark Municipal Airport opened in 1928, 10 years after Teterboro, and immediately became the center of aeronautical commerce in New Jersey.

Balchen had no sooner become settled in his Hasbrouck Heights apartment when a call came for him to return to the Antarctic. The cargo ship *SS Viking* had foundered on the polar ice floes and Balchen flew a Sikorsky amphibian with supplies to the stricken ship.

The Bergen County Chamber was also instrumental in helping Balchen claim his U.S. citizenship. Prior to his flight to France in 1927 as co-pilot of Cmdr. Byrd's Fokker, *America*, Balchen had to apply for U.S. citizenship because Rodman Wannamaker, the flight's sponsor, had said that only Americans would fly his plane on the historic international air mail flight. During the five-year waiting period for citizenship, prospective Americans are not supposed to leave the country. In Balchen's case that was almost an impossible covenant for he was constantly asked to fly on historic expeditions or missions of mercy. With the urging of the Bergen County Chamber, New York Congressman Fiorella LaGuardia (later the famed mayor of New York City) pushed a special bill through Congress granting Balchen full citizenship, the first person so honored by the U.S. since Lafayette.

Before Balchen could pick up his citizenship papers on June 22, 1931, he was in and out of the country on various flights, thus confusing the resident rule even further. At that point Jacob Binder and other Chamber members went to bat for him before Bergen County Common Pleas Judge William M. Seufert, and the matter was finally resolved in Balchen's favor. The Chamber of Commerce celebrated Balchen's citizenship by holding a dinner in his honor at the old Swiss Chalet in Rochelle Park. More than 600 guests attended and heard the explorer say, "I never would consider living on the other side again. I am used to living here." At that time, the pilot was living in a rented apartment in Hasbrouck Heights with his Norwegian wife, whom he married in October 1930. His best man had been Peter J. Siccardi, Bergen County's flamboyant police chief.

Balchen's next adventure began in 1932 when explorer Lincoln Ellsworth was organizing an Antarctic expedition, and hired him to fly his plane. In October 1933, the pilot flew to the West Coast and brought Ellsworth's low-winged Northrop Gamma, named the *Polar Star,* back to Teterboro and began making final preparations for the flight.

Lincoln Ellsworth, whose wealthy father had died and left him a fortune, planned to make a 2,500-mile-round-trip flight between Little America and the Weddell Sea on the other side of the continent. Along with Balchen, he hired Sir Hubert Wilkens, the veteran explorer, as the expedition's manager.

In December, the expedition arrived in New Zealand aboard the cargo vessel, *Wyatt Earp.* The group immediately jumped off for Little America where Balchen test flew the plane. One night, the ice in the Bay of Wales broke up and seriously damaged the moored plane.

The accident forced the expedition to postpone its plans and return the damaged plane to the Northrop factory in California for repairs. This period permitted Balchen to fly back to Bergen County where he spent a great deal of his time speaking to service clubs and other interested groups.

In the early fall of 1934, the Ellsworth expedition returned to Antarctica with a revised plan. They would take off from Deception Island and fly to Little America. Because of the change, Balchen became the first man to establish a base at Deception Island in the northwestern portion of Antarctica. Foul weather, more mechanical problems and a dispute between Ellsworth and Balchen forced the expedition to abandon the plan for the remainder of 1934. At that point, Balchen resigned as chief pilot.

Before the U.S. entry into World War II, Balchen served on patrol and ferrying missions for the Royal Norwegian Naval Air Force. In 1941, he transferred to the U.S. Army Air Corps and for two years commanded Task Force 8 in Greenland, building and commanding the secret Sondre Strom airbase used as a stopover for military flights to Europe.

Balchen's pilots also performed dozens of rescue missions in Greenland, including the month-long rescue of survivors of a B-17 crash. During that period, Balchen himself made 55 flights into the interior searching and dropping supplies. Three times he had to land his plane on its belly. Balchen's most dangerous wartime missions were his flights over northern Europe. He evacuated 2,000 Norwegians, 900 Americans and 150 others from neutral Sweden. He also helped evacuate 70,000 Russians from a labor camp in northern Norway.

In addition, he helped form an aerial lifeline which parachuted espionage agents, arms and supplies to the Norwegian underground and military supplies to Denmark. Balchen was awarded the Legion of Merit, a special Congressional Medal and other decorations from the United States, Norway and Sweden.

Following the Ellsworth adventure, Balchen had taken the position of operations manager of Norwegian Airlines. He was the president of the company when it merged into Scandinavian Airlines (SAS) after the war. The early over-the-pole flights by SAS were pioneered under Balchen's watchful eye.

In his later years, he began to paint with watercolors, and a number of his works of art now hang in prestigious halls around the world.

Balchen died in 1973 at the age of 73.

Endurance Record Set
Louis T. Reichers

Inducted Aviation Hall of Fame of New Jersey, 1989

In July of 1930, two Kearny, NJ, residents planned to break the endurance record established by the Army Fokker C-2, *Question Mark*, the previous year.

Aircraft mechanic, John McPhail had convinced Lou Reichers that he should attempt to set the endurance

Smithsonian collection

Lou Reichers

flight record. Reichers had learned to fly in 1928 with the Army Flying Corps. He was employed then as personal pilot to Bernarr McFadden, publisher, physical culturist and all- around eccentric. They joined in the venture with Capt. John S. Donaldson, a World War I Flying Ace, founder and president of the Newark Air Service based at the fledgling Newark Airport. Donaldson also ran a Manhattan-based firm, New York and New Jersey Endurance Flight, Inc., organized to help sponsor flyers who sought to establish endurance records.

Donaldson convinced the Stinson Aircraft Corp. to lend two of their high-winged monoplanes with Lycoming radial engines for the flight. Reichers and his co-pilot Robert Black were to receive $3 per hour for every hour in the air. Reichers and McPhail knew that flight had to last at least two weeks to better the mark of 150 hours and 40 minutes established by Maj. Carl Spaatz and Capt. Ira Eaker.

After several weeks of practicing crude plane-to-plane refueling techniques over Roosevelt Field, Long Island, Reichers and Black began their airborne quest. The co-pilot's seat had been removed from the enclosed cabin and an air mattress stretched on the floor in its place. One of the early air-to-ground voice radios had been installed. There was also an aluminum 80-gallon auxiliary gas tank in the cabin. It had a filler neck stuck up through the fuselage beside a narrow trap door that was just large enough for a man to stand erect with his head and shoulders protruding outside the plane in order to grab the refueling hose and fit it into the filler neck.

On either side of the fuselage extending from the landing gear struts to the engine, were two catwalks for servicing the motor in flight. The valves had to be oiled twice a day, as did the rotating cam shaft. In addition, all the spark plugs would have to be replaced at least once during the flight. Between flying the machine, refueling every four hours and climbing about on the plane's engine, the two men would have their hands full 24 hours a day.

For the first few days, the flight was uneventful. Then one of the wing tanks sprung a leak, forcing the pilots to refill the good tank from the auxiliary tank every two hours. Meanwhile on the ground, Capt. Donaldson added new sponsors for the flight. Fuel and engine equipment companies and clothing and watch manufacturers supplied equipment and signed contracts authorizing the pilots to say the products with-stood the rigors of long endurance flights.

On the eighth day of the flight, Black put too much grease on the magneto cam shaft and the plane's engine began running roughly. Both men knew that within four hours the engine would be vibrating so badly it might break loose from its mount. It seemed as though the endurance record was out of their reach. After a consultation by radio with McPhail and an engine expert from Lycoming, the pilots decided that they would have to change the entire breaker assembly in flight. It was necessary to turn off the engine while Black struggled to replace the defective part. They began the procedure at 9,000 feet and the plane glided earthward at approximately 1,200 ft. a minute so Black had less then eight minutes to make the repair. At the six-minute mark, with Black still working frantically on the engine, Reichers turned toward the field and prepared to make a dead-stick landing. Just 500 feet above the grass strip, Black yelled, "O.K. Lou! Switch on!" and the engine caught. The endurance flight would continue.

After 313 hours and 35 minutes, the Stinson's engine gave out and the two men were forced to land on a golf course several miles from Roosevelt Field. They had flown almost 31,350 miles and established a new endurance record.

McPhail a Maintenance Expert

At the age of nine, John D. McPhail had come from Scotland to New Jersey with his family in 1905. After schooling in Trenton, he joined the Royal Canadian Air Force in 1915 where he served as a First Class Air Mechanic.

For two years following the World War I Armistice, he barnstormed across the country, flying every type of aircraft built at that time. In 1921, he settled back in New Jersey and began a colorful career in civil aviation.

Throughout the early 1920's, he worked at Teterboro for the Wittemann brothers and Anthony Fokker. As a chief mechanic, McPhail was aboard most of Fokker's test and demonstration flights including the 12-city Ford Reliability Tour in the fall of 1925 that propelled Fokker's reputation upward in the United States. He was "loaned" by Fokker to help prepare Richard Byrd for his 1928 Antarctic expedition. Three years later, McPhail was hired as an Eastern Airlines mechanic at Newark Airport.

In 1936, entertainer Harry Richman and Eastern's chief pilot, Dick Merrill, were attempting to fly from England to Newark in a Vultee monoplane *Lady Peace*. A loss of fuel forced them to land in Newfoundland. Capt. Eddie Rickenbacker, president of Eastern, organized a rescue party that included McPhail. He and another mechanic, Jake Neuenhaus,

made repairs to the Wright Cyclone engine and replaced the propeller that had been damaged on landing. The *Lady Peace* was soon again airborne on her final leg to Newark.

Following World War II, he became the airlines' chief inspector and conducted a 27,000 mile, six-week tour of 76 Eastern bases in the U.S. and Mexico. That trip was followed a few years later by a 54,000-mile journey to Eastern bases.

McPhail retired from Eastern in 1951.

Solo Across the Atlantic

When Bernarr Macfadden acquired a new, sleek Lockheed Altair monoplane, Lou Reichers decided it was the perfect machine for him to fly across the Atlantic. He broached the subject to his boss and was turned down. Not discouraged, Reichers decided on a different approach which he described in his book *Flying Years*.

Contrary to public opinion, Bernarr Macfadden did not live entirely on Grape-Nuts, buttermilk and carrots. He existed on those, but actually lived on publicity. To keep his name before the public, he invaded the New York newspaper field, publishing the Evening Graphic, *a picture newspaper of questionable ethics that was finally forced to suspend publication due to libel suits that ran into millions of dollars.*

The Depression had hit the publishing world, and hit it hard. Money that Macfadden was using to bolster the Evening Graphic *was money poured down the drain. In the magazine field* True Story *was the only Macfadden publication enjoying handsome profits, but this profit was being used to keep his nickel magazine,* Liberty, *alive. The* Evening Post *and* Liberty *needed publicity. In the case of* Liberty, *this publicity would have to be nationwide if it was going to help its ailing circulation figures, and this was probably the psychological time to make Mr. Macfadden a proposition.*

Reichers used the need for publicity in his pitch to Macfadden for financial assistance, and the ploy worked.

In April of 1932, as a preliminary test flight, Reichers decided to fly the Altair from Montreal, Canada to Havana, Cuba. The basic planning was done at Newark Airport and modifications to the airplane, including the installation of additional fuel tanks, were completed at the Aeromarine Plane and Motor Co. hangar at Keyport, with the blessing of Ingliss M. Uppercu, president of Aeromarine.

Reichers left St. Hubert Airport outside of Montreal at 9:22 a.m. in the Altair named *Miss Liberty* for the occasion. Nine hours and three minutes later, he landed at General Machado Airport, 20 miles inland from Havana, and became the first man to accomplish that 1,800 mile nonstop flight.

Prior to leaving Montreal, Reichers had cabled his expected time of arrival to a friend, Facundo Bacardi, in Havana, and had suggested that Bacardi welcome him with the largest daiquiri ever assembled. When he taxied to the hangar line in Havana and cut the engine, a small Cuban boy, dressed in a white uniform, walked up to the plane and presented him with a huge, frosted drink. Having run out of drinking water some three hours earlier, Reichers enthusiastically welcomed the chilled drink. With two hands, he hefted the glass and shouted "Saludo" to the waving crowd.

Reichers couldn't remember when a drink tasted more refreshing. Down it went in a few long gulps and suddenly his fingers and toes began to tingle. By the time he reached Cuban customs, he could hardly complete the forms. His friend Bacardi had delivered the goods. Reichers was smashed!

During his three days of relaxation in Havana, Reichers was introduced to President Machado by Bacardi, and, by chance, met the president's appointment secretary, a young, stocky sergeant major named Batista. Just three months after the airman returned to Newark, Batista overthrew Machado and proclaimed himself as the island's leader. Subsequently, he was elected president, a position he held until he too was banished by Fidel Castro.

At Newark, the Altair was given a thorough inspection by Macfadden's mechanics and Wright engine experts at Teterboro, while Reichers awaited favorable weather forecasts for the first leg of his flight to Newfoundland.

At two minutes past midnight on May 12, Reichers waved good-bye to his wife and son, pointed the Altair north, and six hours later, landed at Harbour Grace, Newfoundland. On landing, he damaged the horizontal stabilizer. With the help of local fishermen/mechanics, he was able to devise a patch out of sail clothe and glue it over the hole. Nothing was going to postpone his date with destiny.

It was ironic that as Reichers was poised to become the second man to fly solo across the Atlantic, his adventure shared the front page of the *New York Times* with the tragic story of the kidnapping of Lindbergh's baby.

Reichers' transatlantic flight would have been picture perfect had he not underestimated his fuel consumption. Approximately 15 miles from the Irish coast, he concluded that he didn't have enough fuel to fly across the Emerald Isle to Dublin on the east coast and to his knowledge there were no airports near the west coast. As he flew over the passenger liner *SS President Roosevelt,* he had to make a quick decision. Should he

take a chance and land on the rough, rock-walled Irish countryside or ditch in the ocean beside the ship and hope to be rescued. He chose the latter.

After circling the ship several times, the Altair splashed down on the rough sea. Reichers was knocked unconscious on landing, but fortunately the plane stayed afloat long enough for the ship's chief officer, Harry Manning, and a lifeboat crew to come to his rescue. The only injury the airman sustained was a broken nose. Macfadden's Lockheed was lost to the churning sea.

Reichers was welcomed aboard the *President Roosevelt* by Capt. George Fried. When the vessel arrived in New York, the press swarmed aboard to interview the pilot and his rescuers.

An editorial in the *Virginia Pilot,* a Norfolk, VA, newspaper had this to say about Reichers' flight.

...While Lou Reichers' attempt to hop the Atlantic at high speed ended in a wetting, he was near enough to his goal when Captain Fried rescued him to have demonstrated that substantial progress has been made toward bringing the continents closer together...that outcome of this flight is evidence that a dawn-to-dusk crossing is not far off.... Devil-may-care chaps like Reichers will continue to add to our knowledge of transocean flying but the rest of us will be content for some time to come to patronize the [liner] Leviathan...

Twenty years later, Captain Harry Manning commanded the superliner *SS United States* on a record-setting Atlantic crossing between New York and Southampton, England. Just sixteen years later, the great ship was tied up at a Norfolk pier, never to sail again, because people like the editorial writer and his readers, had discovered the convenience of jet travel to and from Europe.

Those early devil-may-care pilots had emphatically proven their point, although the majority of them weren't alive to announce proudly "we told you so!"

The Flying Car

In January 1935, Lou Reichers again made headlines when he flew a promotional stunt for the Sun Oil Company.

Sun had developed a new high-test, non-premium gasoline that they claimed would start an automobile engine in less than a second at zero degrees. To prove their claim, they wanted to have a new model car carried up to an altitude of one mile, where the temperature was zero, and have the car started for the edification of unbiased observers.

The only airplane with a landing gear wide enough to permit an automobile to fit between the wheels was Vincent Burnelli's UB-20 Flying Wing, that he had created at Keyport. A 1935 Ford roadster was strapped under the fuselage of the UB-20. Then

Reichers carefully piloted the plane off the runway at Floyd Bennett Field in Brooklyn. When the plane reached 6,000 feet, a race car driver, Zeke Meyer, dropped through a trap door in the floor of the airplane, plopped into the seat of the roadster and started the engine. All the while, a chase plane had a motion picture photographer aboard to record the event for posterity.

Again, a New Jersey-built plane piloted by a Jersey native had performed a "first" in the annals of aviation that was to become commonplace less than 15 years later. During World War II, Reichers had an active career as a transport pilot. (See 1942)

Youngest Pilot

Joseph Sheehan

In the mid-20s, the Bureau of Air of the U.S. Department of Commerce established flying rules to regulate civilian aviation. One thing they didn't specify was a minimum age for pilots. That oversight set the stage for another New Jersey first. Joseph Sheehan, age 12, soloed at Teterboro Airport in the summer of 1930, thus becoming the youngest pilot to solo in an airplane.

His instructor, Okey Bevins, was a former Gates Flying Circus birdman. Historian Bill Rhode described what happened in an article that appeared in the June, 1988 edition of *Air-List-Ads*:

He [Okey] put a small box under the youngster's seat and extensions onto the rudder bar of the aircraft, an open cockpit BIRD biplane powered by a WWI-era Curtiss OX-5, watercooled engine. After a number of hours of dual instruction and many landings on the old sod field, Okey Bevins climbed out of the front cockpit, and told little Joe Sheehan he was to make his first solo flight.

The 12-year-old boy pulled his goggles back down over his eyes. He taxied without wheel brakes to the end of Teterboro, blasted the biplane around and took off. He made a beautiful circuit of the field and a fine three-point landing on wheels and tailskid.

A few days, later Bevins took Sheehan to Roosevelt Field, LI, then the showcase airport in the east. After informing the cadre of reporters and photographers who were constantly on duty at the field of his intention of letting a 12 year old fly solo, Bevin took the boy up and pointed out the landmarks. Once back on the runway, Bevins climbed out of the plane and the youngster again demonstrated his flying ability. The stunt brought little Joey national media coverage.

As so often happened in those days, that event stimulated others to attempt a similar stunt. A year later at the West Hampton Airport on Long Island, 11-year-old Jackie Chapman soloed, placing Joey

Sheehan's accomplishment second in the book of records.

After several other youngsters had soloed over the next two years, the Bureau of Air banned solo flying for anyone under the age of 16.

That didn't stop Al Bennett, a well known Piper Distributor at Hightstown, NJ, prior to World War II and a Taylorcraft dealer following that war. He had taught his 13-year-old daughter to fly, but she couldn't solo for three years. Undaunted, Bennett took her and a Taylorcraft to Havana, Cuba, and let her fly alone at the Jose Marti Airport.

Bennett was an innovative salesman during the Depression when money was extremely tight. In the mid-'30s, government and the aviation industry were exploring ways to encourage private flying. A number of plans were put forth and Bennett's was accepted by the CAA.

The program called for payments of $50 by the government to student pilots when they soloed and an additional $50 when the new pilot had completed 10 hours of solo flying. There is no report on how successful Bennett's plan was, but he became known as a super salesman. In the *1940 Aircraft Year Book*, Bennett was praised for his sales ability:

Private airplane merchandising, a field barely touched since the boom days following the Lindbergh flight to Paris, received new attention. Distributors increased. Typical of the men developing fresh sales appeal for the general public was Alfred B. Bennett of Hightstown, NJ, who studied the problem of airplane sales as a part of his college course. Distributor over a wide area in New Jersey, Pennsylvania and New York for one make of light plane, he was credited in 1939 with selling more commercial planes than any other individual in the world. Explaining private plane sales, Mr. Bennett reported: "The problem must be solved either from the standpoint of more private airplanes to create the demand for more airports, or from the standpoint of more airports to provide the merchandiser with a selling point. An airplane for the private owner is only as useful as the number of airports at his disposal. The demand for highways was created by an increasing number of automobiles. It is logical to assume that the demand for more airports will be created by mass ownership of planes. Private flying, as such, needs no subsidy from anybody. It is in the midst of its own boom. But private flying, in terms of maximum utility, must find an earlier avenue of expansion than would be provided by the normal course of events as typified by the slow, gradual growth of motoring."

In pursuit of a definite sales plan, Mr. Bennett, with 10 years experience as an airplane distributor, progressively sold whole communities on flying by demonstrating the ease of airplane operation. With the help

of civic bodies, he offered rides to entire populations of small communities on weekends, using ordinary hay fields on the town limits as improvised airports.

1931
State Aviation Director
Gill Robb Wilson

Inducted Aviation Hall of Fame of New Jersey, 1980

Gill Robb Wilson was named the first State Director of Aviation for New Jersey and was assigned an office in the State Police Building in Trenton.

Wilson had flown in France with the Lafayette Esquadrille during World War I and returned home with the rank of Captain and the French Croix de Guerre, among other combat decorations.

Following in his father's footsteps, Wilson had become a Presbyterian minister after the war. In 1921, he was assigned to a church in Trenton.

He became active in the American Legion and was named chairman of that organization's Aeronautics Committee.

Wilson's initial task as State Director of Aviation was to survey the state's aeronautical situation and to recommend appropriate laws and regulations that would mesh with early federal aviation laws.

His first move was to ground all unapproved aircraft and require airports to establish minimum conditions before obtaining a license to operate. Many historic and rare aircraft were grounded, never to fly again. It was estimated that at least half the aircraft in New Jersey disappeared from the flying fields, were moved into barns for safekeeping or put to the torch.

Arch Maddock of Trenton became Wilson's first airport inspector. Maddock had been a flying instructor, a co-pilot for T.A.T. Airlines, manager of William Penn Airport in Philadelphia, and operator of a branch of the Newark Air Service for Bob Copsey. Maddock and Wilson warned all pilots to avoid South Jersey because of the dearth of decent flying fields. Atlantic City and Camden were the exceptions.

Under Wilson's leadership hundreds of rooftop markers were painted on factories throughout the state and highway route numbers were printed in large figures along the state's roadways. The markers were the only aerial quidance system in those early days, and were credited with saving countless lives and aircraft.

In two short years, Wilson had established himself as one of the most aggressive and progressive aviation officials in the nation. He was named to the Department of Commerce Advisory Committee on Aviation in 1937. There he had the opportunity to affect aviation safety throughout the U.S. In 1936, he made the first national airport survey.

He served four terms as president of the National Aeronautics Association and in 1937, became the president of the National Association of State Aviation Officials. At that organization's annual convention, Wilson summarized the general attitude of state officials toward flying despite the downturn of business during the Depression decade. He stated optimistically: "The development of aviation will dominate the history of the world for the next half century."

In a plea for the creation of a strong national aviation policy, Wilson said, "The public welfare is vulnerable through lack of a national aviation policy. The report of the President's Aviation Commission gathers dust in the files. Budgets are inadequate to guarantee the public safety. Unhealthy conditions force our air transport systems to such fierce competition that the savor is gone from the game. Where aviation should be sounding the keynote to a fresh prosperity, it lolls in the doldrums of uncertainty and fear. Federal agencies are a house divided against itself in a struggle for prestige of control of aviation.

"Aircraft develop without the least relationship to airports. Aids to navigation are totally inadequate, especially in sparsely settled sections of the land where they are most needed. Great metropolitan areas develop their facilities without strategic rhyme or reason. Unsatisfactory airports are maintained in existence by other than sound aeronautical judgement. Procurement routine and budget red tape run far behind the immediate and imperative necessities of present traffic. Government personnel are too few to do the work they are represented as doing. No policy for airport construction has ever been inaugurated. Unnecessary regulation for private pilots discourages the entire group. Political pressure is forced upon the weather bureau, while half-paid, unqualified, part-time star gazers hope they guessed right in visibility."

His recommendations included creation of a Bureau of Federal airports, granting air transport companies route certificates assuring them permanency, an increase in the budget for the Weather Bureau, representation in the Bureau of Air Commerce for the private flier, additional funds for the Bureau, ratings for aviation trade schools, invocation of laws of eminent domain for the removal of obstructions around airports, intensification of air-marking towns and cities, coordination of Red Cross and flying activities for disaster relief, construction of a new wind tunnel for the National Advisory Committee for Aeronautics and establishment of a Joint Committee on Aviation in Congress.

Although he was active on a national level, Wilson kept abreast of aviation matters in the Garden State. In a 1936 editorial in the *Bergen Evening Record*, entitled " A Public Job Well Done," he was lauded:

There was more than one smile when the Legislature created a State Aviation Commission with a paid director at a salary of $5,000 a year. Critics believed this was just another soft bit of patronage for a favorite son. The smiles ceased, however, after Gill Robb Wilson who was appointed to the position, had been working for a time. His work has been so good and has created so much attention that it is doubtful if the State will be able to hold him indefinitely.

Bergen County's interest in Wilson would seem to be negligible. He has never made any serious effort to publicize his labors. Yet, he has been one of the central figures in the effort to bring a new industry to Teterboro Airport, a program which, if realized, would bring thousands of new families here. He has participated effectively in conferences with important industrial leaders, and this is but one of his many contributions in the promotion of the State's interests. The Teterboro transaction may or may not be consumated; but if it is, Director Wilson will have earned his annual salary many times over.

Wilson has just returned from a month's visit to Germany. While there he studied the aviation industry in all its phases, bringing back much information that will be helpful to him in New Jersey. At the same time, he furthered the proposal to have New Jersey selected as the site for a permanent landing field for the German Zeppelin Company's dirigible. Permission to use the Navy's field at Lakehurst cannot be continued indefinitely. Some other site along the Atlantic seaboard will have to be selected. It is admitted that this would be desirable for New Jersey, not alone for the

employment it would provide, but also because it would give the State desirable advertising.

Bids for a Zeppelin Company terminal have been made by several cities, but it is believed that New Jersey has the advantage of proximity to the metropolitan district. Wilson's activities along such lines have been helpful. He believes that trans-Atlantic dirigible service has come to stay, and his opinions are respected; He is not given to idle chatter.

Wilson could have taken life easy at Trenton had he so desired. The creation of an Aviation Commission was at best an experiment, with few people believing that it would justify the expenditure. Thanks to Wilson's initiative and energy, it is now soundly established on a permanent basis. New Jersey could use more men of that type in its other departments; but they are found rarely in governmental service, and when they are, the better inducements offered by private industry soon take them away. Recognition of the State Aviation Director for a job well done has been long overdue.

It was during his trip to Germany that Wilson realized the need for a coastal defense system. While being wined and dined by his Nazi hosts, a blithe remark made by a World War I submarine commander struck a discordant note.

"Your east coast is the best submarine hunting ground in the world," said the submariner. Wilson knew that if America became involved in a war, the Army and Navy did not have the aircraft or manpower to defend coastal shipping from submarine attacks. Why not, Wilson asked himself, enlist the help of civilian airmen?

At that time, private planes were forbidden to fly beyond a gliding distance of the shore. Wilson knew the regulation could be extended seaward to cover coastal sealanes without any great hazards. Then, too, small planes could maneuver at wave-top altitude in murky weather much better than heavy military planes.

To get the backing necessary to organize the first Civil Air Defense Service (CADS) in New Jersey, Wilson went to his friends in industry who owned private or corporate aircraft and understood the need for a sound air defense system. They included Guy Vaughn of the Curtiss-Wright Corp., George Merck of Merck Chemical, Walter Kidde of the Kidde Company, Gen. Robert Wood Johnson of Johnson & Johnson, Henry DuPont of Wilmington, DE, Ferdinand Roebling, his Trenton neighbor, and perhaps a dozen more.

Wilson wrote in his book, *I Walked With Giants!*:
I was fed up to the ears by the apathy of our national administration concerning airpower and the general public outcry of 'Peace, peace!' when there was no peace. We got out descriptive literature [on the CADS] outlining the nature and function of the project. We

Charles "Casey" Jones and Gill Robb Wilson

compiled pilot and aircraft rosters, flew experimental patrols, simulated emergency situations, ran tests for cross-country navigation and conducted numerous indoctrination classes.

In 1940, Wilson created his own civilian air corps in New Jersey while most Americans didn't believe the country would become involved in war.

"I made my Fairchild-24 available for instrument training," he explained, "basing it at Hadley Field near where Fred Jones, a TWA captain, lived. Fred had offered to teach the rudiments of instrument flight to any member of the CADS who cared to take instruction. He had his hands full.

Originally, we had some 300 CADS members, but of course many members were available for military call, and after Pearl Harbor eventually left for regular service."

Wilson, as president of the National Aeronautics Association, used that Washington office as the center of CADS activity.

While involved in organizing the CADS and overseeing the state's division of aeronautics, Wilson found the time to write poems (a favorite avocation) about aviation. In 1938, a book of his poems entitled *Leaves From An Old Log*, was published. It received excellent reviews. With the passage of time, his book has become a collectors' item.

Seeing the need to protect the U.S. coastline and patrol the vital war shipping lanes, Wilson sold his idea to Fiorello H. LaGuardia, director of the U.S. office of Civil Defense and the former New York City mayor. The program attracted the backing of Army Air Force Gen. H.H."Hap" Arnold and the Civil Air Patrol was born. Wilson became the CAP's first executive officer.

It was also at his urging that the Civilian Pilot Training program was organized in 1940 in anticipation of future military need.

All of Wilson's oratory and writings urging the government to increase air power attracted the attention of the *New York Herald Tribune* and he was hired as the paper's aviation columnist. During the war years, he traveled to every front as a war correspondent.

At war's end, he served one more year as New Jersey's Director of Aeronautics and then became editorial director of *Flying Magazine*. There he established one of the magazine's more popular features—his descriptions of the beauty of flight in colorful verse, illustrated by striking photographs.

In 1957, some of the verses and photographs were published by Random House in a volume titled *The Airman's World*. He retired as the magazine's publisher in 1963.

Over the years, Wilson's vision and energy seemed to have had no bounds. He not only conceived and cre-

ated the Civil Air Patrol and the National Association of State Aviation Officials, but he was also a founder of the Aircraft Owners and Pilots Association and the prestigious Wings Club, based in New York City.

His pursuits were many and diverse—preacher, pilot, poet, philosopher, promoter, publisher and war correspondent. New Jerseyans can be proud to call him a native son,

Charles Healy Day

Inducted Aviation Hall of Fame of New Jersey, 1981

Charles Healy Day

In January 1931, Charles Healy Day surprised everyone by resigning as an officer of the New Standard Aircraft Corp., based at Teterboro. He said at the time that he wanted to be free to pursue the simple pleasures of life. Within six months, he and his wife were flying around the world.

In a *National Geographic Magazine* article, published in June, 1932, Mrs. Gladys M. Day gave a graphic description of their journey:

The idea of the trip originated one evening in January, 1931. We were sitting across a dinner table from one another discussing what we should do with our temporary freedom.

Charles Healy Day had just terminated his duties with the airplane company for which he had been working. It seemed to me that the time had come to break away from routine life. If I could help it, we were not going to spend the year 1931 living in a three-room apartment in Ridgewood, New Jersey.

We discussed flying around the United States. "Why not the world," I said, "if we can get a plane?"

"Get the plane? Why not build it?" said Charles Healy. And that is the way our adventure began.

Day built a stagger-wing open cockpit biplane of his own design in the back room of an automobile paint shop in Paterson. In April, the plane, powered by a 100 hp Cirrus engine manufactured in Belleville, was flight-tested by Homer Fackler at Teterboro, and Day announced that he and his wife were planning a leisurely flight around the world.

The airplane, christened the *Errant*, cost $500 to build. The stagger-wing design produced an extraordinarily stable plane. Its maximum speed was 105 mph and it had a cruising speed of 85 mph. It could land at the unusually slow speed of 30 mph, which became extremely important in areas of the world where there were no air fields.

Comfort was an important feature of the ship. Day had arranged a side-by-side cockpit instead of the usual two cockpits fore and aft. Mrs. Day said the togetherness made it "easy for us to talk to each other in flight and communicate concerning maps and routes. In addition, we could appreciate the humor of many of the events that befell us together."

Following the flight tests, the wings of the plane were removed and it was shipped to New York and put aboard the *S.S. American Shipper.* On May 8, the Days sailed to England with their airplane, which was reassembled at Heston Airport and the flight was begun.

The couple flew from England to France and Germany and then over the Balkans to Istanbul. From Turkey they flew to Palestine, Persia (Iran) and on to India. Just as they were flying up the China coast to Shanghai, a war between Japan and China broke out in Manchuria, so they decided to ship their plane back to the United States. Once back in San Francisco, the intrepid couple flew across the American continent, arriving back at Newark Airport on Dec. 20.

They had traveled more than 24,000 miles — 16,000 by air—and the total cost of the trip was less than $6,000. Although they did not fly across the two great oceans of the world, research has revealed that Gladys Day of Ridgewood was the first woman to fly in a fixed-wing aircraft around the world.

She concluded her *National Geographic* article with this observation:

Our small plane had shown us the contours of the world, far places and foreign people, the splendor of the Syrian Desert and the Persian Gulf at dawn, the cathedrals of Europe and the Taj Mahal of India, Englishmen, Frenchmen, Germans and primitive Burmese tribesmen, the Orient troubled by war, and last of all, the stable American Continent and our own country. It was time for the Errant, *home from its wandering, to rest.*

When the Days returned to Ridgewood they were enthusiastically received and a banquet was held in their honor.

Naval Disasters
U.S.S. Akron, U.S.S. Macon

The Navy's lighter-than-air program grew by leaps and bounds during the 1929-1931 period. Spurred by plans to double the size of the Navy's airship fleet and the establishment of a new West Coast airship base at Sunnyvale, CA, scheduled for completion in 1933, the Navy had rapidly expanded its aeronautical personnel. Large groups of student airship aviators went

into training at the Naval Air Station at Lakehurst to prepare for service aboard the new airships. The prospects for long careers in lighter-then-air vehicles had never been brighter before or after.

As far back as 1926, a parachute-rigging school had been established at Lakehurst. Chief Petty Officer Lyman Ford was in charge of the program.

Once the young sailors learned the rigging trade, they were required to make a jump using a parachute they had packed. The men jumped from Navy blimps stationed at Lakehurst. Ford became nationally known, and in later years traveled throughout the United States and Europe demonstrating the art of parachute rigging and jumping.

In early 1927, a Lt. T.G.W. Settle, a Navy balloon pilot assigned to the Naval Air Station, flew a 19,000 cubic foot balloon from Lakehurst to Lisbon Falls, MI. The nonstop flight took 21.5 hours and covered 478 miles.

In 1930, the unusual Metalclad Airship ZMC-2 arrived at Lakehurst and was flight tested throughout the year. The *Aircraft Year Book of 1931* reported on the progress of the tests.

During the 16 months of its operation, it was flown more than 300 hours and, according to naval officers, functioned satisfactorily as an experimental and training ship. It was reported that the ship had come up to expectations, that it has high structural strength and maneuverability, and has demonstrated its ability to retain helium with less leakage than fabric covered airships of similar size.

The ZMC-2 has a capacity of 200,000 cubic feet of helium and is powered with two air-cooled engines totaling 450 horsepower, giving it a top speed of approximately 70 miles an hour. The only change in the ship since its delivery to the Navy was the substitution of a landing wheel underneath the pilot's cabin for the skid originally used.

The hull covering the ship consists of thin aluminum alloy sheets .0095 inch thick. Hence the name Metalclad. The seams of these sheets are gas tight, the metal hull thus serving as a direct container for the buoyant helium gas as well as carrying all shear stresses and to a large extent the tensile stresses also.

The ZMC-2 remained in service for 12 years. She was scrapped in 1941 after more than 2,200 hours of flight time.

U.S.S. Akron Christened

In August of 1931, the President's wife, Mrs. Herbert Hoover, christened the first of the Navy's new airships *Akron* at the Goodyear Zeppelin Corp. hangar in Akron, OH. It was the second airship named Akron and both came to tragic endings.

The new *Akron* was 780 ft. long and had a maximum diameter of 135 ft. Her top speed was announced at

U.S.S. Macon over Hangar #1, Lakehurst

80 mph and she was designed to carry five fighter planes in a hangar within her hull.

Under the command of Cmdr. Charles Rosendahl, a survivor of the *Shenandoah* crash in 1925, the *Akron* was flown to Lakehurst and commissioned Oct. 27, 1931.

In November, the *Akron* carried 207 passengers on a 10-hour flight, the largest number of passengers ever carried in a single aircraft.

While the nation's attention was focused on the activities of the *Akron,* another unique airship made its first flight at Lakehurst. Designated the *K-1,* the blimp was the first to be fitted with a belly mooring, the first to burn a propane-type gas instead of liquid fuel and the first to have an internally suspended control car. The K-1 was the prototype of blimps used so successfully during World War II.

In January of 1932, the *U.S.S. Akron* left Lakehurst to join the Navy's Scouting Fleet in the Atlantic Ocean. While on maneuvers, the dirigible rendezvoused at Hampton Roads, VA, with the *U.S.S. Potoka* (a Navy tanker) and was moored to the *Patoka's* mast for the first time.

In May, the *Akron's* trapeze gear for the recovery of small aircraft was installed and several practise aircraft recovery missions were achieved. Later in the month the airship flew to San Diego, CA, to participate in naval maneuvers on the west coast. In July, the huge dirigible returned to the east coast after a hazardous flight over the Rocky Mountains. That summer Cmdr. Alger H. Dresel relieved Rosendahl as the commanding officer of the Akron. The following January, Cmdr. Frank C. McCord replaced Dresel.

On April 3, 1933, the *Akron* left Lakehurst at 6:30 in the evening and headed toward New England to assist in calibrating radio direction finders.

The night was black and stormy off the New Jersey coast as Cmdr. McCord advised his helmsman to follow a course due east. McCord hoped to maneuver around the rapidly moving squall line which had not been predicted when the airship departed Lakehurst, just an hour before.

Aboard the pride of the Navy's lighter-than-air fleet was Rear Adm. William A. Moffett, chief of the Bureau of Aeronautics and America's greatest advocate of the airship program.

Just a few minutes past midnight on April 4, the *Akron* was caught in a severe downdraft. McCord immediately had ballast dropped, and for a short period, the *Akron* stabilized. With a great rush, it climbed to 700 feet, only to be hit again by gusting winds.

Dropping at 14 feet per second, the ship's commander ordered his elevator man to increase the rate of climb and at the same time he set the ship's eight engines at full speed. The maneuver didn't work and the tail of the 200-ton dirigible smashed into the churning ocean. The vessel crashed down 20 miles southeast of Barnegat Light. Of the 75 men aboard, only four were saved. Both Moffett and McCord were killed.

Macon Joins Fleet

The previous March, Admiral Moffett's wife had christened the *Akron's* sister ship at the Goodyear-Zeppelin airship dock in Akron. The new air colossus was named the *U.S.S. Macon*

Only 17 days after the loss of the *Akron*, the *Macon* made its maiden flight, achieving a speed of 70 knots. Following subsequent tests, three-bladed, adjustable-pitch propellers were installed, replacing the two-bladed wooden props that had been part of the original equipment.

The *Macon* was commissioned by Rear Adm. Ernest J. King, who had assumed Adm. Moffett's position. Cmdr. Dresel commanded of the new ship.

On June 23, it left Akron on its delivery flight to Lakehurst. Aboard were Paul W. Litchfield, president of Goodyear Zeppelin Corp., Dr. Karl Arnstein, the company's chief engineer and Adm. King.

Like the *Akron*, the *Macon* was equipped with an aircraft recovery trapeze that permitted it to launch and reclaim small Curtiss F9C-2 Sparrowhawk biplanes that were stored in the dirigible's hangar space. Throughout the summer, there were repeated hook-on drills in the skies over Southern Jersey, until the procedure became routine.

On Oct. 12, the Navy's newest airship departed Lakehurst on its first transcontinental flight to Moffett Field, the Naval Air Station near San Francisco. The citizens of South Jersey would never see the huge silver ship of the sky again.

For the remainder of 1933 and all of '34, the *Macon* participated in Navy maneuvers. On an east bound transcontinental flight to Opa-Locka, FL, in April of 1934, it encountered severe turbulence that caused the buckling of diagonal and inter-ring girders. Repairs were made and it continued on the mission, returning to Moffett Field in May of that year. In July, Lt.Cmdr. Herbert Wiley became the skipper of the *Macon*.

It was while on a minor fleet exercise off the Santa Barbara islands on Feb. 11 and 12, 1935 that the *Macon* came to the same sad end as its sister-ship two years earlier.

On the flight back to Moffett Field the airship's upper fin broke loose and the loss of gas in the rear of the ship made it fly nose up. Ballast was immediately dropped and the *Macon* shot up to a height that tripped the automatic valves, releasing valuable lifting gas. Twenty four minutes after the fin ruptured, the *Macon* splashed down in the Pacific. Thirty minutes later, it sank.

Only two sailors of the 83-man crew lost their lives in the tepid Pacific waters. The Navy never attempted to build another dirigible.

Aviation Greats at Teterboro

The grounding of Fokker F-10s following the crash that killed Notre Dame's coach Knute Rockne in April of 1931 had brought a feeling of frustration and despair to the Flying Dutchman's workers at the Teterboro and Passaic plants, but the small airfield continued to be a magnet for the great and near-great aviators throughout 1931. The Wright Aeronautical Corp. hangar where the engines of legendary aircraft had been installed or fine tuned—Byrd's *Josephine Ford* and *America*, Lindbergh's *Spirit of St. Louis*, Chamberlin's *Columbia* and Earhart's *Friendship*-- attracted flyers from around the world who had dreams of conquering new horizons.

In April, Clyde E. Pangborn, the former general manager of the Gates Flying Circus, and Hugh Herndon Jr., a wealthy young man, arrived at Teterboro in a red Bellanca monoplane and announced they planned to fly around the world in a record time. At the same time, a Texas pilot, Wiley Post, and an Australian navigator, Harold Gatty, were making similar preparations.

Pangborn and Herndon hired Lew Yancey to accompany them on a round-trip flight to Puerto Rico to teach them both instrument flying and navigation.

And during the same month, Bert Hinkler, a well-known British test pilot, who was leisurely flying around the world, landed at Teterboro for an engine tune-up.

In early May, a Danish pilot Holgar Hoiriss and Otto Hillig, a studio photographer from Liberty, NY, set their silver Bellanca, *Liberty* down on Teterboro's sod and announced their intention of flying to Denmark. The Wright experts fine-tuned the Liberty's engine and on June 18, Hoiriss and Hillig, who was financing the trip, took off from Teterboro heading for Newfoundland and finally to Denmark.

Also in June, two little known pilots, Russell Boardman and John Polando, flew their Bellanca into Teterboro for a Wright engine check in preparation for a flight from Newfoundland to Turkey. They were aiming at the nonstop distance record set the year before by Frenchman Dieudonne' Costes of 5,000 miles from Paris to Manchuria.

As June gave way to July, both the Pangborn-Herndon and Boardman-Polando teams were ready for their record-breaking attempt. Wiley Post and Harold

Gatty had begun their round-the-world flight two weeks earlier, so Pangborn and Herndon had new speed standards to shoot for. Post's Lockheed Vega *Winnie Mae* eventually circled the globe in eight days, 10 hours and 51 minutes, 12 days faster than the previous record established by Germany's *Graf Zeppelin* in 1929.

Boardman and Polando flew successfully nonstop from New York to Istanbul, topping Costes' record by just 12 miles. When the Bellanca's Wright engine was switched off by Boardman in the Turkey capital, there was only a pint of fuel left in the tanks.

Pangborn and Herndon flew to Wales on the first leg of their around-the-world flight. They moved on across Europe and the Middle East. They were only slightly behind the Post-Gatty time when their plane was badly damaged while landing on a soft field in Siberia. At that point, all hope of breaking the record vanished.

The activity continued at Teterboro during the summer months of 1931 and Bernt Balchen was hired to manage the airfield.

Frank Hawks, who flew for Texaco, and Lou Reichers were having their planes prepared to break inter-city speed records. Navy Lt. Maj. Carleton Champion, who had established an altitude record in 1927, and the former Russian stunt flyer, Alexander P. DeSeversky, also visited the Wright maintenance facility. Pilot Johnny Miller and his Pitcairn autogiro were in and out of Teterboro regularly between air show appointments and test flights for the Pitcairn executives. Miller had built a reputation for his daring by becoming the first man to "loop" an autogiro.

A Persian, Ali Shirazi, who was a U.S. resident, brought his open-cockpit Avro Avian to Teterboro and announced plans to fly to Persia (Iran). He named his plane *New York to Tehran* which was a misnomer for he intended to sail with the plane on a cargo ship across the Atlantic and then fly on to the Persian capital.

After much hoopla, Shirazi flew from Teterboro to Washington, DC, to pick up a letter of good wishes from President Herbert Hoover. While attempting to land at the Washington-Hoover Airport, he inadvertently set his little plane down on top of a hangar. The accident dashed Shirazi's travel plans.

Although the historic flights in 1931 did not have the impact of those in 1927, the year did mark extraordinary accomplishments for that era. The *Trenton State-Gazette* in an editorial on July 31 entitled "Great Summer for Aviation" summed up the season's record of aeronautical achievements.

On to new heights of achievement—that has been the record of aviation during the Summer of 1931.

First it was Post and Gatty with a record-smashing flight around the world. Then it was Herndon and

Pangborn with their successful trans-Atlantic venture as the preliminary journey in an attempt to shatter the Post-Gatty mark.

And now it is Boardman and Polando with a remarkably sensational nonstop dash to Istanbul, Turkey, a distance of some 5,500 miles from their starting point, New York.

With Colonel Lindbergh and his wife in the early stages of their flight to Japan, it is none too soon to observe that the 1931 trans-oceanic and international flying season contains an unusual amount of splendid accomplishments.

The Boardman-Polando feat, incidentally, is perhaps the outstanding instance of adherence to a lengthy flying schedule since Lindbergh blazed the aerial trail from New York to Paris.

Boardman and Polando, after the long-distance record, set out for Turkey. They reached their destination almost exactly in the time and the speed estimated in advance. They shattered the previous mark of 4,912 miles with a facility of performance which challenges the imagination.

These new chapters in the record book of aviation seem to indicate improvements all along the line. It appears that airplane construction, mechanical equipment, pilot skill and meteorological data are rapidly reaching a stage of development which will give great impetus to the various branches of commercial flying.

Certainly it can be said that American aeronauts who dared the great expanse in the Summer of 1931 have contributed immeasurably to the advancement of the art and science of aviation.

Across The Pacific
Clyde Pangborn

Inducted Aviation Hall of Fame of New Jersey, 1973

In October, while Clyde Pangborn and Hugh Herndon were having their Bellanca, *Miss Veedol*, repaired in Siberia, they heard that a Japanese newspaper *Asahi* was offering 50,000 yen (about $25,000) for the first flight across the Pacific Ocean from Japan to the United States mainland. Then the city of Seattle created an extra incentive by offering a $28,000 prize for the first flight from Tokyo to Seattle. The aviators had already sunk $50,000 in their adventure (most of it Herndon's family money) so they jumped at the chance to recoup some of their losses.

Pangborn and Herndon flew immediately to Tokyo unmindful that they needed special entry papers. The Japanese officials accused them of being spies and put them in jail. It cost Herndon's family $1,000 to bail them out. Immediately, the aviators made plans to leave Japan. At 7 a.m., Oct. 4, the overloaded

Pangborn and Herndon

monoplane took off from Smushiro Beach, about 280 miles north of Tokyo, and headed out over the Pacific.

To lighten the load, Pangborn had fashioned a cable release to the landing gear that when pulled would cause the gear to fall off. As soon as they were out over Atsukeshi Bay, Herndon pulled the cable and the gear dropped off. But trouble continued to haunt the flyers.

When Pangborn looked out his window, he could see two bracing rods still attached to the fuselage. He realized that when they attempted a belly landing in Seattle, the two rods would crash through the plane's under belly and perhaps badly injure one or both of the pilots.

Miss Veedol flew across the Pacific at 18,000 feet in turbulent, below-freezing weather. As darkness began to fall over the Bering Strait, Pangborn decided to do something about the bracing rods. He turned the controls over to Herndon, opened the window above his seat, and climbed out onto the Bellanca's wide-starboard wing strut. Then, as he had done so many times as a barnstorming acrobat, he wrapped his legs around the strut and hung down below the fuselage to unscrew the wheel rods. Within seconds, Pangborns fingers and feet began to freeze and the bucking plane made his task seem almost impossible. But with great effort, he loosened the left rod. Almost too stiff to move, Pangborn climbed back into the cockpit, warmed up a bit and then performed the same feat on the right strut.

It was still dark as they passed over the Aleutians. They huddled together for warmth in the freezing cabin and flew on toward the Gulf of Alaska. It was 3 a.m. when they finally reached Seattle, but it was too dark to land. For three hours, they flew around Mt. Rainier debating their next move.

The cloud cover over Washington was low as usual, but at dawn it was time to land, so Pangborn turned the small plane toward his home town of Wenatchee, WA. Once the plane was lined up on the familiar dirt strip just outside of town, he landed the Bellanca slowly and the plane skidded along on its belly until

it came to an abrupt stop when a gust of wind blew the tail in the air. A small crowd, including Pangborn's mother and brother, Percy, and a Japanese man with a $25,000 check, greeted them.

Clyde Pangborn, one of America's leading barnstorming pilots, and Hugh Herndon, a wealthy young man who enjoyed flying, had become the first men to fly 4,600 miles nonstop across the Pacific Ocean. Their flight took 41 hours and 13 minutes.

Because they didn't land in Seattle, just 100 miles away, that city's fathers refused to give them the additional prize money.

Pangborn became enthralled with airplanes the first time he saw one fly over his parent's farm in Wenatchee. He was 13 then. Every time an early barnstormer would pass through the area, Pangborn would drop his farm tools and run to get a closer look at the flying machine. His willingness to help a pilot paid off in free rides.

In 1917, he became an air cadet with the Army Signal Corps and within a few short weeks, he was deemed a pilot. After World War I, he barnstormed along the west coast until he joined Ivan Gates as a partner in the Gates Flying Circus.

When the Circus disbanded in 1929, Pangborn was listed among the top five American pilots who had flown in excess of 10,000 hours by the Air Bureau of the Department of Commerce. Then a Hackensack, NJ, resident, he flew as chief test pilot for the New Standard Aircraft Corp at Teterboro.

In 1933, he and pilot Bennett Griffin planned to fly around the world and set a new flight record, but expected finances never materialized and the project was scrapped.

The MacRobertson Race

Looking for new adventures in 1934, Pangborn teamed with Roscoe Turner, the colorful racing pilot to fly in the MacRobertson race from England to Australia. They chose a twin-engine, low-wing, Boeing 247 passenger plane because of its range.

An Australian chocolate manufacturer, Sir MacPherson Robertson, had put up $75,000 and a gold cup for the three-continent race. Awards were to be made in two categories: open speed and handicap.

The plane was shipped to London on the deck of the *SS Washington*. Sixty entries from 12 countries were received but only 20 planes competed. Although they had an oil leak in one of the B-247's engines and were forced to make unscheduled landings along the way, Pangborn and Turner finished third in the 11,000 mile race. The people of Melbourne, Australia were disappointed to discover that Turner had not brought his pet lion, Gilmore, along on the flight.

At a Congressional Committee hearing in Dec. 1935, Pangborn told what he and Herndon had observed while they had been in Japan. "America is threatened by only one enemy," he said. "That enemy is Japan. Japan is prepared to deal America a tremendous blow. Japan has perfected man-operated torpedoes. Thousands of Japanese have already volunteered for the honor to die as pilots of these bombs."

Six years later, the Japanese bombed Pearl Harbor.

During World War II, he ferried bombers across the Atlantic to Great Britain to help reinforce the British Royal Air Force. When the war ended, he continued to fly but ill health finally took him out of the sky.

In 1958, Pangborn died in New York City at age 62.

Teterboro Depressed

The preparations for the ocean flights of 1931 were the last gasp for the glamour days at Teterboro Airport. By the early spring of 1932, the Fokker plant had closed and the Wright engineers, now part of the Curtiss-Wright organization, were busily transferring their equipment to a new service hangar at the Curtiss-Essex Airport at Fairfield, NJ.

Coupled with those losses was the fact that the New Jersey Aviation Board had grounded all unlicensed aircraft, leaving Teterboro with only a few airworthy planes. The Depression was taking a terrible toll. Pilots were hard put to make a living and barnstorming returned with a flourish. The former Fokker hangar was converted into an arena where weekly boxing matches and marathon dances were held.

Wendell G. Randolph, a chemical engineer with a masters degree from Columbia University, rented a small, unheated hangar at Teterboro and, with an uncle, began producing aircraft dopes. By 1935, Randolph Products was successful enough to move to a Carlstadt facility, where it grew to some 60,000 square feet of office space, manufacturing facilities and scientific laboratories. The company went on to become a leading producer of industrial paints for the aerospace industry.

During World War I, Randolph was credited with developing the gas masks used at that time. Decades later, his company developed the high-tech putty used on the space shuttle.

In the 1980s, Randolph's son, John, took over the daily operation of the business, but the old man stayed on as chairman of the board until the time of his death in August 1990 at age 94.

Browne Flies Atlantic

In May of 1932, Amelia Earhart, Nate Browne and Stanley Hauser were all at Teterboro preparing their aircraft for transatlantic flights before the Wright maintenance hangar closed.

Nate Browne, a test pilot for Aeromarine Klemm and Vincent Burnelli at Keyport Airport was one of the few adventurers able to find backing for a record flight. He flew his Fokker Universal monoplane into Teterboro to have its Whirlwind engine serviced prior to his successful flight across the Atlantic Ocean.

Upon his return from Europe, Browne flew to Seattle, WA, to prepare for a transpacific flight. His plans called for refueling while in flight because he didn't feel the Fokker could carry sufficient fuel to complete the nonstop journey to Japan. A veteran parachute jumper, Frank Brooks of Oregon, was hired to accompany Browne to handle the refueling hose while in flight. During a practise session over the Seattle, it took three attempts to retrieve the hose that dangled below the refueling plane. Once the hose was inserted into the Fokker's tank and fuel began to flow, the hose became entangled on the plane and a fire developed. Both fliers had to bail out over Puget Sound. Browne's dream of becoming the first man to fly west to east across the Pacific had gone up in smoke.

Stanley Hauser, a Linden, NJ, pilot, attempted to duplicate Browne's Atlantic flight. Engine trouble forced him to turn back, but it didn't dampen his enthusiasm. After repairs were made, he took off again and disappeared over the Atlantic. For six days, his family and friends were tormented by his loss, until a radio report from a steamship told of his rescue at sea.

She Conquers Atlantic
Amelia Earhart

Inducted Aviation Hall of Fame of New Jersey, 1973

In the early spring of 1932, as Amelia Earhart prepared her red Lockheed Vega monoplane for a solo flight across the Atlantic to Europe, she was arguably the most famous woman in America. Since her first transatlantic flight in 1928 as a passenger aboard the Fokker trimotor *Friendship,* she had been a leader in promoting women's roles in aviation.

In 1929, she and other leading women aviators of the time, promoted a Women's Air Derby, a cross-country competition run in conjunction with the National Air Races held in Cleveland, OH. The race was open to women holding a pilot's license with a minimum of 100 hours of solo flying time. Earhart estimated there were less than 30 eligible candidates in America. The first Derby course was from Santa Monica, CA, to Cleveland. Louise Thaden, one of the best known aviatrix in the country, finished first. Earhart was third. Humorist Will Rogers dubbed the race "The Powder Puff Derby." Immediately after the first derby, Earhart and 25 other licensed women pilots met at Curtiss Field in Valley Stream, Long Island, to form an association. It was called The Ninety Nines for the number of charter members who had joined. In the past 60 years, the Ninety Nines has increased its membership a thousandfold and has chapters throughout the world.

Although she was a shy person, interested only in proving that women could compete in the air with their male counterparts, Earhart was constantly called on by advertising agencies, movie producers, writers and promoters of every ilk to endorse their products or participate in stunts of various kinds. It was all more than the young, former social worker could handle alone, so she asked George Palmer Putnam, the man who had discovered her, to help sort out the endorsements and other proposals.

She wrote a book *20 Hrs, 40 Min* which was published by Putnam's company. She became the aviation editor for *Cosmopolitan* magazine, and endorsed a number of aviation products and Lucky Strike cigarettes even though she was a nonsmoker. Many staid Americans were perturbed by that latter association.

Soon, the aviatrix and the publisher developed a close bond of friendship. In 1929, he asked her to marry him. She politely declined until, two years and six proposals later, she gave in. Just prior to the ceremony, she handed him a note that read:

"Dear G.P., You must know again my reluctance to marry, my feeling that I shatter thereby chances in work which mean so much to me. I feel the move just now as foolish as anything I could do. In our life together, I shall not hold you to any medieval code of faithfulness to me, nor shall I consider myself bound to you similarly. I may have to keep someplace where I can go to be myself now and then, for I cannot guarantee to endure at all times the confinements of even an attractive cage. I must exact a cruel promise, and that is you will let me go in a year if we find no happiness together. I will try to do my best in every way."

Thus, the marriage began. The couple moved into his house in Rye, NY, and the husband/agent continued to promote his restless wife. The team became so successful that enough money was raised to underwrite other flying adventures. Through it all, however, A.E., as she liked to be called, hated the commercialism that she faced almost daily.

It is said that one morning over coffee at home early in 1932, A.E. asked Putnam if he would mind if she attempted to fly solo across the Atlantic. He agreed, for he knew that she had already become determined to be the first woman to accomplish that feat.

To prepare for the flight, the flier turned to her friend Bernt Balchen, who called Teterboro his home base.

She brought her Lockheed Vega to the Jersey airport, so that Balchen and Ed Gorski, a former maintenance

supervisor for Fokker, could prepare it for the long journey. They strengthened the plane's fuselage, added extra fuel tanks and ordered a new Pratt and Whitney engine from the East Hartford, CN, plant. Gorski, who retired to Kennelon, NJ, after a 60-year career in aviation, vividly remembered those early days:

"We flight-tested the Vega for hours on end over Teterboro," he recalled with nostalgic fondness. "We would load the little plane with sandbags to simulate the weight of the fuel that would have to be carried over the Atlantic, and then fly around the Meadowlands. When it came time to land, we had to rid ourselves of the weight, so I would push the sandbags out while Bernt flew in circles. People thought we were dropping bombs. Today, those bags would have landed right on Giant Stadium in East Rutherford."

Both Balchen and Gorski accompanied Earhart to Harbour Grace, Newfoundland, and stayed with her until the weather predictions over the Atlantic were favorable. Balchen remembered those last days before the flight.

"She arrives at the field in jodphurs and leather flying jacket," he wrote, "her close-cropped blond hair tousled, quiet and unobtrusive as a young Lindbergh. She listens calmly, only biting her lip a little, as I go over with her the course to hold and tell her what weather she can expect on the way across the ocean. She looks at me with a small lonely smile and says, 'Do you think I can make it?' and I grin back: 'You bet.' She crawls calmly into the cockpit of the big empty airplane, starts the engine, runs it up, checks the mags, and nods her head. We pull the chocks, and she is off."

Earhart left Harbour Grace on May 20, 1932 — exactly five years to the day that Charles Lindbergh had

Gorski, Earhart and Balchen

become the first person to fly nonstop from New York to Paris. When she landed in a field in Culmore, Ireland, 14 hours and 54 minutes later, her blithe greeting to the first astonished Irish farmer who met her was, "Hi! I've come from America."

Upon return from Europe she was honored with a ticker-tape parade up Broadway in New York City. She told friends that she at last felt vindicated for her "uselessness" on the *Friendship* flight of 1928.

Although she was world famous, Earhart never seemed impressed with herself. As Ed Gorski recalled, "Amelia was a very nice lady. She was never the least bit pretentious."

Once the Atlantic was conquered, Earhart began planning a more ambitious flight. She wanted to become the first woman to fly an airplane around the world. She again went back to Lockheed and purchased another Vega, selling the red Atlantic plane to the Franklin Institute in Philadelphia.

The Vega's unique monocoque design had attracted many men and women eager to set new records or fly to some impossible place. The monocoque construction was originally developed by John Knudsen Northrop, a Newark, NJ, native, who worked for Lockheed in 1927. A year later, Northrop formed his own aircraft corporation and built his first experimental flying wing and a series of all-metal planes called "Alpha," "Beta" and "Gamma." The latter became extremely popular with pilots looking for dependable long-distance aircraft. The planes he developed over the years, including the first successful flying wing in 1939, are legendary. Before he retired in 1952, he gave our nation the first inertially-guided intercontinental ballistic missile, the "Snark."

Earhart and her husband moved from Rye to the West Coast and found a backer who was willing to sponsor a flight from Hawaii to the U.S. mainland. So she, Putnam and Paul Mantz, a Hollywood stunt pilot who had become her adviser, sailed to Hawaii. She flew back to the mainland in 18 hours and 15 minutes. Another record flight had been easily accomplished.

On May 8, Earhart flew nonstop from Burbank, CA, to Mexico City. Following several days of celebrations, she flew from the Mexican capital to Newark in 14 hours, 18 minutes and 30 seconds—the only woman to fly the route in both directions.

Her Last Flight

Preparations for the round-the-world flight began while Earhart served as a visiting aeronautics adviser at Purdue University in Indiana. An Amelia Earhart Research Foundation was established at Purdue and money was raised for a "flying laboratory" for her use. The plane chosen was a twin-engine, low-wing Lockheed Electra built to accommodate 10 passengers. The cabin space would permit her to carry the necessary extra fuel and instruments for the global flight.

Two men were chosen to be the navigators on the flight. Harry Manning, a captain with the United States Lines, and Fred Noonan, an aviator with a great deal of navigational experience. Earhart, with co-pilot Mantz and her two navigators, flew from Oakland, CA, to Honolulu on March 17. Two days later, the same crew, minus Mantz, were set to take off for Howland Island in the Pacific, but the Electra hit a rut that sheared off the plane's undercarriage and the flight was cancelled. They returned to California with the plane aboard a cargo ship, and then sent the Electra to Lockheed in Burbank for repairs. While the work was underway, Manning withdrew from the project because of other commitments.

When the plane was again air worthy, Earhart and Noonan decided to reverse the direction of the flight. Their new route took them to Miami, FL, Puerto Rico, Venezuela, Brazil and then across the South Atlantic to Africa. They traversed Africa and Asia and then flew on to Port Darwin, Australia. Their last successful flight was to Lae, New Guinea. At that point, they had circumnavigated three quarters of the earth's surface.

The next leg of their journey would take them to Howland Island, a mere dot on the charts of the Pacific Ocean. Before taking off from Lae, Earhart wrote a note to her husband:

"I wish I could stay here peacefully for a time and see something of this strange land. The whole width of the world has passed behind us—except this broad ocean. I shall be glad when we have the hazards of its navigation behind us."

Earhart's apprehension concerning the most dangerous portion of the flight was not unfounded. With the limited navigational equipment available to Noonan in 1937, the aviators and their supporters knew Howland would be difficult to locate.

On July 2, 1937 (July 1 across the international date line on Howland Island) at 10 p.m., Earhart guided the Electra down the 3,000 foot jungle runway and lifted off toward Howland where the United States Coast Guard had stationed the cutter *Itasca* as a navigational aid.

The following morning aboard the *Itasca*, Commander Warner K. Thompson and his crew of spotters strained their eyes in search of a small silver plane that might be shrouded in a distant cloud bank hanging ominously in the western sky. The plane was then an hour overdue.

At 7:42 a.m. (Howland time), more than 21 hours after their departure from Lae, Earhart's voice was heard clearly in the radio room aboard the cutter.

"KHAQQ calling *Itasca*." she said. "We must be on you but cannot see you; but gas is running low. Have been unable to reach you by radio. We are flying at 1,000 feet."

Cmdr. Thompson and the spotters redoubled their efforts to make visual contact with the Electra, but to no avail.

They heard from the aviatrix again about 15 minutes later. She reported that the Electra was circling, but could not hear the ship's reply. Frantically, the sailors in the radio shack sent a series of Morse-code dots and dashes which were heard on the plane. "We are receiving your signals," she replied. "Please take bearing on us and answer on 3105 kilocycles." Try as they could, the radiomen simply could not get a fix on the plane's position. It was becoming obvious to Cmdr. Thompson that what had begun as an upbeat mission for his ship was swiftly turning into a tragedy.

The frantic voice of Amelia Earhart was heard for the last time a 8:45 a.m. "We are on the line of position 157-337. We are running north and south." Then silence.

When it became apparent that the aircraft was down, the Coast Guard cutter set out in search of the missing Electra with no exact location for guidance. Soon, an armada of rescue vessels and aircraft was launched to search for the pilots. Nothing was ever found of the airplane or of the flyers' personal belongings.

More than 50 years have passed since Earhart and her navigator vanished somewhere over the South Pacific. If she is still alive, as some speculative journalists have claimed, she would now be more than 90 years old.

The sad truth is that no one will ever know what became of the cheerful lady with the tousled hair and invincible spirit. Nonetheless, the memory of her tenacious determination and unequaled achievements will continue to be an inspiration to women throughout the world for years to come.

One of the verses that appeared in Gill Robb Wilson's book, *The Airman's World*, published by Random House in 1957, was entitled *Amelia*.

Somewhere, a fin on a lazy sea
And a broken prop on a coral key;
Somewhere, a dawn whose morning star
Must etch dim light on a broken spar;
Somewhere, a twilight that cannot go
  Til it misses the surf with after glow;
But here, only silence and weary eyes
And an empty hangar and empty skies.
Somewhere, the toss of a tousled head
In the street of the angels overhead;
Somewhere, a smile that would never fade

As the score reversed in the game she played;
Somewhere, a spirit whose course held true
To do the thing that it wished to do;
But here, only silence and weary eyes
And an empty hangar and empty skies."

Casey Jones School
Charles S. "Casey" Jones

Inducted Aviation Hall of Fame of New Jersey 1984

In 1932, Charles S. "Casey" Jones and Lee Warrender, both former employees of the Curtiss-Wright Corp., along with World War I flying ace Col. George Vaughn, then president of the Eastern Aeronautical Corp. at Newark Airport, established the Casey Jones School of Aeronautics in Newark. The school was the first to be licensed by the Aeronautics Branch of the Department of Commerce (now the Federal Aviation Administration) as a technical school. Jones served as its first president.

The initial curriculum was a master mechanic's course of 14 months duration. Later it became a two-year course. Shortly after the mechanics program was begun, an aeronautical engineering program was instituted under the direction of Walter M. Hartung. In the first 18 months, the school expanded its facilities in Newark. An Aeronautical journal reported, "With 180 students enrolled, the school has become one of the largest non-military schools in the world for aeronautical mechanics and engineers."

In 1937, the school took on the ambitious project of building its own airplane. It was a two-place pusher amphibian conceived by Lee Warrender and built under the supervision of Walter Hartung. In test flights at North Beach Airport in Jamaica, NY, the amphibian lifted off the water in 26 seconds and flew at a cruising speed of 80 mph.

Jones, Vaughn and Warrender also organized the JVW Corp., a subsidiary of the school, which operated a hangar at Newark Airport and was the sales and service representative for Stinson Aircraft and Link Trainers.

Jones had seen an amusement park ride which gave patrons a chance to experience "piloting" a plane. The ride had been invented by Ed Link of the Link Pipe Organ Co. of Binghamton, NY. Jones met with Link and suggested that a Sperry gyroscope be installed in the ride so Army mail pilots could be taught to fly with instruments without ever leaving the ground. That suggestion led to the highly successful Link Trainer.

When La Guardia Airport opened in 1939, Jones and his partners established a second technical school adjacent to the airport. They named it the Academy of Aeronautics and offered master mechanic and design courses.

When President Franklin Roosevelt announced his proposed program for the construction of 50,000 airplanes in 1938, it was obvious that the Air Corps would need assistance in the technical and mechanical field of instruction. Jones, with a group of executives from flight and technical schools, approached the Air Corps with a proposal for the establishment of both flight and technical instruction at their schools. The proposal was enthusiastically accepted.

Just prior to and during World War II, more than 17,000 Air Corps technicans were trained under the program at expanded facilities at Newark and La Guardia.

After the war the Newark school was closed. The Academy of Aeronautics (now the College of Aeronautics) has continued to prosper over the years. Since its beginnings in Newark, the school has graduated more than 55,000 students, thought to be the largest number from any institution of its kind.

Casey Jones was born in Castleton, VT, in 1894. He graduated from Middlebury College, VT, in 1913. In the fall of 1914, he took the position of Physical Education Director of Montclair Academy, Montclair, NJ. While there, he met and married Marjorie Williams of West Orange, NJ. Within the year, he had enlisted in the Aviation Section of the Army Signal Corps. Later, he served in France as an instructor and combat flyer with the French Escadrille Spad 96.

Upon his discharge from the service in 1919, Jones became affiliated with the Curtiss Corp., organizing the Curtiss Exhibition Co. which conducted flying schools and a charter passenger service. Later, the company became the Curtiss Flying Service with a chain of 40 flying fields located throughout the United States. He became a vice president of the Curtiss-Wright Corp. in 1929, a position he held until 1932.

In addition to his administrative duties, in the early 1920s Jones became interested in airplane racing. The "clipped wing" Curtiss Oriole biplane he designed was a popular attraction at all the races in which he participated.

At the time of his death in 1976, Charles "Casey" Jones was one of the most highly respected aviation personalities in the United States.

Colonel George A. Vaughn

At the end of World War I, Col. George A. Vaughn, a Staten Island resident, was second only to America's ace of aces, Capt. Eddie Rickenbacker, when it came to the number of enemy aircraft destroyed in aerial battles over France. Rickenbacker was credited with 26 "kills" and Vaughn had 13. Several other American flying aces had more kills than Vaughn but they did not survive the war.

A graduate of Princeton University, Vaughn was an astute businessman who remained in the field of aviation for his entire career. He was one of the founders, and for 19 years, the commander of the New York Air National Guard. He remained active with that group throughout his lifetime. Several years before he died in the summer of 1989, Vaughn had described what a "dogfight" between German and American fighter planes had been like. He had scored seven victories while attached to the British Royal Flying Corps and six more with the American Expeditionary Forces.

"Most people seem to think a dogfight is just two airplanes going round and round for several minutes at a time until one shoots the other down," he said. "As a rule, it didn't work out that way because there were so many in the sky that you jumped from one to the other, and two or three of them shot at you, not just one. You shot at four or five, anybody you could get your sights on — and then another one. It was usually just two or three bursts, and then maybe somebody was on you by that time. That's the way it was.

"The atmosphere was more or less a sporting one in those days. I suppose it was the last time that there would really be such a thing as, you might say, hand-to-hand combat in the air. Although we flew in formation, when the actual combat came it was strictly a one-man proposition. Everybody was by himself."

The close associations made during those days naturally carried over into private and business relationships after the war. Many former combat pilots worked together on various projects throughout their lifetimes. George Vaughn, a gentle, quiet man, was always one around whom his former flying buddies rallied.

Walter M. Hartung

Inducted Aviation Hall of Fame of New Jersey, 1990

Walter M. Hartung

Born in New York City and raised in Westwood, NJ, Walter M. Hartung spent more than 50 years in the field of aeronautical education. Upon graduating from the Guggenheim School of Aeronautics, New York University, with Bachelor of Science and Aeronautical Engineering degrees in the mid-1920s, Hartung's career began in 1928 as an aircraft designer with Aeromarine-Klemm in Keyport, NJ. When the 1929 stock market crash forced the company to close, he worked briefly for aircraft designer Vincent Burnelli and the Merrill Aircraft Corp. He began his teaching career in 1931 as dean of aeronautical engineering at Beckley College in Harrisburg, PA. During his summer vacations, he traveled to Massachusetts to work for the Granville Aircraft Corp. He was one of three engineers who designed the Gee Bee Racer in which James Doolittle won the coveted Thompson Trophy in 1932.

In 1933, he joined the newly formed Casey Jones School of Aeronautics as chief engineering instructor. He served in that capacity at both the Newark school and its expanded facility, the Academy of Aeronautics. Early in World War II, he supervised the training of Army Air Corps mechanics and contributed his talents to the Airline War Training Institute. More than 16,000 men and women were trained at the Casey Jones facilities as mechanics for wartime service.

Hartung joined the Air Corps in 1943 as a captain and served with the Air Transport Command overseeing aircraft maintenance in both the European and Pacific theaters of operation. When discharged, he held the rank of of colonel.

Returning to the Academy of Aeronautics, he was named executive vice president and dean of the institution, a position he held from 1946 to 1963. During that period, he earned his PhD in education administration from New York University.

In 1961, as chairman of the U.S. technical education delegation, he led a group of college officials on a tour of Russian educational facilities.

Under his leadership, the academy became a nonprofit institution in 1963, and he was named president in 1964. He became chairman of the board in 1984.

A two-term mayor of Tenafly, NJ, Hartung joined the board of the Aviation Hall of Fame of New Jersey (AHOF) in the mid-1980s and served a three year term as president of the board from 1983-85. It was during his administration that the AHOF's Educational Center was constructed. He also served a term as the president of the prestigious Wings Club headquartered in New York City.

In 1990, his lifelong dedication to aeronautical education was recognized when he was inducted into the Aviation Hall of Fame & Museum of New Jersey.

George W. Brush

Hartung was succeeded as president of the Academy of Aeronautics in 1984 by George W. Brush, a native of Boonton, NJ. In 1986, Brush was instrumental in having his school achieve college status in New York State.

Brush began his aviation career as a student at the Casey Jones School of Aeronautics and graduated with an aircraft maintenance certificate. In 1939, he became an experimental machinist for the Curtiss-Wright Corp. in Paterson where he worked until he was drafted into the field artillery in 1942. He became the first director of training at the Teterboro School of Aeronautics in 1947, and joined the Academy of Aeronautics at La Guardia Airport in 1950 as Senior Administrator, a position he held until he was named president of the school 35 years later. Over the years, Brush earned a bachelor of science degree in business administration at Fairleigh Dickinson University in Teaneck, NJ, and a doctorate in higher education administration at New York University.

The long time Maywood resident, served with a number of professional educational organizations. He was a charter member of the New York Board of Regents External Degree Faculty and a member of the Accreditation Visitors, Middle States Association of Colleges and Schools and the Aeronautical Advisory Commission, New York Board of Education, just to name a few.

In 1990, Brush retired from the College of Aeronautics but planned to remain active in educational programs in both New York and New Jersey.

Teaneck High School

The first high school aviation course in the nation became part of the Teaneck, high school curriculum in September of 1933. When the program was approved by the New Jersey State Board of Education and the Commissioner of Education, a World War I pilot, Major Arthur G. Norwood of Teaneck was granted the first aviation teacher's license in the Garden State.

Students interested in the coed aviation program had to be 15 years of age. The course consisted of a two year curriculum. First year students met five periods each week during school hours. Second year students met three times a week at the high school and an additional two hours at Teterboro Airport, where a two-seat Aeronca was based. The airplane had been purchased by Norwood from Ed Gorski for $1,890.

The aviation course had sprung from an extra-curricular activity begun in 1930 by several students interested in flying. A glider club was organized under the direction of Major Norwood, and a glider was built. The motorless craft flew 1,400 hours, mostly down a slope behind the school. It made 8,000 take-offs and landings without an accident.

The success of the aviation course attracted nationwide attention. Inquiries concerning the program were received from 15 states. Leslie F. Neville, a Teaneck resident and managing editor of *Aviation*

1932 - Teaneck High School glider. Left, Bill Robertson and "Skid" Johnson; 6th from right Maj. Arthur Norwood, 5th George Rosenberg, 4th Larry Muller.

Magazine, said of the course "its work is phenomenal and unprecedented." In September 1934, Lord and Lady Henry Tate visited the school. Lady Tate was a member of the British House of Commons and chairperson of the Civil Air Committee. She was vitally interested in seeing how the students had progressed.

On May 5, 1934, George Rosenberg of the 1933 graduating class made his first solo flight. In September of 1934, Fred Gloeckler soloed followed a month later by Bill Robertson. The following year, at age 18, Robertson became the first person in the nation to obtain a license to fly passengers after learning to fly in a high school aviation class.

By early 1936, 11 students had soloed and were working toward a flying license. They were Lawrence Muller, Fack Cafafelli, Allen Price, Patricia Thomas, Lawrence Sottonsanti, Arnold Johnson, Dorothy Fulton, Harry Rutherford, Louis Rohr, Henry Scheff and Carl Hilbers.

The aviation industry was also attracted to the Teaneck high program. Major Norwood received a letter from the Luscombe Aircraft Corp. of West Trenton, offering to take two boys from the graduating class and train them in sales and manufacturing.

Norwood said at the time, "It is gratifying to receive offers from the various aircraft companies, because it proves that the aviation classes are worth more than just publicity for Teaneck High School."

Lawrence Muller received his private pilot's license in May of 1936 at Roosevelt Field, LI., and, at age 21, was invited to teach an aviation class at State Street Junior High School in Hackensack. In his first year, he had 24 students in the class that met once a week.

That same year, Patricia Thomas received her license and was believed to be the youngest woman pilot in the nation, and the first to be licensed following instruction in a high School aviation course. She went on to acquire both instructor and commercial licenses.

In May of 1937, Major Norwood's flight training was credited with saving the life of 19-year-old Dorothy Fulton when the propeller of the school's airplane dropped off.

Fulton, who had received her private pilot's license in August of 1936, had taken off from Bendix Airport, climbed to 2,000 feet and was flying over Cedar Lane in Teaneck when the accident occurred. She later explained what happened. "It was so hot I decided I would fly over Teaneck a while to cool off. I usually practice shooting landings, but this time I decided I'd just stay up a while. I heard the motor speed up. Right away I cut the switch. That is drilled into us at school. And then I saw the propeller moving away from the ship. I suppose I should have got scared, but I didn't have time."

The propeller crank shaft had broken and the propeller was swinging around toward the wing. "I just had time to lift the wing so the prop could get past," Fulton further explained. "If I hadn't, the propeller would have torn the wing apart and I probably would have crashed. Then I dropped the nose of my plane to keep up my flight speed, which was about 80 miles an hour. The problem was to stay in the air for five miles, the distance to the airport. Luckily, at school we learned our gliding angles well, so I made it."

At the time of the incident, Fulton had soloed 95 hours.

Major Norwood was quoted as saying he was proud of his young student and that the old idea that women didn't know anything about machinery and motors was untrue. Dorothy Fulton had proven his point.

Flight training was abandoned during the 1937-38 school year and Norwood resigned as the aviation instructor. In the four years that he taught aviation theory and flying at Teaneck, more than 300,000 miles were flown and 32,500 takeoffs and landings were accomplished without injury to the plane or students. When he left Teaneck, Norwood could proudly point to the fact that from his graduating classes one student had a transport license, another worked in the design department of an airplane factory, six were attending engineering colleges and five others had nearly accumulated enough flying hours to become transport pilots.

Joseph Rosen, who had graduated from New York University's Guggenheim School of Aeronautics in New York City with a Masters' Degree in Physics and an aeronautical engineering degree in 1934, became the aviation instructor in 1939.

The aviation course flourished under Rosen's tutelage. He taught six classes daily. The subjects covered were aerodynamics, aircraft structure, meteorology, navigation and power plants. During World War II, the enrollment in the aviation program reached 35 students.

Six students who would have graduated in the spring of 1944 dropped out of class to enlist in air units of the various services. Four others left to work in war plants.

One former Aviation Club member, Cpl. Robert A. Rockefeller, was killed in the South Pacific on a mission as an aerial photographer. Another, Arnold R. "Skip" Johnson, won a Silver Star for gallantry. As a B-17 pilot in the Pacific, his crew had been credited with downing 10 Japanese planes and the sinking of

a submarine in 1942. When he returned to Teaneck in December of that year, the Teaneck V.F.W. and a citizens committee honored him with a dinner. Of the women who took flight instruction, Patricia Thomas, Dorothy Fulton and Kay Menges joined the WASP and ferried war planes to ports of embarkation around the United States.

In a newspaper interview in 1944, Joseph Rosen estimated that more than 350 students had taken classroom instruction in theory and principle of aviation. Of that number 40 per cent were in military aviation either as pilots, mechanics or ground crew workers. Most of the remainder, he said, were working in aviation war plants, many as engineers.

In the same article, the Teaneck high principal, Charles Steel, claimed the highest representation in the military air forces of any New Jersey school on a percentage basis, and more skilled aviation workers in factories than any other school. By 1945, aviation was being taught in 14,000 of the 25,686 high schools in the nation.

Following the war, the flying aviation course was dropped because of lack of student interest and Joseph Rosen took his aviation program to Bergen Junior College which later became the main campus of Fairleigh Dickinson University in Teaneck.

When he was two months old, Rosen's family moved from Brooklyn, NY, to Perth Amboy where he attended a one room school house. The family later moved to Hudson County, and Rosen went to high school in Hoboken and West New York.

He worked for several aviation manufacturers before becoming a junior aeronautical engineer at the Naval Aircraft factory in Philadelphia. During the period he worked for Teaneck High School, he taught pilot training and advanced engine courses at New York University. He retired from his professorship at Fairleigh Dickinson in 1975, but was still active at age 81 in 1990.

Byrd Back to Antarctic
Isaac "Ike" Schlossbach

A native of Neptune, NJ, Isaac "Ike" Schlossbach, a former Navy commander and pilot, was the navigator aboard the ship, *Bear of Oakland,* that carried Richard E. Byrd's second scientific expedition to Antarctica in 1933.

Schlossbach graduated from the U.S. Naval Academy at Annapolis, MD, in 1915. The following year, he became one of the first students at the Navy's submarine school in New London, CT. During World War I, he served aboard a submarine off the coast of Europe.

Surviving the war unscathed, he decided to become involved in another new field—aviation. In 1921, he volunteered to be a Navy pilot and was assigned to the Navy's flight school at Pensacola, FL. Schlossbach was in the first class of regular Navy men to earn their wings. He had flown just 65 hours prior to being assigned to fly a twin-engine flying boat attached to the U.S.S. Wright.

In the late '20s, Schlossbach developed problems in the optic nerve of his left eye which eventually had to be removed, forcing him to retire. At age 38, he was at loose ends until he read of Sir George Wilkins' proposed plan to sail a submarine under the polar ice pack. He volunteered to join the expedition and sailed as first officer and navigator aboard the sub *Nautilus*. Although they were never able to find their way under the ice to the North Pole, they did prove it was possible to sail safely under the Arctic ice.

In 1932, Schlossbach's next adventure took him into the tropical jungles of Central America in search of fertile soil for the cultivation of bananas for the United Fruit Co. A year later, he was back in the frozen Antarctic region with Byrd. At Byrd's Antarctic base, Little America, Schlossbach found the Fairchild airplane that had been flown by another Garden State pilot, Dean Smith, on the first Byrd expedition and then abandoned. Determined to make the plane fly again, although it had spent five years under the snow, Schlossbach and several colleagues, dragged the old ship across the frozen tundra and rebuilt it under a wind-torn tent. Months later, the *Fairchild* again flew.

It was during this second Byrd expedition that the admiral decided to spend the five winter months alone in an advance weather station 123 miles from Little America. After two months in solitary confinement, Byrd realized that a poorly ventilated oil stove was slowly poisoning him. It took two days by dog sled for a rescue party to travel to the Advance Base. There they found Byrd weak and incoherent. Two months later, Byrd was strong enough to travel and Ike Schlossbach flew to the base to transport the admiral back to Little America.

The Byrd expedition returned to the United States in 1935. Three years later, Schlossbach's contribution to the project were recognized in Trenton when Governor A. Harry Moore presented him with a special Congressional Medal of Honor.

There had been a delay in presenting the medal because Schlossbach had left for the Arctic in 1937 as a member of the Clifford MacGregor Arctic Expedition. Schlossbach and MacGregor, a meteorologist at Newark Airport, had met at the Explorers' Club in New York City and decided to explore the regions of Greenland that were still unknown. They recruited nine young men for the expedition and when they left Port Newark on a three-masted schooner, Schlossbach was the only experienced explorer in the group. During the 15 months in Greenland, the Neptune native made 20 airplane flights over the unexplored land and was the first to fly over Ellesmereland.

Other New Jerseyans on the low-budget expedition were John Johnson of Farmingdale, Bob Inglis of Trenton, Murray Weiner of Bradley Beach, Francis Laurence of East Orange, Robert Furlong of Upper Montclair and Roy Fitzsimmons of Newark. Most of the crew members contributed something toward the expenses of the trip. One member, a Bob Danskin, reportedly gave a four-place Waco 220 airplane.

In 1938, the old Navy commander decided to establish an airport on his property in Neptune. He called it "Jumping Brook." It became the first home of the Jersey Aero Club which Schlossbach had helped establish. The flying club idea was novel at that time, but because of joint ownership of aircraft many people had an opportunity to learn to fly during those Depression days.

A quote from an article written by a local pilot Steve Giegerich in the *Asbury Park Press* in 1983, emphasized Schlossbach's importance to the aviation buffs in the New Jersey shore area.

... he was a mentor, a teacher and a friend to countless area residents who learned the joy of flying under his tutelage and guidance.

At the outbreak of World War II, Schlossbach was again in Antarctica with Admiral Byrd (1939-1941) when President Franklin Roosevelt decided to establish airfields in Labrador, Greenland and Iceland. He was recalled to active duty and, along with other Arctic pioneers like Bernt Balchen, he headed off to Labrador to build an airbase at Fort Chimo. When the job was completed, Schlossbach was sent to Guadalcanal in the Pacific, which he called the "hottest place I've ever been." Later, he returned to the north country for another tour of duty at Argentia, Newfoundland. When the war ended, Schlossbach, then 56, participated in the Ronne Antarctic Research Expedition (1946-48), the last private American expedition to go to the Antarctic.

The expedition mapped 450,000 square miles. A cape that he discovered was named Cape Schlossbach.

The original Jumping Brook Airport was later renamed Schlossbach Field and then the Asbury Park Air Terminal. In 1973, the airfield was sold to developers.

The Jersey Aero Club, the oldest and largest continually active flying club in New Jersey, is now based at Ed Brown's Allaire Airport. In 1963, the club honored Schlossbach for his services to the non-business pilots of the Garden State.

The tribute read:

"All aviation people in New Jersey owe much to 'Ike' Schlossbach who was a pioneer in aviation and helped so many youth to fly, at no profit to himself."

Ike Schlossbach died at age 93 in 1984.

In September of 1988, the Jersey Aero Club celebrated its 50th anniversary with an Air Fair at Allaire Airport. It was the second air fair in the club's history, the first had been held 42 years earlier.

Along with Ike Schlossbach the original founders were Bruce Larrabee, Dan McLain, Richard Hicholas and Richard Wallace. By April 1939, 70 members were listed in the Articles of Incorporation. Records indicate there are only three older clubs in the United States.

During the first half century, the club owned 37 aircraft (14 purchased new) and some 1,500 members have participated in club activities. In 1988, only Stanley Herbert, one of the first to join in 1938, remained a club member. The active flying members with the longest tenure were Don Hurley and Abe Gindoff, who both joined in 1947.

The first woman member, Ruth Fewsmith, joined in April 1940. Since then, there have been 30 women members.

Richard Evelyn Byrd

No American explorer was as highly revered as Richard Evelyn Byrd. His exploits in the Arctic regions of the world were international news. He was an heroic figure who had a flair for accomplishing feats that were beyond the comprehension of the people of his time.

Byrd was born in Winchester, VA, in 1888. His well-to-do parents were able to send him to the Shenandoah Military Academy, the Virginia Military Institute and the University of Virginia, prior to his entering the U.S. Naval Academy in 1908. Graduating with the Class of 1912, he was commissioned an Ensign. In March 1916, he was transferred to the Navy's retired list with the rank of Lieutenant (jg) because of a leg injury. In May of the same year, he was recalled to active duty just months before the United States declared war on Germany. After serving with the Navy's Bureau of Navigation for several months, he was assigned to the Naval Aeronautic Station, Pensacola, FL, for aviation training. He earned his Navy wings in April 1918.

Byrd became the commanding officer of the U.S. Naval Aviation Forces in Canada for the remainder of the war.

After the Armistice, he served in the Office of the Director of Naval Aviation, Bureau of Navigation, and in April and May, 1919, he participated in the navigational preparation for the transatlantic flights of the NC planes. Over the next decade, he organized and participated in a series of historic flights.

In the spring of 1925, byrd organized and assumed command of the Naval Flying Unit which accompanied the Polar expedition of Donald B. MacMillan. A year later, he and Floyd Bennett became the first men to fly over the North Pole.

In 1927, he commanded the Fokker trimotor *America* to Europe that carried the first official sack of mail between the continents.

In 1928, word was received that Byrd, Bernt Balchen and Harold June had flown over the South Pole, the United States Congress advanced him to the rank of Rear Admiral "in recognition of his extensive scientific investigation and extraordinary aerial explorations of the Antarctic continent, and the first mapping of the South Pole and polar plateau by air." Following the Second Antarctic Expedition on which he was accompanied by Ike Schlossbach, Congress authorized the Second Byrd Antarctic Expedition Medal which was presented to Byrd and all members of his expedition.

By the mid-1930s, Byrd's life was inexorably connected with Antarctica. He was the commanding officer of the U.S. Antarctic Service Expedition in 1939-1941; during World War II, he assisted with the development of cold climate clothing and served with the Bureau of Aeronautics, Navy Department in the South Pacific; in 1946-47, he commanded the Navy's Antarctic Expedition, the largest ever to explore that frozen world; in 1949 he became the founding chairman of the Iron Curtain Refugee Campaign of the International Rescue Committee, a nation-wide effort to bring assistance to escapees from communist tyranny; and in 1955, Byrd headed the U.S. Antarctic expedition, Operation DEEP FREEZE, which was to be responsible for the Antarctic phase of the United States participation in the International Geophysical Year (1957-1959).

His participation in Operation DEEP FREEZE was two-fold. He acted as senior U.S. representative in charge of the political, scientific, legislative and operational activities which comprised the total U.S. Antarctic program, and his duties also required him to report and make recommendations to the Secretary of Defense on all matters pertaining to the U.S. Antarctic program.

In 1957, he was awarded the Medal of Freedom by the Secretary of Defense on behalf of the American people, as well as the Secretary of Defense and the many key officials of the government who recognized Admiral Byrd's very great achievements and contributions in polar, scientific and geographic exploration.

At the time of his death on March 11, 1957, Byrd had received more than 36 medals..

Blacks Fly Transcontinental
Dr. Albert E. Forsythe and
C. Alfred Anderson

Dr. Forsythe Inducted Aviation Hall of Fame of New Jersey, 1986

Alfred Anderson and Dr. Albert E. Forsythe

Another significant event had its beginning at Atlantic City's Bader Field in 1933. Two black men, Dr. Albert E. Forsythe and C. Alfred Anderson, became the first of their race to accomplish a transcontinental flight. Flying a 95hp Fairchild 24 monoplane, *The Pride of Atlantic City,* the two men left Bader Field in July and made 50 stops across the country on their way to Los Angeles. Years later Forsythe explained: "I got interested in flying in 1932, and bought a plane toward the end of the year. I had no previous flying experience before that."

Forsythe, who was practicing medicine in Atlantic City, said that Anderson had gone to a flight training school outside of Philadelphia — one of the few in the nation that would train blacks — and recommended that Forsythe receive his training there.

"At the time, the War Department and most everyone else refused to train blacks to fly. Anderson had a U.S. government transport license before I even started to fly, but he was unable to get a job. That was partly the inspiration for me to develop this program that consisted of a series of three flights never made by black men," Forsythe recalled.

The only instruments in the plane were a compass and altimeter. "The trip was purposely made to be hazardous and rough," the doctor explained, "because if it had been an ordinary flight, we wouldn't have attracted attention. We had no radio, no lights and no parachutes because we didn't have the money to buy those things."

They made the 2,500 mile flight following a Rand McNally road map until it blew away. At night they used flashlights to guide their way. The flight to Los Angeles took two and a half days and upon their arrival, they were greeted by an applauding crowd of 2,000 -- mostly blacks. Forsythe said he hoped he and Anderson had set a standard for other blacks to emulate.

Prior to the flight the mayor of Atlantic City, Harry Bacharach, endorsed the project as a promotional stunt for the city. His letter to Forsythe read:

Dear Dr. Forsythe:
It is with much pleasure that I have been informed of your plans for a transcontinental round-trip flight sponsored by the Atlantic City Board of Trade.

Such an enterprise will reflect great honor on the citizens of our resort, and as Mayor of our city, I am certainly greatly impressed with the splendid initiative of your group in encouraging this project in order to bring added publicity to our city which is known throughout the land as the World's Playground.

With best wishes for a most successful flight,

> *I beg to remain*
> *Sincerely,*

When they returned to New Jersey, the aviators were honored with a parade in Newark that attracted 15,000 people.

In November of 1933, the two men became the first blacks to fly across international borders from Atlantic City to Montreal, Canada. Dr. Forsythe had earned an advanced degree at McGill University Medical School in the French Canadian city.

Born in Nassau in the Bahama Islands in 1897, Forsythe came to the United States in 1912 to study architecture at the Tuskegee Institute directed by the legendary black educator Booker T. Washington. In addition, he took a class in chemistry with black inventor George Washington Carver which stimulated him to become a doctor rather than an architect.

He hung out his shingle in Atlantic City and developed a thriving medical practice. His prominence in the city's black community and his financial stability made it possible for him to underwrite the flights and garner support from both black and white groups.

In 1934, Forsythe and Anderson planned a more ambitious flight — island hopping 12,000 miles in the Caribbean.

Forsythe purchased a Lambert 90hp Deluxe Monocoupe, for the proposed Pan-American Goodwill Flight and took it to Tuskegee to have it christened the *Booker T. Washington* with the entire faculty and student body present. With the staunch support of New Jersey's director of aviation, Gill Robb Wilson, permission to land in the countries on the airmen's itinerary was granted by the various embassies. Then detailed information regarding the venture was sent to President Franklin D. Roosevelt, the U.S. State Department and the aviation branch of the Department of Commerce. All proffered their support of the undertaking.

Prior to the Caribbean trip, Forsythe and Anderson flew into St. Louis to pick up a friend, and there they met Charles Lindbergh. Forsythe remembered that meeting. "We were planning the flight through the West Indies and other islands and he had been there. He was telling us about the various airports, the problems we might encounter during the flight, and the equipment we needed. He was very pleasant to us."

The first stop on their goodwill tour was Nassau. The *Booker T. Washington* was the first plane ever to land there, and because they arrived after dark, and attracted a large crowd, they almost didn't make it. With Anderson at the controls, they were forced to make several passes over the proposed landing site before the enthusiastic citizens realized they had to make way for the plane. Cars, with headlights blazing, were hurriedly lined up to illuminate the landing strip. Then the plane touched down easily. As would be the case at each stop along the way, the aviators were enthusiastically received.

The next stops were Cuba and Jamaica. Anderson recalled that they flew through a tropical rain storm that was so dense "we had to get right down over the water to fly. The rain peeled the paint off the struts."

Their Caribbean adventure took them to Haiti, the Dominican Republic, Grenada, Trinidad and Guyana in South America. At every stop the presidents and governors of the various countries arranged special receptions for them.

In 1935, Forsythe gave up flying and concentrated on his medical profession. For 20 years, he cared for the sick in Atlantic City before moving his medical practise to Newark in 1952. He retired in 1977.

Following the historic flights, Anderson worked as a flight instructor in Virginia and with the outbreak of war in Europe, Tuskegee Institute hired him to teach flying.

A year later, the nation's first lady, Eleanor Roosevelt, visited the institute to inspect its infantile paralysis clinic. While there she heard of the pilot training program and was introduced to Anderson. She told him she'd always heard that colored people couldn't

fly planes and was amazed to find one who could. Anderson invited her for a flight in his Piper Cub and she accepted, much to the chagrin of her staff members. That well reported flight pushed Army brass to consider blacks for Air Corps duty and a Civilian Pilot Training (CPT) program was established at the institute, called the Tuskegee Experiment.

Although they were constantly hassled by local citizens, the press, white Army flight instructors and even the Ku Klux Klan, enough blacks earned their wings to form the all black 99th Pursuit Squadron. (see 1942-45)

Gorskis Operate Teterboro
Edward and Julia Gorski

Inducted into Aviation Hall of Fame of New Jersey Edward, 1973; Julia, 1978

In 1933, Ed Gorski of Lodi, NJ, made perhaps the two most important decisions of his life. On the professional side, he assumed control of Standard Aviation Flying Service at Teterboro Airport following the departure of George DeGarmo. He enhanced his private life by marrying Julia Chizacky of Garfield, NJ.

The Depression years were a poor time for a young couple to take on the task of running an aviation business, but with the backing of Henry M. Bogert of Hackensack, they took the plunge. Fifty-five years later, Gorski told friends; "Those were lean years, but I was a bit hard-nosed and we paid off all the bills and did whatever was necessary to keep the business running."

The "necessary" he mentioned was working with Julia seven days a week, 14 to 16 hours a day. They hangared and maintained aircraft in the old Fokker hangar where Gorski had worked for almost a decade. They organized weekly air shows on summer weekends and sold airplane rides for $1 each. They became a leading dealer and distributor of Stinson and Aeronca airplanes. Eventually, they developed a reliable charter service, flew aerial photography missions and

Ed and Julie Gorski

operated a thriving student pilot training program.

Ed Gorski began his aeronautical career at the age of 15 helping Clarence Chamberlin assemble surplus World War I aircraft on a corner of the marshland that the Wittemann brothers had purchased from Walter Teter. Each day, Ed would ride his bicycle from his Lodi home to the lowlands that was then a section of Hasbrouck Heights.

In 1924, when Anthony Fokker moved his Atlantic Aircraft Corp. into the Wittemann plant, Gorski went to work for the Dutchman as a mechanic and soon became a supervisor. He had a hand in assembling or maintaining many historic Fokker aircraft including the Fokker trimotors Cmdr. Richard E. Byrd flew to the North Pole in 1926 and across the Atlantic in 1927. He also supervised the assembly of the Fokker *Friendship* in which Amelia Earhart became the first woman to fly across the Atlantic in 1928. In 1930, when Fokker introduced the largest passenger plane in the world, the F-32, Gorski did extensive testing of the high-winged monoplane.

Gorski first soloed in 1926 flying a World War I "Jenny." He recalled that his first personal airplane was an "elephant eared" OX-5 powered Travel Air biplane. No matter the plane's appearance, it was a day to remember, he flew his own biplane for the first time.

He was "between jobs" in 1932 when he and Bernt Balchen helped Amelia Earhart prepare her red Lockheed Vega for the first solo transatlantic flight by a woman. The two pilots accompanied Earhart to Harbour Grace, Newfoundland, where she took off for Europe. It was a proud moment for both men when word was received that the tousled-haired aviatrix had landed safely in Ireland.

Many well-known personalities such as big-game hunters Martin and Osa Johnson, were regular users of Teterboro during the Gorski years. Publisher and physical culturist, Barnarr Macfadden kept his company plane, *Miss True Story* at Teterboro. Gorski remembered that Macfadden would pay him to test fly the Vega prior to each Macfadden flight because the publisher feared the plane would be sabotaged. Being Macfadden's test pilot almost cost Gorski his life in 1939. The following account of a lucky escape appeared in the May 9 issue of the *Passaic Herald-News.*

Edward Gorski, 32, general manager of Standard Aviation Inc., at Bendix Airport, escaped with bruises and shock yesterday afternoon when an airplane he was flying alone crashed to the ground when the motor failed.

The plane is owned by Bernarr Macfadden, the publisher who lives in Hackensack.

Gorski, who lives at 354 River Drive, Garfield, was pinned in the overturned monoplane for 20 minutes before it could be lifted sufficiently to pull him out. Henry M. Bogert of Hackensack, president of Standard Aviation, said Gorski had just taken off for a flight to Roosevelt Field and was about 100 feet in the air when the motor died. He guided the ship to the ground but when the wheels struck the soft earth and bushes it somersaulted, landing on its back.

Although he was not pinned beneath the machine, Gorski was trapped because the top hatches are the plane's only mode of entrance and exit. It was necessary to lift the ship clear off the ground to get the flier out.

A fire broke out in the motor but was promptly extinguished by field mechanics.

The plane, a Northrup semi-cabin type, is the one Macfadden entered in the Bendix Trophy Race last year but withdrew at the last minute. The plane is kept at the Standard Aviation hangar at Bendix Airport.

Gorski is in charge of the training of 30 New York University students in the Civil Aeronautics Authority's program to qualify youths to man the nation's increased air force,"

Explorer Lands with a Bang

Billy Diehl taught Martin and Osa Johnson to fly at Teterboro. H.E. Brennert, writing for the November 1949 issue of *American Helicopter* magazine told this tale of Martin's first solo flight in 1935:

It was at Teterboro. Johnson had had seven or eight hours dual, was doing good (sic), and seemed anxious to solo. Bill [Diehl] thought he was doing good too. So one morning after a few trips around the field together, Bill stepped out of the ship and told Johnson to go around by himself.

"There's gas for about 45 minutes," cautioned the instructor, "so come right back."'

Johnson's face showed a little surprise at Bill's sudden decision, but he recovered himself, nodded more affirmatively and gunned the little trainer out across the Teterboro dust-bin and onto the runway.

The takeoff was okay. At 600 feet, the explorer leveled off and cut a long, shallow 360 that brought him back in line with the runway below. Things went fine up to that point. Then, just as Johnson was about to close the throttle for his glide back to terra firma, the usually intrepid fellow suddenly began feeling more 'terra' than 'firma.' The idea that he was about to land an airplane for the first time, unaided and alone, struck him rather negatively. He was scared, even as you and I are sometimes. The trigger hand that always held steady in the face of a charging rhino or lion was now trembling on the throttle of a mere airplane. Martin

Johnson was a most embarrassed man. He was really confused, discomposed, and involved in difficulty!

But there was one thing he was sure of. He didn't want to land — not just yet, anyway. And leaving the throttle open, he began another 360 around the field. He repeated it again and again and again while Bill, watching from below, sensed what was going on in Johnson's mind.

"The gas will eventually run out," observed Bill in one of his quiet outbursts of humor. "It won't be necessary to shoot him down, or anything drastic like that." After about 40 minutes of this cruising, and with about a pint of gas left, Johnson got hold of himself sufficiently to attempt a landing. Down he came until he was about 30 feet over the runway and then he began leveling off. His judgement was pretty well lost. Holding the nose high as he came across the field, the upset fellow quickly squandered the last few lift-sustaining mph's, and while 20 feet high, the little biplane stalled and fell flatly to the runway with a resounding smash. The ship wasn't damaged too much, nor was Johnson, but his face was a little flushed for a time after. The experience, however, didn't prevent him from eventually becoming one of the best amphib pilots.

Goodyear Blimp Hangar Built

In 1938, New York City was constructing a fair ground in Flushing Meadows to be the site of the 1939 World's Fair. At the same time, the Goodyear Tire and Rubber Co. was building a large blimp hangar on the northeast side of Teterboro Airport to house the airship *Mayflower*. The huge structure standing beside Route 6 (now 46) and the constant coming and going of the airship became a major attraction for the airport. New jersey citizens came from far and wide to take a $5 blimp ride over Manhattan.

The blimp hangar remained at the airport during the war years, and then was dismantled. In 1947, Bill Odom, who twice flew around the world on record flights, built his hangar and restaurant on the blimp hangar's foundation.

Goodyear blimps have visited Teterboro in the summer months most every year since then. They no longer offer rides to the general public, but are in evidence in the skies above any national sporting event that takes place in the New York area.

Wartime Restrictions

Just before America's entry into World War II, Standard Aviation was among the first fixed-base operators on the East Coast to be awarded the Civil Pilot Training (CPT) Program by the U.S. Government. Gorski and his staff instructed hundreds of students from several colleges in the basics of flying. In the spring of 1942, Teterboro Airport was closed by the Air Corps because of its proximity to the Atlantic

Coast, forcing the Gorskis to move their operation to Warwick, NY. There they continued to fulfill their contractual obligations with the CPT program.

During that period, Standard Aviation taught several thousand students to fly. While Ed Gorski supervised the training, Julia handled the documentation of the complex program. She filled out endless forms and reports, maintained all student flight and aircraft records and handled the business accounting and weekly payrolls. Her administrative duties left little time for flying, which she enjoyed. The business could not have flourished without her.

Soon after the contracts were satisfied, Ed Gorski joined the Air Corps as a ferry pilot and flew runs across the Pacific. While he was away, Julia ran the FBO operation until the shortage of fuel and customers forced her to sell most of their aircraft and equipment and await Ed's return.

"...he always used the Spiro Agnew school of diplomacy and told the pilot to 'get that dirty airplane off my airport'..." --Ben Rock"

In 1946, the Gorski's purchased a small airstrip in Lincoln Park, NJ, and developed it into one of the finest general aviation airports in the state. Pilot Ben Rock, who Gorski taught to fly at Teterboro, recalled how pristine the Gorskis kept Lincoln Park.

If anybody ever landed at Lincoln Park with a dirty airplane, he always used the Spiro Agnew school of diplomacy and told the pilot to 'get that dirty airplane off my airport.' Ed always ran one of the cleanest, safest and strictest operations on the East Coast."

Ed and Julia Gorski continued to work as a tireless team until they retired in 1979. Ed had spent 57 years in the aviation business, and Julia had been an aviation executive for 45 years, a remarkable accomplishment for a woman of any era.

Throughout the 1980s, Ed Gorski was a familiar face at Lincoln Park. Each time he saw something going on at the field that didn't suit him he'd complain to management. He might have sold the field, but his spirit never left. He died in 1989.

Many young men who had spent their teenage years at Teterboro running errands for the Gates Flying Circus troupe or working part time for Anthony Fokker were among the pilots and performers Gorski used as flight instructors or charter pilots who also worked weekends taking passengers on short sightseeing flights around the Court House in Hackensack for one dollar. They included, Bill Diehl, Bob Golem, Sam Barnitt, John Thomson, Warren Smith, Bill Rhode, Lou Ranley, Ben Rock, Bill Picune, Ned

Smith, Tony Barone and Charles "Slim" West. All went on to distinguished aviation careers.

Samuel C. Barnitt

Inducted Aviation Hall of Fame of New Jersey, 1977

Sam Barnitt

Sam Barnitt, a lifelong resident of Hasbrouck Heights, began his aviation career as a teenager washing Clarence Chamberlin's airplanes and running errands for the Gates Flying Circus. At the age of 20, Barnitt was a pilot with the Jones Flying Service and by 1936 he was flying for Standard Aerial, George DeGarmo's Hackensack-based company. He developed a system of flying on instruments to obtain accurate aerial photographs for mapping.

In 1939, Barnitt became a commercial pilot with Colonial Airlines which merged with Eastern Airlines in 1956. During his 35-year career with the airline, he was involved in many "firsts" for the company. He made the inaugural flight of the four-engine, prop-jet Lockheed Electra on the New York-Miami run and flew the first DC-8 and B-747 jets in the Eastern fleet.

During the Vietnam war, Barnitt made eight flights to the Far East carrying troops from New Jersey's McGuire Air Force Base.

Those trips made a lasting impression on him.

"On the way over, those kids seemed to be in a fog. They just didn't know what was in store for them. But coming back, when we touched down on McGuire's runway, they would let out a cheer that shook the cockpit. They were sure glad to be home," he recalled.

When Barnitt retired in 1974, he was 11th in seniority among 4,368 Eastern pilots and had logged nearly 40,000 hours of flight time.

Ironically, he died in 1979 at Newark Airport while awaiting an Eastern Airline flight.

William J. Picune

Inducted Aviation Hall of Fame of New Jersey, 1979

In 1932, at the age of 16, Bill Picune, then working for a New York City camera store, decided to jump from an airplane with a movie camera attached to the knee pocket of his coveralls. That he had never jumped before didn't faze him.

He went to Roosevelt Field, Long Island, took one jump lesson and the following day he bailed out at 1,500 feet. As planned, he took pictures all the way down.

That was the beginning of an outstanding career as a jumper and commercial pilot.

After that first jump, Picune became enamored with aviation, and by early 1933, he was at Teterboro Airport jumping regularly to the delight of weekend audiences.

"I made a deal with Ed Gorski to give me flying instructions in return for two jumps a week," he told the author. "I can't remember who came out on top however, I think Ed did."

As soon as he learned to solo, Picune bought an Aeronca C-2 and began accumulating flying time, but continued to jump and teach jumping to support himself.

In all, Picune made 336 jumps while barnstorming throughout the northeast with pilots and jumpers Quentin Cudney, Chet Faller and Joe Levine. Following each jump, his friends would pass the hat among the captivated onlookers. Once, they collected a total of 15 cents. In the summers of 1935 and 1936, Picune competed in the jumping contest at the National Air Races at Cleveland.

He developed the first bat wings to help stabilize his descent. "The bat wings proved successful in stopping my body spin in delayed jumps," he explained. "They allowed me to do loops, slow my descent and glide myself wherever I wanted—that is, within a mile or two."

In 1939, he joined Eastern Airlines as a co-pilot flying DC-2s to Miami, and a year later, he went with United Airlines. By the summer of 1941, he had been promoted to captain.

During the war years, he flew the Chicago-Fairbanks-Juneau run for the Air Corps under a United Airlines military contract. And during the Vietnam war, he spent a year and a half carrying military personnel and cargo to the Far East.

In July of 1955, between flights, he worked for Warner Brothers Productions on the motion picture *The Spirit of St. Louis,* flying various vintage airplanes.

Picune flew the nonstop New York to Honolulu run during his last six years with the airline. He remembered a particularly bittersweet flight in 1974.

"The most exciting, yet sorrowful time in my career was having General Lindbergh and his family on my trip to Honolulu, which was his last flight. I believe I am one of the last to be fortunate enough in having one of General Lindbergh's autographs."

Upon his retirement in 1975, Picune and his wife Adelaide moved from their home in Mahwah, NJ, to

Golden, CO, where their daughter Patricia lived. In 1986, he was strickened with Alzheimer's disease and passed away in 1988.

John E. Thomson

Inducted Aviation Hall of Fame of New Jersey, 1979

By his own admission, John Thomson had been a habitual truant in the Hasbrouck Heights school system even though his father was the town's Superintendent of Schools. In 1929, his father, Professor Jay Earle Thomson, authored a school book called *Aviation Stories*. Young John's interest in flying was encouraged at home even if his truancy was dealt with harshly at times.

In the summer of 1927, at age 15, Thomson made his first solo flight in a home-made hang glider. Once that experiment proved successful, he began flying in gliders powered by motorcycle engines. They worked fine going up, but the only way to stop them was by making what he called "semi-controlled crash landings."

Thomson soloed his first airplane in 1931 under the watchful eye of Ed Gorski. He then went to work for the Gorskis as an instructor and pilot, carrying passengers for $1 a ride. Within a few years, he had logged over 1,6000 hours in the sky. During the 1930s, he also worked for the Wright Aeronautical Corp., Taylor Aircraft, and the Curtiss Aeroplane Co. in Buffalo.

Bill Picune and John Thomson

In the early 1940s, Thomson joined Trans World Airways. During World War II, he flew C-47s and C-53s as part of TWA's military contract with the Air Transport Command. For the next 32 years, he piloted every type of airplane in the TWA fleet from DC-2s to Boeing 707s.

When not flying commercially, Thomson kept his hand in general aviation. His favorite plane was a modified Lockheed Lightning P-38 that was christened *The Teterboro Special* by Fred Wehran.

Thomson flew the P-38 at closed-course, low-level air races around the country. In 1947 he finished in 4th place at the National Air Race in Cleveland.

At this writing, he has retired from TWA, and keeps busy rebuilding antique airplanes and historic aircraft engines at his small airfield on the west coast of Florida called Dixie Sky Ranch.

Henry P. Geleski

Inducted Aviation Hall of Fame of New Jersey, 1977

Henry Geleski

It can be said that Henry Geleski was a lifelong resident of Hasbrouck Heights and Teterboro Airport. From the time he was old enough to ride his bicycle from his home on the hill in Hasbrouck Heights to the meadowlands below, Geleski could be found at Teterboro Airport. He was a skinny, 14-year-old kid when he first became a "go-fer" for the airmen of the Gates Flying Circus. His interest in mechanics and engines was encouraged by "Slim" West who took the youngster under his wing. Geleski developed his skills working on the old Standard airplanes flown by the Gates troupe and soon had a reputation as a master mechanic.

When the circus folded, Geleski worked with Bill Hartig on Clarence Chamberlin's planes for a year before again joining West at the Pioneer Aviation Company.

During World War II, he worked for the Ridgefield Manufacturing Corp., building troop-carrying gliders that were used in the invasion of Europe.

Following the war, Geleski went to work for Ted Hebert's Safair Corp. at Teterboro and remained with the company for 30 years. In later years, he held the position of service manager at Teterboro and Caldwell Airports. He died in 1978 just prior to his induction into the Aviation Hall of Fame of New Jersey.

Morro Castle Burns

It was just before dawn on Sept. 8, 1934 that tragedy struck the oceanliner *Morro Castle* as it passed off the shore of Sea Girt, NJ. While the majority of her 318 passengers and 240 crew were still sleeping soundly on the last night of a eight-day Caribbean cruise, a flash fire broke out on board. Within minutes, the four-year-old cruise ship was a blazing inferno.

Before the fateful day was over, 134 people lost their lives and the *Morro Castle* had drifted onto the Asbury Park beach. The fatality list might have doubled had it not been for the valiant efforts of New Jersey shore residents. One of those selfless people was pilot Matty Zeleski.

Early that morning, Zaleski, the manager of the Shore Airport at Brielle, received a call from the Manasquan First Aid Squad telling him of the disaster that was unfolding off the coast, They asked if he could fly to the stricken ship to search for survivors. Zeleski agreed unhesitatingly.

"The weather at this time was very stormy. A strong northeast gale was blowing with a very low ceiling which delayed my taking off," Zeleski remembered. He had chosen a two-cylinder, 38hp Aeronca monoplane for the mission because of its maneuverability.

"I knew it would be a terribly rough ride, but I was confident that the little ship could weather the storm and I could actually do more good with the Aeronca, for if there were survivors in the area I could hover over them and yell words of encouragement."

As Zeleski prepared to take off, two men had to hold the little plane's wings so the gusting wind didn't blow it over before it was airborne.

Using the billowing black smoke rising from the liner's hull as a beacon, Zaleski pointed his tiny craft eastward and slipped and bounced through the menacing dark clouds over the raging sea.

Circling above the strickened ship, just three miles off the coast, Zeleski came upon a horrible sight.

"I could see large numbers of both living and dead floating in the high waves and rough water," he recalled.

"My first thought was to let them know that they had been seen, by flying a few feet over the water, yelling, and waving to them with the thought of keeping up their spirits and encouraging them."

Rescue boats had not been dispatched because the Coast Guard believed the sea was too rough for anyone to survive, but when Zeleski arrived back at Sea Girt and told them what he had seen, the boats were dispatched immediately.

Once back in the air, Zeleski directed rescue operations by leading boats to groups of survivors. "The bodies of the dead were so numerous that we didn't do anything about them. We concentrated only on the living," he explained. "I saw many pitiable sights in the water and the vision of the living struggling along with the dead was the worst scene I had ever witnessed. I hope never to see or hear of such a tragedy again."

Throughout the ordeal, Zeleski thought only of finding the survivors, and getting them to safety.

"The thought of danger never entered my mind." he said. "To me, it was another flight. You don't think, you just get all riled up."

Altogether, 64 passengers and crew were saved by the dauntless efforts of Zeleski, the Coast Guard and a number of other citizens who owned boats. They had risked their lives on the stormy sea to rescue the desperate survivors of the *Morro Castle*. For the part he played in the adventure, Zeleski received a commendation of the Navy that stated:

"Your skill and intrepidity during this disaster were undoubtedly instrumental in saving a number of lives. Your gallant disregard for personal safety in flying a land plane over the sea under such adverse conditions upholds the best traditions of the Navy."

Modestly, Zeleski described his role:

"It was purely accidental. I was simply the one who was there. It was one of those things, when you did what had to be done because you knew it was right."

1935

Luscombe to West Trenton

In February of 1935, Don A. Luscombe, one of the most innovative builders of pleasure aircraft, moved his entire aircraft company from Kansas City, KA, to Mercer County Airport in West Trenton. The Luscombe Airplane Development Corp. brought with it the prototype of the first all-metal structured airplane called "Phantom."

The West Trenton plant was organized on a production line basis, similar to those used successfully in the auto industry, a revolutionary concept for that time. Luscombe then farmed out much of the small, formed or pressed metal parts to local companies and concentrated his employees' efforts on the construction and assembly of aircraft. Eventually, the plant was producing a fuselage in two hours using four men. Eight complete aircraft were coming off the line each week.

The Phantom had a price tag of $6,000, extremely high for the 1935 economy. To capture a portion of the mass market, Luscombe accepted the design for a 50 hp light, metal-framed airplane from two of his young engineers, Howard Jong and Frank Johnson. He began mass producing the "Luscombe 50." This small sport plane became certified as the "Luscombe 8."

Jules De Crescenzo, who lived in Oradell, NJ, remembered when Luscombe first came to New Jersey:

"Don arrived in Trenton in 1935. He contacted Joseph D'Annunzio the owner of the D&W Blue Print Company, an architectural engineering and drafting supply firm. Since Don was short of funds, they made a deal that D&W Blue Print would furnish all the necessary equipment to set up an engineering department. Since Mr. D'Annunzio is my brother-in-law, the deal included a place for me with the company because I had some previous aeronautical engineering experience."

In 1936, to help ensure that a constant source of qualified workers would be available, Luscombe established the Luscombe School of Aeronautics. Classrooms were located in one of the company's three small buildings next to the hangar, and a CAA approved curriculum prepared students for an airframe and engine license. Approximately 80 per cent of the graduates went to work for Luscombe.

One of the early students turned employee was Bill Shepard. While in college, Shepard was told that Luscombe was looking for engineers. He went to Trenton and applied for a job.

"Don interviewed me," Shepard said. "I was trying to impress him with my talents and he was trying to convince me to attend his school for $500 for a six-month course." Luscombe won the debate and Shepard began classes with 15 other candidates. They each paid $50 for the on-the-job training program. We'd work on the aircraft most of the day and spend just an hour or so on classroom work, " Shepard recalled. "Don paid us $15 per week, so we recouped $360 of our tuition money."

The first instructor was Cy Terry. Later Frank Johnson ran the school.

Shepard and the other Luscombe bachelors—Les Lynch, Bill Force and Jong — roomed at the "Jolly Roger," a large three-story, multi-room mansion owned by Roger Johnson, a Luscombe vice president. It was alleged that the mansion had served as a brothel during the Revolutionary War for Hessian troops.

Nick Nordyke, a master craftsman with a power hammer, was highly respected by all the young engineers. Shepard remembers him as being a bit strange.

"All the sheet metal work was done by hand," he explained. "An old German, Nick Nordyke, was an expert at pounding out curved metal panels. He always worked behind closed doors. He didn't want to show us how he did the job."

Shepard worked four years for Luscombe as an engineer in charge of production control. His personal recollection of Don Luscombe were enlightening.

"Don had an attractive personality and engaging manner. Primarily he was a salesman, not an engineer or designer in the engineering sense. He would conceive an idea of the plane he wanted, or adopt someone else's concept, and monitor the progress of the design as his engineers worked on it. He was a man who worked with words rather than figures.

"Luscombe was a natural leader and was at his best when working up a new venture, finding backers, gathering a nucleus for an organization and generating enthusiasm among the employees. He was not very interested in, or good at, setting up the detailed organizational structure or running it after things became routine."

Don Luscombe was born in Iowa City, IA, May 25, 1895. During the first World War, he left the University of Iowa to drive an ambulance for the French Army and later for the American Expeditionary Force. He became involved in aviation by hitching rides with French pilots as they ferried aircraft from airfield to airfield.

At war's end, he operated an advertising agency in Davenport, IA, where he designed the Monocoupe airplane which became extremely popular. By 1933, after just seven years, Luscombe had established himself as a recognized and respected name in the business of manufacturing airplanes.

The Monocoupe Corp. produced 465 aircraft in 13 different models.

Restless and disillusioned by a continually declining Depression economy, Luscombe tendered his resignation to Monocoupe in 1933 and moved to Kansas City. There within a year, he conceived and built the prototype of the all-metal-framed "Phantom I" and again moved his base of operations, this time to West Trenton.

The first two years in West Trenton were a financial struggle. The company grossed only $160,000. But by mid 1939, 230 aircraft had been sold and the year-end gross income was $450,000. The plant was producing 32 planes a month and couldn't keep up with the backlog of unfilled orders.

The need for additional capital to finance necessary expansion became obvious in 1938. To solve the problem, a large block of Luscombe stock was put on the market. An Austrian, Leopold Klotz, purchased the shares, plus those of two elderly New York City ladies, thus effectively reducing Luscombe's majority control in the company.

The Klotz involvement in company affairs had a dramatic effect on the decision-making process. Leopold not only became involved in the day-to-day policy making process, but brought his own production manager, Henry Boller, into the West Trenton plant. Jules De Crescenzo explained how Boller controlled the work force.

"Henry was a Prussian stereotype with an air of superiority,." De Crescenzo wrote. "He was a pilot of some kind; I never knew his aeronautical background. He immediately set up a control room in the center of the small hangar. This room was surrounded by glass windows so he could watch the men working. He also installed a time clock and we had to punch in and out. Most of us were being paid about 39 cents an hour. The morale of the workmen hit bottom. When an expensive aircraft bolt or part fell from the work bench, we didn't bother picking it up—it was left to the sweepers. This, of course, upped the cost of building the aircraft."

Luscombe, a free thinker and a man of determination, found life becoming unduly complicated. In April 1939, after 12 innovative and productive years, Luscombe sold his stock to Klotz and at age 44 retired to a farm in Ambler, PA.

Jules De Crescenzo

Inducted Aviation Hall of Fame of New Jersey, 1983

DeCrescenzo collection

Jules De Crescenzo

When he left Luscombe in 1939, Jules De Crescenzo went on to a distinguished career in aviation. That same year, he became the director of training and chief instructor of the Rising Sun School of Aeronautics in Philadelphia. A year later, U.S. Air Corps Technical Training Command assumed control of the school and De Crescenzo remained as the chief instructor.

In 1942, he joined the Civil Aeronautics Administration as an air safety officer, a position he held for 32 years. Although his base of operations was Teterboro Airport, his area of responsibilities included northern New Jersey and the lower portion of New York state east of the Hudson River.

He had been born in Philadelpia, PA, in 1905 and began his career as an apprentice mechanic for Parkin Brothers of that city in 1921. For the next 14 years, he worked for several aircraft and automotive organizations in the Philadelphia area.

While he was employed by Luscombe, he learned to fly, and in 1937, he purchased a C-3 Aeronca monoplane from Ed Gorski at Teterboro. Right after the World War II, he spent a great deal of time at Teterboro certificating surplus military aircraft being flown by the fly-by-night freight carriers operating there.

In 1952, he was permanently assigned to the Federal Aviation Administration's General Aviation District office at Teterboro. For 23 years, he became one of the most familiar faces at airports and aircraft repair stations throughout his assigned New Jersey and New York district; inspecting aeronautical facilities and aircraft and certifying them to operate under the strict FAA standards.

"There were only three inspectors in those days and we spent most of our time on the road," De Crescenzo recalled. "Now the Flight Standards office at Teterboro has 32 inspectors. Only three cover general aviation activities, the others oversee the commercial carriers at Newark Airport."

In the 1960s, he had the FAA establish an aviation mechanic safety award for the state of New Jersey. Each year, mechanics would be asked to submit ideas that would make aircraft safer to fly, and then a panel of judges would choose the one they thought was the most important new safety development of the year, and the creator would receive a certificate for his efforts. Generally, the state's governor would make the presentation to the honoree.

De Crescenzo retired in 1975 but continued to work as a consultant to aviation schools, airlines, and airport management companies. In 1990, at age 85, he was still active in the field.

Although he has won dozens of awards during his career, the one he received in 1980 from the Flight Safety Foundation best sums up his contribution to aviation: "For his personal efforts, dedication, and contributions in promoting the recognition of the aircraft mechanics role in aviation."

First to Norway
Thor Solberg

Inducted Aviation Hall of Fame of New Jersey, 1985

The man who worked diligently on the awkward looking Loening Amphibian "Air Yacht" biplane in a Floyd Bennett Field (Brooklyn) hangar was tall, trim and erect. He had spent countless hours preparing his flying boat for a flight he had been planning since he was a teenager in his native Norway — to follow the route, in reverse, of the legendary Viking Lief Ericsson from the New World to Norway.

Thor Solberg's inspiration to become an aerial pathfinder was the noted Norwegian explorer Roald Amundsen, who electrified the world in 1906 by becoming the first man to travel the Northwest Passage in the Arctic. Solberg, then 13, was determined to emulate his hero. His parents hoped he would join the family construction business in their native city of

Thor Solberg

Flora, but Thor, then a young adult, wanted to choose his own career and make a name for himself.

Following World War I, he went to Germany to learn to fly. Upon his return to Norway, he began planning for a flight to the United States. Then, a chance meeting with Roald Amundsen, changed most of his plans, if not his life. He enthusiastically explained his plan to the old explorer who suggested that the young man go to America where he could find people willing to underwrite his adventure. But, most important of all, Amundsen told him, plan your trip carefully. Have accurate charts. Learn navigation. Be prepared for any emergency.

Solberg came to the United States in 1925 at age 32 and opened a frame shop in Brooklyn, NY. The business was an immediate success. In 1930, he became a U.S. citizen and two years later he used his meager savings and borrowed money to purchase a Bellanca Airbus for an attempted flight to Norway. He planned to follow Lief Ericsson's route, stopping in Canada, Newfoundland, Greenland and Iceland before crossing into Norway.

He took off from Floyd Bennett Field and made it as far north as the Bay of Fundy in Nova Scotia before heavy ice on the Bellanca's wings forced him to set the land plane down on the raging Atlantic waters. Fisherman towed the plane ashore, but while he spent a comfortable evening in a fisherman's cottage, local souvenir hunters stripped fabric and engine parts from his plane.

Deeply disappointed but not discouraged, Solberg returned to Brooklyn and immediately began planning another flight. It took three years to gather the necessary resources and by the summer of 1935, his plane was ready.

On July 18, in the Wright Cyclone-powered Loening amphibian, christened "Lief Eriksson," and with Paul Oscanyan of Bogota, NJ, accompanying him as a radio operator, Solberg began the 5,300-mile journey that took him from Jamaica Bay in New York to the Norwegian city of Bergen in 29 days.

He was warmly welcomed in his native land. King Haakon invited him to court and bestowed upon him the Order of St. Olaf, one of Norway's highest honors. He is still regarded as Norway's premier aviator.

But ironically, on Aug. 15, 1935, the day before he and Oscanyan arrived in Bergen a stunning air tragedy occurred. Wiley Post, who had flown around the world in 1931, and world famous humorist Will Rogers, were killed when their plane crashed in an Alaskan lake. For almost a week, Post and Rogers were on the front pages of newspapers throughout the United States, pushing Solberg's achievement to inside coverage.

"Nobody knew my real reason for making the flight or why I took my time in Greenland and Iceland," Solberg was quoted 20 years after the flight. "My reason was that I felt there were great possibilities for the future of aviation in Greenland and Iceland. But I knew it would be necessary to build airports and radio stations there before commercial and military flying services could be established.

"It was with this in mind that I wrote to President Roosevelt after Norway was invaded by Hitler's army. The President called me to Washington in the fall of 1940. During my conversation with him in the White House, I gave him my opinion as to why the Germans had invaded Norway. It was my idea that they were on their way to the United States and I felt we had to protect in Greenland and Iceland before the Germans could get to those places. I went into detail with President Roosevelt about the danger of the Germans establishing airports so near us from which they could operate bombing planes to the United States."

The President took Solberg's advice. About three weeks after their meeting, U.S. Coast Guard vessels were sent to the east coast of Greenland. There, they found a German military expedition on the offshore ice. The Germans were taken into custody and interned in Boston. The installation of U.S. air bases followed shortly thereafter at Julianehaab and Angmasalik, Greenland. Those towns were two of the stops on Solberg's flight. The bases in Greenland, Iceland and Labrador were used extensively by Allied forces during World War II to ferry war planes, equipment and troops from the U.S. to Europe.

Later, President Roosevelt sent a thank-you letter to Solberg for his contribution to national defense in which he called him a "great American."

That same year, Solberg purchased 70 acres of land in Readington, Hunterdon County, NJ, where he founded the Solberg-Hunterdon Airport that officially opened in July, 1941. "It was a struggle," he said in 1958. "Now I have 1,400 acres, the largest privately owned airfield in the East."

During the war years, he trained more than 5,000 military pilots without a single mishap.

Solberg's contribution to aviation and exploration were recognized by various organizations over the years. In 1936, the Explorer's Club named him a Life Member. In 1953, the U.S. Board of Geographic

Names authorized the naming of a bay on the east coast of the Palmer Peninsula in Antarctica "The Solberg Inlet." And in 1985, a street in Readington Township was named "Thor Solberg Road" in his honor.

Thor Solberg died in 1967, having achieved the fame he sought as a child. His airport is now run by his son, Thor Jr., and two daughters, Lorraine and Suzanne. Throughout the 1980s, one of the outstanding balloon festivals in New Jersey was held yearly on the Solberg property.

The Rocket *Gloria*

In late February 1936, more than 700 people huddled together against a bitter cold wind that swept across the thick ice on Greenwood Lake, NY, to witness a historic aeronautical event—the flight of the first mail-carrying rocket. The group represented nearly half the year-round residents of the New York and the New Jersey towns that encircled the lake.

Although they were becoming impatient with the long wait, the onlookers were excited by the presence of newsreel cameramen, reporters and photographers from news services throughout the New York metropolitan area. The rural lake area was seldom privy to such historic events.

Standing before them was a 16-foot-long rocket plane with a 16-foot wing span. It was attached to the top of a wooden catapult that had been designed and constructed by a local craftsman, Mike Morin of Sterling Forest, NY. Beside the ramp was a similar plane awaiting its turn to be launched. The planes were christened *Gloria I* and *Gloria II* in honor of the daughter of John Schleich, a sponsor of the experiment. When it came time for young Gloria Schleich to swing the champagne bottle and christen the rocket planes, she discovered the liquid was frozen, so she threw snow on the two strange contraptions instead.

Support for the Project from Stamp Collectors

The flight was an undertaking of the Rocket Airplane Corporation of America; the aerodynamic design of the wings and fuselage was a contribution of the Guggenheim School of Aeronautics. Support for the project came from a number of stamp collectors' clubs. Fred Kessler, who represented the New York City based rocket corporation had arranged for a first-day cover to be created and 6,149 of the covers bearing a 16c stamp and addressed to stamp collectors far and wide, were stored in a fireproof mail sack and placed in the nose cone of *Gloria I*.

Then the moment the crowd had been awaiting for more than two hours arrived. Dressed in an oversized, white fireproof suit, Dr. Willy Ley of Berlin, Germany, the inventor of the rocket engine, ignited the fuel with a large torch. For a brief second, the *Gloria I* trembled atop the catapult. Then, with a great rush, it sprang into the air, flew above 125 yards and nose-dived into the ice.

Undaunted by the performance of the first Gloria, Dr. Ley and his associates transferred the mail to Gloria II, and without using the catapult, Ley ignited the plane's rocket. It skidded some 50 feet across the ice before becoming airborne. Reports say it flew 300 yards before sliding back onto the ice in Hewitt, NJ. The first air mail delivered by rocket—albeit across a lake—had arrived in the Garden State.

Hewitt Postmaster Walter White retrieved the sack of mail and took the letters to his post office where they were cancelled.

In the May 1936 edition of *Popular Mechanics Magazine,* the editors were very impressed by the short flight.

Although it covered only a few hundred feet, the recent flight of the Gloria, *America's first air mail rocket, at Greenwood Lake, NY, may in time be considered as significant as that first historic flight of the Wright brothers at Kitty Hawk, which covered an even shorter distance.*

Despite the short distance covered, the rocket mail flight has been termed a success because it proved certain basic principles important to the world-wide research program. It proved a rocket motor can lift and propel a loaded airplane fifty times as heavy as the motor itself. It also proved a rocket airplane can maintain a safe stability while in the air.

Following World War II, Dr. Ley became an important advisor in the United States' space program.

The fuel for the planes, canisters of highly volatile liquid oxygen, had been delivered all the way from Jersey City by Jack Welchman. Skidding and sliding on the icy roads along the way, Welchman was unaware of the danger of transporting that type of fuel. One bad bump could have blown the truck, canister and Welchman skyhigh.

Mike Morin wasn't paid for the construction of the catapult, so he confiscated *Gloria II.* The little silver bird stayed in the Morin family for 50 years. It was stored in a barn at Ringwood Manor, Ringwood, NJ, until an Aviation Hall of Fame of New Jersey trustee, Dave MacMillan, and the author discovered its whereabouts. With an assist from Bert Prol, the curator of the Manor, and with consent of the Morin family, the *Gloria II* was released to the Aviation Hall of Fame for a brief display at the AHOF's museum in 1987. It was then given to the Lincoln Park Airport Experimental Aircraft Association Chapter 501 for a complete restoration. When completed, the *Gloria* will be permanently displayed in the New Jersey museum, thanks to the Morin family's generosity .

Hindenburg Arrives

On May 9, 1936, the giant airship *Hindenburg* arrived at the Naval Air Station, Lakehurst, on its maiden voyage from the Rhein-Main Airport outside of Frankfurt, Germany. The Hindenburg, the largest airship in the world, had established a new transatlantic speed record of 62 hours, almost 20 hours less then the previous record set by the *U.S.S. Los Angeles* in 1924.

Millions of New York and New Jersey residents witnessed the maiden flight of the great silver Zeppelin, with the black swastika painted on its red tail, as it glided down the New Jersey coast toward Lakehurst.

The *Hindenburg* was the creation of Dr. Hugo Eckener, Germany's leading proponent of lighter-than-air travel. He had been one of the earliest disciples of Count Ferdinand von Zeppelin, the father of Germany's successful airship program who died more then 20 years before the Hindenburg flew. The successful flights of the *Graf Zeppelin*, in the late '20s and early '30s to north and south America had demonstrated Germany's ability to build large passenger-carrying airships, that like ocean liners, could keep a reliable schedule of service.

The *Hindenberg* was 803 feet long and its diameter of 135 feet was considerably larger than the *Graf*.

It had four engines and accommodations for 50 passengers housed in the hull rather than the gondola. The cabins and public rooms were comfortably furnished and the service was first class.

Prior to beginning service to the United States, the *Hindenburg* made a transatlantic crossing to Brazil in March of 1936. Although there had been some engine problems, that maiden ocean flight was considered an outstanding success.

Charles F. Hanser of Red Bank, NJ, flew on the maiden flight from Lakehurst, May 11, 1936. His traveling companion was Dr. William Scholl, president of the Scholl Manufacturing Co., a client of Hanser's advertising firm.

According to his son Paul of Ramsey, NJ, Hanser, an aviation enthusiast who had made an Atlantic crossing on the *Graf Zeppelin* in 1930, attempted to be on the maiden flights of all commercial aircraft right up to the Boeing 747.

On the first west/east *Hindenburg* flight, Hanser wrote the following letter to his children:

May 12, 1936

My Dear Audrey & Paul:

Well, I suppose both of you were surprised when you found out that I got a place on this great ship after all. I didn't give the possibility of such a thing much thought after I got to the office on Monday and didn't know I had a chance until about ten minutes before departure. One chap didn't show up in time and that clinched it for me. I was told that thousands wanted to go, but no one thought of going to the hangar and taking pot luck as I did. So here I am!

It isn't noon yet and we are far out over the Atlantic, sailing along at a 90-mile-an-hour clip as smoothly as anything in the world. There is no sway, no vibration, none of the bumps and noise of a plane. We expect to land in Frankfurt tomorrow night late.

The ship is really luxurious and has every possible convenience; good beds and good grub. I got quite a thrill last night as we shot up Broadway past Times Square, only a thousand feet up. The whistles of the boats in the river were shrieking their bon voyage and below us we could see automobiles at a standstill. I suppose we must have made a great sight zooming along so close to the ground.

Uncle Junie had a fit over my going. I never saw him so nervous and upset. Perspiration stood on his forehead in beads. He begged and argued I must back out. He sure was scared. If he were up here with me now, he would certainly get a great kick out of it.

I met quite a few interesting people. In small quarters on a ship like this, you are seeing the same faces all the time and soon you get to know the different ones.

My one regret is that I can't come back in this bag Saturday night. It's full up, otherwise I'd hop straight back and be home next Tuesday night. Anyhow, I'll make it snappy on the other side and beat it as soon as I can.

I saw a most interesting sight just now. Down below on the water I saw a pencil line of foam streaking along with the ship. Then it was joined by another. For ten minutes or more that kept up and then the two streaks shot under the ship and were lost to view. I'll bet they were a couple of big fish attracted by us up here!

All my love,

Daddy

P.S. The envelope and stamp will be of some value some day, as it shows it's the first flight of this ship. Save it.

That letter and Hanser's *Hindenburg* ticket, which cost $400, are on display in the New Jersey Aviation Hall of Fame & Museum at Teterboro Airport.

The Paterson Evening News hired Bob Golem, a former Teterboro stunt pilot, who had formed Paterson Airways and flew out of Murchio Airport in Wayne, to follow the *Hindenburg* down the Jersey coast to Lakehurst so that Roy "Doc" Simpson could photograph the arrival. The photographs that appeared in the *News* on May 9, 1936 were among the first printed in the United States.

Ten Round-Trip Crossings

The *Hindenburg* made a total of 10 round-trip Atlantic crossings during the summer of 1936. Surprisingly, the schedule of arrivals and departures was met on almost all the flights. Passengers departing from Lakehurst would be flown in a DC-3 from Newark Airport and boarded the airship a half hour before departure. A retractable stair lowered from the airship's underside led up to B deck where the officer's quarters, lounge, crew mess and galley were located. Two inner stairways, one on either side of the ship, led up the 25 double berth passenger cabins (each five by six feet), the dining room, lounge and writing room. Large windows, angled out to conform with the outer contour of the Zeppelin, provided passengers with a panoramic view of the land and sea below. The flights to America averaged 65 hours and the return trip to Germany took 52 hours with a boost from the prevailing winds. That speed bested by a full day-and-a-half the time of the ocean liners *Queen Mary* and *Normandie*.

Before the *Hindenburg* left on her last 1936 flight, she carried 84 leading American businessmen on a 700-mile tour of the northeastern states. The resulting enthusiasm for lighter-than-air travel among the American movers and shakers indicated that business would continue to flourish in 1937.

U.S. Refuses Helium to Germany

The one major flaw in the *Hindenburg's* makeup was the highly flammable hydrogen gas that filled the gas cells in its superstructure. The only country to possess an abundance of nonflammable helium was the United States, but due to Adolph Hitler's saber-rattling in Europe, U.S. government officials refused to sell helium to the Germans because they felt the *Hindenburg* could become a weapon of war.

In order to appease the Americans and perhaps change their minds concerning the sale of helium, Dr. Hugo Eckener asked that the red swastikas, the symbols of the new Germany, be removed from the tail of the *Hindenburg*. His pleas fell on the deaf ears of Adolph Hitler and his advisors. Eckener's conservative views were not popular with Hitler's gang.

Airship's Last Voyage

In the late afternoon of Oct. 9, the leviathan of the sky lifted gently from its mooring at the Lakehurst Naval Air Station, turned toward the sea and quickly faded from view in the mist of a rainy night. She carried 50 passengers, bringing the total passenger count for the summer's 10 round- trip flights to over 1,000.

That was the beginning of the German's airship last eastbound voyage.

Chester J. Decker

Inducted Aviation Hall of Fame of New Jersey, 1985

Chet Decker

In June of 1936, 19-year-old Chester Decker of Glen Rock, NJ, became the National Soaring Champion at the National Soaring competition at Elmira, NY. At the meet, Decker established a new soaring record of 246 miles from Elmira to Atlantic City. His championship was based on accumulated points gained over three days of flying in a German-built Bowlus-Albatross glider.

Decker, a graduate of Ridgewood High School, entered his first national soaring contest in 1932, flying a homebuilt intermediate glider. Though not a winner, he learned a great deal from watching older pilots perform and recognizing the importance of the equipment used.

He had begun soaring in 1928 using a homemade glider that was shaped from a spar of a Fokker trimotor monoplane that he found on a junk pile behind the Fokker factory at Teterboro Airport. His first flights were on the grounds of the old Ridgewood Country Club. To get airborne, he would be towed by a 1928 model A Ford. Those early flights didn't last more than 30 seconds. He also practiced soaring at Murchio and Arcola airports and at Teterboro where he remembered Ed Gorski — then the fields manager — being very cooperative.

In 1935, he took his Franklin Glider back to Elmira for the national meet and finished in a tie for first with Richard DuPont of the Wilmington, DE, clan who was flying the more sophisticated Bowlus-Albatross. It was at that contest that Decker decided to acquire the German glider and go head to head with DuPont on equal terms.

In the 1936 national contest four launching methods were used: airplane tow, auto tow, shock cord and winch. The first three had been used in previous years, but the winch launch method was introduced to the Elmira flyers by the Associated Gliding Clubs of New Jersey. It had been designed and was operated at the championship contest by Gustave Scheurer of Jersey City, a vice president of the New Jersey glider organization.

Decker finished out of the money at the 1937 and 1938 nationals, but in the latter year, he flew his motorless craft 183 miles from Elmira on one day of the meet.

At the 10th Annual National Soaring Contest in 1939, Decker almost made a clean sweep of the various categories. During the 15-day event conducted by the Soaring Society of America, the New Jerseyan won the Edward S. Evans National Soaring Championship Trophy and was the co-winner of the A. Felix DuPont altitude award. Decker also established a new American record for a distance and return flight of 40 miles round trip.

Warren Merboth, also a Glen Rock resident, placed third in the 1939 championships.

In September of that year, a banquet was held in Glen Rock for Decker. He received the Governor A. Harry Moore Trophy for the best flying of the year by a New Jerseyan.

"Gliding is a wonderful way to learn to fly." --Chet Decker

Years later, upon his induction into the New Jersey Aviation Hall of Fame, Decker explained his fascination with soaring.

"Gliding is a wonderful way to learn to fly. The air is your friend — you're not fighting the elements but going with the rising air currents or 'thermals'—it's just coasting downhill on the air like on a sled in winter. There is, I suppose, a certain degree of fanaticism connected with it; you have to really love to fly."

Because of his gliding expertise, Decker had soloed in an Aeronca C-3 in 30 minutes at the age of 18 in 1932, and received his pilots license.

In 1940 at the national championship contest, Decker was leading all contestants when he was called into the service. With a college equivalency exam under his belt, he went into flight testing at the Wright-Patterson Air base in Dayton. He helped develop the use of tactical aircraft to tow gliders in battle. Once the glider was released over a given target the towing plane, either a fighter or bomber, would attack the enemy. Toward the end of the war, Decker developed the concept of modifying Douglas C-47s (DC-3s) as gliders capable of carrying 50 troops.

Although he kept his pilot's license current after the war, Decker did very little flying, concentrating instead on his large car dealership in Hawthorne, NJ. During his flying career, Chet Decker won more than 20 trophies in soaring competitions, all lost in a fire at his car agency years later. The Bowlus-Albatross glider he used to win the 1936 championship is now exhibited in the Elmira Soaring Museum.

He had been born in Brooklyn, NY, and moved with his parents to Glen Rock at the age of three. He was a West Milford resident when he died in 1985.

Amazon Jungle Search
Charles F. West

Inducted Aviation Hall of Fame of New Jersey, 1977

Charles "Slim" West

In November 1936, Charles "Slim" West, Art Williams and Ed Hill began a search for Paul Redfern, a pilot who had been lost over the jungles of Brazil 10 years earlier.

In August of 1927, Redfern had taken off from Brunswick, GA, in a Stinson-Detroiter on the first attempt to fly nonstop to Rio de Janeiro, Brazil. Had he completed the 4,600 mile journey, he would have set a new nonstop record, outdistancing Chamberlin's 1927 flight to Germany by 700 miles.

Redfern's plane had no radio, and although there were reported sightings of the Stinson-Detroiter as far south as Trinidad, nothing was ever heard from him again.

But over the years, the Redfern legend remained alive. Reports from Brazilian natives told of a white man living in the jungle along the shore of the mighty Amazon River. West, Williams and Hill felt the rumors were valid enough to make a search worthwhile. The three adventurers had convinced themselves that the time and money expended for their expedition was well spent for if they found Redfern they would reap the benefits of motion picture, radio and book rights, not to mention a sizeable bonus from the company that built Redfern's plane.

The three airmen flew to British Guiana and from there made eight nonproductive flights over the dense forest bordering the river. Determined to find the elusive white man, they abandoned their seaplane and with an interpreter traveled more than 300 miles in eight days by foot and canoe to a village deep in the jungle. They met with the elders of the tribe who indicated that they had seen a white man who flew like a bird. Then they would say no more.

Deciding their cause was lost, the three explorers began the long trek back to British Guiana and ran into trouble. Rushing river currents upset their canoes and left them without provisions. Their interpreter suggested a short cut over the mountains, which turned out to be a journey none of the men would ever forget. For three days the party suffered from hunger and exposure, causing painful sores on their bodies. All required hospitalization when they finally arrived in Guiana. West remained there for 30 days before leaving for home.

His stay in Hasbrouck Heights was brief. He purchased another plane and he and Art Williams again flew south, determined to find the white man. This time they were successful. They spotted a white man surrounded by natives in a village clearing. West dropped a note asking if he were Redfern. No reply was received. The search was ended.

Off to Alaska

Upon his return to Hasbrouck Heights West was approached by Roger Q. Williams, a friend of many years, to join him in an Alaskan search for six missing Russian fliers who had attempted a trans-polar flight. Williams assured him they would be paid for their efforts by the Russian government through the White Pass & Yukon Airways of Alaska.

The two men flew from Floyd Bennett Field, to Seattle, WA, in a giant-winged Curtiss Condor owned by the Alaskan company. In Seattle, the airplane was fitted with special gas tanks to enable it to remain aloft 20 hours a day. Williams and West then flew on to Nome, the base of the search operation. After weeks of futile flying over the frozen wasteland, the project was abandoned.

West was born in San Francisco in 1896. In 1914, he soloed in a home-built airplane and thus qualified as an Early Bird of Aviation (those who flew before 1916). He joined the Gates Flying Circus in 1925 as the-supervisor of maintenance and worked long hours keeping the old World War I airplanes in the air. When the circus moved to Teterboro the following year, West moved east with them.

In August of 1927, West married Helen Romano of Lodi, NJ, in a Fokker trimotor while flying above Bergen County during the Flying Circus' first air show at Teterboro. Newspapers throughout the New York metropolitan area covered the unusual event.

When the circus closed late in 1928 due to new government regulations that decreed its aircraft unsafe, West opened his own aircraft repair shop in Rochelle Park, NJ, the Pioneer Aircraft Co. In 1930, the company moved to Teterboro Airport and West's brother-in-law, Frank Romano, became a partner in the business. The shop was among the first government approved aircraft maintenance centers in New Jersey and throughout the 1930s maintained all the Standard Aviation planes based at Teterboro.

In 1935, West sold his half of the company to Romano and then became involved in the Brazilian and Alaskan adventures. Charles and Helen West moved to Oakland, CA, in the 1950s, where he died in 1972.

1937
Tragedy Strikes

At 4 p.m., Thursday, May 6, 1937, the weather at Lakehurst was turbulent. Dark, low-hanging clouds pushed by swirling winds, gusting up to 30 mph, drove rain squalls through the area. Cmdr. Charles Rosendahl, the commander of the Naval base, radioed Capt. Max Pruss, the commander of the *Hindenburg,* that it would be prudent to stay clear of Lakehurst until the weather moderated.

This first flight of the huge zeppelin that year had not been a pleasant one. Strong head winds across the Atlantic and down the American eastern coast from Canada had reduced its speed from a usual 90 mph to only 60 mph, and Capt. Pruss admitted to a passenger that the flight was one of the worst the airship had encountered since it had begun operations the previous year. The 6 p.m. arrival time was already 12 hours behind schedule.

Capt. Pruss flew the *Hindenburg* over Lakehurst, continued south and circled slowly off the tip of New Jersey until, at 7:10 p.m., when he received word from Rosendahl of improved conditions. Moving at 84 mph, 590 feet above the naval base, the *Hindenburg* made a pre-landing check of conditions. It circled the field slowly and began landing procedures. Below were 138 civilian and 92 Navy ground handlers standing by to catch ropes that would be dropped from the airship so they could manually pull it to the mooring mast.

The lines were dropped at 7:20 p.m. when the airship was still 200 feet in the air and approximately 200 yards from the mast. The ground crew seized the lines and began guiding the tremendous silver hulk toward its docking mast. Cmdr. Rosendahl later said everything was proceeding routinely.

Passengers could be seen waving down from the large promenade windows to relatives and friends below, along with several hundred other people who rou-

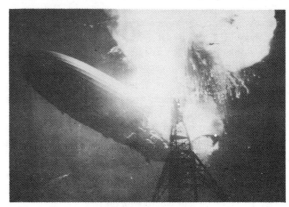

Tragedy at Lakehurst.

tinely journeyed to Lakehurst to watch the arrival of the mammoth airship.

One of those was Florence D. Toohey of Harrison, NJ, who took her nine-year old niece, Doris, and her son, John, age two, to witness the arrival. They had left home under sunny skies, but when they reached Lakehurst, a drenching thunder and lightning storm greeted them. The *Hindenburg* would be late arriving they were told, so they left the field to have a bite to eat.

They got back to the naval base in time to watch the *Hindenburg* circle in preparation for landing. Years later Florence Toohey recalled what they happened next.

"The mooring ropes were dropped and the ground crew was attempting to secure the ropes when the ship appeared to turn blue and then burst into flames," Mrs. Toohey wrote.

"We watched people falling from the airship to the ground screaming, and (the smell of) burning flesh permeated the air. A reporter, who had befriended us while we were waiting, picked up my son and ran for the safety of the big hangar with my niece and I in hot pursuit, since I had never seen the man before. Once we were safely inside the hangar, I tried to reach a telephone, but all of them were in use by the reporters and I roamed around until I met Cmdr. Rosendahl who permitted me to use the telephone in his office so I could let my family know we were all safe."

Doris McGill Lindstrom, the nine-year-old niece, now of New Milford, NJ, remembered being very excited standing behind a chain link fence to the left of Hangar # 1 as the huge airship arrived.

"Just as it was about to dock, I saw a purple streak race through the aircraft and yellow sparks shoot out. I thought it was a fireworks display, but just then the whole ship burst into flames. As we ran away, I could feel the heat at my back. The ground seemed to shake from the explosions."

According to Mrs. Toohey, automobiles were coming from every direction following the blast.

"When we tried to return home," she said, "I drove the car over people's lawns trying to get back to the highway. Cars were all headed in one direction using both sides of the road. We arrived home safely, but it is something I will never forget."

Ed Carr, who lives near what is now called the Naval Air Engineering Center, was one of many local residents hit hard by the Depression in 1937, who were paid one dollar as ground crew to haul the giant zeppelin down and onto its mooring mast. He remembered the event vividly:

"There was one explosion and then another one that dropped me to my knees. Nobody realized how big it was. It was like the world was on fire.

Carr doesn't remember actually seeing the explosion, "I was too busy running. I just ran and ran, and I haven't been back since." During his mad dash from below the flaming inferno, Carr suffered minor burns from being hit by pieces of the wreckage.

The man who made the historic broadcast of the disaster was fired by his superiors because he became overwhelmed by the tragedy he witnessed.

Herb Morrison, a young radio announcer from station WLS in Chicago, was at Lakehurst to report on the *Hindenburg's* first transatlantic arrival of the new season. His account of that momentous event has become a classic in broadcasting.

"Here it comes, ladies and gentlemen, and what a sight it is, a thrilling one, a marvelous sight." Morrison began. Then he continued to describe the pre-mooring routine with colorful prose until a flame was spotted.

"It's burning, bursting into flames," he screamed, "and it's falling on the mooring mast and all the folks. This is one of the worst catastrophes in the world...

"Oh, the humanity and all the passengers..." he then sobbed and went silent. His is the only recorded report of the accident.

Fifty years after the tragedy, Eleanor Enssle Zarr recalled that evening in May of 1937. Her mother's brother, Eugen Schauble, was a member of the *Hindenburg* crew and Eleanor had become friendly with a young cook named Alfred Groezinger. Following each arrival of the *Hindenburg,* the Enssle family would take the uncle and several crew members to their home in Roselle Park, NJ, where the crewmen would spend their few days off while in New Jersey.

Zarr said after the explosion her family became separated. She explained what happened then:

"I finally located my parents near the hangar. My mother was hysterical and my dad was crying. As some of the survivors were ushered into the hangar by Navy personnel, we spotted some crew members and inquired about my uncle. Several of them said they saw him jump from one of the engine catwalks, as the ship started to roll that way, another said he ran back into the ship to help, and still another remembered seeing him run about in a confused state.

"We frantically searched and waited for further news. Ambulances and fire trucks came from all the surrounding towns, there was horror and confusion everywhere. After waiting what seemed an eternity, a Navy man suggested we go to the base hospital where the wounded had been taken and perhaps we would find Eugen there.

"We found our car and started to drive the long road to the hospital with people running in the street in every direction. It was dark so we had our headlights on and suddenly the lights shone on a figure wandering aimlessly through the weeds along the road. My mother screamed, 'Stop the car! That's Eugen up ahead.' Sure enough it was my uncle who was in a state of shock. As soon as he saw my mother he started crying. We took him to the hospital.

"That hospital was a sight I will never forget as long as I live. There were survivors everywhere in every condition from slightly injured to severely burned. They were working on Capt. Lehman getting him ready to transport to another hospital. It was then that I learned that Freddy Groezinger had survived, but had burns and was already in another hospital. The doctors checked my uncle who had some burns on his face but he was discharged in our care. His tight leather helmet and jacket had saved him from more severe burns.

"It was difficult to console Eugen because he had lost so many comrades, especially Willie Dimmler who took his place in the control room so that he could go out on the catwalk of the gondola to look for us. It was from there that he jumped to the ground.

"Needless to say, it was something that none of us could ever forget. It left a scar forever.

"I forgot to mention that my uncle had a ticket for me to fly to Germany on the next trip of the *Hindenburg.*"

It had taken only 32 seconds for the huge zeppelin to burn and crash to the ground.Miraculously, 35 of the 97 passengers and crew aboard the airship survived the disaster. Thirteen of the dead were passengers.

The explosion of the *Hindenburg* brought the era of the great airships to an end. But in the few short years they flew, they had established Lakehurst as the nation's first international airport.

Airship Proponent
Charles Emery Rosendahl,
Inducted Aviation Hall of Fame of New Jersey, 1979

The spectacular and tragic demise of the German airship *Hindenburg* did nothing to blunt the enthusiasm of Cmdr. Charles E. Rosendahl, our nation's greatest expert on lighter-than-air ships. He spoke out for a continued airship program but the Congress would not fund it. He was quoted as saying:

"The United States is missing a bet. Why? Because we as a nation are not taking advantage of the rigid airship — a form of transport that only the United States can have, and which more than a decade ago proved its ability to fly greater pay loads over greater distances than the best airplanes of today."

He pointed out that the U.S. monopoly of helium, the non-inflammable lifting gas, made it possible for the nation to develop airships that could carry tremendous cargos around the world easily and safely.

He stayed on as commander of the Lakehurst Naval Base while a year-long inquiry into the cause of the *Hindenburg* disaster was held. It upset the commander when the media would state that the *Hindenburg* exploded. "The *Hindenburg* burned," the dynamic commander said. "I don't give a damn what anybody else says."

When a film depicting the *Hindenburg* burning as an act of sabotage was released in 1976, Rosendahl, then retired and living in Toms River, said in an interview in the *Atlantic City Press* that he inclined toward the sabotage theory, but even 40 years after the event he hadn't reached a definite conclusion.

He had been very close to Dr. Hugo Eckner and he pointed out that Adolph Hitler and other Nazi leaders didn't like Eckner because he was non-political and had protested when Hitler ordered large swastikas emblazoned on the airship's tail. But he said emphatically, "I don't know of any Nazis in the (Zepellin) organization."

In September, 1938, Rosendahl became the executive officer aboard the *U.S.S. Milwaukee,* but was back ashore by 1940 working on lighter-than-air (LTA) projects. It had become apparent to the Navy brass that the best way to patrol the U.S. coast lines and to protect ship convoys from submarine attack was with the use of non-rigid airships known as Blimps. Rosendahl was a leader in the development of the non-rigid program and by the time he assumed com-

Dr. Hugo Eckener and Adm. Charles Rosendahl.

mand of the cruiser *U.S.S. Minneapolis* in September of 1942, the Goodyear Tire and Rubber Co. was producing five blimps a month and less than a year later the monthly number had jumped to 11.

Two months after taking command of the *Minneapolis,* the ship was severely damaged during the battle of Guadalcanal in the Pacific. Eighty feet of her bow had been blasted away by Japanese torpedos and three of the ship's four boilers were nonfunctional. Despite a 30 degree list to the port side, Cmdr. Rosendahl ordered his big guns to keep firing all through the night. The following day, the cruiser made its way into Tulagi Harbor and the commander ordered his crew to cut down palm trees and fashion them into a temporary bow. With the wooden bow, Rosendahl and his crew made their way back to the United States for repairs. The commander received the Navy Cross for his heroic leadership.

Rosendahl was then promoted to Rear Admiral and put in charge of Naval airship training at Lakehurst, a position he held until the war's end. He would proudly state that not a single ship was lost in a convoy protected by the Navy Blimps.

It took an act of Congress in 1947 before the Admiral received the long delayed Distinguished Flying Cross and Distinguished Service Medal. A controversy within the Navy Department delayed the awards until after Rosendahl retired as a Vice Admiral. He received the DFC for bringing the storm-torn bow section of the airship *Shenandoah* to safety in 1925, saving the lives of six crewmen, and the DSM for directing the anti-submarine blimp training program.

Rosendahl was born in Chicago in 1892 and graduated from the Naval Academy in 1914. He was the only man to twice receive the prestigious Harmon Trophy from the President of the United States as the world's outstanding airship pilot.

In his later years, Rosendahl was the driving force behind the establishment of an airship museum. On Oct. 27, 1976, he received by the authority of the Secretary of the Navy the deed to a 13-acre tract on the Lakehurst Naval Air Station to be used as the site for a public museum. Six months later, the Admiral died at age 85, and the project was scrapped. Upset by the lack of interest in the museum, his widow turned his valuable papers and awards over to the University of Texas; a day New Jersey did not deserve.

Seaplane Bases Abound

Although Fokker had used the river in the 1920s to test his amphibians and Ed Gorski had an Aeronca C-3 seaplane based there in 1936, the AFA Seaplane Base became the largest and best known of all the operators on the Hackensack River.

Founded in December 1937 by Bill Mellor, John Howard and Harold Lentz, the AFA Seaplane Base began operating along the Overpeck Creek, near its confluence with the Hackensack River. In the first six months, Lentz sold his interest in the business to Mellor and began his own flight-training program.

Putting in long hours and running an efficient operation, Mellor and Howard were able to expand their facility to become the largest seaplane base in New Jersey, renamed Mellor-Howard Seaplane Base.

Early in 1940, the government began underwriting flying lessons for college students. The plan, which cost $480 per student/pilot, was to train civilians to fly should the United States become involved in the conflict then raging in Europe. Mellor-Howard received a government contract to teach students from Bergen Junior College, Teaneck, under the auspices of the Civil Pilot Training Program (CPT). The partners immediately built a hangar and expanded their fleet. One woman, Arlene Wilder of Bogota, NJ, was among the first 15 student pilots who soloed after just two weeks of training.

When additional flight training contracts were received from New York University and St. Peters College in Jersey City, Mellor-Howard's roster of instructors was increased. The new pilots included Dick Weed, John Zottorelli, Mel Taylor, Harry Kornhiser and Michael Malino.

A few months after the Japanese attacked Pearl Harbor and the United States had declared war on the Axis powers, civilian flying was banned within 50 miles of the U.S. coastline thus forcing eastern New Jersey operators to look for bases inland.

Mellor and Howard found Lake Susquehanna, near Blairstown, NJ, and leased an adjacent cornfield. They flattened the field and set up a training base.

John Howard loads a package aboard a floatplane flown by Kay Hilbrandt. Andy Erback looks on.

The seaplanes were flown into lake, then hauled from the water, to have their floats replaced with land gear. In less than a week, the flight training program was going strong again.

That was the beginning of Blairstown Airport which was still in operation 50 years later.

In 1943, both Mellor and Howard joined the Air Transport Command as second lieutenants. They spent the next two years ferrying aircraft, delivering supplies and evacuating wounded troops in both the European and Pacific theaters of operation.

Following the war, Mellor and Howard reopened their original base at the foot of Eucker Street in Ridgefield Park and were among the first schools certified to give flight training under the G.I. Bill, a government subsidized education program for veterans. They expanded to include courses for private, commercial, instrument and instructor licenses as well as seaplane ratings. They greatly increased their staff of instructors, all of whom had flown for the various services during the war. The roster included Karl Kloeppel, Dan De Cicco, Herb Barthman, Ernie Golub, Justin Davis, Cal Bowater, Jack Dentz, Andy Erbeck, Harold Sauter, Ed Johnson, Bob Harrell, Joe Vasilenko, Jim Durie, Ken Stein, Ray Lehman and, the only woman instructor, Kay Hilbrandt.

Karl Kloeppel, who went on to a 34-year career with Eastern Airlines, recalled in a letter to the author how Mellor-Howard coped with unfavorable, winter weather conditions.

"During the winter of '39-'40, the Overpeck Creek froze solid. Mellor-Howard continued dual flight instruction and supervised solo flights off the frozen surface while others on larger bodies of water like the Hackensack River and Newark Bay were forced to close down during most of the heavy winter months.

"One novel idea was used in 1940. The frozen surface became smooth glare ice that offered very little braking friction to the metal float bottoms. Volunteer students and instructors on ice skates waited a sufficient distance down the frozen creek surface to catch the struts on both sides of the seaplane and drag their skates as brakes. Novel as it was, it worked and permitted Mellor-Howard to continue some limited operations. During the winter of 1945, when I was employed as instructor, I had the pleasure of giving quite a bit of dual instruction with both float-equipped ships and with land planes for a 10-day period over the Christmas holiday off the frozen Overpeck.

"Perhaps the greatest period was after the record snow that fell on the 26th of December 1947. Mellor-Howard continued what amounted to the best winter on record, operating four Cubs on wheels, two on skis and the remainder of the fleet on floats. We were able to continue operation without interruption for a six-week period and during that time managed to give almost 60 students a land plane rating."

During that post-war era, the waters of the Hackensack River were alive with seaplanes. The area was called "EDO Meadow" by both *Flying* and *AOPA Pilot* magazines which referred to the manufacturer of the floats then used on a majority of seaplanes. There were more than 50 seaplanes operating in the area from six bases, including Mellor-Howard.

Tony Barone, in partnership with W. Gaito and R.P. Hahn, began operating the North American Flying Service in 1937. Barone's operation was closed during the war and he moved to Wurtsboro, NY. At war's end, he hired Bob Chalmers to operate the base, and when Chalmers died, Barone sold it to Louis Hasselbeck. Hasselbeck was killed in 1970 and his wife Ethel took over the business which eventually was turned over to her son-in-law, Bruce Dunham, who remained as one of the few operators on the river in the 1990s.

Across the river in Ridgefield Park, Frank Garafalo, Ed Zoeller and Harry Emery established the Modern School of Aviation. In 1941, they sold the business to George Lambros, Nat Cutler and two other financial backers. The base, renamed the Metropolitan School of Aviation, was almost immediately closed by wartime restrictions, but Lambros re-established it as the Lambros Seaplane Base in 1946. His was the only school in the area to offer multi-engine land and seaplane training. Lambros flew a large Grumman Widgeon. Eventually, he retired to Florida and leased the base to Rolf Nelson, who later became a flight examiner.

Bill Kurtz and Leo Vanderwahl ran the Dawn Patrol flight school on the river. Harold Lentz had Sky Harbor, and the Jersey City Skyport on Newark Bay was operated by Ed Binder.

By the end of the 1940s, Mellor and Howard were forced to make some serious decisions. The G.I. Bill flight-training program was drying up, forcing all the operators to scramble for business. In addition, they knew that flying from their base on the Overpeck Creek would be greatly inhibited by the state's plan to build a turnpike from the George Washington Bridge south to the Delaware border, which included a bridge across the creek that would obstruct aircraft movements.

They decided to gradually phase out the flight-training program and promote a seaplane charter business that could be flown off the unrestricted Hackensack River. John Howard remained as part of the team for a few months and then left the flying business and went into construction.

Over the next few years, Bill Mellor developed a thriving charter business, operating 12 seaplanes and amphibians as well as several land planes out of

Teterboro Airport. Many times, he had more customers than pilots to fly them. Even when he reduced his fleet to a more manageable size, he continued to prosper until he retired in 1959.

Both Mellor and Howard lived most of their lives in Ridgefield Park, where they died in the 1980s.

Harold J. Lentz

When Harold Lentz left the Mellor-Howard partnership in 1937, he became involved in an unusual adult education project established by the Works Project Administration (WPA) in Bergen County. It was an aviation school.

The classroom study was done at the Broadway School in Hackensack and flying instruction took place on the Hackensack River.

More than 600 WPA students were taught the art of flying by Lentz, including 10 young girls and women. The most extraordinary pupil was Mrs. Catherine Hinkel, a 65-year-old Westwood, NJ, widow, who passed the aviation course with honors. She earned her wings in 1938.

Following his graduation from Ridgewood High School, Lentz served in the Marine Corps from 1932 to 1934. When he left the Corps, he headed for Ethiopia to fight for Emperor Haile Selassie against the Italians. Greatly outnumbered by the efficient Italian Air Force and handicapped with obsolete equipment, the volunteer pilots were restricted chiefly to observation and supply work. Finally, in February 1936, after four months of service, Lentz tired of the comparative inactivity and returned to the U.S. to head the WPA flying project.

In 1939, Lentz made headlines by taking off from a dry field with pontoons attached to his plane. He flew a new Piper J-3 Cub, powered by a Lenape Papoose engine, to Red Bank Airport. Following his landing on conventional gear, Lentz had the wheels removed and replaced with pontoons. The job was accomplished with the help of Lenape Engine Co. mechanics. Lenape, based in Matawan, was owned by New Jersey aviation pioneer Joe Boland.

Then Lentz was faced with the problem of taking off from an airport with a seaplane. The first attempt was made on greased pontoons, but the ground was too dry and hard. Next Lentz and several airport mechanics built a dolly of wheels from an emergency compressor and a temporary axle to extend between the pontoons. The men on the field steadied the wing tips and tail by running with the plane for about 50 feet, then Lentz signaled, and the ship took off in about 100 feet. The take-off was believed to be the first from an airport by a seaplane equipped with emergency wheels.

Lentz opened a modern seaplane base in the Hackensack River on the East Rutherford/Carlstadt line in July, 1940. With the largest group of women flying students ever gathered in New Jersey in attendance, the Mayors of East Rutherford, Carlstadt and Secaucus officiated at the dedication of the Sky Harbor Seaplane Terminal in honor of the Women Flyers of America. Twenty potential women pilots, most wearing Civilian Air Corps uniforms, began their flying instructions later in the afternoon .

Women Flyers of America was formed by Edith E. Keating of New York. The original group numbered 210 women between the ages of 16 and 37, eager to fly. They were pledged to supplant men in all aerial war duties except those of actual combat.

Alice Jean May, a 20-year-old Englewood resident, had completed her training and was presented with her "wings" at the dedication ceremony. She later went on to become a WASP.

Harold Lentz joined the Army Air Corps during World War II as a Ferry Command pilot. After the war, he decided to make the military his career and sold the seaplane base to John Zdenzel, who carried on the operation until 1965.

Lentz retired from the service as a Colonel in 1970 and moved to St. Petersburg, FL.

In the late 1940s, Ted Roman operated a seaplane base from an unused pier along the Perth Amboy waterfront. He flew a small fleet of Piper Cubs off the Arthur Kill.

Improved air traffic control and stricter FAA regulations in the New York metropolitan area doomed float plane flying along the northeast coast of New Jersey. The FAA wanted all planes to fly under its electronic umbrella.

Karl Kloeppel described the remarkable safety record on the river in the late 1940s and early '50s.

"All the seaplane bases were within 3,500 feet of each other. Air traffic operating off the Hackensack River and Mellor-Howard traffic off the Overpeck Creek crossed each other at right angles, but in a 22-year period there never was a collision or even a near miss!

"Pilots before 1956 or so were taught to watch out for other traffic. This was true just about everywhere prior to a change in most flight school curriculums to enable aspiring aviators to pass the new flight test requirements of the FAA. Instead of learning to control your own destiny in the cockpit, more emphasis has been placed on attention to instruments, radio navigation, flying in a controlled environment under airways or tower traffic control.

"I've flown with pilots in recent years who never look out of the cockpit window. Their eyes are glued to their instruments. There is no joy in that," he said.

Bendix to Teterboro

An upturn in New Jersey's aviation industry developed in 1938, when Eclipse Aviation, a Division of the Bendix Aviation Corp., moved from East Orange, NJ, into a large new plant on property adjacent to the old Fokker plant at Teterboro Airport. During World War I, the property on which the three new buildings stood had been used for a large victory garden. The Bendix plant had approximately 350,000 square feet of floor space that included a hospital unit.

The economic shot in the arm so impressed Teterboro's 21 residents, they renamed their borough "Bendix" a year before the plant opened. As a part of the change, Bendix Airport was incorporated in Trenton. Bendix officials announced plans to make the airport a major center for research and private flying. The new corporation officers were Vincent Bendix, president, Harry A. Bruno, vice president, Louis F. Mitten, treasurer and Harold Hofman, secretary.

The official opening was Oct. 24, 1938 and less than a month later the Pioneer Division of Bendix moved its operation to New Jersey from Brooklyn, NY, to form single Eclipse-Pioneer (E-P) Division. Raymond P. Lansing, the general manager of the new division, remembered how the move was accomplished.

"The small businesses in East Orange and Brooklyn were under great pressure to make deliveries. One of our biggest problems was to move with a minimum amount of shutdown. This was accomplished by good planning. We moved department by department, shutting down on Friday night so that men could report for work at Teterboro on Monday morning with machine tools ready to run and work laid out.

"People were happy to move into the sparkling new plant with adequate room and light," Lansing continued. "The growth of our business was assured far beyond the capacity of our East Orange and Brooklyn plants. The move to Teterboro, into plant facilities that represented the newest and best of Bendix, was accepted by all as a major step in real and deserved progress."

During one of the weekend moves, the fog was so bad along Highway 17 (then called Route 2) that the moving vans were held up in Carlstadt for two days.

To promote the new Bendix facility, Vincent Bendix added a second lap to the Bendix Trophy race that he began in 1931. The race from Los Angeles to Cleveland was held in conjunction with the annual National Air Races in Cleveland. The first pilot to fly to Cleveland and on to Bendix Airport would receive a bonus of $1,000. Frank Fuller Jr. crossed the wide white finish line that had been laid down across the sod New Jersey runway. He was greeted by several thousand enthusiastic fans.

An amusing incident occurred just prior to Fuller's arrival. One of Ed Gorski's pilots, Bob Golem, landed at the Bendix field flying a low-wing Ryan training plane similar in appearance to Fuller's Seversky monoplane, and the waiting crowd rushed across the field to give him a heroes' welcome. There was barely enough time to clear the runway before Fuller thundered in to establish a new transcontinental speed record of nine hours, and 35 minutes.

In 1938, aviatrix Jacqueline Cochran won both legs of the race at a average speed of 242 mph.

With the outbreak of war in Europe, the Bendix plant was an immediate success. European nations began placing significant orders for instruments. The annual sales of $75,000 in 1938 grew to more than $3 million in 1941.

During World War II, Eclipse-Pioneer expanded to some 29 facilities totaling more than 1.7 million square feet of floor space. Subsidiary plants were operated in North Bergen, Little Falls, Hackensack and Philadelphia, PA.

The impact of the war on the American civilian population is hard to conceive unless one lived through those times. Men and women became totally dedicated to the war effort. At the Bendix plant employees worked 72-hour, six-day weeks on night and day shifts. Restaurants, diners and even nightclubs were open 24 hours a day to accommodate all shift workers. The instruments that were developed and built by both the Eclipse and Pioneer workers included electric aircraft starters, sextants, generators, drift meters, voltage regulators and fuel flowmeters. The Bendix Gyro Flux Gate Compass was considered so revolutionary, it was used by the military for two years before an announcement of its existence was made to the general public.

Five years after the borough of Bendix was established, its citizens voted to return to the borough's original name, Teterhoro. The principal complaint was that the post office was confusing the giant plant facility with the borough itself and mail was being misdirected.

Following the war, there was an immediate drop in military contracts, but Eclipse-Pioneer was able to quickly change priorities. E-P engineers continued to develop instruments that fit the needs of the aviation industry. In 1947, a PB-10 electronic autopilot was installed on a Chicago and Southern Air Lines DC-4 to become the world's first electronic autopilot to be used on commercial aircraft.

Later that same year, the first post war airliner, the DC-6, established a new airline speed record from Los Angeles to New York in six hours, 47 minutes and 13 seconds using a full complement of Bendix instruments and accessories. How well the company survived the post war business doldrums is clearly illustrated in employment figures. In December 1945 the Teterboro plant had 3,295 employees. By 1949, the figure had risen to more than 4,200.

Royal French Ryder

Inducted Aviation Hall of Fame of New Jersey, 1979

All newly developed Bendix instruments had to be flight tested and that job was undertaken by Royal French Ryder in 1944. Before joining the Bendix staff, Ryder had been a test pilot for two years with the Eastern Aircraft Division of General Motors in Trenton where he flew Grumman Avenger torpedo dive bombers used by the Navy.

In the Eastern Aircraft department were civilian test pilots Will Villwock, William Dirlam, Ronald Roth, Hank Albertmeir, Ray Higgins and Everett Vreeland. Gunnar Wallen was the director of flight operations and he was assisted by Harry Seymour.

With Bendix, Ryder tested instruments of all types in the company's varied fleet of aircraft; a Tri-Pacer, a F-82 fighter plane, an open-cockpit Stearman biplane and a B-25 bomber. It was in the bomber, flying out of the Naval Air Station at Pomona, just outside Atlantic City, that Ryder, with co-pilot Mike Bachik of Ramsey, first tested the Bendix automatic approach and landing systems.

"Frequencies were fed into a computer to program configurations," Ryder explained. "I'd just sit back and fold my arms. The system was hooked into the automatic pilot and had a triple check. It got so I didn't want to fly or land myself."

Bachik remembered that they made nine hands-off landings that first day. "I guess altogether, we landed the B-25 500 times in Pomona and Florida without touching the controls." he said.

In the 1920s, Ryder worked for various automobile firms as a mechanic, but he soon discovered that a "grease monkey" gets no respect even if his name is Royal French Ryder. He reasoned, that in the avia-

Ryder and Bachik.

tion business, a man of his good looks, natural flare and regal name could attract attention and make a good living at the same time. He took up flying in the late 1920s and by the mid 1930s was a flight instructor for Lowell White's Flying Service at Caldwell-Wright Airport at Fairfield. With the approach of World War II, he began training young student pilots for the government-sponsored Civil Pilot Training program first at Caldwell and then with the Staten Island Flying School at Martin's Creek, PA.

In 1942, he joined General Motors and two years later moved to Bendix, a job he held for 21 years. When he retired, he returned to Caldwell as a flight instructor, and eventually logged over 16,000 hours.

Always a man with a keen wit, Ryder kept an apartment in Hasbrouck Heights that he called "the office," and handed out cards at the age of 76 that offered potential customers, mostly women, "Specialized Flight." He'd laugh each time the author would say his name sounded like an exotic after-shave lotion. Because of his helpful interest in the All-Womens International Air Race (the Powder Puff Derby), it was rumored, but never confirmed, that Ryder was the only male member of the Ninety-Nines, the organization of women aviators.

Following the war, Aron Fabian "Duke" Krantz, the former Gates Flying Circus wing-walker and parachutist, became the head of the Bendix flight department. In addition to Ryder, the company pilots were Paul Arnold, who served in the Army Air Corps for three years and then flew for American Overseas, Alaskan and Colonial Airlines; Steve Bannister, another World War II flying veteran and a charter pilot; and Mike Bachik, the Bendix chief of maintenance and former Air Transport Command pilot.

When Krantz took over, a DC-3 "Flying Showcase" was added to the fleet and flown to aviation events around the country to display Bendix products.

In those early years, the aircraft were housed in the old Wright Aeronautical hangar, located behind the Bendix plant. While traffic was held up along Teterboro's Industrial Avenue, the aircraft were taxied down the long hangar ramp, across the road and onto an airport taxiway. Later the operation was moved into the new, large Atlantic Aviation hangar, built by the Brewster Construction Co., and in the early 1970s to the company's own hangar on the east side of the airport.

Krantz and Ryder became immediate friends, and following their retirement, were inseparable. Anyone who met the two dapper gentlemen, with their finely trimmed, waxed mustaches and mischievous eyes, never forgot them. They were a unique twosome.

When Krantz retired in 1962, the flight department was headed by Arnold of River Edge. His five-man staff consisted of Bachik, Mike Stenvers, Earl Frederickson, John Cirri and Ed Striegel.

The great characters who worked for Bendix over the years weren't all confined to the flight department. Addis Kocher who spent his career as a field engineer for the company, had a varied and colorful career. He described himself to Jack Elliott during an interview that appeared in the *Newark Star-Ledger* on Jan. 14, 1990, as *...the janitor in the back room when history was being made. Most of the time you didn't know it.*

In his unique position with Bendix, there were very few of the legendary aviators of the 1930s that Kocher didn't come in contact with. His total recall and comic wit made him a much sought after speaker well into his 80s. And it was obvious to his audience that Gen. Jimmy Doolittle was the favorite of all aviation celebrities he met over the years.

Upon graduating from the Massachusetts Institute of Technology, Kocher began his career working with his father. When the Depression struck, his father fired him, and in late 1931, he went to work for Bendix for $18 per week. A year later, he met Doolittle when he installed the first aircraft de-icing device on Doolittle's Lockheed Orion, a racing plane.

Kocher amused his audience by telling how Doolittle arranged for his first raise with Bendix. "Jimmy flew into the Curtiss Wright Airport at Caldwell with his instruments filled with oil," Kocher said. "He was madder than hell at me 'cause he thought I made a mistake. I discovered that a pump had been installed backwards by someone else and Jimmy felt so bad he wrote to my boss and insisted I get a raise. He even threatened to hire me away from Bendix." Kocher received a $4 raise.

Kocher remembers being with Doolittle and the Major's wife Jo at a meeting when Doolittle suddenly left for the Wright-Patterson Air Force Base in Dayton. Although neither Mrs. Doolittle or Kocher knew it at the time, Maj. Doolittle was picking up orders to bomb Tokyo.

Over the years, Kocher worked on aircraft flown by "Wrong Way" Corrigan, Amelia Earhart, Howard Hughes, Igor Sikorsky, Roscoe Turner and Giuseppe Bellanca. But he told Elliott, the two airmen he admired most were Doolittle and Wiley Post.

He called Doolittle "a very humble man" and about Post he is quoted as saying "the most honest person I ever knew."

He explained his connection with Post in Elliott's column.

In 1933, after he completed his around-the-world solo flight, Post had a contract with TWA to make the first stratospheric flight across the United States. I had to put an auxiliary Bendix supercharger on his Lockheed Vega so he could climb from 22,000 to 32,000 feet.

He had the first pressurized suit. I inflated it for him in the Standard Oil hangar at Newark Airport, which was run by Ed Aldrin, father of astronaut Buzz Aldrin.

Kocher, a life-long resident of Boonton, retired from Bendix in 1972. In 1989, he was still going strong as a story teller with the knack of making the aviation heroes he knew come alive.

When the space age dawned, Bendix kept pace. Guidance systems of all types were developed and New Jersey-built instruments could be found on Pershing missiles, Saturn booster rockets and the lunar module, used to land the first men on the moon. In 1966, Eclipse-Pioneer became known as the Navigation and Control Division of the Bendix Corp. In 1974, three new divisions were split off from Navigation and Control—the Test Systems Division, the Guidance Systems Division and the Flight Systems Division.

In 1982, the company merged with the Allied Corporation and two years later another merger with the Signal Corporation created the Allied-Signal Aerospace Company. In the early 1990s, the Teterboro operation was known as the Bendix Test, Flight and Guidance Systems Division of Allied-Signal.

1939
A Momentous Year

Those who lived through 1939 will remember that it was a year of great achievement and the beginning of one of the darkest periods in history.

In January, a small article that appeared in daily papers announced that a German physicist, Otto Hahn, had created an atomic explosion. The average American cared little and knew less about the event.

In February, General Francisco Franco was recognized as the leader of Spain after a bloody civil war.

In March, the German Army occupied Czechoslovakia, and nylon stockings were first introduced to American woman.

In April, President Franklin Roosevelt opened the New York World's Fair, and Italy invaded Albania.

In May, Pan American's "Yankee Ciipper" flying boat inaugurated the first transatlantic passenger service, and Italy and Germany signed "a pact of steel."

In June, 907 Jews aboard the Hamburg-American liner *St, Louis* were denied landing rights in Cuba, and New Jerseyan Chester Decker won his second national soaring championship at Elmira, NY.

In July, Lou Gehrig, the New York Yankee first basemen, retired after playing 2,130 consecutive games. Three years later he would die of amyotrophic lateral sclerosis, now commonly known as Lou Gehrig disease.

In August, the largest peacetime order for warplanes was announced by the U.S. War Department, and the classic motion picture *The Wizard of Oz* opened in theaters around the country.

In September, the Nazis invaded Poland and World War II began. For the next six years nothing would be the same anywhere in the world.

CHRONOLOGY OF OTHER AERONAUTICAL EVENTS AND ACHIEVEMENTS
1930 to 1939
1930

- Newark Airport became the busiest in the world.

- The New Jersey Board of Commerce and Navigation refused to permit Frank A. Morgan on Nolan's Point, Lake Hopatcong, NJ, to operate a flying boat between the lake community and New York City. This decision was protested by the Aeronautical Chamber of Commerce and the National Aeronautic Association (NAA). In October the Board of Commerce and Navigation announced a far less sweeping injunction against inland water flying that satisfied all parties.

- The Laretto Aero Club was formed at Teterboro Airport by Charles Hascup, John Burns, Joseph Schialampo, Tony Barone, Phil Mazzola, Sam Gains, Frank Garafolo and Tony Minelta. The club remained active until 1948.

1932

- Ivan Gates founder of the famed Gates Flying Circus, committed suicide in New York City at age 42.

1935

- At the Caldwell-Wright Airport, the Curtiss Flying Service subleased its facility to pilot Lowell White, who established the White Flying Service.

- A new Art Deco administrative building at Newark Airport was formally opened by Amelia Earhart.

- Jersey City Airport closed.

1936

- Col. Coyle, the New Jersey firewarden, convinced state officials that aircraft could effectively protect the 2.9 million acres of statewide forest from fires. In 1936, the state established Coyle Airport at Warren Grove, NJ. The Forest Fire Service first used a Stearman biplane piloted by Wesley Smith in which Coyle flew as an observer.

- Nic Vuyosevich established Clifton Airport beside the Passaic River in Delawanna, NJ. He hired George Ray as a flight instructor and Eddie Allen as the field's mechanic. Local protests closed the airport in 1939.

- The Socony-Vacuum Oil Co. of Paulsboro, NJ, produced the first 100 octane aviation fuel by a catalytic crackingmethod invented by Eugene Houdry.

1937

- Amelia Earhart and navigator Fred Noonan were lost off Howland Island in the Pacific while on a flight around the world.

- The Camden Central Airport, which had become the principal air terminal for Southern Jersey and Philadelphia, was doomed when a new municipal airport opened in South Philadelphia. All the major airlines, regularly using Camden, moved to the new facility.

- The Noxema Airship flew from Lakehurst to the Miami Air Races. Built at Atlantic City by Capt. Anton Heinen, who had been a consulting engineer for the *Shenandoah,* the airship was the first built to be moored to a mast without a ground crew. The loss of the airships *Akron, Macon* and *Hindenburg* killed the publics interest in airships. Stanley Washburn Jr., who later became a Pan American Airline executive, was Heinen's partner.

- Pan Am's chief pilot Ed Musick, at the controls of a Sikorsky flying boat, was lost when the plane explodes over the Pacific.

1938

- "Ike" Schlossbach established an airport on his property in Neptune, NJ, called "Jumping Brook." It became the first home of the Jersey Aero Club.

- Walter and Margaret Laudenslager purchased Red Bank Airport from John Casey and operated it until 1966.

1939

- A Pan American Airways flying boat, "Bermuda Clipper," made an emergency landing off the shore of Cape May, NJ. Fast changing weather conditions were blamed for the diversion of the flight from Baltimore, MD, the intermediate stop between Hamilton, Bermuda and New York City. There was a crew of seven aboard but no passengers.

- John M. Miller flew an Eastern Airline Pitcairn autogiro from the roof of the Philadelphia Post Office and delivered mail to the Camden Central Airport. The Pitcairn made the round trip in 14 minutes.

- The war in Europe began to effect New Jersey as warplanes were flown to Newark Airport, disassembled and shipped from Port Newark for Britain and France.

- Anthony Fokker, pioneering designer and manufacturer, died of meningitis at age 49.

1940

Although the war in Europe did not have an immediate effect on the normal lifestyle of most Americans in 1940, the year did mark the beginning of the largest industrial buildup in the nation's history. Those vibrations of war in Europe and Japan's aggression in the Far East, played a major role in the growth of the aviation business in New Jersey.

The Curtiss-Wright Corp. in Paterson, the Bendix Corp. at Teterboro and the Luscombe Airplane Corp. in West Trenton expanded their facilities at a tremendous rate to produce the aircraft, engines and instruments necessary to supply Allied forces, and later, American troops.

Curtiss-Wright at War

The echoes of war in Europe played a major role in the growth of the Curtiss-Wright Corp. in North Jersey. On July 14, 1940, the company dedicated a new plant on Getty Avenue in Paterson. The building was completed in the spectacular time of 57 working days.

The outstanding feature of the 2.3 million square foot building was the design of the production line for aircraft engine parts. Raw materials entered the plant at one end, flowed through various manufacturing operations and emerged as completely fabricated units. A single-row Wright Cyclone engine required 5,000 labor hours, 37,000 manufacturing operations and 5,500 separate parts.

Curtiss-Wright had another large factory in Fairlawn, and by early 1941, two other plants in Caldwell and Clifton manufacturing Curtiss electrically controlled propellers. In May of 1941, C-W had achieved a new high monthly output of Cyclone and Whirlwind engines on the redesigned assembly lines. The men and women of Wright could assemble an engine every 25 minutes.

In 1943, an enormous Curtiss-Wright plant opened in Wood Ridge, NJ. It employed almost 20,000 people at its peak of engine production during World War II.

Curtiss-Wright's President, Guy Vaughan accepted the challenge from the U.S. military to produce six types of aircraft, four types of power plants and five types of propellers. During that period, C-W produced and delivered more aeronautical equipment than any aircraft company in America.

Curtiss propellers were used on such fighter planes as the Lockheed P-38 Lightning, the Bell P-39 Aircobra, the Curtiss P-40 Warhawk, the Republic P-47 Thunderbolt, the North American P-51 Mustang, to name a few. The Curtiss C-46 Commandos, the work horses of the air, were used by the Army Transport Command to achieve new heights in air transportation,

making countless numbers of flights over the Himalayan mountains between India and China.

The B-17 Flying Fortresses that flew on endless bombing missions over occupied Europe were powered by Cyclone engines. Four Cyclones also propelled the B-29 *Enola Gay* on its flight to Hiroshima, Japan, when the first atomic bomb was dropped.

From 1940 to 1945, the year the Japanese surrendered, Curtiss-Wright had produced 281,164 aircraft engines in plants in Paterson, East Paterson, Wood-Ridge, Fairlawn and Cincinnati OH; 146,468 propellers at plants in Clifton and Caldwell, and 29,269 planes, including 15,000 fighters for 28 Allied nations, in Buffalo, NY, St. Louis, MO, and Columbus, OH. The New Jersey work force totaled 46,000 men and women. During the peak war years, Curtiss-Wright was the second-largest manufacturer in the United States and its sales topped $1 billion two years running.

Whirlwind engines were also used in General Sherman tanks and M-7 tank destroyers. Bennett Fishler, the former publisher of the Ridgewood (NJ) Newspapers and the third president of the New Jersey Aviation Hall of Fame Association, spent the war in Europe as a Sherman tank commander. He vividly remembered the Whirlwind engines in the tanks under his command.

"The Whirlwinds had one drawback," he explained. "They required a sophisticated experienced driver who could drive by the tachometer. He could never let his RPMs go below 800, even while shifting. This required double clutching and a neat sense of timing. Many a Whirlwind burned out because the driver couldn't manage the job.

"Because of that fact, engine replacement was commonplace and all tank companies had maintenance platoon facilities in the field. A good crew could manage a replacement in five hours. One of the reasons for this short time was the fact that the Whirlwind was air-cooled and had no complicated cooling system to disengage."

Robert E. Johnson

Inducted Aviation Hall of Fame of New Jersey, 1991

Throughout the 1930s and '40s, Robert E. Johnson held the position of Chief Field Engineer for the Paterson C-W division. His entire 40-year career was devoted to overseeing engine installations, flight testing and training both commercial and military pilots on the intricacies of flying C-W Whirlwind or Cyclone engines. He spent hundreds of hours working with maintenance and flight crews of most of the world's great early commercial aircraft — the Douglas DC series of planes, the Boeing 314 flying boats and 307 Stratoliners, and the Lockheed Lodestars and Constellations.

Robert Johnson

Increased speed required improved engine efficiency and special operating techniques. Using his knowledge and experience of airplane performance, gained by working for the Curtiss Airplane Division in Buffalo early in his career, Johnson pioneered a technique of maximizing cruise performance in multi-engine aircraft that became standard procedure on both commercial and military planes. His work with the manufacturers and the airlines in developing efficient operating techniques earned him the title "Father of Cruise Control."

Just prior to World War II, Johnson was promoted to Chief Field Engineer. He developed a field organization of 35 engineers who were selected for their technical talent as well as customer relation skills. The team set a standard for the industry. His engineering group members were assigned to various aircraft manufacturers and military air commands around the world where, they in turn, taught the intricacies of maintaining C-W engines. Johnson estimated that he spent 75 percent of his time in the field during the war years.

He established the Air Force winterization program in Alaska in 1942. That same year, he developed the power and air speed settings for the B-25 bombers Maj. Jimmy Doolittle and his flight crews flew off the deck of the aircraft carrier U.S.S. Hornet for the surprise bombing raid on Tokyo, Japan.

In 1944, he served on the B-29 Engine Committee, headed by Gen. William Irvine, USAF. This committee planned and directed the successful launching of the long-range bomber carrying the first atomic bomb. Johnson was on the island of Saipan to witness the take-off of 111 four-engined B-29s on the first saturation bombing mission of Tokyo.

Johnson's field engineers stayed on the run during the war year. Frank Lary, who joined Wright in 1941, told of the part he played in Doolittle's Tokyo raid.

"It all started routinely enough, just a one-day visit to Wright Field at Dayton [OH] with Bob Johnson, talking to an Air Corps colonel and a couple of majors. This session quickly escalated into a fantastic two-week adventure when the colonel said, 'Take this stuff to Eglin Field (FL) and contact Major Jimmy Doolittle.' Its full impact didn't hit me till a couple of months later when the news broke that Jimmy Doolittle had led the bombing raid on Tokyo.

"Prior to that time [Feb. 1942], pilots had set engine power by parameters other than maximum fuel economy. Bob Johnson knew many of the top pilots and saw the possibility of improving range by 20 percent through a more rigorous approach. He wanted the crews to use a simple but effective cruise control to get the maximum range. The Air Corps was interested in Bob's concept and had sponsored a project with North American Aviation to develop this for the B-25C bomber with Wright R2600-B engines. Bob and I spent two weeks in Los Angeles doing an analysis and obtaining flight test data with North American."

Using Johnson's formula, North American flew a B-25C from Los Angeles to Ft. Worth, TX, and back thus proving the engines could increase their range by applying Johnson's cruise control method. The information was exactly what the colonel at Wright Field needed to tell Major Doolittle.

"Getting to Eglin Field wasn't easy from Dayton," Lary recalled. "Two flights to Pensacola [FL]. No rental cars there. Bus to Fort Walton Beach and hitchhike to Eglin.

"I had read about Jimmy Doolittle as a 'Gee Bee' pilot and winner of many closed course air races. I certainly didn't expect to find a Phd in Aeronautical Engineering from the Massachusetts Institute of Technology, which Doolittle was. He reviewed the cruise control curves and all supporting data in great detail and with an understanding equivalent to those who produced them. This race pilot was impressive!

"In addition to engine management procedures to obtain optimum airplane range, Major Doolittle expressed a seemingly casual interest in the maximum overboost the R2600-B could tolerate at take-off power, without an unacceptably high risk of catastrophic failure. However, there was no talk of the nature of the mission. I quickly understood that this just wasn't discussed even though it was obvious that they were fitting each airplane with special, internal fuel tanks.

"Part of the adventure, different from most of my engineering assignments, was living 10 days in the same suit and shirt with only spare undershorts. Fort Walton Beach boasted no clothing stores, so I made do by washing and using a borrowed iron in the motel room at night. My appearance after a few cycles of this didn't enhance the early morning hitchhike to the base.

"The high point of the whole experience was my departure from Eglin. As I was bemoaning the prospect of the arduous trip back to New Jersey, made doubly difficult by wartime travel restrictions, Maj. Doolittle offered me a ride in his B-25 to Bolling Field (Washington, DC) the next day, which I eagerly accepted. It was then just an easy train ride to Newark where my car was parked.

"Adventure is an absorbing and unexpected experience and the two weeks spent with Bob Johnson and Jimmy Doolittle was that. The best of it all was my contact with Doolittle. You don't forget him and you feel inspired by the experience."

Lary learned within three months what his and Bob Johnson's efforts had accomplished. Maj. Jimmy Doolittle led a squadron of 16 B-25s off the deck of the aircraft carrier Hornet 650 miles from the shore of Japan and successfully bombed the capital city of Tokyo. All the aircraft were able to deposit their bombs and fly on to China because of Johnson's cruise control methods which, ironically, he had calculated on a Japanese slide rule.

After the war, Johnson returned to the Curtiss-Wright plant in Woodridge and became assistant to the president for commercial airline problems. He retired in 1965 at age 66 and moved from his home in HoHoKus, NJ, to Green Valley, AZ.

In retirement, he wrote countless articles on aviation history relating to his hands-on experiences.

Johnson died on Nov. 1, 1989 at age 86.

Herbert O. Fisher

Inducted Aviation Hall of Fame of New Jersey, 1983

Another Curtiss-Wright employee who had an active career overseas during World War II was Herbert O. Fisher, the chief test pilot of the C-W airplane division in Buffalo, NY. Fisher had flown 2,499 P-40 Warhawk fighter planes and approximately 1,000 C-46 transports before their delivery to the U.S. Air Corps and its Allies. He then went to the China-Burma-India (CBI) theater of operations to work out bugs in the C-40s.

The twin-engine transports, conceived and built during the war, had practically no service experience prior to being delivered to the military and problems developed in many of the internal systems. Fisher's assignment was to find the problems and teach military field mechanics how to solve them.

During his 14 months with the Air Transport Command in the CBI, Fisher flew 96 high altitude missions over the treacherous Himalaya Mountains, the "Hump" route to China. He flew when icing conditions and other weather phenomena were the severest to test the performance and load-carrying capabilities of the much maligned C-46. The engineering and flight techniques he initiated with ground and air personnel were credited by the Air Corps with the saving of hundreds of crewmen's lives.

He also lectured and conducted P-40 flight demonstrations at almost every fighter base in the CBI theater. As a civilian test pilot, Fisher flew 50 combat missions to prove the performance of the P-40 under actual combat conditions.

Herb Fisher

After the war, he became the first living civilian pilot to be awarded the Air Force Air Medal by President Franklin D. Roosevelt. He also received Command Pilot Wings and was given the rank of full colonel by Gen. Szeto Fu, commander-in-chief of the Chinese Air Force of Taipei, Taiwan.

Following the war, Fisher was transferred to the Curtiss Propeller Division at Caldwell as chief test pilot and a sales engineering representative. His experimental flying at Caldwell did much for the advancement of aircraft safety.

Curtiss-Wright developed the first successful reversing propellers used in conjunction with aircraft brakes to stop forward motion on landing. Fisher made hundreds of landings to test the efficiency of reverse propellers.

When planes were first pressurized in the late 1940s, they were not equipped with oxygen masks as they are today. Therefore, if a loss of oxygen occurred in an aircraft flying at 30,000 feet, the passengers would suffocate before the plane could descend to a lower altitude. In an attempt to quicken the descent, C-W engineers concluded that if the propellers were reversed in flight, the plane would descend rapidly and thus save lives.

Flying a four-engine Boeing C-54, Fisher, with Bill Furlick as co-pilot, flew up to 30,000 feet and reversed all four propellers simultaneously, The big ship dropped 15,000 feet in four seconds, but at a relatively low forward rate of speed. His wife, Emily, remembered being in the chase plane with the news photographers, and watching her husband's plane suddenly disappear.

"We were flying side-by-side," she said, "and suddenly the C- 54 was gone. It dropped like a stone. Watching it drop rapidly made some of the people on our plane air sick."

Fisher made 150 high-speed dives evaluating thin transonic and supersonic propellers on a P-47 Thunderbolt at speeds in excess of 600 mph. For the Navy, he took on another risky experiment. The program called for vertical or zero lift dives of a Grumman F-8-F Bearcat using reversing propellers as a dive brake. Beginning the dive at 25,000 feet, the rates of descent were up to 37,000 feet per minute. The Navy wanted the techniques perfected for vertical dive bombing on a target.

Few problems Fisher faced during his years of experimental flying were planned. On a routine night ferry flight of a C-46 from Caldwell to the C-W plant in Columbus, OH, with Bob Kusse in the right seat and flight engineer Don Bond aboard, the control column suddenly yanked out of Fisher's hand and fell forward against the instrument panel. Mysteriously, the C-46 kept flying straight and level as if nothing had happened. Immediately, Fisher notified the airway traffic control in Allentown, PA, over which they were flying, and ordered his crew to strap on their parachutes. Then, gingerly, he pulled the control column all the way back and discovered there was no change in the plane's flight attitude. It just droned on without a hint of trouble. It was obvious that all controls had somehow become completely detached from the elevator. To gain more altitude in case they had to bail out, Fisher asked Bond to slowly move back in the plane to shift the center of gravity aft ever so slightly. The nose began to rise and soon they were flying at 6,000 feet.

Fisher found that the ailerons and rudder controls were unaffected by the mishap, so he began a slow, wide 180 degree turn back to the Caldwell area. Then Fisher began experimenting with the throttles and discovered that by reducing power slightly, allowing the nose to drop several degrees, and then advancing the throttles, the plane would descend approximately 1,000 feet, then return to level flight.

At Caldwell, Robert Earle, the Propeller Division's vice president and general manager, was in contact with members of his engineering staff attempting to pinpoint what had gone wrong with the C-46, all to no avail. At 2 a.m., he awoke the company's president, Guy Vaughan, to report the critical situation. Vaughan said, "Tell them to take the plane out over the Atlantic and bail out." Fisher and his crew decided they would rather attempt to ride the plane in than take a chance on drowning in the Atlantic.

An emergency landing was planned on the long runways at Newark Airport. After a 15-mile approach, the plane was brought down slowly by reducing power and then pushing it back up to 150 miles per hour. When the plane was just a foot off the runway, Fisher reversed the propellers. The big ship touched down and came to a dead stop within 700 feet. When the plane was examined, investigators discovered that mechanics had failed to replace two clevis pins in the empennage during maintenance on the elevator control system. Subsequent testing showed that the spring-loaded control system would function properly without the pins 17 times, but on the 18th move of the control column, the linkage would separate.

In 1953, Fisher resigned from Curtiss-Wright to join the Aviation Department of the Port Authority of New York and New Jersey as chief of the Aviation Development Division. During his 23 years with the Port Authority, he flew the British Comet, the first commercial jet transport in England, and subsequently flew every U.S. commercial and business jet, including the B-747, DC-10 and L-1011 transports, prior to their landing at Port Authority airports in the New York area.

In his later years, the plane he enjoyed flying the most was a P-40 brought into Teterboro by a West Coast restauranteur. It was the 2,500th P-40 in which he had flown.

During his 60 years of continuous flying, Fisher spent 19,351 hours in both propeller and jet powered aircraft without an accident or violation. When friends congratulated him on his skill as an aviator, he was always quick to add, "You have to be lucky too."

In March of 1990, at age 81, Fisher was still active in numerous aviation organizations. with his wife of 50 years in their home in Smoke Rise, a section of Kinnelon, NJ, he told the author, "If I had to do it all over again, I wouldn't change a thing. Life has been good to me."

After a short illness, Herb Fisher died in July 1990.

Dr. Cornelius J. Kraissl

Inducted Aviation Hall of Fame of New Jersey, 1989

A man who vividly remembered the hazards of flying the Himalayan "Hump" was Major Cornelius J. Kraissl, MD, a flight surgeon with Clair Chennault's famed Flying Tigers in China.

"My first sight of Kunming was a C-46 impaled in some Chinese buildings," he said, "which proved to be a prophetic omen. The Hump pilots had my deepest respect. Flying over rugged mountains from the Assam Valley to Kunming day in and day out, mostly at night, in all kinds of weather — this took intrepid tireless men."

Cornelius Kraissl

He was assigned to an air base in Hsian, China, only 30 miles from the Japanese lines. "Arriving at Hsian, I saw them taking bodies out of a C-47 that had just crashed on take-off, he recalled. The horizontal stabilizer locks were still in place. My job was to identify bodies."

His hospital was a two-room adobe building and he was the only doctor. His staff was two Mexican-trained Chinese nurses, four enlisted men and two house boys. On a daily basis, American and Chinese pilots showed up in Hsian in need of help.

The base was 6,000 feet high, hot and dry, not ideal conditions in which to fly an airplane. "The C-47 was a great airplane once it was airborne," the doctor explained. "but with a 500-pound bomb under each wing, and heavily loaded with ammo, it had difficulties getting off the ground. There were many 'fireballs' at the end of the runways. Flying bullets and the likelihood of the bombs exploding, made it hazardous for the rescue teams."

Kraissl, who flew over the Hump on a number of occasions, had first hand knowledge of the treacherous weather conditions the pilots and crews had to face. It only strengthened his determination to be available to help all those courageous men 24 hours a day.

He told of his most memorable experience while in the combat zone:

"While chatting with Lt. Pennington in Hsian," Kraissl related, "He said 'We're going to bust some bridges this morning, Doc, do you want to come along?' I said it sounded great and asked Pennington what he wanted me to do. 'Just sit beside me and watch the fun.' he replied. I told him that in the National Guard I used to fire the flexible gun. 'I only have eight strafers fixed in the nose,' he said. 'Why don't you fly with Harry De Pew on my wing? He has a flexible gun.'

"When we got to the target at Fengstsun Bridges, we noticed four flak towers and numerous trenches and foxholes. Each B-25 went in individually at 300 feet to strafe and skip bomb. The mission was highly successful and when we got back I went to Ops (operations) to ask if Pennington had gotten back yet. The officer turned around and looked at me with disbelief and said 'He isn't coming back — we thought you were with him!'"

Six months later, Kraissl's luck ran out. He was sent to a large Army hospital in Kunming, China with a slipped disc in the neck and amoebic dysentery.

He recalled the day the Pacific armistice was signed as the Chinese celebrated V-J Day with their fantastic dragons.

The decorations he brought back to the United States included a Bronze Star, Air Medal, China Medal of Honor, Distinguished Unit Citation and a CIB campaign ribbon with three stars.

Born in 1902 to American parents in Austria, Kraissl was brought to River Edge, NJ, at the age of two months and has lived at the same address on Kinderkamack Road ever since. He attended Park Ridge and Hackensack schools and then went on to Brooklyn Poly Technic and the Columbia College of Physicians & Surgeons where he received his medical degree in 1927.

In 1929, he joined the New York Air National Guard (NYANG) as a Medical Corps First Lieutenant and was promoted to captain in 1933. A year later, he became a Civil Aeronautics Administration medical examiner and for 56 years gave thousands of pilots their annual physicals. By the late 1980s, he was the unchallenged dean of medical examiners in New Jersey.

At the outbreak of the Korean War, he was recalled to active duty as the commander of the March Air Force Base Hospital in California. Later, he established the Plastic Surgery Center at Travis Air Force Base.

He returned to NYANG as the State Air Surgeon with the rank of Brig. General. Over the years, he has served on the Air Force Surgeon General's Reserve Medical Advisory Council and the Air National Guard Medical Advisory Council, Washington, DC.

As one of the leading plastic surgeons in North Jersey, Kraissl served as director of surgery at Bergen Pines County Hospital, Paramus; chief of the plastic surgery department at the Hackensack Medical Center, and on the surgical staffs at Valley Hospital, Ridgewood, and Pascack Valley Hospital, Westwood.

Throughout his career, he stayed active with the NYANG, and in 1990, at age 88, he was conducting medical checks for pilots in the area.

Army Commands Newark Airport

In 1940 Edwin E. Aldrin Sr. became the superintendent of Newark Airport which had lost its airline business to the newly opened LaGuardia Airport in Flushing, NY, because the Newark city council and the airlines could not come to an a agreement on renewing a long term lease. So the airport was closed.

By early 1941, Aldrin had worked out a compromise between the city and the airlines that enticed them all to return.

With the United States' entry into World War II, Newark became an active center for the transportation of aircraft and war materiel to Europe. The Army Air Corps took command of the airfield. Additional land was reclaimed from the meadows. Longer, paved runways and a modern lighting system were installed, along with new hangars, cargo buildings and warehouses.

By the war's end, the federal government had invested more than $15 million in airport improvements. Archie Armstrong, the airport engineer supervised the bulk of the work.

At an air show at the airport in the fall of 1941, historian Dave Winans remembered witnessing some of America's military aid to our nation's friendly forces overseas. "In between scheduled air show events, tiny gray fighter planes made constant flights in and out of Newark's giant new north hangar area where they had been assembled, " he explained. "As each one came in, a swarm of mechanics prepared it for overseas shipment by stenciling inverted orange triangles on wings and fuselages. They were then dismantled and crated for delivery by ship to Malaysia.

"They were Brewster Model 339s, the export versions of our Navy's F2A-2 Brewster "Buffalo" fighters, destined for the Dutch East Indies Air Force. Unfortunately, most of those that did arrive safely were shot down by superior Japanese "Zero" fighters during the invasion of Malaysia a few months later."

Hangar #55, which had been built in 1940 to accommodate the aircraft of the major carriers who fled Newark for Mayor LaGuardia's new facility, had been leased to the Brewster Corp. for the assembly of the "Buffalo," which was the first monoplane used by the U.S. Navy. More than 1,100 employees worked at the hangar which is still referred to as the "Brewster Hangar" by airport personnel.

G.M. Builds Aircraft

Within weeks after the Japanese attack on Pearl Harbor, the large General Motors assembly plant at Linden, NJ, shut down its automobile assembly lines in preparation for the wartime challenge.

On Jan. 21, 1942, the Eastern Aircraft Division of GM was formed. Immediately, orders for the Navy's Grumman F4F "Wildcat" fighter planes were received, and the assembly lines were moving again at Linden. At the same time, the West Trenton GM plant began assembling the Navy's torpedo bomber, the Grumman TBF "Avenger." The GM Bloomfield plant supplied parts and sub-assemblies to the main plants.

By 1945, New Jersey men and women had turned out 13,500 of the famous Grumman fighter planes. In 1944, they had reached a production peak of 20 planes each working day.

The airports beside the two plants had been especially constructed as test fields. Other wartime airfields were opened in Morristown and Millville, NJ.

More than One Million Receivers Produced

Aircraft radios designed and developed by New Jersey technicians at the Aircraft Radio Corp. (ARC) in Boonton were used almost exclusively in both Army and Navy aircraft during the war years. They were designated as SCR-274-N. The "N" stood for "Navy" and it was the only time the Army would so designate an aircraft radio. With the help of sub-contractors, Western Electric, Colonial Radio and Stromberg-Carlson, ARC produced nearly 1.4 million receivers, transmitters, modulators and other individual items of the basic system, known as the "command sets."

In Ridgefield, NJ, 162 Waco-designed 15-seat, troop-carrying gliders, used in the invasion of Normandy and other major battles, were built in a small plant. Much of the work was supervised by Henry Geleski, a former Teterboro mechanic.

Every industry with an interest in aviation participated in the eventual Allied victory. The English might have lost the Battle of Britain had it not been for the efforts of Standard Oil of New Jersey's (now EXXON) chemical engineers who worked at the Bayway, NJ, and Baton Rouge, LA, refineries.

When World War II began both the British Royal Air Force (RAF) and the German Luftwaffe were using 87-octane aviation fuel. The German Messerschmitt fighter planes could climb faster and were more maneuverable than the RAF's Spitfires and Hurricanes, even though they flew at a slower speed.

During the Battle of Britain, it was important that RAF planes climb above German fighters and bombers in order to attack the superior force. but the RAF planes could not achieve top speeds on takeoffs and climbs burning 87-octane fuel.

The Standard Oil engineers developed a 100/130-octane aviation fuel that gave the RAF fighters 30 percent more power and a superiority over the Germans.

By mid-1943, the Bayway Refinery was producing 20,000 barrels of high octane fuel a day and delivered more avgas than any other refinery during the war.

Despite the turmoil in which the world was thrown in 1940, there were still people setting records of various kinds in the field of aviation.

Jumps With Five 'Chutes
William E. Rhode

Inducted Aviation Hall of Fame of New Jersey, 1984

It was a bright May Sunday in 1940, when Bill Rhode, one of New Jersey's most daring professional parachute jumpers, strapped on five parachutes and climbed into a Ryan B-5 monoplane, piloted by Roy Van Houten. He was determined to establish a new parachute jump record.

The small plane lifted off from the grass strip at Murchio Airport in Preakness and flew in tight circles above a fascinated crowd until it reached an altitude of 4,000 feet. Rhode swung out of the plane's small door, adjusted his many 'chutes and jumped into space. He immediately opened the first 'chute and as soon as it billowed fully, he opened another—then another and another and another. At 500 feet the five large, white parachutes seemed to hold him motionless in the sky.

As soon as he touched down, well wishers mobbed him. He had a new world's record for a multi-chute jump. The previous number of 'chutes opened on one jump was four. Had the parachutes become entangled, Rhode would have plunged to his death. The record still stood in 1990.

Jumping from airplanes had become second nature to Rhode. He began his jumping career at age 20 and was just 25 when he made the record jump. By then, he had jumped 150 times.

Rhode was born and raised in Jersey City. His family moved to Leonia in 1928, and in that year, at age 13, he discovered the excitement of Teterboro Airport and the Gates Flying Circus. Like so many youngsters of that time, he became friendly with the Gates pilots, and fell in love with aviation the first time he flew with Clyde Pangborn.

He was a quiet, inquisitive kid who sat for hours in Vic's Airport Inn, located behind the Curtiss-Wright hangar at Teterboro, listening to the endless adventure yarns spun by men who would become legends.

He first jumped in 1936, and began performing at Ed Gorski's weekend air shows at Teterboro. He took his act to Murchio in 1938, where a hat was passed among the spectators after each jump for nickels, dimes and quarters. Those meager funds combined with his weekday factory wages, enabled him to survive in the Depression years. "After all, in those days a loaf of bread only cost a dime." Rhode said.

At the Cleveland Air Races in 1938, Rhode took second place in the spot-jumping competition. In October of 1939, pilots Lee DeWitt, Shorty Keough and Rhode flew to the southeastern states to barnstorm for the

Bill Rhode - the jumper.

winter months. They staged mini air shows and took passengers for airplane rides for a few dollars a person. That was the last summer of fun and frolic for the three aviators; as the rumble of war became increasingly louder.

During World War II, Rhode flew as a B-24 and B-17 tail gunner on 35 missions over France and Germany.

He recalled that his bomber squadron lost more than half its original personnel. "It was sad when the Quartermasters would come into the barracks (quonset huts) and pick up the personal items of each crew that went down and ready them to be sent to their homes. By the Grace of God, our crew made it home by boat."

Rhode vividly described his arrival in New York. "Those coming home boasted that they would sing and dance on the ship as we saw the Statue of Liberty. You know what? As we sailed up the Bay at 4 a.m., the 'big town' was blacked out. We all stood on deck in the darkness as the ship passed the shadowy outline of the statue. Every guy cried his eyes out. Big ones and little ones. It's very hard to describe the emotions of men coming back to the U.S. from combat and leaving buddies back there. All the things we take for granted, day by day, come back to haunt us. The sight of men crying in the darkness just passing the statue is a sight I'll never forget. It's riveted into my brain."

He returned home without a scratch only to be badly injured in a jump over Sussex (NJ) Airport. His emergency parachute had become tangled with a faulty primary 'chute and he suffered a broken back on landing. At age 30, the doctors told him he'd never walk again. His fiancee, Mildred Klopp, refused to believe it and urged him to stand and walk. After eight painful months, he was back on his feet.

He flew again too, even did some aerobatics at air shows. His principal income in those years came as a parachute rigger, a profession he had learned early in his career. "When you use them all the time," he said "You feel better when you've packed them yourself."

In 1951, Rhode began a new career as a flight instructor. His permanent base of operation became Hanover Airport, Hanover, NJ, where he stayed until the airport closed in the late 1980s. Before he quit, he had flown more than 30,000 hours and taught almost 550 students to fly.

Rhode, a prolific New Jersey historian, has authored two books: *Baling Wire, Chewing Gum and Guts* tells the history of the Gates Flying Circus. Much of his research had been conducted at Vic's Airport Inn as a teenager. *The Flying Devils* recounts his months of barnstorming through the south in 1939. He has had countless magazine and aviation personality articles published.

He wrote a particularly poignant piece concerning his almost fatal jumping accident, called "God Bless the Women," which appeared in *Air-List-Ads*, a magazine for pilots, published in Stewartsville, NJ. He told of his struggle to walk again and how he never would have made it without the support of his helpmate, Mildred; how they were married, bought a home and raised five children, and how he stayed in aviation throughout his life with Mildred's support and understanding.

In that article, he said goodbye to flying this way: *Recently [1985], at the ripe old age of 70 years and with several decades as a flight instructor, I retired from the "bounce and go" routine and now spend my time writing books and articles about aviation as it was. After 40 years of marriage, five wonderful kids and three frisky grand-kids, I look back upon life as it was and I have to admit to the truth of the adage, "Behind every successful man is a persevering woman."*

What Mildred saw in me — a plain-looking guy — I don't really know, but I saw and found a lot in her. I'd still vote for her in any beauty contest. I still open doors for her and help her into her coat and I'll stand for a mild bit of carping from her because I was lucky finding her.

I never did get my own airport, but I found everything else of value. My logbooks read of 50 years of flying, with a total of 32,851 flying hours and now I watch the

younger boys push aviation higher and farther and there, lurking nearby, are the women they need. "God bless the women."

1941
Civil Air Patrol

The Civil Air Patrol (CAP) was established under presidential executive authority on Dec. 1, 1941. The civilian flying corps was the brainchild of New Jersey's Director of Aeronautics Gill Robb Wilson. On a visit to Germany in 1936, Wilson became alarmed by the Nazi's military might. He realized how vulnerable the long U.S. Atlantic coastline was to submarine attacks, like those that had taken place during World War I. He knew the Army Air Corps and the Navy didn't have sufficient aircraft or pilots to police even the New Jersey coast, so he conceived the idea of having a civilian coastal patrol established in the Garden State.

The New Jersey group, formed in 1940, was named the New Jersey Civil Air Defense Service (CADS). Groups of pilots and their aircraft were organized throughout the state. Plans to use the CADS to patrol the Jersey coastline, to guard dams and reservoirs, to search for missing aircraft, and to move people and equipment rapidly from place to place were drawn and approved by Governor Harold Hoffman. In a surprisingly short time, the organization had 300 members.

The statewide "Wing", was headquartered in Trenton. The Wing was divided into three geographical regions called "groups." Individual units in each region were known as "squadrons." There were 12 squadrons in all, located at Caldwell, Newark, Somerset, Hightstown, Bridgeport, Atlantic City, S. Plainfield, West Trenton, Red Bank, Vineland, Asbury Park and Palmyra. George A. Viehmann of Summit, became the first Wing commander.

Seven days before the Dec. 7, 1941 Japanese attack on Pearl Harbor, U.S. Civilian Defense Director Fiorella LaGuardia signed a formal order creating a national Civil Air Patrol, with an organizational chart similar to the CADS. Gill Robb Wilson became the CAP's Executive Officer.

In New Jersey, Viehmann continued as Wing commander and the membership grew. While the CAP was essentially a paper organization throughout the nation, the New Jersey Wing was already trained and equipped with pilots, mechanics and airplanes. The New Jersey (CAP) base, one of three along the Atlantic coast, was opened at Atlantic City on March 6, 1942, commanded by Capt. Gill Robb Wilson. Once the operation was running smoothly, Major Wynant Farr of Monroe, NY, became the commander.

By early 1942, German U-Boats were sinking ships almost daily along the Atlantic coast, and CAP pilots and their single-engine land planes were put to the test. In the year and a half that the CAP operated out of Atlantic City, 13 New Jersey aviators crashed at sea, but all survived. The only fatality occurred when 1st Lt. Ben Berger lost control of his plane during a proficiency flight on Easter Sunday, 1943.

CAP Sinks German Sub

In the 50-year history of the CAP, few flights have been as significant as that of the Grumman Widgeon NC 28674.

It was a sunny, early July day in 1942, when the Atlantic City Coastal Patrol Base 1 was instructed to investigate a submarine contact report. Base 1 launched a number of aircraft to search for the elusive enemy. Among them was Widgeon NC 28674, piloted by John B. Haggin, who was accompanied by Commander Farr.

Flying 300 feet above the waves, some 24 miles off the Absecon (NJ) Lighthouse, observer Farr sighted globs of oil on the water. Closer investigation revealed the long ghostly shape of a submarine moving below the surface at approximately two knots. The Widgeon was one of the few armed civilian aircraft. It carried two aerial depth charges under its wings, each filled with 300 pounds of TNT.

Having never flown a combat mission, Haggin and Farr were apprehensive about bombing the submarine prematurely. So for more than four hours, they stalked the undersea marauder waiting for the opportunity for a sure kill. That time came when the sub's commander made the fatal mistake of rising closer to the surface.

Haggin dove the Widgeon to a scant 100 feet above the waves with Farr sighting through the crude bombsight. Finally things were right and Farr pulled the rope attached to the makeshift bomb rack release and sent the "ash can" on its explosive way. And explode it did, striking only a few feet off the submarine's bow, creating a shock wave that made the Widgeon shake violently. As a result of the first attack, the sub's bow-high attitude surrounded by an ever-widening oil slick made it an easy target. With new-found confidence, Haggin and Farr closed in for the kill.

The Widgeon swooped low at full speed to avoid the resulting concussion as Farr released the remaining depth charge. Again, they were right on target. Pieces of wood that floated to the surface were later identified as having come from the submarine's gun deck.

Although this incident is not listed as a confirmed sinking in U.S. Navy records, there is little doubt that the Widgeon deserved to be credited. It was one of two German submarines sunk by civilian aircraft during World War II.

The Widgeon NC 28674, was still flying in 1985 in western Alaska and the Aleutian Islands for Neal and Company of Homer, AL.

On Aug. 31, 1943, the Atlantic City Coastal Patrol was transferred to Hadley Field in S. Plainfield and became part of a multi-state unit that towed targets for military gunnery practice. Other units around the state assisted in courier missions, missing aircraft searches and in providing security personnel at local airfields. Members of the Asbury park Squadron flew "attack" flights on Fort Monmouth to test a new device called "radar" that was being developed at the Monmouth County military base.

At the war's end, the Civil Air patrol became a non-profit corporation and on May 26, 1948 it was designated as an official auxiliary of the United States Air Force. Although CAP pilots no longer had to search for German submarines or tow aerial targets, they maintained an active search and rescue and disaster relief organization. A cadet program that prepared young men and women to fly or become active in other aviation endeavors was established and has continued to flourish.

In the late 1940s and early 50s, the New Jersey CAP was commanded by Lt. Col. Frank Carvin, Lt. Col. B. Hunt Smith and Col. Irving Feist.

Col. Nanette M. Spears

The "Dragon Lady"

In 1956, Colonel Nannette M. Spears was named the CAP Wing Commander. She served in that capacity for 13 years and became a legend in her time as a no-nonsense leader of both men and women. One of only three women Wing Commanders in the nation, she was affectionately known as the "Dragon Lady."

The striking brunette with the ready smile, was constantly on the move. She attended hundreds of CAP and other aeronautical functions from Cape May on the southern tip to Sussex county in the northwest corner of the state, preaching the importance of aviation education to high school and college students.

At 17, she was a concert pianist, a graduate of the Cincinnati Conservatory of Music and had her own radio program. When she married Albert K. Spears in the mid-30s, she became an accomplished horsewoman and owned several spirited hunters and polo ponies. Flying didn't come until 1939. Spears explained how that happened in a 1969 *Newark Star-Ledger* article:

I first took up flying as a sport in 1939, while on a visit to California. My husband hadn't been happy with my previous hobby which was playing polo and riding horses daily. He didn't think it was safe. When I wrote him about my new hobby, he sent me a 22-page letter trying to dissuade me. Nevertheless, when I returned to New Jersey, I continued with my flying lessons at Newark Airport. After a year, Col. E.E. Aldrin [then the airport manager] came to me and asked me to answer letters from people wanting to learn how to fly. He set up a desk for me at Newark Airport.

Soon, Gill Robb Wilson, director of aeronautics for the State of New Jersey, started to organize civil pilots, realizing that a war was imminent. When the Civil Air Patrol was activated, just one week before Pearl Harbor, I became its first recruiting officer.

From then on, Spears served on all levels of staff from squadron to wing. Just prior to her promotion as Wing commander she became the first woman to receive the Civil Air Patrol's highest decoration, the Distinguished Service Award. The award was presented by Maj. Gen. Lucas V. Beau, CAP National Commander and Col. Fiest, the New Jersey wing commander. Feist's recommendation read:

Colonel Spears' activities with this wing show a record of continuous and uninterrupted service since the very inception of the Civil Air Patrol. This officer has continually demonstrated exceptional ability and, through her exercise of logical reasoning and sound judgment has become the keystone to the administrative structure of the entire wing.

Colonel Spears is never hesitant to accept duties of great responsibility and, in the assumption of these duties, has repeatedly demonstrated an exceptional degree of individual and moral stamina which has contributed in high degree to the success and steady growth of this wing.

In 1962, Spears met Milt Caniff, the nationally renowned cartoonist who created the popular comic strip "Terry and the Pirates." One of the leading characters of the strip was the "Dragon Lady." Three weeks after their dinner together, Caniff sent a painting of the "Dragon Lady" with the inscription "The C.O. is the D.L."

Just a year after she stepped down as Wing Commander, having held the position longer than any other New Jersey commander, Spears died of cancer while visiting her brother, Dr. Abner Moss of North Hollywood, CA. She was 56.

Following her death, the New Jersey Wing adopted the name "The Dragon Wing" in her honor.

Over the years, the New Jersey CAP has hosted youth from around the world. And has been an active participant in the International Air Cadet Exchange program. The New Jersey cadets have excelled in their training, while senior members have provided radio communications and a chaplain's program that has been rated among the best in the nation.

Adult members throughout the state continue to participate in search and rescue missions, both actual and practice. Experiments have been conducted jointly with the Navy and Air Force to determine if CAP planes could still be used to detect modern submarines as they did during the war.

Through all of this activity, only one fatal accident occurred. On Nov. 15, 1961, a plane, piloted by Peter A. Danzo of the Teterboro Composite Squadron, crashed in a swamp near Morristown, killing him and Robert C. Klein of the North Hudson Squadron and Walter Sibi, a Union City, police officer who had gone along as a freelance photographer.

Despite anti-militaristic feelings during the Vietnam War, the CAP thrived in New Jersey. With the coming of the space age, aviation studies became "aerospace education." The cadet program was redesigned and New Jersey cadets began to excel in the study of the new criteria.

When Col. Spears retired in the late '60s, Col. Walter M. Markey of Chester, NJ, became Wing commander. During his administration, the CAP purchased a fleet of six Cessna 150 aircraft. The single-engine monoplanes were used for everything from teaching cadets to fly, to search missions, to the formation of a Wing Flight Team, "The Dragonflies," organized by Lt. Col George Bochenek.

Markey was succeeded by Col. Frederick Bell, who moved the Wing headquarters from the Lakehurst Naval Air Station to McGuire Air Force Base. A yearly cadet flying summer encampment was begun at McGuire AFB during Markey's tenure as commander.

Col. Ri Nakamura of Lakewood, NJ, took command of the CAP in 1976 and the New Jersey CAP Wing returned to its original format of three groups.

In 1977, Maj. John O'Hara, a teacher from Kearny High School, became director of the CAP's aerospace education program. Over the next few years, anywhere in the state that there were CAP cadets, O'Hara could be found building gliders, launching model rockets or letting some lucky cadet wear a NASA spacesuit in one of his demonstration shows.

When Col. Bochenek of Linden became Wing commander in 1980, the officials at McGuire AFB announced that barrack space for the cadet summer encampment program was no longer available. Under the direction of Maj. Harold Thorp, Lt. Col. Mary Bennette, Lt. Col. Stephan Lovas and many former cadets, a bivouac-style encampment was pioneered. A small tent city was built at Fort Dix including a command post, a field sick bay, classrooms, sleeping quarters and a full field kitchen. After an intensive week of training, the camp was disassembled and stored until the following year.

The '80s introduced a new field of electronic search. The increasing use of Emergency Locator Transmitters on private planes and boats meant new training for air and ground search teams. The number of missions per year soared to an average of 80. In 1986, New Jersey Wing won both the North East Region Search and Rescue Competition and the national championship at Whiteman Air Force Base in Missouri. Air Force officials were so impressed by the New Jersey team's work, they invited them to the air Rescue and Recovery Center at Scott Air Force Base in Illinois to demonstrate their techniques in electronic search. The outstanding efforts of the team won the Wing a Unit citation from the National Civil Air Patrol.

In 1987, Col. Frederick Camenzind of S. Hampton, NJ, became Wing Commander. He increased the size of the wing from three groups to four. The Cessna 150s were replaced with the three Cessna 172s, a Cessna 182 and a Cessna 152. A new emphasis was placed on the cadet program under Maj. Beverly Camenzind, and cadets applied for special activities in greater numbers than ever.

In 1989, the New Jersey Wing cadet drill team won the Northeast Region Cadet competition commanded by Capt. Kenneth Hawthorne. And as the 50th anniversary of New Jersey's Civil Air Defense Service, the forerunner of the CAP, was being celebrated in 1990, the cadet drill team hoped to bring the national championship back to the Garden State for the first time since 1949.

The men and women of the New Jersey Civil Air Patrol have voluntarily served the state and nation for 50 years. Their accomplishments deserve the applause of every New Jersey citizen. For five decades, they have protected our nation's coastline in time of war, saved numerous lives by their search and rescue efforts, trained young men and women in the art of flying and have brought special recognition to the Garden State.

Navy Blimps Protect Coastal Shipping Lanes

The importance of the Civil Air Patrol's role in policing the nation's coastline is emphatically clear when one realizes that on Dec. 7, 1941, the Navy had an airship program on the planning boards, but no fleet airship unit in service. Although four successive chiefs of the Bureaus of Aeronautics, from Admiral William A. Muffett in the early 1930s to Admiral J.H. Towers in 1940, had unequivocally endorsed a nonrigid airship (blimp) program, no congressional support had been forthcoming until a provision for 48 blimps was tacked onto a bill that became known as the "10,000 Plane Program," passed on June 15, 1940.

When President Roosevelt declared war on Japan, the Navy had ten blimps, only six of which were large enough for service at sea. There was 5,000 miles of coastline on both the Atlantic and Pacific Oceans to be patrolled by the six blimps from one operational airship base at Lakehurst.

Just 13 days after war was declared, a Japanese submarine sank the *SS Medio* off the coast of Eureka, CA. The prospects for merchant shipping were bleak.

To make matters worse, Japanese submarines were striking at land targets. On Feb. 23, 1942, a daring Nippon sub attacked oil derricks just north of Santa Barbara, CA.

In 1942, a staggering total of 454 merchant ships were sunk off the Atlantic coast with only 13 airships on patrol. The losses dropped dramatically the following year: 65 ships sunk. Fifty three blimps were on patroll by then. Only 11 ships were sunk in 1944 and 1945 when the Atlantic airship submarine-patrol fleet numbered 68 vessels. In all, 532 ships were sunk in the Atlantic and Gulf coastal waters of the United States and in the Caribbean and South Atlantic during the war. But not one vessel was sunk by enemy submarines while under escort.

Lakehurst became the headquarters of Fleet Airship Wing, that had eight-blimp squadrons located at four operating bases at South Weymouth, MA, Weeksville, NC, Glynco, GA, and Lakehurst.

Moffett Field in California became the headquarters of the airship wing that patrolled the Pacific coastline. There were three main operating bases: Santa Ana and Moffett Field, CA, and Tillamook, OR.

On May 15, 1943, Rear Admiral Charles E. Rosendahl returned to Lakehurst from the Pacific theater to become Chief of Naval Airship Training and Experimentation. The programs he established were used to train the majority of 1,500 pilots and 3,000 air crewmen who manned the airships during the war.

The Lakehurst facility was expanded to accommodate the anti-submarine blimps. Four additional hangars were built and by 1944 the Navy had 130 blimps patrolling the United States' coastal waters.

L1 and L4 blimps were used for training at Lakehurst. On board the small non-rigid training airships, one man handled both the elevator and rudder. Once they became proficient at flying the trainers, they were transferred to K-ships, the larger blimps used for convoy duty. The "Ks" were 270 feet long and had a top speed of 72 knots.

Painting by Keith Ferris

A Civil Air Patrol Grumman "Widgeon," piloted by Ray Higgins with Wynant Farr as observer, attacked and sunk a German submarine off the Absecon lighthouse July 1942

The cadets graduated from the training program as ensigns in the Navy. Normal patrols averaged about 10 hours a day. On escort duty, the blimps flew an average of 15 hours.

The lighter-than-air program remained at Lakehurst until 1960, when three new Naval schools moved into the vast facility. Lakehurst became known as the Naval Air Test Facility. The sailors tested and evaluated aircraft launching and recovery systems. There were five test tracks, one a mile and a half long. In the huge Hangar 1, the deck of an aircraft carrier was constructed for training purposes.

In 1972, an engineering center was opened at the New Jersey site, creating more than 1,200 civilian jobs. The Navy's Boatswain's school and the Marine Aircraft Launch and Recovery school also moved to Lakehurst to train Navy, Coast Guard, Marine and Allied military forces.

Although the Navy dirigibles and blimps are now a technology of the past, Navy veterans and those people who lived in the Lakehurst area during the heyday of the lighter-than-air activities, still come together on occasion to celebrate the anniversaries of various former Lakehurst activities.

Mission to Moscow
Louis Reichers

On May 29, 1941, the Air Corps Ferrying Command (ACFC), later named the Air Transport Command, was created by Gen. "Hap" Arnold and became a vital supply and communication link between the United States and Great Britain. Col. Robert Olds commanded the new service.

Ferrying American-built bombers to England was not the only mission of the ACFC. Col Olds also ran a shuttle service from Washington, DC, to the United Kingdom. His pilots flew military and civilian officials between the two countries in modified B-24 bombers. The shuttle became known as the "Arnold Line."

When it became obvious that America would eventually become actively involved in World War II, Louis Reichers, the Kearny resident who flew the Atlantic in 1932, re-enlisted and was assigned to the Ferrying Command. Because of his Atlantic flight experience, Reichers was assigned to fly the top secret "Harriman Mission" to Moscow.

W. Averill Harriman, a valued diplomat of that period, was asked by President Franklin Roosevelt to visit Moscow to discuss a $1 million lend lease arrangement with Russian Premier Josef Stalin. Wooing Stalin away from Adolph Hitler, with whom he had signed military agreements in the late 1930s, was important to the European war effort.

Longest Over-Water Flight

In September of 1941, less than three months before the attack on Pearl Harbor, Reichers flew the Harriman party to Archangel, Russia, via Gander, Newfoundland, and Prestwick, Scotland. The final 2,775-mile leg of the eastbound flight was the longest over water up to that time. For his accomplishment Reichers was toasted by Josef Stalin at a state dinner in the Kremlin.

On the return flight, Reichers pioneered a southerly route back to the United States, flying from the Russian capital to Washington over the Mid-East, Africa, South America and the Caribbean islands. He was awarded the Distinguished Flying Cross.

Reichers successful South Atlantic Flight brought him another top secret mission late in 1942. Then a Lt. Colonel, he was named the commander of the KIT Project which involved the delivery of 36 A-20 twin-engine bombers from Morrison Field in West Palm Beach, FL, to Algiers. It was the first tactical ferrying of a combat group to an active front by their own crews.

Unlike the experienced ACFC pilots, the young airmen of the 68th Group had never undertaken a flight of 8,000 miles.

Military Build-up Begins

The majority of the A-20 pilots were 10 years younger than Reichers and had been flying aircraft for only a year or two. With the veteran pilot in the lead, all 36 of the bombers made the transatlantic crossing successfully. The military build up for the invasion of Italy had begun.

Reichers left the service in 1947 and went to work for Cushing & Newell, Inc., a product design and development firm in New York City. Calling on his engineering background, he specialized in technical writing and project design. Much of his work had to do with manuals for missiles and was considered highly classified.

When a project was completed Reichers and his wife, Lee, were able to take long vacations. "We usually prowled around Europe," Mrs. Reichers explained.

In 1956, he wrote an autobiography *The Flying Years* that detailed his many adventures as a barnstormer, record setter and military aviator. A year later, he established an office for Cushing & Newell in Denver, CO, with a small staff. The pressure of the job became too much for him, and in 1962, he died of a heart attack at his mountain retreat in Estes Park, CO. He was 61 years old.

World War II

Thousands of gallant New Jersey men and women aviators and ground support personnel served with the Air Corps, Navy or Marines during World War II. In his or her own way, each contributed to the final victory in Europe and the Far East. Although pilots and flight crews received headline recognition for their accomplishments, it took a super-human cooperative effort between those on the ground who maintained the aircraft and those who flew them to create a winning team.

The stories of sacrifice and heroism are endless. Here are a few that are representative of all Garden State residents who served in the aeronautical branches of the various services.

Only three New Jersey airmen were awarded the Congressional Medal of Honor, and only one, First Lt. Kenneth A. Walsh, survived to accept it. Brig. Gen. Frederick W. Castle and Major Thomas B. McGuire were selected for medals for heroism on the day of their deaths.

Brig. Gen. Frederick W. Castle

Inducted, Aviation Hall of Fame of New Jersey, 1988

Gen. Fred Castle

In April 1944, Col. Frederick Walker Castle of Mountain Lakes, NJ, was given command of the 4th Combat Wing, the largest in the 8th Air Force, headquartered at Roushham Air Base near Bury St. Edmunds, England. On Christmas Eve 1944, during the height of the Battle of The Bulge and only a few weeks after he had been promoted to Brigadier General, Castle headed a bombing mission of 2,032 B-17 Flying Fortresses against Von Rundstedt's ground forces and key German airfields. The attacking bomber force, protected by 800 fighter planes, has been described by historians as the greatest air armada ever assembled.

The citation accompanying his Medal of Honor read: En route to the target, the failure of one engine forced him [Castle] to relinquish his place at the head of the formation. In order not to endanger friendly troops on the ground below, he refused to jettison his bombs to gain speed and maneuverability. His lagging, unescorted aircraft became the target of numerous enemy fighters which ripped the left wing with cannon shells, set the oxygen system afire, and wounded two members of the crew. Repeated attacks started fires in two engines, leaving the Flying Fortress in imminent danger of exploding. Realizing the hopelessness of the situation, the bailout order was given. Without regard for his personal safety he gallantly remained alone at the controls to afford all other crew members an opportunity to escape. Still another attack exploded gasoline tanks in the right wing, and the bomber plunged earthward, carrying Gen. Castle to his death. His intrepidity and willing sacrifice of his life to save members of the crew were in keeping with the highest traditions of the military service.

Castle had been born Oct. 14, 1908 at Fort McKinley, Manila, Philippines, during the first foreign service tour of his father, Col. Benjamin F. Castle of the 29th Infantry. Young Castle received his early education at schools in Tientsin, China, Washington, D.C., Paris, France and Mountain Lakes, where the family resided for many years after World War I.

Following his graduation from Boonton (NJ) High School and Storm King (NY) Military Academy, Castle took the New Jersey National Guard competitive exam for an appointment to the U.S. Military Academy and ranked No. 1. He entered West Point in July of 1926 and graduated seventh in the cadet class of 1930.

As a second lieutenant, he took Air Corps training at March Field, CA, and Kelly Field, TX, and became a pursuit pilot at Selfridge Field, MI. In 1934, he resigned from the service and for the next seven years, worked for the Allied Chemical and Sperry Gyroscope Companies.

Immediately after the bombing of Pearl Harbor brought the U.S. into World War II, Castle returned to active duty and soon was assigned to Gen. Ira Eaker in London to help create the 8th Air Force. After two years on Eaker's staff, he asked for active duty and took command of the 94th Bomb Group based in Suffolk, England. Over the next nine months, he led many important bombing missions to western Europe. The fateful Christmas Eve 1944 flight was his 30th mission.

Major Thomas B. McGuire Jr.

Inducted Aviation Hall of Fame of New Jersey, 1982

It was just 13 days after the death of Gen. Castle that Major Thomas B. McGuire, a Ridgewood native, flew his last mission over the Phillipines.

McGuire was leading a group of four P-38 "Lightning" fighter planes over the Japanese-held airstrip on the Phillipine Island of Los Negros. As Japanese fighters bounded into the air to meet the challenge, the airmen scattered. An enemy fighter zeroed in on one of the American planes, and the pilot radioed for help. McGuire was quick to respond. Flying practically on the tree tops, the major manuevered his twin-fuselaged fighter in pursuit of the enemy and, in his excitement, he forgot to release his wing fuel tanks. Suddenly in a tight turn, the plane stalled and dived straight into the jungle below. Like Castle, McGuire died making a noble attempt to save the life of a fellow airman.

With 38 enemy aircraft to his credit, Thomas McGuire was the second leading all-time American flying "ace." Richard Bong who also flew in the Pacific, had 40 Japanese kills to his credit when he was recalled to the states. The New Jerseyan had been determined to surpass Bong's record before he returned home, but fate stepped in to halt the quest.

McGuire, born on Aug. 1, 1920, attended the Georgia School of Technology. He entered the Army Air Corps in 1941 and was commissioned a second lieutenant in 1942 with a pilot's rating.

He was assigned to Alaska as a fighter pilot and it wasn't until early 1943 that he transferred to the South Pacific. At the time, he had not flown in combat or even seen a Japanese plane. It wasn't until August

Somewhere in the Pacific - Charles Lindbergh and McGuire

of that year, flying with the 431st Fighter Squadron, 475th Fighter Group, that McGuire began to chalk up his combat victories.

While flying top cover for bombers striking at Wewak on New Guinea, he shot down three Japanese aircraft and, a day later at the same location, he got two more. He had become a flying "ace" in his first two air battles.

Over the next year, McGuire kept adding to his number of victories. It soon became obvious that he would challenge Bong for the top spot in the annals of American combat aviators. But it was not to be.

During his brief career, McGuire received the Congressional Medal of Honor along with the Distinguished Service Cross, three Silver Stars, six Distinguished Flying Crosses and 15 Air Medals.

First Lt. Kenneth A. Walsh

The "Fighting Irishman"

The third New Jersey recipient of the Medal of Honor was Marine 1st Lt. Kenneth A. Walsh of Jersey City. With 21 enemy aircraft to his credit, Walsh was also New Jersey's second leading flying ace of all wars.

The citation accompanying his Medal of Honor states:

For extraordinary heroism and intrepidity above and beyond the call of duty as a pilot in Marine Fighting Squadron 124 in aerial combat against enemy Japanese forces in the Solomon Islands area. Determined to thwart the enemy's attempt to bomb Allied ground forces and shipping at Vella LaVella on August 15, 1943, First Lieutenant Walsh landed his mechanically disabled plane at Munda, quickly replaced it with another and proceeded to rejoin his flight over Kahili. Separated from his escort group when he encountered approximately fifty Japanese Zeros, he unhesitatingly attacked, striking with relentless fury in his lone battle against a powerful force. He destroyed four hostile fighters before cannon shellfire forced him to make a dead-stick landing off Vella LaVella where he was later picked up. His valiant leadership and his daring skill as a flier have been a source of confidence and inspiration to his fellow pilots and reflect the highest credit upon the United States Naval Service.

Walsh was born in Brooklyn, NY, on Nov. 24, 1916. His family moved to Jersey City in the mid-1920s and he graduated from Dickinson High School in that city in 1933. In December of the same year, he enlisted in the Marine Corps and underwent recruit training at

Parris Island, SC. He spent the next two years as an aviation mechanic and radioman at the Marine Corps base at Quantico, VA.

In March 1936, Walsh was selected for flight training at Pensacola, FL, and won his wings as a private in 1937. While doing scout and observation flying for four years aboard the aircraft carriers *Yorktown, Wasp* and *Ranger,* he was promoted through the enlisted ranks to Marine gunner, equivalent to the rank of warrant officer.

In October 1942, he was commissioned a second lieutenant, became a first lieutenant in June 1943 and a captain six months after he received his Medal of Honor. He scored all his 21 victories in Vought "Corsair" F4U fighter planes.

He remained in the service after the war and again went overseas at the outbreak of the Korean Conflict in 1950. He served in Korea until July 1951, and was awarded a gold star in lieu of his 15th Air Medal, "for outstanding performance of duty in aerial flight against the enemy in Korea."

He retired from the Marines in 1962 as a lieutenant colonel No greater tribute could be paid to Col. Walsh than when the Marine Corps referred to their fourth-ranking ace of World War II as "the Fighting Irishman of Marine Aviation."

Including McGuire and Walsh, New Jersey had 32 flying aces during World War II. Each ace flying in either Europe or the Pacific, had shot down five or more enemy aircraft in air-to-air combat. Many of them had destroyed numerous enemy aircraft on the ground and badly damaged others during deadly aerial dog fights. Here listed alphabetically are the Garden State's flying aces, their home towns and the number of enemy aircraft they were credited with downing. Unless otherwise marked all the flyers were members of the United States Air Force.

NAME	HOME	SCORE
Aron, William E.	Oakland	5.00
Baumler, Albert J.	Bayonne	5.00
Bostrom, Ernest 0.	East Orange	5.00
Brezas, Michael	Bloomfield	12.00
Ceuleers, George F.	Bridgeton	10.50
Drake, Charles W. (USMC)	Martinsville	5.00
Duffy, James, E. Jr.	N. Caldwell	5.20
Frazier, Kenneth (USMC)	Burlington	12.50
Gerard, Francis R.	Lyndhurst	8.00
Godson, Lindley W. (USN)	Colonia	5.00
Graham, Lindol F.	Ridgewood	5.50
Hart, Cameron M.	Westfield	6.00
Hill, Frank A.	Hillsdale	7.00
Jackson, Michael J.	Edison	8.00
Jones, Frank C.	Montclair	5.00
Jones, John L.	Paterson	8.00
Lamb, Robert A.	Waldwick	7.00
McCormick, Wm. Jr. (USN)	Somerset	6.00
McGuire, Thomas B. Jr.	Ridgewood	38.00
Paskoski, Joseph J.(USN)	Millville	6.00
Petach, John E.	Perth Amboy	5.25
Pisanos, Spiros	N. Plainfield	6.00
Poindexter, James	N. Millville	7.00
Popek, Edward	S. Hackensack	7.00
Stanch, Paul M.	Audubon	10.00
Strait, Donald J.	East Orange	13.50
Sutcliffe, Robert C.	Trenton	5.00
Sykes, William J.	Atlantic City	5.00
Walsh, Kenneth A. (USMC)	Newark	21.00
Warner, Arthur T. (USMC)	Newark	8.00
Williams, Gerard M.(USMC)	Berkely Hgts	7.00
Young, Owen D. (USN)	Tenafly	5.00

Flying Tiger
John E. Petach, Jr.

It has been said that the pilots who joined Claire Chennault's American Volunteer Group (AVG) in China just prior to the Japanese sneak attack on Pearl Harbor in 1941, were perhaps the most colorful and celebrated airmen of that war. They were former Army, Navy and Marine pilots who had resigned from the various services to fly as mercenaries to protect the Burma Road, the key supply route into Western China from Burma and India.

It had taken a special "executive order" signed by President Franklin Roosevelt to permit recruiters to surreptitiously offer military personnel an opportunity to fly for the Chinese government with the understanding that they could return in one year to their American military units.

The recruits salaries ranged from $250 to $750 a month plus 30 days paid leave and expenses. The pilots were told they would get an additional $500 for each enemy aircraft destroyed. For an aggressive fighter pilot, it was an opportunity to make some big bucks (in those Depression years) and put the flying skills they had honed in mock battles to the test.

The special combat force that migrated to China, carrying false passports that identified them as missionaries, musicians and artists, numbered 330 — 75 of them were pilots. Two of that number came from New Jersey, pilot John E. Petach Jr. and crew chief George Tyrrell, both of Perth Amboy.

Although the AVG flyers, nicknamed the "Flying Tigers" by the admiring Chinese, were badly outnumbered and flew slower, less maneuverable aircraft than the Japanese, they officially destroyed 297 enemy planes in the seven months they flew together with a loss of only four American pilots killed in combat. Unofficially, the Tigers are credited with crippling perhaps as many as 600 Japanese planes. Petach had an official "kill" total of six, which qualified him as an "ace."

The AVG emblem — a winged Bengal tiger vaulting through a "V" for victory was created by the Walt Disney Studios. But the Tiger's most lasting insignia, the menacing shark teeth painted on the cowlings of all their Curtiss P-40 aircraft, was first drawn by AVG pilot Eric Shilling. He had seen a photograph of a similar ornamentation on a German Messerschmitt 110 based in the Mediterranean.

When American air forces moved into the China, Burma, India (CBI) theater of operations, with an overbearing commander who outranked Channault, the battle-weary Flying Tigers decided to pick up their option and head home. Chennault urged the fliers to remain, but the majority left, and the AVG was disbanded on July 4, 1942.

One of the five pilots who remained was Johnnie Petach. He had been asked to stay a bit longer to train the newly formed 23rd Fighter Group, commanded by Col. Robert L. Scott. Despite the fact that he had recently married one of the two AVG nurses and she was waiting to accompany him back to the states in Chungking, he felt duty-bound to work with the new pilots.

On July 10, 1942, Petach volunteered to lead a group of P-40s on a bombing raid ver a lake near Nanchang where Japanese gunboats had been seen. He made a dive-bomb run on a gunboat and was hit by ground fire, causing his plane to explode. He never did return home.

John E. Petach was born in Donora, PA, on July 15, 1918, but spent his formative years in Perth Amboy. His family home was at 98 Market Street. Upon graduating from Perth Amboy High School as an honor student in 1935, Petach matriculated to New York Univesity where he was president the Psi-Vpsilon fraternity. In 1939, he received a degree in chemical engineering and immediately entered the Navy's flight program. He received his wings and was assigned to a Scout Bomber Squadron aboard the *U.S.S. Ranger*. It was in mid 1941 that he was recruited for the AVG.

After his death, he was awarded the Distinguished Flying Cross. It wasn't until 1984, that the official announcement was received by his family, and that year his mother Julia and former wife Emma Jane Hanks, received the medal at a special ceremony at the McGuire Air Force Base.

After the ceremony, George Tyrrell said: "I knew him very well. I was glad he got the award. I think he deserved it."

Tyrrell pointed out that he and Petach were in the same Flying Tiger squadron during their time in China. Then referring to the award, he added, "I didn't know anything about it. I guess it (the medal) got lost in the shuffle of paperwork. It happens. Sometimes it takes 42 years to find out a man is a hero."

Tyrrell's job in China was to keep a minimum of five P-40s in combat condition at all times. "We were sent over as guinea pigs," he said. "but we got quite a bit of schooling from General Channault. It was my job, like anything else. The military was attractive to me at that time. I believe then and I believe now that if you're going to live in this country, then you must be willing to defend it. I did my small part."

In 1945, a film version of Gen. Robert L. Scott's book *God is My Co-Pilot* was produced and actor Dane Clark portrayed Petach. Following his fiery death, there is a scene in which his fellow flyers dive headlong at the enemy shouting, "This one's for Johnnie Petach!"

First American Fighter Victory
Captain Frank A. Hill

Inducted Aviation Hall of Fame of New Jersey, 1992

An associated Press report dated August 20, 1942 that appeared in the New York Herald Tribune read:

England — Capt. Frank A. Hill, twenty-three years old, of Hillsdale, NJ, shot down a Focke-Wulf 190, the German's fast new fighter, for the first American fighter victory of the war, but did not see it crash and so reported only a 'probable.'

The United Press International reported the same incident: *Capt. Frank A. Hill of Hillsdale, NJ, was the hero of one American formation in the air battle over Dieppe yesterday, which was reported to have hit bad luck when it was jumped by an overwhelming force of Focke-Wulfs.*

The formation was not able to get help from other Allied squadrons which were driving off German bombers, and had to wage a lone fight against some of Germany's top pilots.

Hill was quoted as saying: "Just like all these fellows [pilots in his squadron], it was my first real taste of combat. I was leading my flight over Dieppe when several Focke-Wulfs came down from the clouds behind us. We were just turning to meet them when one crossed my sights. I gave him a four-second burst with cannon and machine-guns and he acted like he was hit pretty bad.

"I must have got both the pilot and the engine. He smoked a little and spun down. He came out of the spin near the ground but then fell off again. His pals were still around though so I had no chance to watch him all the way."

Frank Hill went on to fly 166 combat missions and accumulated eight victories, three shared with his wing man, for a total of six and a half enemy aircraft shot down, four probables and more then eight damaged. His official total was seven "kills."

The Aug. 31, 1942 issue of *Time Magazine,* under a page heading "U.S. At War," discussed these early confrontations of Americans with the war machine of Nazi Germany. The article read in part:

The first American boys looked at the Nazi earth, into the Nazi guns, into Nazi faces. The war drew on toward the ultimate focal point: millions of Americans facing millions of the enemy.

But the novelty of 'firsts' was still fresh. Capt. Frank A. Hill won the first U.S. dogfight victory over Europe by shooting down a Focke-Wulf 190 in the skies over Dieppe (modestly he claimed only a 'probable' victory, because he did not have time to watch the plane crash). Capt. Hill was 23, from Hillsdale, NJ. He had been a high school athlete, had worked as a plumber's helper. Now his picture showed him at a British airport after the battle, grinning toothily from his cockpit like a youngster tickled about his first solo.

At that point in history, Frank Hill was America's favorite hero of the European war.

At the age of 18, Hill, with a group of Hillsdale boys, had rebuilt and flown a glider purchased from a New York City storage company. Some of the more active members of the Pascack Valley Gliding Club were John Olley, Ed Staubach, Dick Selgroth and Bob Blauvelt. They flew as often as possible from an open field in River Vale, NJ, near the old Kocember's nine-hole golf course.

"Fourteen of us learned to fly it, and none of us got hurt, although the glider was often in the shop for repairs," Hill recalled.

Hill praised the efforts of an adviser to the teenage aviators, Gordon Detweiller, as "a man dedicated to flying and to youth."

In a 1942 *New York Herald Tribune* interview, his proud mother, Mrs. Frederick L. Hill: said "He was always and forever a boy to fool around with airplanes. Why, he even used to hang his models around on the electric light fixtures."

Hill later had fond memories of his first airplane flight at age eight with pilot Billy Diehl. They took off from the sod runway at old Arcola airfield in Rochelle Park.

In 1933, he and a buddy volunteered to do odd jobs for Ed Gorski at Teterboro. The boys weren't doing the chores out of the goodness of their hearts. Like so many other teenagers of the time, they hoped a pilot would offer them a ride. Bob Soehners, who was a friend of Hill's older brother Fred, took the boys on numerous flights over Bergen and Passaic counties. Little did the pilot know that he was stimulating the interest of a young boy who was to become an American flying ace.

Hill joined the Air Corps in 1939 and due to his glider experience, received his wings in 1940. While flying with the 31st Pursuit Group a year later, the engine of his P-39 failed on takeoff causing the plane to crash. After six months recuperating from back injuries, he was back in the cockpit of a P-39 flying long-range missions in New Hampshire in preparation for a flight to England. But there was a change of plans.

"At the last moment, Gen. H.H. 'Hap' Arnold decided that flying P-39s across the Atlantic by way of Greenland and Iceland was not the safest thing to do. Hill said, "So we left all our equipment, even flying suits and helmets, in the U.S., and our complete fighter group, along with the 52nd Fighter Group, was sent to England by ship. We went in convoy during the month of June 1942. I later learned that during that month, we lost the most shipping of the entire war to German submarines."

In England, Hill and his fellow pilots were given British equipment and the famous Spitfire V fighter planes. They had just one month to become acquainted with the Spitfires before they flew into action. It was on his first mission that Hill shot down the first of seven enemy aircraft. He later flew cover for Gen. George Patton's troops in North Africa. He became the commander of the 31st Fighter Group while flying missions over Sicily and Italy during the Allied invasion of those areas.

Hill remained in the Air Force following the war and fulfilled assignments in various parts of the world including Germany, France and Greenland. He was promoted to colonel in 1951. He retired from the service in 1969.

He and his wife, Linda, operated the Hillson Real Estate Co. in Denville, NJ, for many years. The family home is in Pompton Plains.

Four "Kills" in 12 Minutes
Francis R. Gerard

Inducted Aviation Hall of Fame of New Jersey, 1983

Although he had watched airplanes from Teterboro and Newark Airports fly over his home in Lyndhurst during his formative years, Frank Gerard had never flown until he began his U.S. Army Air Corps basic flight training in Jackson, MI, early in 1943.

His first flight was in a Stearman biplane which he described as being "very disappointing." He had thought there would be a greater sensation of speed and "more excitement,"

Over the next two years, Gerard experienced enough excitement in the air to last a lifetime. The Belleville, NJ, native flew 420 combat hours and downed eight

Flying aces meet - back row: WW II aces Frank Gerard, Donald Strait, Frank Hill. Front: WW I aces Ray Brook s and George Vaughn

enemy aircraft during dogfights over France and Germany.

He had graduated from Lyndhurst High School just five months before the Japanese attack on Pearl Harbor and immediately went into war work at the Newport News, VA, shipyards as an apprentice shipbuilder. It was during that brief period that he decided on a flying career.

"Seeing those ships so close, I knew they were too confining for me," he explained. "I certainly didn't want to become a doughboy."

Gerard was commissioned a second lieutenant and received his pilot's wings at Craig Field, AL, 10 months after his enlistment in October 1942. A few months later he was flying with the 8th Air Force in Europe. On D-Day 1944, and the succeeding two days, he flew eight missions over the beachheads in France and began chalking up enemy aircraft "kills."

"At the beginning, I was both excited and scared as hell," he admitted.

In one aerial encounter over Liepzig, Germany, Gerard shot down four German fighters in just 12 minutes.

"We were flying cover for an armada of 800 U.S. bombers deep in enemy territory," Gerard recounted. "We had 14 P-51s in our squadron and were suddenly jumped by 100 German fighters. I got the first one rather quickly, and then dived down into the the bomber formation and got my second one. The last two were dogfights in which I was lucky enough to come out on top."

The P-51s Gerard flew on 91 missions were hit 13 times during his two tours of duty in Europe, but he was only forced to ditch his plane once.

"My plane was hit over Belgium, but I was able to find a fairly smooth field to set her down in. The English found me and got me back to my base in England."

When he returned to civilian life, Gerard entered Lafafette College in 1947 and joined the New Jersey Air National Guard (NJANG) that same year. Subsequently, he attended John Marshall Law College, received his degree and hung out his shingle in Lyndhurst in 1951. Later that year, he was recalled to active duty because of the Korean War.

Following his second tour of duty, Gerard continued to serve with the NJANG.

In 1961, he was named Chief of the New Jersey Bureau of Aviation, (formerly Department of Aviation) succeeding Robert Copsey. Copsey had become the state's second director of aviation in 1946 when Gill Robb Wilson left the post to pursue a publishing career.

Just a few months after assuming his new state position, Gerard was again called to active duty during the Berlin Airlift as director of operations with the 108th Tac Fighter Wing. Jerry McCabe assumed the position of acting chief of the Bureau of Aviation until Gerard returned in 1963. By then, the bureau was again designated as a department of aviation.

As director, Gerard was concerned with the development of programs for public safety, the progress of aviation in New Jersey and the licensing and regulating of all airports, heliports and fixed-base operators within the state. Aeronautical education and the implementation of a state and regional defense airlift plan to cope with a national, regional or state emergency were always among Gerard's priority concerns.

He was particularly active in an effort to establish another major airport in the state.

Gerard headed the aviation department until 1978, but during the 1970s, he was twice assigned active duty tours in the Pentagon. Five men served as acting director for various periods in his absence: James E. Varanyak, Stephen Link, Thomas W. Coyle, Joseph C. Haines and Campbell Jackson.

In September of 1978, Walter D. Kies replaced Gerard permanently as director.

Gerard was past president of the Army Air National Guard Association of New Jersey, a member of the American Association of Airport Executives, served as president of the National Association of State Aviation Officials and a host of other committees.

In 1982, Governor Thomas Kean appointed Maj. Gen. Frank Gerard as chief of staff for the New Jersey Department of Defense, putting him at the top of the state's National Guard and Civil Defense organization. He was the first Air National Guard officer to hold that position. At his swearing-in ceremony, the Sea Girt, NJ, resident said he believed "in letting the commanders command, in delegating responsibility and authority, and trusting my people."

Gerard retired from that post in 1990 at age 65.

A Double Ace

Captain Donald J. Strait

Inducted Aviation Hall of Fame of New Jersey 1989

In 1940, Donald J. Strait joined the 119th Observation Squadron of the New Jersey Air National Guard (NJANG) as an airman. Mobilized by Presidential Order in September of that year, his first assignment was as an aerial gunner.

In 1942, he entered flying school as an Aviation Cadet and after completing advanced training in January of 1943, he was assigned to the 361st Fighter Squadron, 356th Fighter Group at Westover Field, MA. His Group was deployed to England in August of 1943 with the 8th Air Force.

Over the next two years, Strait flew P-47 and P-51 fighter planes for 430 hours on 122 combat missions. He began his combat flying as a duty pilot but his flying ability quickly brought him more responsibilities. He served as Flight Commander, Squadron Operations Officer and Squadron Commander of the 361st during his time in Europe.

Strait was credited with 13 1/2 enemy aircraft and is listed as a "double ace" by the Air Force.

At the war's end in 1945, Major Strait returned to the United States as Chief of the Fighter Section Evaluation Branch at Winston-Salem, NC. In November of that year, he was discharged and a year later joined the 108th Fighter Wing, NJANG, at McGuire Air Force Base as Group Operations Officer. By February 1951, he was the Wing Commander.

Recalled to active duty for the Korean War in March of 1951, Strait served as Director of Operations, 108th Fighter Bomber Wing (Strategic Air Command) and then Commander 108th Fighter Bomber Group. When he returned to reserve status in 1952 as a Colonel, he became the Commander of the 108th Tactical Fighter Wing and had the additional responsibility of Commander, New Jersey Air National Guard. In 1956, he was promoted to Brigadier General in the reserves and was asked to serve in the civilian position of Deputy for Reserve and ROTC Affairs in the Office of the Secretary of the Air Force, Washington, DC.

He became a Command Pilot (Jet Qualified) in August of 1959, and the following year, commanded the Air National Guard Tactical Air Force during summer exercises.

The New Jersey Wing was again mobilized by Presidential Order in October 1961 during the Berlin Crisis. Strait personally led the deployment of the 141st Tactical Fighter Squadron's F-84F jet fighters to Chammont, France. When the 108th was returned to state control in August 1962, Strait resumed his duties as commander.

He was back on the Federal payroll in October of 1962 during the Cuban Crisis at the request of the Commander, Tactical Air Command. He was assigned to the office of the Assistant to the Commander of Reserve Forces in Washington.

Promoted to Major General, Strait became the Assistant Chief of Staff for Air for the New Jersey Department of Defense, and was responsible for all tactical fighter, airlift and supporting units of the NJANG. He held that position until he retired in 1971.

When not serving his country on active or reserve status, Strait worked for Republic Aviation in Farmingdale, L.I. When he retired in 1975, he was a senior vice president of the Fairchild Hiller Corp., and general manager, Republic Aviation Division.

He was born in East Orange, NJ, in 1918, and graduated from Henry B. Whitehorne High School in Verona, NJ, in 1936. He and his wife, Louise, retired to Jackson Springs, NC.

14 Enemy Destroyed

Major Michael J. Jackson

Michael Jackson of Plainfield volunteered for flight training in 1941. Upon graduating from flight school, he became a flight instructor. He was among the first 50-man cadre sent to Stewart Field, Newburgh, NY, to teach the art of flying to cadets at the U.S. Military Academy. When the first class graduated with wings in June of 1943, Jackson asked for combat duty. Six months later, he was assigned to the 56th Fighter Group in England and became operations officer of the 62nd Fighter Squadron.

By December 1944, he had become a Squadron leader with the rank of major, and already had destroyed six enemy aircraft in the air and on the ground. In the book, *Fighter Aces of the U.S.A.* written by Raymond Toliver and Trevor Constable, Jackson told how he and his squadron of P-47s surprised pilots flying in Me-109 Messerschmitts, which were then the scourge of the skies over Europe.

On Christmas Day, 1944, Jerry was making every effort to support the Battle of the Bulge. I had my squadron up on a sweep between Bonn and Frankfurt. Ground controller vectored us to a bogie, and while flying at 30,000 [feet] near Bonn, we spotted numerous Me-109's at about 24,000. I maneuvered to get into the sun, and looking them over, saw they were flying the same battle formation we were flying — three flights of four aircraft each, almost line abreast.

I gave the order to drop tanks, and, in a diving turn onto their rear, gave instructions that I would take the man on the far end and each of my squadron was to "cue up" on the 109 corresponding to his own position. It was the prettiest sight a fighter pilot could ever wish to see.

Those poor German pilots never knew what hit them. My target blew up in front of me at 150 yards range. My wingman got his, and so right down that beautiful line. All twelve Me-109's went down in pieces or flames on that one spectacular pass. After having been at the 109s mercy for so long during the war, it was a wonderful feeling to have been able to pull this off.

By the war's end, Jackson had downed eight enemy aircraft, destroyed six on the ground and damaged five others.

He left the service in 1946 but continued flying with the Air Force Reserve and the 108th Fighter Wing, New Jersey Air National Guard. By the time he retired from the reserves in 1975, he held the rank of brigadier general. When he wasn't flying, Jackson worked in the advertising field for several major companies and publications, retiring from the business world in 1984. He lived in Linden, NJ.

18 Kills in One Day

Lt. William J. Sykes

On Sept. 17, 1944, 1st Lt. William J. Sykes of Atlantic City destroyed a German plane in aerial combat and accounted for two more on the ground, helping his fellow P-51 Mustang pilots establish a new combat record for a single fighter squadron by destroying 18 German planes while escorting heavy U.S. bombers over Kassel, Germany.

Sykes had achieved his first "kill" the previous month and received the air medal "for meritorious achievement in aerial combat." He got two more on Nov. 4 in what was described as "the biggest air battle ever fought" in the sky over Leipzig, Germany, boosting his score to six. He was then a "flying ace." He accounted for three more enemy planes on Dec. 22, and two days later he was missing in action.

It wasn't until Jan, 27, 1945 that his wife Constance Rogers Sykes, who he had married during flight training in Pargould, AK in April 1944, received a POW letter from him postmarked "Stalag XIIA, Deutschland." It read:

"Dear Connie, How do you like Atlantic City? I've been under ether on the table again to cut something. Anyway, I'm keeping the leg, but it sure is a job. I hope to be on crutches in a month. Still can't sleep. How are you and Bill [their infant son] feeling? I worry more about Mom and Dad than anything else. I wish I could have carried Bill's picture with me. If the leg heals good, I may be able to make a break. It snows every day and is cold. Hope you get your money OK. Love to you and Bill and the family — Bill."

He had been shot down on Christmas Eve 1944. Just a few days before, he had rejected a rotation furlough home, having long exceeded the 50-mission mark.

Later, his father received a letter telling how a shell fired by a German pilot had exploded in his plane, shattering his leg. A second shell struck his gunsight in a burst of flame that virtually blinded him. When he managed to bail out he explained, "God must have done it for me as I only had 1,300 feet and couldn't see or know what I was doing."

When he returned to the United States, Sykes weighed 110 pounds, down 45 from his normal weight. While recuperating from his leg wound in an Army hospital in Pawling, NY, he saw his son for the first time.

Sykes, born in Atlantic City, was a sports hero at Holy Spirit High School. He enrolled at Villanova University and became a flying cadet. Three days after Pearl Harbor was attacked, he enlisted in the Army Air Corps. After getting his wings and taking advanced training at various bases around the United States, he was assigned to the 378th Fighter Squadron in England. Nine days later he recorded his first kill over Germany.

Sykes, then a captain, remained in the service until 1947. When he finally retired, he had logged more than 6,000 hours in the air. He and his family lived in Margate, NJ, when he died in 1987.

Sons Missing in Action

Lindol and Donald Graham

The spring of 1944 was a tragic time in the household of Mr. and Mrs. George C. Graham of Ridgewood. In April, the couple received word that their oldest son, Capt. Lindol Graham, a fighter pilot, was missing in action in Europe. Two months later, their anxiety was further heightened when they received a notice from the war department that their younger son, Lt. Donald Graham, a B-24 bomber co-pilot, had also been shot down and was missing.

On August 21, the Grahams received a bitter-sweet postcard from Donald:

"Am prisoner of war, being treated good. Just finished a delicious meal furnished by the Red Cross Got clean clothes, cigarettes, etc. Am not wounded. German intelligence looked up Lindol. He was killed and buried by his plane in March. This is temporary address. Will write from permanent camp. Call Timmie. Give her my love.

Love,

Don

Both Graham boys had spent a short time in combat before tragedy struck. Lindol was shipped overseas to England in August of 1943, but spent two months in the British Isles awaiting his P-38 fighter plane to arrive by ship. It was January before Graham's squadron was ready to fly missions over Nazi occupied Europe. Graham immediately made his presence felt. On Jan. 29, 1944, he shot down three enemy planes during a raid over Frankfurt, Germany. The feat earned him a commendation from Gen. Ira Baker, the Allied Air Commander in England, who

stated it was the greatest number of planes any fighter plane had shot down in one day in that area.

He was credited with two more enemy "kills" on Feb. 20, bringing his total to five which qualified him as an ace. He increased that total by one on his last fateful mission on March 18. In three months, he had six enemy aircraft to his credit and had been awarded the Distinguished Flying Cross for his "aggressiveness and superior flying skill displayed in destroying three enemy aircraft on one mission."

The letter the Graham family received from Maj. Gen. J.A. Ulio, Adjutant General, confirming Capt. Graham's death read:

"I realize the great suspense you have endured and now, the futility to those hopes which you have cherished for his safety. Although little at this time may be said or done to alleviate your grief, it is my fervent hope that later, the knowledge that he gave his life gloriously for his country may be of sustaining comfort to you."

Lt. Donald Graham's combat flying time was even shorter than his older brother's. In a March 1990 letter to the author, Don Graham succinctly related his overseas experience:

"We went to Topeka, KS, to pick the new plane that would carry us to South America, Africa, Tunisia and finally Italy (near Foggia) for about 10 days. My last mission was over Munich (Germany) where I went down. The date was June 13, 1944. I roamed the countryside for two days before I was picked up. After that I was interrogated at a prison near Frankfurt for two weeks. Then to Stalag Luft 3, Sagan, Germany. This camp was near the Polish border."

Lt. Graham had left the United States on May 14, 1944, and was captured by the Germans one month later. Ironically, Graham's B-24 had not been shot down, it was rammed by another bomber flying out of control. Although both the tail and nose of Graham's plane had been torn away, he was able to bail out safely. He was liberated by Gen. Patton's Third Army on April 29, 1945.

Donald Graham and his wife now reside in Pawleys Island, SC.

Nazi Jet Outmaneuvered

Lt. George F. Ceuleers

Lt. George F. Ceuleers of Bridgeton, NJ, was the only American fighter pilot during World War II to shoot down a German ME-262 jet fighter, then the fastest airplane in the world.

Flying a P-51 Mustang, Ceuleers and four other Mustang pilots had just completed a successful mission flying cover for a B-17 Flying Fortress bombing strike

Lt. George F. Ceuleers

against Hamburg, Germany. As he and his fellow pilots of the 364th Fighter Group, 8th Fighter Command were heading back to their base, Ceuleers spotted a formation of Liberator bombers on the way to drop a bomb load on Hanover, Germany. Flying high above overcast skies, the bombers were being attacked by eight German jets, the newest planes in their arsenal.

As he watched in horror, he saw a jet knock down two Liberators on one pass with deadly bursts from its four 30mm cannons. With Ceuleers in the lead, the four P-51s raced to the rescue, flying at 29,000 feet. Although the jets had a 150 mph a advantage on the P-51s, the determined Americans drove them off and the Me-262s turned tail and ran. Still anxious to do battle, Ceuleers decided to chase the jet.

The German pilot turned his plane down toward a hole in the cloud cover, and Ceuleers knowing he couldn't catch the faster plane on a straight run, pushed his stick forward and dove almost vertically through the clouds, thus increasing the speed of the P-51 beyond its maximum capacity. The race covered 250 miles in approximately 20 minutes. When the P-51 and the Me-262 were at 500 feet over Leipzig, the P-51 closed the gap. The American pilot fired 600 50 cal. machine gun rounds into the streaking jet. Suddenly, one of the two jet engines burst into flames and its pilot jumped to safety. The wounded bird dove into the ground and exploded with a roar.

American airmen had destroyed German jets prior to Ceuleers' victory, but those victims were either caught taking off or landing. The Bridgeton native's victory was the only one in World War II achieved in aerial combat.

Ceuleers was already a USAF flying ace when he downed the German jet. By the war's end, he was

credited with 10.5 enemy planes destroyed, achieved in 103 combat missions.

The ace was a 1938 graduate of Bridgeton High School. He attended the University of Illinois for two years prior to enlisting in the Army Air Corps in 1941. Following primary, basic and advanced flight training, he was commissioned a lieutenant and assigned a P-38 to fly. Twice during his training period, he narrowly escaped death. In 1942 over Ontario, Canada, his plane exploded, but he escaped by parachute. Six months later, while flying a P-38 over Hollywood, CA, his left engine caught fire and Ceuleer again bailed out.

Following the war, Ceuleers chose to remain in the service. When he retired with the rank of colonel, he and his wife moved to Georgetown, CO.

Troop Carrier Command

Fred Roth

For every flying ace in the various services, there were thousands upon thousands of pilots flying aircraft of all descriptions, from four-engined bombers to light reconnaissance planes. Fred Roth of Jersey City enlisted in the Air Corps in 1942 with thoughts of becoming a bomber pilot. After he received his wings and commission as a second lieutenant, he was assigned to a squadron training in twin-engine B-25 low altitude bombers.

But in 1944, there was a greater need for pilots in the Troop Carrier Command, so Roth was shipped to Austin, TX, where he checked out in C-47 transports. Within months, Roth was flying his twin-engined plane in short hops across the Atlantic — Goose Bay, Newfoundland, Reykjavik, Iceland, and on to Prestwick, Scotland. Upon reaching the British Isles, Roth began flying gasoline and supplies to General George Patton's Third Army as it pushed its way across France. He remembered that when he set his C-47 down at Orleans, France, which had just been liberated, the airfield was still smoldering from recent bombardment.

On Sept. 17, 1944, the Troop Carrier Command was assigned the task of transporting paratroopers to Holland as part of the British-planned armored strike through that country, known as "Operation Market Garden." Roth carried troops of the 82nd Airborne and dropped them over Mijmegen, Holland, in the lead assault designed to capture five key bridges over the Rhine River.

After a successful drop, Roth's aircraft was hit by German anti-aircraft fire and, with both engines disabled, he was forced to ditch his ship in the North Sea, just off the Dutch coast. None of his five-man crew was hurt and all were captured by the Germans after

P-51

desperately rowing their rubber raft against a strong tide for five hours.

For a month, he and other allied prisoners were forced to march across Holland and Germany to Stalag Luft I in Barth, Germany, where they remained until the camp was liberated by the Russians on May 1, 1945. Ironically, when the liberation was announced in the world press, only the fighter aces at the Barth camp made the headlines.

Fountain's Follies

In the summer 1985 edition of the New Jersey Aviation Hall of Fame's quarterly publication *Propwash*, historian Henry M. Holden told of the adventures of combat glider pilot Fred Fountain of River Vale, NJ. Fountain flew on three of the five glider combat missions in the European Theater of Operations during World War II and miraculously survived them all.

No World War II aircraft were more vulnerable than the plywood and fabric combat gliders and the life expectancy of their pilots was 50-50 at best. They were among the unsung heroes of the war. Flying 48-foot long WACO CG4-gliders (many built in Ridgefield, NJ), they endured enemy flak, foul weather and aircraft that occasionally shed parts in flight. Landing the silent, motorless giants, loaded with 13 men or an artillery piece, behind enemy lines was described as no more than a controlled crash.

The glider had only the most basic flight instruments — air speed, vertical speed, turn and bank indicators and a compass. Glider pilots said the compass was superfluous since "there was only one place we were going to navigate to by ourselves and that was down."

The pilots shunned parachutes because none of the troops they carried wore them. On a combat mission their destiny was a one-way trip. Only the tow plane pilot had any chance of making it back to base that day.

There were six major glider missions in World War II: Burma, Sicily, Normandy, Southern France, Holland and the Rhine.

The history of the 101st Airborne describes the glider pilots as "the most uninhibited individualists in the Army who successfully defied all attempts at organization."

The glider jocks had little use for military convention, and ignored most military courtesy. They loved flying, drinking and women, not necessarily in that order. They felt that if they were going to be killed in combat, there was no point to being polite, disciplined or sober.

Fred Fountain was 28 years old when World War II broke out. He was considered too old for Air Force cadet training so he volunteered for the little-known Glider Pilot Program (GPP). The daily routine as

Fountain described it was "book work and frill in the morning, and flying in the afternoon." Each day 25 men were cramped into a school bus built for 20 children and driven 60 miles from Bergen Junior College in Teaneck [now Fairleigh Dickinson University] to the Solberg-Hunterdon Airport in Readington, NJ, for flight training. Fountain said there was so much classroom work that it even continued on the bus. "It was a typical Army operation. The food was bad, bunks too small and the drilling a joke".

Forty-five days later Fountain graduated, but the Army had changed its mind about the GPP, so all the new pilots were returned to the Army as buck privates. Later, the Army reversed itself and Fountain went for more flight training wearing his sterling sliver wings. First came the small power planes, then the two-place gliders. From there, he went on to the four-ton WACO CG4A heavy glider.

Fountain's first combat mission was on Aug. 15, 1944 to Southern France with the 436th Troop Carrier Group, 79th Squadron. "Fountain's Folly" was the 37th of 40 gliders in the first lift. As often happened, the telephone line between the tow plane and the glider tore away on take-off. Fountain, his cargo of English Tommies and their jeep were in the air 4 1/2 hours and out of contact with the tow plane. He remembers that during the long hours his British passengers relaxed and brewed themselves some tea. Near the Landing Zone (LZ), Fountain watched as several gliders crashed. One fell apart in mid-air, its human cargo falling helplessly into the sea.

On the landing approach, Fountain's copilot prayed instead of reading the air speed indicator and operating the spoilers.

Fountain screamed at the man to no avail, so he landed the glider himself.

As the frail troop carrier came to rest, a deadly spray of German automatic fire tore through its wooden fuselage. In his haste to vacate the craft, Fountain lost his gun and forgot to destroy the glider.

"Our airborne guys took care of the machine gun nest," he said, "and since I was too tired to dig a foxhole, I crawled under a British 57mm field piece. That was a mistake. When it fired, tears came to my eyes and I went deaf for awhile." Fountain's next mission to Holland took place on Sept. 18, 1944. This time there was no copilot in Fountain's Folly #2. The mission fleet consisted of 1,500 gliders and he and his human cargo spent more than three and a half hours in the air. Solo flying with a full load was an exhausting job. Fountain had to struggle to keep the glider from oscillating. If his ship didn't fly above the tow plane's slip stream, the ride was worse than a rowboat on a storm-tossed sea. And if the glider had structural defects, there was the distinct possibility of it breaking up in flight.

Five minutes from the LZ, Fountain's Folly #2 was hit by a German 40mm shell that tore a huge hole in the fabric skin and missed the main wing strut by inches. Two of his passengers were badly wounded, but the pilot was able to keep the smoke-filled glider airborne.

Fountain crash landed in a field, amid the rubble of wrecked gliders and dead cows.

He stayed in Holland for four or five days before working his way back to England. He remembers being in Brussels but has no recollection of how he got back to England. As usual, all the surviving glider pilots had gotten drunk. Fountain estimated that 90 percent of a glider pilot's time was spent getting drunk and raising hell, and 10 percent was spent flying. "And if the big brass didn't like it, they could always try to find someone else to fly the damn gliders."

The Rhine Mission on March 24, 1945 was Fountain's last. Fountain's Folly #3 was double towed for more than three hours carrying a jeep trailer, heavy machine gun and six airborne troops. This time, he had as a copilot, a former P-51 pilot who had never seen the inside of a glider.

The Rhine Mission saw 906 WACO gliders launched. The landing zones were in disputed territory, and artillery, mortar, machine gun and rifle fire greeted the hapless pilots as they tried to land their silent giants. "Less than one-quarter of the gliders that reached the assault area came through undamaged," said the official report.

As he headed down to the LZ, Fountain began to think his luck had run out. First his tow plane exploded in front of him right after he cut loose; then as he flew into the smoke shrouded LZ, suddenly he saw high tension wires cutting across his glide path. Sideslipping and with full spoilers, he narrowly missed the wires. The glider plowed through a number of fences and slammed into a tree. Before he could climb out of the wreck, another glider smashed into what was left of his craft. When the dust settled, Fountain and his copilot ran for cover through a hail of machine gun fire and dove behind a hedge row. "With our faces in the dirt," he remembered. "We said several quick prayers." A rumbling noise caused Fountain to look up in time to see a glider skidding toward them. Miraculously, the wheels missed them by inches but crushed Fountain's carbine. Again he was without a gun in the middle of a fire fight. Desperately, he crawled into a gully to wait for the shooting to stop. He survived, but never saw his co-pilot again.

Glider pilots and their giant silent birds were a creation of World War II. When the war ended, they faded from the scene.

Fred Fountain came home to New Jersey and established a successful insurance business in Hackensack. He died of cancer in 1986.

A Mid-air Collision
—Score; U.S. 1: Nazis 0.

On Feb. 1, 1943, Elton Conda of Burlington Township, NJ, was the belly gunner aboard a B-17, that was rammed by a German fighter plane over North Africa. The intrepid Flying Fortess flew 1,500 miles without its left horizontal stabilizer and left elevator. A gash in the fuselage penetrated two thirds of its girth just in front of the tail section.

In the Jan. 31, 1982 edition of the *Burlington Country Times*, Carol Suplee, the paper's feature page editor, interviewed Conda and wrote the following condensed version of his adventure.

The Messerschmidts came screaming out of the sky, intent on downing the American B-17, part of a squadron which had just bombed German emplacements in North Africa. It was Feb. 1, 1943, and 23-year-old Elton Conda of Burlington was at his post in the belly gun turret of the bomber.

With guns blazing, the lumbering bomber defended itself against the faster, deadly German fighter planes. As he dived for the attack, one German pilot miscalculated, or was hit, and his plane collided with the B-17 with such force that the rear of the bomber was nearly severed. The Messerschmidt fell to a fiery end.

Conda spun his turret around after the shock of the collision and realized the tail section was gone and the entire rear of the plane was hanging by a few shreds of metal. He didn't have time to ponder his immediate future since the bomber was still under attack. With only manual controls left and his guns useless, Conda "faked it," revolving his turret and moving his guns manually, pretending to fire back at the marauding German fighters.

"They didn't know the difference," he grinned, remembering the day.

A B-17 literally flying on a wing and a prayer.

Later, they were to find bits of the doomed Messerschmidt inside the fuselage of the B-17. The impact had sheared off one entire stabilizer, part of the tail was missing and cables providing power to the turrets had been cut.

When they were clear of enemy territory, Conda climbed up out of his turret into the plane, still miraculously aloft after the collision. Even more amazing, the tail gunner had also survived and was left in his flapping, shaking turret wondering if the whole assembly would soon follow the Messerschmidt to the desert below.

The pilot was later to receive a citation for his skill in bringing his plane and crew back safely. 'It appeared to be an impossibility,' said the official document.

Conda admitted the crew didn't appreciate their luck until minutes after the plane had landed and the whole tail assembly fell onto the runway with an unceremonious thump. The weight of curious onlookers was too much for it.

Conda followed a circuitous route to that fateful day. As the nation and the world moved inexorably toward that cluster of events which were to signal the start of World War II, there was little on the minds of many Burlington County youths except, as Conda readily admitted, "raising hell."

On the Thursday before the attack on Pearl Harbor, Conda decided he'd better change directions and enlisted in the Army. The growing war talk may have affected his decision, but he claimed that he had no special reason. It was something new he wanted to do.

Conda had never flown before he was assigned to a B-17, but he knew guns inside and out and so up he went.

"It was on my second mission," he said, "when our wing plane (one of the bombers in a formation of three) blew up in mid-air that I finally realized someone could get hurt." Conda was suited to his assignment. He was short ("Still am," he joked) and could curl up in the almost impossible position needed to operate the hand and foot controls in the belly turret.

His presence on the lucky crew that Feb. 1 was accidental. He was cleaning his gun one day and a new pilot approached him, saying he was looking for a volunteer to replace one of his gunners who was sick.

"Can you fly the damn airplane?" the cocky Burlingtonian snapped—"Yes," shot back the pilot. "Can you shoot the damn gun?"

Conda, who had had 25 missions under his belt by that time, said, "We have a deal."

Conda said he did notice later that day that the young pilot (it was his second mission) could, indeed, fly the damn airplane. A Collier's magazine dated April 20, 1943, recounts that Conda approached the pilot after

he had completed his miraculous landing and wordlessly pumped his hand for several seconds.

Was he afraid during those hours when his life, the crew's and the plane itself hung by a slim, steel thread? "We didn't have fear in our minds" Conda said "You were too busy looking for fighters and trying to do your job."

And although he wonders now, as he occasionally did then "what I was doing there"in company with other youths of such tender age and experience, there is no doubt in his mind about one lesson:

"I learned," he grinned, "that it's dangerous to volunteer."

Edward "Lucky" Stevens

Love sometimes entered into a man's heroics during the war. That was the case with Sgt. Edward "Lucky" Stevens of Mountain Lakes. At age 22, he established a record in the Pacific Theater of Operations by flying 155 missions and spending 1085 combat hours as a nose gunner in a B-17 Flying Fortress.

It was usual for a gunner to fly 50 missions or 300 hours, then pack his duffle and head back to the States. But Stevens had a special incentive — Gladys Irene Edgar of Sydney, Australia, a member oi the Australian Women's Army Service, who he met while on leave.

On all his missions, Stevens carried a photo of the pretty girl. He wouldn't have thought of flying without it. Once, he held up a mission while he ran back to his tent to retrieve it.

After each flight, Stevens painted a bomb on the back of the photo and dated it.

Stevens' missions were not all routine. On one, his plane ran out of gas and was forced to crash land on an uninhabited Pacific Island. Supplies and relief were not forthcoming for more than a week. Stevens claims his good luck photograph was a "lucky charm" for his entire crew.

When the armistice with Japan was signed, "Lucky" Stevens and Gladys Edgar were married. And 50 years later, they were still living happily in New Jersey. Lucky still carries his "good luck" photograph of Gladys.

New Jersey WASP

Prior to World War II, very few women held pilots' licenses. Aviation in America was dominated by men and it was commonly accepted among the male flying fraternity that women were not capable of piloting sophisticated aircraft. Male pilots conceded that there were exceptions to their rule--Earhart, Nichols, Cochran and a few others seemed talented enough to fly anything with wings, — but the majority of women, it was thought, were not big enough or smart enough to handle the souped-up military and commercial planes that were then being flown.

The performance of women in military aviation during the war greatly changed that attitude and introduced flying to a large number of women who might never have pursued aeronautics as a profession or a hobby. Their contribution to the war effort was significant.

Pilot Jacqueline Cochran, who established numerous flying records in the 1930s, was the leading advocate of women military pilots. Prior to their being accepted by the U.S. military, women, recruited by Cochran, were voluntering to fly for the British Air Transport Auxiliary (ATA). In Britain, women pilots ferried new and old aircraft from factories and repair depots to active squadrons at airports throughout the British Isles. Altogether, Cochran recruited and trained 24 pilots for the special duty.

Two New Jerseyans were among the group; twenty-two-year old Virginia Farr of West Orange, who had learned to fly at age 18 and became an instructor at Al Bennett's Central Jersey Airport in Hightstown, and Myrtle Allen of Hawthorne. Both joined the British ATA in the spring of 1942 and flew an assortment of aircraft from Spitfire fighters to Wellington bombers.

To be eligible for ATA service, women had to have a minimum of 300 hours of flying time. When Allen volunteered to serve she had been in the air only 175 hours but was determined to qualify, so she flew nonstop until she accumulated the necessary hours.

"I sat in the air from dawn to dusk," she said in a 1942 interview in the *Rochester (NY) Times-Union* "Even if they get a similar service in the United States," she added, "I've signed a contract with Britain and will stick unless our government says otherwise. British protection has been a Godsend to us in the past and I want to do all I can to help."

Farr had taught 100 men to fly at Hightstown and most of them had joined the U.S. Air Corps. In the spring of 1943, many of them were fighting in the skies over North Africa. When they were given a short leave, they flew to London and staged a party in Farr's honor. By then, she had attained the rank of First Officer.

In the fall of that year, Farr received a leave of her own and sailed back to the United States to surprise her parents, Mr. and Mrs. Barclay Farr. The British, impressed with her flying skills, offered her the opportunity to fly as a co-pilot aboard a bomber being ferried to England. She readily accepted.

The work of the British flying women also impressed U.S. Air Corps Gen. H.H."Hap" Arnold and he asked Cochran to form a similar group in America. Many New Jerseyans joined the Women's Auxiliary Ferrying Squadron (WAFS) organization, which later became known as the Women's Airforce Service Pilots (WASP). They were given basic training at Avenger Field, Sweetwater, TX. Classes of 100 women received the same cadet training as male pilots. They flew single-engined planes from Piper Cubs to P-38, P-39, P-47 and P-51. They learned to handle twin-engined Mitchell B-25 bombers and the larger four-engine B-17s and B-24s.

Like their British counterparts, they flew planes from shore to shore across America. In addition, they took on the more dangerous task of towing targets for aerial gunnery practice.

A 1980 roster of former WASP identified the following New Jersey women as having flown as service pilots (Maiden names are in parenthesis. The home towns listed are where the women resided when the roster was published.)

Alston, Lucy (Gladson)	Cranford
Brick, Katherine (Menges)	Fall Brook, CA
Carney, Evelyn (Hoagland)	Wayne
Cronan, Selma	Wood-Ridge
Daughady, Alice	Bridgeton
Focht, Izydora (Bochanek)	Columbia
Gray, Majorie	Oyster Bay, NY
Gladney, Patricia (Thomas)	Los Altos, CA
Haydu, Bernice (Falk)	Riviera Beach, FL
Hilbrandt, Kathleen	Hasbrouck Heights
Johnson, Aleta (Grill)	Pemberton
King, Kittie (Leaming)	Tuckahoe
Kline, Emily (Porter)	Kinnelon
Macrae, Ruth (Kahl)	Haddonfield
Maier, Melvina	Lakehurst
McCracken, Dorothy (Ehrhardt)	Morristown
McGlinn, Marge (Bergh)	Marmara
Potter, Maureen (Maloney)	Kendall Park
Rosenthal, Ruby (Hibbler)	Toms River
Ryder, Phyllis	Wildwood Crest
Starr, Alice-Jean (May)	River Vale
Whims, Suzanne (Sivade)	Ventnor

Two WASPS listed as deceased are Helen Mary Clark, formerly of Englewood, and Helen Jo Severson, former address unknown.

Helen Mary Clark had been a member of the first class of WAFS. She reported for duty at New Castle Army Air Base, DE, on Sept. 12, 1942. The initial group of 28 women was trained at Houston Municipal Airport in Texas under squadron commander Nancy Harkness Love and Jacqueline Cochran.

Born in Cincinnati, OH, in 1909, Clark moved to Englewood with her family in 1916. She learned to fly at Suffolk Airport on Long Island in 1934 and took advance training with Lowell White at the Caldwell Wright Airport in Fairfield.

She received her instructor's license in 1940 and by the time she joined the WAFS, she had a total of 756 flying hours. For a month in the spring of '42, Clark flew with the Civil Air Patrol on submarine search missions out of Atlantic City. When the WASPs were disbanded in December 1944, she had added another 697 hours to her flight log.

After the war, she married Gerould Clark, a realtor, who later became the mayor of Englewood. In 1950, she joined the Air Force Reserves with the rank of major. She was assigned to the Military Air Transport Service Flying Division (MATS) based at Andrews Air Force Base near Washington, DC.

She kept her plane at Teterboro Airport until 1956. She died in 1979.

The majority of New Jersey WASP pilots kept an active interest in aviation either as members of the world-wide women's pilot association, The Ninety-Nines, or as active flyers.

Marjorie M. Gray

Inducted Aviation Hall of Fame of New Jersey, 1992

Marjorie Gray

Majorie Gray of Cliffside Park first soloed in 1938 and earned a commercial certificate in 1942. Later that year, she accepted Cochran's invitation to enter the first class of women to receive Air Corps flight training at Ellington Field, Texas. "We were the guinea pigs," she recalled.

She served as a ferry pilot with the Air Transport Command until the WASPs were deactivated in December 1944. During that time she flew 19 types of military aircraft, from L-4 Cubs to B-25 bombers more than 750 hours. In 1950, she accepted a direct commission in the Air Force Reserve and retired as a Lt. Colonel in 1972.

When she left the service in 1944, she began instructing at Westfield Airport. Some time later, she moved to Teterboro and with Dick Gederra set up a flight school for Robinson Aviation. She stayed with Robinson for 18 months. Then in August 1947, she went into business for herself.

Gray became one of the first woman fixed based operators in the U.S. when she established Marjorie M. Gray Aero Services at Teterboro Airport. At that time owning and operating a FBO was described as a "young man's game." But, in a short time, she was holding her own with the boys.

She offered clients flying lessons, a charter service and aircraft for hire. One of her instructors was Bill Voorhis of Grantwood, NJ. Not one to sit behind a desk, Gray taught many of the fledgling pilots to fly and, as a flight examiner, she tested applicants for pilot certificates.

At first, she had three planes but no hangar and had to buy gas at the retail price. Working seven days a week, Gray built her clientele. Within a year, she had a 60 x 80 foot hangar and a portion of a quonset hut for her office and shop. She had also made arrangements to buy fuel in bulk. Twenty years after Gray moved on to other pursuits in 1951, her maintenance chief, Al Moldenhauer, recalled the years he worked for her as "some of the most pleasant I've ever spent. She was a very competent instructor and swell to work for."

Leaving the FBO, Gray joined the Curtiss-Wright Corp. as a senior technical writer. The following seven years, she served as an associate editor with *Flying* magazine working for Gill Robb Wilson. In the early '60s, she joined the International Electric Corp. in Paramus as a technical writer.

She then moved to Long Island as a documentation analyst for the Kollsman Instrument Corp. Later she held a similar position with the Grumman Aircraft Corp.

In 1956, Gray was awarded the Lady Hay Drummond-Hay Trophy for "outstanding achievement in aviation" by the Women's International Association of Aeronautics.

She was made a life member of The Ninety-Nines' Long Island Chapter, where she lived after leaving Cliffside Park, and served as the NY-NJ chapter's governor in 1946.

In 1947, Bernice (Bee) Falk (Haydu) became part owner and director of operations of the Ruscoe Flying Service at the Woodbridge (NJ) Airport. During the war, her three partners, James Ruscoe of Avenel, Edward Carr of Irvington and James Stine of Fanwood had flown supplies over the "hump" between India and Burma. Other members of the staff were Edward Salmon of Newark, Vincent Coppola of Westfield, Carl Rasmussen and Rollin Williams of Iselin and Stephen Galaida of Avenel, all veterans.

In 1948, the company left Woodbridge Airport when a highway was cut across the runway, and moved to Hadley Field. The competition there eventually drove them out of business in 1949.

In the 1970s, Falk, then Mrs. Haydu, led a battle in Washington for veteran benefits for WASP. The women aviators had flown under Civil Service status. She pointed out the WASPs were part of the military in nearly every sense — from boot camp training to dangerous flying missions — but they were not part of the Air Corps. Haydu told Congress that from 1942 to 1944, the 1,074 WASP pilots flew military aircraft 60 million miles.

Thirty eight WASPs lost their lives on missions that included breaking in new planes and engines, ferrying combat-weary craft to American airfields, towing target sleeves for gunner practice and teaching male cadets how to strafe, drop bombs, lay smoke blankets and track enemy aircraft.

The facts concerning the accomplishments of WASPs did not sway the Congress to change the law even though Senator Barry Goldwater of Arizona was squarely on the side of the women. Most bills supporting the WASP cause presented in both the House of Representatives and the Senate died in committee hearings, causing Haydu to give up the fight.

Selma Cronan said her mother influenced her decision to become a pilot. Soon after she had obtained her pilot's license in 1943, she joined the WASP.

"At the time, I was all fired up on the war effort,"she said. "I was going to join something. I was a pilot and here was an opportunity to enlist. I said okay and I went."

After the war, Cronan continued to fly and participated in numerous air races. At the same time, she began writing aviation articles for various trade publications. Her children's books on the subject, published by Random House, brought her national recognition. She became a popular lecturer at colleges and universities across the country and in Europe and the Orient. For her accomplishments, Cronan was awarded the Amelia Earhart Medal by The Ninety-Nines in 1960.

Tuskegee Airmen

In March of 1941, the 99th Pursuit Squadron was activated at Chanute Field, Rantoul, IL, and on June 4, six aviation cadet enlistees reported to Chanute for specialized training in maintenance engineering, armament and communications. They were the initial cadre of the first all-black pursuit squadron of the Army Air Corps.

Black leaders had been pushing for the elimination of discrimination in the national defense systems as early as 1938. It took almost two years to convince the Army and Navy to change their policies but the Air Corps continued to refuse to accept blacks. A threatened law suit by the National Association for the Advancement of Colored People in January of 1941, and at the urging of Eleanor Roosevelt, the president's wife, who flew with the Tuskegee Institute's flight instructor, Chief C. Alfred Anderson, that same year, forced the Air Corps officials to change their policy. In April, the War Department announced that it would establish an air unit at the

Tuskegee Airmen — Calvin Spann, Andrew Keyes, Charles Washington, Thomas Rock, Harold O'Neal.

Alabama institute where black airmen would be trained. Thus began the Tuskegee Experiment.

In July 1941, the first class, designated 42C, began with 12 cadets and one officer — Capt. Benjamin O.Davis Jr., a 1936 West Point graduate. Immediately after the Pearl Harbor attack, the ground support cadets, who had completed their training at Chanute, were transferred to the Tuskegee Army Air Base that had been constructed in less than five months.

Nearly all of the 2,000 black airmen who fought in World War II were graduates of Tuskegee.

The 99th, commanded by Davis, began flying strafing missions on June 2, 1943 in North Africa. Later they were joined by three other squadrons that were combined into the 332nd Fighter Group.

In February 1944, Tuskegee Airmen began operations in Italy. They played a leading role at Anzio, where in aerial dogfights with Hitler's master race pilots, they shot down eight enemy planes in one day and 17 over the course of the hard-fought invasion. A year later, the 332nd earned a Distinguished Unit Citation for "extraordinary heroism" while flying bomber escort missions to Berlin.

The Airmen were called "Schwartze Vogelmenschen" (Black Birdmen) by the Germans and the white American bomber crews reverently referred to them as "The Black Redtail Angels."

Some 40 years after World War II, Dr. William G. Wilkerson of Orange, NJ, remembered how he became a member of the 332nd Fighter Group.

"I guess I was born to fly," he explained, "for at a very early age, perhaps six or seven, I would walk 10 miles from my family home in south Jersey to Camden Central Airport every Sunday just to watch the planes. At 13, I was lucky enough to find someone interested in teaching me to fly. Upon entering college, I signed up for the CPT program and continued to fly all through college. I gave several demonstrations as the CPT's youngest stunt pilot."

When the United States declared war on Japan and Germany in 1941, Wilkerson immediately joined the Air Corps. He successfully passed an Air Corps written exam and later learned that he was the first black to do so. But he wasn't called for duty immediately.

"I had to wait until they could build a field to train black pilots," he said.

Upon completing his training, he was assigned to fly P-40s and became the first black test pilot in the Air Corps. When the 332nd was shipped overseas, Wilkerson was the senior test pilot. He flew as a bomber escort in Africa and Italy. "Our group never lost a bomber to the enemy while we were escorting," he said proudly.

In 1944, Wilkerson was shot down when he went to the aid of a stricken bomber. The big plane made it back to base, but he was forced down and badly injured. The local underground picked him up and within a few weeks he was transferred to an American hospital in Naples.

"I finally came home as a basket case," he said. "I'll never forget the men and women of the underground. They were the real heroes."

Wilkerson recovered from his injuries and went on to a distinguished medical career.

In 1943, Calvin Spann didn't know much about racism and segregation while growing up in Rutherford. At age 17, he volunteered for Air Corps duty and was sent by train to Biloxi, Miss. When the train rolled below the Mason-Dixon Line, the black waiter in the dining car suggested that he pull the curtain closed so he wouldn't get shot while eating dinner.

At Biloxi he discovered that black pilots couldn't train with whites. He could earn their wings only at the Tuskegee Institute, he was told.

Fifty years later, he remembered those days. "I guess I was politically innocent. I hadn't experienced much discrimination in my life. And I didn't know about the Army's segregation. I just wanted to be a pilot. I didn't know that was unusual. I got sent to Keesler Field in Mississippi and waited around for a week in civilian clothes. They told me they didn't have the facilities to train black pilots."

Spann completed 26 missions in P-51s from Italy before the war ended. The majority of the time, he and his Tuskegee comrades flew cover for bombing raids over Germany and Austria. The flight he remembered best was a 1,700-mile trip from Italy to Berlin and back. It was the longest mission in the history of the 15th Strategic Air Force.

"We [the fighter pilots] came back running on vapors," Spann said. "Some of the boys really struggled to get those planes back to the bases."

By the war's end, the 450 Tuskegee Airmen had accumulated 150 Distinguished Flying Crosses and Legions of Merit. Sixty-six were killed in action and 32 others were shot down and held as prisoners of war.

When he came home, Spann couldn't get a commercial flying job, so he became a chemical plant supervisor and later a medical salesman for Hoffman-LaRoche in Clifton.

The following is a partial list of the New Jerseyans who participated as Tuskegee Airmen and their home towns.

Pilots/Navigators

J. Bruce Bennett	Lakewood
R. Augustus Bynum	Montclair
Victor L. Connell	Nutley
Ellwood Driver	Newark
Charles Dryden	Matawan
LeRoy Gillead	Elizabeth
Claude B. Govan	Newark
Thomas L. Hawkins	Glen Ridge
Edward Jenkins	Nutley
Roy E. LaGrone	Somerset
Charles E. Malone	Montclair
James O. Plinton	Rahway
Louis Purnell	Camden
Price D. Rice	Montclair
Daniel Rich	Rutherford
Tomas Rock	East Orange
Henry Scott	Jersey City
Calvin J. Spann	Rutherford
James H. Smith	Newark
Thomas W. Smith	Plainfield
Thomas C. Street	Springfield
Robert Terry	Newark
Daniel Tindall	East Orange
George E. Wanamaker	Montclair
Spann Watson	Hackensack
William G. Wilkerson	Orange
Raymond Williams	Jersey City
Wendel Williams	Paterson

Ground Personnel

Harry Banks	Newark
Samuel A. Black	Plainfield
George Bolden	Cherry Hill
Earl Brown	
Whittier English	Teaneck
Cass Freeman	Newark
Sam Gibson	Montclair
Walter P. Hawkins	Rutherford
William Hester	Toms River
Michael A. Hill	Edison
Andrew J. Keyes	Succasunna
Harold O'Neal	Springfield

Ground Personnel continued

Vincent Jay Mason	Orange
Armour McDaniels	Newark
George Reed	Montclair
Samuel Scott	Jersey City
William Walker	Atlantic City
Charles E. Washington	Kearny
George Watson	Atlantic City
Leonard R. Willette	Belleville

First Atom Bomb
Capt. Robert A. Lewis

A New Jerseyan played a leading role in bringing an end to the bloodiest war in the history of man. He was Robert A. Lewis of Ridgefield Park who was the co-pilot aboard the B-29 *Enola Gay.*

As the giant four-engined bomber lifted off the runway on the Pacific Island of Tinian in the Mariana Island chain, Lewis wrote in his special log. "August 6, 1945; We got off the ground at exactly 0245."

The flight was named "Little Boy Mission #1," in honor of the most destructive single weapon in the world, the atomic bomb, which was housed in the belly of the plane.

Lewis had been asked to keep a log of his thoughts during the momentous flight. A copy of that 10-page handwritten document is now in the archives of the Aviation Hall of Fame of New Jersey at Teterboro. The pilot of the aircraft was Col. Paul W. Tibbets of Miami, FL.

The huge bomber flew at 4,000 feet over the Pacific Ocean heading toward the Japanese mainland and a city Lewis hadn't heard of prior to the mission, Hiroshima.

At 0420, the ship's navigator "Dutch" Van Kirk reported that they would be over Iwo Jima at 0552, and Lewis commented in his log "...so we'll just check on him." They hit their check point exactly on schedule, and Tibbets pushed the airplane to 9,000 feet.

At 0730, Lewis wrote "we are loaded, the bomb is now alive and it's a funny feeling knowing it's right in back of you. Knock wood."

They climbed to 30,000 at 0740 and Lewis stated, "...well folks, it's not long now."

At 0830 Lewis reported, "Right now we are 15 miles from the Empire [Japan] and everyone has a big hopeful look on his face."

A few more minutes passed, and Lewis scribbled, "There'll be a short intermission while we bomb our target."

The morning was bright and clear and there was no enemy resistance as Lewis wrote, "We turned off our IP and had about a four-minute run on a perfectly open target. Tom Ferebee [the bombardier] synchronized on his briefed A.P. and let go — for the next minute no one knew what to expect. The bombardier and the right seat jockey or pilot [Lewis] both forgot to put on their dark glasses and therefore witnessed the flash. There were two very distinct slaps on the ship. Then that was all the physical effect we felt. We then turned the ship so we could observe results, and there in front of our eyes was without a doubt the greatest explosion man has ever witnessed!!!"

The world's first atomic bomb had been detonated. Three days later, a second bomb was dropped on Nagasaki and the Japanese government surrendered. The most devastating war man had ever created had come to an end.

New Jerseyan Bob Lewis and his fellow crew members were national heroes, and more than two million GIs who were preparing for the invasion of the Japanese mainland breathed a collective sigh of relief.

As early as March of 1945, plans had been formulated for a massive invasion of Japan. Gen. George C. Marshall told President Harry S. Truman that there could have been a half-million American casualties during the projected year-long conflict. The Japanese military had coined a new slogan, "One Hundred Million Die Together," and rallied the civilian population for a last stand. They had 2.3 million troops ready to defend the beaches and nearly four million civilians who could be formed into a militia for the big showdown.

The successful flight of the *Enola Gay* may have saved hundreds of thousands American lives.

Although 30-year-old Col. Tibbets, a tough, demanding officer, commanded the 509th Composite Group at Wendover Air Base in the desert on the Utah-Nevada border, all of the B-29s flight tests and the training of the *Enola Gay's* crew were conducted by Capt. Robert Lewis, a brash young man of 26. It wasn't until the crew had transferred to the island of Tinian, that Lewis discovered Tibbets planned to fly the B-29 on the mysterious mission. Lewis, now demoted to co-

Enola Gay crew - Col. Paul Tibbets, pilot; Capt. Tom Ferebee, bombardier; Bob Lewis, co-pilot; Ted Van Kirk, navigator.

pilot, angrily asked Tibbets for an explanation. Tibbets replied that he was responsible for the historic mission and if mistakes were going to be made, he preferred to make them.

Lewis and the B-29 Superforts were closely linked during his wartime service. In 1943, he flew more than 50 missions in an experimental B-29, and in 1944 was an instructor pilot for such top brass as Gen. Curtis LeMay, Gen. Frank Armstrong and their staffs at the Grand Island A.F.B. in Nebraska. That same year, he established an altitude record for a four-engined plane of more than 38,000 feet at Alamogorda, NM.

In a note to the author, Lewis told of an exciting encounter:

"Big thrill! On Jan. 21, 1944, Col. Charles Lindbergh asked me if he could go up with me in the B-29 which I was testing. The answer, of course, was yes, yes. He was my boyhood hero. He brought along John Myers, test pilot for the Northrop flying wing. On Jan. 22, we flew out over the Gulf of Mexico and I received a first-class flying lesson from the best ever."

Lewis returned from the service, married Mary Eileen Kelly and they raised a family of four boys. For a while, the former Air Force captain flew for American Overseas Airline, but soon found he could make a better living as an engineer. Over the years, the family lived in Maywood, Old Tappan, Matawan, Sparta and in 1981, when he retired as a project engineer with the Estee Corp. of Parsippany, he and Mary Eileen moved to Virginia where he died in 1983 at age 65.

New Jersey Companies that Contributed to the War Effort

The 1946 edition of the *Aircraft Year Book* listed the following airframe, engine and accessory manufacturing companies in New Jersey that contributed to the war effort during the 1941 to 1945 period.

AIRFRAMES: Eastern Aircraft Division of General Motors, Linden and West Trenton; Brewster Aero Corp., Newark Airport; Luscombe Airplane Co., West Trenton; Ridgefield Manufacturing Corp., Ridgefield.

ENGINES: Curtiss-Wright Corp., Paterson, Wood-Ridge, East Paterson and Fairlawn

PROPELLERS: Curtiss-Wright Corp., Prop. Div., Caldwell.

ACCESSORIES, TOOLS, FINISHES: Aeromark Co.; Elizabeth Aircraft Radio Corp.; Boonton American Oil & Supply; Newark American Transformer Co., Newark; Breeze Corp., Newark; Continental Electric Co., Newark; Crouse Manufacturing Inc., Newark; Crescent Insulated Wire & Cable Co., Trenton; Daven Co., Newark; De Caval Turbine Co., Trenton; Diehl Manufacturing Co., Somerville; Eclipse-Pioneer Div., Bendix Corp, Teterboro; Thomas A. Edison, Inc., In-

strument Div., West Orange; Edison-Splitdorf Corp., West Orange; Charles Engelhard, Inc., Newark; Standard Oil of New Jersey, Bayway; Finch Telecommunication, Inc., Passaic; Gaybex Corp., Nutley; Hanson-Van Winkle-Nunning Co., Matawan; Heineman Circuit Breaker Co., Trenton; Irvington Varnish & Insulator Co., Irvington; Kidde Manufacturing Co., Belleville; Okonite Co., Passaic; Palnut Company, Irvington; RCA Victor Div., Radio Corp. of America, Camden; Radio Frequency Labs, Inc., Boonton; Resistoflex Corp., Belleville; John A. Roebling's Sons Co., Trenton; Switlick Parachute Co., Trenton; Titanine, Inc., Union; U.S. Varnish Co., Hasbrouck Heights; Vimalert Co., Ltd., Jersey City; Lawrence Engine & Resistors Corp., Linden; A.W. Faber, Inc., Newark.

1946
Aviation Takes a Back Seat

When Guy Vaughan retired as the Curtiss-Wright Corporation's chairman of the board, he was succeeded by Paul V. Shields. Roy T. Hurley was named president. It's significant that Hurley's expertise was in low-cost industrial production. He had been director of manufacturing engineering for the Ford Motor Co. and vice president in charge of manufacturing for the Bendix Aviation Corp.

In order to keep an acceptable profit margin the company branched out in the production of other products such as plastics and textile roller bearing spindles. The officers of the company weren't interested in spending money on research, but over the next ten years they developed research projects financed by the government.

Hurley became chairman and president in 1951, following the resignation of Shields. It was during his administration that several decisions were made concerning the future powerplant needs of airlines that effectively put C-W out of the commercial engine business.

At the outbreak of the Korean War in 1951, the company did not have a jet engine design of its own to offer to the military, so a deal was made for the rights to manufacture two English jet engines, the Armstrong-Sidley J-65 Sapphire and the Olympus, now used in the Concorde. The J-65s were installed in such fighter planes as the Republic F-84F Thunderstreak and the FJ-3 Fury.

A former Curtiss-Wright public relations consultant who asked to be anonymous told the author his version of the downfall of the company.

"The main cause of C-W's fall from the heights was a wrong guess on the part of Hurley on the immediate future of the pure jet engine as against a turboprop. Wright had a good early jet, and could go either way for airline use, but (logically, if not strategically) decided that the most economical and effective version for airline use was the turboprop. It could lift heavier loads, save runway and fuel on takeoff, and be much more economical all around for commercial flight — but at a considerable penalty in speed.

"We prepared for him [Hurley] an elaborate presentation with charts, tables and I don't recall what else to show to the airlines, which had just about topped off with the DC-7 and wanted the next step up. He demonstrated his philosophy to all major airlines, but it fell flat. They wanted top speed and performance no matter what the cost. Boeing came out with its pure jets and Pratt & Whitney, GE and others took over the engine business. Of course now, super-efficient propjet transports are on many drawing boards — Hurley was about 30 years ahead of his time.

"He had earlier put on an elaborate exhibition at the Waldorf Astoria which introduced to this country such overseas developments as ultrasonic inspection (now used industry wide), the Wankel rotary engine, which was installed in experimental aircraft, and in all, some 19 exhibits of other new developments, some of which are only resurfacing today."

One of those was a flyable ramjet that is now being toted as the power-plant for the 21st-century *Orient Express,* a transport that could fly between New York and Tokyo in two and a half hours.

Another success story that never went beyond the experimental stage was the first throttleable rocket

Richard Dehmel looks into simulator as Curtiss-Wright president Guy Vaughan (left) and a pilot exam flight training manual.

engine in the world. Designed by Dr. Robert H. Goddard, who is considered to be the "father of rocketry," at the Propeller Division in Caldwell, it was flown by Lt. Col. Frank Everest in the Bell X-2 in 1955, 10 years after Goddard's death. The speed of the X-2 exceeded that of the X-1, the first plane flown faster than the speed of sound, which had engines built by Reaction Motors of Denville. It is a fact that the first three successful rocket powered aircraft, the X-1, X-2 and X-15, were propelled by engines designed and built in New Jersey.

The former public relations consultant remembered the highly publicized demonstration of the Curtiss-Wright Air Car in 1959. The large automobile-like C-W car was designed to fly on a cushion of air over any unobstructed terrain. It became a major attraction.

"The demonstration, held at Radio City Plaza in Manhattan, attracted attention all right," the consultant explained. "It was attended by news and cameramen from all over. The car had been brought to the plaza on a truck, so when the engine was started and the air cushion developed, it blew all the dust in the Plaza into the eyes and lungs of anyone in the area, and believe me, the following press reports blew the Air Car out of serious consideration forever. But now, as you know, air cushion vehicles (not by Curtiss-Wright) are used over water, and occasionally land, with worldwide success."

First Electronic Flight Simulator

Richard C. Dehmel

Inducted Aviation Hall of Fame of New Jersey, 1991

In 1943, Richard C. Dehmel licensed C-W to produce flight training devices under his patents. The simulators were the first of their kind, and after five years of research, they went into production. By 1951, an electronics division was formed and a modern plant in which to produce the simulators for military and civilian use was opened in Carlstadt, NJ. The plant also produced remote pilots, engine and propeller controls, guided missiles, recording equipment and related devices.

In that first full year of operation, the value of the Electronic Flight Simulator was proven during 13,000 hours of simulator time in which Pan American World Airways trained 125 crews of its own, 40 crews for British Overseas Airways and 85 Military Air Transport crews. It was reported in the C-W 1951 annual report that "Use of the simulator enabled Pan American to reduce crew training costs by 60% and cut in-flight training time from 21 to eight hours per crew."

Born in San Francisco, CA, in 1904, Richard C. Dehmel received a B.S. degree from the University of California. He moved east in 1927 and went to work for Bell Laboratories in New York City. He was sent back to the West Coast by Bell Labs in 1937 and while there earned his pilots license at Telegraph Atlantic Airport outside of Los Angeles. Knowing of Dehmel's electronic skills, Don Reese, the operator of the airport, suggested that the engineer develop an electronic simulator that would be an improvement on the Link trainer then being used to teach pilots to fly. Dehmel took on the challenge and developed the first electronic simulator in the world. When he retired in 1965, as the C-W vice president, corporate engineering research, he owned 44 patents concerning the simulator, many of which are being used in the highly sophisticated simulators of today.

Living in retirement in Short Hills, NJ, Dehmel has stayed active as a lecturer.

The X-19 VTOL

All the military services were interested in the development of a vertical take off and landing (VTOL) aircraft designed with a tilt propeller. The first design, designated the X-100, had a single engine and a propeller on each wing. To achieve a vertical take-off the props could be turned straight up and once the plane was airborne, they were turned for horizontal flight. By 1962, C-W had a flyable experimental model with four propellers on two wings attached to the forward and aft section of the fuselage. It was called the X-19. The plane was large enough to carry six people and could fly as fast as 450 mph for more than 600 miles.

Preliminary test flights were made at the Caldwell Wright Airport in Fairfield, each followed by months of modifications. During the summer of 1965, the airworthiness tests were moved to the FAA's National Aviation Facility, Experimental Center in Pomona, NJ. A total of 49 flights were completed. On the 50th flight, on August 25, 1965, the X-19 crashed, and test pilots James Ryan of Smithtown, NY, and Lt. Col. Bernard Hughes of Brigantine, NJ, narrowly escaped with their lives.

"There we were at 1,600 feet," Hughes, the co-pilot said later, "and the aircraft went into a violent roll. I noticed two propellers were coming off as we headed down. There was only about a second to act. We were already at 400 feet when we pushed the eject button. I was thrown straight down toward the ground. Fortunately, the parachute caught just before I hit the field. All I got were a few cuts and bruises. The other test pilot wasn't seriously injured either."

A World War II fighter pilot, Hughes had worked as a test pilot for more than 15 years. In addition, he was the commanding officer of the 119th Air National Guard Tactical Fighter Squadron.

Following the X-19 crash, the military lost interest in the project and C-W never flew the second machine they had built. In the 1990s, VTOL aircraft, similar to those created in New Jersey, are flying and airline executives believe they may be the inter-city transports of the future.

Curtiss-Wright went out of the engine business in the 1980s although their aircraft and engine designs during the 1940s, 50s and 60s were ahead of their time. Historians can only speculate as to where C-W would be today if they had been willing to privately finance and build the various experimental products they developed during that period.

Aftermath

Although they were no longer in the aircraft or engine business, it would be assumed that the management of the Curtiss-Wright Corp. of the mid-1980s would have been proud of the contributions their company made to the advancement of aviation. Yet, the complete opposite is true.

When the Aviation Hall of Fame & Museum of New Jersey wanted to honor C-W in 1982 for its 60 years of engine and aircraft development, the AHOF trustees were told that C-W was no longer in the engine business and were not interested in receiving the honor. Some weeks later, they changed their position and were presented with the AHOF's prestigious Aviation Achievement Award.

Of course, the vast majority of C-W's management of the 1980s had not spent the greater part of their lives in the field of aeronautics. That, however, was not true of the employees who banded together to form a C-W Retired Employee Association. The group, numbering more than 200, is first, dedicated to the preservation of C-W's heritage, which also happens to be their own, and second, good fellowship.

The former employee with the most seniority among the retirees is Joseph A. DeMona of Wyckoff. In 1917, DeMona went to work for the Wright-Martin Aircraft Corp. in New Brunswick as a tool room employee. He left the company in early 1919, the same year Wright and Martin went separate ways, and the Wright Aeronautical Corp. was established in Paterson.

DeMona returned to Wright in October of 1921 as a lathe operator. Seven years later he was appointed as Jobsetter and became the foreman a year later. He continued to work his way up the production ladder and eventually became the Manufacturing Manager responsible for all manufactruing departments, and the engine assembly and engine test departments. He had more than 8,000 employees reporting to him.

In 1955, DeMona was transferred to the Works Manager's office as the assistant works manager. His assignment was to establish a special department dedicated to cost reduction and scrap control. "During the five years before I retired in 1960, my department saved millions of dollars for the company," he said proudly. When he left Wright, DeMona had spent the better part of 52 years in aircraft engine production.

When the Wood Ridge C-W plant closed in 1983, Gerard A. Abbamont of Teaneck, who spent 43 years in the engine test field with the company, realized that management had no interest in preserving the incomparable C-W history. Determined not to let that happen, Abbamont began collecting every scrap of information, every artifact and photograph and finally every full-sized example of the engines produced by the company.

Once he ascertained how many types of engines were available from the John Deere Company, which had taken over the Wood Ridge plant, and other sources, Abbamont contacted Thomas Peters, the director of the City of Paterson Museum, and asked if he (Peters) would be interested in a C-W historic exhibit. Peters enthusiastically agreed to make space available. Abbamont then asked former C-W engine experts to help him restore the engines and to create pictorial displays. The restoration team consisted of Andrew Smith, Kenneth Bell, Frederick Bossler and William Fogg.

In May of 1986, the "Year of Aviation Display — a tribute to the workers" was opened.

After a year's "run," a new home was needed for the exhibit — no small task when one considers that the smallest engine weighed over 1,000 pounds.

Abbamont approached the New Jersey Aviation Hall of Fame & Museum about housing the collection at the Teterboro facility. The AHOF's trustees accepted the offer, although it was understood that space would not be available immediately to display the entire C-W engine collection. Anthony DiStefano, di-

rector of the Teterboro School of Aeronautics, offered to donate storage space for the engines until the museum could be expanded.

Abbamont was named the AHOF's curator of engines and power plants. By the late 1980s, the museum had acquired the finest collection of C-W historical documents and artifacts in the United States. The entire cataloged collection will be preserved in the AHOF's Educational Center library and the equipment, some one of a kind, was to be exhibited upon completion of the Center's proposed expansion.

The World's Busiest Air Freight Terminal
Frederick L. Wehran

Inducted Aviation Hall of Fame of New Jersey, 1972

In 1940, the Riser Land Company, the owner of Teterboro, was looking for buyers for the airport. It appeared that the 300-acre tract would eventually be sold as an industrial park site. Frederick L. Wehran, a Union City, NJ, native, envisioned the airport, just eight miles for New York City, as the perfect site for an air freight terminal. At that time, only dreamers thought of using the airplane to move large quantities of material. Wehran was one of those.

He was one of a handful of men with experience in air freight hauling. He had spent the previous seven years in Western Canada in search of gold, silver and lead, buying and selling lumber and drilling for oil in remote regions. He needed men and supplies at his projects, so he began an air freight service with six airplanes. Soon, his bush pilots were flying freight as far north as Alaska.

Eventually, he made a fortune in mining stocks, but in 1939, when Canada joined England and declared war on Germany, the Canadian government banned the transfer of securities out of the country.

"I was sunk," Wehran explained. "Everything I had was frozen in Canada."

Returning to New Jersey with just $10,000, he discovered Teterboro was for sale. "I looked at the New York skyline across the river and all that activity and thought, 'This is it. It has to be. There's going to be an air freight industry, and right here is the place for it."

Using his $10,000 and borrowing $40,000 from friends, Wehran arranged for a $400,000 mortgage, and in 1941 bought the Meadowland's acreage. Following his uncanny instincts and business acumen, Wehran made arrangements to borrow $1 million from Standard Oil of New Jersey (now EXXON) to put down runways and build hangars. But before he could get the projects underway, the United States declared

Aviation pioneers at Teterboro 1955: Ruth Nichols, Clarence Chamberlin, Fred Wehran and Blanche Scott.

war on Japan and Germany, and the Army took control of Teterboro because of its proximity to the Atlantic coastline. Wehran had to put his dream on hold for four years.

In 1916, Wehran took his first airplane ride at age 16 with the Canadian Air Force. But when the authorities realized he was under age and not a Canadian citizen, they sent him packing back to the United States. He eventually became a World War I Marine.

His dexterity with a dollar, like his aptitude for flying, had brought him a fortune during the 1920s. Before his 30th birthday, he owned two New Jersey homes, a 160-acre summer estate in Monroe, NY, several expensive cars and four airplanes--a Sopwith Camel, a British Avro, an Avian, and a Thomas Moore Scout.

He first discovered Teterboro the hard way. In 1924, the Avro's engine quit at 500 feet over the airfield. In the inevitable crash, his co-pilot was killed and Wehran might have died if Clarence Chamberlin hadn't pulled him from the wreck.

That wasn't the first plane he had "totaled." While flying in a snowstorm over Caldwell, his Sopwith Camel went into a 1,000-foot spin. He crawled away from the crumpled wood and canvas wreck with just a few broken ribs.

"It's amazing how many crashes I survived," Wehran mused years laters. "I was a good pilot, but one thing after another seemed to happen to those little ships."

The Avian lasted until 1926 when the wings snapped off and it crashed into a cornfield in Warwick, NY. He was later quoted in a Warwick newspaper:

"It was worth a smashup to get acquainted with such a fine community. I've never been treated better in my life."

The most damaging crash, however, came in October 1929 when the bottom fell out of the stock market. Wehran was able to ride out the initial plunge, but by 1932, he was broke like everyone else.

"I watched a fortune melt away like snow in April," he recalled. That's when he and his wife, Peggy, left for Canada, made a second fortune, endured a second economic crash, and bought another return ticket to New Jersey.

The Army had used Teterboro throughout the war, so it wasn't until V- J day that Wehran was able to begin building his freight center. The movement of supplies and personnel by air during the war years proved that airplanes could compete with rail and water transportation in moving priority goods swiftly and safely. Former military airmen returned home, bought surplus C-46 and C-47 transports, and began looking for airfields where they could setup shops. Wehran had just the place for them.

Wehran was relentless in his quest to develop the best air freight terminal in the nation. "We went pounding away at it," he said. "Pounding away to get runways in; up to our neck with problems to solve; going to see people like Standard Oil and Bill Brewster and telling them we needed money to make it work. They had to see it. They had to believe it."

Wehran was convincing. Standard Oil gave him $1 million for exclusive rights to sell its fuel at his airport. It turned out to be a good deal for both parties. Wehran got his runways, and by the middle of 1947, an average of 250,000 gallons of fuel were being consumed monthly.

The Brewster Construction Company, based in Bogota, NJ, was one of the largest in the state. That company got the contract to pave the runways and Wehran convinced owner Bill Brewster to invest in hangars and other buildings.

To help him oversee the work being done and to collect rents from his various tenants, Wehran hired two ex-Air Force flyers as his assistants. Henry A. Conway, a former 15th Air Force B-24 navigator, was named secretary-treasurer of the company and Douglas C. Wolfe, who had flown P-39s and Spitfires over North Africa, was assistant airport manager. Tom Lineaweaver supervised an eight-man maintenance crew.

George Hicha was another early employee, and became the airfield's first air traffic controller. He recalled: "When I arrived Teterboro in April 1946, the airport covered 500 acres with one sod runway 3,000 feet long. Under construction were three new paved runways. Two were 4,500 feet long and 100 feet wide running north and south. The east-west runway was 80 feet wide. The new runways weren't finished until late in '46."

The air freight business was already in full swing even before the paving was complete, although heavily loaded DC-3s and DC-4s had trouble taking off and landing when the sod was wet.

In those post-war years, there were four flying schools based at Teterboro — Rausch, Safair, Whites and Robinson. The air freight service included Flying Tigers, Willis Air Service and Meteor Air Transport. There were even two small airlines, New Hampshire and Robinson. All told, 50 operators used the air terminal during its first year of operation.

George Hicha

Inducted Aviation Hall of Fame of New Jersey, 1979

George Hicha volunteered for military service in 1942 with the U.S. Marines. After basic training, he was sent to the CAA Control Tower Operator School at Ft. Worth, TX. He received a CAA diploma and control tower operator certificate in 1943. As a noncommissioned officer, he served at Marine control towers

George Hicha

throughout the United States and in the South Pacific.

Upon leaving the service, he was hired by Wehran and moved to Passaic. He began controlling air traffic from sunrise to sunset, standing atop the operation's office roof and using a light gun to direct aircraft in and out of the airport. Late in 1946, a tower "cab" was built on the roof to protect Hicha from inclement weather. That cab was eventually perched on a tall wooden stand and placed at the junction of the runways.

Hicha worked with Wehran to revise the air traffic patterns in order to alleviate the noise of aircraft flying over residential areas, a problem that still faces every busy airport in the world.

Once the paved runways were completed, Hicha was handling 1,200 movements (landings and takeoffs) a day. Teterboro was ranked as the ninth busiest airport in the nation. In early 1947, Wehran hired six more controllers to relieve the pressure. Later that year, the CAA took command of the tower and surplus radio equipment was installed. Hicha became a government employee working under tower chief Walter Buechler.

An article in an October 1947 issue of the *Bergen Evening Record* reported that Wehran was relieved to have the CAA assume the air traffic control duties. He was quoted as saying that it was a "near miracle that there has never been a serious accident at the field although we've had more than 300,000 aircraft movements since the end of the war."

Wehran kept the business coming. he charged less for fuel than Newark or LaGuardia airports and by not charging landing fees, he lured all the ex-GIs to his modern facility. There were 25 tent offices on the field in the Spring of 1946 but soon they were replaced by quonset huts and hangars.

He liked the spunk of the veteran airmen. "Nobody could tell them they couldn't make a go of it," he remembered. "Give them 99 reasons whey they can't, and they'll give you one reason they can—and you've lost the argument.

"At first it was the survival of the fittest, " Wehran continued. "They came to Teterboro, Army and Navy pilots, and they were just babies. They didn't know how to run a business. But some of them learned the

value of a buck and grew up overnight. I saw them grow up. It was fun to watch."

Charles F. Willis Jr.

One youngster Wehran observed was 24-year-old Charles F. Willis Jr. who, with George A. Enloe, had begun an air freight business in Baltimore, MD, following the war. Both ex-Navy pilots, Willis and Enloe moved their budding freight and aircraft maintenance business to Teterboro in late 1945 and set up shop in two surplus Army tents. During their first year in New Jersey, the freight line flew 1,241,765 ton miles of cargo.

Willis, who was president of the company, possessed an enviable naval aviation record. He had flown 134 combat missions in both the Pacific and European theaters of operation, earning three Distinguished Flying Crosses. His duties had also included organizational work in training squadrons and establishing and operating seaplane bases in the Pacific, valuable experience with which to begin his own business.

Willis entered the Navy in 1939 and obtained a commission as an ensign in 1941. He was stationed at Pearl Harbor when the Japanese attacked on Dec. 7, 1941 and suffered wounds of the arm and hand.

Enloe was the company vice president in charge of engineering. During the war, his pilot duties were augmented by the construction and management of Pacific naval bases. The new company's maintenance service was his chief concern.

In late 1946, Lt. Cmdr. Bob Rose, joined the company as executive vice president.

The Willis maintenance group used a Brewster-built hangar, the first major structure to be built at Teterboro since the 1920s, to service Mohawk Airlines' fleet of DC-3s, Lehman Brothers' converted B-23s, SAS and Aramco's DC-6s, Argentine Airlines' DC-4s and the personal DC-6 of Mrs. Juan Peron, wife of Argentina's dictator.

In March of 1947, Willis founded the Teterboro School of Aeronautics and hired Don Hulse Sr., Dave Van Dyke Sr., George W. Brush Jr. and Tony DiStefano to run the operation. "We had only six students enrolled," DiStefano remembered.

From that meager beginning, the school prospered. It was a government-approved airframe and engine mechanic school certified by the Civil Aeronautics Administration and the New Jersey Department of Education. Many of the schools' graduates joined the maintenance staff of Willis Air Service, which grew to more than 200 workers.

Meanwhile, the ton-miles flown by Willis cargo planes had almost doubled the previous year. The October 1947 issue of *Airport* magazine noted that

Willis and Flying Tigers were among the top five air freight carriers in the United States.

Early in 1953, Willis sold his Teterboro businesses to Hulse and Van Dyke and moved to Washington, DC. During Gen. Dwight D. Eisenhower's campaign for president, Willis had co-founded a group called Citizens for Eisenhower, and when the General was elected president, Willis was asked to join the White House staff as director of personnel.

After Willis left Washington, he became president of Alaska Airlines. Years later, he returned to Washington as a consultant and lobbyist.

Lou Ranley

Inducted Aviation Hall of Fame of New Jersey, 1977

No one came back from World War II better prepared to fly Teterboro's rundown surplus aircraft than Lou Ranley. While serving in New Guinea with the Air Transport Command, he remembered, "I got all the strays to fly — all the banged-up ships. I became an air/sea rescue officer and all I saw were mountains, ocean and Japs."

When he joined the Army Air Corps at age 30, Ranley had already flown 1,500 hours. He was assigned by the Army to teach potential Navy pilots to fly at Purdue University. "That got boring," he said, " so I raised a fuss and got into the Ferry Command and that became boring. I wanted to go overseas so I fussed again and ended up in New Guinea. I flew

Popular Lou Ranley cartoon by Milt Neal.

every kind of wreck there. I was lucky to get out alive."

Back at Teterboro after the war, Ranley became the chief pilot for the Rausch Flying Service. Because of his "wreck" flying experience, Larry Rausch would send him to various parts of the country to pick up disabled planes.

"Rausch thought he was an engineer, " Ranley said, "so he'd buy old wrecks and rebuild them for resale. One of his creations was half a Lockheed Lodestar and a Hudson bomber that he connected together . We called it the Hudstar. The darn thing flew."

Ranley's co-pilot on many of those flights was Edmund Nelle, who eventually became president of Butler Aviation, based in Montvale, NJ. Tony Lembo, Vince Revelle, Fred Huettenmoser, Gene Orlando, and Wally Traver were others who worked for Rausch.

In 1917 at age five, Ranley sat in his first airplane in Paterson. "The plane was in a church yard on Main Street. My mother bought Liberty Bonds so they let me sit in the ship," he said.

The Ranley family moved to Clifton in 1926 and that's when the 14-year-old boy first heard of Teterboro.

"I set out to find the place. I walked there and saw airplanes. Then I was given a bike and I rode to Teterboro until someone stole my bike, " Ranley chuckled. "So it was back on foot again."

He became one of the many young "go-fers," running errands for the Gates Flying Circus pilots who paid for the favors with airplane rides. Ranley's first flight was with one of the greatest pilot/stuntmen of them all, Clyde Pangborn.

Ranley bought an Aeronca C-3 and learned to fly in the early 1930s. "My instructor had no license," he said, "but that didn't bother anyone." He then had a series of planes and taught flying at the North Jersey Airport, Franklin Lakes, Murchio Airport, and Teterboro, His students included Fred Wehran and entertainers Arthur Godfrey and Johnny Carson.

In 1946, Ranley became a CAA flight examiner, flight testing potential pilots and then approving or disapproving the issuance of a license. His territory covered New Jersey from Trenton north, southern New York State and eastern Pennsylvania.

Over a 40-year period, he estimated that he licensed more than 8,000 pilots for private, commercial, instrument and multi-engine land and sea aircraft. He became the chief pilot for John and Tony Habermann's Teterboro Fight Academy in 1974 and had flown more than 30,000 hours as an examiner and teacher when a heart problem grounded him in 1987.

By 1990, Lou Ranley was still the undisputed dean of the Teterboro community.

Philip J. Landi

Inducted Aviation Hall of Fame of New Jersey, 1986

Philip J. Landi, one of the young men who worked with Fred Wehran as an assistant manager, went on to a distinguished aviation career with the Port Authority of New York and New Jersey. In September of 1976, he flew a helicopter into the *Guinness Book of World Records*.

At the controls of a twin-engine, four-passenger Boelkow helicopter, Landi left Teterboro Airport and flew to the World Trade Center in Lower Manhattan, becoming the first person to land and take off from the highest building helipad in the world.

He landed on a 20-by-20-foot platform, raised 20 feet above the center of the Trade Center's south Tower roof, 1,385 feet above the bustling streets below. Once the helicopter rotor stopped whirling, Landi's two passengers, William J. Ronan, Port Authority chairman, and Caesar B. Pattarini, director of aviation, climbed out and went down to their offices below.

Later, a similar landing pad was opened on the Trade Center's north tower to allow emergency assistance to be flown in.

Following three years of service with a B-29 Bomber Group in the Pacific during World War II, Landi, a Rockaway, NJ, native, majored in airport management and operations at the Sparton School of Aeronautics in Tulsa, OK. While there, he learned to fly.

Port Authority receives new Bell 222U helicopter. L-R: Philip Landi, Mgr. P.A. heliports, Robert Aaronson, P.A. director of aviation and Richard White, chief, helicopter maintenance.

He returned to New Jersey in 1948 and began working for Wehran. "One of my jobs was to collect the monthly rents from the 50-some operators at the field, " Landi recalled. "It was a thankless job. Most all of them had a new excuse each month for not being able to pay."

When the Port Authority assumed control of Teterboro in 1949, Landi joined the agency. As helicopters became accepted as a viable means of transportation in congested metropolitan areas, Landi's expertise as a pilot and a manager earned him the title of Manager, Helicopters & Heliports Operation. Soon he became recognized as a leading expert in heliport construction and helicopter operations and was asked to consult with industry representatives and government agencies from Canada to Washington, DC, concerning helicopter acquisitions and heliport development.

During the 36 years that Landi managed the Port Authority's helicopter operation, he and his staff pilots flew more than 57,000 hours, covering in excess of six million miles without a fatal accident. For that achievement, his department received 12 bronze safety awards from the Helicopter Association International.

In 1973, Landi received the Max Schumacher Memorial Award from the Helicopter Association of American for "distinguished service to the commercial helicopter industry through the advancement of the use of helicopters in urban area operations."

In 1981, Landi was chosen by the State Department, with British Embassy approval, to flight-check Queen Elizabeth's helicopter pilots prior to their flying Prince Charles over the New York/New Jersey area. He than accompanied the Prince on his aerial tour, pointing out the sites of interest along the way.

Landi was always proud of the fact that he greeted every U.S. president, from Eisenhower to Reagan, who came to New York on official business.

When he retired in 1988, he was lauded for having done more to promote the use of helicopters in the New York metropolitan area than any other advocate. Before he retired, he had supervised the design and construction of the Port Authority's modern heliport on Manhattan's East River. The new port accommodates tilt-rotor aircraft, considered the commuter aircraft of the future.

Atlas Sky Merchant

In 1946, a large, four-engine DC-4 owned by the Atlas Supply Company, a subsidiary of Standard Oil of New Jersey, arrived at Teterboro under the command of Col. Edwin E. Aldrin, who had organized Standard Oil's flight department at Newark Airport in 1928. He had been hired by F.H. Bedford Jr., the president of Atlas Supply , to create a flying show room in which

Atlas products could be exhibited. Aldrin bought a war-surplus C-54 (a DC-4 in civilian use) for $75,000. He had its interior fitted with shelves to accommodate Atlas tires, batteries and accessories, plus 16 passenger seats, two bunks, a galley and a motion picture projector.

Christened the *Atlas Sky Merchant* on Nov. 11, 1946 by Mrs. Robert E. Wilson, wife of Standard Oil's board chairman, the plane made its first flight that afternoon. In a month's time it flew around the country from coast to coast and border to border. In January 1947, the plane began a 12-city southern tour.

The *Sky Merchant*, one of the first of its kind, was an immediate success. New products were shown to local merchants and dealerships were arranged at each stop along the way. The silver plane, with a red stripe running the length of its fuselage and red tail fin with the word "Atlas" emblazoned on it, attracted crowds wherever it landed, for it was one of the largest flying at that time.

Bill Foster was the first pilot and Jeff Powell, an Atlas tire representative, flew as co-pilots. In 1947, Louis J. Vanmansart, a Paterson resident who had served in the Air Corps with Aldrin, joined the Atlas team as chief pilot.

Bedford and Joseph Partenheimer, his vice president and general manager, then planned an ambitious round-the-world flight for the flying show room. Aldrin, who commanded all the flights, worked out the schedule that would take the plane to 26 countries and 45 cities in South America, Africa, India, Asia, Australia and the United States.

The flight began at the Miami air races where the plane was opened to the public. In two days, more than 12,000 people walked through it. Then 100 days and 44,500 miles later it returned to Teterboro. There were 13 passengers and a crew of six. E.M. Harvey was Vanmansart's co-pilot. The other crew members were F. Ferraro, flight engineer, J. Nielsen, engineer and steward, T.A. Lewis, navigator and A.W. Albright, radio operator.

Convinced they had found a winning formula to sell their products, Bedford sent the *Sky Merchant* around South America and then to 22 cities in North Africa and Europe. It continued as a flying show room until 1953, when Aldrin sold it for half a million dollars to the non-scheduled California-Eastern Airlines. On its first flight from San Francisco to Tokyo, an engine failed 300 miles from the west coast and it was forced to ditch in the Pacific. It floated for six hours and the crew was rescued before it sank.

Aldrin retired when he left Atlas and Vanmansart went with the New York Rubber Co., flying a twin-engined Beechcraft based at Teterboro.

Other Early Operators

Many other businesses were attracted to Teterboro. **Air Associates** arrived in Teterboro in 1940. The company constructed a half-million dollar plant, adjacent to the old Fokker hangar, and began manufacturing aircraft hydraulic and pneumatic equipment. Following World War II, it became the largest manufacturer of aircraft seat belts in the United States. The Teterboro plant was closed in the 1970s.

Van Dusen Aircraft Supplies, a Minnesota-based company, moved its eastern operation to Wehran's facility in 1946 and was purchased by Aviall in 1987. Doug Jesch of Wayne, who worked for Van Dusen for 36 years and had managed the Teterboro operation for 20 years, retired when the new management assumed control. In the late 1980s, he owned and operated The Pilot Shop, just a block from the end of the airports runways.

A former Pan American Airways check pilot, James Starr, founded the **Air Facilities Corp.** at Teterboro in late 1945. The company was the eastern states distributor for Fairchild and Bellanca aircraft. They also ran a charter service into the mid-1950s.

Robinson Aviation operated out of two large hangars on the south-west side of Teterboro where eight aircraft flown by Robinson Airlines were maintained. The New York state regional carrier and the New Jersey maintenance base were controlled by Mr. and Mrs. C.S. Robinson, who held the positions of president and treasurer. Eventually, Robinson Aviation became Mohawk Airlines, then Allegheny, and in the '80s, it joined the giant USAir family.

In October 1946, **Mallard Air Service,** which had begun at Newark Airport as a Navion aircraft dealership, moved its headquarters to Teterboro. Robert Hewitt was president, Frank Kane, vice president of sales and Ken Forester, vice president of engineering. Jim Taylor headed operations, assisted by Bob Boettger. Alice Jean May, a former WASP pilot, was the company's secretary.

During the Korean war years, Mallard did a thriving business buying and selling DC-3s for conversion as executive aircraft. Ken Forester Sr. recalls that the company could purchase a DC-3 for approximately $30,000, make some repairs and sell it almost immediately for $100,000.

"At one point we made $3 million in seven months," he said. "My brother-in-law (Hewitt) thought we could do better if we converted the DC-3s ourselves. So we set up a big conversion operation in Bridgeport, Connecticut and within a year went bankrupt."

Forester didn't leave Teterboro. In 1955, he organized a small fixed-base operation that he called General Aviation. Under the watchful eye of Forester and his son, Ken Jr., the business flourished. In the late

1980s, they built a modern hangar/terminal complex and bought a Million Air franchise.

The Atlantic Aviation Corp., a subsidiary of the Delaware-based Dupont Corporation, came to Teterboro as a distributor of Beechcraft planes and Bendix radios. Sydney Nesbitt was the first president. As the corporation expanded to other airports, the president's headquarters was moved to Wilmington, DE. Watson Richards became general manager at Teterboro. He was followed by Bill Patrick, who eventually became the company president, Gene Larimer, Bill Crawford, Henry Esposito and Bob Kuter. In those formative years, Neal Fulton Jr. headed the flight department and personally demonstrated the capabilities of the aircraft. Fulton went on to become a corporate pilot.

During the 45 years Atlantic has been at Teterboro, it has distributed numerous types of aircraft including Bell and Agusta helicopters, DH-125 Hawkers, and the Israel-built Westwind and Astra jets. Moving into the 1990s, the company is the largest fixed-base operator at the airfield and in the mid-80s opened a modern terminal/hangar building as the centerpiece of a four-hangar complex. The large hangar No. 3, built by Brewster Construction in the late 1940s, has the first FAA control tower attached to it. When the controllers left that tower in 1976 and moved to a new structure on the east side of the airfield, the top three floors became the first museum of the Aviation Hall of Fame of New Jersey.

Henry J. Esposito

Inducted Aviation Hall of Fame of New Jersey, 1986

Henry "Hank" Esposito spent his entire adult life promoting general aviation. In 40 years as an executive with Atlantic Aviation, he became New Jersey's most recognizable personality — a friend of corporate aviators and their passengers throughout the United States. No request was too trivial for him to fulfill whether it be from a president of the United States or the weekend pilot who occasionally pulled onto Atlantic's ramp at Teterboro. Over the years, he became a confidant of HRH Prince Bernhard of the Netherlands, entertainer Arthur Godfrey and a host of aviation personalities. He has seen to the needs of four U.S. presidents, countless government officials, corporate executives and entertainers from the stage, screen, television and radio.

Following three years in Europe during World War II, Esposito, who was born in Jersey City and raised in Hasbrouck Heights, joined Atlantic Aviation's accounting department in 1949. Five years later, he became manager of customer relations and began building his reputation among the general aviation community as "Mr. Teterboro." In 1963, he was named manager of Atlantic's flight department and,

Hank Esposito (right) and friends: John Mendes, director aviation, A.I.G.; Ray Tourin, director aviation, Philip Morris; Joe Panetta, manager & chief pilot, Gulf & Western; Frank Manno, chief pilot, Volkswagon

in 1970, became general manager of the Teterboro facility. In the 1980s, Atlantic's management in Wilmington asked Esposito to become the division marketing manager responsible for developing new business for the company's six fixed-base operations from coast to coast. The new position kept him in the air commuting between Teterboro and Atlantic's bases as far away as Long Beach, CA, and as close to home as North Philadelphia, PA. But he never lost his one-on-one relationship with corporate pilots from all corners of the country.

Those personalities who based their aircraft at Atlantic's terminal included Godfrey, actors Cliff Robertson and Christopher Reeves, and comedian Bill Cosby. Esposito says Cosby is a naturally funny person who calls him "Uncle Hank."

"One time he was going to Europe. The finest food was aboard his private Gulfstream II jet," Esposito remembered. "He said he felt like having a couple of chili dogs. So I went out and got him a couple of 'dogs' before he took off."

In the 1950s, Esposito was responsible for coordinating perhaps the largest Republican gathering ever held in New Jersey, when President Richard Nixon's followers held a campaign rally in Atlantic Aviation's hangar #3 which is as large as a football field. In subsequent years, he greeted and assisted Vice President George Bush and Senator Ted Kennedy on numerous occasions as they passed through Teterboro on the campaign trail. And Frank Sinatra, the kid from Hoboken who lived in Hasbrouck Heights for a few years, was seen regularly on the Atlantic ramp when he came to the area for concerts.

Esposito's sense of humor and his ability to laugh at himself endeared him to friend and foe alike. He has been a member of the International Order of Characters for many years. In 1985 he was chosen for the Character of the Year Award, putting him in fast company. Previous winners had been the legendary pilot Roscoe Turner and Senator Barry Goldwater.

Fred W. Bohlander

Inducted Aviation Hall of Fame of New Jersey, 1974

Fred Bohlander

Another Teterboro pioneer who was usually present to greet and assist the great and near-great personalities passing through the airport was Police Chief Fred Bohlander. One of only 21 citizens in the tiny Teterboro municipality, Bohlander became its police chief by default. When the Bendix Corp. moved into the borough in 1938, its management requested police protection. Bohlander recalled, "I was the only eligible man in town. All the other residents were over age. I started it as a favor to the municipality on a part-time basis."

Bohlander began his aviation career in 1922 as a mechanic with Anthony Fokker's Atlantic Aircraft Corp. The following year, he received his airframe and engine license and worked with Bill Hartig as a detail aircraft assembler. He said he made last-minute repairs on Charles Lindbergh's airplane, *Spirit of St. Louis,* just before the Lone Eagle's solo flight over the Atlantic Ocean.

"I worked to reset a mirror for the periscope," he told a reporter. "The *Spirit's* front windshield was blocked off by an auxiliary gas tank preventing Slim from seeing straight ahead without using the periscope."

During the 1930s, Bohlander sold automobiles in Rutherford, NJ, and had no inkling that he'd become a one-man police force before the end of the decade. For 28 years, he formed Teterboro's entire force and an effective one. In the early 1950s, he recovered $500,00 in silver bullion on its way out of the country via Teterboro Airport.

Whenever a high government official was scheduled to arrive at the airport, he coordinated the efforts of the Secret Service and county and state police who would escort the VIP to his or her North Jersey destination.

As the borough's industrial development grew and the airport expanded, in 1967, the borough council gave Bohlander a four-man force to keep patrols on the roads 24 hours a day. He retired in 1973 and after serving as a councilman for one term, he retired from public life. But he never spent more than a week away from the airport that had been the focus of his life. He passed away in 1981.

Consolidated Instrument Co.

The **Consolidated Instrument Company** that produced tachometers, altimeters, temperature and pressure gauges for most American aircraft as far back as the 1920s, moved to Teterboro following the war.

George Renz moved his business into one corner of a corrugated hangar and immediately began servicing the instruments of the more than 50 operators who had moved into Wehran's facility.

In 1949, O.B. Johannessen joined the company as an expert in the repair of consolidated auto pilots and gyros. In 1960, Johannessen became the president of the company.

As a design, engineering and manufacturing facility, the company's list of firsts to the industry include: the Course-find Syncro Tester, used on the original PB20 Auto Pilot; the Combustion Monitor, today called EGT; the D.C. powered Standby Horizon; the Twin Mechanical Tachometer and 26,000 single, dual and triple tachometers. Another Consolidated innovation was the Dayglo Orange highlighting of horizon bars which was eventually adopted by every aircraft and automobile instrument manufacturer in the world.

Eric Johannessen, O.B's son, joined the company and rose through the ranks to the position of vice president.

As the 1990s dawn, Consolidated occupies a building across from the airport that houses 30 employees who manufacture and service instruments and avionics for aircraft owners around the world.

World Airways Arrives

In 1950, two war-surplus C-46 twin-engine passenger planes arrived at Teterboro, the sole assets of a defunct Long Island airline called World Airways. They were owned by Edward J. Daly, a hard-drinking maverick entrepreneur. It was said that Daly, then a 27-year-old ex-GI, raised $50,000 in a poker game to acquire the aircraft and all rights to the airline. The cost of gate space at LaGuardia Airport was more than Daly could afford so he moved into Teterboro. At the same time, he and his family set up housekeeping in Tenafly, NJ.

Phil Landi remembered Daly as a "tough guy to do business with, but he was a tireless worker and the innovator of low cost air travel."

Daly's thinking was ahead of its time. He envisioned his small airline as the first efficient, low-cost charter operation, ready and eager to serve millions of people who had never flown. In the 1950s, a commercial airline seat was expensive which prohibited the average person from flying. Within a year of his move to Teterboro, Daly had secured military and cargo contracts. His airline was soon transformed into a major carrier for the U.S. Military Airlift command out of Teterboro and McGuire Air Force Base. That year, with a staff of 33 employees, World Airways carried 13,000 passengers. The following year, the passenger count almost doubled when Daly inaugurated a coast-to-coast charter fare of $85.

In 1956, the airline's headquarters was moved from Teterboro to Oakland Airport in California, but it continued its service to the East Coast out of Newark.

During the Vietnam War, World Airways secured government contracts to carry troops in and out of the war zone. Newsmen began referring to Daly as "pistol-packin', rough talkin' Ed." His employees said it was well deserved. For, while Daly was busy overseeing the safety of his passengers, cargo and aircraft, he wore a six-shooter strapped to his hip, and he threatened to use the gun on anyone who attempted to interrupt the airline's Vietnam flights.

Although Daly died in 1984, World Airways, the airline that began in New Jersey, continued its inexpensive transcontinental flights into the late 1980s. It was eventually driven out of business by the many discount airlines nurtured by airline deregulation.

Meteor Air's DC-4

Throughout the 1950s, Meteor Air transport, owned and operated by Bob Morrow, acquired contracts to run passenger charter flights from the U.S. to various parts of the world.

In 1949, Irving "Ike" Stanton joined Meteor as a captain and check pilot on DC-3, C-46 and DC-4 equipment. For the next 10 years, he made numerous ocean crossings, flying both passengers and cargo charters. In 1957, he flew a DC-4 around the world.

On June 20, Stanton set off from Newark Airport with the DC-4's 77 passenger seats filled by English war brides returning to their homeland to visit relatives. Stanton had a crew of seven aboard, two pilots, two navigators, a flight engineer and two flight attendants. The scheduled flying time to London was almost 19 hours, including short stops at Gander, Newfoundland and Shannon, Ireland.

From London, the DC-4 flew to Hamburg, Germany, to pick up a load of German passengers emigrating to Australia. For Captain Stanton, that flight was a real diplomatic challenge. Ben Heinzen described the flight in an article in the *Nutley Sun*

On the world-circling flight, Stanton ran the gamut of international politics and revolutions. He stopped in

A Nose hangar: cold weather engine maintenance.

democracies like England and West Germany, flew over downtrodden and Communist-controlled Eastern Europe, bypassed troubled Cyprus for calmer Lebanon; negotiated with the American-suspicious, pro-Moscow Syrian Government for fly-over permission; put down in striving rival republics Pakistan and India and got entangled in the revolutions in the five-island Indonesian republic."

It was after the DC-4 had departed from Calcutta, India, that Stanton flew into a monsoon which he called "The worst storm I've ever had to fly through. The plane was like a leaf in a storm, and came close to being turned completely over at least three times."

From Australia, Stanton flew the DC-4 across the Pacific and 10 days later arrived back at Teterboro "a bit older and a helluva lot wiser," he said.

In 1930, Stanton operated an auto-repair garage in East Orange. He received his first flying lessons in exchange for overhauling aircraft motors. He continued operating the garage throughout the '30s and flew charters on the side. In 1940, he became an instructor in the Civilian Pilot Training program, leaving the garage business behind forever. He joined the Navy Air Transport command in 1942, ferrying New Jersey-built Grumman Hellcats and Wildcats from the east coast to San Diego, and flying damaged planes back for repairs.

When he left the service in 1946 as a lieutenant commander, he took a job with Air Cargo Transport flying out of Newark. That year, he made a pioneering "survey flight" in a DC-3 from Newark to Liberia, Africa, via the West Indies and South America. When his co-pilot quit in Miami, he piloted the long overwater hops single handedly, taking some short breaks by letting his navigator and engineer fly the plane.

The plane received a gala welcome in Liberia and the crew was feted by the country's legendary president William S. Tubman.

Following his years with Meteor, Stanton joined Zantop International Airlines and moved his family from their Nutley home to Canton, MI, where he eventually retired.

John E. Swart, the Meteor maintenance superintendent, was the man who kept the over-used World War II aircraft airworthy for Morrow and his pilots. Swart spent almost as much time in foreign locations repairing crippled aircraft as he did in Teterboro. In 1955, he spent several months in the Arctic repairing a DC-3 that had landed on its nose while delivering supplies to the technicians who were installing the U.S. early warning radar system. Once the plane was repaired, Swart flew it back to Teterboro. A few weeks later, he was in a steaming Central American jungle rescuing another Meteor plane. It was all part of the job.

Swart, a Wayne resident, became the service manager for Atlantic Aviation at Teterboro in 1960. He retired in 1983.

Wehran Sells to
the Port Authority

In 1949, seven years after Fred Wehran began operating Teterboro, *Aero Digest* magazine called it "the busiest privately owned air freight terminal in the world" and presented him with its Commendation Award: "The individual airport operator who contributed the most to the development of the air freight industry."

By 1949, the Port of New York Authority (now the Port Authority of New York and New Jersey) had assumed the management of LaGuardia and Newark Airports. As part of a lease with both cities, the agency agreed to make millions of dollars of improvements to the commercial ports. To accomplish this goal, the bi-state agency found it necessary to increase fees to commercial airline tenants, who protested vehemently. The airlines threatened to move from both airports.

As an alternative to LaGuardia and Newark, the air carriers began discussions with Wehran about moving their operations to Teterboro. Realizing that they might lose this battle of wills, the Port Authority also sent emissaries to deal with Wehran. He was flattered by all the attention, and eventually accepted a Port Authority offer of more than $3 million for his airfield. He left with no regrets.

Wehran remained in the land development business — acquiring and selling vast tracts on the border of New Jersey and New York. And he built airports. He later sold the Mahwah, NJ. facility to the Ford Motor Company as a site for an automobile assembly plant. Another in Greenwood Lake, NJ, is still in existence, but Wehran had sold it to a motion picture studio as an adjunct to a wild animal park.

In 1966, at age 66, Wehran decided to learn to fly helicopters, not a simple task for fixed-wing pilots half his age. His first machine was a Bell-47G4A which he used to commute from his farm in Mahwah to his office in Wyckoff, and to survey his many conservation projects in the desolate Ramapo Mountains. Four years later, he advanced to the more powerful Bell JetRanger helicopter.

In 1982, at age 82, Wehran talked about the versatility of a helicopter. "I can go up, down, backward, forward, and I can land on a dime. I won a trophy at an air show in Monticello, NY, in my JetRanger for being the oldest pilot in the show and for doing a helicopter dance — hovering maneuvers, actually. That's why helicopter pilots are called 'hover lovers'."

What the Monticello audience didn't know was that they were watching the oldest, active, certified helicopter pilot in the United States and perhaps in the world perform.

Wehran's helicopter flying days weren't without problems. One day he was practicing an "auto-rotation" (power-off emergency landing technique) in his JetRanger, when his controls jammed and he couldn't regain full power. He was forced to complete his descent all the way to the ground. The jarring impact on the muddy field threw the 'copter off balance and true to its nickname, the machine did some wild "chopping." The blades were smashing against the ground and cutting off pieces of the tail boom. Wehran, trapped inside, feared an explosion. Later, when asked what he was thinking as he awaited his fate, he said, "I couldn't help it. As I watched that last big piece of the tail fly by, I thought, 'My God, there goes $50,000'."

Wehran continued to fly solo to age 86, then one day after a particularly hard landing on his Mahwah helipad, he decided to hire a younger man to fly with him. Shortly thereafter, he was strickened with a heart attack and except for a few joy rides in an open-cockpit biplane, piloted by his friend Dave Mac-Millan, he gave up flying.

In May of 1986, the man with the Midas touch donated $250,000 to the Aviation Hall of Fame & Museum of New Jersey for the expansion of the Garden State's aviation museum's Educational Center. In 1988, the center was named the Fred L. Wehran Pavilion in his honor.

Wehran, at age 91, lives quietly on his Mahwah estate but still enjoys participating in Aviation Hall of Fame affairs.

Port Authority Makes
Improvements

The Port Authority didn't let its new possession wither on the vine. The agency purchased additional meadowland acreage to increase the airport's size to 915 acres. The two north-south runways were extended to 5,000 feet, and by 1955, $7.5 million had been spent on the field. Then the Authority invested $10.5 million to convert Teterboro into a first class general aviation airfield. This again included lengthening the runways and equipping one with instrument landing facilities.

John B. Wilson, a 27-year veteran of the Port Authority, became manager of Teterboro in 1953 and supervised its growth for 15 years. When he retired in 1968, Teterboro was among the nation's busiest airports, handling 279,146 aircraft movements, significantly more than Newark, New Jersey's principal commercial air facility.

In 1970, the Port Authority leased Teterboro to the Metropolitan Air Facilities Division (MAFD) of Pan American World Airways (now Pan Am World Services). In the early 1960s, Juan Trippe, Pan Am's chairman, envisioned the need to create reliever airports in order to siphon ever-increasing business air traffic away from major commercial airports where passenger aircraft were forced to wait in long lines before taking off. Trippe reasoned that if the smaller planes had their own facility they wouldn't be competing with commercial airliners for runway space.

The airline and the Port Authority reached an agreement in 1965 which New Jersey Governor Richard J. Hughes called "ingenious." It emphasized that ownership of the airport should remain in the hands of the Port Authority, but that Pan Am would assume full responsibility for its operation as a public airfield for a period of 30 years. It also stipulated that there would be no operation of fixed-wing aircraft on regular transport schedules. After a number of legal challenges were circumvented, Pan Am officially became the operators on Jan. 1, 1970.

O.J. Studeman was the vice president of the Metropolitan Air Division. A former Pan Am captain, the tall Texan, had been Pan Am's Western Division chief pilot in the early 1940s. During world War II, he was in charge of Pan Am's operations under contract to the Navy in Alaska and the Aleutians. Later, he handled the Pan Am Navy operations in the entire Pacific Theater. Prior to his MAFD assignment, he had managed the company's Latin American operation for 15 years and then was put on special assignment at Pan Am's Guided Missile Range Division at Cape Canaveral, FL.

Under Studeman's supervision, Teterboro's two runways were lengthened and four modern hangars were built at the south end of the airfield. That initial construction opened the airport's south end for further growth as a business aircraft center.

Richard Smith, the first Pan Am Teterboro manager, had spent 25 years in airfield management around the world for Pan Am. Smith's staff included Fred Gammon and Phil Engle who, 20 years later, became Pan Am World Services' vice president and the airport's manager respectively.

The Pan Am Business Jets Division moved its headquarters to Teterboro in 1970, headed by Charles C. Fleming. The division marketed French-built Dassault Falcon Jet business aircraft in the Western Hemisphere. As the then public relations director for both Teterboro-based Pan Am divisions, the author watched the airport and Business Jets grow rapidly, fulfilling Juan Trippe's last imaginative dream of servicing the needs of corporate executives, their aircraft and crews.

Studemann retired in 1972, and was replaced by John P. Kennedy. Under Kennedy's leadership, Teterboro became one of the nation's finest and busiest airports catering to corporate aircraft. In 1983, the FAA reported that Teterboro was not only the busiest (286,184 aircraft movements) airport in New Jersey, but ranked 33rd among all airports in the nation. It was the nation's fourth busiest general aviation facility.

Kennedy had spent the previous six years as the System Director, Facilities and Planning for Eastern Air Lines. He was responsible for the development of plans and implementation of programs to meet Eastern's operating requirements at 94 airports in the United States and Mexico.

During the Kennedy years, Falcon Jet and Aero Services, founded by Orlando "Dit" Panfile, built extensive hangar/office facilities at the south end of the field, and Atlantic Aviation and Teterboro Aircraft Service expanded their facilities along the west side of the historic airport.

More than two dozen Fortune 500 companies house their aircraft at Teterboro and another 200 use the airport's runways on a regular basis. Teterboro is home base for almost 500 business and private aircraft.

Because Teterboro Airport is located in a highly populated area and shares the skies with air traffic from both LaGuardia and Newark Airports, a modern air show in the tradition of the Gates Flying Circus is no longer feasible. The last public aerial demonstration was held at Teterboro in 1973, attended by more than 25,000 people. The highly successful two-day event was organized by a committee of airport operators under the able direction of John Lambiase, the chief of the FAA Flight Service Station, who had served at Teterboro for 15 years.

Teterboro Aircraft Service and School of Aeronautics Prosper

Two organizations that were off-shoots of the Willis Air Service, the Teterboro Aircraft Service (TAS) and Teterboro School of Aeronautics (TSA) continued to grow into the 1990s. As the only two Teterboro tenants with roots that go back to the early days of Fred Wehran's ownership, they are still owned and operated by the same families.

David Van Dyke, was a rough and tumble aircraft mechanic who had spent four years before World War II on the frozen tundra of Alaska, repairing Lockheed 12s and tri-motor Fords for aviation pioneer Noel Wein's Alaska Airlines. Van Dyke and Donald Hulse, whom Van Dyke called "the best accountant to hit this part of the country," were the principal partners in the school, aircraft maintenance shop and flight school that had belonged to Charles Willis. Hulse was president of the school and Van Dyke ran TAS.

Their first move was to trade the large hangar (that Willis had occupied, but the new team couldn't afford) to Bob Morrow, president of Meteor Aircraft, for one considerably smaller. From there, they ran the three businesses. "We were badly cramped for quarters," Van Dyke recalled, "but we began making money and once the Port Authority agreed to let us expand, we built the present TAS hangar."

At that point, Tony DiStefano was the school's director, assisted by Joe Bischoff. Carl Grimpe was the flight school's chief pilot, assisted by the Johnson brothers, Charles and Hank. Lou Ranley had office space as the FAA flight examiner.

In 1971, following the redesigning of a large factory building at the south end of the airport by Pan Am World Services, the Teterboro School moved into 44,000 square feet of the new facility, known as the Pan Am Building, more than doubling its previous space.

Hulse and Van Dyke severed their partnership in 1973, the same year the school received accreditation by the National Association of Trade & Technical Schools. Hulse continued as president of the school.

In January of 1974, the school enrolled its first students in a newly formed electronic division and in 1981 a joint program between TSA and Bergen Community College leading to an Associate Degree in Applied Science was begun. More than 12,000 technicians have graduated from TSA since its meager beginning in 1947.

In 1975, Van Dyke began negotiations with the EXXON corporation to become the third AVITAT terminal in North America. The TAS hangar was expanded in 1976. It provided complete ground services for pilots, executives and aircraft to the standards of excellence EXXON required of all AVITAT installations.

In January 1975, the flight division, which had operated out of the TAS hangar, was sold to John and Tony Habermann, operators of the Teterboro Flight Academy. The flight school was then moved to the east side of the airport in the early 1980s.

Now both well into their fourth decade as viable entities at Teterboro Airport, TAS and TSA continue as family-run businesses. When Don Hulse died in 1979, Don Jr. assumed the presidency of the school. Dave Van Dyke continued as the head of TAS, but his sons David and Frank manage the daily operation.

John M. Habermann

Inducted Aviation Hall of Fame of New Jersey, 1991

Thousands of private, commercial and military pilots were trained and licensed by John Habermann since 1966 when he and his brother, Tony, established a flight school at Morristown Airport with just three aircraft. The operation moved to Teterboro Airport in 1968 and over the years, their fleet increased to 25 planes.

In 1971, John Habermann was appointed as an FAA Pilot Examiner, authorized to conduct private, commercial, instrument, multi-engine and airline transport pilot rating exams. In 20 years, he licensed more than 3,500 pilots and conducted in excess of 2,500 safety and bi-annual flight checks.

Born and raised in Guttenberg, NJ, Habermann began his aviation career in 1950. After a stint aboard a Navy destroyer during the Korean War, he worked at various North Jersey airports as a charter and corporate pilot and flight instructor. For a short period in the early 1960s, he flew C-46s throughout the mid-west for Zantop Air Transport, located in Detroit.

Teterboro veterans: Tony and John Habermann, Lou Ranley and Ben Rock.

Upon returning to New Jersey, he became chief pilot for Chatham Aviation at Morristown Airport and developed the largest flight training school in the northeast. He also began a charter department that served many international corporations in the area, and one of the first commuter airlines in the country, connection Morristown with the major New York airports.

As the co-owner of the Teterboro Flight Academy, Habermann and his pilots participated in numerous fund raising and community events and took an active role in promoting aviation in local schools.

In 1989, the Habermann brothers sold the flight academy ad established Metro Aviation Testing, an FAA authorized organization that gives flight and written exams to pilots who wish to upgrade their ratings.

Pan American Sells World Services

In May of 1989, Pan American World Airways sold its World Services Division to Johnson Controls, a Milwaukee-based conglomerate. The new Johnson Aviation Division was still known as World Services and Fred Gammon remained as operational vice president.

1946
Second Director of Aviation
Robert L. Copsey

Inducted Aviation Hall of Fame of New Jersey, 1981

Early in 1946, Robert L. Copsey became the director of the New Jersey Bureau of Aviation succeeding Gill Robb Wilson who had held the post since the bureau was founded in 1931. The tall, raw-boned Nebraska native, came to New Jersey in 1928 as vice president of the Newark Air Service and the first manager of Newark Airport. A founding member of the 119th Observation Squadron, New Jersey National Guard, the former World War I pilot served first as the organization's operations officer and later as its commander.

In 1926, he gave up barnstorming across the nation to become one of the first Bureau of Air Commerce (BAC) inspectors. His pilot's license was the 29th issued by the BAC.

Copsey was with Charles Lindbergh on the night before the Lone Eagle's historic flight across the Atlantic in May of 1927 attempting to convince his old friend not to make the dangerous flight. This is how he remembered that night:

"I knew Slim — that's what we called Lindbergh — when he was flying the mail from St. Louis to Chicago. On the night of May 19-20, before he took off, I was with him in the Half Moon Hotel at Coney Island. I was in his room until about two in the morning, and I did my damndest to keep him from going. I was absolutely positive he wasn't going to make it. It was going to be a long flight, with uncertain weather, and he would be riding on a flying fuel tank."

At 7 a.m. on the morning of the 20th, Copsey and other friends at Roosevelt Field, pushed the *Spirit of St. Louis* up a dirt ramp at the runway's end to give the plane extra momentum on take off.

"He couldn't have had more than three or four hours of sleep," Copsey remembered, "but he was going in spite of all hell and high water. Even using the ramp, his plane barely cleared the electric wires as it lifted off."

Recalled to active duty in 1942 as a lieutenant colonel, Copsey became the commanding officer of Baer Field at Fort Wayne, IN. A year later he commanded the 1st Troop Carrier Command, headquartered in Indianapolis.

After the war, he returned to his family in Summit, NJ, and accepted the job with the Bureau of Aviation when his predecessor, Wilson, became an aviation columnist with the *New York Herald Tribune*.

Copsey took a leave of absence from his post to go on active duty with the Air Force during the Korean War, this time with the rank of major general. He served until 1955, first as chief of reserve affairs at the Pentagon in Washington, DC, and then as base commander at the Fort Bragg Air Base in North Carolina. During his five-year absence, Frank E. Kimble was acting director of the Bureau.

Humorist Will Rogers and Bob Copsey.

In 1955, he retired from the Air Force and returned to his duties in New Jersey. He stayed on until 1961 when he retired permanently to Colorado Springs, CO, the home of the United States Air Force Academy. There he played golf and watched proudly as young airmen matured as pilots flying in pressurized cockpits, surrounded by a galaxy of instruments in super-charged aircraft.

"At times it makes me a little sad to see the evolution of pilots from individualists into today's highly disciplined and controlled monitors of electronic devices," the Hall of Fame pioneer said a few years before he died in 1987 at age 91. "I have the greatest respect for their ability, but they will never know the freedom that was so precious to the men who flew the Jennies."

Airwork Corporation

In May of 1946, the secretary of War issued an interim permit to the city of Millville, NJ, to use the former Millville Air Base, opened during World War II, as a municipal airport. At the same time, two former veterans of the war were looking for an airport to establish an aircraft engine overhaul station that would become known as the Airwork Corporation.

The idea for an engine overhaul facility was born in the mind of Major Josiah Thompson II, while serving in the Army Air Corps at Wright Field in Dayton, OH. Thompson, a graduate of Yale University and Babson Business School, foresaw that there would be thousands of transport aircraft in the skies immediately after the war, but only government-owned overhaul facilities. He also knew that aircraft engine manufacturers were planning to enter the jet age and had little interest in supporting wartime piston engines.

Immediately upon discharge, Thompson surveyed the airlines and discovered a desire on their part to subcontract engine overhaul work. His original idea seemed to have merit, so he convinced Francis L. Hine, who later became president of Airwork, to join in the project. They were soon joined by Captain Thomas Dickson Jr., a former maintenance officer in the 4th Ferrying Division, and David Dows Jr., who was a captain and pilot in the Air Transport Command, and a close friend of Thompson. Col. Paul D. Meyers was next to join the group. He held pilot's license No. 23, was a former pilot in the French Aero Squadron in World War I, and a member of Gen. Claire Clennault's staff as base commander in Kunming, China during World War II. By coincidence, he had served as the commanding officer of the Millville Air Base before being sent to China.

How Millville became the Airwork base of operations shows that truth is stranger than fiction at times. Thompson and Hines were in the Millville area in the summer of 1946 looking for a suitable site for their embryo company. They stopped in Kreamer's Pharmacy on Main Street, for a soft drink. At the counter they discussed a number of possible locations they had already surveyed. The clerk over hearing their conversation, mentioned there was a former military airport just outside of town now run by the city. When they arrived at the site, they found a deserted $5 million former fighter base with two 5,000 foot runways in excellent condition. The men worked out a 15-year lease with the city on several warehouses full of cobwebs and dust, and with a large amount of hope and youthful enthusiasm began preparing their facility for a November 18, 1946 opening.

Because there were few experienced aircraft mechanics in the Millville area, Tom Dickson and "Mac" McKercher set up a classroom in the shop, heated by a pot-bellied coal stove, and began teaching on borrowed engines.

The toughest job fell to Paul Meyers. He had to sell the first engine overhaul job by the untried firm with the nation's most inexperienced crew to a corporate customer. But sell it he did, and Airwork was on its way.

Airworks first volume contract for the overhaul of TWA's Pratt & Whitney engines came in March 1947. The engines were used on DC-4s which were flying the Atlantic in 17 hours at that time. Business continued to grow and in 1949, Jerry Church opened the first Airwork distribution branch in Miami, FL. In the 1950s, they expanded their operation to include overhaul of turboprop engines and by the mid-1960s, the company moved into the pure jet field.

In 1968, Airwork Corp. was sold to Purex Corporation, Ltd. and the name was changed to Airwork Service Division of the Purex Aviation Group.

Moving into its 45th year of operation, Airwork still maintains a fly-in service hangar at Millville Airport for the convenience of its customers. Each month more than 50 airplanes fly into Millville for engine service work. In addition, Airwork has overhaul and repair facilities in Miami, Westbury, Long Island; Dayton, OH; Wichita, KS and Houston, TX. There are more than 700 Airwork employees, approximately 550 of whom are in Millville, which makes the company a leading employer in the city.

Airwork holds engine troubleshooting and line maintenance schools that attract over 1,000 mechanics to Millville every year to refresh and upgrade their capabilities.

More than 80 leading Fixed Base Operators throughout the United States and Canada are part of the company's Turbine Service Network, authorized to sell and service engines from Airwork.

Airwork has built its nationwide reputation on prompt efficient service and a willingness to go beyond the normal to service its customers. In Millville, they tell the story of a phone call that came after plant hours from an aircraft operator who needed an engine. Because all but the executive staff had left, the president drove six hours to deliver the engine in the company's old truck which was originally used in a coal mine.

Morristown Assumes Control

Morristown had another of the airports that had been constructed during World War II, although it had been in the planning for more than a decade before.

As early as 1931, Morristown's mayor, Clyde Potts, and the Town's Aldermen, were aggressively seeking help from the Department of Commerce to construct a municipal airport in an area known as the Normandy Water Company tract. Although there were numerous studies done throughout the 1930s, including an examination of the area by Dr. Hugo Eckener, the president of the German Zeppelin Co., as a possible international dirigible landing site, the airport did not become a reality until the Army Air Corps leased the land and constructed an air base there.

In 1946, the facility was turned over to the city. At the official opening, three military pilots, all residents of Morristown, flew AT-6s from Washington, DC, and landed in formation on the new municipal runways. The pilots were Malcolm McAlpin, B.E. Billings and Edward K. Mills, who became the airport's first manager.

Early Operators

The first operators to use the new facility were: the Morristown Airport Corp., headed by Mills, Macrombie Airways, under the direction of McAlpin, the Colonial School of Aviation, managed by Charles Becker, John Hilton's Flying Service, and Morristown Airways, operated by Thomas Wear.

Allan Heinsohn became the airport's manager in the late 1940s, a position he held for a decade. It was during that period, that Edward Mills served as mayor of Morristown.

Corporate Facilities

In the late 1980s, the 625-acre airport was the third busiest in New Jersey. As more and more corporations moved their headquarters from congested cities to the more rural areas like those surrounding Morristown, aircraft representing corporate giants like AT&T, Schering-Plough, Warner-Lambert and Nabisco used the airport as a home base. Chatham Aviation, a fixed base operator at the field, was owned by George Mennen of the Mennen toiletry company.

As the last decade of the century dawns, airports like Morristown, Teterboro, Atlantic City, and Essex County, along with Newark, seem to have the best chance to survive the ever expanding building boom in the Garden State.

1947
Sound Barrier Shattered
Captain Charles Yeager

It was a cool, clear morning when the specially modified B-29, carrying a small, orange plane under its wing, lifted off the desert runway at Muroc Air Force Base, CA. The huge bomber climbed easily to 35,000 feet with its strange cargo, and once it had leveled off, Capt. Charles "Chuck" Yeager of the U.S. Air Force climbed down from the bomb bay, buffeted by a 240-knot slipstream, and settled into the tight cockpit of the plane with the words "Glamorous Glennis" emblazoned on its needle nose. When his harness was securely fastened, Yeager signaled and the Bell X-1 was released from its mother craft.

The little bird dropped like a bomb until Yeager put the powerful 6,000-thrust, liquid oxygen-alcohol rocket engine into motion. Then it shot ahead at an amazing rate of speed.

Propelled by a single rocket engine developed and built by Reaction Motors in Denville, the X-1 became the first aircraft in history to fly faster than the speed of sound. Considered an invisible wall in the sky, the "sound barrier," that many men of science had thought to be impenetrable had finally been shattered by one brave man, an exceptionally aerodynamic airplane and a rocket engine created by New Jersey engineers and technicians.

Yeager said years later, "People were real surprised that we had done it, and to find that my ears didn't fall off or anything else."

The fascinating details of Yeager's historic flight through the sound barrier have been told in several books and motion pictures. By the time he retired from active duty with the Air Force in 1975 as a two-star general, he had become a legendary figure. Not only had he flown the volatile X-1 faster than the speed of sound, he did it with several broken ribs.

Two nights before his powered flight in the small orange rocket plane, Yeager and his wife Glennis had gone to Pancho Barnes' "The Happy Bottom Riding Club" for dinner. Barnes' club, a favorite hang-out of the test pilots stationed at the Muroc Air Base (now Edwards Air Force Base), was a dude ranch, and following dinner, Yeager asked his wife if she'd like to go for a horseback ride into the Mojave Desert.

They rode for about an hour before deciding to race back to the stable. Yeager was in the lead at an all-out gallop as they approached the gate to the ranch property which someone had closed while they were away. In the darkness Yeager didn't see the gate and his horse ran headlong into it. He was thrown roughly to the ground, and as he explained later "I was knocked silly."

Glennis Yeager realized her husband had broken a rib and insisted he go to the base hospital for repairs. He refused for fear of being grounded by the flight surgeon. The next morning, Glennis took him to a private doctor who strapped up his ribs. He then reported to the base and told his best friend and fellow test pilot, Jack Ridley, his problem. By using a short piece of a broom stick, they devised a way for Yeager to shut the cockpit door of the X-1 after he had climbed down the ladder from the mother ship.

In his autobiography, *Yeager,* published by Bantam Books, Inc. in July 1985, he described what happened at that point.

"Going down that damned ladder hurt. Jack was right behind me. As usual, I slid feet-first into the cabin. I picked up the broom handle and waited while Ridley pushed the door against the frame, then I slipped it into the door handle and raised it up into lock position. It worked perfectly. Then I settled in to go over my checklist. Bob Cardenas, the B-29 driver, asked if I was ready.

"Hell, yes," I said. "Let's get it over with." He dropped the X-1 at 20,000 feet, but his dive speed was once again too slow and the X-1 started to stall. I fought it with the control wheel for about five hundred feet, and finally got her nose down. The moment we picked up speed I fired all four rocket chambers in rapid sequence. We climbed at .88 Mach and began to buffet, so I flipped on the stabilizer switch and changed the setting two degrees. We smoothed right out, and at 36,000 feet, I turned off two rocket chambers. At 40,000 feet, we were still climbing at a speed of .92 Mach. Leveling off at 42,000 feet, I had thirty percent

Reaction Motors' XLR 99 rocket engine production line, Denville, NJ. Engine powered X-15

of my fuel, so I turned on rocket chamber three and immediately reached 96 Mach. I noticed that the faster I got, the smoother the ride.

"Suddenly the Mach needle began to fluctuate. It went up to .965 Mach — then tipped right off the scale. I thought I was seeing things! We were flying supersonic! And it was as smooth as a baby's bottom: Grandma could be sitting up there sipping lemonade. I kept the speed off the scale for about twenty seconds, then raised the nose to slow down."

Breaking the sound barrier was a top secret accomplishment. No announcement of the event was made to the general public for eight months. Then Yeager became a national hero and major publications offered to buy his story. His superior officer, Col. Albert Boyd, strictly forbade any of the test pilots from accepting remuneration from commercial ventures, so Yeager continued to survive on his Air Force pay.

If Yeager couldn't cash in on his personal achievements and the success of the X-1 flight, Reaction Motors could. In just six short years, the New Jersey firm had created a rocket engine that could be controlled by man. Supersonic aircraft designers were knocking at the company's door looking for bigger and better engines to propel their planes. The Denville company was riding high.

Reaction Motors Inc.

Just nine days after the Japanese attack on Pearl Harbor, four men incorporated a company they named Reaction Motors, Inc. (RMI). The corporation's sole asset was one Liquid Fuel Rocket Motor, developed by one of the partners, James H. Wyld. The name of the company had been chosen by Wyld, who hoped his rocket company would eventually be compared to General Motors.

"The analogy was not very close," he said in later years, "as we had scarcely two nickels to rub together and our plant consisted mostly of half of the upper floor of John Shesta's [another partner] brother-in-law's garage in North Arlington, NJ, which was about as large as a rather spacious outhouse."

Lovell Lawrence Jr., H. Franklin Pierce, Shesta and Wyld were rocket enthusiasts in the late 1930s who had come together through the American Rocket Society. Many of their early rockets were fired in a concrete block house they had constructed in Franklin Lakes, adjacent to the 800-foot runways of Nelson's Airport.

Lawrence was named president of the new company. He was a graduate of Montclair State College and had worked for years as an engineer with IBM. Pierce, the new vice president and head of test engineering, had been a machinist in the U.S. Navy and with the New York City Interborough Rapid Transit subway system. John Shesta, a graduate of Columbia University, was the company's treasurer and director of research and engineering. He had taught engineering and worked in that field before joining RMI. Wyld, a Princeton University man, was the company's secretary and chief research engineer.

In early 1942, the partners sold a 445 N (100 lb.) thrust, liquid oxygen-alcohol rocket engine to the Navy for $5,000 and established their new business in a rented building in Pompton Lakes. Their first employees were Louis Arata, Charles Dimmick, Leslie Collins and Kirt Fischer.

By November of that year, they had developed an engine with 4,450 N (1,000 lb.) thrust to fulfill another Navy contract. Years later Lawrence described those times as "a hectic era that can never be duplicated."

"Can you imagine men working for months on their own time at their own expense to build a rocket that blew up during its first two seconds of testing?" he asked. "We were chased by the police (when testing the noisy engines), caused grass fires and sometimes drew crowds when the word got out there might be a test firing.

"We had our rocket test stand on a two-wheel trailer so we could move it from place to place by automobile to stay away from the police," he recalled.

The high point in their early experiments came in 1941 when Wyld tested a regenerative engine — a rocket that uses fuel for cooling. "It ran three times at two minutes each," Lawrence explained. "Up to that time 30 seconds was a long run. That is when we decided there was a future for rockets. Our idea was that they could give a fighter plane or bomber a short burst of speed to get out of trouble."

Realizing their facilities were completely inadequate for their growing business, the partners moved into a three-story building in Pompton Plains that had been a silver factory dating back to the late 1800s, and later, a former night club called "The Silver Circle." Behind the building, they constructed three test stands to fire their rockets and continued to use the old block house in Franklin Lakes for other experiments. It was there that they began testing the four-chamber, 26,700 N (6,000 lb.) thrust aircraft engines that would eventually bring them worldwide recognition. By then, Al Africano, Roy Healy and Bob Truax had joined the small staff of experimenters.

During that period, Reaction Motors was asked to solve a critical problem in cleaning and repairing aircraft superchargers. "It only took us a couple of weeks to design the equipment," Lawrence remembered. "Then the Army Air Corps offered us a $20 million contract to produce it."

The partners had no idea how to set up a production line so Lawrence turned down the $20 million offer.

A rocket motor plant is not the best neighbor, and soon the roar of the test engines brought complaints. A petition was circulated among the neighbors demanding that the testing be stopped. The town council agreed that rocket testing was not appropriate in a residential area. So in 1946, the company moved into two large buildings adjacent to the U.S. Naval Ammunition Supply Depot at Lake Denmark, NJ, a completely secluded area near Dover, insulated by thousands of acres of government property. Three years later, the RMI administrative, personnel, finance and manufacturing components of the company moved to nearby Denville. At that point, RMI had 650 employees, a substantial staff when compared with the 20 employees on the payroll in 1943.

From a humble beginning, RMI established many "firsts" in the world of rocketry. It was the first American corporation dedicated solely to the development of liquid rocket engines and accessory equipment; the first to develop a regenerative cooled liquid rocket engine generating 1,000 pounds of thrust using liquid oxygen and alcohol propellants and the first to develop a similar engine generating 3,000 pounds of thrust using liquid oxygen and gasoline propellants. That rocket JATO unit was first used by the Navy in 1943 on the Martin PBM flying boats as an assist-take-off unit.

"Those rockets we made in New Jersey are the ancestors of the rockets that were used in the Apollo program," Lawrence said. "The 150-pound thrust regenerative engine we first tested was the same type engine used to develop 7.5 million pounds of thrust in a Saturn 5 missile."

"We also developed the first throttleable rocket engine. This is what the astronauts used for the moon landing, varying their power as they looked for a landing site."

From 1946 through the early 1960s, RMI introduced more powerful engines on a regular basis. It was a 6,000 pound thrust engine that pushed Chuck Yeager through the sonic barrier.

Four years later a RMI 6,000 series engine powered the Navy's piloted research aircraft, the "Skyrocket," to over 1,200 miles per hour and up to an altitude of 80,000 feet. The Air Force Bell X-IA exceeded 1,650 miles per hour in level flight in 1953.

In May of 1958, RMI merged with The Thiokol Corporation.

A year later in June, another "famous first" took place at Edwards Air Force Base in California. An experimental aircraft designated the North American X-15, equipped with two 6,000 series liquid rocket engines, was launched from the wing of an Air Force B-52 bomber. That first glide flight was flown by civilian test pilot Scott Crossfield. Three months later Crossfield flew the X-15 at Mach 2.11 (1,393 mph) on its first powered flight. The first 20 flights of the X-15 were made with the 6,000 series engine while the men and women in Denville put the final touches on the large XL99 throttleable engine that pushed the sleek black plane to even greater heights.

When the new engine was installed in the X-15, Crossfield flew the ship at 1,960 mph to an altitude of 81,200 feet in November of 1960.

In his book, *Always Another Dawn*, Crossfield described the awesome power of the XL99 engine: *The one fact that made the X-15 far from conventional was the power-plant. It was not shown in detail on the drawings, but the entry on the specification sheet told all: "ENGINE. REACTION MOTORS, INC. XLR-99. THRUST 57,000 POUNDS AT 40,000 FEET ALTITUDE." Like the engine in the X-2, this engine was to be throttleable; it had nine times the power of the Reaction Motors engine in the X-1 or skyrocket. It would generate nearly one million horsepower, or as much power as seven Navy cruisers. On a shallow, ballistic-flight profile, it would hurtle the X-15 to a maximum speed of 7200 feet per second, which is over a mile and a quarter a second, 75 miles a minute, and better than 4500 miles an hour or about Mach 7.0, twice as fast as man had ever flown. On a "zoom," or steep ballistic-flight profile, the powerful engine could boost the X-15 to an altitude above 250,000 feet, twice as high as man had ever flown. In between those extremes, the X-15, could explore more unknown areas than all the research airplanes in history, and then some.*

Over the next two years, the X-15, powered by New Jersey engines was flown in excess of 4,000 miles per hour and into the lower reaches of space by NASA pilots Crossfield, J.A. Walker and Air Force Major R.M. White.

On June 27, 1962, Walker flew at the incredible speed of 4,104 mph. On July 17, 1962, White flew to an altitude of 313,750 feet, the first aircraft flight above 300,000 feet (59.6 miles). That achievement qualified White as an astronaut because he flew more than 50 miles into the atmosphere. A year later, Walker flew up 354,200 feet (67 miles) so America had two astronauts before the first spacecraft was launched thanks to the scientists and engineers in Denville, NJ.

Around the World in Piper Super Cruisers

The *New York Times* reported the take-off of the round-the-world flight of Clifford Evans and George Truman from Teterboro Airport in its Sunday Edition, August 10, 1947:

Two light single-engined planes of a type that usually venture no farther than the next airport took off from the Air Terminal here this morning en-route to Goose Bay, Labrador, on the first leg of a round-the-world flight.

At the controls of the red-and-cream Piper Cub Super Cruisers were George W. Truman, 39, of Los Angeles, and Clifford V. Evans, 26, a former Army Air Force pilot of Washington.

Mr. Truman's tiny plane left the ground at 11:10 a.m. and was followed seconds later by Mr. Evan's plane. The two aircraft circled the field once, dipped their wings to a group of well-wishers alongside the runway and turned northeast for the 1,050-mile flight that was to take about ten or eleven hours, the fliers estimated.

If not for the newsreel cameramen and the fact that both pilots kissed their wives good-bye, it would have been difficult to distinguish the takeoff from the scores of flights from here daily by private pilots, many of whom putt-putt around the metropolitan area in the same model airplane. Another difference was the takeoff itself, when the planes used considerably more of the runway than used normally by light planes.

At takeoff, the planes' gross weight was 2,108 pounds, exceeding the routine takeoff gross load of the model by 430 pounds. Most of the extra weight was the fuel. Each plane carried 138 gallons, 100 more than standard.

Both pilots took along sandwiches and a bottle of coffee. There was no room for parachutes, although each plane carries an emergency life raft.

The two fliers expect to circle the globe from four to six weeks. Their 22,000-mile route will carry them to Iceland, England, France, Italy, North Africa, Iraq, India, Burma, China, Japan and back to the United States by way of Alaska.

Cruising at an economical speed, the pilots plan to push along at about 100 miles an hour. The planes are powered by 100-horsepower Lycoming engines. This is about half the horsepower of Lindbergh's Spirit of St. Louis.

The tiny cockpits of the air "flivvers" were crammed with radio equipment navigational aids and chart cases. The pilots plan to fly close together, one monitoring the other's course for added safety and economy in fuel.

The planes have a range of 2,600 miles. The longest overwater flight along the route is the 1,850-mile hop from Hokkaido, northern-most island in the Japanese chain, to Attu in the Aleutians. Other stages of the flight vary in length from 200 miles to 1,000.

"We're going to take our time and see the sights," Mr. Evans said this morning. "Like regular tourists"

On December 10, the two Piper Super Cruisers landed back at Teterboro at 10:12 a.m. Evans and Truman had flown 25,162 miles around-the-world in 123 days, a feat that had never been accomplished in light airplanes. The small planes had been escorted into Teterboro by nine AT-6 aircraft belonging to the Air Force Reserve based at Newark Airport. Fred Wehran, the owner of Teterboro, and Col.Robert L. Copsey, the New Jersey Director of Aviation who represented Governor Alfred Driscoll, were among the throng of 2,000 people to greet the intrepid fliers.

Evans and Truman reported that they had made 49 stops and visited 23 nations during the circumnavigation of the globe. The first flight around the world in 1924 by three Douglas World Cruisers, one of which was flown by Leslie Arnold, took 175 days to travel 27,553 miles.

Teterboro was chosen as the starting point of the flight because Safair Inc., the leading Piper distributor on the East Coast, had a fixed base operation at the airport. Safair mechanics under the watchful eye of owner, O.P. "Ted" Hebert, and maintenance supervisor, Henry Geleski, prepared the two planes for their long flight.

Evans and Truman, both Air Force veterans, were working as flight instructors for the Brinckerhoff Flying Service at College Park Airport in Maryland when they decided to attempt the long flight. After months of careful planning and the donation of two used Super Cruisers by the Piper Aircraft Company, the two men, who Piper president, William T. Piper asked, "Why in the hell do you fellows want to make a fool trip like this?" left Teterboro confident that they would accomplish their mission. At least six times during the long flight, the duo were buffeted by gale-force winds, including a typhoon over the Formosa Straits which grounded them for six days.

Following the flight Truman was quoted as saying, "There are probably 10,000 pilots in the country who could do what we have done if they were careful. That's about all we were trying to prove."

While in Shanghai, China, the intrepid airmen spent a few days with Gen. Claire Chennault, the former commander of the Flying Tigers, who had retired from the Air Corps and was directing China's Civil Air Transport. The general asked them to stay in China and fly with his airline. At the time, they declined, but in less than a year, Evans returned to China and flew for Chennault. He died in 1975. His Piper, *City of Washington,* is on display in the National Air and Space Museum's Garber Facility in Suitland, Maryland. Truman died in 1986.

O. P. "Ted" Hebert

Inducted Aviation Hall of Fame of New Jersey, 1975

O.P."Ted" Hebert learned to fly at Calstrom Field, FL, in 1921 while serving in the U.S. Army Air Corps. The following year, he graduated as a 2nd lieutenant from flight school at Kelly Field, TX. Assigned to the Aberdeen Proving Grounds in Maryland, he flew an as-

"Ted" Hebert

sortment of World War I planes while working on the development of ordinance and weapons. It was during that period that Hebert first visited the grass strip at Teterboro Airport to accept DH-4s that had been modified by the Wittemann Aircraft Corp.

Upon leaving the military in January 1929, Hebert joined the Curtiss Flying School in Michigan as an aerobatic instructor. In 1933, he co-founded the Pacific Seaboard Airline, a West Coast commuter air service, and the following year, he won the bid for the first commercial air mail route between Chicago and New Orleans.

He moved east in 1935 and established Safair, Inc., a flight school, at Roosevelt Field, Long Island. During that period, he instructed Thor Solberg, prior to Solberg's flight from New York to Oslo, Norway in 1935. He also gave instrument and navigational training to Douglas "Wrong Way" Corrigan, the young man who flew the Atlantic without government approval in 1938.

His operation stayed on Long Island until 1942, when wartime flying restrictions forced him to move the flight training program to Blairstown, NJ, and Sunbury, PA. At those locations, he ran a government sponsored Civilian Pilot Training program in conjunction with New York University.

At war's end, Hebert moved Safair to Teterboro Airport. Over the years, the company was the distributor for Piper, Republic Seabee, Globe Swift, Rockwell Commanders and the Stinson line of aircraft.

In the 1970's, Hebert expanded his operation to the Essex County Airport in Fairfield, NJ. Both FBOs were disbanded when he retired in the early 1980s.

When one of his veteran employees was asked what he remembered most about Ted Hebert, he replied: "Tell them that this man in 46 years as an aviation entrepreneur never failed to meet a payroll."

O.P. "Ted" Hebert died in May of 1989.

McGuire Air Force Base

On Sept 17, 1949, the Fort Dix Army Air Base was renamed the McGuire Air Force Base in honor of Thomas B. McGuire Jr., a Ridgewood, NJ, native, a World War II Medal of Honor winner and America's second all-time leading flying ace.

The air base had its beginnings in 1937 as a single sod runway on property owned and maintained by the U.S. Army, adjacent to Fort Dix, near Wrightstown, NJ. As war clouds loomed on the horizon in 1940, the Army acquired 17,000 additional acres for the airport and paved runways were installed.

By 1942, the Fort Dix Army Airfield was a beehive of activity. The Anti-Submarine Command's B-25s moved onto the field, and the base provided for the overhaul, servicing and preparing of aircraft for overseas shipment. Parachute jump training and a secret mission for the development of guided missiles were all part of the activity.

In 1945, the air base was the western terminus for the return of wounded military personnel from Europe, and for returning veterans, who were then flown to separation centers throughout the United States.

When the field became the McGuire Air Force base in 1949, the 91st Reconnaissance Squadron occupied the field until the 52nd Fighter Interception Squadron moved in. Then the air base became the home of the 611th Military Air Transport Wing (MATS). In 1954 C-118 aircraft arrived with the 18th and 30th Air Transport Squadrons.

By the late 1980s, McGuire Air Force Base occupied 4,000 acres in Burlington County. Like a small city, it had a population of 5,200 military and 2,000 civilian personnel with approximately 8,500 dependents. One of the 22 major tenant organizations based at McGuire was the New Jersey Air National Guard. The Guard had been organized at Newark Airport and was based there until 1965.

An appropriate memorial to Major Thomas McGuire, a P-38 fighter plane painted with the same markings as those on the plane he flew in combat, was erected on a pedestal in the center of a traffic circle near the main gate of the base .

It had been through the determined efforts of William J. Demas of Wrightstown, that money was raised for the memorial. Demas had negotiated with the Smithsonian's Air and Space Museum for the P-38, one of only five left in the world in flying condition. It was flown from California. Then, under the direction of Lt. Patricia Harem at McGuire, the fuselage was stripped to its original aluminum finish. The words "Pudgy V" (a term of endearment to McGuire's wife) and 38 Japanese flags representing the planes the ace shot down were painted on the fuselage. The plane was then ready to mount.

On May 5, 1982 the P-38 memorial was dedicated. Present at the ceremony were U.S. Secretary of Defense Caspar W. Weinberger, U.S. Rep. H. James Saxton, (R-13) Gov. Thomas H. Kean and Marilynn Beatty, formerly Mrs. Thomas B. McGuire.

Standing on the sidelines that day was F.J. Kish, who had been McGuire's crew chief in the Pacific. To reporters he told the story of McGuire's last evening alive.

"Tommy was due to go back to the States in a week," he said. "He had hoped to bag enough Japanese planes the next day to assure himself of the 'leading ace' title.

"He told me that he wasn't taking his own plane up, but some other fellow's, and I said to him 'Major, why change horses in the middle of the stream?' You know what he said to me then? He said he thought he'd pushed his luck in 'Pudgy' and that his number might be up."

Kish was at another airfield the next morning when McGuire took off. When Kish returned later, a fellow mechanic called him over, placed a hand on his shoulder and said, "Your boy's not coming back."

The year the memorial was dedicated, the people of Ridgewood, under the leadership of Dr. Anthony Cipriano and Gerald DeSimone, raised funds for the creation of a bronze bust of McGuire and donated it to the small museum dedicated to the ace's memory in the Welcome Center at the Air Force base. At the presentation, in January of 1983, Col. Larry D. Wright, Commander of the 438th Military Airlift Wing Command, said:

"A country which has no heroes is wanting. A country which has heroes but forgets them is sorry. With this presentation here today, we can be assured that this hero will not be forgotten."

Hawaii to Teterboro Nonstop

William P. Odom

On March 7 and 8, 1949, newspapers across the nation followed the exploits of William P. "Bill" Odom as he attempted to fly a small, single-engine Beech Bonanza more than 5,000 miles nonstop from Hawaii to the Teterboro Air Terminal on the East Coast of the United States. He had first attempted the flight in January of 1949, but a fuel problem forced him to abort the flight in Oakland, CA.

He had left Honolulu on his record-breaking flight at five minutes past midnight on March 7. Thirty-four hours later, as he passed over Cleveland, OH, he reported he had just finished shaving and changing his suit. "I feel pretty good at the moment," he said, "I've never had to fight sleep as I have this time."

When the Bonanza "Waikiki Beech" set down on the wide Teterboro runway at 12:05 p.m. March 8, exactly 36 hours after its departure from Hawaii, there was less than 16 gallons of fuel remaining in its tanks. The airplane had flown a total of 4,957 miles to establish the international distance record for light airplanes.

When the bonanza rolled to a stop, Odom was almost mobbed by a welcoming crowd of thousands. "If it had not been for the fuel-consuming detour over the Rockies, necessitated by weather, we could have flown an additional 1,000 miles," Odom told the exuberant crowd. "The Waikiki Beech functioned perfectly throughout the entire flight. In spite of the extreme conditions through which we at times flew, there was never a time when the slightest mechanical difficulty was experienced."

Later in the month, the National Aeronautics Association in Washington, DC, declared that Odom's flight was the greatest nonstop, solo flight in history. He exceeded Wiley Post's New York-to-Berlin flight by almost 1,000 miles.

Odom, a World War II pilot, was no stranger to long distance flights. In April of 1947, he had flown around the world in a modified Douglas A-26 twin-engine bomber. The flight had been sponsored by Milton Reynolds, a Chicago pen manufacturer. Reynolds and flight engineer, Carroll "Tex" Sallee, accompanied Odom on the flight.

The A-26, christened "Bombshell," had been modified at Teterboro Airport. Both Odom and Reynolds supervised the work. The long flight began and ended at Chicago.

The Bombshell established a record of 78 hours, 55 minutes and 26 seconds — 12 hours faster than the previous record set by Howard Hughes and his crew of four in 1938.

Odom was at the controls of the bomber every minute of the flight and he did all the navigating. Frederick Graham, a *New York Times* columnist said of Odom, "He must be considered a great pilot and navigator and one of the iron men of the cockpit."

In mid-August of the same year, Odom broke his own record by again circumnavigating the world in the Bombshell. This time it was a solo flight completed in just under 73 hours.

The dapper Odom had become New Jersey's leading aviation celebrity. He established the Bill Odom Aviation Corp. in a modern hangar/office building with its own restaurant, on the northeast corner of Teterboro Airport where the Goodyear blimp hangar once stood. His executive charter fleet consisted of three Beech Bonanzas and a Lockheed Lodestar.

George Kaminus was the company's chief pilot. A troop transport pilot in the Pacific area during World War II, Kaminus had three years experience flying for American Airlines. "Tex" Sallee was Odom's maintenance head.

The 1949, Hawaii to Teterboro flight added to Odom's fame and he began planning for a round-the-world flight from Pole to Pole. Long distance flights were

Bill O'dom

what he did best and they kept him in the spotlight, helping to bring business his way.

Then in September of 1949, Odom agreed to do something he knew very little about — to fly in the closed-course race at the National Air Show in Cleveland, OH.

Famed aviatrix Jacqueline Cochran had purchased a radically modified P-51 Mustang fighter plane to enter in the annual Thompson Trophy race at the National Air Show. Women were prohibited from flying in the Thompson race, so Cochran hired Odom to fly her green machine called the "Beguine."

Built specifically to fly at great speeds around the pylons, the Beguine was redesigned with one wing 18 inches shorter than the other to negotiate the sharp turns more readily. Odom's lack of experience in flying World War II fighter planes and the strange configuration of the Beguine proved to be his downfall.

As the planes took off, Odom was in seventh position. But as they passed the stands on the first lap, he had moved into third place. Flying low and fast, the competing planes headed west toward a far pylon and those in the stands lost sight of them. As the roaring racers approached the stands on the second lap, the *Beguine* was not among them. Startled, his friends asked aloud, "Where's Odom?" Then, in the distance, they saw smoke rise. Fear clutched at their hearts. Tragedy had struck in the small Ohio town of Berea, where one of the pylons was positioned. Odom's plane flipped over on its back and then plunged into the new home of Bradley and Jeanne Laird, driving itself like a firebomb through the roof and deep into the cellar floor. Jeanne Laird and her 13-month son were killed. Odom was mangled beyond recognition.

Eyewitnesses said that Odom had mistakenly turned inside the course and when he saw he was inside the pylon, he tried to compensate by turning into the short wing which caused the P-51 to roll over.

Chuck Tracy, the aviation editor of the *Cleveland Press*, wrote: *It was a high-powered engine, I flew a P-51 for a while during my last tour in the Air Force. The torque, the engine noise, and the heat from the engine just scares the hell out of you.*

A non-fighter pilot who finds himself suddenly upside down quickly panics and starts pulling back on the stick, which is fatal. yet, I don't think he (Odom) had a choice, anyway, because it happened in a flash. When an airplane hits a high speed stall, everything stops working for a while. The wings don't lift. It (the plane) just flips out of control.

CHRONOLOGY OF OTHER AERONAUTICAL EVENTS AND ACHIEVEMENTS

1940 to 1949

1940

- In Matawan, NJ, Lenape Aircraft Motors began producing a five-cylinder radial, 95 hp engine called "Brave" to power the heavier sport planes being used for student pilot training. Joseph J. Boland designed the engine.

- The 500 member Penguin Flying Club, comprised of Brewster Aeronautical Corp. employees at Newark Airport, was believed to be the largest flying club in the nation. James Coburn was its first president.

- Frederick H. Rohr, founder of the Rohr Aircraft Corp., was born in Hoboken, NJ, in 1896. His natural genius formulated advanced concepts for mass production of aircraft sub-assembly components, advanced drop hammer forging, over-pressed forming of parts and the use of stainless steel and honeycomb construction.

1941

- In the May issue of *Aero Digest* it was reported: "The first model produced by the Zodiac Aircraft Corp. of Lodi, NJ, the Libra-Det, was successfully test-flown last month by Romer Weyant. The new airplane is a low-wing monoplane powered with a 130 hp Franklin engine, and constructed of plywood." The company was headed by Harley L. Clark, Horace Keane, vice president, and Rex L. Uden, secretary/treasurer.

- On December 7, 1941, the Japanese attacked Pearl Harbor and the United States declared war on Japan and Germany.

1942

- Thomas and Robert Bittner, twins from Hamilton Township, NJ, were both flying bombers to England for the U.S. Air Corps. They gained their pilot's licenses at age 16 and their transport and instructor's ratings at 19. Prior to joining the service, they had worked for the Luscombe Airplane Corp. at Mercer County Airport.

- Frederick Kuhnert, the Hackensack florist who built the first Aerodrome in New Jersey, died in his Hackensack home.

- Two American bombers that played a vital role in the war effort were designed by Isaac M. Laddon, a Garfield native. In 1939, the B-24 Liberator Bomber was delivered to the U.S. Army Air Corps, and in 1945, Laddon's B-36 which had a maximum speed of more than 435 mph was flown. The B-36 inspired the slogan "peace through air power."

- Anthony G. Barone of Little Ferry purchased Wurtsboro Airport in New York State and taught flying under the CPT program. He had previously owned and operated the North American Flying Service at the seaplane base in Little Ferry. When he died in 1986, he had been an FAA flight examiner for 40 years.

- Lt. Arnold (Skid) Johnson of Teaneck, was honored at a testimonial dinner at the Swiss Chalet in Rochelle Park, NJ, in December 1942. Johnson, a B-17 Flying Fortress pilot in the Pacific Theater of Operation, and his crew were credited with downing 10 Japanese aircraft and sinking an enemy submarine.

1943

- The United States Navy officially commissioned a Naval Air Station on property leased from Atlantic City for the duration of World War II.

-

- Lt. Joseph B. Boyle of Teaneck was the co-pilot aboard the B-17 *Dry Martini* that shot down 10 German fighter planes on a single raid of the Renault plant outside of Paris. The previous record by a single bomber was seven set on Nov. 1942. The pilot of the *Dry Martini* was Allen V. Martini of San Francisco, CA. Lt. Boyle had been decorated for bringing the Dry Martini back from a raid in the fall of 1942 when Maj. Tom Taylor of Eugene, OR, piloting in Capt. Martini's absence, was killed. A 20-millimeter shell had exploded in the B-17's cockpit killing Taylor and momentarily blinding Boyle.

1944

- The first helicopter mission of mercy was flown on Jan. 3, when a U.S. Coast Guard Sikorsky R-4 flew through a severe storm from New York City to Sandy Hook, NJ,. where an explosion caused injuries aboard the destroyer *U.S.S. Turner*. Transporting much needed blood plasma, the historic helicopter mission was credited with saving more than 110 lives.

- An Air Corps fighter plane was named *Spirit of Atlantic City* because the resort's citizens had sold

War Bonds to pay for the airplane. The Republic P-47 was flown by Major Walker "Bud" Mahurin, a Californian, who became a flying "ace" with 24.5 enemy aircraft downed in Europe Following his tour of duty in Europe, Mahurin and the P-47 were brought back to the U.S. for a bond drive. A huge celebration was held in Atlantic City.

- Former Princeton University classmates, Col. Robert Love, deputy chief of staff of the Air Transport Command, and Major Malcolm E. McAlpin, his assistant, a Morristown resident, became the first men to fly a twin-engine DC-3 to Punta Arenas, Chile, then the southern most airport in the world. A few months later, the two pilots flew a DC-4 to La Paz, Bolivia, 11,910 feet above sea level, the highest airport in the world. It was the first time a four- engine aircraft had landed and taken off at such an altitude.

1945

- On March 8, the first powered flight of a rocket-powered *Gorgon* air-to-air missile was launched from a Navy PBY- 5A aircraft off the coast of Cape May.

- It was estimated that Norman A. Hortman of New Brunswick, made more than 50 transatlantic flights during World War II as a member of the Air Transport Command. In those days of propeller-driven aircraft with limited range, that number of Atlantic flights were impressive.

- Airline Captain James J. Polizzi, an Englewood resident, was named operations manager of Trans-World-Airways for all of Europe. Based in Paris, he held the position for two years. In the mid-30s, he flew for the Crusader Oil Co. of Bayway, NJ. For the airline, he flew everything from DC-2s to Boeing 747s

- In April, Arch Maddock and Charles Payton opened Pennington Airport in Pennington, NJ, on Payton's farm. They sold the airport in 1951.

- In Camden, the aircraft carrier *USS Wright,* named for Wilbur Wright, was christened and launched by Mrs. Harold S. Miller, Wright's niece.

1947

- Capt. Glenn Honeck flew cargo into Teterboro Air Terminal from Burbank, CA, in a record coast-to-coast delivery time of 24 hours and 10 minutes. The cargo? Two thousand recordings of Francis Craig's rendition of *Near You.*

- One of the first woman helicopter pilots in America, Anne Shaw, went to work for the Metropolitan Aviation Corp. which operated an air taxi service out of Teterboro Airport.

- The 154th Anniversary of the first balloon flight in America was duplicated on Jan. 9th, by a helicopter owned by Helicopter Air Transport. The chopper took off from the company's base at Camden Airport, circled the Penn Mutual Insurance Co. building in Philadelphia, site of the old Walnut Street prison where Jean-Pierre Blanchard began his balloon voyage in 1793, and it then flew 15 miles to the southeast and landed in Deptford Township where Blanchard had ascended.

1948

- The Port of New York Authority began operating Newark Airport for the City of Newark.

- A $65,000 commercial air terminal building was opened at the Naval Air Station at Atlantic City.

- A Signal Corps balloon was released at Belmar, NJ, and rose to an altitude of 140,000 feet.

1949

- American Helicopter Magazine reported in it's March issue that in three years the Navy would have helicopter squadrons operating from coast-to-coast. The Helicopter Utility Squadron Two, stationed at the Naval Air Station, Lakehurst, was designated as the helicopter pilot training base.

1950

The 1950s ushered in aviation's jet age, and as the decade opened, North Korea's army swept into South Korea unhindered. Within months of the invasion, President Harry Truman committed America's support to the South Koreans.

The Korean conflict was the first in which jet aircraft were used extensively. On Nov. 7, 1950, a U.S. F-86 jet fighter downed the first Russian MIG-15 piloted by North Koreans. Four Curtiss-Wright cyclone piston engines, built in Wood Ridge, NJ, powered the B-29 Superfortresses that bombed North Korea on a daily basis.

Many New Jersey men and women who had served in World War II were called back to active duty, but only one Garden State resident achieved the statue of flying ace during the three-year conflict. He was Major Stephen L. Bettinger.

Bettinger, a Newark native, was a dedicated fighter pilot. In 1942, he enlisted as a private in the Army Air Corps, perfected his flying skills and was commissioned a second lieutenant in late 1943.

He joined the 12th Air Force, 57th Fighter Group in Italy and Corsica, and flew propeller-driven P-47s on more than 100 missions as a fighter-bomber pilot. During that period, he was credited with shooting down one German ME-109.

At the outbreak of the Korean War, Bettinger volunteered for combat duty and flew another 95 missions. Serving with the 4th Fighter Wing out of Seoul, Korea, he shot down five enemy MIG-15s, probably destroyed another, and severely damaged two more. He was the 38th and last "jet ace" of the war,

On a mission late in the war, he was shot down and taken prisoner by the Chinese. At the war's end, he returned to the U.S. and remained in the service. He retired in 1973 as a full colonel, and moved to Kirkland, WA.

Katherine A. Menges Brick

Inducted Aviation Hall of Fame of New Jersey, 1978

On the home front, a former WASP from New Jersey was elected as the international president of the Ninety-Nines, the women's pilot organization founded in 1929 by Amelia Earhart and 98 other early women pilots.

Through the decades of the '40s, '50s, '60s and '70s, no New Jersey woman was more involved in aviation activities than Katherine "Kay" Menges Brick. In 1961, as the executive director of the All-Woman Transcontinental Air Race, commonly known as the "Powder Puff Derby," Brick established that organization's national headquarters in the Safair

Kay and Frank Brick

hangar at Teterboro Airport. She held that position for 14 years.

As a teenager in the 1930s, Brick had taken the aviation course at Teaneck High School. Upon graduating with a BS degree from Sargent College, Boston University, she received her Pilot's license at Teterboro in 1941. The following year, she joined the WASP (Women's Airforce Service Pilots) and graduated from the Advanced Ferry Command Pilot program in 1943. Over the next two years, she flew 15 different types of military aircraft across the country.

After the war, she stayed at Teterboro as an aircraft salesperson, instructor and aviation publicist. It was during that period that she married Frank R. Brick Jr., her flight instructor before the war. They moved to a home in Norwood, NJ, where they had a daughter, Canivet, who also became a pilot.

Kay Brick flew in six Powder Puff Derbies, but for the most part, she spent her time directing the countless details of each year's race—finding sponsors, establishing transcontinental flying routes and overseeing the race itself.

"The Powder Puff Derby made the public realize that flying was safe, and women could do it — and do it well," Brick explained. "Many girls, even today, fly with their pilot husbands. With the Powder Puff, they can say, 'I can do it on my own'"

During her active career, Brick served on the Powder Puff Derby board for 25 years, on the FAA Advisory Committee for three years, on the National Pilots Association board for six years, on the P-47 Thunderbolt Pilot's Association board for eight years and a host of others.

For her contributions to aviation, Brick received the Amelia Earhart Medal from the Ninety-Nines in

1949, 1960 and 1976. She was the recipient of the Paul Tissandier Diploma, FAI (an international award) in 1973, and the "Pioneer Women's" Award for 1981" by the OX-5 Aviation Pioneers. She was included in *Notable Americans of the Bicentennial Era, Who's Who of American Women 1972 and '73; Who's Who in the East 1974-75* and the fourth edition of the *World Who's Who of Women.*

"What I've done over the years has been terribly exciting, and I found that aviation was a very, very interesting world," Brick said from her Fallbrook, CA, home where she had moved in the late 1970s. "People who fly have a young, youthful outlook. They are intensely interested in everything they do."

In May of 1987 at age 78, Brick with her friend and sister-pilot, Pam Vander Linden, two years her junior, were detained in Puerto Vallarta, Mexico, as suspected drug runners. Somehow, the plane had been placed on a U.S. Drug Enforcement Agency (DEA) "black list" and the Mexicans, who were accused by the DEA of not cooperating on drug enforcement, decided to hold the Bellanca owned by Vander Linden, until the DEA cleared them. The "jailing" of the "two grandmothers" made international headlines, although in truth, the women spent their five additional days in Puerta Vallarta on the beach.

"Had Pam not been the mother-in-law of Charles Schulz, the creator of the Peanuts and Snoopy cartoon, I'm sure the incident would never have gone international," Brick said. "We even had a clipping from Yugoslavia."

At this writing, she was still flying to various parts of the world. She has visited all 50 states and flew as Copilot to Australia.

Brick saw no reason to stop as she began her fifth decade as a pilot. "When you're flying, you really feel like a bird. You have this complete feeling of freedom," she said, "so why stop?.

Frank Reeve Brick Jr.

Frank R. Brick Jr. was born in 1887 in Jersey City. He graduated from Stevens Technical Institute in Hoboken with an electrical engineering/communications degree. During World War I, he joined the Navy and checked radio communication equipment on ships of the Atlantic Fleet.

In 1917, while flying from ship to ship off Guantanamo Bay, Cuba, Brick's pilot became ill so Brick took the controls and flew safely to their destination although he had never taken a flying lesson. Brick stayed in the Navy for six years and during that time, he became a pilot.

After the war, he flew and handled engineering duties for the Radio Corporation of America in New York City. Most of his time was spent demonstrating radio

and direction finder equipment at Roosevelt Field, Long Island.

In the early 1930s, Brick moved to Elizabeth and became vice president and chief engineer of Finch Telecommunications. In developing the company's products and testing facsimile patents, he flew a Fokker Super Universal monoplane, based at Teterboro.

With the outbreak of World War II, Brick became an officer in the Bendix Civil Air Patrol squadron and later commanded CAP Group 221. With Finch, he worked on secret electronic developments for the government, including radar.

After the war, he formed the Brick Electronic Co., married Katherine Menges and they moved to Norwood. He died in 1976 at age 89.

The Powder Puff Derby

The annual All-Woman Transcontinental Air Race (AWTAR), known as the "Powder Puff Derby," was the oldest, longest and largest speed air race for women in the world. It was the only race endorsed by The Ninety-Nines, Inc., the international organization of more than 6,000 licensed women pilots founded in 1929.

Each year, a route with specific stops was laid out between two cities which had bid for the honor of hosting the start and finish of the race. Two New Jersey women served on the AWTAR's Board of Directors for many years.

Kay Brick, 1951 to 1977 and Alice Hammond of Millville 1961 to 1967. Brick was chairman of the group from 1961 to 1974.

Only two aircraft and three pilots entered the first race from Palm Springs, CA, to Tampa, FL, in 1947. Thirty years later, 1977, racing between the same two cities, 150 aircraft and 331 pilots and passengers participated. That was the last year the Derby was flown.

New Jersey hosted three races. In 1952, Teterboro Airport was the terminus for 41 aircraft and 68 pilots. Actor Robert Taylor was the honorary starter in Santa Ana, CA, and television and radio personality Arthur Godfrey met the women as they arrived at Teterboro. The 1961 race began in San Diego, CA, with 101 aircraft flown by 201 pilots, and it terminated in Atlantic City. The 1963 race again ended in Atlantic City after a 2,460 mile flight from Bakersfield, CA.

Patricia Thomas Gladney, the Hoboken resident who was the first female graduate of the Teaneck High School aviation course in 1935 to receive a pilot's license, flew in 24 Powder Puff Derbies, a total equaled by only two other women who participated in the race over the years. Alice Hammond flew in 16 races, more than twice as many as any other New

Jersey aviatrix, except Gladney, who has resided in California since the end of World War II.

Those New Jersey women who participated over the 30 years of racing are listed with their home towns and the years in which they raced.

POWDER PUFF DERBY

30th Anniversary
1947-1977

AMSTER, Carrie Grace '68, '70   Rockaway
ANGELINI, Claire '76-77p.   Howell
BARLIN, Betty '72   Oakland
BELLINO, Clarice M. '75-77   North Caldwell
BLACKBURN, Janis '76   Old Bridge
BLEVINS, Karwyn '76   Mt. Arlington
BRICK, Kay A. '55-59, '77   Norwood
CAGGIANO, Diana '76-77   Pompton Lakes
CRONAN, Selma, '60-61, '63   Hasbrouck Heights
CRUMP, Margaret '69-70   West Caldwell
ELLIS, Helen '64   Haddonfield
GLADNEY, Patricia Thomas '49,'51,'53,'56-58,'60-73
          Hoboken
HAMMOND, Alice '53-57, '59-65, '67-70
          Millville
HAYDU, Bee Falk '67, '71   Newton
HILBRANDT, Kathleen '60   Hasbrouck Heights
HITCHINGS, Alma '70, '72, '76-77 Howell

KERNS, Mary Jane Loch '64   Hamilton Square
LOUDENSLAGER, Marguerite '65
          Lincroft
LIBONATE, Mary Jane '77   Bricktown
MAHER, Gay '63, '64   Princeton
MEISENHEIMER, Alice '62,'63, '69
          Cherry Hill
MYERS, Mary Roes '73, '75, '77   Atlantic City
NAUMANN, Peggy Shinn '68-70, '72-73, '75
          W. Caldwell
NELSON, Geraldine '76   Montclair
PANKOW, Kitty '76   Haddonfield
PEAKE, Margaret '77   Kinnelon
RASMUSSEN, Leslie '64   Boonton
ROBERTS, Jerry '68, '70, '71, '76   Haddon Heights
SCHAPIRA, "Ellie" '71-72   West Orange
SHAW, Nancy '73, '75-77   Wildwood
SHOEMAKER, Barbara '52   Hackensack
SMITH, Dorothy J. '66   Matawan
STEINFIELD, Nancy '77 p.   Howell
STEWART, Katherine Palmer '59, '64
          Atlantic Highlands
STRUZINSKI, Kathleen '67   Riverside
THOMAS, Edith "Micki" '69-73, '75-77
          Pompton Lakes
WILSON, Priscilla "Pat" '63, '66, '71-73, '77
          Bedminster NJ

Hyphenated years are inclusive. p.-passenger '77 Commemorative Flight only.

Powder Puff pilots Barbara Maddock and Alice Hammond

1951
Three Accidents Close Newark

The airport was returned to the City of Newark in 1946 and a consulting firm was hired to study the operation and future development of the facility. The consultants recommended that both the airport and seaport development and operations be placed under the administration of the Port Authority, thereby relieving the Newark taxpayers of the financial burden of supporting the transportation centers. As a result, the Port Authority began operating Newark Airport in March, 1948. Archie Armstrong was named the manager.

The bi-state agency immediately began plans to expand the air terminal. By the early 1950s, the airport area covered 2,300 acres, and a new instrument runway was completed.

But just as that third decade of service dawned rather brightly, three tragic airline accidents claimed 119 lives.

The first was in December 1951. A non-scheduled Miami Airline C-46 crashed in Elizabeth, just after take-off, killing the 56 people aboard. It was the second worst air disaster in U.S. history. (Fifty-eight had perished in a Lake Michigan crash the previous year).

Just a little more than a month later, an American Airlines plane crashed into a residential section of Elizabeth killing all 23 aboard, including former Secretary of War Robert P. Patterson, and five on the ground. Ironically, the 33-year-old pilot of the stricken plane, Capt. Thomas J. Reid, lived only three blocks from the crash site.

On February 10, 1952, a four-engine National Airlines DC-6 slammed into Elizabeth killing 25 passengers and four residents of a 52-family apartment. The Port Authority immediately closed the airport and Elizabeth's mayor James T. Kirk said his city was "living under an umbrella of death." All three accidents had occurred within a one mile radius.

The airport remained partially closed for eight months as the accidents were thoroughly investigated. The instrument runway, the only one with an approach light system at the time, was closed to satisfy city officials in both Elizabeth and Newark.

More Expansion

In 1953, an $8.5 million, ultra-modern passenger terminal was opened under the management of Archie Armstrong. Lt. Gen. James Doolittle, one of the great air heroes of World War II, addressed the large crowd at the opening day ceremony, calling Newark "one of the best and safest airports in the world." But the new facility did not significantly increase the passenger traffic at Newark, and in the late '50s and early '60s, the terminal restaurant "The Newarker" seemed to attract more public enthusiasm than the aircraft. Both in passenger traffic and airplane movements, Newark ranked a poor third among the three New York metropolitan airports — LaGuardia and Idlewild (later J.F. Kennedy Airport), the newly opened international airport in Jamaica, NY, were the other two. The Port Authority managed all three.

When airlines replaced their piston-driven aircraft with large capacity jets, it became obvious to Port Authority planners that the 1950s terminal was not designed to handle the larger aircraft, so plans were drawn for a completely new central terminal area that would be located along the west side of the major runways. Joseph L. Vanacore, was the PA's chief of planning for the enormous undertaking, and in 1971 became the airport's manager. The new central terminal consisted of three separate terminal buildings each with three circular satellites that could accommodate a total of 55 jet aircraft. Terminals A and B

opened in 1973, while terminal C remained nothing more than a steel skeleton. At the same time the airport was renamed "Newark International Airport" which caused some snickering among the spectators who assembled for the opening ceremony. Did flights to Bermuda and the Bahamas really warrant the new name?

The tide began to turn for Newark in the late 1970s when the federal government deregulated the airline industry. Within four years, Newark's fortunes rose to all-time heights, and if the Port Authority's crystal ball is correct, the airport will never fall on hard times again.

Vanacore had been replaced by John J. Dickerson Jr., a life-long resident of Palisade Park, NJ, in 1978, just as an influx of new airlines came on the scene. All were anxious to compete in the lucrative New Jersey/New York market, but found that gate space was tight at both LaGuardia and Kennedy Airports, so they flocked to under-utilized Newark International. Dickerson recalled those busy times. "There were any number of fledgling airlines coming through the door, it was like a revolving door of potentials, a lot of them made their own assessments and never came back. Others, who I would call neophytes, they really didn't know what it took to run an airline. They had no idea what space cost at an airport and they had a rude awakening when they went out to buy an airplane. Most of them were under-capitalized and they couldn't hack it."

Perhaps the most unique new carrier was PEOPLExpress which immediately became the leader of the pack of newcomers. As the first major airline founded in New Jersey since the early 1930s, the non-union, employee-owned airline lured passengers to New Jersey with fares that were in most cases half the amount charged by their seniors

Dickerson remembered Donald Burr, the president of PEOPLExpress, as a visionary young man. "Burr could see the potential of the old North Terminal. For very little expense, he could move his airline into the North Terminal facility and with the three airplanes he owned start carrying passengers. By the time we had signed an operating agreement with him, he had five planes and was climbing. Space did not limit him because he had the entire terminal building."

By the mid-1980s, Newark passenger traffic had grown at a phenomenal rate. The airport accounted for virtually half of all domestic travel at the three NJ/NY airports. Over the three-year period—1983-1985—passenger traffic increased yearly at an average of almost 30% while the national average for airports handling more than 10 million passengers was just seven and a half percent.

The airport's unprecedented growth put a tremendous strain on its facilities. The Central Terminal

Area (CTA), designed to accommodate 18 million passengers handled 17 million in 1986. But in 1987, Continental Airlines merged with New York Air and PEOPLExpress and moved its entire operation from the old North Terminal into Terminal B. The CTA now had 22 million people moving through its gates. What had been a leisurely airport to fly from had became a traveler's battle zone.

Under the direction of Dickerson's successor, Vincent Bonaventura, a graduate engineer, adjustments were made in the passenger flow, additional parking lots were opened and the roadway system was widened to temporarily relieve the congestion.

In 1984, the Port Authority had created an international arrivals center in one third of Terminal C, and at the same time signed an agreement with PEOPLExpress to complete the remaining portion. Following the merger, Continental continued with the expansion program. Terminal C was opened in May of 1988.

"Terminal C is dramatically different from Terminals A and B," Bonaventura said with pride. "Instead of 19 gates, Continental now has 41. There are only 55 gates in A and B combined, so we've had a 75 percent increase in gate space."

Terminal C has 95 check-in locations, 14 moving sidewalks, two Presidential Clubs, and 19 eating locations, plus shops of various kind. Its centerpiece is a glass-domed atrium with an 80-foot skylight and a waterfall running down its walls. The 855,000-square-foot building is the largest single terminal in the New York metropolitan area.

Once Newark had been discovered by the traveling public, airlines from around the world were suddenly interested in flying out of New Jersey. In the early '80s, PEOPLExpress and Virgin Atlantic airlines began service from Newark to London, England, and many of the domestic airlines flew to destinations in Mexico and the Caribbean, but it wasn't until 1989 that the big boys came to Newark to compete for a piece of the international pie. They included Air Canada and City Express servicing several Canadian cities; Scandinavian Air System (SAS) flying to Copenhagen, Stockholm and Oslo; TAP (Air Portugal) to Lisbon; UTA French Airlines to five provinces of France and both United and Northwest airlines to several Asian capitals. By the end of '89, Newark had 340 foreign departures to almost 40 international destinations.

To provide for the new business, the Port Authority spent $11 million to redesign Terminal B's Satellite 3 as an international arrivals and departure area, replacing the two-gate international arrivals area in Terminal C. Space was set aside for U. S. Customs and Immigration and an international baggage handling area.

"Ole Redhead"

During the first three months of 1990 British Airways, Lufthansa, TWA, Air France and El Al (Israel's airline) began international service.

Entering the last decade of the 20th century, Newark is again the busiest airport in the New York area. By the year 2,000, Bonaventura estimates that 45 million passengers will pass through Newark's three terminal buildings annually. He and his airport designers are already planning for another significant expansion program they've named "Newark 2,000."

1956
Teterboro Floods the
Airwaves
Arthur Godfrey

Inducted Aviation Hall of Fame of New Jersey, 1976

There was a brisk crosswind blowing in the clear early evening of Jan. 7, 1954 as the air traffic controllers were changing shifts in the Teterboro tower. The two late-shift controllers had just arrived as a familiar voice requested permission to takeoff to the west on a short runway that was aimed directly at the hill in Hasbrouck Heights. The controller on duty turned to tower chief Dan Kaplan and said, "Godfrey wants to takeoff on runway 32." Kaplan shook his head.

"Tell him takeoffs are not permitted in that direction by request of the airport's management."

The message was relayed to entertainer Arthur Godfrey, who was at the controls of his twin-engine DC-3, and permission was granted to takeoff on runway #1, which extended toward the northwest.

Twenty years later, Kaplan recalled what happened then: "About halfway down the strip, he (Godfrey) flew at low altitude veering over waiting aircraft and headed for the control tower. The four men in the tower dashed for the stairwell. We could have counted the plane's rivets as it roared over the cab."

Asked by radio if he was in trouble, Godfrey replied "that was a normal takeoff for Teterboro."

The tower chief wrote a report to his superiors citing the incident as a clear violation of the rules. The Federal Aviation Administration (FAA) said that Godfrey's pilot's license would be revoked if he couldn't satisfactorily explain why he had "buzzed" the tower.

That set off a feud between Godfrey and the FAA that brought Teterboro to the attention of Godfrey's 40 million listeners. Although he eventually lost his license for six months, the entertainer chastised the FAA and Teterboro for years on both his daily radio and television shows. At that time, he was arguably the most popular entertainer in the United States.

Ironically, he had been given the DC-3 in 1950 by a group of aviation executives headed by his old friend Eddie Rickenbacker, the president of Eastern Airlines, because of his constant promotion of aviation — private, commercial and military. He would tell his listening audience, "Everybody should learn to fly. It can't be too hard," he'd chuckle in a familiar deep baritone. "After all, if I could learn, anyone can."

Godfrey, born in New York City in 1903, had moved with his family to Hasbrouck Heights at an early age. His parents were poor and he worked after school as a baker's delivery boy. He once told the author that he trapped muskrat in the meadows below the Hasbrouck Heights' hill long before an airport was even considered.

He joined the Navy in 1920 at age 17 and flew for the first time. For more than 30 years, he kept an assortment of airplanes at Teterboro and, at the peak of his popularity, he commuted regularly between New Jersey and his farm in Virginia.

In 1966, Godfrey participated in a record-setting flight around the world. He and Dick Merrill, Eastern Airlines' most celebrated captain, put together the logistics of the flight. With Fred Austin, a TWA captain, and Karl Keller, a Rockwell Standard Corp. test pilot, they circumnavigated the globe in a Rockwell "Jet Commander" business aircraft. The 23,333 mile flight, which included 20 refueling stops, was made in 55 hours and 30 minutes flight time at an average speed of 423 mph.

Because of his close friendship with U.S. Air Force General Curtis LeMay, Godfrey became such an ardent supporter of the Air Force that he resigned his commission as a commander in the Naval Reserve and accepted a retired commission in the Air Force Reserve. All through the '50s and the '60s, he was permitted to fly in highly sophisticated Air Force aircraft. And on the civilian side, he flew all the generations of commercial aircraft up to the B-747.

For his own enjoyment in later years, he had a Beech Baron D-55. In the aviation industry the tail letters "NIM" became almost as famous as he was. In July 1974, he flew solo from New Jersey to Point Barrow, Alaska and back 12,000 nautical miles in 62 hours.

Although known mainly as a radio and television star, Godfrey appeared in three Broadway shows — 1945 with Ray Bolger in *Three to Make Ready;* 1965 opposite Maureen O'Sullivan in *Never Too Late* and 1967 on the summer circuit in Generations with James Coco. In 1966, he co-starred with Doris Day in the film *Glass Bottom Boat.*

During his 40-year career, Godfrey received awards from military and civilian organizations for his aviation achievements and for his promotion of flying during a period when the average citizen had a deep-seated fear of airplanes. When he died in 1983, he left his aviation awards and memorabilia to the Aviation Hall of Fame and Museum of New Jersey. Those trophies, plaques and models are on display in the AHOF's museum in the tower that he had made famous almost 30 years before. At the time of the 10th anniversary of the AHOF in 1982, Godfrey wrote to his close friend, Henry Esposito, the general manager of Atlantic Aviation where Godfrey had always kept his plane, "Despite a closet full of aviation trophies, the only feat for which I will probably be remembered is allegedly buzzing the tower at Teterboro."

Esposito said that is probably a fitting epitaph to his aviation career. "He was one of a kind. There will never be another Arthur.

"He liked to say 'If it isn't fun, the hell with it!'" Esposito said, "We don't have as much fun since he's gone."

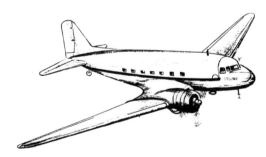

DC-3

1958

New Jersey's Largest Aircraft

The largest aircraft ever built in New Jersey was test-flown in 1958. Designed and built by Michael M. Stroukoff at Mercer County Airport in West Trenton, The YC-134A amphibian with 18-foot water/snow skis had a maximum gross weight of nearly 41 tons. Like Stroukoff's earlier model, the YC-123E, the huge plane could take off from rough or smooth runways or from ice, snow, mud or water.

A little known aircraft designer, Russian born, Michael M. Stroukoff emigrated to America in 1923. Unable to find employment as a civil engineer, he held various jobs until he became an airplane designer.

During World War II, he designed a series of gliders, the first of which were built in New York City by the Chase Aircraft Company. When the original owners of Chase backed out after losing money on their U.S-Air Force (USAF) contracts, Stroukoff became the defacto president. Still known as the Chase Company, the firm was moved by Stroukoff to West Trenton in the fall of 1946.

Stroukoff maintained the interesting philosophy that his future designs for powered aircraft should first be proven air worthy as gliders. His 1947, 32-seat glider, the CG-14B, was redesigned with an all-metal skin as the YCG-18. Two prototypes and five production models were delivered to the USAF. One of the two prototypes was fitted with detachable wing pods, each mounting 1200hp Pratt & Whitney engines and flown as the XC-122 CA medium cargo carrier. Nine were sold to the USAF and remained in service for a decade.

Stroukoff was then requested by the USAF to design both a glider and powered transport to be approximately twice as large as the C-122. The new SC-123 was completed and flown in October 1949, while the new XCG-20 glider appeared during March 1950. With USAF approval, plans were made to place the XC-123 into production.

In 1951, one of the two big gliders was converted into America's first jet transport by having two twin-jet J-47 engine pods fitted to its outer wings. It became known as the YC-123 and was flight-tested at Mercer County Airport.

It was then Stroukoff was informed by the Air Force that unless his plant facilities at Trenton were enlarged, he would not be awarded a large contract for the C-123B transports. With his back against a wall,

he was forced to merge with the Henry J. Kaiser interests which purchased 49% of the Stroukoff stock to enable him to expand his operation in 1952. Kaiser, at that time, was building Fairchild-designed C-119 transports at the former Ford Willow Run bomber plant in Michigan. A parallel assembly line for the C-123Bs was set up for mass production.

Stroukoff Aircraft was reorganized with Kaiser's son, Edgar, installed as president, and Mike Stroukoff as vice president in charge of research. In all, only five C-123Bs were built at Trenton while parts and sub-assemblies were shipped to the Kaiser Michigan plant. Trenton was relegated to the development of the new YC-123E heavy transport amphibian previously mentioned. The plane was designed with his so-called "Pantobase" system which called for a waterproofed fuselage, wingtip pontoons, and retractable water skis and wheels.

Just as the Stroukoff/Kaiser enterprise became a reality it was struck by scandal. Congress learned that the Kaiser interests were charging the Air Force a half-million dollars more for C-119s than those built by Fairchild. The contract was cancelled immediately. Along with it went the contract for the C-123Bs. This left Stroukoff high and dry until he forced Kaiser to buy him out for $2.2 million.

At that point, Stroukoff built New Jersey's largest airplane, but no contracts were forthcoming from the Air Force, which had re-awarded the C-123B contract to Fairchild. That company built 303 of Stroukoff's creations from 1954 to 1957. They were known as "Providers" and served well in Vietnam.

From all indications, Michael Stroukoff deserved better from his adopted country. There are neither records (which he had burned) nor surviving aircraft (which he had scrapped). He died in 1974 at age 90, a much embittered man.

1959

First Air-Cushioned Flying Machine

Charles J. Fletcher

The late December day was windy and raw as Charles J. Fletcher, an aeronautical engineer from Sparta, NJ, struggled with the controls of his latest invention, the Glide-Mobile, attempting to make it lift off the runway at the Andover-Aeroflex Airport in the hills of Sussex County. The engine of the strange contraption roared as its propeller pushed air down under the 182-lb. machine. Anxiously, Fletcher moved the con-

Charle Fletcher and his Glide Mobile.

trol stick back and forth in the small cockpit, determined to make it lift off the pavement.

Suddenly, the Glide-Mobile rose a half-foot and slithered across the runway. Fletcher, dressed in his Navy flight jacket and wearing a crash helmet, smiled happily and one of his engineering assistants was heard to say, "Ridiculous! It actually works."

The first air-cushioned vehicle in the nation had successfully flown.

The 36-year-old Fletcher, founder and president of the Fletch-Aire Company, based in Newton, NJ, hoped to interest the military in his invention for use as a flying jeep. He also felt there was a good market in the automotive field for his tire-less flying car.

The Glide-Mobile, which looked like a small car mounted on a Coast Guard rescue raft, had a lightweight tubing frame, covered by aircraft wing fabric, and was painted green and white. In order to fly, air had to be sucked in through an opening in the top of the engine housing by a whirling propeller and driven with great force toward the ground. A fabric apron around the bottom of the vehicle captured the air causing it to lift the car. The movement of the control stick caused rudders inside the air-car to channel the rapidly moving air through a series of louvers and vanes which pushed the vehicle fore or aft, left or right at the pilot's discretion. The inventor said his air-car could travel at "almost 50 miles an hour" and expected advanced designs to reach speeds of 70 or 80 mph. At that time, he estimated the cost of the air-cars would be approximately $3,000. He told reporters it would take no more than 20 minutes to teach someone to operate his aircraft.

A friend and fellow engineer, Hartman Kircher of Sparta had helped the designer build the strange contraption in Fletcher's garage on Cherry Tree Lane in Sparta.

At the time of the Glide-Mobile's first flight, both men worked for the Reaction Motors Division of the Thiokol Chemical Corp. in Denville. Fletcher had made major engineering contributions to the development of the rocket engine that powered the supersonic X-15 into space and worked on other Reaction Motor's projects such as the Viking missile and the EX-10 torpedo.

Prior to that, he had been a flight test engineer for the Piasecki Helicopter Corp. in Morton, PA.

Following his graduation from Franklin High School in 1941, Fletcher attended the General Motors Institute Teterboro Airport. At the outbreak of World War II, he joined the Navy's pilot training program and received his wings in 1944. He flew Grumman Hellcats from the Essex-class carrier *USS Bennington* in the Pacific theater of operations. In 1950, he graduated from the Academy of Aeronautics as an aeronautical engineer, and returned to the Navy during the Korean War. He was assigned to the Navy's Bureau of Aeronautics, based in Norfolk, VA. It was during those years that he developed the concept of the Glide Mobile.

"The machine spent nine years on the drawing boards and 87 days in my garage [while being built]," he explained years later.

Fletcher had been unable to patent his invention because the United States invoked a secrecy agreement used to protect items of military value. Apparently, however, a leak had sprung in the secrecy agreement and England and France began building Glide Mobile-type vehicles that eventually became hovercraft.

In the late 1980s, both England and France sued the U.S for $12 to $15 million claiming their engineers invented the machine. Fletcher's early drawings and a 16mm film of the Glide Mobile in action, taken by Kircher, were used by Justice Department lawyers as evidence that the New Jersey-built machine flew years before similar craft in either European country.

The Glide-Mobile was never produced commercially and the prototype vas eventually stripped by vandals outside Fletcher's Franklin, NJ, office.

Should the government at some time in the future prove that Fletcher's air-car was the first flying model of an air cushioned flying machine in the world, the Sussex County engineer, who holds 23 aerospace, product and Navy patents, will have a special niche in the world of aeronautics.

In 1989, Fletcher, then president of the Aerosystems Technology Corp. of Franklin, and Kircher discussed the possibility of restoring the Glide Mobile's frame for display in the Smithsonian Institution, Washington, DC.

CHRONOLOGY OF NEW JERSEY FLIGHTS
1950 to 1959
1950

- The Harmon International Aviation awards committee named Gen. James H. Doolittle aviator of the decade. A similar award was bestowed on Jacqueline Cochran as the outstanding aviatrix, and Vice Admiral Charles E. Rosendahl of Toms River, as the top aeronaut (lighter-than-airman),

- Alice Jean May of Englewood, flying a Ryan Navion at an average speed of 140 mph, won the 178-mile All Woman Cross-Country Race at the 11th annual Reading, Air Show. She was a secretary/pilot with the Mallard Air Service, Inc. at Teterboro Airport.

- Charles Lanier Lawrence, the man who designed and developed the air-cooled engines that powered many noted long distance airplane flights, died at the age of 67 at his home in East Islip, Long Island.

- Marine Lt. Robert Longstaff of Jersey City received the Silver Star for a daring helicopter rescue in Korea. While flying a reconnaissance mission over Seoul, he intercepted a radio message for help from three pilots downed behind enemy lines. Flying through heavy flak, Longstaff hovered over the crash scene while the pilots hoisted themselves aboard his helicopter. The Marines referred to helicopters as "the most useful gadgets in the war."

- Tom Murchio, founder of Murchio Airport, died.

1951

- A device to simplify air navigation was introduced by the Hammond Hap Company of Maplewood, NJ. The compact plotter that showed all the required navigational data at a glance was called the Hammond's Ground Speed and Directional Plotter.

1952

- The largeat, non-rigid airship, ZMP-1, arrived at the Lakehurst Naval Air Station from the Goodyear plant in Akron, OH.

1953

- Alice Hammond of Millville, NJ, flew in her first of 16 Powder Puff Derbies.

1954

- The amazing 12-month, round-the-world journey of 62-year-old Marion Hart came to a conclusion at Teterboro Airport on July 11. Having learned to fly at age 54 at Teterboro, she flew her single-engine Beechcraft Bonanza 35,000 miles to 25 countries.

- Bert Acosta, "Aviation's Bad Boy", died in a Denver, CO, sanitarium at age 59.

- New York Airways inaugurated Helicopter passenger service from Trenton, Princeton, and New Brunswick to LaGuardia and Idlewild Airports in New York.

- Aircraft designer Charles Healy Day died at age 77.

1955

- President Dwight D. Eisenhower designated the site of the former Naval Air Station, Atlantic City, as the National Aviation Facilities Experimental Center (NAFEC) to be managed by the newly established Federal Aviation Agency (FAA).

- 1st Lt. Albert V. Hodges of Nutley became the first New Jerseyan to fly faster than the speed of sound. Hodges flew well over 720 mph in a F-100 Saberjet at George Air Force Base in Victorville, CA. He had flown 93 missions during the Korean War.

1956

- At age 76, Joseph Boland, who with his brother Frank, built and flew the first fixed-wing airplane in New Jersey, presented a hand-made model of his tailless biplane to Paul Garber, curator of the National Air and Space Museum in Washington, DC.

1957

- An Air Force F-IOOF, christened *Spirit of St. Louis II*, was flown by Maj. Robinson Risner from McGuire Air Force Base to Paris, France, to commemorate the 30th anniversary of Charles Lindbergh's solo Atlantic crossing. The original *Spirit* took more than 33 hours to make the crossing. *Spirit II* did it in six hours and 37 minutes.

- Explorer, Adm. Richard E. Byrd, died in Boston at age 69.

1958

- The world's first talking satellite, *Score,* developed at the Signal Labs, Fort Monmouth, was launched into orbit.

- Thor Solberg purchased 70 acres of land in Readington, Hunterdon County, NJ, and built the Solberg-Hunterdon Airport.

- Clyde Pangborn died in New York City at age 62.

1959

- Lt. Col. Kenneth D. Frazier of Hatboro, NJ, a highly decorated veteran of World War II and the Korean War was killed on July 17, when his Navy jet fighter crashed and exploded on a farm in Hillsboro Township, Somerset County, NJ. The 39-year-old Marine reserve officer was credited with 12.5 Japanese planes destroyed during World War II which made him a double-ace.

- Aircraft designer Robert B.C. Noorduyn, who helped Anthony Fokker establish his aircraft business in New Jersey, died in Canada.

1960

The late 1950s set the stage for the space age that would dominate the next decade. In October 1957, the Soviet Union surprised the the world by launching a satelite into space. Suddenly *sputnik,* the Russian name for the sphere, became an international word. The United States' space experts were astonished that the satellite weighed 184 pounds, eight times heavier than the one they planned to launch the following year. A month later, the Soviets launched a dog into space in a vehicle that was six times heavier than the original sputnik.

In February of 1958, the U.S. launched the 30.8-pound *Explorer 1* satellite and the nation was in the space race.

Almost a year later, the first seven American "astronauts were named. Among them was Navy Commander Walter Schirra of Oradell, NJ. The following month, April 1959, as a prelude to a U.S. manned space flight, the National Aeronautics and Space Administration (NASA) launched two monkeys into space to ascertain what effects space travel would have on them.

Four months later, the X-15 rocket plane made its first powered flight propelled by engines built by Reaction Motors of Rockaway Tounship, NJ. Piloted by Scott Crossfield, the X-15 climbed 10 miles above the Mohave Desert (CA) flew at 1,400 miles per hour, twice the speed of sound. By the end of March 1961, the X-15 had flown to an altitude of 31.25 miles into space and exceeded speeds of 2,650 mph.

In April of the same year, the Russians shot Major Yuri Gagarin into orbit and brought him back to earth. In May, American Navy Commander Alan B. Shepard Jr. spent 15 minutes in a Mercury space capsule 115 miles above the earth, and at the same time, President John F. Kennedy announced a program to send a man to the moon.

In July of 1961, Air Force Capt. Virgil I. "Gus" Grissom flew to a height of 116 miles in 16 minutes — the second astronaut in space. Six months-later on Feb. 20, 1962, Lt. Col. John H. Glenn Jr. became the first man to orbit the earth.

In May of 1962, M. Scott Carpenter circled the earth three times, followed by a six-orbit flight by New Jerseyan ----

Walter M. Schirra Jr.

Inducted Aviation Hall of Fame of New Jersey, 1982

"This is Mercury Control," NASA spokesman Col. "Shorty" Powers said calmly. "Five, Four, Three, Two, One....blast off....Wally Schirra is on his way!"

Walter M. Schirra Jr.

NASA Photo

As he watched the spacecraft's escape tower blow away, the effusive Schirra said, "This tower is a real sayonara."

The date was Oct. 3, 1962. The United States' fifth, manned spacecraft was in orbit. Schirra would stay buttoned up in this spacecraft *Sigma 7* for nine hours and 13 minutes before splashing down in the Pacific Ocean.

Known as "rah-rah" because he was an enthusiastic prankster, Schirra thoroughly enjoyed finding a sandwich and a gag ignition key mounted by spacecraft technicians on the right-hand attitude controller when he squeezed into the *Sigma 7* cockpit.

While flying over South America, the astronaut was asked to say something in Spanish which would be broadcast live around the world. He cracked, "Buenos dias, y'all."

Although he had a carefree attitude, Schirra knew the danger of his new profession and often said, "Levity is appropriate in a dangerous trade."

Born in Hackensack Hospital on March 12, 1923 to Mr. and Mrs. Walter M. Schirra Sr. of that city, young Walter and his family moved to Oradell during his formative years. At age 13, he took his first airplane ride with veteran Teterboro pilot Billy Diehl. Schirra Sr. had flown with the Army Air Corps during World War I, and after the Armistice, he and Mrs. Schirra had barnstormed throughout the Eastern United States, so it was natural for them to encourage their son toward the field of aeronautics.

Upon graduating from Dwight Morrow High School in Englewood, Schirra was accepted as a midshipman at the U.S. Naval Academy at Annapolis, MD. When he graduated in 1945, he was assigned to the Naval Test Station, Pennsacola, FL, for flight training.

During the Korean war, Schirra was assigned as an exchange pilot with the United States Air Force's 154th Fighter Bomber Squadron. He flew 90 missions in F-84 aircraft over North Korea, receiving the Distinguished Flying Cross and two Air Medals for his Korean service.

After Korea, Schirra became a test pilot and took part in the development of the Sidewinder missile at the Naval Ordnance Training Station at China Lake, CA. He once launched a Sidewinder while in flight, saw it suddenly go berserk and turn back in pursuit of his own plane. Keeping his cool, Schirra outmaneuvered the deadly missile until it ran out of fuel and crashed.

He was also the project pilot for the F7U-3 Cutlass and an instructor pilot for the Cutlass and the FJ3 Fury. He flew F3H-2N Demons while assigned as operations officer of the 124th Fighter Squadron on board the carrier *Lexington* in the Pacific.

By the time he was selected for the first astronaut team, Schirra had accumulated more than 4,000 hours of flying time, with 3,300 hours in jet aircraft.

Like the four astronauts who had preceded him in space, after his successful flight, Schirra was sent back to his native state to be honored by its citizens. Upon his arrival at Teterboro Airport, he discovered that the old airfield had been renamed "Walter M. Schirra Airport" to commemorate the occasion. A parade from Hackensack to Oradell was arranged and an estimated 40,000 people lined the six-mile route shouting "Wally! Wally! Wally!" "

More than 10,000 people screamed enthusiastically as the astronaut entered the River Dell Regional High School stadium in Oradell.

Schirra told the crowd he was more thrilled by his welcome in Bergen County than he had been during the countdown for his historic flight. "It's a great treat to realize that I can, after all this time, still come back to so many friends," he said. "The charm I remembered for so long is still here. It would take a week to take it all in."

Discussing the space program he said, "You people are so enthusiastic about the space program that I will tell you that we are dead serious about this program, too. There are frontiers to challenge in space and we hope the aura of mystery is fast disappearing. In Oradell today, it has been proven that we are all on that satellite and it is the best satellite."

He told the audience that there had been considerable misunderstanding about the astronauts volunteering for the space mission. "We didn't volunteer," he stated. "We were called to Washington where it was explained to us what we were going to do with the space capsules. Later, we changed the name to spacecraft to make it sound better. But then we were told we would work and improve the spacecraft. We would be the communicators between the pilots and engineers. That sounded more interesting. That's what we did. How to get there and back was the mission. A lot of people forget about the 'and back' part."

Accompanying Schirra were his wife and two children and his parents, who had moved to California several years earlier.

The tribute was arranged by Mayor Frederick Wendel of Oradell. Gov. Richard J. Hughes, Sen. Clifford P.Case and Congressman William B. Widnall participated in the parade.

A Second Trip in Space

On Dec. 15 and 16, 1965, Schirra made his second journey into space as the command pilot of the *Gemini 6* flight. The history making mission accomplished the first rendezvous of two manned, maneuverable space vehicles.

Accompanied by Thomas Stafford, Schirra maneuvered *Gemini 6* to within six inches of the *Gemini 7* spacecraft which had preceded Schirra's ship into space. The two spacecraft flew in the same orbit for five-and-a-half hours. At no time was the distance between them greater than 100 feet. The astronauts aboard *Gemini 7* were Frank Borman and James Lovell.

Although Schirra would again fly in space during NASA's Apollo series of flights, he told an audience of more than 700 guests at the time of his induction into the Aviation Hall of Fame of New Jersey in 1982 that the *Gemini 6* flight was his most satisfying. Referring to the rendezvous of two spaceships he said, "The Russians haven't been able to do that to this day. We did it with manual controls."

The two spacecraft had flown completely around each other, back and forth, over and under — a technique that had to be developed for the planned manned flights to the moon. *Gemini 6* did most of the maneuvering. Schirra and Stafford had prepared two years for the adventure.

On the day *Gemini 6* was launched, with all systems set to go, a two-inch electrical plug dropped two seconds too soon from the base of the rocket as it was about to blast off. The dropped plug sent false signals that the rocket was lifting prematurely. Not feeling any motion, Schirra didn't overreact. Instead of immediately pulling the rings that would have ejected them from the craft, Schirra and Stafford sat tight. The lift-off went perfectly.

"Schirra, the test pilot, did what no electronic device could do," said flight director Chris Kraft after the launch. "He arrived in a split second at the right decision. He got a lift-off cue, but felt no motion. He ignored all signals."

Known as a "textbook" pilot, Schirra remained in the in both the Mercury and Gemini spacecraft following their splash-downs. He was the first astronaut to be brought aboard the recovery ship twice in that manner.

On the morning of Dec. 16, Schirra and Stafford startled the Mission Control team in Houston by describing in great detail a large object flying below them on a north-to-south trajectory. They said they feared the brightly-lit UFO might collide with Gemini 6. When they had the engineers and technicians in a fit of panic, they began playing "Jingle Bells" on a harmonica and a set of bells they had smuggled aboard the spacecraft. There were no worldly restraints on Schirra's practical jokes.

Another New Jersey Spaceman

Edwin E. "Buzz" Aldrin Jr.

Inducted Aviation Hall of Fame of New Jersey, 1980

On Nov. 11, 1966, Edwin E. "Buzz" Aldrin Jr. of Montclair, and James Lovell were launched into space aboard the *Gemini 12* spacecraft, the last flight of the *Geminis*. During the four-day journey, Aldrin established a new record for extra vehicular activity (EVA) by spending more than five-and-a-half hours outside the spacecraft.

When Lovell and Aldrin had arrived at the launch pad a sign greeted them saying, "Last Chance! No Reruns! Show will close after this performance!" Then as they walked past the sign and headed toward the spaceship, photographers saw that the astronauts each had a word imprinted on the seat of their pants — "THE" and "END."

The first major accomplishment of the flight was the third-revolution rendezvous with the previously launched *Agena* spacecraft. When a radar failure occurred, the back-up computations that Aldrin had assisted in pioneering a year earlier, based in part on his Massachusetts Institute of Technology (MIT) thesis, proved to be invaluable in executing the rendezvous successfully.

During his umbilical EVA, Aldrin attached a tether to the *Agena* and retrieved a micro-meteorite experiment package from the unmanned spacecraft. He also evaluated the use of body and foot restraints designed for securing aetronauts to the spacecraft while completing work tasks outside the vehicle.

After undocking from the *Agena,* Gemini remained attached to the Agena by a 100-foot tether which Aldrin had put in place. In the next three orbits, Lovell and Aldrin demonstrated for the first time that a spacecraft could be controlled to remain vertically above a free-flying object.

The *Gemini 12* made the first fully automatic, controlled re-entry into the earth's atmosphere and splashed down in the Atlantic two-and-a-half miles from the prime recovery ship *USS Wasp.*

Born in 1930, Aldrin was raised in Montclair. His father, Edwin Sr., was the pioneer aviator who organized and directed the Standard Oil of New Jersey flight department for many years. Aldrin acquired his nickname because during childhood one of his sisters pronounced the word "brother" as "buzzer." Aldrin later said, "I had already decided when I was a young boy that I didn't want to be known as Edwin. So when I got the nickname 'Buzz' it just stuck."

Aldrin played soccer in high school and his teacher Rita Holden remembered his determination. "He was the shortest student in the class, but he always got that ball through the goal."

Aldrin attended the United States Military Academy at West Point, and graduated third in his class of 473 cadets in 1951. A year later, he received his Air Force wings in Bryon, TX, and was sent to Korea. There, he flew 66 combat missions in F-86 fighter jets and destroyed two Russian-built MIG-15s.

Upon returning from Korea, Aldrin was assigned to numerous Air Force posts, including the position of Flight Commander of the 36th Tactical Fighter Wing in Bitburg, Germany. Once back in the U.S., he entered MIT and worked toward a doctorate by doing a thesis on guidance for manned orbital rendezvous. After being forced to prove his theories correct during his *Gemini 12* flight, Aldrin tutored other astronauts in the intricacies of space rendezvous and became known as "Dr. Rendezvous."

He had joined the space program in October of 1963, among 13 new astronauts in the third group named. His first important assignment was as backup pilot for the *Gemini 9* mission.

In 1968, he was named the backup command module pilot for the *Apollo VIII* flight. A year later, he would become the first man to land a vehicle on the moon.

Schirra Commands First Apollo Flight

The first manned flight of the third generation of United States spacecraft was commanded by Wally Schirra. As the triumphant 11-day mission of *Apollo 7* soared into orbit on Oct. 11, 1968, Schirra reported, "She's riding like a dream."

With command module pilot Donn F. Eisele and lunar module pilot Walter Cunningham, Schirra executed maneuvers enabling the crew to perform exercises in the transposition, docking and lunar orbit rendezvous with the S-IVB stage of their Saturn IB launch vehicle. The various tests were done in preparation for the lunar landing in July of the following year.

The spacesuits worn by the three astronauts weighed 32 pounds, were individually tailored, contained layers of fireproof fiberglaas and aluminized plastic.

Shirra said "They each cost $100,000 with just one pair of pants."

The men were the first to suffer colds in space. Their space craft was dubbed the "ten-day cold capsule."

Prior to their flight, Schirra and Cunningham were arrested for drag racing in Coco Beach, FL. Despite pleas of innocence, they couldn't convince the officer to drop the charges. Their court appearance was postponed until after they had orbited the earth. Following the successful flight, the judge forgave them.

A few months after the mission, the entire *Apollo 7* crew was presented with a special EMMY award for making the first live network television broadcast from space.

At the completion of the Apollo flight, Schirra had become the only astronaut to fly in all three generations of space vehicles — Mercury, Gemini and Apollo. Soon after the flight, Schirra resigned from the space program saying "The space age devours people. I have been completely devoured by this business."

His major awards include the U.S. Distinguished Service Medal, three Distinguished Flying Crosses (one earned while flyng in Korea) with two Air Medals, the Collier Trophy, the Harmon Trophy and others.

The author's most vivid and revealing recollection of Wally Schirra's humanistic personality occurred at his Aviation Hall of Fame induction dinner in 1982. A group of ten youths, members of the Rev. Russell White's Eagle Flight Explorer Scout troop, based in East Orange, NJ, were invited to the dinner by the Hall of Fame president Bennett Fishler.

The teenage boys and girls, all in uniform, were seated at a table near the dais. Wally, sitting on the dais, was chatting with several local politicians, when Rev. White asked me if I thought Wally would shake hands with one of his boys who had just been accepted to the Air Force Academy. I said I was certain he would, and interrupted Wally to introduce the boy. Wally not only shook the boy's hand, but spoke to him for five minutes about the wonderful experience the boy would encounter at the Air Force Academy. While the boy was there, the politicians took a back seat.

During his space flight career, Schirra was being paid according to a military scale. When he retired, he was earning $18,000 a year. "I read that news commentators were getting a million dollars to report on what we were doing," he said with a smile. "That's pretty dangerous — they might fall off the stage in the broadcast studio. I guess astronauts were on a pay scale of old time professional ball players.

"But we enjoyed our work immensely. You couldn't buy what we were doing, although a lot of people would have liked to."

Schirra said that he has no regrets about not flying to the moon. He explained that he preferred his pioneering role and his opportunities to contribute engineering and planning ideas.

Schirra, his wife Jo and two children lived in Denver, CO, when he retired. Several years later, the family moved to Rancho Santa Fe, CA.

First-Human Spacecraft
Russell L."Rusty" Schweikart

NASA Photo

Russell "Rusty" Schweikart

During the 10-day voyage of the *Apollo 9* capsule into space, March 3 to March 13, 1969, astronaut Russell "Rusty" Schweickart, a Neptune, NJ, native, became the world's first self-contained human spacecraft.

His two-hour space walk in a completely self contained space suit was cancelled due to a sudden attack of nausea that overcame him. When he recovered, he climbed out on the "front porch" of the orbiting lunar module for a view of earth from 147 miles up, while his fellow crew members, command pilot Col. David R. Scott and Col. James A. McDivitt kept the spaceship on a steady course.

Schweickart spent 40 minutes outside the spacecraft, taking pictures and successfully testing the garments and life-support apparatus that future astronauts would use to walk on the surface of the moon. It was the first time an American astronaut had left his orbiting craft and depended solely on a back pack for his oxygen, air conditioning and communications rather than on "umbilical hoses" leading from the vehicle.

The space suit cost $2 million. The two back packs weighed a total of 125 pounds, bringing the total weight of the suit and backpacks to 180 pounds, 19 pounds more than Schweickart's weighed himself. .

The red-headed New Jerseyan, code named "Red Rover" for radio communications, stood on the porch-like platform attached only by the "golden slipper" foot restraint, that had been tested by Astronaut Buzz Aldrin on the *Gemini 12* flight. He had left the capsule at 12:07 p.m. Eastern Standard time, as the vehicle passed over the Pacific ocean at sunrise. He climbed back in as the sun was setting over Africa. "Boy, oh, boy, what a view!" Schweickart exclaimed.

In an October 1983 article in the *Pan Am Clipper* magazine, Schweickart recalled his thoughts while riding through the blackness of space:

I realized that I wouldn't have a time like this again, so I said to myself, "Hold on, what's going on? Why am I here? What does it mean?" I became a total sponge. I felt that mankind had come to this point and I was up there for all the millions of people on earth, not for

Rusty Schweickart. I began thinking, "What's my responsibility?" I didn't generate a lot of answers, but I opened up to a lot more [of the experience] than just reading dials and throwing switches.

On the fifth day of the flight, McDivitt and Schweickart took man's first flight in the lunar module (LM), the spiderlike vehicle that would eventually land men on the moon. The spacemen climbed through a small hatch that connected the two orbiting vehicles, clamped the door shut, unhooked from the command ship and rocketed off more than 100 miles away. Then, primarily relying on radar, the astronauts maneuvered back to a smooth rendezvous and link-up with the *Apollo* capsule piloted by Scott.

As the bug-like space vehicle approached the small space capsule, Scott radioed "You're the biggest, friendliest, funniest-looking spider I've ever seen."

McDivitt and Schweickart reported that they were blinded by the bright sun as they guided the LM on its final approach to the docking. When Scott excitedly radioed "I have a capture," McDivitt commented, "Dave, that wasn't a docking, that was an eye test. Okay, Houston, we're locked up."

Another successful test had put man closer to the moon.

Schweickart, one of a few civilian astronauts in those early days of space flight, said he felt honored to have been part of the space program.

"There's one moment in history when humanity emerged from the earth." he said, "and the moment happened in our lifetime. What a privilege to take part in it."

In his book, *Carrying the Fire,* published in 1974, Apollo 11 astronaut Michael Collins described Schweickart as "a blithe spirit, eager, [with an] inquisitive mind, quick with a cutting retort, not appreciated by the 'old heads.' Mildly nonconformist, with

First men to travel to the moon - Armstrong, Collins and Aldrin.

a wide range of interests, contrasting sharply with the blinders-on preoccupation shown by many astronauts."

Schweickart left NASA in 1977 and went to work for California Governor Jerry Brown. He then became a member of the California Energy Commission and made his home permanently in Sacramento. In 1985, he organized the Association of Space Explorers. It is an exclusive group. Approximately 200 men and women who have flown in space are eligible to join. By 1988, there were 52 members from 16 countries including the United States, Soviet Union, Bulgaria, Cuba, Czechoslovakia, East and West Germany, France, Hungary, Mexico, Mongolia, the Netherlands, Poland, Romania, Saudi Arabia and Vietnam. The purpose of the group is "to encourage the exploration and development of space for the benefit of humankind."

The Day The *Eagle* Landed
Aldrin, Armstrong and Collins

An entire nation held its collective breath as Charles Duke, NASA capsule communicator in Houston, began the countdown. "sixty seconds," he said and the massive television and radio audience began counting with him.

Through the crackle of the atmosphere came a reply from Edwin "Buzz" Aldrin Jr., the pilot of the strange spider-like spacecraft. "Down two and a half (feet per second). Forward, forward. Good. Forty feet, down two and a half. Picking up some dust."

Duke said, "Thirty seconds," and the entire listening audience stopped breathing completely. Aldrin reported matter-of-factly, "Contact light!" That was followed by Neil Armstrong's long awaited announcement: "Tranquility Base here. The *Eagle* has landed." Man had safely reached the surface of the moon.

In every city and town in America the collective sigh of relief was almost audible. Then the shouting, laughing, bell ringing, whistle blowing celebration became ear shattering. The deed had been accomplished and Americans had a right to be proud.

Nowhere was that feeling of pride and joy more evident than in Aldrin's hometown, Montclair, or in the Jersey shore community of Brielle where the elder Aldrin and his wife had retired. It's interesting to note that the astronaut's mother's maiden name was Moon.

In the pioneering spirit of so many Garden State residents before him, Aldrin, with the help of thousands of engineers, technicians and fellow astronauts, had taken a quantum leap for mankind and the field of aeronautics.

The Eagle had touched down at 4:17:43 p.m. EDT, Sunday, July 20, 1969. Aldrin, Armstrong and module pilot Michael Collins had been traveling in space some 103 hours. Although Armstrong was the first man to step onto the moon's surface, all photographs showing the first man on the moon are of Aldrin. Armstrong carried the camera.

Not many remember Aldrin's words as he took his first steps through the moon's deep, powdery surface. "Beautiful... magnificent desolation" is the way he described it.

The astronauts spent two hours and 20 minutes on the moon, proudly planting an American flag, collecting moon rocks and setting up scientific instruments. The space suits and oxygen/air conditioning packs the men carried weighed a total of 180 pounds, but the men found they could easily take large leaping steps in the low gravity pull of the moon.

Although the landing on the moon had been breathtaking, it seemed comparatively easy once they were down. But the men at the NASA control center and those in space knew that if the lifting engine failed to perform or the rendezvous with the Columbia could not be accomplished as planned, Armstrong and Aldrin would be stranded in space with less than a day's supply of food and water. Those were extremely tense moments.

To make matters worse, as the two moon walkers climbed back into the *Eagle*, one of their bulky space suits caught on the arming switch for the ascent engines, breaking it off. After a quick conference with the engineers at the Houston space center, the astronauts were advised to retract the point of a ball-point pen and use the hollow end to reach the metal strip inside the broken switch. To the relief of everyone, it worked. The zero-g pen had cost $1 million to develop, little did the designers know that it would become a lifesaver and worth every penny.

The LM lifted off the moon with little difficulty and began its search through the vast blackness of space for the command module *Columbia*. Module pilot, Michael Collins, had been circling the moon every two hours awaiting the *Eagle's* return. It was now time for Buzz Aldrin, "Dr. Rendezvous," to put the theories to the acid test. They worked perfectly.

Apollo 11 splashed down in the Pacific Ocean at 12:50 p.m. on July 24, 1969. The astronauts were picked up and taken aboard a raft. There, they were scrubbed clean before being lifted aboard the *USS Hornet* where they were placed in isolation. President Richard M. Nixon was on the aircraft carrier and chatted with the new American heroes through a glass window in the quarantine van. The three spacemen stayed in the van for 18 days.

When he faced the press or well-meaning fans, Aldrin would see red when asked how it felt to be the second man to land on the moon. His pat reply was, "We both landed at the same time."

Thomas J. O'Malley and Samuel Romano

Two other former New Jersey natives who played a leading role in the space program were Thomas J. O'Malley, the Kennedy Space Center's first launch director and Samuel Romano, who headed the Delco Electronics' vehicle systems group that developed the Lunar Roving Vehicle.

O'Malley, a former resident of Clifton and Packanack Lake, spent 20 years with his right index finger poised above a button that made space history during the first two decades of our nation's space program. It was he who pressed the button igniting the Atlas booster under John Glenn, hurtling the first American into Earth orbit. In all, he oversaw more than 50 launches, from ballistic missiles to Apollo spacecraft. He had 2,200 technicians working under his supervision.

A 1937 graduate of the Newark College of Engineering, O'Malley began his career working for Curtiss-Wright in Wood Ridge, NJ, testing turbo prop engines. Nineteen years later, he joined the Air Force Atlas program, assuming he'd work as a rocket specialist. Soon he was in charge of ballistic missile launches.

"I had one blow up on the pad, and one blew up after a flight of 60 seconds. I began to wonder if I'd made the right move from New Jersey to Florida."

Others believed he made the right move. In 1981, O'Malley was named "Man of the Year" by the Space Congress.

At age 65 in 1982, he reminisced about the progress that had been made during 20 years he had spent in the space program. "In the early days, we had to do everything manually, including loading the fuel. Everything involved switches. Today, most of it's done with computers."

Launching the first manned spacecraft in February 1962 was O'Malley's most rewarding accomplishment. The decision to "go" with the Mercury spacecraft launch was his and his alone.

"We kept delaying it for a month because of high seas in the recovery area," he recalled. "We were very anxious to get it off."

During the delay, O'Malley and astronaut John Glenn, whose life was on the line, became close friends.

"He paid me the greatest compliment I've ever received when I started explaining the abort procedure a few days before his mission," the Jersey native said." Glenn just said he had the greatest faith in the world in me and walked out of the room."

U.S. Senator John Glenn of Ohio attended the Space Congress award ceremony honoring O'Malley.

O'Malley believes ordinary citizens don't understand what benefits space travel can provide for humankind.

"Just think about the possibilities of space," he said. "There's all the energy we'd ever need out there, but the damn problem is people don't understand that progress is what makes us go forward. They want to stay where we are. People have lost the drive to go where we've never been before."

Just prior to his retirement, O'Malley was involved in the space shuttle program. In 1981, he was at Edwards Air Force Base in California to watch the return of the first space shuttle flown into orbit and back to earth.

"It came back in much better shape than we expected." he said. "When future generations look back on this exploration, they'll compare it to the voyage of Columbus."

In the late '80s, the momentous decisions are behind him and he enjoys the good life in Florida. Every so often, he travels north and looks up old friends from those early days at Curtiss-Wright.

Samuel Romano

"Okay, we're moving forward, Joe. Whew, hang on. We're coming around left, heading directly south right now to miss some craters off to our right."

Those were the words of Apollo 15 astronaut Jim Irwin as he clung to the passenger seat of the first Lunar Roving Vehicle (LRV) and reported the progress he and the vehicle's driver, astronaut David Scott, were making in their open-air moon buggy. He was speaking to Joe Allen at the Mission Control Center in Houston, TX.

The success of the LRV brought a smiles to the faces of New Jerseyans in Santa Barbara, CA, and several towns in Bergen County. Samuel Romano, a 44-year-old native of Jersey City, headed the Vehicles Systems Group at the Delco Electronics Division of General Motors in Santa Barbara, and was responsible for the design and development of the LRV. Romano's parents, Dominick and Josephine of Rutherford and his brother Frank, a Ridgefield Park resident, were glued to their television sets watching the two astronauts prepare the LRV for its first ride on the moon.

The Apollo 15 was the first of three lunar missions to include a Lunar Roving Vehicle as a payload. The mission began with the launch of a Saturn V rocket on July 26, 1971, from the Kennedy Space Center.

The rover was carried to the moon in the descent stage of the Lunar Module, with wheels neatly folded against the chassis to save space. After landing the astronauts unfolded and set up the unusual craft.

During their 67-hour stay on the moon, Irwin and Scott used the LRV to make three separate motor trips to explore the rim of Hadley Rille, the edges of deep craters, and the slopes of the Apennine Mountains. They covered approximately 15.7 miles, almost four times the distance traveled by astronauts on all three previous lunar missions combined when the moon explorers had been walking.

Meanwhile, astronaut Al Worden conducted scientific experiments and observations from the orbiting Command Module.

Romano, a 1955 graduate of the Newark College of Engineering, joined the General Motors Defense Research Laboratory in Santa Barbara in 1960 and became manager of vehicle systems development. In 1966, he was named Project Manager, Lunar Roving Vehicle Program for GM's Delco Electronics Division. His team of 320 employees conducted studies and hardware development on a wide range of vehicles for operation on the lunar surface. The vehicles included small, remote-controlled types to large, mobile laboratory-sized systems. Those studies, which covered more than 10 years, culminated in the design and development of the LRV.

As program manager for the LRV, Romano was awarded the 1971 NASA Public Service Award for the successful development of the LRV, used on the Apollo 15, 16, 17 moon landings. The lunar dune buggies had greatly extended the radius of exploration by the astronauts and permitted them to gather a larger number of moon samples for scientists to study.

When Romano presented the author with a wheel of the LRV for display in the New Jersey Aviation Hall of Fame's museum, he said: "The only other place you'll find one of these is on the moon."

Romano is the nephew of the late aviation pioneer Charles "Slim" West, formerly an aviator with the Gates Flying Circus.

New Jersey Airmen in Vietnam

The success of America's space program shared the headlines throughout the 1960s with the Vietnam War, one of the ugliest chapters in U.S. military history. As it had been in all the 20th century conflicts, New Jersey airmen played both leading and supporting roles in the war effort. Hundreds of Garden State airmen were recognized for their gallant efforts. Three outstanding ones were Navy Lieutenant Hugh Dennis Wisely of Wayne, Air Force Lt. Col. Albert R. Howarth of Westfield and Army Captain George Meade of Elmwood Park.

Hugh Dennis Wisely

Maj. Dennis Wisely

On Dec. 19, 1966, while serving aboard the aircraft carrier *USS Kitty Hawk* off the coast of Vietnam, Hugh Dennis Wisely shot down his first enemy aircraft. He described the action in a letter to his parents Mr. and Mrs. Hugh E. Wisely of Wayne.

"You must have heard by now that I shot down a plane the other night. I almost got it on my birthday. I was on CAP [planes ready to be launched by catapult] from 0030 to 0239. At about 0212, as I was engrossed in a WW II novel JAS [Jan, his wife] had sent me about the RAF, I heard them announce over the loudspeaker 'Launch the CAP!' Two minutes later I was in the air going almost 600 knots at low altitude.

"They had some bogies [enemy aircraft] just out over the water near Than Hon (North Vietnam), about 90 miles away. I kept thinking, I hope they don't run before I get there. We were flying over a low overcast and I didn't want to go zipping in over the beach and get a few SAMS [ground launched missiles] shot at me.

"As we got within 15 miles, they turned and started to run. I fired my missile at three miles, just in from the beach. After it exploded, I hauled out to sea again. What a happy moment! I did aileron rolls all the way back to the ship!"

In May of 1967, Wisely shot down a second MIG, thus becoming the first American airman credited with downing two enemy aircraft during the Vietnam conflict. Air Force Colonel Robin Olds was the second. Wisely stayed aboard the carrier *Kitty Hawk* for three tours of duty, a total of 27 months.

During that time, it wasn't all victories for the Jersey native. On his 209th mission over a heavily defended target a few miles south of the North Vietnam capital of Hanoi, his F-4 Phantom jet was hit by enemy ground fire causing the plane's hydraulic system to become inoperative. He and his radar intercept officer, Jim Laing, ejected at what he described as "a hot 400 knots." He landed in a tree in a dense jungle. He said later, "You get real scared at a time like this. Prayer seems important. I said a few 'Hail Marys'"

Using a survival radio he carried in his flying suit, Wisely kept in contact with other F-75s circling above the spot where he had gone down. It took several hours for rescue helicopters to reach him and to find Laing. Within two days they were back on the *Kitty Hawk* and Wisely was flying again.

When he left Southeast Asia, he had flown more than 350 missions and had logged in excess of 4,400 flight hours.

Born in Kearny, NJ, in 1940, Wisely was seven when he took his first airplane ride at Teterboro Airport. In 1950, his family moved to Wayne where he graduated from high school. In 1961, he joined the Navy's NAVCAD program and learned to fly.

The ejection from the Phantom over Vietnam was not his first. In October of 1966, while on maneuvers off the coast of San Diego, CA, his Phantom jet, with Lt. (j.g.) G.L. Aderson as the flight officer, collided with a A-4 Skyhawk attack bomber piloted by Lt. Comdr. J.C. Eichinger. All three airmen ejected safely from their crippled aircraft and were picked up by helicopters from the *Kitty Hawk*.

In Command of the Blue Angels

In December of 1979, Wisely was chosen to lead the Navy's famous Blue Angel aerobatic squadron. He told the press that the assignment was the fulfillment of a lifelong dream. "It was a real thrill. To be named the commander of the Angels is something of which I'm quite proud," he said.

The appointment, following a stringent, four-month selection process, made Wisely the 18th officer to assume command of the Navy's most prestigious air squadron. He had 12 officers and 70 enlisted men under his command and during his two-year tour in command, he and his men traveled extensively throughout the United States.

The Blue Angels flew McDonnell Douglas F-4F Skyhawks of which Wisely said, "It's an older plane but it carries a powerful engine." In the two years he flew with them, the Blue Angels gave more than 140 exciting demonstrations of the art of aerobatic jet flying.

When he left the Angels in 1981, Wisely became the executive officer of the carrier *USS America*. He then spent two years as the executive officer with the Air Test and Evaluation Squadron in California. His group tested air-to-air missiles and air-to-ground missiles flying an assortment of naval aircraft. His work earned him a membership in the exclusive Society of Experimental Test Pilots.

In the fall of 1985, Captain Hugh D. Wisely was appointed commander of the aircraft carrier *USS John F. Kennedy*. He took the carrier on patrol with the U.S. fleet in Mid-Eastern waters.

Lt. Col. Albert R. Howarth

Capt. Albert Howarth

One of the most coveted awards in aviation, the Air Force's Mackay Trophy, was presented to Lt. Col. Albert R. Howarth of Westfield by Air Force Chief of Staff, Gen. John. P. McConnell at the Pentagon in Washington, DC.

A career officer, Howarth was cited for his action while piloting a disabled A-26A on a combat mission over Vietnam on Dec. 14, 1966.

While attacking enemy anti-aircraft gun positions, one of his aircraft's two engines was hit by enemy fire and burst into flames. Unable to control the fire, Howarth ordered his two navigators to bail out. The first jumped clear of the burning ship, but the second man became entangled in a seat belt mechanism.

The citation described the seriousness of the event: An explosion was imminent, but despite the critical situation and diminishing chances for his own survival, Howarth, while maintaining firm control of the aircraft, physically assisted the remaining navigator in getting disentangled and only after ensuring his safe egression, did he parachute to safety.

For his heroic action, the 40-year-old colonel received the Silver Star prior to being named as the Mackay Trophy winner.

The trophy, established in 1912 by Clarence W. Mackay, a member of the Aero Club of America, is given to an Air Force individual or unit for the most meritorious flight each year. The silver cup is three feet high and when it was created, cost $65,000. Today, its replacement might be 10 times that amount.

Some of America's greatest military aviators are among the names engraved on the silver cup — names like World War I ace Eddie Rickenbacker; Benjamin Foulois, one of the first officers to operate a military aircraft purchased from the Wright brothers; General of the Air Force "Hap" Arnold; Capt. "Chuck" Yeager, the first man to fly faster than sound; and Lt. Leslie P. Arnold, a former Leonia resident, who was a member of the first round-the-world flying team in 1924.

Born in Newark, Howarth graduated from Union (NJ) High School His family lived in Union for 25 years. He entered the Army Air Corps in 1944 and was commissioned in-1946. During the Korean War, he was a B-26 pilot with the 3rd Bombardment Wing

George Meade

flying out of Kusan Air Base. He flew 55 combat missions and spent 214 hours in the air. He also was designated a "locomotive ace" for destroying nine trains and damaging seven others.

While in Southeast Asia, Howarth flew 483 combat hours on 96 missions in less than two years. When he returned to the United States, he was named a Command Pilot.

After 30 years of service, he retired to Fort Myers, FL.

George Meade

While flying more than 1,000 combat missions as an Army helicopter pilot, Captain George Meade was awarded the Air Medal for Valor, a Bronze Star and 20 additional Air Medals during his tour of duty in Vietnam.

He had graduated from Pope Pius High School in Passaic, NJ, and gone on to earn a B.A. degree from Seton Hall University. He learned to fly through the Army R.O.T.C. flight program and went into the service immediately after his college days. Following his years in Southeast Asia, he continued to fly as a traffic reporter in New York metropolitan area for WOR radio in New York City. For 20 plus years, Meade has been heard each morning on the popular *Rambling with Gambling* show. He was one of the pioneers in the field of helicopter traffic reporting and the best known in Northern New Jersey.

Ironically, Meade became a traffic reporter by accident. "After I was discharged from the Army in 1968, I was lucky and found a helicopter pilot job with Butler Aviation at La Guardia Airport," he explained.

"The traffic pilot who flew for CBS [radio] was sick one morning so I flew for him.

"I stayed with Butler for a year and then got the job at WOR. In 20 years of flying the traffic, I estimate I've flown 12,000 hours and done more than 8,000 reports. Knock wood, I've never had an accident."

His working day begins at 6:15 a.m. at the Port Authority hangar at Teterboro Airport, where the familiar Bell Jet Ranger helicopter, with "WOR 710" emblazoned on its side, is housed. Once the machine is thoroughly warmed up, the Oakland, NJ, resident lifts off the ramp to fly for three hours over New York City, Northern New Jersey and portions of Westchester County, NY. One might think that reporting the traffic for 20 years from a thousand feet above the pavement could become boring, but Meade has found that traffic can become snarled for many reasons. The most common are simple fenderbenders and overturned tractor-trailers. The more colorful have been cattle running loose on the New Jersey Turnpike when a truck carrying them overturned; a scantily dressed woman walking her dog beside a highway and a 10-mile backup on the Palisades Interstate Parkway when a water-main broke near the George Washington Bridge.

When he isn't flying, Meade spends a great deal of time speaking to various groups about his job and promoting aviation. A fine photographer, his excellent collection of aerial slides have been well received by school groups or business organizations throughout New Jersey. He and John Gambling, the host of the WOR morning show, have always been willing to promote important local events during their lighthearted exchanges before and after the traffic reports.

Over the years, he has been recognized for the public service he provides. RKO General, the owners of WOR named him "Newsman of the Year," the Bergen County (NJ) Safety Council gave him the President's Safety Award, and from the New York City Police, he has received a Commendation Certificate and Commendation Bar. St. John's University bestowed an honorary Doctorate of Humane Letters on him.

When asked about aviation safety, Meade always answers "the most dangerous part of my job is driving to the airport from Oakland."

Stunt Pilots Killed

While men in space and at war dominated the thoughts of Americans throughout the 1960s, men who flew just a few thousand feet above the earth were also attracting the public's attention. Two Garden State natives, Clifford Werner and Edward Mahler, were among that exclusive group.

In September 1962, Clifford Werner (known professionally as Cliff Winters), a former Brick Township, NJ, resident and professional stunt pilot, wing walker and parachute jumper, died in the crash of a Ryan biplane when the engine quit while he was attempting to pick up a handkerchief from the ground while hanging from the wing at an air show at Chino, CA. It seemed the 33-year-old daredevil had a death wish that came to pass.

When questioned earlier by the media concerning his dangerous occupation, he answered glibly, "It's a matter of time, but that's [performing a stunt] the way I want to go."

Born in Orange, NJ, Werner received his education in West Orange and New Providence, NJ. He first flew in a homemade glider at age 15.

He joined the military and gained his paratrooper wings. Later he earned a commercial pilot's license under the GI Bill. He then joined an aerial circus in the southeast and learned aerobatics.

Back in New Jersey, he supported himself by crop dusting and performing at air shows with his friend and fellow parachutist, Hanz Schmidt.

An extremely handsome and personable young man, Werner was lured to California to be a movie stunt man. It was then that he adopted the show business name of Winters. He became famous for his ability to purposely crash a plane. After spending two years perfecting the stunt, Werner crashed through prefabricated buildings, barn doors, flaming walls and even living trees.

A member of the Screen Actors Guild, Werner was a stand-in for Peter Lawford in *Never so Few* and appeared in *Beyond Glory*. He was a regular stunt stand-in on the syndicated television show *Ripcord*. During one episode, two planes accidently collided and Werner's plane lost its tail assembly. He had to bail out, but he didn't have a parachute on. He scrambled around the cockpit floor for the parachute and then jumped with it in his hands. While he was free falling, he hooked the chute to his harness. Howard Curtis, who piloted the other plane, described Werner's actions as "about like trying to change a tire while your car is still moving." Werner fell two thousand feet before his chute opened.

There were other crashes in California at Porterville, Riverside, a pair at Lake Elsinore and two into the Salton Sea. In addition, there was a deliberate one for cameramen off the coast of Avalon on Catalina Island.

Television cameras were recording his last stunt. The cameras had been positioned in a trench below the ground so they could catch the action. Werner successfully picked up the handkerchief before the plane dove into the ground. His final act was shown on "Wide World of Sports," but the crash was cut from the sequence.

Hanz Schmidt remembered his friend as being completely fearless and ready to take on any challenge. "I guess his time just ran out," he said, sadly shaking his head. "But I think he ought to be remembered. He was one of a kind."

Edward Mahler

The skies were bright and clear above the Experimental Aircraft Association (EAA) museum at Oshkosh, WI, when Ed Mahler of Pittstown, NJ, put his red, white and blue PJ-295 biplane through a rigorous aerobatic routine. His faultless performance that day won the approval of the judges and Mahler was crowned the EAA's aerobatic champion. That victory was a culmination of a dream that began in the mid-1950s when he worked as a lineboy at Basking Ridge Airport in Somerset Hills, NJ. There, he pushed planes in and out of hangars, did minor maintenance and anything else Rick Decker, the operator of Decker Flying Service, requested. During those years, he received his private pilot's license and was working toward a commercial ticket.

Historian William Rhode, then a flight instructor for Decker, remembered Mahler as a hard working, tall, ruggedly handsome man. "Ed had a special relationship with airplanes," Rhode said. "He seemed to talk to them. Over the years, he perfected his flying skills and became one of the best stunt pilots in the nation."

Mahler's first aerobatic plane was an Air Force surplus North American AT-6. "As far as I know," said his brother, Bob, "Ed is still the only pilot to fly an advanced air show routine in an AT-6. He would snap roll it on takeoff."

In 1964, Mahler and Lee Weber of Somerset, built the PJ-295 and soon Mahler became a familiar air show participant flying both the AT-6 and the colorful little biplane. Engine failure at a show in Maryland caused the AT-6 to crash, but Mahler escaped with only superficial cuts. He sold the wreck and continued performing in the PJ-295. His most famous trick was flying up-side-down, just a few yards above the ground, and then snatching a flag strung between two poles.

Tom Bianco, who maintained Mahler's planes, described his boss warmly. "He isn't a publicity-hound stunt man like Evel Kinievel. He's an aerobatic man," Bianco said.

Mahler and his wife, Valerie, bought a home on the edge of Sky Manor Airport in Pittstown. There, he and Sonny Everett formed an air show team called Airshow America. Mahler also flew one seaeon for Jim Bede as part of the Bede jet team.

He and fellow pilot George Mennen, the men's toiletry magnate, came up with a novel stunt. They mixed Mennen after-shave concentrate in the smoke oil that Mahler released during his show. One low pass over the grandstand would permeate the air with a pleas-ant spice odor. They named the plane the "Mennen Special."

In 1968, at an air show at Suffolk County Airport on Long Island, Mahler was killed in a tragic accident.

While practicing over the field, he heard something snap in the rear of his plane. Upon landing, he discovered that a stiff metal brace under the aircraft's stabilizer had sheared off. He mistakenly thought the plane was designed to fly without the brace, so he removed a similar one on the opposite side of the fuselage to correct the plane's balance.

When he was again airborne, he began a slow roll at about 200 feet above the airport's runway. Suddenly, the tail assembly came apart and the plane spun into the ground. Mahler died instantly.

Bob Mahler said, "There was nobody better. That's not my opinion — that's the opinion of the professional pilots he flew with and the opinion of the people who saw him fly."

Bianco paid this tribute to Mahler:

"Ed was a fantastic man. He had an effect on people. He'd be gone for a weekend to do a show and when he came back, he'd buzz the house to let us know to meet him at the airport and help him push the plane in the hangar. We listened for it every weekend. I'm gonna miss the man."

CHRONOLOGY OF OTHER AERONAUTICAL EVENTS AND ACHIEVEMENTS
1960 to 1969
1960

- The Courier 1-B communications satellite, developed by ITT's Federal Labs at Nutley, NJ, was successfully launched from Cape Canaveral, FL. It received a transcribed message by President Dwight D. Eisenhower, transmitted from Fort Monmouth, NJ, and retransmitted the message to Puerto Rico.

- Aircraft designer Giuseppe M. Bellanca died at age 70.

- Record-setting aviatrix Ruth Nichols died at age 59.

1961

- Max Conrad, known as the "Flying Grandfather," holder of several world distance records for light planes, took off from Teterboro Airport in a twin-engine Cessna on a mission of mercy. The plane was being donated by entertainer Arthur Godfrey to the African Research Foundation which operated hospitals in Africa. For Conrad, it was his 78th flight across the Atlantic.

1962

- Col. William R. Blair, USA (ret), died at Fair Haven, NJ at age 87. He was known as the father of Radar I. Blair, who served in the Army from 1917 to 1938, was chief of research and engineering at the Army Signal Corps laboratory Fort Monmouth from 1930 to 1938. Radar was developed there under his direction. He conceived the idea of radar prior to 1930, when he realized that ground troops could not fire at planes traveling 300 miles an hour on detection based on sound, but they could be detected by means of radio. The patent office gave him the base patent rights for radar in 1957.

- Louis Reichers, who flew across the Atlantic in 1932, died in Estes Park, CO.

- Telstar, a three-foot, 170 pound satellite developed by the Western Electric Co. of Hillside, NJ, began transmitting live television across the Atlantic Ocean.

- Joseph Boland, who with his brother Frank built New Jersey's first flying machine in 1909, died on Sept. 10 at age 85.

1963

- On his 16th birthday, Philip I. Laudenslager soloed in five different airplanes from the Red Bank Airport. The son of W.R. Laudenslager, owner of the airport, had amassed 100 hours of dual instruction in all types of aircraft. The five airplanes were a 1946 Piper J3 Cub a 1962 Piper Colt, a 1960 Piper Tri-Pacer, a 1962 Piper Cherokee and a 1961 Piper 250 Comanche. "Had I owned more airplanes," said Philip's father, "he would talk me out of them too."

1964

- Navy Commander William V. Lassen of Bloomfield, NJ, and Lt. James T. Osborne flying from the Naval Air Test Center at Patuxent River, MD, accomplished a unique feat. They flew a Navy jet coast-to-coast and photographed a 2,700-mile-long corridor, four miles wide, across the United States. The single continuous strip of film was 200 feet long. When he retired as a naval aviator in 1976, Lassen had flown 4,868 hours in 30 years.

1965

- Gay Dalby Maher, a mother of three of Medford, NJ, became the first person to fly a helicopter from coast to coast. She flew a three-place Hughes helicopter with no radio. Maher left Culver City, CA, on Feb. 6 and arrived at the National Aviation Facilities Experimental Center in Pomona, NJ, on Feb. 16. She was in the air approximately 40 hours flying at 80 mph and made 33 fuel stops. A flight instructor at the Flying W Ranch, Maher was famous for her flying attire — a large black cowboy hat and boots to match.

- Walter Gingrich sold the 77-acre North Brunswick Airport to developers.

- The day after Christmas 1965, a sputtering engine forced 19-year-old Phillip Ippolito Jr. of the Bronx to land his small airplane on the George Washington Bridge. He and Joseph Brennan of Hackensack, were on a flight from Ramapo Valley Airport in Spring Valley, NY, to Red Bank (NJ) Airport. The engine began acting up south of the bridge and the pilot made a 180 degree turn while he decided what to do. "I was just plain scared" he admitted. He considered ditching in the river, but Brennan, a Navy veteran, said he couldn't swim and was terrified of water. That left no alternative but the bridge. Luckily, it was a Sunday morning and traffic was light. "As I came over the roadway," Ippolito explained, "I did a left side slip and after 50 feet I went into a forward slip. This brought the plane directly over the roadway, but my flying speed was almost double the normal 40 to 45 miles-an-hour landing speed. I kept worrying about the people on the bridge up until the moment I hit the pavement." The plane rolled along the span until the right wing tip struck a truck, spinning it around. The two men suffered only minor injuries.

1966

- Aeronaut Tracy Barnes landed his balloon "Big White" in Rio Grande, on the western edge of the Cape May peninsula on September 11, thus completing the first transcontinental crossing of the United States in a hot air balloon. Barnes had begun his historic flight on April 9 from San Diego, CA, in a balloon named *Firefly 90*. At Wrightsville, PA, the balloon struck a power line and burned. At that point, Barnes transferred to *Big White* to complete his five month odyssey in New Jersey.

- The unique, experimental three-hulled powered airship *Aereon III*, which was 85 feet long, 53 feet wide and 18 feet high was destroyed while undergoing test flights at Mercer County Airport. Designed and built by the Aereon Corp. of Princeton, the *Aereon III* was flipped over on its back by a 15-knot crosswind. Its two pilots escaped injury.

1966

- Gill Robb Wilson, New Jersey's first director of aviation died at age 73 in California.

1967

- Selma Cronin of Leonia, NJ, a pilot and author, and the recipient of the 1960 Amelia Earhart Medal, was presented with the 1967 Lady Drummond-Hay Trophy for her accomplishments in flying and devotion to education.

- Maj. Gen. Benjamin D. Foulois, the first pilot to become Chief of the Army Air Corps, died at age 87. He had retired from military service in 1935 and moved to Ventnor, NJ. Foulois was among the first pilots to test the Wright Flyer for the Army in 1908.

- Thor Solberg, the first man to fly from New York to Norway, died in Hunterdon County, NJ.

1968

- Chauncey Julius Strickland, retired president of the Newark Air Service died at age 76. Strickland joined the Newark Air Service when it was founded in 1928 at Newark Airport. He became the company head in 1934 and held the position for 20 years. He was a graduate of Roselle (NJ) High School and Lafayette College.

1969

- Hangar #1 at the Lakehurst Naval Air Station was designated a National Historic Site by the National Park Service.

- The New Jersey State Police Helicopter Patrol Bureau was established at Mercer County Airport, Trenton. Police superintendent David B. Kelly initiated the program directed by Sgt. William Burke and trooper Gary Knight. The initial training was performed by Ronson Helicopters, Inc. Fourteen troopers took the 50-hour course.

First Astronaut Team - Front L-R: Walter M. Schirra, Donald K. Slayton, John H. Glenn, Scott Carpenter; back row: Alan B. Shepard, Virgil I. Grissom and L. Gordon Cooper

A Gathering of Eagles - (L-R) Gen. James Doolittle, Edwin "Buzz" Aldrin, Capt. Eddie Rickenbacker, Lowell Thomas and Edwin Aldrin Sr.

Thomas O'Malley at Atlas Launch console circa 1960s.

1970

While men were still exploring the surface of the moon in the early 1970s (the last Apollo moon flight occurred in December of 1972), the adventurous publisher of *Forbes Magazine,* Malcolm S. Forbes of Far Hills, NJ, was planning a balloon flight across the United States that would establish numerous international ballooning records. At the same time, Donald G. Borg, the publisher of the *Bergen Evening Record,* and the author, then the public relations officer for two divisions of Pan American World Airways based at Teterboro Airport, were recruiting five prominent North Jersey industrial and civic leaders to support the creation of the first state aviation hall of fame in the United States.

Aviation Hall of Fame
Donald G. Borg and Pat Reilly

Borg Inducted Aviation Hall of Fame of N.J., 1974

In April of 1972, seven New Jersey civic Leaders met in the office of Donald G. Borg, publisher of the *Bergen Evening Record,* to explore the possibility to organizing an aviation hall of fame to honor the men and women who played a part in the unparalleled history of Teterboro Airport. They were: attorneys, Horace F. Banta and John J. Breslin Jr.; banker, Edward A. Jesaer Jr.; realtor, Alexander Summer; industrialist, Fairleigh Dickinson Jr.; Borg and the author, then an airline publicist.

The group unanimously agreed to form an organization to be called the Teterboro Aviation Hall of Fame (AHOF). They set forth the the purposes of the new historic association:

° To receive and maintain funds for charitable and education purposes;

° To honor aviation leaders, pilots, teachers, engineers, inventors, government leaders and other individuals who contributed to the fame and development of Teterboro Airport;

° To perpetuate the memory of such persons and record their contributions and achievements by suitable memorials;

° To promote a better sense of appreciation of the origin and growth of Teterboro Airport and the part aviation in general has played in the changing aspects of the community and nation;

° To establish and maintain a library and museum preserving for posterity the history of those honored by the Teterboro Aviation Hall of Fame.

Officers of the fledgling association were elected.

Founding fathers - Breslin, Banta, Dickinson, Jesser, Reilly, Borg and Summer.

Borg was named president; Summer, vice president and the author, secretary/treasurer. Banta agreed to draw up the necessary papers to establish a non-profit association.

The idea of organizing an aviation hall of fame at Teterboro had first been seriously discussed two years earlier at a 50th anniversary party commemorating the commercial opening of Teterboro. The affair had been organized by Don Baldwin, Texaco's chief pilot, Henry Esposito of Atlantic Aviation and the author,

The aviation pioneers present were Clarence Chamberlin, Aron "Duke" Krantz, Blanche Noyes, Fred Wehran, Roy Ryder and Billy Diehl, who was the first itinerant pilot to land at the airport in August of 1920. Others honored but not present were Charles Lindbergh and Bernt Balchen.

More than 500 people attended the "Wing Ding." Among the guests were Mr. and Mrs. Donald Borg and their son, Gregory. The Borgs were long-time aviation buffs. As a young man, Donald had flown with Floyd Bennett in the 1920s.

As the evening progressed, the Borgs and the author, a former Bergen Record employee, discussed the great aviation pioneers who had been a part of Teterboro's unique history and agreed that the airport's heritage was worth preserving for the edification of generations to come. It was more than a year later that the author again broached the subject to Borg who enthusiastically endorsed the idea of an aviation hall of fame.

Early in 1973, Wilton T. Barney, Bennett H. Fishler Jr., Fred L. Wehran, David Van Alstyne and Robert A.M. Coppenrath were added to the board, and a committee of aviation pioneers nominated the first 10 men and women for induction into the first state aviation hall of fame in the nation.

Those nominated were Floyd Bennett, Clarence D. Chamberlin, William Diehl, Amelia Earhart, Edward Gorski, Aron Krantz, Charles A. Lindbergh, Fred L.

Wehran and the three Wittemann brothers, Charles, Paul and Walter, as a single entry.

Ill health forced Borg to withdraw as president of the association, and Wilton T. Barney was elected to replace him. Barney held that position for seven years. The author became the executive vice president and director. Under Barney's leadership, the AHOF prospered. More than 800 aviation enthusiasts became members of the association.

The first dinner held in April 1973 at the Tammy Brook Country Club, Cresskill, attracted more than 600 guests who not only welcomed the first batch of inductees, but were entertained by a 20-minute multi-media presentation concerning the careers of the men and women who were honored. Entertainer Arthur Godfrey was the special guest speaker.

The 1974 dinner, honoring Frederich Bohlander, Anthony Fokker, William Hartig, Jack Webster, and the special election of Donald Borg, who had died that year, was held in the Atlantic Aviation hangar. A mini airshow flown by many of the finest airshow performers in the country was the entertainment for the evening.

In 1975, a new air traffic control tower was constructed on the east side of Teterboro Airport, and the author convinced John P. Kennedy, then the vice president of Pan Am World Services, the operators of the airport, to permit the AHOF to use the top two floors of the old control tower as a small museum. The space was used to display the bronze inductee plaques and an assortment of artifacts that had been donated to the organization. Late in the year, with the concurrence of Atlantic Aviation, which held the lease on the tower building, Barney and Kennedy signed a lease agreement for $1 a year for the tower-top space. Tosh Sakov, a local museum designer, donated the services of his staff to create the interior design of the two small tower rooms.

More than 10,000 visitors attended the opening of the museum and another mini airshow.

By 1978, the Teterboro Aviation Hall of Fame had become the most viable, historic aviation organization in New Jersey. Aviation historians and enthusiasts from around the state approached the author with the idea of forming a state-wide aviation hall of fame and museum.

President Barney and the trustees, which now numbered 36, asked State Senator Matthew Feldman of Teaneck to introduce a bill in the State Legislature that would officially recognize the Teterboro Aviation Hall of Fame as the Aviation Hall of Fame & Museum of New Jersey.

On July 3, 1979, with Ted Barney at his side, Governor Brendan Byrne signed Senator Feldman's bill into law at the State House in Trenton. Thus, the Aviation Hall of Fame had become the official repository for all documents, photographs and artifacts concerning New Jersey's distinguished aeronautical heritage. The governor mandated that the AHOF be an educational center for New Jersey's young citizens.

"We are extremely pleased that Governor Byrne and the State Legislature have recognized our efforts to preserve New Jersey's illustrious aviation heritage," said Barney. "No state in the nation has played a more important role in the development of aviation than New Jersey, and the Governor's signature on this bill is an important first step toward the permanent preservation of our aviation heritage. We hope that in the future, our schools will include the history of New Jersey's aeronautical achievements in their curriculum."

State Senate bill No-3005 read:

°   An act to designate the aviation hall of fame and museum at Teterboro Airport as the Aviation Hall of Fame and Museum of New Jersey.

°   Whereas, Historic aviation achievements and events in New Jersey are unparalleled by any other state in the Union;

°   Whereas, These world acclaimed aviation accomplishments have not been properly memorialized;

°   Whereas, Such an oversight of this important New Jersey historic heritage is an injustice to all the citizens of the State;

°   Whereas, An aviation hall of fame and museum has been established at Teterboro Airport;

°   Whereas, There is now interest in creating a greatly enlarged museum at Teterboro that would encompass the entire history of aviation in this State;

°   Whereas, Such a museum would serve an important educational role among the children of this State;

°   Whereas, Such a museum would be a major tourist attraction that would enlighten New Jersey's visitors to the importance of the State's role in the development of aviation; now therefore, be it enacted by the Senate and General Assembly of the State of New Jersey:

°   1. The aviation hall of fame and museum at Teterboro Airport is designated the Aviation Hall of Fame and Museum of New Jersey.

°   2. This act shall take effect immediately.

First State-Wide Induction Dinner

At the same time, Henry Esposito, the general manager of the Atlantic Aviation facility at Teterboro, agreed to permit the AHOF to use a third floor in the old tower as administrative office space. With the help of conscientious volunteers, the office was opened full time under the author's direction.

The first induction of aviation pioneers from throughout the state was held in May of 1980. Although the AHOF bylaws specified that, except for the first election, only four pioneers could be inducted each year, the AHOF trustees waived the requirement for a two-year period in order to recognize a greater number of the state's aviation personalities. That year Edwin E."Buzz" Aldrin, Dr. Solomon Andrews, A. Raymond Brooks, Adm. Charles E. Rosendahl, Gill Robb Wilson and the three Boland brothers, as one entry, were honored.

In addition, the trustees agreed to establish two other awards, one to honor New Jersey organizations that had contributed to the growth of aviation in the state and nation, and another to pay special tribute to aviation personalities for a particular yearly accomplishment, or for long and meritorious service or in recognition of the contributions of AHOF volunteers. The awards were called "The Fred L. Wehran Aviation Achievement Award and the Distinguished Service Medal."

Also in 1980, Bennett H. Fishler, Jr., the publisher of the Ridgewood Newspaper chain, succeeded Barney as president. A year later, he signed an agreement with John Kennedy to lease a plot on the east side of Teterboro Airport for the construction of an AHOF educational center. It was stipulated in the lease that the AHOF was required to build a structure on the property within 18 months or the lease would be voided.

Trustee Raymond Wells, a prominent Bergen County architect, created plans for a hangar/museum building and a fund-raising campaign, chaired first by Robert Coppenrath and then Henry Becton, was begun under the author's direction.

It became obvious that the $1.2 million needed to build the museum could not be raised in the allotted time so the author asked Kennedy if the lease would be valid if a small building were constructed on the site. Kennedy agreed, and again architect Wells stepped forward to draw plans for what became known as the Phase I museum building.

Walter M. Hartung was elected AHOF's president in 1983 and in the spring of the following year, ground was broken for the Phase I building. The $250,000 museum was opened in March of 1985, just two months after William D. McDowell had become president of the AHOF association. The interior design of the museum, from the paint on the walls to the construction of exhibits, was accomplished by volunteers working weekends during January and February and every night in March. That faithful, hard working troupe included: Bill Baumann, Pete Huesmann, Irv

Koetting, Frank Romano, Harry Gooding, Bob Morris and Bob Ennerson. Interior designer Robin Ringrose Albracht supervised Baumann and the author in the proper placement of artifacts, photographs and illustrations.

The next major project undertaken was the reassembly of a 1950 Martin-202 airliner that had been donated to the museum by the Associated Products of America (APA) in memory of Arthur deDomenico, the former president of APA. Trustee Dave MacMillan took on the monumental project that was underwritten by a grant from the Emil Buehler Fund. Once the plane was assembled, Koetting and Gooding rewired the interior to accommodate 110 V current. Harry and Evelyn Liming completely repainted and restripped the exterior. In September 1987, the Martin was christened *The Spirit of Arthur deDomenico* by June Freemanzon, the president of APA.

With the urging of the AHOF administration, the airport road leading into the AHOF Educational Center was changed by airport management in 1986 to "Fred Wehran Drive" in honor of the man who had made Teterboro the busiest, privately-owned air freight terminal in the world following World War II. At the 1987 annual induction dinner, John Harden, then the airport manager, announced the name change. Wehran then moved to the microphone and donated $250,000 to the museum building fund. It was a dramatic evening.

In recognition of his gift, the Educational Center was named the Fred L. Wehran Pavilion and a plaque was unveiled in the spring of 1988.

Although the AHOF had the money to expand the Wehran Pavilion, a three-year ban on building at Teterboro was imposed by the Department of Environment Protection. William Moxley, who was elected president for a three-year term in 1988, insisted that an outside agency be hired to do an environmental study of the land surrounding the Wehran Pavilion to determine the exact limits of the wetland. That study was completed in the fall of 1989. It clearly showed that the proposed expansion building would not infringe on wetlands.

The study was sent to the New Jersey Department of Environmental Protection (DEP) in late 1989 requesting permission to expand. At the same time, trustee Wells donated the Phase IA architectural plans and trustee Harold Spaeth contributed the lighting and heating plans for the proposed building. The completed set of drawings were then sent to the Port Authority for their approval.

As the century's last decade dawns, the trustees remain confident that the expansion of the Wehran Pavilion will be completed in the early 1990s.

The Aviation Hall of Fame Educates

Aside from the more than 200,000 interested citizens who have visited the AHOF museum since it opened in 1976 and had an opportunity to absorb at least a portion of New Jersey's distinguished aeronautical history on exhibit, the AHOF has had an active outreach program. Volunteers and staff members have presented well in excess of 600 lectures to various groups from senior citizens to grammar school students. At schools, they have presented career day programs and participated in numerous aviation programs and exhibitions. The staff has worked closely with student interns.

The series of yearly AHOF lectures have brought some of America's best known aviation authorities to the AHOF's lecture hall or to the annual induction dinner. The list includes Paul Garber, the "father" of the Smithsonian's aeronautical collection; astronauts Wally Schirra, Buzz Aldrin and Bob Cenker; Pan American presidents Juan T. Trippe and William Seawell; entertainer/pilot Arthur Godfrey, historians Harvey Lippincott, Dr. John Lattimer and Dr. Douglas Robinson and artist/pilot Keith Ferris, just to name a few.

In 1991, the AHOF received the Federal Aviation Administration's regional and national awards for "excellence in aviation education." Later that year, a Sikorsky amphibian helicopter was donated by the U.S. Coast Guard.

The life blood of any museum revolves around the dedicated volunteers who give hundreds of hours each year to the operation of the facility. When the tower-top museum opened in 1976, the first volunteer was 14-year-old Nick Presti of Hackensack. Each weekend he would open the tower and invite guests to view the displays and watch the aircraft activity at the airport. Presti went on to earn his private and commercial pilot's license and in the late 1980s flew as an American Airlines co-pilot.

In the 1980s, Viola Wills has held the position of volunteer chairperson, responsible for providing guides and party planners on a weekly basis. Volunteer William Baumann Sr. is the exhibit designer, Gerard Abbamont holds the title of curator, engines and propulsion and Lt. Col. Harry Liming is the CAP liaison.

Artists Fred Cassens and Joyce Huber have handled the design and layout of the AHOF's various publications since 1972 and historians Bill Rhode, Dave Winans and Bill Ryan have provided countless articles concerning New Jersey's pioneer aviation personalities for the AHOF's quarterly publication "Propwash."

Other volunteers who have given of their time for a number of years include: Peter Huesmann, Frank Romano, Erik Lindstrom, Dave MacMillan, Harry Gooding, Irv Koetting, Derek Long, Bob Morris, Louis Welfare and Art Bares.

The staff has included Lillian Terlizzi, executive administrator, Dorothy Gulino and Karen Careri as administrative assistants and the author has been the director since 1972.

The trustees are particularly proud of the student interns who have volunteered for various periods of time over the years. Many have become active in the field of aeronautics.

The constant support of the Port Authority of New York and New Jersey, Johnson Controls World Services (formerly Pan Am World Services) and Atlantic Aviation have made it possible for the AHOF trustees to operate and expand the state aviation museum over a period of two decades.

A complete list of Hall of Fame inductees and those organizations and individuals who have received the Aviation Achievement Award and Distinguished Service Medals follows:

New Jersey Aviation Hall of Fame Inductees 1973-1990

1973

Floyd Bennett	Clarence D. Chamberlin
William Diehl	Amelia Earhart
Edward Gorski	Aron "Duke" Krantz
Charles A. Lindbergh	Charles Wittemann
Clyde Pangborn	Paul Wittemann
Fred L. Wehran	Walter Wittemann

1974

Frederich W. Bohlander	Anthony H.G. Fokker
William A. Hartig	Jack O. Webster

Donald G. Borg (Special Election)

1975

Bernt Balchen	O.P. "Ted" Hebert
Juan T. Trippe	Roger Q. Williams

1976

Bert Acosta	George DeGarmo
Ivan Gates	Arthur Godfrey

1977

Samuel C. Barnitt	Louis G. Ranley
Ben B. Rock	Charles " Slim" West

1978

Kay A. Brick	Henry Geleski
Julia Gorski	R.B.C. Noorduyn

1979

George Hicha	William J. Picune
Royal French Ryder	John E. Thomson

1980

Edwin E."Buzz" Aldrin Jr.	Dr. Solomon Andrews
Joseph Boland	Gill Robb Wilson
Frank Boland	Arthur Raymond Brooks
James Boland	Charles E. Rosendahl

1981

Ralph S. Barnaby	Robert N. Buck
Robert L. Copsey	Charles Healy Day
Charles F. Durant	Kenneth R. Unger

1982

Leo Loudenslager	Thomas B. McGuire Jr.

Walter M. Schirra

1983

Jules DeCrescenzo	Herbert O. Fisher
Gen. Francis R. Gerard	Thomas A. Murchio

Thomas W. Robertson

1984

Robert J. Collier	Harold Curtis
Charles S. Jones	William E. Rhode

1985

Chester J. Decker	Malcolm S. Forbes
Dr. Albert E. Forsythe	Thor Solberg

1986

Jack Elliott	Henry J. Esposito
Philip J. Landi	Dean C. Smith

1987

Silvio Cavlier	Paul Garber
Oliver Simmons	Kathyrn Sullivan

1988

Frederick W. Castle	John T. McCoy
Ruth R. Nichols	Harry A. Nordheim

1989

Cornelius J. Kraissl	Louis T.Reichers
Donald J. Strait	Stanley Switlik

1990

Edwin E. Aldrin Sr.	William J. Conrad
Walter M. Hartung	Frederick Kuhnert

Fred L. Wehran
Aviation Achievement Award
1979 - 1990

1979

Bendix Corp.

1980

Curtiss-Wright Corp.

1981

Switlik Parachute Co. Airwork Corp.
Bell Laboratories

1982

Aircraft Radio Corp.
Teterboro School of Aeronautics

1983

Atlantic Aviation

1984

Exxon Corp.	Allaire Airport

Reaction Motors

1985

Air Cruisers Co.	Dowty RFL Industries
Hadley Airport	Somerset Air Service

1986

Butler Aviation	Sussex Airport
Ronson Aviation	United Airlines

1987

Port Authority of NY & NJ	Randolph Products Co.

Southern Jersey Airways

1988

Linden Airport	Lincoln Park Airport
Pan Am World Services	Teterboro Aircraft Service
Singer-Kearfott Systems Div.	

1989

American Airlines	Bader Field
Jet Aviation-EAF	Texaco, Inc.

1990

East Air Corp.	Air List Ads

New Jersey Civil Air Patrol

Distingnished Service Medal
1982 - 1990

1982

Horace F. Banta	John J. Breslin Jr.
Donald G. Borg	Fairleigh Dickinson Jr.
Edward A. Jesser	H.V.Pat Reilly

Alexander Summer Sr.

1983

Henry P. Becton	Robert A.M. Coppenrath

Raymond R. Wells

1984

Frederick Cassens	Sen. John Russo
Joseph Supor	

1985

Henry Esposito	Sen. Matthew Feldman
Irving Koetting	Viola Wills

1986

Arlene B. Feldman	William Baumann
Robert D. Hunter	Lillian Terlizzi

1973

Across America in a Hot Air Balloon

Malcolm S. Forbes

Inducted Aviation Hall of Fame of New Jersey, 1985

Only 15 months after he took his first ride in a hot air balloon, Malcolm S. Forbes, a native of Englewood, NJ, launched his blue and gold, 65-foot high balloon, *Charteau de Balleroy,* at Coos Bay, OR. Thirty-four days later, he landed in the Chesapeake Bay off the coast of Maryland. The flight was the first from coast-to-coast in one hot air balloon. He had flown a total of 21 days and traveled 2,911 statute miles.

Six world records were established on Forbes transcontinental crossing of the United States, They were set in the three largest hot air balloon classifications for both duration and distance. Forbes established the official world record for duration on Oct. 22, 1973, flying from Sioux Lookout, NE, to Esbon, KS, in 13 hours and 5 minutes. He broke the world record for distance on Oct. 25 on a flight from Tecumseh, NE, to Clover Bottom, MO, covering 312 miles.

In 1966, Tracy Barnes had been the first person to fly a hot air balloon across the United States. His original balloon caught fire along the way and he ended his flight in Rio Grande, NJ, in a balloon barrowed from a friend.

In an April 1979 issue of *Playboy Magazine* interview, Forbes had this to say about ballooning:

PLAYBOY: *How did you react to your first balloon ride?*

FORBES: It was such a novel experience, a kind of

Publisher/balloonist Malcolm Forbes

Peter Pan thing. It's so different from flying; it's not flying. You're right in the wind and the air and the clouds — all those forces in nature that come together and have an impact on you and the balloon. You're floating and you're never sure where you're going. In a plane, you gun the engine and flip your flippers and you go up or down and right or left, and it's an immediate response. In a balloon, your sole source of power is a blast of heat, and there's a 15-second interval between the blast and when the heat reaches the top of the balloon and you float up. If you stop to think about it, it's like driving a car that doesn't accelerate until 15 seconds after you hit the gas. Try that sometime. Getting the feeling of the timing in a balloon is one of the extraordinary challenges, and one that captivated me that first day.

You have absolutely no control over your direction. As the wind goes, so go you. It's a unique feeling, combined with the fact that you're seeing a view of the landscape floating slowly beneath you that is different from any view you've ever seen. The whole thing is such a huge turn-on that I have not, with rare exceptions, found ANYBODY who's done it who doesn't love it. You can float just above the treetops, everybody waves at you and yells up, wanting to know where you're going. Well, you don't know where you're going, and even that's an unusual sensation in itself.

On a motorcycle, you sense that not everybody is happy to see you and your mode of transportation going by, but a balloon turns everybody on, with no exceptions. It's a happy thing. People on the ground enjoy seeing this beautiful, unusual thing floating by. What is it? The fact is, it makes no sense. It isn't something to GO anyplace in. You get in it and go no place in particular. With a balloon, getting there isn't half the fun; it's ALL the fun. The trip is the whole trip. The vehicle itself is the thing, the end in itself, not the means of getting somewhere. And all those sensations happen to you the first time you're in one.

PLAYBOY: Less than a year and a half after your first balloon ride, you set six world records in your cross-country flight. Obviously, you plunged into it.

FORBES: Sure. Once I got into it, I wanted to do the things that hadn't been done. It wasn't just competitive zest. I thought that if you're going to do it at all, you might as well mobilize your resources and have more fun doing what nobody else has done. To keep flying day in and day out you have to have a lot of ground support. You don't know where you're going to land. You fly until you're out of fuel, then you have to have trucks that can get to you. I was dropping tanks to reduce weight — they weigh 20 pounds even empty — and somebody had to retrieve those with a helicopter. Amazing lot of logistics. People can do it on a less expensive scale, but it's harder and takes longer. And what we were doing was taking off from where we landed. That hadn't been done before. You can say you're going to go from West to East, but you can't say you're going from Milwaukee to St. Louis. You can't pick your towns.

PLAYBOY: How did your family react to what you were doing?

FORBES: Enthusiastically. It was an exciting adventure and everybody was in on putting the logistics together. Two of my boys filmed it. A guy named Tracy Barnes had gone cross-country over the period of a year, but it really hadn't been done as a consecutive trip. It was pioneering. I decided it would be fun to try doing it and had the balloon built. The thing got a lot of press coverage because it excited people, and it was the kind of thing where day by day you could follow the progress, or the lack of it, and it did a whole lot to make people aware of the sport.

Later in 1973, Forbes founded the world's first balloon museum at the Forbes-owned Chateau de Balleroy in Normandy, France.

Following his successful transcontinental flight, Forbes and his advisers began planning a transatlantic flight. A great deal of effort and more than $1 million went into the project. But in the predawn hours of Jan. 6, 1975, the dream of flying the Atlantic suspended from a cluster of superpressure balloons was dramatically shattered when the thirteen 33-foot balloons broke free of their tethers and disappeared into the atmosphere.

Forbes and his systems pilot, Dr. Thomas P. Heinsheimer, a distinguished aerospace scientist, were already in the spherical aluminum gondola, *Windborne*, ready for their flight from Santa Ana, CA, when the four clusters of three balloons each began lifting prematurely. The flight from California to the East Coast at 40,000 feet was to be a trial run, allow-ing all systems to be checked prior to a commitment for an Atlantic crossing.

What happened on that early morning was vividly described in an article by Dick and Donna Brown in the 1975 Spring issue of *Ballooning Magazine*:

Hangar One became a scene of bustling activity as Windborne and her entourage of silvery balloons proceeded out the hangar door and into the chilly Pacific air. Sealed within the gondola were aeronauts Malcolm Forbes, Tom Heinsheimer and Tlalos, a miniature representation of the Mexican God of the Wind.

The lead balloon and first cluster were raised with no problem. As the second cluster was being raised, the release mechanism slipped and the cluster shot abruptly into the air. With instant reflexes, the ground crew jumped on the third cluster's cart to prevent a chain reaction. It was 4 a.m. and a hold was announced while the crew assessed the situation. At this time, the ground breezes were on a slight increase. There was an air of apprehension as four large searchlights (one aimed at each balloon cluster) plus several banks of floodlights cast an eerie glow across the launch site. A host of fellow aeronauts and special guests huddled near the lights for warmth, anxious to see Windborne get off the ground so they could return to a warmer place to monitor the skyship's aerial progress.

For nearly an hour, Windborne sat on the launch pad with its lead balloon and top two tiers already waving in the breeze. Then, suddenly a gust caused the remaining two clusters to drag their weighted carts! To the horror of the spectators and ground handlers, the balloons clattered and banged into each other as they tore away from their mooring! Jean Pierre [Jean Pierre Pommereau was the launch director] jumped onto the top of the tumbling gondola and without a second to spare cut the balloons free! While searchlights played on the soaring clusters, the crowd surged forward.

Immediately the aeronauts unbuckled their safety harnesses, opened the hatch and escaped without injury. The area was quickly evacuated for fear that the liquid oxygen tanks might rupture.

Immediately after the mishap, Forbes credited Jean Pierre with saving the pilots' lives. At great danger to himself, he had activated the emergency quick disconnect which cut the balloons from the gondola. If the launch had not been aborted, the capsule would have been severely damaged and perhaps lifted in that condition into the stratosphere.

Undaunted by failure and with tremendous enthusiasm, Forbes announced that he and Dr. Heinsheimer would try the flight again within six weeks. But, alas, the second attempt to span the Atlantic never materialized.

Later that year, Forbes was awarded the coveted Harmon Trophy as the Aeronaut-of-the-Year for his transcontinental flight two years earlier and the aborted attempt to fly the Atlantic that same year. In just a two-year period, Forbes was credited with having done more to promote the sport of ballooning than anyone in the 20th century.

Every year since 1973, Forbes has sponsored an international balloon festival in Balleroy, France. The event is attended by leading balloonists in the world.

Eagle Flight Founded

A Baptist minister in Orange, NJ, organized an Explorer Scout troop he called Eagle Flight, dedicated to teaching inner-city youngsters in East Orange the rudiments of flying an airplane.

The Rev. Russell White's program was believed to be the nation's only flight training school for black teenagers.

Explaining the importance he placed on the program, White said: "I wanted these youngsters to look toward the sky in their lives, to keep their chins up, and not to be limited in their aspirations. Many of these kids did not know of anything beyond the streets. The academy is not about flying; it's about life."

He began his aviation training program with just seven youngsters age 11 to 18 in 1977 and since then more than 500 have participated. Discipline is the backbone of the Reverend's flight academy. Youngsters who wish to participate must learn to take orders, keep passing grades in school and be respectful. When a new candidate applies for membership in the Eagle Flight, he or she must come to the meeting place with a parent to meet the Reverend and his officers. As was pointed out in the August 10, 1986 issue of the New York Times, Rev. White pulls no punches when addressing potential members. He was quoted as saying:

"Ladies and gentlemen. I hope that you are here because you want to be here. If you would rather be running track, then go do that. If you feel that you may miss a meeting here because you have something more important to take its place, leave now because here we train pilots.

"The first time any of you get out of line, show the slightest disrespect to myself or a fellow officer or I hear that you talked back to your parents, you're out. It's as simple as that. For each one of you here, there are five others waiting to take your place.

"I'll tolerate no drugs or drinking here. Don't even think of trying it because I'll know from your eyeballs and your body language whether you're straight or not.

"Do you understand me?"

"Yes sir." the students replied in unison.

Anyone who has ever spent time around the Eagle Flight Scouts are used to hearing "yes sir." repeated time and time again not only to the Reverend and the adult advisers who assist him, but to the Eagle Flight cadet officers as well.

The program has paid off handsomely for those youngsters who participated. More than a dozen former Flight members have enrolled in he Air Force and Naval Academies, and others, like Irving Carter of East Orange, became airline and commuter line pilots. When Carter flew for People Express at age 24, he was believed to be the youngest minority pilot flying for a major airline in the country.

The cadets wear U.S. Air Force Academy uniforms donated by the Air Force and fly a Cessna 150 that was also donated. Each week they drill and spend hours studying meteorology, flight dynamics and map reading. When they fly, it's at the Essex County Airport. although they are not required to take flight training, 50 percent of them have over the years.

To add to their knowledge, Rev. White has arranged for trips to the Air and Space Museum in Washington, the EAA air show in Oshkosh, WI the Air Force Museum in Dayton, OH, the Air Force Academy at Colorado Springs, CO, and a number of other universities that have active aviation programs.

When he visits local high schools looking for recruits for his program, White's talks are inspirational.

"Set your sights high, young people," he urges. "Look up, not down at the wine bottles on the sidewalks of East Orange. Instead of crack and Qualudes, made something of yourself, You can learn to fly an airplane if you join my program. But it isn't easy. You have to work hard. Nothing is easy. You have to earn it. There is no such thing as can't. You have to keep your grades up. The discipline is tough. But the rewards are unbelievable. Imagine flying your own airplane. Imagine being up in the sky, seeing forever, seeing things you have never seen before.

"You can be somebody. Learn how to sit up straight. Lift up your head. Act like somebody. You are somebody. You can do it. Brush your teeth. Comb your hair. Press your clothes. Taxi out and wind up your engine...."

Everyone New Jerseyan in the field of aviation can be proud of the job being done daily by Rev. Russell White and his volunteers by using aeronautics to inspire inner-city kids to reach for the stars.

CHRONOLOGY OF OTHER AERONAUTICAL
EVENTS AND ACHIEVEMENTS
1970 to 1979
1970

- Col. Nannette Moss Spears, former commander of the New Jersey Wing, Civil Air Patrol, died.

- George Moffat Jr., an English teacher at the Pingry School, Elizabeth, NJ, won the International Gliding Championship at Marfa, TX, besting 80 contestants from 25 countries.

- Emile Burgin, the first man to fly an airplane around South America died at his New Egypt, NJ, home.

- John Olcott, a consultant with Aeronautical Research Associates of Princeton, flew the "Aereon 26," a delta-shaped, wingless, experimental aircraft at the FAA's NAFEC facility in Pomona, NJ.

1971

- George J. DeGarmo died at age 73 in Red Bank, NJ.

- The first running of the National Air Races at Cape May County Airport was marred by two separate mid-air collisions. In a seven-plane race four crashed, killing the pilots, and another was damaged but landed safely. The following year, the State Division of Aeronautics turned a down a request by the National Air Race Association to again hold the races at Cape May.

- William McE. Miller Jr., president of the Aeron Corp. of Princeton, flew his stubby, fat, delta-shaped airship he called an *Aerobody,* over Atlantic City. Author John McFee, became fascinated with the strange contraption and wrote a book concerning the men involved in the development of the craft called *The Deltoid Pumpkinseed.*

1972

- Charles West died in Oakland, CA, where he and his wife, Helen, had moved in the 1950s.

- Peggy Nauman of West Caldwell and Betty Barlia of Oakland were the top scorers among the New Jersey entrants in the 1972 Powder Puff Derby from San Mateo, CA, to Miller Airpark at Toms River, NJ.

- The Curtiss-Wright flight school, maintenance and charter service at Caldwell-Wright Airport in Fairfield, NJ, closed. The 278-acre airport was put up for sale by the Curtiss Wright Corp.

- At the beginning of the fall semester, the Mercer County Community College began offering several aviation courses including: flight technology and aviation electronics and instrument technology.

1973

- Arthur Zimmerman of Lake Swannanoa, NJ, began producing a Standard Class, fiberglass sailplane which was the first to have flaps. He sold them for $9,000 each.

- Two South Jersey aviatrixes, Diane Shaw of Wildwood and her co-pilot Rose Myers of Atlantic City, drew the post position in the 1973 Powder Puff Derby. The two New Jerseyans were the first off the runway at Carlsbad, CA. They were out of money when they landed at Elmira, NY.

- Kurt Hofschneider of Colonia, NJ, few a Tiger Moth biplane, that he and Paul Jordon had spent two and a half years to restore, from Alexandria Airport in Pittstown to the annual EAA convention in Oshkosh, WI, and won championship for the best Wrold War II aircraft. Both Hofschneider and Jordan are former airline pilots.

- Bernt Balchen, the first man to fly a plane over the South Pole, died at age 73.

- Leslie E. Neville, Sr., a leading aviation journalist, died at his home in Teaneck.

- A street at Teterboro Airport was named in honor of pilot Billy Diehl, the first itinerant pilot to land there in 1920.

- Tragedy struck as the Navy's precision flying team, the Blue Angels, arrived over the Lakehurst Naval Air Station on July 26. The team had come to New Jersey to appear at the annual "open house" weekend at the historic base. The four F7F Phantom jets were performing an arrival maneuver to familiarize themselves with the terrain. One plane, flying upside down, brushed the plane above it. Both planes crashed in the pine forest that surrounds the base. Three of the four airmen ejected from the jets and their parachutes deployed. Only one survived.

- Aircraft master mechanic William Hartig died at age 78.

1974

- The Curtiss-Wright Corp. sold the Caldwell-Wright Airport to the Essex County Improvement Authority.

- The 50th anniversary of the first transcontinental air mail flight was commemorated on July 1, when Thomas W. "Bill" Tinkler, a retired United Airlines pilot, accepted three freshly postmarked letters and boarded his 1948 Luscombe 8F at Newark Airport and began a flight to San Francisco. The original flight left from Hadley Field South Plainfield and took 34 hours and 20 minutes. Six pilots participated. Tinkler had the three letters postmarked at each of the 17 towns and cities in which he stopped enroute to San Francisco.

- Aron "Duke" Krantz, one of New Jersey's most colorful pioneer aviators, died while on vacation in Florida.

- Clarence Chamberlin, age 81, died at his winter home in Fort Myers Beach, FL.

- New York Airways inaugurated 20 daily, scheduled helicopter flights from Teterboro Airport to Newark, La Guardia, Kennedy and Morristown Airports.

- Ben Rock, chief of the Teterboro Engineering and Manufacturing District Office (FAA), presented 30-year service pins to FAA Teterboro employees. The recipients were: Dan Kaplan of Montvale, chief of the Teterboro tower, 33 years; George Hicha of Franklin Lakes and Michael Rowny of Whitehouse, NJ, both assistant tower chiefs, 32 years; Jules DeCrescenzo of Oradell, principal maintenance inspector, 31 years, and Edyth Pohl of Hackensack, assistant flight service chief, 31 years.

- The Asbury Park-Neptune Airport was closed and the property sold to developers by Isaac (Ike) Schlossbach who first opened the field in 1938. Billy Leigh Gibson had operated the field for Schlossbach.

- The National Business Aircraft Association named Jack Elliott, the aviation editor of the *Newark Star-Ledger,* as the 1973 winner of the Lois Henry Journalism Award for the most outstanding newspaper aviation column.

- Charles Augustus Lindbergh died of cancer on the Hawaiian island of Maui. He was 72 years old.

- While attempting to fly his balloon across the Atlantic Ocean, 46-year-old Bobby Berger died when the helium filled sphere burst at 6,000 feet over Barnegat Bay. Authorities did not know that Berger had no previous ballooning experience until he was standing in his gondola ready to take-off from the Naval Air Station at Lakehurst. He told reporters: "What got me into ballooning was the challenge and the glory and I felt there might be some fame and fortune in it for me. I'm not without fear. It's more of an anxiety. I've been given an opportunity to get off my duff and do something exciting." The excitement lasted about 20 minutes.

- William C. Machorek Jr., a 32-year old Air Force Major from Teaneck, NJ, flew as navigator aboard an Air Force SR-71 Lockheed high-altitude strategic reconnaissance plane, piloted by Capt. Harold B. Adams, from London to Los Angeles. The 5,645-mile route over the North Pole established a speed record of just under five hours.

- An illustrated history of Curtiss-Wright Aircraft from 1903 to 1965, entitled *To Join With the Eagles,* was written by two New Jerseyans, Richard M. Goldman of West Orange and Murray Rubenstein of Teaneck. More than 20,000 first edition copies were sold.

- Charles J. Kupper, owner of the Kupper Airport in Manville, NJ, died at age 72. Born in Hoboken, Kupper lived for many years in Piscataway, NJ.

- Warren Marsh of Edison, NJ, received his commercial glider pilot's license and in the next 10 years made more than 4,000 flights. Known as the *Ambassador of Soaring,* March encouraged hundreds of his passengers to take soaring lessons. March flew out of Sky Manor Airport in Pittstown.

- Edwin E. Aldrin Sr. died in Brielleat age 78.

1975

- Police escorted the *Spirit of '76,* a huge twin- engine Martin 202A airplane, along local roads from Cape May County Airport to its new home at Moreys Pier in North Wildwood. The 40-passenger aircraft was then lifted onto a hydraulic pedestal. By combining a sensation of movement, created by the hydraulic system, with films and aircraft sounds, the airplane became a popular amusement ride. The brainchild of Fred Mahana Jr., the plane had been purchased from Arthur deDomenico, president of Associated Products of America. The novelty air plane ride lasted for two seasons and was then dismantled and scrapped.

- Marion Rice Hart, a 83-year-old "flying granny" who piloted her single-engine Beechcraft from Bedford, MA, to Shannon, Ireland, became the oldest woman pilot to cross the Atlantic alone. She had learned to fly in 1945 at Safair, Inc. at Teterboro Airport, and soloed after 10 hours of instruction.

1976

- In commemoration of the United States' bicentennial, Constance Wolf, a 70-year-old balloonist, ascended in a helium-filled balloon from Independence Mall in Philadelphia, and landed an hour later in Shamong, NJ. She was attempting to duplicate the flight of Jean Pierre Blanchard, the first man to fly in the Western Hemisphere 183 years earlier. Blanchard had landed in Deptford Township, NJ.

- Charles "Casey" Jones, founder of the Casey Jones School of Aeronautics, died.

- Roger Q. Williams, the first man to fly from New York to Rome, died in California at age 85.

- Henry B. Tonking, a Mt. Hope, NJ native, at age 81 was the oldest, active glider pilot in the United States.

1977

- Joe Colombo of Wayne, entered his home-built Scorpion helicopter in the Experimental Aircraft Association's annual rotorcraft championship competition. His craft was chosen as the grand champion of its class.

1978

- Transfair '78 was held Aug. 16-20, at the National Aviation Facilities Experimental Center in Pomona. The fair featured all forms of transportation and the air show portion was heralded as the largest in the U.S.A. The U.S. Air Force Thunderbird and the Golden Knights parachute jumping team performed along with such national figures as Art Scholl, Bob Hoover and "wing walker" Joe Hughes.

- Henry Geleski died just prior to his induction into the Aviation Hall of Fame of New Jersey.

1979

- Samuel C. Barnitt died at age 65 at Newark Airport while awaiting an Eastern Airline Flight.

- New Jersey state police superintendent Clinton L. Pagano initiated a helicopter Med-Evac service. The flying troopers transported 31 Med-Evac patients in the first year of service.1980

- Frank Hareslak of Old Bridge, NJ, a man with an abiding interest in aerospace, founded the American Academy of Aerospace Education in his home town. The motto of the non-profit organization is: to teach, to guide and to encourage. For more than 12 years, Hareslak and his volunteer members have taught hundreds of youngsters the techniques of aircraft model building. They have guided Boy Scouts and Cub Scouts toward aviation or space exploration merit badges. They have encouraged, young people to expand their horizons beyond the present through essay and award programs. Those who worked on programs during the 12 years the academy has been in existence are: Bill DeFrance, Sarah Tamsula, Fran Hareslak, Al Mizenko and Bill and Paula Sandritter.

1980

During the decade of the '80s, New Jersey men and women were demonstrating their aeronautical skills in contrasting ways. Some were establishing aerobatic records while others were making their mark flying in aircraft reminiscent of those flown by the Wright brothers. Still others continued to explore outer space in the first reusable spacecraft. The crews of New Jersey-based civilian and military jet aircraft generated media attention following historic flights

during the busy decade, and the first airline established in the Garden State in more than 50 years began service from Newark Airport.

PEOPLExpress Airline

When three PEOPLExpress Airline Boeing 737s left the ramp of the old North Terminal at Newark International Airport in April of 1981, the event marked one of the fastest takeoffs of an airline in history. People's three initial routes were to Buffalo, NY, Columbus, OH, and Norfolk, VA. By the year's end, the airline had 13 planes flying to ten cities from its Newark hub.

Three young entrepreuers — Donald C. Burr, L. Gitner and Melrose Dawsey, all former Texas Air International employees — founded the new cut-rate airline. Spurred by governmental deregulation of the airline business in the late 1970s, the three young executives quickly built a following by offering flights at rates considerably below the established air carriers. Passengers were required to pay $3 to check their luggage and there was a charge for food served aboard the flights. But most of the early People passengers didn't miss these amenities because many were first-time fliers or young folk who could tolerate three hours in flight without a meal.

The PEOPLExpress success in the air was matched by its remarkable employee relations program on the ground. Burr, who was elected chairman, ran the company without traditional supervisors, secretaries or even organizational charts. All the 250 original non-union employees were expected to perform a variety of jobs. "Cross-utilization," Burr called it. Employees all held stock in the company and shared in the profits. Pilots and flight attendants worked in the office and at ticket counters when they weren't flying and, it was reported during the inaugural year, Burr and Gitner could be found hustling baggage.

Business analysts were skeptical of the horizontal-management style that Burr preached and were expressing doubts about the company's future growth. Never-the-less the airline expanded to 4,000 employees, more than 60 aircraft and assets of a half-billion dollars by the end of 1984.

John J. Dickerson Jr., the airport manager at the time, had a great deal of respect for Don Burr. In discussing the rapid growth of PEOPLExpress, Dickerson said he and his staff never thought the airline would be so successful.

"It was a new experience for us," he said. "We didn't know it then, but it was the beginning of ' hubbing,' [all flights leaving and returning to the same ' hub' airport] which is now a common word in the airport lexicon. It was a high concentration of flights by one airline from a single airport. That was the beginning of the 'hub' concept and we had no way of knowing in advance."

The unique management concept of Burr's airline also fascinated Dickerson. "Everyone was supposed to do everything," he recalled. "They had no secretaries. They seldom wrote letters because they had no one to type. As an example, one of their international pilots was in charge of garbage. That's how diverse they were. Everybody could implement any plan that they wanted, which, of course, raises problems when you're managing a building — fire codes, public occupancy, ramp safety — a whole plethora of unique problems. We had a passenger explosion in the North Terminal. I shudder to think how many people were in that building at one time during the height of their operation. Everything an airport expects to have when there is a three- day snowstorm, they had every hour of the day. Bodies all over the place, just waiting for flights. The discount prices brought a new kind of passenger to the airport. It took people out of their cars and buses driving to Florida. Greyhound [bus company] must have really been affected, because that's the kind of people they were attracting."

Dickerson remembered Burr as a dramatic and inspirational speaker who seemed to have little trouble selling his management concept to both financial backers and potential employees.

"He prided himself on knowing the first names of all his employees," Dickerson said. "That was fine at the beginning, but when he suddenly had 4,000 people working for him, he lost that one-on-one connection. Once old and new employees couldn't any longer participate in the daily decision making process, they became discontent. But obviously, he couldn't have 4,000 people all doing their own thing."

In June of 1983, PEOPLExpress began service from Newark to London, England. The one-way fare was $149, or little more than half the lowest regular coach fare of $275 being charged by competitive airlines. The new service to London filled a void left after Sir Freddie Laker's airline went bankrupt in 1982. That entrepreneur had pioneered low-cost transatlantic flights ($236 round trip) with his Skytrain service in 1977.

In the fall of 1983, two PEOPLExpress women pilots became the first to command a Boeing 747 on transcontinental and transatlantic flights. They left Newark International Airport within hours of each other. Capt. Beverly Burns was at the controls of the 3:30 p.m. 747 flight to Los Angeles and Capt. Lynn Rippelmeyer was in the left cockpit seat for the 7:30 p.m. flight to London. According to the International Social Affiliation of Women Airline Pilots, they were the first regularly assigned female captains of 747s.

Both women began their aviation careers as flight attendants for other airlines, but had inner desires to become pilots. They learned to fly and began their commercial piloting careers with small commuter and cargo lines. The women joined PEOPLExpress in 1981 as co-pilots and were promoted to captains of B-727s and B-737s the following year.

Rippelmeyer, a Sparta, NJ, resident, said at the time of her Atlantic flight, "People go out of their way to show how proud they are of you. They bring their little girls over to the cockpit and show them. It's real neat."

In August of 1985, PEOPLExpress had 400 non-stop daily flights throughout its system, 200 of them originating from Newark. Their 72 aircraft served 43 destinations in 23 states, Montreal, London, and Brussels. In addition, they were awaiting delivery of five new 727-2005 and three Boeing 747-200s in the spring of 1986.

Late in 1985, PEOPLExpress acquired the financially troubled Denver-based Frontier Airline and two New England commuter lines, Britt Airways and Province-town-Boston Express. It was about this time that the early predictions of failure due to over- expansion by Wall Street analysts began to become a reality. People's stock, once worth $25½ had fallen to below $10 on the market. In the first quarter of 1986, the airline had a record $58 million loss. PEOPLExpress tried to sell Frontier to United Airlines but the deal fell through and in June of 1986, the financial wizards were saying that the airline would have to sell a portion of its fleet to survive.

In September of 1986, the Houston-based Texas Air Corporation, under the leadership of Frank A. Lorenzo, acquired PEOPLExpress in a stock transaction worth an estimated $122 million. Texas Air already owned Continental Airlines and New York Air, and was attempting to take over Eastern Airlines. In mid-January 1987, Lorenzo announced that both PEOPLExpress and New York Air would be merged with Continental Airlines.

The creation of PEOPLExpress had a profound effect on the growth of Newark International Airport.

In 1981, the year PEOPLExpress began operations, LaGuardia Airport, a smaller facility then Newark, handled eight million more passengers then the newly expanded international airfield in New Jersey. Then suddenly, the flying public discovered the airport in the New Jersey Meadowlands when they came in search of the rock-bottom prices offered by PEOPLExpress.

The airport managers during the period of growth in the early 1980s, Dickerson, and Vincent R. Bonaventura, expended a great deal of effort in establishing reasonable ground transportation costs and in convincing customers that Newark was a convenient alternative to LaGuardia. The end result was that in 1986, Newark's total number of passengers surpassed both LaGuardia and John F. Kennedy Airports.

In a Feb. 1, 1987 article, Nick Fox, a staff writer with *The Record* wrote, "It was the airline that was cheaper than a bus. Than it became the airline that was more trouble than a subway. Now it's just the airline that was."

On that date, PEOPLExpress was absorbed by Continental Airlines, and the airline passenger business might never be the same.

World Aerobatic Champion
Leo Loudenslager

Inducted Aviation Hall of Fame of New Jersey, 1982

Leo Loudenslager

Led by Leo Loudenslager of Sussex, NJ, the United States Aerobatic team won the world championship in August of 1980. The contest, called "The Olympics of the Air" by aerobatic enthusiasts, was held at Wittman Field in Oshkosh, WI. It was the first time in the sport's 20-year history that the championship was held in the United States. As champions, team members received the Nesterov Trophy emblematic of the championship which they had previously won in 1970 and 1972.

Loudenslager, who won four gold and two silver medals during the competition, competed against the world's best pilots on teams from Australia, Canada, Great Britain, France, Italy, New Zealand, Republic of South Africa, Romania, Spain, Switzerland and West Germany. The Soviet Union and Czechoslovakia did not attend the competition.

Up to that time, Loudenslager had won a record five consecutive national championships and in the years that followed he won two more national titles — the only person ever to accomplish that feat. He was the U.S. team captain at the World Championships in Russia in 1976, Czechoslavakia in 1978 and Austria in 1982.

In 1981, he won the Victor Award which is presented yearly to the "Most Outstanding Sports Figure." This

"Oscar" of the sports world had never been awarded to a pilot before.

Loudenslager's most disappointing world championship competition was the year he led his fellow fliers to Russia. In his book, *Above & Beyond, Eight Great American Aerobatic Champions* Lt. Col. Mel R. Jones described the situation at the Russian contest:

"The contest was so blatantly rigged through manipulations of scoring devices, Soviet protests and delaying tactics that Henry [a U.S.team member, Henry Haigh] observed that it was like watching one contest and then seeing the scores for another contest posted."

Loudenslager, the U.S. champion, finished 23rd.

It was while serving as a U.S. Air Force B-52 mechanic at the Travis Air Porce Base in California in 1963, that Loudenslager learned to fly. He joined the base flying club and then worked up to nine hours at a gas station after his normal eight hour day, to earn money for flying lessons. The grueling schedule, sometimes allowing only three hours for sleeping, would have discouraged most people, but the more he flew, the more he wanted to. He also decided early on that aerobatics would be his specialty.

Things didn't change much after he left the service. He found a job as an American Airlines' pilot in 1966 and spent all his spare time constructing an airplane that he felt would be a winner. Although the majority of aerobatic pilots prefer biplanes, Loudenslager decided on a monoplane. For five years in his home and at Sussex Airport, he modified a small, sleek Stephens Akro, until all semblance of the original design disappeared and a craft he called the "Laser 200" was born.

When asked by a reporter for *Aviation Convention News,* a monthly magazine published in Midland Park, NJ, why he preferred a monoplane, he replied, "I've always had one theory in aerobatics and that is, all other things being equal, the prettiest airplane would probably have some advantage in getting the nod in the score. But the problem is to make the monoplane perform as well as a biplane. All the Lasers were taken from a Stephens Akro, which involved modifying and clearing up the performance and also bringing my own talents to a level sufficient to do it. I'm there now, and now it's time for them to imitate me.

"You know, so much is always given to the airplane. In this business, 70 percent machine and 30 percent the driver. We're kind of reversed. You've got to get a pilot who can get in that thing and make it go."

When asked how he prepared himself for aerobatic competition, he replied, "Physically, I don't do a thing, except stay in good shape. I don't do anything supernatural, but I do jog, and so forth. But the primary part of the preparation is mental, and the mental preparation in my case is isolation.

"During that time my mind is back up in the sky. Of course, you have to memorize the maneuvers, but you also have to think about how the wind will affect it; what you're going to do one way or another; really going over and over things, mistakes that you've been making, to try and correct in your mind so that the next time you climb into the cockpit there's no mistake."

Loudenslager is known as an obsessive competitor and consummate performer. During the air show season, he and other U.S. team members, including New Jerseyan Jim Roberts, criss-cross the nation performing at air shows from California to New Jersey to raise money to cover the cost of attending the world championship competition. His blue and white Laser 200 is always a favorite among the spectators.

In the mid-1980s, Loudenslager and his family moved to Tennessee, but once a year he returns to New Jersey to perform for his old friend, Paul Styger, at the annual Sussex Airport air show, the finest in New Jersey.

James Roberts

A fellow airline pilot, Jim Roberts, worked with Loudenslager in building the Laser 200 and acted as a coach during the endless hours of practice flying over the Sussex County farmlands. Roberts built a Laser 200 for himself and became so proficient as an aerobatic pilot, that just two years after entering the National Unlimited Aerobatic Competition, he placed fourth in the United States. In 1981 and 1982, he flew with the U.S. Aerobatic team and traveled to Austria in the latter year to compete for the world title.

Roberts, a West Virginia native, was raised in Flemington, NJ. He learned to fly in 1960 at Sky Manor Airport, Pittstown. He became a U.S. Army pilot in 1961 and when he was discharged in 1965, he joined American Airlines as a 727 captain.

When he and his family moved to Lake Hopatcong, NJ, Roberts became involved with Loudenslager in the development of the Laser 200. In 1977, he began constructing his own Laser and a year and a half later he flew it for the first time.

In the mid-1980s, Roberts began flying a 160 hp Long Eze in airshows in addition to the Laser. It was the only Long Eze airshow act in the world at that time.

Into the 1990s, both Loudenslager and Roberts remain popular flying acts throughout the United States.

Paul Styger became manager of the Sussex Airport in 1946, following his discharge from the Army Air Corps. In 1955, he bought the country airfield and, 10

years later, organized the first Sussex County Air Show. All of the great air show performers in the nation have appeared at the Sussex show over the years.

William H. Voorhis Sr.

Inducted Aviation Hall of Fame of New Jersey, 1992

Bill Voorhis Sr.

For 50 years, William H. Voorhis Sr. taught men and women to fly. In 1991 at age 78, he was the oldest active flight instructor in New Jersey, flying daily at Sussex Airport.

Born in Fort Lee, Voorhis learned to fly at Pinebrook Airport in 1931, but didn't become seriously involved until 1941, when he earned his commercial instructor's license. That same year, he became an instructor with the Civil Pilot Training program, and joined the U.S. Air Corps Reserves. The following year, he was transferred into the war training service in Bloomsburg, PA, where he taught pre-Navy pilots to fly.

After the war, he taught flying under the G.I. Bill for Wiggins Airways in Norwood, MA. In 1948, he returned to New Jersey to teach at Murchio Airport prior to joining the Marjorie Gray Aero Service as an instructor at Teterboro Airport. When Gray gave up her business in 1951, Voorhis stayed on and ran the flight school until 1958.

Having spent his entire adult life in aviation, in 1983, he established a permanent base at Sussex where he continued to teach for the remainder of that decade.

A talented aviation artist, several of Voorhis' paintings are on display at the New Jersey Aviation Hall of Fame & Museum.

Somerset Airport
George Walker

Inducted Aviation Hall of Fame of New Jersey, 1991

Somerset Airport is another that has been owned and managed by the same family for more than 40 years. George Walker, who spent more than 55 years in the aviation business as a mechanic, teacher and pilot, purchased Somerset in 1946. His partners were John Beekman and Sam Freeman.

Located on 200 acres in Bedminster, NJ, the Somer-

George Walker

set Air Service has thrived as a family-run business because of Walker's diligent management and service to his customers.

Born in Fraserburgh, Scotland, Walker arrived at Ellis Island at age seven. His family settled in Rahway where he attended public schools. In 1927, he joined the Army Signal Corps and upon discharge tried his hand at farming in Florida during the early Depression years. Unable to make a living, he returned to Rahway, and while working on a local estate, he attended night classes at the Casey Jones School of Aeronautics in Newark. When he graduated with an A&P license, Walker was hired as an instructor during World War II, teaching both civilian and military personnel. In the latter part of the war, he maintained 12 aircraft for the Civil Air Patrol at Solberg and Basking Ridge airports.

In the 1990s, Walker's son, Dan, and his daughter, Mrs. Ellen Parker, are both active in the management of the airport. However, George continues to oversee the entire operation.

1981
Ultralight High Flying
Jim Campbell

The grueling flight seemed endless — circling again and again above the long runways at the Naval Air Engineering Center at Lakehurst, climbing higher and higher just a few feet at a time, the craft with its 30 hp engine strained to carry Jim Campbell of Oakland, NJ, to a new ultralight altitude record in 1981.

It became colder with each turn upward and when the motor-driven hang glider reached 21,210 feet, the estimated temperature was 50 degrees below zero. The altitude record had been set.

The small machine descended rapidly, and landed safely, but the pilot couldn't stand up. He was covered with ice and literally frozen stiff. Family members, friends and well-wishers helped him out of his ultralight. He soon warmed and recovered fully.

One of the well-wishers was Patricia Trusty of Westfield, MA, who had been attending the flight program at Mercer County Community College. She brought Campbell a hot cup of coffee and the two became immediate friends. Campbell was later quoted in the Washington Post as saying: "I looked up and there she was, grinning down at me. Her smile filled my entire universe — on that day I thawed from the inside out."

In September 1982, Campbell and Trusty completed the first transcontinental flight by Ultra aircraft. They flew in two aircraft, each christened *Kindred Spirits*. The flight took three months and covered 3,800 miles. "It could've taken 24 days," the 26-year-old Campbell told the press," but we wanted to learn the skills we would need to fly around the world. The United States was really a classroom."

The 24-year-old Trusty said, "This barnstorming adventure is about living life to its fullest."

The two flimsy aircraft were constructed of heavy dacron spread over a frame of steel and aluminum tubing. They each weighed 250 pounds and were powered by 37 hp engines. They could cruise at 60 mph using regular automotive gasoline. Campbell described the flight from Watsonville, CA, to Oakland, in glowing terms and immediately began promoting a transatlantic flight.

"What we have here is a plain, old-fashioned adventure. Like the old barnstorming days, we've flown across this country with the wind at our back and the birds as companions. We've seen the deserts, the mountains and the plains. And we've met thousands of people across this land. Although it's only going to be the two of us crossing the Atlantic, all the people who've helped us on our way, who invited us to their homes for meals, who offered us showers and who wished us well will be with us in kindred spirit."

Campbell made his first solo flight in a glider at the age of 14. He soloed in a single-engine airplane at 16. He became a commercial pilot and flight instructor with an instrument rating for single and multi-engine aircraft. By the time he had become a devotee of ultralights, he had flown more than 8,000 hours, in all types of aircraft from from balloons to jets.

Born in Beacon, NY, Campbell grew up in Oakland. While attending high school, he joined the U.S. Air Force reserves and served with them for four years.

"Flying took hold of me early," Campbell told the *Ridgewood News*. "As a kid I used to sit on a fence at Lincoln Park Airport and bum rides. When I was 11, I won first prize in a subscription drive contest that the *Ridgewood News* ran for its paper boys. The prize was a trip to Japan. It was the biggest trip I'd ever taken. I visited some relatives I had over there and the experience made quite an impression on me."

Campbell evoked admiration for his adventurous spirit, determination and his special knack for self-promotion. The around-the-world flight was planned for the summer of 1983, the same year that the Air and Space Bicentennial celebration was being held. In need of sponsors and publicity to attract them, Campbell and Trusty flew their ultralights from Liberty State Park in Jersey City to the base of the Statue of Liberty. The well-publicized flight brought out a large press delegation. They watched as Campbell landed smoothly on the lawn in front of the statue. He and John Iannone, who was the director of the proposed round-the-world flight conferred. Campbell found that the downdraft of the helicopters hovering over Liberty Island had given him trouble landing, so he radioed Trusty to land immediately. She landed a bit long on the grass and it appeared that she might run into the sea wall surrounding the statue. Campbell tried to catch her right wing and pivot the plane, but instead was knocked flat and had to be taken by helicopter to a Manhattan hospital where he was treated for several broken teeth, a broken nose and a deep cut on his right cheek.

Because of financial considerations, the round-the-world flight never materialized.

Jim Campbell and Pat Trusty moved to California and eventually parted ways. Campbell joined the staff of *Sport Pilot Magazine* and in the late 1980s became its editor. In July of 1989, he moved to Winter Haven, FL, and began his own publication called *Aviator*.

The Racing Attorney
Seymour Gelzer

When Seymour Gelzer, an East Brunswick attorney, participated in the Air Transit Race in June 1981, it was his second long-distance race in a decade. The race course included a round-trip transatlantic flight. The participants flew from Le Bourget Airport outside of Paris, France, to Bridgeport, CT, and back across the Atlantic to Beauvais Tille, France.

Gelzer and his co-pilot, Roland E. Jeffords of Cranbury, NJ, spent many hours in their twin-engine Piper Aztec monoplane over the always treacherous Atlantic, making two roundtrip flights in order to participate in the race. The New Jerseyans finished seventh among the twin-engine aircraft that competed, although the first four places were won by turbo-charged planes.

One race plane and crew had been lost off the coast of Ireland and 10 of the original participants withdrew from the race because of weather conditions.

When the two adventurers returned to the United States, Gelzer was quite nonchalant about their achievement. He described the flight as "quite un-

eventful except for the poor weather which was anticipated."

In July of 1971, Gelzer had flown his Piper Aztec in the London-Victoria Air Race, commemorating the 100th anniversary of Victoria, British Columbia. The former World War II Navy navigator and bombardier again had to fly across the Atlantic twice and twice across the American continent.

The race, which began at the Abbingdon Royal Air Force base outside of Oxford, England, was divided into seven individual legs, the longest being Abbinsdon to Quebec, Canada. It was, at that time, the second longest sanctioned handicap race, covering more than 5,800 miles.

Gelzer finished near the bottom in his class. However, the difference between the first plane on the ocean leg of the flight and Gelzer's, which ranked 22nd, was only two miles per hour, based on actual speed versus handicap speed.

In 1988, Gelzer flew to Moscow with Claudio Tonini of South River and Gerald Gordon of Edison in Gordon's twin engine Cessna 210. They left from Monmouth County Airport and flew north through Canada, Newfoundland and on to Bergen, Norway, where they rested for a few days. The next stop was Helsinki, Finland, before flying into Moscow. The round trip took 26 days.

"In those days, before 'glasnost' had really caught on in Russia," Gelzer said, "we were one of very few private aircraft permitted into the Soviet Union. It wasn't difficult to make arrangements once you found the right connection."

Born in Jersey City in 1925, Gelzer took up flying at Teterboro Airport in 1955. As the 1990s dawned, he estimated that he had logged more than 3,000 hours at the controls of various aircraft.

When it was suggested that he was a glutton for punishment in making long-distance flights, he replied, "It isn't bad just making four-hour runs a day. It's possible to keep to that schedule when you fly the northern route."

Roland E. Jeffords and Seymour Gelzer.

He did admit that while flying the London to Victoria race, he stayed awake for 40 hours. "But if I could find someone to go with me, I'd fly around the world tomorrow," he concluded with a chuckle.

He is a long time resident of Jamesburg, NJ.

1982
Around The World in 47 Hours
Harold Curtis

Inducted Aviation Hall of Fame of New Jersey, 1984

A Gulfstream-III owned by the National Distillers and Chemical Corp. took off from Teterboro Airport at on Jan. 8, 1982 and flew around the world in 47 hours, 39 minutes to establish a new speed record for corporate aircraft of its weight classification. The Teterboro-based G-III shaved almost 10 hours off the mark of 57 hours, 20 minutes set by professional golfer Arnold Palmer in a Lear-36 in 1976.

The airplane, christened *Spirit of America* in honor of the 100th anniversary of National Distillers' Old Grandad bourbon distillery, was the first production model of the Gulfstream-III. The commander of the flight was Harold Curtis, manager of the company's air transport division. William Mack of Upper Saddle River, was chief pilot and Robert Dannhardt of Sparta, flew as the assistant chief pilot. Air Force Capt. L. Scott Curtis, Harold's 27-year-old son, went along as the official observer for the National Aeronautic Association which sanctioned the flight. G. Lee

Pilots Bill Mack and Harold Curtis flank Gulfstream American Corp. chairman Allen Paulson.

Weems, also of Upper Saddle River, the transport division's chief of maintenance, doubled as chef on the historic flight.

The G-III made five scheduled refueling stops on its 23,490-mile circumnavigation of the earth. The first was at Geneva, Switzerland, followed by quick stops in Bahrain, Singapore, Guam and Hilo, Hawaii.

In 1966, another New Jerseyan, entertainer/pilot Arthur Godfrey, had established a 'round-the-world record in a corporate Jet Commander.

The actual flying time of the *Spirit* was 43:39:06 hours. Those flight times and other records claimed were sent to the National Aeronautic Association in Washington, DC, and the Federal Aeronautique Internationale in Paris, France, to be reviewed. They were certified as new records.

In addition to the 'round-the-world record, Harold Curtis and his crew had set 12 new ones for time flown between designated cities.

Curtis said that the cooperation they received from ground personnel throughout the world was outstanding.

"If we had been Air Force One, we couldn't have been handled any better or faster,"Curtis explained. "And if politics of the world were run by the air traffic people around the world, there wouldn't be any wars."

As the G-III was on its final approach to Teterboro a crew member said, "Don't ever let anyone tell you it's a small world."

When Harold Curtis began flying corporate aircraft, he was one of a new breed of pilots in business suits who traveled around the nation and the world in planes designed for speed and comfort. For Curtis, the flight of *Spirit of America* was the culmination of a long career as a corporate pilot. His Teterboro-based flight department was the first to fly the Grumman Gulfstream I across the Atlantic and the first to put the Gulfstream II and III into corporate service.

He remembered a humorous incident that occurred in 1958 on one of the first European flights in the propeller-powered Gulfstream I

"Our first G-Is were flown to Europe almost immediately," he said. "They (Europeans) were surprised to see an American airplane that wasn't an airliner. One day over Paris, we were spotted by a TWA Constellation. One of its pilots asked us over the radio 'Hey, isn't that airplane made in Long Island? How'd you get it over here, in a boat?'"

When National Distillers received the first Gulfstream II in 1967, they immediately sent it on a tour of Europe with top company executives aboard. At the time, the G-II was the only corporate aircraft able to fly nonstop from America to Europe. Flying with the jetstream from New York, the large twin-engine jet made the flight to London easily, but on the return trip, Curtis had to put down in Burlington, VT, because the jet had only 30 minutes of fuel remaining in the tanks.

Born in New York City in 1921, Curtis grew up in Brooklyn. As a teenager, he worked at Floyd Bennett Field on weekends in exchange for flying lessons. Before the United States became involved in World War II, he worked as an engine mechanic for Pan American Airways at LaGuardia Airport. During that time, he organized a local flying club.

His flying career began in earnest when the U.S. declared war on Japan and Germany. He moved to Florida and became a flying instructor at the Royal Air Force school in Clewiston. When he began instructing in 1942, his logbook indicated that he had flown 300 hours. By 1944, he had flown several thousand hours.

Following the war, he piloted amphibian aircraft on charter flights in the Bahamas, before joining the Anaconda Mining Co. flying a war surplus Grumman Goose amphibian on exploration flights in Brazil.

On a ferry flight of the Goose to Belem in northern Brazil, Curtis was detained several days in Cuba and again in Haiti, while local revolutions were in progress. "There was much shooting and excitement," he said. "We just kept our heads down and waited for it to stop."

In Brazil, he spent "four wonderful years" flying metal engineers on gold and lead explorations throughout the country and into British Guyana and Venezuela.

The Korean War brought an end to the South American operation, so Curtis returned to the U.S. and joined National Distillers. In 1951, he bought a home in Upper Saddle River, and later moved to Franklin Lakes.

On Aug. 31, 1982, Curtis retired from National Distillers and moved with his wife La Verne to her home town, San Antonio, TX. When he was inducted into the Aviation Hall of Fame of New Jersey in 1984, he said, "Imagine being paid for something you love to do. These have been fabulous years, flying the best equipment to the best places all over the world, and flying for the best company."

William L. Mack

All of the flight planning for the 'round-the-world flight was done by Bill Mack. He worked closely with Gulfstream Aerospace representatives to assure that the requirements of both companies were met. It was important to Gulfstream's management that the airplane flew long segments, thus demonstrating its flying stamina. Mack personally piloted the plane for almost half of the 47-plus hours it took to circumnavigate the globe.

Mack, a Long Island City, NY, native, began his career in 1942 as a 17-year-old Navy aviation machinist mate and served in the Pacific theater of operations during World War II. He applied and was accepted for Naval aviation training but before he joined the program, the war ended and he was discharged.

In 1946, Mack worked as a mechanic with American Airlines based at LaGuardia Airport. He left the airline in 1948 as a senior mechanic when the overhaul base was moved to Tulsa, OK.

That same year, he became a crew chief with the newly formed 102nd Radar Calibration Squadron of the New York Air National Guard based at Westchester County Airport in White Plains, NY. But he still wanted to fly, so in 1951, he qualified to join the U.S. Air Force pilot training program at Perrin AFB, Sherman, TX. He took his multi-engine training at Reese AFB, Lubbock TX.

Mack's first corporate job was with the Federal Telecommunications Laboratory of Nutley, NJ, in 1952, flying a DC-3, a R3D and a B-17 for electronic flight evaluation. Following brief stints with the flight departments of Cluett, Peabody and the American Oil Company, he joined National Distillers at Teterboro in 1960. He became the company's chief pilot in 1976, a position he held until the company was sold to the Quantum Chemical Corp. in 1986. When the flight department was disbanded, Mack continued to fly leased aircraft for Quantum, based at the large Atlantic Aviation complex at Teterboro.

1983
First All-Female Military Flight Crew

In May of 1983 at McGuire Air Force Base, the first all-female crew flew a large military transport across the Atlantic Ocean to evacuate seriously ill military personnel. Although the Air Force admitted that the flight of the Lockheed C-141B Starlifter was arranged for recruiting purposes, it did prove that women could handle the 100-ton aircraft as efficiently as men.

Capt. Giuliana Sangiorgio of Sergeantsville, NJ, commanded the crew of six specialists.

Albert J. Parisi, a *New York Times* reporter, filed the following story on the historic flight:

As the big Lockheed C-141B rose from the runway at McGuire Air Force Base here [Wrightstown], climbing

All-woman crew: L-R: Capt. Guiliana Sangiorgio, S. Sgt. Denise Meunier, Capt. Barbara Akin, Sgt. Mary Eiche, 1st Lt. Terri Ollinger and Airman Bernadette Botti.

into the night sky and out over the Atlantic, the fact that the flight was making military history was secondary in the pilots mind.

Instead, course headings and fuel-consumption ratios were the first priorities for the mission of nearly five hours to the American air installation at Lajes Field in the Azores, and then to Rhein-Main Air Force Base in Frankfurt, West Germany.

The two pilots and five crew members were women, making this the first trans-Atlantic military cargo flight with an all-female crew. Its members were drawn from the same unit, the 18th Military Airlift Squadron, which is based at McGuire.

"I don't know if this earns us a place in the Guinness Book of World Records," said 29-year-old Capt. Giuliana Sangiorgio of the Hunterdon Country community of Sergeantsville, "But it's a big first for the service, and certainly a big accomplishment for us."

The purpose of the three-day military exercise, which began May 11 was the evacuation of seriously ill American service personnel and family members from West Germany to specialized-treatment facilities in the Washington area.

More specifically, said Air Force officials, the mission was an effort to demonstrate the importance of women in airborne operations and to further the public's awareness of military airlift capability in a service that is placing more women in jobs that have been traditionally male.

"Each crew member here is an expert in her field." said Lt. Col. William Brem Morrison, commanding the 18th Military Airlift Squadron." In the days to come, you will see more and more missions of this nature flown by all-women crews or integrated crews, which is being done at present.

"What we're trying to stress here is that the Air Force is offering an equal opportunity for women.

"It is hoped," Colonel Morrison added, " that recruiting efforts will be helped by the historic flight."

Although the women aboard refused to liken their mission to Charles A. Lindbergh's solo trans-Atlantic flight in 1927, they emphasized that their pioneering effort would make it easier for women to be accepted as pilots and flight-crew members at United States Air Force bases around the world.

"The Air Force has come a long way in accepting women in job fields where only men have been considered in the past," said co-pilot, First Lt. Terri Ollinger, 29, of Cincinnati. " The Air Force has a long way to go yet in continuing to place women in positions of responsibility and career fields, but everything has to start with a crawl before it can move on to a run "

That progressive step, say some women pilots, must include an increase in their ranks. At McGuire's l8th Military Airlift Squadron, for example, only 3 percent (pilots and aircrew members) of the unit's 230 personnel are women. And of the 275 active-duty pilots stationed at the field, the home base of the 438th Military Airlift Wing, only 12 are women with varying degrees of flying experience.

According to military officials at McGuire and the Defence Department in Washington, fewer than 4 percent — 1,225 — of nearly 23,100 Air Force pilots are women.

"I'm certain that in time the numbers will change for the better," said Captain Sangiorgio, a graduate of Embry-Riddle Aeronautical University in Daytona, FL, one of the few colleges in the country devoted to aviation.

Women pilots were introduced to military service in the early 1940's, when they ferried combat aircraft from the U.S. to Army Air Corps bases in England, via Greenland. Their service as military pilots during World War II was termed necessary because of a shortage of qualified fliers, but they were not permitted to engage in combat or to enter combat zones.

Such regulations, supported by Congressional action, still apply. Women pilots and crew members fly routine transcontinental and intercontinental missions and exercises, just as their male counterparts do; however, in a war or critical situation involving life-threatening risks, women are excluded.

Women's rights advocates have called such restrictions hypocritical, even though women pilots and crew members draw the same flight pay and basic salaries as men.

"It's a Congressional restriction that we have to abide by, not an Air Force policy," Colonel Morrison emphasized. He noted that before 1980 there were no women in his unit.

Women pilots believe that, the more visible they be-

come in their career field, the quicker they will be accepted by male service members and the public.

"Many of us felt not too long ago that we were in a goldfish bowl and were being constantly studied and scrutinized," said Captain Sangiorgio, who has logged nearly 1,600 hours of flight time and was one of the first women pilots assigned to McGuire.

But the novelty of women flying will wear off in time, and we'll be better off when it does.

The crew members had logged a total of 10,700 military flying hours among them. In addition to Capt. Sangiorgio and First Lt. Ollinger, the other crew members were: first pilot Capt. Barbara Akin of Dallas, TX, who, while in New Jersey lived in Willingboro; Instructor flight engineer Tech. Sgt. Donna Wertz of Baltimore, MD, who lived in Browns Mills; flight engineer Staff Sgt. Denise Meunier of Westfield, VT, also a Browns Mills resident; loadmaster Sgt. Mary Eiche of Lakehurst, FL, a Bordentown resident, and loadmaster Airman First Class Bernadette Botti of Buffalo, NY, who resided on the McGuire base.

The entire round-trip flight of the Starlifter was exactly on time. The flight was a giant step for womankind in military aviation.

First Woman Aviation Director
Arlene B. Feldman

New Jersey governor Thomas H. Kean named Arlene B. Feldman the director of aeronautics on June 1, 1982, succeeding acting director John J. Santarsierro, who had replaced Walter D. Kies, when Kean had moved into the state house in 1981. Feldman, a lawyer and pilot, thus became the first woman director of aeronautics in the United States.

Upon assuming her new post, Feldman's principal concern was to save New Jersey's airports that were closing at an alarming rate because the owners were financially unable to maintain and improve their facilities. With the backing of State Senator John Russo, an Ocean County democrat, himself a pilot, she and her staff conceived "The New Jersey Airport Safety Act of 1983." The proposed legislation was considered the most sweeping change in New Jersey's airport/aircraft regulations since the division was formed in 1931.

The bill, introduced by Russo in the State Senate and by Assemblyman John Market, a Bergen County republican in the Assembly, contained the following provisions:

1. Elimination of the state aircraft registration fee.

2. Financial aid to both private and publicly owned airports.

3. State loans below the prime rate to privately owned airports and an authorization to make outright grants when appropriate.

4. The elimination of the power to license pilots which had been on the book for many years but never exercised.

5. To empower the state to purchase land for clear zones to protect approaches at privately owned airports.

6. The power to purchase private airports if they were in danger of being closed, but not the power to operate the airports.

7. The state would no longer license fixed-base operators at the various airports throughout the state.

8. To support the program, the tax on aircraft fuel would be raised by two cents a gallon.

The bill passed both houses of the legislature and Gov. Kean signed it into law. Jack Elliott described the action in his *Newark Star-Ledger* column, titled *"A Shot in the Arm for Airports,"* that ran July 17, 1983.

Over the years, aviation people in New Jersey have watched one airport after another close, eliminating the accessibility of key areas in the state — mostly urban areas — by fast, efficient general aviation aircraft.

The new law resulted in large measure from the efforts of Arlene B. Feldman, who took over as director of the Division of Aeronautics on June 1, 1982.

She recognized the urgent need for such legislation, outlined its parameters and assembled a team which wrote the measure, with the help of key people on the Governor's staff, and with the advice and counsel of the bill's sponsors, Assemblyman John Market (R-Bergen) and Sen. John Russo (D-Ocean).

In the past, New Jersey has lost millions of dollars in federal funds because no matching state funds were available. (Usually, the federal government contributes 90 percent and state or local government agencies are required to provide 10 percent under the airport improvement program, which includes runways, navigation facilities, lights, etc.)

The signing in the Governor's office on Monday attracted a number of top aviation officials, including William F. Shea, the FAA's associate administrator of airports, who flew up from Washington, and Joseph H. Del Balzo, former director of the FAA Technical Center in Atlantic City, and currently director of the

FAA's Eastern Region headquartered at Kennedy Airport.

Del Balzo called the New Jersey Legislation "a big step forward."

"The beauty of the program in New Jersey," Shea said, "is in the high emphasis it places on the importance of airports to our national, multi-model transportation system."

All the reasons why nothing could be done about it were recited and reiterated a hundred times over. Every time another airport died, it was accepted as inevitable.

It changed with the stroke of the pen of Gov. Thomas H. Kean when he signed into law The New Jersey Airport Safety Act of 1983.

Essentially, the new law changes the role of the state Division of Aeronautics from that of policeman to that of doctor. Under the new law, the division will have the power to save airports and the medicine ($$$$) to do it.

The legislation is history-making inasmuch as it enables the state to provide financial aid to privately owned public use airports, as well as publicly owned facilities.

New Jersey is the first state to take this step, according to Joseph G. Mason, executive vice president of NASAO (National Association of State Aviation Officials), who flew up from Washington to attend the signing of the historic legislation.

Prior to this measure, New Jersey was one of only three states (Colorado and Nevada are the other two) which provided no funds whatever to any airport within its borders.

Kean said it all at the signing ceremony when he stated, "we're not going to bring up the tail end anymore. We're going to be the leaders."

General aviation airports provide a gateway to an area. They have a tremendous influence on businesses and on employment in an area.

Feldman resigned from her state job in August of 1985 and became the Acting Director at the Federal Aviation Administration (FAA) Technical Center at Atlantic City. In 1988, she became the highest ranking woman in the FAA when she was named the Deputy Director of the Western-Pacific Region which include FAA activities in Arizona, California, Hawaii, Nevada and the Pacific area. The region has more than 5,000 FAA employees.

Feldman was replaced as New Jersey's aeronautical director by Catherine A. Nickolaisen, who held that post until 1989, when Paul Baker became the acting director.

Voice of N.J. Aviation
Jack Elliott

Inducted Aviation Hall of Fame of New Jersey, 1986

Jack Elliott

For more than a quarter-century, Jack Elliott has written a weekly aviation column for the *Newark Star-Ledger* he calls *Wings Over Jersey*. The column includes activities at New Jersey airports, interviews with aviation pioneers, unusual accomplishments of contemporary pilots and, most important of all, stories concerning the survival of general aviation facilities throughout the state. His columns became a rallying point for those concerned by the constant threat of government regulations and suburban development to the vitality of the state's aviation industry.

His tireless efforts have brought him many awards. His articles on the state of business aviation in New Jersey for the *Star-Ledger's* annual business review section *Outlook*, won the Lois Henry Journalism Award of the National Business Aircraft Association (NBAA) twice in national competition. Elliott was the only aviation writer or broadcaster to win the coveted NBAA award twice.

He has also received numerous citations from the Air Force Association and in 1982 was named "Man of the Year" by the Union-Morris Chapter 195.

Other citations have been presented to the newsman by the Aviation/Space Writers Association, the FAA, and the New Jersey Division of Aeronautics.

His column in the Nov. 12, 1989 *Sunday Star-Ledger*, six years after the New Jersey Airport Safety Act was passed, clearly defined general aviation's plight. It read as follows:

The paper was yellowed, but the headline was still bold and clear: 'AVIATION CRISIS IN '72: DWINDLING AIRPORTS.'

The date: Feb. 6, 1972. The newspaper: The Sunday Star Ledger. *The byline: The same one that appears above this column.*

"I found it when I was going through some stuff in the attic," said Cas Gubernat of Dunellen, as he handed us the story that ran more than 17 years ago.

The story quoted an official of the New Jersey Division

of Aeronautics as saying that 34 of the state's 85 airports were in jeopardy. If all 34 were lost, that would leave the state with 51 airports. Incredibly, that is precisely the number we have left in the state today (not counting three seaplane bases).

If we continue to pursue the same course in the future that we have in the past, 17 years from now New Jersey will be virtually inaccessible to general aviation aircraft. These are aircraft which carry millions of inter-city passengers and billions of dollars worth of merchandise annually, in addition to life-saving missions such as transport of human organs for transplant, rare blood and rare pharmaceuticals.

New Jersey would not be the same state without these facilities.

None of the 34 airports lost in the past 17 years can ever be replaced. There is no land available to replace them. And an average general aviation airport requires little more than the equivalent of a half a mile of suburban road.

The state has lost 40 percent of its general aviation airports in the past 17 years. Imagine if we had lost 40 percent of our highways. You can't imagine it because it's unthinkable.

To anyone who appreciates what a general aviation airport contributes to the economy of an area and to the economy of the state, the loss of 40 percent of our airports is just as unthinkable, even though it is a fact.

There is no way that the effect of that loss will not impact on the economy of the state eventually, and by the time that fact is recognized it will be difficult, if not impossible, to do anything about it.

Going back to the article of 17 years ago, it quoted an official of one of New Jersey's top Fortune 500 companies as comparing a good airport to a bird feeder. It attracts new business to a community, he said. The only difference between then and now is that general aviation is performing a much greater variety of missions than it did then.

The mayor of Lewiston, MT, was quoted as saying, "It's as if we were cut off from the world. We can't even get salesmen in here to sell us things anymore."

The article 17 years ago states that 92 percent of the airports in the United States are not served by airlines. The figure in 1988 was 92.5 percent, according to statistics provided.

Demand for general aviation airports and the services they provide is growing according to the Aircraft Owners and Pilots Association.

These airports are now the major source of airline pilots of the future. Years ago, the military was the major source. That is no longer the case.

Owners of the airports, which have survived in the unfriendly climate they find themselves in here in New Jersey, have tried to meet the increasing demands placed on them by the closing of so many airports. But every time any of them tries to improve or expand its facilities to accommodate those demands, it is met by opposition at every level of government. The fact that we have lost 40 percent of our airports in 17 years speaks for itself.

One of the major problems is a lack of recognition of the role general aviation airports play in our economy. General aviation is a significant part of the nation's transportation network. It is an economic resource. If we lose sight of that fact, we won't pay the price for it. Our children will

Elliott, a Warren Township, NJ, resident, holds a commercial pilot's license with instrument, seaplane and glider ratings. He has logged more than 2,000 hours, most of it in pursuit of articles for *Wings Over New Jersey*.

Remembering the Lost Airports

Historian Bill Rhode was asked to recall some of the pioneers who struggled for years to develop and maintain their airports in New Jersey and a few of the aviators who would have been considered regulars at each field. His letter to the author was a rich source of information.

In 1945, Bruce Huppert took over Ocean County Airport at Breton Woods, from its builder. Bruce was an early barnstormer flying out of the Jersey City Airport from 1933 until it closed in 1936. Then he flew one of Chamberlin's Condors, hopping passengers around the country, until 1940. He was a machinist at Bendix during the war. Then, he and his wife operated at Breton Woods until the airport closed about 1965.

Ike Schlossback's Jumping Brook Airport at Neptune was built on his farm and later became the Asbury Park Air Terminal. It lasted from 1935 to 1975. There was also an Asbury Park Airport in Deal. It was started by Jack Casey in 1922 and when he left for Red Bank, Al Morton became the operator. Many of the early barnstormers who worked the Jersey shoreline in the summer months could be found in Deal. Gus Michaelson, Paul Green, Joe Blodgett and Harry Fielder are a few that come to mind. The field closed in 1956.

Jack McGuire opened the Toms River Airport in 1947. It folded about 1954.

Somerset Hills Airport at Basking Ridge lasted into the '80s. George Walker with Bob Litts were the first operators in 1932 and after the war Paul Housel, who owned a publishing company, took over. Economics forced it to close in 1983.

There were two Princeton airports. The Princeton Air Park was located along Route 1 and was also known as Nassau Air Park. Witt Savage operated it from

1945 to 1956 when the ground became too expensive to keep.

Princeton Airport along route 206 began in 1945 and is still a busy field. Bart Bartholomew operated it from 1956 to 1960, then Dave Van Dyke, owner of the Teterboro Aircraft Service, took it over. He finally sold it to Webster Todd, the son of the Todd Shipyard magnate.

Hightstown also had two airports. Al Bennett set up shop along Route 1 at Windsor in 1930. He sold hundreds of planes and taught countless numbers to fly. The field closed in 1942. Al died in 1989.

The other Hightstown Airport was in Hightstown. Jerry Fielder operated there first in the 1930s. After the war, Al Eckhart ran the place until progress closed it in 1960.

From 1945 to 1960, there was a North Brunswick Airport in North Brunswick that was run by Mr. and Mrs Walter Gingrich, she was the sister of Tom Robertson who operated Hadley Field for several decades.

Westfield Airport, which was located in Clark, opened in 1928, and by 1930 became a beehive of activity for teenage pilots learning to fly with Charles Dann. Alex Garofalo, Frank Goldsborough and Bob Buck all set international teenage flight records out of Westfield. Other regulars at the field were Harry Gordon and Rick Decker. The airport was gone by 1955. Decker later operated flight schools at Hadley Field, Somerset Hills and Kupper Airports.

I don't imagine there are too many people around who remember the Dawn Patrol seaplane base that operated from 1946 to 1950 at Secaucus.

Nelson Airport in Franklin Lakes, which Don Nelson opened in 1930, was a favorite of Frankie Hammond, Johnny Hupschmidt, John Trinca and Margie Gray. It closed in 1941.

Arcola Airport in Rochelle Park was located next to a large amusement park owned by Moe Katzman. It began operating as an airfield in 1927 and such well-known pilots as Silvio Cavalier, Bill Diehl, Freddy Weisher, Bruce Huppert, Bill Strong, Johnny Hupschmidt and Fred Trautwein, whose father owned the property, were regular users until it closed in 1936.

Horace Landers opened Mahwah Airport beside Route 17 at Mahwah in 1948 and bowed out to Fred Wehran in about 1954. Fred sold it four years later to the Ford Motor Co. and they built a huge assembly plant there.In the western part of the state there was Phillipsburg Airport, first operated by the Warren County Aviation Co. and later by Ted Phillips (1945-50); Eckels Autogiro Field in Washington where Eckels flew several autogiros from 1933 to 1939, crop dusting, instructing and doing promotional work;

Budd Lake Airport, known as the highest (1,050 feet) in New Jersey, operated for 10 years beginning in 1946, under Bart Bartholomew's management. I (Bill Rhode) instructed for him for two years. Ireland Field in Pine Valley, was operated in the '20s by Harry Rogers. Others we lost were Pine Brook Airport at Pine Brook, started by Roland and Chet Neumann in the late '20s. It had to close in 1938, when Route 46 was re-routed down its grass runway; Sussex Martin Airport at Sussex was begun by Frank Hammond. Frank Lees and Bill Hopkins were regulars there. It was abandoned in 1944, when the present Sussex Airport opened. There was also a Totowa Wayne Airport at Wayne, operated by Jake Brain from 1945 to 1963, and of course, Tom Murchio's Airport in the northern section of Wayne that opened in 1919, as one of the first in the state. It went out of business in 1956.

Camden Central Airport at Camden was originally called Crescent Airport run by the Walz Flying Service. In the 1930s, it was the major airport servicing Philadelpihia and a number of early airlines flew regularly scheduled flights from there. Johnny Miller flew the mail from Camden to the roof of the post office in Philadelphia using an autogiro.

I instructed at Hanover Airport in East Hanover for 28 years before it closed in 1985, almost 50 years after it opened. It had been started by Abe Steppel. Other instructors there over the years were Ted Spatz, Rolf Nelson, and Bob Alois.

When World War II began, the New Jersey National Guard Airport at Sea Girt closed. It had been the NJNG's encampment field and the site of the Governor's summer estate in the '20s and '30s.

Keyport Airport at Keyport, began as Walling Field and lasted from 1933 to 1955. Forsgate Airpark at Jamesburg failed about 1952, and the Newark-Elizabeth Airport at Elizabeth, where Billy Hughes held forth, closed at about the time Newark Municipal Airport opened in 1928.

The list of lost airports seems sadly endless. Charles Kupper's Kupper Airport in Somerville, Harry Nordheim's Flying K Airport in Margate. Kroelinger, Pitman, Bridgeport, Cumulus Ridge, Flanders all closed in the 1980s. It was really an epidemic.

I'd like to plug a few of the boys behind the scenes — the mechanics. They work hard to keep the rest of us flying. I'm talking about guys like Ward Oakley, Bill Bischak and Bill Gallagher at Lincoln Park and Hanover. And Slim West, Frank Romano, Bill Hartig, Henry Geleski and Ken Boedecker who were at Teterboro. Also let's not forget Toni Farrell, R.J. Mathews, Larry Young and Harry Emery. They were always around when needed.

1984
First Woman to Walk in Space
Kathryn D. Sullivan

Inducted Aviation Hall of Fame of New Jersey, 1987

Kathryn Sullivan

NASA Photo

On Oct. 11, 1984, Kathryn D. Sullivan, a native of Paterson, became the first American woman to walk in space. On shuttle flight 41-G aboard the spacecraft *Challenger*, she and astronaut David C. Leestma performed an in-space simulation of refueling another spacecraft in orbit.

Bundled in spacesuits, costing $2.1 million each, and tethered to the shuttle by safety lines, the two astronauts spent three hours and 27 minutes in the *Challenger's* open cargo bay. During the entire time outside the shuttle, Sullivan and Leestma shouted happily to each other as they floated weightlessly 130 miles above the earth.

Sullivan assisted Leestma as he attached a refueling line to a fitting on a tank half filled with volatile hydrazine, a fuel used by satellites to maintain their orbit and attitude toward Earth. They became so involved in their chore that the shuttle's commander, Robert Crippen, finally had to ask them to rejoin the rest of the crew.

"Good job," he said. "Time to come in."

The actual fuel transfer was done by remote control, a day after the "walk," from within the *Challenger's* cabin. While she was outside the spacecraft, Sullivan floated over the side of the vehicle and grasped a handrail in one hand while using the other to repair a broken data transmission antenna in time to beam television pictures of the space walk back to earth. "Orbital repair strikes again," she said, as she dangled over the side of the ship at a 90-degree angle helping Leestma align the loose antenna so pins could be driven into two holes electrically from inside the cabin.

"We're pinned," Leestma reported. "They're locked. They're locked."

Sullivan chimed in, "No sweat. They're solid." She then floated over the top of the shuttle and worked on another antenna that had been causing problems.

The spacecraft had circled the Earth two and a half times while the astronauts performed their extra-vehicular chores. As the ship floated over Paterson, Sullivan said, "Lots of Sullivana down there. I love it. This is really great." *Challenger's* flight 41-G was a mission of firsts:

- The first seven-person crew, one more than on any previous flight.

- The first time two women were on the same spacecraft. Sally Ride accompanied Sullivan.

- The first American woman to make a second space trip, Sally Ride.

- The first astronaut to make four shuttle flights, Commander Bob Crippen

- The first flight of a Canadian astronaut, Marc Garneau.

- The first demonstration of a satellite refueling technique in space.

- And the first spacewalk by a U.S. woman, Sullivan. Sullivan, although born in Paterson in 1951, was raised in California. Prior to leaving New Jersey, her father, Donald, had worked as an aeronautical engineer for the Curtiss-Wright Corp.

In 1973, she earned a Bachelor of Science degree at the University of California at Santa Cruz, and in 1978, she received a PhD in Geology from Dalhousie University, Halifax, Nova Scotia.

Many of her career highlights took place underwater on four marine research cruises from 1973 to 1976. In a vessel atop the Mid-Atlantic Ridge, she helped a oceanographic team map an undersea mountain range, and off the coast of California, she studied crustal faults.

She was chosen as an astronaut candidate by NASA in January 1978 while she was finishing her doctoral studies. In August of 1979, she completed her training and evaluation program and she became eligible to fly as a mission specialist. Prior to being selected for the spacewalk mission, Sullivan had done a great deal of high-altitude photography of the Earth for various geological and agricultural studies.

She hoped to stay with the space program as long as she remained physically able. Perhaps around the year 2000, she will be serving as a chief scientist aboard a permanent orbiting space station or lunar base.

Terry J. Hart

Born in Pittsburgh, PA, in 1946, Terry Hart moved to Long Valley, NJ, in 1968 and went to work for Bell Laboratories in Whippany, NJ. The following year, he went on active duty with the Air Force Reserve and took his pilot training at Moody Air Force Base, GA. As a qualified F-106 jet pilot, he joined the New Jersey Air National Guard in 1973.

In January 1978, he was selected as an astronaut candidate by the National Aeronautics and Space Administration (NASA) and in August 1979, he completed his training and evaluation period, making him eligible for assignment as a mission specialist on future Space Shuttle flights.

When it was announced that he would be a member of the five- man crew aboard *Challenger* shuttle flight 41-C on April 6, 1984, he told the *Bell Labs News,* "Working with NASA was a chance to combine my technical background from Bell Labs with my flying background from the U.S. Air Force. I was anxious to experience the adventure of being part of the space program." Hart made space history when he used a 50-foot robot arm to pluck the crippled Solar Max satellite from orbit. It was the first time the robot arm had been used to snare a rotating satellite in space. Repairs were made to the $75 million satellite while the *Challenger* circled the Earth was restored to service.

Hart also used the robot arm to deploy a bus-size satellite containing a number of experiments, including one involving several varieties of tomato seeds developed at the New Jersey Agricultural Experiment Station at Rutgers University's Cook College. The project's purpose was to determine the effects of space on 20 bags filled with seeds, including the Ramapo tomato and other varieties developed at Rutgers. The satellite was scheduled to be retrieved from space a year later and the seeds were to be distributed to schools across the nation for atudent-run experiments. Coincidentally, Hart received his master of science degree in electrical engineering from Rutgers in 1978.

In a letter to the author dated Oct. 24, 1984, Hart described his space journey:

"After six years of training and talking to crews who had preceded me, I thought I was well prepared for the spectacular experiences of spaceflight," he wrote. "The view is truly as beautiful as everyone has described, but two aspects of it caught me by surprise even after all those years of anticipation. First of all, the blackness of space is so absolute that it is without parallel on the ground. When the Shuttle is in the sunlight, the tiles are gleaming white and the pupils of the eyes constrict considerably. As a result, the contrast between the brilliance of the reflected sunlight and the total absence of any light immediately next to the tiles is startling. No stars, no reflections, no diffusion of light, just total, absolute blackness. It may seem strange, but the only time the stars are visible is on the dark side of the earth and then only when the cockpit lights are turned down. The second surprise is just how thin our atmosphere really is. Two minutes after liftoff the Shuttle is essentially above all of the atmosphere. From an altitude of 300 miles, those few miles of atmosphere are incredibly thin compared to the 8,000 mile diameter of the earth."

Immediately after his space flight, Hart resigned from NASA and returned to Bell Labs as a supervisor of the Military and Space Applications division. He and his family moved to a new home in Morris Plains, NJ.

Robert J. Cenker

Another Pennsylvanian, Robert Cenker, migrated to New Jersey in 1972 and joined RCA's Astro-Electronic Division in East Windsor as an engineer working in advanced stabilization and control. Much of his career was spent in the design and development of communications satellites, including the RCA Satcoms 1 and 2, the GTE Spacenet satellites and the advanced Series 4000 spacecraft. In addition, he was the system engineer on the U.S. Navy NOVA navigation satellite program.

In 1985, he was selected by NASA to serve as the prime payload specialist on Space Shuttle Mission 61-C. His training lasted six months. The first three were part time and consisted of orientation, video instruction, bookwork, physical, physiolosical and security screening. He spent the last three months at the Johnson Space Center practicing normal and anomalous mission operations.

Cenker was aboard the shuttle *Columbia* when it was launched January 12, 1986. While circling the earth, the RCA Satcom Ku-Band-1 satellite was deployed by Cenker. He also performed experiments with an infrared camera developed at RCA's David Sarnoff Research Center in Princeton and manufactured by the Astro-Electronics Division.

Cenker is a native of Uniontown, PA, and received his bachelor's and master's degrees in aerospace engineering from Penn State University. He also earned a master's degree in electronic engineering at Rutgers University. He and his family call East Windsor home.

A number of other New Jersey corporations and institutions have made significant contributions to the space effort. They include Singer Kearfott Guidance and Navigation Division in Little Falls, International

Telephone and Telegraph of Nutley, the Army Signal Corps Laboratory at Fort Monmouth, the Navy Air Turbine Test Center in Trenton, RCA at Holmdel, the Forrestal Center in Princeton, Allied Signal Aerospace Co. at Teterboro, Bell Laboratories in Murray Hill, and similar research and development centers in the Garden State. Again New Jersey has been on the cutting edge of man's conquest of the skies.

1986

Rodgers' Flight Recreated

James Lloyd

James Lloyd, an admitted "bona-fide airplane freak" and an amateur historian, discovered a hero from the pioneering days of aviation in Calbraith Perry Rodgers, the first man to fly an airplane from coast to coast. Lloyd and Rodgers shared a common birthplace, Pittsburgh, PA, although Lloyd moved to Oradell, NJ, when he was in the fourth grade and eventually graduated from River Dell Regional High School. Early in 1986, Lloyd, who had received his pilot's license three years earlier, realized that Sept. 17 would mark the 75th anniversary of Rodgers' history-making flight. He felt it would be appropriate for a fellow Pittsburgh native to recreate the flight.

Rodgers' flight had been supported by the Armour Meat Packing Co. as part of a publicity campaign to promote a new Armour soft drink called "Vin Fiz." The Wright Flyer Rodgers used had been christened *Vin Fiz* and the name was emblazoned on the bottom of the biplane's lower wing.

Lloyd approached the Armour Company for support of his project and received a positive reply. He then convinced Jack McCormack of Peterodactyl Ultralights of Tacoma, WA, to design a craft similar in appearance to the one Rodgers flew, and had Steve Noyes of Newburyport, MA, build it.

Meanwhile, Lloyd contacted the towns across the country in which Rodgers had landed to appraise them of his flight plans. To his surprise, he found a number of the towns and villages were no longer in existence, so alternate landing spots had to be chosen. Although Rodgers had begun his flight from Sheepshead Bay in Brooklyn, Lloyd chose Hoboken, NJ, as his starting point. At 8 a.m. on Sept. 17, the contemporary *Vin Fiz* with Lloyd at the controls sat poised on Hoboken's Sinatra Drive, in the very shadow of Stevens Institute of Technology from where Lloyd

had graduated in 1978 with a Ph.D in Materials Science and Engineering.

As the River Dell Regional High School band played a rousing rendition of "America the Beautiful," the remake of the 1911 Wright Flyer skipped down the drive, lifted into the air and flew out over the Hudson River toward the Statue of Liberty. One reporter compared the sound of the 30 h.p. engine as it passed overhead as "much like a weed-whacker amplified until it's as loud as you imagine it to be when your neighbor starts his up at 8:00 on Saturday morning." The event was seen by an estimated 5.5 millin viewers tuned in to ABC's Good Morning America television show.

Like Rodgers' plane, Lloyd flew below 1,000 feet at a maximum speed of 40 mph. His first stop that day was Middletown, NY. He then flew on to Hancock, NY. Lloyd later said, "The arrival in Hancock was the last time I was on time for the rest of the journey. Bad weather and mechanical problems plagued us for rest of the trip."

In 1911, Rodgers crashed 12 times on his transcontinental odyssey and the Wright Flyer was completely rebuilt by the time he reached Long Beach, CA, 49 days later.

Lloyd arrived in Long Beach on Nov. 12, having spent 57 days enroute. He had flown 98.5 hours and made 101 stops. The modern *Vin Fiz* used four sets of landing gears, four props, two engines and innumerable spark plugs.

"I landed in bean fields, pastures, county roads, unfinished housing developments, high school football fields, municipal parks, golf courses and airports," he reported. "It was quite a trip."

Considering all the trouble that Rodgers had, Lloyd was disappointed that his flight took a few days longer "...but it gives some indication how big this country really is," he pointed out. "We could not reproduce Rodgers problems and we were constrained to land at all of his stops. In addition, we had the worst weather anyone had ever seen. In 30 days, we had four good flying days, the rest were marginal, submarginal or downright stinko."

Lloyd's ground crew following his flight by car consisted of his wife, Susan Oguarian, who acted aa the official photographer for the trip, Pat Keasler, a former New Jerseyan who now resides in Salem, MA, and Jack McCormack.

At the time of the flight, Lloyd made his home in Fishkill, NY, where he worked for IBM.

It is interesting to note that according to Hoboken historians, Lloyd was the first person to take off in a fixed wing aircraft from their city.

Pedal-Powered Flying Machines

Charles K. Paul, a Woodbridge, NJ, attorney, invented a novel human-pedal-powered flying machine. He convinced the Navy to test his invention in Hangar # 1 at Lakehurst claiming it was an ideal rescue vehicle.

The Pedalcopter, as he called it, consisted of a 5,000 cubic foot, helium-filled balloon with a large propeller mounted below it. The propeller was turned by a person pedaling a bicycle with the gear connected to it. Paul could make his unique invention ascend, descend and turn in any direction. But the Navy never accepted the concept.

For several years, Paul could be seen flying his creation over the farmlands of Woodbridge and in 1957, as president of the Pedalcopter Company, he applied to the Civil Aeronautics Administration for an Airworthiness Certificate.

The artist's conception of the Pedalcopter sent to Jules DeCrescenzo, the CAA inspector, indicated that he then conceived his contraption as a flying advertising billboard. His explanation below the drawing read:

"This is an artist's drawing of how the Pedalcopters will look from a distance in the air. In lieu of the word 'PEDALCOPTER,' there will be inserted [on the balloon] the names of local and national products. The balloon revolves in a clockwise motion, approximately 20 revolutions per minute, therefore, anyone will be able to read the advertisement from any location. The blades move counter clockwise about 100 revolutions per minute with normal pedaling speed, making the machine easy to operate for extremely long periods of time."

Years later, DeCrescenzo was asked what ever happened to the Pedalcopter. He had no answer. Paul reportedly had never called to arrange an appointment for the airworthiness flight test.

Muscle-Power Flight
Paul Osadchy

It was in 1973, while attending the Reading (PA) Air Show that Paul Osadchy's son, Tommy, saw an article in an aviation magazine telling of a $125,000 prize put up by British industrialist, Henry Kremer, for the first human-powered flying machine. The rules stated that the contraption had to fly 10 feet above the ground and perform a figure-eight over a two-mile course. Osadchy, an industrial engineer from North Arlington, NJ, became fascinated, or perhaps a better word is obsessed, with the idea. He began designing and building a muscle-powered aircraft in the basement of his home. Soon parts were all over the house — a wing in the kitchen, the tail in Tommy's bedroom, the fuselage in the living room. It was a family affair and his wife, Norma, was as enthusiastic about the undertaking as were the men in her life. The pioneer designer spent an entire year of his life and most of his meager savings on the project before it was ready to fly. He christened it the *Wing Charmer*."

In 1975, Osadahy moved his operation into a hangar at Orange County (NY) Airport in preparation for the solo flight. By then, the media had found him and he became as instant celebrity. Visitors from as far away as Iceland and Tokyo passed through the hangar door marked "Paul Oaadchy's Manpowered Aircraft." The 300-lb. flying machine was unique. It had a 60-foot wing constructed of Canadian spruce and styrofoam, covered with a thin vinyl fabric. The streamlined fuselage and the oversized tail were made of the same material. The undercarriage was constructed of welded, light metal tubing which held a single bicycle wheel, a seat for the pilot and the framework where the propeller was mounted.

The first flight was scheduled for July 13, but Osadchy found the weather to be perfect the night before, so he decided to try a preliminary flight before the crowds arrived the next day. His adrenalin was running high as he began pumping the bicycle gear leading to the propeller up to full speed. Soon the machine was moving down the runway with his wife and son running along side supporting the fragile wings. As the tail skid scraped along the pavement, Osadchy pumped even harder.

"I could feel the tail getting lift as I knew it would," he said later.

Then suddenly, there was a sickening grinding noise and the propeller stopped turning. The gears had stripped. Sadly, the family rolled the big bird back to the hangar and stayed in seclusion the following day when more than 400 spectators showed up to witness the solo flight.

The failed first flight didn't dampen the Osadchy family's spirits. Within a month, adjustments and reinforcements were made. The *Wing Charmer* was ready to fly again.

With the help of two strangers, a pilot and a local onlooker, Osadchy was able to determine the ground speed necessary to get his creation airborne. The local man brought his car onto the runway and, with the pilot sitting in the trunk holding a rope attached to the front of the plane, he began driving slowly down the pavement. As the car's speed increased, the *Wing*

Charmer, with its 51-year-old inventor at the controls, lifted off the pavement, yanking the rope from the startled pilot's hand.

"I was in a state of shock," Osadchy told his family. "It was so sudden that nobody knew what happened, like the scene of a crime where all the witnesses describe a different event. But I flew! I flew!"

Over the next six years, he constructed six more of the large-winged craft, each an improvement on the previous model. By 1981, the *Wing Charmer II* weighed only 55 pounds with a 50-foot wingspan. Osadchy had used strong, light-weight materials like fiberglass tubing, graphite and a Mylar covering. This one flew. A young man, Samiar Patel, pedaled it airborne in 1982 at the Monmouth County Airport.

But it was too late to recoup his investment. By then, Paul MacCready, a Californian, had built a pedal machine he called the *Gossamer Albatross,* that not only flew the two-mile, figure-eight course, but successfully traversed the English Channel, piloted by Bryan Allen.

In *ERADCOM,* the company publication of ERADCON's Electronic Warfare Laboratory, where he worked, Osadchy was quoted as saying:

There were quite a few detractors. They thought I was a crackpot and always associated my idea with perpetual motion and those items that were, to them, unrealistic. I even had someone mention Evel Knievel to me once and imply that I was attempting to a sensationalist quick buck. However, those who questioned me from the beginning are coming back and saying, 'Gee, there was something to your ideas.' And something has indeed been accomplished, even though I did not accomplish it.

In 1989, Osadchy was still working on pedal-power flying machines when a heart problem forced him to undergo open heart surgery. While he recuperated at home, he designed a muscle powered helicopter that he plans to build. Comments written in his guest book from those early years in Orange County indicate that others believe in dreamers too. People wrote: "...to see human progress" and "...to see the glory, say a prayer" and the one of which Osadchy is most proud "...to see a man of courage."

Piasecki's Heli-Stat

On July 1, 1986, a 75-foot-tall flying machine, consisting of a blimp and the parts of four helicopters, crashed and burned during a test flight at the Naval Air Engineering Center at Lakehurst, killing pilot Gary Olesfski of Bordentown, one of five crew members aboard. Witnesses reported that the strange machine, called a Heli-Stat, got 40 feet off the ground, then tilted backward and fell to the ground in flames.

The Heli-Stat was conceived by Frank M. Piasecki, the inventor of the tandem rotor helicopter, which was the second successful helicopter to fly in America. The huge flying machine was designed to have a vertical lift of 25 tons, nine tons greater than U.S. military helicopters of that time.

The construction was being financed by the U.S. Forest Service for use in harvesting timber in areas where there were no roads.

The program was started in mid-1979 as a proof-of-concept test vehicle. It consisted of four Navy surplus Sikorsky helicopters, powered by Curtiss-Wright engines, mounted on a giant aluminum open-truss frame that was attached to a Navy surplus 343-foot, one-million-cubic-foot, helium-filled airship. The ungainly contraption was longer than a football field, wider than an aircraft carrier and stood 12 stories high.

Piasecki claimed that his machine had great potential in many areas. Aside from timber harvesting, it could be used for high-rise construction, laying large pipe lines in inaccessible areas or off-loading containers from ships near the shore.

As the chief of the FAA's Teterboro Engineering and Manufacturing District office, Ben Rock became involved with Piasecki's oversized dream. He worked with Piasecki as a government employee until he retired in 1984, and then continued as an airworthiness certification consultant and FAA coordinator.

The unusual looking airship used a combination of the lifting power of the helium and the four helicopters. When Heli-Stat's dacron gas bag was filled with helium its lifting power offset the weight of the four helicopters, the aluminum frame and the dirigible itself. Thus the airborne weight of the entire structure was near zero, allowing the total lifting thrust of the helicopter rotors to be applied to lifting a useful load of 25 tons.

The machine was flown by four pilots. One controlled the Heli-Stat from the rear left helicopter where he had the best view of the suspended load hanging from the center. The other three cockpits were manned by

Frank Piasecki and Ben Rock stand below the Heli-Stat.

dual-rated helicopter/airship pilots who functioned as flight engineers and were capable of operating the controls if necessary. The airship could fly 165 miles and had a maximum speed of 65 mph.

The Heli-Stat made more than 60 test flights, both tethered and untethered before it was destroyed by fire less than a half-mile from where the German dirigible *Hindenburg* exploded in 1937.

Nick Grand, the public information officer at the Naval installation described the accident.

"The Heli-Stat made a rolling takeoff, and its wheels were 15 to 20 feet off the ground when the right rear helicopter separated from the rest of the craft," Grand said. "Then almost instantaneously, a large amplitude vibration was created. The other three helicopters almost simultaneously separated [from the structure] and old mama gravity took over. Everything came crashing down."

The accident climaxed a controversy that had begun in 1979 when Piasecki proposed to build the airship and the Forest Service accepted the offer.

Piasecki was awarded a $10-million contract with a 1982 deadline to finish the project. Delays, technical problems and rising costs pushed the cost of the project to $37 million and brought on a congressional inquiry.

In a 1982 letter, a general accounting office analyst W.H. Sheley told then-Secretary of Agriculture John Block that the estimated cost of the program had risen to more than $31 million and that the truss support of the Heli-Stat was flawed by shoddy workmanship, and that few timber companies said they would benefit from such a vehicle.

Congress overrode the objections and by 1985 had pumped $30 million into the experimental craft.

Following the accident, an official of the Forest Service said "Unfortunately, the Heli-Stat cannot be reproduced by Piasecki again because it was made from surplus that he used up and from things gathered from the junkyard"

Former Congressman Robert B. Duncan, once the chairman of the House Transportation Appropriations Subcommittee and a supporter of Piasecki's dream, was shocked when he was told of the disaster at his home in Yachats, OR.

"I've always believed we ought to keep pushing back the frontiers of knowledge," he said. "When I heard about the accident, I said 'My God, maybe this is my fault, because I insisted that Frank find surplus blimp parts and use aluminum irrigation pipes. Goodyear told us they could build the same machine for $95 million to $100 million, using carbon-filament for the cantilever structure."

Obviously the Congressman should have let the experts decide on the material to use vhen constructing an elephantine airship like the Heli-Stat.

Ben B. Rock

Inducted Aviation Hall of Fame of New Jersey, 1977

Teenager Ben Rock

Ben Rock was no stranger to helicopters. In 1939, he was employed by the Sikorsky Aircraft Co. in Stratford, CT, when Igor Sikorsky successfully flew the first helicopter in the United States. In 1941, he joined the U.S. Navy's Bureau of Aeronautics as a supervising inspector of all experimental research, development and flight testing, and in 1942 he flew in the experimental Sikorsky XR-4 two place helicopter. The test flights were so impressive that the Army Air Corps ordered several dozen of the flying machines.

Over the years, Rock was involved in certification projects encompassing practically all of the major helicopter manufacturers from that early two-place machine to the Boeing 234 twin-blade passenger helicopter, the world's largest, introduced in 1981.

Rock's fascination with flying started in his preteen years when he would walk to Teterboro Airport from his home in Clifton, NJ.

"Teterboro was my second home," he said. "It was a long walk, but always worth it. Finally, I built a bicycle out of spare parts — we were too poor to afford a new one — and the trip became much easier."

At age 9, Rock took his first flight with Billy Diehl in an open cockpit biplane and his career choice was sealed. When he was 15, he bartered his services with Ed Gorski, Teterboro's operator. He'd work for a week as a line boy in exchange for one hour of flying lessons. At 16, he soloed and became the youngest licensed pilot at the airport.

"If it wasn't for Ed and Julie Gorski's dedication to Teterboro during the Depression years, we wouldn't have an airport today. It was Ed's fortitude, initiative, and hard work that started Teterboro rolling and kept it rolling," Rock said.

In the mid-30s, Rock spent his weekends selling airplane rides for Gorski at Teterboro. For a dollar, passengers would fly from Teterboro around the courthouse in Hackensack (about two miles away) and back. On a good Sunday, the Gorski pilots carried 250 to 350 passengers aloft.

Using a megaphone, Rock would stand on a wooden

box and give a sales pitch that would have made P.T. Barnam proud.

"Ladies and gentlemen, we have a brand new Stinson Reliant that will take you over the city of Hackensack and the courthouse building for one dollar," he'd begin... "You may smoke if you wish, there is an ash tray at your elbow. High or low, fast or slow, any which way you want to go. Old maids sigh for it and children cry for it. Just step right up folks. Only one dollar."

Rock did some of the passenger "hopping" himself. He remembered the quirks often found in the aircraft of those days.

"Some airplanes were not made as well as today's," he explained. "Some had fuel tanks located behind the instrument panel that often leaked into the cockpit. Before taking a passenger up, I would start chewing a whole pack of Beechnut gum and I'd give a pack to the passengers to chew. When they asked why, I told them it was in case the fuel tank sprung a leak. Beechnut gum always stopped the leak. It stuck to the tank better Wrigley's. Some tanks were pockmarked with Beechnut."

At age 18, he learned to drive a car and headed north to Stratford, CT, to work for Sikorsky. His first job was on the huge Sikorsky S-42 flying boats that Pan American Airways used on its first transpacific flights and the S-43 that Howard Hughes flew around the world in 1938.

In 1941, he joined Chance Vought Aircraft as an inspector of Navy dive and torpedo bombers and Corsair fighters used on aircraft carriers.

During the seven years he spent as a supervising inspector for the Navy's Bureau of Aeronautics, his headquarters was the United Aircraft Corp. in Stratford. Rock was particularly proud of the highly classified work he did with Charles Lindbergh who was on special assignment at United Aircraft as a civilian technical representative. Rock was responsible for the airworthiness of Lindbergh's aircraft which was to be used for top secret missions.

One day, Lindbergh took off in a specially equipped Corsair fighter which Rock had approved as airworthy. Once airborne, it was discovered that the Corsair'a landing gear would not retract. Via the radio, Rock and Vought technicians instructed Lindbergh to try various alternative methods of retracting the gear but none worked. Rock knew the gear worked perfectly during retraction tests on the ground and worried that someone had sabotaged the secret project. After circling the airport for 30 minutes, Lindbergh was ordered to land as four fire trucks lined the runway in case the landing gear collapsed on touchdown. To Rock's great relief, Lindbergh gingerly landed the heavy fighter safely. It was later found

that the retract hydraulic valve shaft had failed internally. Remembering those tense moments, Rock said, "Aviation is hours and hours of boredom, punctuated by moments of sheer panic."

In June 1948, Rock transferred from naval duty to the Civil Aeronautics Administration (CAA) as an Aviation Safety Agent. For the next 13 years, he worked with every major aeronautical manufacturer in the CAA's Eastern Region certifying new aircraft and equipment. That dedication to the industry earned him the position of Chief of the Engineering and Manufacturing District Office based at Teterboro. In 1961, he moved back to New Jersey and assumed responsibility for the certification of all aeronautical products within a geographical area of 75,000 square miles in the northeast.

Following a near fatal plane crash in 1950, Rock always told friends he was living on borrowed time. On April 3 of that year, he was flying as a passenger in a CAA Stinson monoplane, piloted by John C. Medford of Elmont, NY. They had left Idlewild Airport (now John F. Kennedy Airport) in Jamaica, NY, at 9:30 a.m. heading for Lock Haven, PA, where Rock was stationed at the Piper Aircraft factory. As they neared the Delaware River, the weather became overcast and a faulty altimeter caused them to crash into the Blue Mountain about 25 feet below the peak. The plane bounced along the hilltop for about 150 yards then smashed and burned in a densely wooded area. Rock had been thrown clear of the Stinson, but Medford was trapped inside and burned to death.

Although the plane was near the village of Penn Argle, PA, the wreckage wasn't discovered for almost two days. A Coast Guard helicopter, one of scores of Coast Guard, Air Force and CAA planes in the search, spotted the wreckage of the CAA plane 28 hours after the crash. Two Air Force medical corpsmen parachuted into the woods and found Rock unconscious 100 yards from the wreck.

Rock regained consciousness long enough to ask for his wife and explain that it was dark when he had regained consciousness after the crash. He tried to build a fire to attract rescuers, but failed. He then scratched a note on a piece of the wreckage and started to crawl downhill but the effort caused him to blackout. The rescuers had to carry him by stretcher three miles down the rugged mountainside. A doctor in Penn Argle predicted that if Rock had been found 10 minutes later, he would not have survived. He was hospitalized for nine months with a fractured spine, a brain concussion and severe burns of the head.

Over the years, Rock and his district office at Teterboro received numerous awards from such diverse groups as the Experimental Aircraft Association and the Air Force Association. He was most proud of the Federal Aviation Administration's (predecessor of the CAA) 1971 Regional Flight Standards Field Office Award. The work of his Teterboro staff was honored over 35 other FAA installations in the United States.

Despite his accident, Rock never gave up flying. Over the years, he owned seven aircraft all named *Daisy*. His plane's tail numbers were familiar at airports throughout the northeast.

When he retired from the FAA in 1984, he became an airworthiness certification consultant and traveled around the world certifying commercial and private aircraft for governments and businesses.

Rock, a Hackensack resident, spends the winter months in Florida, "away from the snow but near an airport."

Hero Test Pilot

Until July 11, 1986, Major Ross E. Mulhare, a River Edge resident, was just one of several hundred New Jerseyans flying in the military services. At 2 a.m. on that fateful day, Mulhare tragically made international headlines when his top-secret Stealth F-19 fighter plane seemed to explode in flight and crash near the base of the 4,100-foot "Saturday Peak" on the western slope of the Sierra Nevada mountains. The crash, which took the 35-year-old major's life, triggered shock waves throughout the Air Force high command.

For several weeks after the accident, the Air Force would not concede that the aircraft was a stealth fighter, constructed of materials that cannot be detected by enemy radar. The crash site was put off limits while a lengthy search was conducted for every part of the supersonic jet.

The Lockheed-built aircraft had been based at Nellis Air Force Base in Nevada, about 210 miles east of where it went down in California.

At the time of his death, his father, Edward Mulhare, said "I just want people to know that we consider our son a hero who was doing exactly what he wanted to do, despite the danger involved. I want to say how proud we are of Ross and what he was doing for his country."

In 1969 when Mulhare graduated with honors from St. Joseph's Regional High School in Montvale, he received the outstanding cadet award from the Reserve Officer's Training Corps (ROTC) program. That was a period when the nation's youth were revolting against the military establishment, but the young River Edge man knew what he wanted and applied to the Air Force Academy where he studied for two years. Air Force Academy students were permitted to attend civilian colleges during their junior and senior

Mr. & Mrs. Edward Mulhare pose before a portrait of their son, Ross, at Aviation Hall of Fame of New Jersey.

years so Mulhare entered Oklahoma State University and received a BA in Business Administration in 1973. That same year, he graduated from Officer Training School and was commissioned a second lieutenant. He then graduated among the top three in his pilot training class and received his wings at Vance AFB, Oklahoma.

Flying F-4 and F-5 fighter planes, Mulhare became an adversary tactics instructor at Nellis AFB. In 1982, he served as a foreign exchange pilot with the Spanish Air Force and helped establish that country's first adversary training program. He then was assigned to the Bitburg Air Base in Germany as a "A" Flight commander in the 525 TFS.

In June of 1985, he was selected to join the 4450th Tactical Group at Nellis.

Mulhare's assignment as the Stealth test pilot was so top secret he never discussed it with his wife, the former Mary Eithelbach of River Edge, or other members of his family. Every three months the Air Force gave him a lie-detector test to prove it.

Throughout his career, Mulhare garnered praise from classmates and superiors. Brother Peter Russell, principal of the St. Joseph Regional High School remembered him as "an exceptional student and an obvious leader." A classmate, John Bykowsky, now a New York attorney, said "This guy really had guts. Rem (Mulhare's nickname) was number one."

At the time of his death, Lt. Col. Roger Locher, Mulhare's squadron commander, stated "he had the desire to excel. Ross Mulhare was the type of a guy you wanted in your outfit. Flying was what it was all about for him. When he was flying, he was happiest."

Mulhare, a devout Christian and devoted father of four, once wrote to his wife in anticipation of his death: "What ever happens, let's turn it for the glory of the father. Take this loss as an opportunity to praise the Lord...praise him for taking me from this earth and bringing me home to him. The Lord in his divine wisdom has said it's time."

Major Ross Mulhare had celebrated his 35th birthday

on July 4th, 1986, just seven days before he and his highly technical machine crashed in California.

In Search of the *America*

In September 1986, the author, and photographer Robin Ringrose-Albracht received an assignment from the editor of *Pan Am Clipper* magazine to travel to Ver-sur-Mer, Normandy, France, in search of pieces of the Teterboro-built Fokker trimotor *America*. The plane had flown from Roosevelt Field, Long Island on June 29, 1927, with a crew of four commanded by Lt. Cmdr. Richard E. Byrd. It carried the firat official sack of mail flown between North America and Europe. After 42 hours in the air, and running dangerously low on fuel, the *America* crash-landed in the English Channel off the Normandy coast in the early hours of July 1 (see 1927).

The article telling of our discoveries was published in early 1987 to commemorate the 60th anniversary of the historic flight.

We flew aboard a Pan Am 747 to Paris and with the full cooperation of the French National Railroad and the French Tourist Office, made our way to Caen in the Calvados district of Normandy. There, a local French tourist official escorted us to Ver-sur-Mer, a village of 1,000 citizens, where we were greeted by Mayor Jacques Ronnaux-Baron and an entourage of local citizens at a small seaside auditorium.

The walls of the room were lined with newspaper and magazine articles describing the 1927 flight. There were photographs of the *America* submerged in the English Channel, individual and group pictures of the plane's crew and others of the subsequent celebration in Paris. Gilbert Angenault, the village tourist official, had located a small section of the Fokker's fuselage fabric and a hand pump, built by the Bendix Corporation, that had been used to transfer fuel from auxiliary five-gallon gas cans to the Fokker's wing tanks.

We had expected to find more artifacts, but instead we discovered something significantly more important to our story. We met people who had played a role in the *America* saga 60 years earlier. There were the Lescope sisters, daughters of the 1927 lighthouse keeper; the Coiffier brothers, sons of the deputy mayor, who had given up their beds to Byrd and his radioman, George Noville, on the day the *America* unexpectedly arrived; Jacques Houze, who had gone to the beach with his father in the pre-dawn hours and had sat in the plane's cockp!t. As nine-year-old Jacques played with the instruments, his dog ate a chicken sandwich which had been dropped by Bernt Balchen when he hurriedly took control of the plane during an in-flight emergency. And there was Mrs.

Julienne Leledier, a charming, delicate woman, who recalled with tears of joy how, as a 14-year-old, she picked her garden clean of its loveliest blooms to present to Lt. Cmdr. Byrd at an official village ceremony.

Also present was Emile Tanugi de Jongh, a retired ambassador-at-large who had served under three French presidents. DeJongh and his American-born mother had acted as interpreters for the airmen following their arrival.

Tanugi de Jongh and his mother had spent three months each summer in Ver-sur-Mer for 11 years to escape the heat in Paris. But none were as memorable as those days in early July 1927. Sixty years later, he remembered that his mother was very upset when she heard that Lt. Cmdr. Byrd and the *America* were racing toward Paris. "It's too bad," she told her son. "If I were in Paris I could see them, but here I am in this little village on vacation." Less than half a day later, Mrs. Tanugi de Jongh and her son were awakened by a member of the Coiffier family and asked to meet Byrd at the Coiffier house to interrupt.

During our 1986 visit, several of the leading newspapers of Calvados and the province of Normandy sent photographers and writers to report on our visit. Unwittingly, we had become celebrities. Following the reception at the beach-front auditorium, we were taken to visit the lighthouse and then the vacant, centuries-old Coiffier farmhouse where Byrd and Noville had slept. The building is centrally located in the village and had stood empty for several years. Robin and I casually mentioned that it would make an excellent museum to commemorate the arrival of the first international air mail in Europe.

The suggestion received an equally casual response.

We were to leave Normandy late in the afternoon of the second day of our visit to Ver-sur-Mer, but a provincial television crew arrived just before our scheduled departure and asked to do a news piece on our visit. It was while we were retracing our steps with the TV crew that we met Jean-Pierre and Nany Dupont. Jean-Pierre had been raised in Ver-sur-Mer and owned a vacation home there. He and Nany worked for Air France and lived in a suburb of Paris. Dupont, a dedicated historian, had heard of our visit to Normandy from friends and immediately drove 200 miles from Paris to meet with us. He enthusiastically embraced the museum idea and we discussed how it could be accomplished.

When Robin and I returned to the United States, we found that the Board of Trustees of New Jersey's Aviation Hall of Fame & Museum, which I direct, were interested in helping the citizens of Ver-sur-Mer create a museum. Approximately, $10,000 was raised in cash and services to create exhibits for a potential Byrd/America museum. Some special gifts were set aside for the village school children who were participating in essay and poster contests which Dupont had arranged with the local school director.

The following September, Robin and I returned to Ver-sur-Mer with cartons of display items and gifts. We were greeted enthusiastically. The presentation ceremony was attended by a provincial senator, the U.S. air attache from the American embassy in Paris, a number of other dignitaries and several hundred villagers. At that point many were seriously discussing the creation of a museum.

In May 1988 at my invitation, Jacques Ronneaux-Baron and Jean-Pierre Dupont and their wives traveled to the United States to attend the Aviation Hall of Fame's annual induction dinner. They sat on the dais as honored guests, and when introduced, the two men explained their desire to create a museum to honor the four American airmen who had crash-landed off the shore of their village 61 years earlier.

In the audience was Anneliese Gillespie, the director of the Emil Buehler Fund, established by the late Emil Buehler to underwrite aeronautical projects. Mrs. Gillespie encouraged the mayor and Dupont to apply to the fund for a grant to purchase the Coiffier home in Ver-sur-Mer to use as a museum.

Six months later, a $50,000 gift was approved and in the early spring of 1989, the house became the property of the "Musee America," the name the French association had adopted. Some immediate repairs to doors and windows in the house were made using funds raised in France and the United States.

During the same period, William N. Moxley, president of the Aviation Hall of Fame Association, and Hal Knapp, principal of the Richard E. Byrd grammar school in Glen Rock, NJ, encouraged New Jersey students and their parents to become involved in a hands-across-the-sea project. As the Ver-sur-Mer students had done the previous year, the Glen Rock children created posters depicting the pre-dawn arrival of the *America* in the village. A contest was held and prizes, donated by the Aviation Hall of Fame and the French Consulate in New York, were awarded. The winning posters were displayed at the AHOF museum at Teterboro Airport.

More importantly, the students on both sides of the Atlantic began exchanging letters as a first step toward a student exchange program. In addition, an advanced French class at the Oradell/River Edge middle school initiated a letter exchange program with their counterparts in Normandy that culminated in reciprocal student visits a year later.

In May of 1989, Robin and I returned to Ver-sur-Mer for the first meeting of the Musee America Association. More than 100 village residents attended to elect the officers. Jacques Ronneaux-Baron was elected president, Dupont and I were named vice presidents.

We then spent our remaining days in Normandy working in the house with a small group of adults, led by Michel Etore, and two dozen children. We chipped the crumbling plaster from the two-foot-thick stone walls of the old house and removed wallpaper from the bedrooms on the second and third floors. The renovation had become a unique community project.

It is not common for Europeans to volunteer their services. because most hospitals, museums and other public places are supported by government funds. So when we first suggested that the men, women and children of Ver-sur-Mer volunteer to help create the museum, the idea was met with skepticism. But the enthusiasm of the five adults who went to work on the building inspired the children and during that short stay in the village, a great deal of cleanup work was accomplished.

Over the summer months, weekend workers, adults and children, continued to make improvements to the building in preparation for a September visit of the Buehler Fund trustees.

In September of 1989, Robin and I, accompanied by Gloria Acosta, the daughter of the *America's* pilot, returned to the village just prior to the Buehler trustee visit. We found the building brightly decorated with flags and welcome messages. During the three-day visit of the Buehler trustees, there were a number of ceremonies, banquets and tours of the 1944 D-Day invasion beaches.

There is still a great deal of work to be done on the Musee America building before it can officially open as a public museum, but the French trustees were confident it will be ready to accept visitors in the early 1990s.

Writers, Artists, Historians Abound

Over the years, some of the finest writers, artists and historians have made their homes in New Jersey. They have chronicled and illustrated the growth of aeronautical industry from its infancy to the advent of space exploration. Their incisive coverage of events and personalities has helped to glamorize the industry and encourage the expansion of commercial and general aviation.

Arguably, the best known of all the early New Jersey aviation newspaper writers was the man who conceived the Aviation Writers' Association, **Richard W. "Dick" Kirschbaum.** He had joined the editorial department of *The Newark News* in 1929, and six months later began reporting aviation news.

Throughout the 1930s, a period commonly referred to as the Golden Age of aviation, Kirschbaum covered New Jersey and national aviation events. During that period, Newark Municipal Airport was the focal point of commercial aviation's growth in the United States and Kirschbaum was there to report the record events and latest developments in the world of aeronautics. His column, *Air Lanes,* which appeared weekly in *The News* was highly regarded by the aviation community.

Kirschbaum, born in Newark in 1894, graduated from Newark's Barringer High School in 1913 and went to work for the *Newark Sunday Call* as a cartoonist. Over the next seven years he worked for the *New York Press,* the *The Newark Ledger* and *The Newark Star-Eagle.* Those newspaper assignments were interrupted by two years of military service during World War I. Kirschbaum's artistic ability added a special flare to his aviation column. Each week he'd feature a drawing of a well known aviation personality to illustrate his column. In 1941, the cartoons were published in a booklet, *Fifty Famous Flyers.*

Kirschbaum regularly covered national air shows and other newsworthy aeronautical events and became acquainted with every aviation personality of the time, from Lindbergh to "Wrong-Way" Corrigan.

In 1942, Kirschbaum was commissioned a captain in the Army Air Corps and eventually served with the 14th Air Force in China, under Maj. Gen. Claire L. Chennault. Kirschbaum, who lived with his wife in Lake Hiawatha, NJ, had a heart attack in October of 1948 while attending the annual National Aviation Clinic in Detroit, MI. His good friend Jacqueline Cochran, the internationally famous aviatrix, made arrangements to fly him back to Newark. He died two months later at Doctors' Hospital at age 54.

E.B. "Mannie" Berlinrut

A contemporary of Kirschbaum's, E.B. "Mannie" Berlinrut became a full-time reporter at the *Sunday Call* in 1929. He covered local news and began writing a weekly aviation column, *Air Lines,* as well as a regular piece on model building and glider flying.

In the early 1930s, he was a founder and officer of the New Jersey Glider Association, which sponsored an annual glider competition at Liberty Corner, NJ. The participants flew primary and secondary gliders, mostly home-built. Sixty years later, Berlinrut remembered that Chester Decker of Glen Rock won the first two championships. "The gliders were very primitive," he said. "The development of soaring gliders that Decker used to win the National Soaring Cham-

pionship in the late '30s, were only in their infancy. We had huge crowds for our contests. They'd come out to watch the flights, each of only a few minute's duration."

Berlinrut was also one of the founding members of the Aviation Writers' Association. "There are now some 1,000 members of the Aviation/Space Writers Association worldwide," he said proudly.

In June of 1942, he entered the U.S. Air Corps as a second lieutenant and served as a public information officer at various U.S. Air Corps installations. He was discharged as a major in 1946 and went into the public relations business with a New York consultanting firm. In 1975, he opened his own firm in New York City which he ran until he retired in 1985.

Roger C. Garis handled the aviation beat at *The Newark News* for several years and later joined the *New York Times Magazine* staff. **Al Skea** followed Garis as the *Newark News* aviation writer and was highly respected throughout the state. When *The News* folded, Skea joined the staff of the *Herald News* in Passaic. During those romantic years of aviation, **Frank Buchner** covered the aeronautical news for *The Star Ledger.* In the 1970s, **Henry Frank** created an aviation column in *The Bergen Evening Record* in Hackensack. Frank's beat was Teterboro Airport, although he covered important events at Newark and other North Jersey airports. Right after World War II, **Bill Larsen,** a military flier, wrote an aviation column for the *Herald News* that featured the grass root pilots from various North Jersey airports.

Leslie E. Neville

When Leslie E. Neville of West Englewood, NJ, died in 1973, he had spent almost 50 years writing about or publicizing aviation. Upon graduating from Leonia (NJ) High School and Columbia University, Neville began his career in 1924 with the *New York American.* In 1929, he went to the magazine *Aviation,* as technical editor. During World War II, he edited *Wings* magazine, an Army-Navy publication designed to stimulate aircraft production.

Neville authored or co-authored a number of technical books including *The Coming Air Age, The Aviation Dictionary, Jet and Propulsion Progress* and *the Aviation Handbook* for *Aircraft Designers.* He was also aviation editor for *Colliers International Yearbook, Funk & Wagnalls Encyclopedia, Americana Annual* and *Grolier & Co. Encyclopedias.*

He was the recipient of a number of awards from the Air Force and other government defense agencies. From 1950 to 1952, he served as public relations director of the Curtiss-Wright Corp.

Arch Whitehouse

Perhaps no aviation writer before or since has produced as many magazine stories, novels and nonfiction works on flying and aviators as Arch Whitehouse of Montvale, NJ. He was regarded as THE expert on World War I flying, a subject he knew quite well from first-hand experience.

Born in England in 1895, his family immigrated to the United States when he was nine. He attended grade schools in Newark and Livingston, NJ, but to help keep food on the family table he left the classroom at age 14 and went to work in a Newark book store. That was followed by stints in a shoe factory in the Ironbound section of Newark and at the Edison Storage Battery plant in West Orange.

When World War I began in Europe, Whitehouse worked his way to England aboard a cattleboat and joined the British army. He didn't find infantry life to his liking so he requested a transfer to the Royal Flying Corps and became an aerial gunner. "It was a fast transition," he said years later. "One day I was in the trenches, and the next thing I knew I was shooting at targets on the ground, then up in the air for pistol duty. In an hour, I had shot down my first Hun."

In a year's time, Whitehead had destroyed 16 German aircraft and six kit balloons. In 1918, he became a commissioned Sopwith Camel pilot but never flew in combat again.

When he returned to New Jersey in 1919, he found jobs hard to come by. Never one not to keep busy, he became a salesman and for the next three years sold everything from rat poison to automobiles. Along the way he married Ruth Terhune of Rutherford.

In 1922, he heard there was a cartoonist position open on the staff of a Passaic paper, so he applied for it. "I had never drawn anything in my life," he admitted, "but they hired me anyway. They sent me to art school. I convinced them I was worthy because I wrote about sports so well."

A year later, he became the sports editor for the *Elizabeth Daily Journal.* Like so many others involved in aviation at that time, Charles Lindbergh's solo Atlantic flight in 1927, changed the direction of Whitehouse's life. Following the flight, he wrote a column about it. A friend who read the piece suggested he try writing for the aviation pulp magazines that were popular at the time. He submitted a story and received a check of $100 by return mail. The editor was impressed by the authentic way Whitehouse wrote, and asked him to check the facts in other stories that were submitted to the magazine. He began writing fiction based on World War I adventures that proved to be very marketable.

During World War II, he was an accredited war correspondent and took part in the Normandy invasion. At the war's end, he moved to Hollywood as a script writer, but found that too confining, tore up a seven-year contract and moved back east. By then, television had killed the pulp magazine business, so he began writing novels. The first one was published in 1959; 37 books followed.

He once bragged that he wrote 3,000 words every morning before taking a noontime-stroll along Magnolia Avenue in Montvale, a routine he followed right up to the time of his death in 1979.

H.K. "Budd" Davisson II

Budd Davisson, a Nebraska boy who moved to Butler, NJ, in 1968, made a significant contribution to the aviation industry through his writings and photography. He estimates that he has written 700 to 800 aviation articles for national magazines and his photographs have graced the covers of more than 300 of those magazines.

From 1982 to 1990, 55 of his photographs filled an 85-foot wall in the National Air & Space Museum's Pioneer of Flight Gallery in Washington, DC. Many of his aviation photographic masterpieces hang in Chicago's Museum of Science and Industry.

Davisson, with degrees in Aeronautical Engineering and marketing, wrote a column *Grass Roots* in *Air Progress* magazine for 20 years. As a pilot, he spent more than 4,500 hours in the cockpit of a P-38 fighter plane and B-25 bomber. As this account was written, he was teaching aerobatic flying in his own Pitts Special which he kept at Andover Aeroflex Airport, a few miles from his home in Sparta, NJ.

James Holahan

"Tireless, always writing hundreds of pages each month, working long days on an ancient manual typewriter which he used until the 1980s when he was introduced to the personal computer," said Joyce Huber, a former art director of *Aviation Consumer and NBAA Convention News,* on the subject of her former boss, Aviation International News editor James Holahan. "I remember once the old manual typewriter broke down," she continued, "and he still filled hundreds of pages with informative aviation text using a Bic pen."

Holahan, born in Jersey City and a lifetime New Jersey resident, acquired his basic flying skills under the Civilian Pilot Training program run by New York University in 1942. While serving with the Army Air Corps during World War II, he flew P-38s and B-25s, but, as he likes to say, "never fired a shot in anger."

Following the war, Holahan worked at Teterboro Airport as an aircraft radio technician and a pilot for Meteor Air Transport. Later, he went to work for Air

Associates as a radio lab technician and company co-pilot.

In 1948, Holahan joined the staff of *Aviation Age* magazine as an associate editor until he was recalled to active duty during the Korean War. Flying F-80s with the 330th Fighter Interceptor Squadron of the Air Defense Command, he again never fired a shot in anger. But over the years, he did rack up 8,500 hours of flying time.

Returning to Aviation Age, he became the Electronics Editor until 1964, when he joined *Business and Commercial Aviation*. He was the senior aviation editor when he left in 1972 to become editor and co-publisher of the *Aviation Consumer*. With his partners, writers Wilson Leach and Robert Hoffman, they set up shop in the Pan Am Building at the south end of Teterboro Airport.

That same year, Holahan and Leach founded the *NBAA Convention News*. Now known as *Aviation International News*, it is published six times a year along with special show issues at five international air show/conventions. The tabloid magazine has a faithful following of readers.

Holahan, a tireless worker, puts in 12-hour days working on his magazine. He is known to arrive at his office, now in Midland Park, NJ, at seven in the morning and stay past ten at night, writing articles or spending hours on the phone researching a story. "He's a genius at putting technical data into language anyone can relate to, " Huber concluded with great admiration.

The Collins, Father and Son

Beginning in 1958, Richard Collins Sr. published and edited *Air Facts* in his hometown of Princeton. The magazine folded when he died in 1968, the year Richard Jr. became the senior editor of *Flying Magazine,* published in New York City. In 1977, he was promoted to editor-in-chief. Over the years he has authored seven aviation books on the art of flying and contributed countless articles to other publications.

David A. Anderton

Dave Anderton was a multi-talented man who worked as an aerodynamicist, aviation photographer and journalist. During World War II, he was the design engineer for the wings of Grumman's TBF. Later, with General Electric, he was project engineer on two ramjet-powered Hermes cruise missile programs.

He spent more than a decade as associate editor of *Aviation Week and Space Technology* and operated the magazine's office in Geneva, Switzerland.

He authored more than a dozen books and other publications and articles. His widely acclaimed *History of the U.S. Air Force* is a required text for Air Force Academy cadets. His photographs of aircraft around the world also won him national acclaim.

A Ridgewood, resident, Anderton earned an aeronautical engineering degree at Rensselaer Polytechnic Institute, and pursued post-graduate studies at Princeton University and Union College. He was an Associate Fellow of the American Institute of Aeronautics and Astronautics and a former executive vice president of the American Society of Journalists and Authors, plus a half dozen other aviation societies.

He died in 1989 at the age of 70.

Historians

Not all the aviation articles published by the media around the nation are written by staff writers. Many indepth stories are created by aeronautical historians who, for the most part, specialize in a particular phase of the industry or an era of flight. Over the years, New Jerseyans have been leading authorities on varied aeronautical subjects. The most prominent of these is Paul Garber, the renowned historian with the Smithsonian Institution's National Air and Space Museum. Others who have spent endless hours researching aviation history and have written books and papers on a diverse range of subjects include:

Douglas H. Robinson, MD, of Pennington, the German Zeppelin and USN dirigible programs.

William H. Althoff of Whitehouse Station, USN lighter-than-air program.

Peter H. Grosz of Princeton, WW I German and Austrian aircraft.

Neal W. O'Connor of Princeton, WW I aviation history.

Howard A. Bueschel of Trenton, aerospace education.

Gerard J. Cassius of Cearville, aviation in general.

William Rhode of Wayne, William Ryan of Berkeley Heights and David Winans of Colonia, New Jersey aviation history.

Alexander Ogston of Tenafly, aviation fuels.

Kenneth Young of Keyport, history of Aeromarine Co.

Henry M Holden of Randolph, commercial aircraft.

Jack Lengenfelder of Lawrenceville, aviation postcard history.

Artists

Some of the nation's finest aviation artists have made their home in New Jersey. Their work has been seen in galleries and museums throughout the world. Others spent their entire careers as illustrators for aeronautical publications.

To create authentic works of aeronautical art, most artists spend months researching their subjects. Every detail of an aircraft, its location and the circumstance in which it is to be depicted are considered.

John T. McCoy

Inducted Aviation Hall of Fame of New Jersey, 1988

Jack McCoy

The watercolor paintings of historic aircraft created by John "Jack" McCoy encompass aviation history from the Wright brothers to Air Force One.

The Clifton resident learned to fly at Curtiss Field, Long Island, NY, in 1927. Subsequently, he obtained a commercial license with a flight instructor's rating.

As a combat artist during World War II, he flew missions with the 8th and 9th Air Force over Europe. His paintings of combat aircraft in action were exhibited in the first show of Army Air Force art at the National Gallery of Art, Washington, DC. After the war, he remained active in the USAF Reserve and retired in 1969 with the rank of colonel. The year before he retired, he flew nearly 50,000 miles as an air crew member on a Lockheed C-141 jet transport while researching a series on the Military Airlift Command.

At a one-man show in 1967 in the National Air and Space Museum, McCoy exhibited his well known collection of paintings commissioned by Pan American World Airways entitled *Historic First Flights of Pan American Clippers*. Another collection, *American Aces of the First Air War,* watercolors of World War I aircraft in combat as described by four WW I flying aces, were shown in 1982.

"Landfall"

Charles Lindbergh personally explained to McCoy what his first impressions were as he arrived over Dingle Bay, Ireland, on his solo flight from New York to Paris in 1927. The famous painting of the *Spirit of St. Louis* that McCoy created is called *Landfall.*

McCoy's first airplane ride in 1923 in a Curtis JN-4-D Jenny was the beginning of a love affair that carried on throughout his life. By his 80th birthday, he had logged 2,000-plus hours at the controls of more than 100 varied aircraft, all in the name of research. In retirement, he admitted, "They were fun too."

Keith Ferris

Inducted Aviation Hall of Fame of New Jersey, 1992

Keith Ferris

Prior to July of 1976, the work of Keith Ferris was highly respected among the editors of aviation trade magazines and advertising managers of large aeronautical corporations. But when the Air and Space Museum opened that summer with his 25-by-75-foot mural *Fortresses Under Fire,* filling the back wall of the World War II gallery, he became a national celebrity.

With guns poised and Wright Cyclone engines roaring, the huge B-17 bomber, *Thunder Bird,* seems to fly out of the wall into three-dimensional reality so typical of Ferris' work.

In the jet aviation gallery, opened in 1987, a Ferris mural, depicting the evolution of jet aircraft, from the first German jet fighter of WW II to the supersonic Concorde, covers a wall 20 by 75 feet. The two murals are viewed by two million people a year.

Ferris is also an author, historian and pilot. He has flown in most every jet aircraft in the Air Force inventory, including the McDonnell Douglas F-15 and General Dynamics F-16. He has traveled across the country with the USAF Thunderbird Flight Demonstration Team in a F-100 Sabre Jet during a practice demonstration. In 1969, he was named an honorary member of the Thunderbirds, and in 1984 was elected as an honorary life member of the Order of Daedalians, the national fraternity of military pilots.

He authored *The Aviation Art of Keith Ferris* which tells of his experiences, motivation and techniques. It is illustrated by 40 reproductions of his work.

"My paintings are a documentation of history," Ferris said. "When I finish a painting, I do it with the pilot in mind. So if he were to look at the painting, he would say, 'Sure, I remember that mission, that's exactly the way it was.'"

Born in Honolulu in 1929, Ferris is the son of an career Air Force officer and grew up with military aviation at bases throughout the United States and in England. He attended Texas A & M, where he studied aeronautical engineering, then put in stints at George Washington University and the Corcoran School of Art in Washington, DC.

In 1947, he began his art career with the Air Force

Training Publications department at Randolph AFB in Texas. He moved to Morris Plains, NJ, in 1956 as a freelance artist working for aviation manufacturers, their advertising agencies and aviation trade publications. He has been an active member of the Society of Illustrators since 1960 and served as Air Force art chairman from 1968 to 1970.

He was still pursuing an active career in the 1990s.

Jo Kotula

In an *Air-List Ads* article entitled *Portrait of an Artist,* writer Jack Elliott speculated that Jo Kotula should perhaps be in the Guinness Book of Records for his accomplishment of painting every cover for the monthly magazine *Model Airplane News* for 38 years — more than 450 original pieces of aeronautical art.

"The covers Kotula painted include some of the most unusual aircraft ever conceived," Elliott wrote. "Some were never built. Some never got beyond the prototypes"

The first cover he drew in 1938 was of a Seversky TransOceanic Super Clipper, with a double fuselage and five engines.

Over the years, Kotula's art haa been seen in various aviation magazines and he illustrated the book on flying by Wolfgang Langewiesche, titled *Stick and Rudder.*

The Asbury, NJ, resident first flew in a "Jenny" at Latrobe Airport in Pennsylvania. He was 15. Little did he realize then that he would create more than 1,500 airplanes of all shapes and sizes on canvas.

Roy E. La Grone

Roy La Grone, a resident of Somerset, NJ, was born in Pine Bluff, AR, in 1921. Early in life, he had a natural flair for art but didn't take it seriously until he attended the Tuskegee Institute in Alabama where there was an art program. He confided that his true reason for attending Tuskegee was to obtain a pilot's license through the Civilian Pilot Training program, the only one then available to blacks. In 1942, he left college and joined the Tuskegee Airmen, took basic military flight training and was commissioned a second lieutenant in 1944.

As a member of the legendary 332nd Fighter Group, LaGrone served in Italy and proudly proclaimed that while escorting B-17 and B-24 bombers on raids over Germany, his group never lost a bomber to attacking enemy planes. He flew 50 combat missions in P-51s. Before returning to the states, his commanding officer Gen. Noel F. Parish told him "You're going to document this."

After the war, he attended the University of Florence in Italy and graduated from Pratt Institute in 1949 with a degree in Commercial Art and Illustration.

He was appointed to the Air Force Art program with the rank of colonel in 1958, and began fulfilling his commander's prediction. By the late 1980s, he had produced 21 paintings documenting the saga of the Tuskegee Airmen. He has traveled to military installations around the world to capture impressions of Air Force life on canvas. As he explained: "These paintings [created by him and his fellow Air Force artists] have a priceless value, both historical and educational."

Like fellow air force artists, he has had the opportunity to fly in some of the hottest military planes from F-104s to F-15s.

Although he had an outstanding business career with the University of Medicine and Dentistry's Robert Wood Johnson Medical School as art director - graphic coordinator, La Grone said "My life-long project is to paint for the Air Force Art Program, the contribution black pilots have made to military aviation, past and present."

Henry Clark

Hank Clark said his talent of creating cutaway drawings on a monthly basis for *Model Aviation* magazine was a God-given gift. "It's my thing," he said. "How do I know how? It's a gift. Talent? You might more correctly say it's the result of 50 years of development."

In order to recreate any airplane requested by his editors, Clark referred to his extensive library of aircraft photographs. "I shot them all, printing zillions of pix for mail fans around the world from 1930 to 1950," he explained. "My son has that negative file now. There are 3,600 — give or take a few."

During World War II, Clark drew aircraft structures for the Grumman Aircraft Company and created a series of pen-and ink lithos of Grumman fighter planes. Later, the Dumont, NJ, resident provided art to *Air Trails* and *Aircraft of the World.*

His drawings can be found at the National Air and Space Museum and other aviation museums throughout the United States. Hank Clark "went West" in 1987.

Brett Dagnall

One of the younger artists who has dedicated himself to aviation art is Brett Dagnall of North Plainfield. He graduated in the early 1980s from Watchung Hills Regional High. He credits his art instructor, Larry von Beidel, with giving him the freedom to choose his own direction and helping him achieve a three-dimensional feeling in his work. The majority of his early art has been of vintage aircraft from a Jenny to the DC-3.

Barry Bichler

Barry Bichler, a Fairlawn, NJ; resident, has built an outstanding reputation among aviation publishers and art collectors since his graduation from Pratt Institute, NY, in 1983. He has a painting displayed in the *Looking at Earth* exhibit at the National Air and Space Museum and his works of art have been seen at the prestigious Farnborough (England) Air Show (1984) and the Paris Air Show (1985). Two of his creations hang in the Marine Corps Museum in Quantico, VA. His work has appeared in a large variety of publications from *Popular Science* to the *Israel Air Force* magazine.

Frank J. McGinley

Frank McGinley of Toms River, reputed to be a tireless worker, has helped countless organizations raise funds by creating special works of art that are printed as lithographs and sold as limited additions for charitable causes. His depiction of the air mail service at Hadley Field in the 1920s sold out in a record time.

Although McGinley's art is all encompassing, his aeronautical collection was a finalist in the Smithsonian Institution's "Golden Age of Flight" exhibit in 1984.

CHRONOLOGY OF OTHER AERONAUTICAL EVENTS AND ACHIEVEMENTS
1980 to 1989

- New Jerseyans operated the Adirondack Airport at Lake Placid, NY, during the 13th Winter Olympic Games. The Pan Am World Services' project was headed by Phil Engle, assistant manager of Teterboro Airport. Others who spent four months in northern New York state were John Meehan of Point Pleasant, NJ, and Rudy Steinthal of Wayne, both veteran aviation supervisors. Aero Services, headquartered at Teterboro, ran the fixed-base operation at the Olympic airport.

- A bright, gold blimp with the word "Jordasche" inscribed on its side, ascended from the Naval Air Station at Lakehurst on its maiden flight. The 140-foot-long blimp contained 5,700 cubic feet of helium. James B. Buza was at the controls. The airship climbed to approximately 400 feet and for two minutes flew out of control in small circles. The blimp landed roughly in a grove of trees that punctured its air bag, collapsing it like a giant curtain. Buza was unhurt, although the airship was a total wreck.

- Cecil Coffrin of Brooklyn, NY, celebrated his 80th birthday flying banners along New Jersey's coastline from Seaside Heights to Sandy Hook. Flying from Colts Neck (NJ) Airport, Coffrin had spent more than 50 summers banner towing and skywriting. When asked the secret to his longevity, Coffrin told Charles Finley of the *Newark Star-Ledger*, "I work seven days a week, maybe that has something to do with it. My great-grandfather was 104 years old when he died. And I take an optimistic view of life. After all, you only go this way once, you know."

- When the high-wing monoplane with the man standing strapped between the wings landed at Essex County Airport in Fairfield, it completed an odyssey flight from West Germany for Jaromir Wagner, a Czech-born auto dealer. He had successfully completed a transatlantic flight standing atop the plane. To cap the journey on Oct. 8, the plane and its outboard passenger flew down the Hudson and circled the Statue of Liberty before turning west toward Fairfield. The flight had taken 11 days. Over the Atlantic, Wagner endured temperatures as low as 94 degrees below zero. Why did he do it? "I like the risk. It's a thrill ," he said.

- A $50 million FAA Technical Center was opened at the NAFEC facility at Atlantic City.

1981

- Dr. C. Malcolm B. Gilman of Bay Head, NJ, died Aug. 26. Dr. Gilman was a highly respected medical examiner for the FAA, a position he held for more than 40 years. During World War I, he flew with the Army Air Corps and attained the rank of colonel. As a civilian, he retained the initial "C" to denote the rank he achieved. Following the war, he became the first air mail pilot to fly roundtrip between Long Island and Washington, D.C., on the second day of U.S. air mail service. Dr. Gilman was born in Rahway, but lived most of his life in Monmouth County.

- Stanley Switlik, founder of the Switlik Parachute Co., died at age 91.

- Frederich Bohlander, a former Fokker Aircraft mechanic and Teterboro police chief, died.

- Thomas M. Ryan Jr., a graduate of Ridgewood High School, was promoted to a four-star general on July 31. At that time, he shared that rank with only 11 other commanding officers. As commander-in-chief of the Military Airlift Command at the Scott Air Force Base, IL, he was responsible for the planning and performance of airlift missions during periods of crisis.

1982

- The Northeast Division of the Yankee Air Force was formed at Essex County Airport. The first president was Lee Herron. Vice President was Ray Golowach.

- Sixteen years after it mysteriously disappeared, a twin-engine, propeller-driven SP-2A Navy anti-submarine patrol plane was discovered by a geological research team at the foot of Mount Fairweather in British Columbia. Vito Muti of Fairview, NJ, was the radio operator aboard the ill-fated plane that was last seen in Kodiak, Alaska, on December. 14, 1957.

1983

- In celebration of the 200th anniversary of the world's first balloon flight in Paris, France, John Burk of Hainesport, NJ, established a flight endurance record for a one-man hot-air balloon. The March 14 flight lasted five hours and 44 minutes. Burk drifted less than 100 miles during his time aloft. He had hoped to break the distance record for his class balloon of 124 miles.

- Walter Wiechetek, a Bayonne doctor, designed a multi-colored patch that showed Leonardo da Vinci's *The Dimensions of Man,* wearing a space suit. It was announced that all space shuttle astronauts would wear the patch. Wiechetek worked for the Hamilton Standard Medical Center in Windsor Locks, CT, as an aerospace physician.

- Warren Marsh of Edison completed his 4,000 glider flight at Sky Manor Airport, Pittstown. The New Jersey soaring fraternity could not recall a greater total of flights in the Garden State. March, who received his commercial glider pilot's license in 1974, flew as many as 600 people a year in his glider.

- An East Hanover, NJ, resident, Patricia Dennehy, a corporate jet pilot with 3,800 flight hours, set five records for a route from Wichita, KS, to Morristown Municipal Airport on Sept. 22. She left Wichita's Cessna Airport at dawn in a single-engine Cessna 170 and flew the 1,200-mile route in 10 hours of flying time, setting a "world class time" record for such a flight. According to Patricia, she researched 25 years of wind statistics and checked fuel capacities before her trip. Her average speed was 156 miles per hour at altitudes of between 7,500 and 9,500 feet. Obviously, her pre-planning paid off because the Cessna 170 usually cruises between 100 and 110 mph.

1984

- Royal French Ryder, popular test pilot, died.

- Arthur Rees, 85, of Essex Falls, NJ, was honored by Gov. Thomas H. Kean during Older Americans Month as the oldest licensed pilot in the United States.

- Two French flyers, Patrick Fourticq and Henri Pescarolo, landed at Teterboro Airport following a 11 1/2 hour transcontinental flight from San Jose, CA. The Frenchmen flew a single-engine Piper Malibu and claimed a speed record for that class of aircraft.

- Ric Gillespie, a 36-year-old professional pilot from Lindenwold, NJ, announced that his research showed that the French flyers, Charles Nungesser and Francois Coli, had successfuly flown across the Atlantic Ocean 12 days before Charles Lindbergh left for Paris in May of 1927. Gillespie, a self-proclaimed historian, said he had uncovered reports of a woodsman in a remote section of eastern Maine who had heard an aircraft engine overhead at the approximate time the two Franchmen would have reached the American shore. Jack Hansen, vice president of operations for the Flying W. Airport in Lumberton, NJ, volunteered to underwrite an expedition to Maine in search of the remains of the French plane. Gillespie spent several months in Maine, but never found the evidence he was seeking.

- "Ike" Schlossbach died at age 93.

1985

- In a single-engine Cessna 182 Skylane, Daniel Campbell of Tuckerton, NJ, who at age 19, lost both legs in a train accident, flew with Peggy Naumann of Manahawkin in the first Trans-Atlantic Air Rally — 4,226 miles between New York and Paris. Upon their arrival in LeBourget Airport outside of Paris, the pair were informed that they had finished 17th out of 67 competitors. They had begun the race at the Morristown Airport. It is believed that Campbell was the only double amputee pilot with a IFR/Commercial rating.

- On a flight to England aboard the British Concorde in July 1985, Berkeley Heights, NJ, resident Fred Finn made his 558th crossing on the supersonic transport. *The Guinness Book of World Records* lists Finn as the most frequent passenger aboard the high-speed, high-priced aircraft.

- Chester J. Decker, the former national soaring champion, died in West Milford, NJ.

1986

- Todd Johnson, a 13-year-old eighth grader at Hillsborough Middle School in Somerset County, was one of 10 youths from across the United States who returned from the Soviet Union following a tour of the Russian Cosmonaut base, Star City, 30 miles above Moscow. "I was disappointed I had to leave," he said. "The Russian kids were great. There weren't any bad things said to us. They had only good things to say, ideas they wanted to tell us. It made me feel bad to have to leave them."

- The airport at the NAFEC facility in Pomona was named the Atlantic City International Airport. Air traffic had increased dramatically with the advent of gambling in the Southern Jersey resort.

- Capt. Ralph Barnaby died in Philadelphia at age 93.

- Balloon Capt. Patricia Malinak, of Medford, NJ, participated in the International Balloon Race in Saga, Japan. She competed in four races with her balloon *The Jabberwocky,* and placed 11th, 5th, 19th and 7th in a field of 67 balloons.

- Two paraplegics soloed aircraft within a week of each other. Both men were from Scotch Plains, NJ. Alan McCreary flew a Piper Cherokee 140 monoplane under the watchful eye of Paul Charron, an instructor at the Caldwell Flight Academy, based at the Essex County Airport. Ray Temchua soloed a Grob sailplane at Sky Manor Airport through the auspices of Freedom's Wings, an organization started by Irv Soble, a United Airlines pilot, who believed handicapped people should have the opportunity to fly. A year later, Temchus became the only handicapped glider instructor in the nation.

- Dr.Albert Forsythe died in Newark at age 88.

1987

- Dean C. Smith, who made the first night air mail flight from Hadley Field in 1925, died in Easton, MD.

- Gen. Robert Copsey, the first manager of Newark Airport, died in Colorado Springs, CO.

- James MacGowan, a paraplegic from Brooklyn, learned to sky dive at the Sky Dives East School, run by Doug Angel. So he wouldn't hurt himself when he landed, MacGowan jumped into water. He was the first paraplegic in the world to win the Star Crest Award for sky diving. He jumped with 11 other sky divers from two planes and then joined hands to create a star cluster.

1988

- Lutz Lessmeister of Woodbridge flew his single-engine, straight-tail Bonanza from Kupper Airport, Manville, NJ, to Nuremberg, Germany. Art Madden had taught him to fly and he made the trip with only 400 hours of flying experience.

- William J. Picune died in Golden, CO, at age 72.

- Moments after taking off from Marlboro Airport at Matawan, NJ, on a sightseeing flight, Barbara Basile of Reading, NJ, found herself in control of the plane when her pilot, Robert Bunyon of Matawan, died of a heart attack. All Basile knew about flying

an airplane had been learned from watching television. But for 30 terrifying minutes, she managed to make all the right decisions in guiding the plane to a crash landing that she survived. At first she thought of attempting to land in the ocean but was afraid of killing swimmers along the shore. So she flew inland to Wall Township. She then aimed the aircraft toward a field, switched off the engine and let it glide down. As it struck the ground, the wheels dug into a dirt patch and flipped the plane over. Basile suffered only a pelvic fracture.

- *Air-List-Ads* magazine began its 25th year in October of 1988. Edited by Harry A. Hamlen, the magazine had a wide circulation in the Northeast. In the 1960s, Hamlen, as executive director of the Aviation Advisory Council of New Jersey, saved Caldwell Airport from extinction by convincing Essex County Freeholders to purchase the land before it fell into developer's hands.

- Colts Neck Airport, operated for 20 years by Paul and Gerie Wille, was sold to developers. Opened in 1938, the 40-acre airport had been a favorite with local sport aviators, and at one time more than 50 aircraft were based there. It was the Central Jersey Glider Club's headquarters for many years. The airport was a section of a 408-acre parcel owned until the early 1980s by industrialist Armand Hammer.

- Dr. Ed Galkin and Bob Zuber, a police officer, both of Edison, NJ. took off from Morristown Airport in a single-engine Cessna 210 and flew around the world. The two men had taken months to plan their trip and equip the Cessna with the sophisticated instruments needed to assure a safe flight. Almost 80 percent of their flight was over water. The flight was planned for 28 days but took 32 because of equipment problems along the way.

- Joe Colombo of Wayne, won the rotorcraft grand championship at the Experimental Aircraft Association's annual convention in Oshkosh, WI. His home-built entry was an EXEC 500 Helicopter. Having won the rotorcraft championship in 1977, Colombo became the first man to win that division twice.

1989

- Ed Gorski, a veteran pilot, instructor and airport operator died at age 84.

- Two large Sikorsky S76-B helicopters were acquired by the state police and based at Morristown and Voorhis, NJ. They were flying intensive care units.

- Robert Johnson, the Curtiss-Wright "Father of Cruise Control" died in Arizona.

- O.P. "Ted" Hebert, owner and operator of the Safair Flying Service at Teterboro, died.

- Harry Nordheim died in Atlantic City.

- Publisher/balloonist Malcolm Forbes died at his home in Far Hills, NJ.

- Under the leadership of Otto K. Mueller, a retired Air Force major, and members of the New Jersey chapter of Yankee Air Force, a 60th anniversary celebration of Gen. Jimmy Doolittle's first "blind flight" was held on Sept. 24 at the former Aircraft Radio Corp. airfield in Boonton Township NJ. A memorial plaque was placed by the township at the end of the sod runway and a bust of Doolittle, created by Dr. Martin Siegel, was unveiled by Col. John Doolittle, USAF (Ret.), the General's son. Those who played an active role in organizing the day-long tribute to the first instrument take-off and landing of an aircraft included Yankee Air Force members: Herbert O. Fisher, Oscar Nathans, John D. Golderer and Raymond Golowach. Representing the township were: Jean Ricker, Douglas Cabana, Mary Louise Leaming, Oscar Kincaid, N.J. (Kip) Koehler III, Richard Foster, David Wahlberg, Allen Breed, Richard Seabury III, Armand Burghard, Thomas Marotta, Philip Justin, Thomas S. Brackin, Jack Cook, and John Hunter. The honorary chairmen were: Governor Thomas H. Kean, Maj. Gen. Francis R. Gerard and H.V. Pat Reilly.

- John H. Andresen, a Glen Rock native, retired after 50 years as an aircraft engineer. During that period, he worked for the Kollsman Instrument Co., the Bendix Corp. and the Intercontinental Dynamics Corp. of Englewood. He invented 72 patented aeronautical devices that made flying safer for commercial, military and private aircraft.

1990

- Former Curtiss-Wright test pilot Herbert O. Fisher died

- Marion R. Hart, the "flying grandma," died in August at age 98. She learned to fly at age 54 at Teterboro Airport and for the next 30 years flew to various destinations around the world.

ADDENDUM

New Jersey Organizations:

Civil Air Patrol

Wing, Groups, Squadrons	Location
New Jersey Wing	McGuire Air Force Base
Group 221 headquarters	Girl Scout Hq., Butler
Lone Eagle Composite Sqdn.	Morristown Airport
North Jersey Senior Sqdn.	Teterboro Airport
Paramus Composite Sqdn.	Teaneck High School
Picatinny Composite Sqdn.	Picatinny Arsenal
Sussex-Warren Composite Sqdn.	Frankford Township
Wayne Composite Sqdn.	VFW Hall, Wayne
Group 223 Headquarters	Roselle Boro Hall
Bayshore Composite Sqdn.	Fort Monmouth
Gen. Jimmy Stewart Comp. Sqdn.	South Amboy
Union County Composite Sqdn.	Westfield
Newark Composite Sqdn.	Newark
Raritan Valley Composite Sqdn.	Kupper Airport
Plainfield Cadet Sqdn.	Plainfield
Group 224 Headquarters	Lakewood Airport
Allentown Composite Sqdn.	Allentown
Col. M.M.Spears Composite Sqdn.	Freehold
Mercer County Composite Sqdn.	Lawrenceville
Ocean Composite Sqdn.	Miller Airport
Pineland Composite Sqdn.	Lakewood Airport
Twin Pine Cadet Sqdn.	Mercer Airport
Group 225 Headquarters	Burlington Cty. Airport
Cumberland Composite Sqdn.	Millville Airport
Jack Schweiker Cadet Sqdn.	Laurel Springs
McGuire Composite Sqdn.	McGuire Air Force Base
Atlantic City Cadet Sqdn.	Atlantic City Airport
Salem County Composite Sqdn.	Elmer

Experimental Aircraft Association

Chapter	Location
Atlantic City	Marmora
Cross Keys	Cross Keys Airport
Lakewood	Lakewood Airport
Lincoln Park	Lincoln Park Airport
Millburn	Millburn
Nutley	642 Franklin St. Nutley
Ocean County	Ocean Co. Vo-Tech
Pittstown	Alexandria Field
Sussex	Sussex Airport
Trenton	Mercer County Airport

Air Force Association

North Jersey Chapters

Highpoint	Passiac-Bergen
Teterboro Bendix	Sal Capriglione
Garden State	Hudson

Tri-County

Central Jersey Chapters

Wings	Union Morris
Middlesex	Mercer Couty
Hangar One	Aerospace Founders

South Jersey Chapters

Admiral Rosendahl	Currie Memorial
Atlantic City	McGuire
Public Affairs Gen. Castle	

Yankee Air Force (New Jersey Chapter)

Essex County Airport

Winners of the Garden State 300 Air Race

Year	Pilot/Co-pilot
1973	Bill Steinfield - Tom Slocum
1974	Sandra Duma - John Duma
1975	Alexamdra Taylor - Rev. Robert Bryan
1976	Helen G. Zubrow - Anne M. Shields
1977	Donald B. Know - Philip J. Kowalski
1978	Dana Kull - Richard Kull
1979	Cancelled due to inclement weather
1980	Skippy Orlitzki - Dan Orlitzki
1981	Joel Spivak - George Angelini
1982	Helen Zubrown - Anne Shields
1983	Sandra Duma - John Duma
1984	Herbert Greenberg - Bruce Lontka
1985	Mary Helfrick - Betty Pifer
1986	Cancelled due to inclement weather
1987	Harold Berk - Adam Devlin
1988	Gar Burwell - Todd Burwell
1989	Racquel McNeil - Steve Waldman
1990	Frank Cross - Marvin Broder

New Jersey Whirly Girls

Adele Budrow	Lindenwold
Kim Darst	Blairston
Mary DeSimone	Medford
Josie Edmonson	Medford Lakes
Darlene Engelke-Haiduck	Millville
Wini Gronvold	Ocean City
Jane Huppert	Stockton
Suzanne Johansen	Belle Mead
Julie Kelly	Carlstadt
Faith Richards	East Orange
Pat Schaeflern	Pittstown
Carol Timmons	Swendenboro
Gwen Waller	Atco
Kristina Wetzel	Parsippany
Cindy Wilson	Wayne

New Jersey Airports 1990

Airport	Owner or Manager	Location
Aeroflex-Andover	Mrs.B.Lo Re/ Don Eddy	Andover
Alexandria Field	William Fritsche	Pittstown
Allaire	E. Brown/Bruce Mawson	Allaire
Atlantic City	Richard Battaglia	Atlantic City
Bader Field	Edward Goddard	Atlantic City
Blairstown	S.Parker/D. Hackett	Blairstown
Buck's	Joseph Di Orio	Bridgeton
Camden County	Karl Kleinberg	Berlin
Cape May County	Irene Schreiner	Rio Grande
Cross Keys	Albert Lewis	Williamstown
Eagles Hest	John Kummings	West Creek
Essex County	Arthur Cmiel	Fairfield
Flying W.	Don Powell	Mt. Holly
Greenwood Lake	T. Dick/R. Miller	West Milford
Hackettstown	Donald Schwanda	Hackettstown
Hammonton Muni	Mrs D De Cicco/P Ranere	Hammonton
Jersey City Seaplane	Harry Frank	Jersey City
Kroelinger	Fred Bernardini	Vineland
Kupper	C Kupper/P Kupper	Somerville
Lakewood	David O'Brien	Lakewood
Li Calzi Airpark	Alan Li Calzi	Bridgeton
Lincoln Park	Joseph Rendiero	Lincoln Park
Linden	B Seljevold/P Dudley	Linden
Little Ferry Seaplane	A Georgas/B Dunham	Little Ferry
Manahawkin	Mrs. Ethel Haslbeck	Manahawkin
Marlboro	Leonard Genova	Lincroft
Mercer County	John Maier	Trenton
Millville Nunicipal	Lewis Finch	Hillville
Morristown Muni	William Barkhauer	Morristown
Newark Int'l	Vince Bonaventura	Newark
Newton	Mrs. Stella Jump	Newton
Ocean City Muni	Edmund Wood	Ocean City
Old Bridge	William Reilly	Englishtown
Oldmans	Thomas Kurtz Jr.	Pedricktown
Pemberton	Robert Cooper	Pemberton
Piney Hollow	Mrs.D Webb/J. Hartin	Williamstown
Princeton	R Mierenberg/K Nierenberg	Princeton
Red Lion	Ray Daniels	Vincentown
Red Wing	George Dengler	Crosswick
Ridgefield Pk.	J Boyd/John Kiekstad	Ridgefield Pk
Rudy's	Rudolph Chalow	Newfield
R.J. Miller	D.Hennessey/F. Goesser	Toms River
Sky Manor	Kent Linn	Pittstown
Solberg-Hunterdon	Thor Solberg	Readington
Somerset	George Walker	Bedminster
S. Jersey Regonial	Ms. Marianne Worth	Medford
Southern Cross	Edward Carter	Franklinville
Susaex	Paul G. Styger	Sussex
Teterboro	Phil Engle	Teterboro
Trenton Robbinsville	Edward Eget	Robbinsville
Trinca	A. Davidson/Ed. Billows	Andover
Twin Pine	William Weasner	Trenton
Vineland-Downstown	Peter Cugino	Vineland
Woodbine Muni	G.A.Barrett Inc./P.Wanek	Woodbine

NEW JERSEY AIRPORTS CLOSED - 1980-1989

Airport	Location
Bridgeport	Bridgeport
Colts Neck	Colts Neck
Cumulus Ridge	Milford
Flanders Valley	Flanders
Hanover	East Hanover
Lambros Seaplane	Ridgefield Park
Pitman	Pitman
Sky Harbor Seaplane	Carlstadt
Smithville	Smithville
Somerset Hills	Basking Ridge

Index